Chang

Latvians, Lithuanians and Estonians in Great Britain

This book presents the fascinating and untold life histories of Latvians, Lithuanians and Estonians, who were displaced from their homelands during the Second World War, and who came to Britain as participants of two European Volunteer Worker (EVW) schemes, from 1946-50: 'Balt Cygnet' and 'Westward Ho!' Approximately 13,000 Latvians, 6,000 Lithuanians and 5,000 Estonians were recruited by the British government from Displaced Person (DP) Camps in Germany and Austria, to fill post-war labour shortages in Britain. Although the refugees regarded the migration to Britain as temporary, the longevity of the Soviet Union's occupation of the Baltic States, meant that the overwhelming majority remained in Britain, and only a handful returned following the restoration of homeland independence in 1991. It was the intention of the British Government that the refugees would eventually assimilate into British society, and the EVW schemes were designed and implemented with this goal in mind.

This book uses narrative accounts from interviews with first generation Latvians, Lithuanians and Estonians carried out by the author to chart their life stories. Documentary and other sources are also used to show how Latvians, Lithuanians and Estonians integrated, but did not assimilate into British society.

The book also outlines the history of Latvians, Lithuanians and Estonians in Great Britain during other periods of history, including the nineteenth and early twentieth centuries, and more recently since the accession of the Baltic States to the European Union in 2004.

The book will be of interest to Latvians, Lithuanians and Estonians in Great Britain and other receiving nations such as the United States, as well as to specialists of British migration history, the Baltic States and identity and immigration theorists.

Emily Gilbert is a freelance writer and researcher based in Devon.

Changing Identities

Latvians, Lithuanians and Estonians in Great Britain

Emily Gilbert

First published 2013
Printed in the UK
ISBN-13 978-1481875455
ISBN-10 1481875450

About the Author
Emily Gilbert is a social historian, writer and researcher based in Devon, UK. She has worked on research projects relating to work and care among four generation families; homeworking in the UK, museums and social identity; and research relating to Russia and the Baltic Republics. She has worked at the Universities of London, Sheffield and Newcastle, as well as for charities and local government in research and policy related roles. She has a Master's Degree in Russian and East European Studies and a PhD in Social History.

For my children, Isaac and Seth
And for all the Latvians, Lithuanians and Estonians who came to
Great Britain as European Volunteer Workers after the Second
World War

Contents

Acknowledgments

This book has relied upon the generous support of many individuals, organisations and communities, not all of whom I am able to acknowledge here. Firstly I gratefully acknowledge the financial support of the Economic and Social Research Council who funded the research and the Department of History at the University of Sheffield, where I carried out the PhD. In particular I would like to thank Professor Colin Holmes who provided the initial opportunity to carry out the research and who supervised the research. The project would not have been possible without the enthusiastic support and participation of the Latvian, Lithuanian and Estonian communities in Great Britain, who were extremely supportive, and with whom I can honestly say, I spent some of the most enjoyable evenings of my life. I am particularly grateful to everyone at the Latvian clubs in Leeds and Nottingham, the Lithuanian clubs in Manchester and Nottingham, and the Estonian club in Bradford. I would like to thank all the questionnaire and interview participants, and all those who generously gave or lent me a range of community documents, including rare books, personal memoirs, newspapers and journals, which have formed extremely useful source materials for this study. In the Baltic States, I am very grateful to several returnees, one of whom found me accommodation during one of my fieldwork visits, and another who took me on sightseeing visits around Riga, as well as tours of some of Riga's best cafes and pubs

I would also like to thank my partner John and my friends and family who have supported me throughout, and my children, Isaac and Seth who have given me the motivation to get this book published.

July 2013

Preface

This book is effectively a reprint of my original PhD thesis, awarded in 2001, with some reworking and additions to bring it up-to-date. The idea of self publishing the PhD was originally conceived as a way of printing some relatively low cost copies of the thesis for my own use: however, I felt that it may also be of interest both to Latvian, Lithuanian and Estonian communities in Great Britain, particularly second and third generation members of these communities; as well as to Baltic communities worldwide, for example in America and Australia. Many of these groups initially came to Great Britain after the Second World War on the European Volunteer Worker Schemes before later moving onto America and other countries for a perceived better quality of life. I always intended to publish the thesis as a book; however, jobs, children and successive moves overtook these intentions and I now feel that self publishing the original thesis is the quickest and simplest way to enable a wider readership of the thesis at a relatively low cost price to the reader.

Although the thesis was written in 2001, it still has major historical relevance. This is the only book, which makes use of the interviews I recorded with first generation Latvian, Lithuanians and Estonians in Great Britain, most of whom will now sadly have died. This is also the only book which analyses the experiences of Latvians, Lithuanians and Estonians in Great Britain from a life history perspective, and with a focus on issues of identity and cultural maintenance. The more recent migration of Latvians, Lithuanians and Estonians to the UK, along with Poles and other East Europeans as a result of European Union enlargement, has brought the issue of East European migration again to the fore, and makes the publication of this book relevant and timely.

Although it is over ten years since the thesis was written and awarded, the memories and experiences I have of working with the Latvian, Lithuanian and Estonian communities in Great Britain remain with me to this day. It was one of the most incredible experiences of my life to be given access to the lives of these migrants and to share in their fascinating lives and histories. I feel very honoured to have been able to carry out this research and it is with this in mind that I would like to share the work and findings from my study with the communities themselves. I hope that you enjoy this book as much as I have enjoyed writing it and it goes someway to answering your questions about the history of the Latvian, Lithuanian and Estonian communities in Great Britain. If you would like to contact me I can be contacted at: emilygilbertuk@googlemail.com

INTRODUCTION

Although this nation has a genius for absorbing foreigners into its system in small doses, and to the mutual advantage of both parties, the present influx is so enormous…that an especial effort is imperative: the gradual absorption of these thousands of foreigners into our community will not occur automatically.

(Report of an Enquiry into the teaching of English to Foreign Workers, 1949)[1]

A Lithuanian remains Lithuanian everywhere and always.

(Lithuanian Charter, 1949)[2]

BETWEEN 1946 and 1950, approximately 13,000 Latvian, 6,000 Lithuanian and 5,000 Estonian Displaced Persons (DPs) were recruited onto two contract labour schemes - Balt Cygnet and Westward Ho! to provide manpower for undermanned industries in Great Britain.[3]   In total, over 80,000 DPs of many different nationalities participated in these schemes and were known collectively as European Volunteer Workers (EVWs).   The EVW schemes were intended not only as a means of reducing critical manpower shortages in certain key sectors of the post-war economy, they were also implemented as a way of ameliorating the refugee crisis in Europe.   As a result of the Second World War, particularly the war in the east between Soviet Russia and Nazi Germany, millions had been uprooted from their homelands and forced to flee west.   At the end of the war, the refugees had found their way into Displaced Persons' Camps, run by the Western Allies in Germany and Austria.   The redrawing of Germany and Austria into Western and Soviet occupation zones had placed these DPs under the responsibility of British, French and American governments.   Among the displaced were hundreds of thousands of Latvian, Lithuanian and Estonian men, women and children, victims of the Nazi/Soviet battle for the Baltic region.   In 1940, Latvia's, Lithuania's and Estonia's brief experience of independence lasting only two decades, was halted by a first Russian occupation, swiftly followed by a period of German rule from 1941 to 1943, and culminating in a second Russian invasion in 1944. The final Russian onslaught imposed almost five decades of Soviet rule on the Baltic peoples. The more immediate effect of these onslaughts however was the uprooting of hundreds of thousands of inhabitants. Large numbers were conscripted into the Russian or German armies, or became forced labourers in Germany. These groups found themselves displaced at the end of the war. The largest migration occurred in the autumn of late 1944, when thousands fled the advancing Russian army, and travelled west. At the end of the war, hundreds of thousands of Latvians, Lithuanians and Estonians were stranded in Europe, and with the Soviet Union tightening its grip over the homeland, were unwilling to return home. The Baltic refugees joined Ukrainians, Byelorussians, Yugoslavs, Hungarians, Poles, Czechoslovaks, Jews and other nationalities in Displaced Persons Camps, and waited for a solution to their plight.

While the refugee crisis in Europe called for urgent attention, in Britain critical manpower shortages were becoming apparent in key areas of the economy, particularly textiles, agriculture, brick works and coal mining. There was also an acute deficiency of domestic workers in hospitals and sanatoria. Labour shortages threatened to destabilise the fragile post-war economy and hamper peacetime reconstruction. Attempts to fill vacancies through the recruitment of Belgian women for domestic work and the resettlement of Polish ex-servicemen were insufficient to solve the problem.[4] With little experience of large-scale immigration, the British Government implemented the first labour scheme - Balt Cygnet in October 1946. Initially, designed on a small scale, Balt Cygnet was quickly extended, and Westward Ho!, a new scheme, on a much larger scale, was introduced in April 1947.

The EVW schemes were contract labour schemes in which the recruited DPs agreed to remain within the specified employment for one year and thereafter change jobs only with the approval of the Ministry of Labour. In practice, this meant that EVWs were confined to areas of manpower shortage until 1951, when the labour controls were lifted. The EVW schemes drew upon some aspects of previous immigration law and policy, particularly the status of EVWs as aliens upon their entry to Britain, and the restrictions of the labour contract. However, due to the scale and the novel aspects of their design, the EVW schemes represented a milestone in British immigration history. Yet despite the significance of these schemes, discussion of them was largely absent from immigration and general histories of Britain for several decades. The schemes began to be addressed in the 1980's and 1990's, most thoroughly in Diana Kay's and Robert Miles', *Refugees or Migrant Workers?: European Volunteer Workers in Britain, 1946-51* (1992).[5] This study drew attention not only to the mechanics and novelty of design, but also to the racialised hierarchy of labour within the government, through which certain nationalities were prioritised while others were relegated to the bottom of the recruiting list. According to Kay and Miles, ranking in the list was primarily dependent upon designated racialised characteristics, most importantly the potential for assimilation. At the top of the Government's racialised hierarchy were Latvians, Lithuanians and Estonians who were homogenised into one differentiating category - the 'Balts'. The 'Balts' were deemed not only to be the most hard-working of the DPs, and 'of good appearance and habits'[6], they were also regarded to have the highest potential for assimilation.

The goal of assimilation was an integral component of the recruitment of DPs under the EVW schemes. It was only with a firm belief that these 80,000 EVWs of varying nationalities would be 'absorbed' into British society, that they were accepted on the schemes. Government discourse about the schemes reveals in no uncertain terms the Government's plans for the 'absorption' and 'assimilation' of the refugees in British society. According to Kathleen Paul in her study, *Whitewashing Britain: Race and Citizenship in the Post-War Era* (1997):

> Expecting them to fill gaps in the labour force in the short term, policy makers clearly also expected these aliens to become British subjects in both form and substance in the long term.[7]

Of course, this was not a new phenomenon in British immigration policy- the goal of assimilation had always prevailed hitherto in relation to migrating aliens. The labour schemes were designed with this aim in mind, and provisions were made once the DPs had landed in Britain to facilitate the process of assimilation. Despite the fact that the aim of assimilation lacked novelty, it is important to note that governmental discourse relating to assimilation in the late 1940's were formed within a country with very little experience of immigration on this scale.

In contrast to the government's intentions, most of the Latvians, Lithuanians and Estonians who participated on the EVW schemes regarded their migration to Britain merely as a brief *sojourn* before returning to the homeland. A 'myth of return' was first propagated in the DP Camps and promoted the idea that the Western Allies would shortly declare war on Soviet Russia, and oust her from the refugees' homelands, thus enabling them to return home. However, the notion of return proved to be an illusion, and fifty years on, many of the original immigrants remained in Britain.

When Latvian, Lithuanian and Estonian DPs first entered Britain as part of the Balt Cygnet and Westward Ho! schemes, their presence was noted by the media, locals and British labour. As with all the EVW nationalities, since they were participants in the first sizeable immigration scheme to Britain, the Baltic refugees were highly visible, although locals were unable to distinguish between many of the different nationalities. Yet, fifty years on at the turn of the new millennium in 2000, despite the significance and permanency of the Baltic DPs migration to Britain, these nationalities had largely disappeared not only from public attention, but also from history.

This book will piece together the lost history of Latvians, Lithuanians and Estonians in Britain, three very distinct nationalities, whose lives, along with some of the other EVW groups – the Yugoslavs, Hungarians and Czechoslovaks, have yet to be analysed in any depth. The book will examine the experiences of migration and settlement of Latvian, Lithuanian and Estonian DPs. The central research questions posed by the research are: To what extent did the 'Balts' assimilate, as the government intended? Adopting the words of Kathleen Paul, how far did Latvians, Lithuanians and Estonians in Britain become British in form and/or in substance? This book will attempt to answer these questions, by charting the life histories of Latvians, Lithuanians and Estonians in Britain, focusing on both individual lives and community developments.

In the 1950's, several studies examined the progress of the EVWs in Britain. Articles by Elizabeth Stadulis and Maud Bülbring in *Population Studies* in the early 1950s, focused on the EVWs' first years in Britain. In 1958, a former civil servant involved in the planning of the schemes, J A Tannahill, detailed the mechanics of the labour schemes and the evolution of the EVW communities.[8] However, none of these studies examined the different EVW nationalities in any depth. Aside from a chapter on Latvians in Bedford in John Brown's *The Un-Melting Pot: An English Town and its Immigrants* (1970)[9], and reference to the Baltic communities in a few general works, the presence of Latvians, Lithuanians and Estonians in Britain was neglected until very recently, certainly in English language academic works. Work was carried out on some of the more numerous EVW nationalities, most notably Poles[10], and more latterly the Ukrainians[11]. There have also been some in-depth studies of immigrants in individual cities, which have included reference to some of the EVW nationalities. Brown's study of immigrants in Bedford in 1970, was supplemented by a 1982 study by Jeffcoate and Mayor, *Bedford: Portrait of a Multi-Ethnic Town*, and a 1985 Open University textbook about immigrants in Bedford - *Migration and*

Settlement.[12] Sheila Patterson conducted research into immigrants in Croydon in 1968, focusing on the process of industrial absorption.[13] In the 1980's, a large scale oral history project carried out by the Bradford Heritage Recording Unit collected the life stories of hundreds of Bradford's European immigrants, including among others Italians, Ukrainians and a few members of Bradford's Latvian, Lithuanian and Estonian communities. Two edited volumes, *The Peopling of London* (1993) and *London: The Promised Land?* (1997) presented studies of some of London's diverse communities.[14] However, in these city-specific studies and most general studies on immigration to Britain, Britain's post-war Latvian, Lithuanian and Estonian communities were paid scant attention during this period.

An important point worth mentioning in relation to the neglect of the EVW schemes is the fact that many of the Public Records relating to the schemes were only opened in the 1990's. Second, the arrival of thousands of immigrants from the Caribbean and Indian Sub-Continent from the 1950's onwards, beginning with the docking of Empire Windrush at Tilbury Docks, near London in June 1948, has tended to mask the presence of white European immigrants. In contrast to the Baltic and other European nationalities, these groups were highly visible and settled in far greater numbers. Throughout the 1960's and 1970's, the integration of the post-colonial newcomers was a priority of government immigration policy. As this book will show, a majority of the Baltic DPs settled in quickly, learnt English and rapidly became fairly inconspicuous. As a result, by the time of the large-scale arrival of immigrants from Britain's former colonies in the 1960's, the Baltic communities in Britain were barely distinguishable from the local population, marked out only by names, accents, occasional political demonstrations and the physical presence of community social clubs and churches.

During this period, academic literature tended to focus on black and Asian newcomers, to the neglect of earlier groups. Indeed, the neglect of the post-war 'British' Baltic communities in academic literature on immigration formed part of one of the chief characteristics of immigration history in Britain in the first few decades after 1945. Until very recently, immigration history, which in any case has a relatively young history in Britain, paid scant attention to white immigrant groups, perhaps with the exception of the Jewish and Irish populations of Britain.[15] During the 1960's and early 1970's, most studies of immigration to Great Britain concentrated on the more numerous and visible, newcomers from the Caribbean and Indian sub-continent.[16]

However, since the mid-1970's a steady stream of publications appeared covering previously neglected white immigrant communities such as the Germans and Italians.[17] Research was also begun on groups such as the Lithuanian immigrants of the late-nineteenth and early twentieth century, who had fled to Britain to escape persecution from the Tsarist State, or to seek a higher standard of living.[18] Although Indo-Pakistani and West Indian immigration into Britain initially led to a neglect of earlier immigrants and minorities, in later years, it acted as a stimulus to the study of these communities. General histories of immigration to Britain reflected these new trends, and have highlighted continuing gaps. *Race in Britain*, edited by Charles Husband in 1982 revealed the range and diversity of immigration to Britain.[19] A chapter by Tony Rees, 'Immigration policies in the United Kingdom' noted the significance of the EVW schemes within British immigration history.[20] Colin Holmes's *John Bull's Island* (1988) integrated new knowledge about neglected immigrant groups into a general history of immigration into Britain for the first time.[21] In *John Bull's Island*, Holmes was keen to direct attention to neglected groups. Writing about post-1945 immigration, Holmes wrote that, 'Some groups which arrived in Britain after 1945 have been totally or almost completely overlooked'. In contrast, 'a mountain of information has accumulated on those immigrants who arrived from the Caribbean and the Indian sub-content. But this concentration of effort has tended to mask the arrival of other sizeable groups.'[22] In 1994, Panikos Panayi wrote what he described as 'only the fourth general history of immigrants in Britain over any length of time' - *Immigration, ethnicity and racism in Britain, 1815-1945*.[23] Like Holmes, Panayi noted the areas of neglect: 'The history of other minorities, such as Poles, Greeks and Lithuanians, has received patchy attention, while some groups have had virtually no work carried out upon them at all...'[24] Writing in 1996, Marcus Banks agreed with Holmes' and Panayi's assessment. Drawing comparison with the volume of research about 'Blacks' and 'Asians', Banks wrote that 'while large numbers of Poles and other east-central Europeans settled in Britain during and after the Second World War, joining the longer-established Irish and Italian populations, they have been the subject of less academic attention'.[25]

Undoubtedly, the small size of the Baltic communities in Britain in comparison to other ethnic groups, their geographical dispersion and relative invisibility, were important factors in their marginalization in studies of immigration. The existence of the Soviet Union also concealed the Baltic countries from the attention of the Western public and in turn promoted ignorance and neglect of the Baltic communities in Britain.

A number of in-depth studies of the Baltic communities in Great Britain *have* been carried out by the communities themselves, but although a few of these studies are written in English or have English summaries, in most cases, they are written in the homeland language.[26] Furthermore, a majority of the studies focus on the history of local communities, cultural activities and the achievements of individuals, and present little discussion of experiences of settlement or shifts in cultures and identities.[27]

The neglect of certain areas of study has also been a characteristic of academic studies of immigration. In 1994, Panayi drew attention to the 'concentration upon particular themes within British immigration history, to the exclusion of others.' In Panayi's view, 'the history of ethnicity, of the lives of the immigrants, their social institutions, churches and clubs has tended to be ignored.'[28] Work tended to concentrate on the migration process, government policy and the early years of settlement. Because a majority of Britain's immigrants have settled since the end of the Second World War, the possibility to examine experiences of settlement throughout the life course has only recently arisen.

In the 1980's and 1990's, there was a sustained effort to re-address Britain's lost immigration history, and since Panayi's comments in 1994, research into the lives of immigrants flourished. The latter trend was due partly to a transformation in research methodologies, which opened up new areas of investigation. Nor was the writing of immigration histories in Britain during this period was not the sole concern of historians. Sociologists, anthropologists and geographers all engaged in immigration research, and all disciplines including history, benefited from an increasing interdisciplinarity. In many ways, historians were rather late in exploiting the opportunities offered by social science. Studies of immigration today now embrace a wide range of approaches and methods, aided by interdisciplinary research centres which utilise the best approaches and methodologies different disciplines have to offer.

During the 1990s, historians increasingly embraced oral history as a method and approach to study immigrant groups, who might otherwise have been neglected due to a lack of sources. The use of oral history also led to changes in areas of investigation. Indeed, oral history became one of the principal methods adopted among historians, sociologists and geographers alike, to research immigrant lives. Oral history encompasses a variety of methods including the semi-structured interview, biographical interviewing and reminiscence. In recent years, oral history has also come to define a particular approach within the field of qualitative research. Oral history is not a new phenomenon. As Paul Thompson, a key figure in Britain's oral history movement pointed out, 'oral history' is simply a new title given to the interview method which has been used by social investigators for many decades: 'Historians have themselves also used interview material freely, not only in biography, but when printed in classic sources such as Henry Mayhew's London Labour and the London Poor, or the work of Booth and Rowtree'.[29] Neither is its use in immigration research particularly novel. One of the most famous early studies of immigration, using the oral history method was Thomas and Znaniecki's, *The Polish Peasant in Europe and America: monograph of an Immigrant Group*[30]. In Great Britain, oral history experienced a resurgence in 1960's and has flourished ever since. The use of oral history reflected trends towards the study of history from the bottom up, as opposed to the more traditional top down approach. According to Green and Troup, its popularity derived from a new generation of historians steeped in the politics of the New Left, civil rights and feminism:

> These university researchers, drawn from a much broader segment of the population than had been the case previously, wanted to include the experiences of marginalized or social groups. Oral history was perceived as a means to empower women, the working class and ethnic minorities, allowing them to speak for themselves.[31]

Oral history is now one of the most popular methods of data collection among younger historians researching twentieth century history, and was included in a reader of twentieth century history and theory as one of 12 major 'houses of history' in Britain in the twentieth century.[32] Yet resistance from conventional historians continues. In 1985, Eric Hobsbawm described oral history as 'a remarkably slippery medium for preserving facts'.[33] The criticisms of many historians, prompted a phase of self-reflection and re-assessment among oral historians, who were eager to justify it as a reliable and valid empirical method. This situation led to developments in the methods and approaches adopted by oral historians. Until the 1970's, oral testimonies were approached in a very similar way to documentary sources and were used to supply factual evidence, as well as descriptive and explanatory detail. This approach was defined by Roper as 'oral history in the reconstructive mode'.[34] Paul Thompson noted in the 1970's that the major strength of oral history lay in the 'particular facts and detailed accounts of everyday events'.[35] However, during the 1980's, attempts to establish empirical legitimacy and to stave off criticism from more conventional quarters, led to a change of direction, which Roper describes as 'oral history in the interpretive mode'.[36] Interpretive oral history focused on the use of oral testimonies as a source for analysing the subjectivity of individual memories, and for understanding 'the hidden, and often unconscious, structures which inform narratives of the past'.[37] Allied to this approach and informed by recent developments within the social sciences, reflexivity also has a central place in interpretive oral history.

However, over the last two decades, some oral historians have criticised the emphasis on subjectivity and reflexivity. There have been concerns among some oral historians, that by exposing its perceived weakness – the subjectivity of memory, oral historians have done themselves a disservice. There has also been criticism that the abundance of studies about reflexivity and subjectivity has been to the neglect of the writing of history. Thompson argues that there has been 'much more discussion' of the bias in the interview method 'than of the bias similarly inherent in all written documentation'.[38] Despite a growing awareness of subjectivity in all historical sources, retrospective and contemporary, suspicion of oral history, as opposed to newspaper reports or private letters for example, remains. In some ways, by over-emphasising reflexivity and the place of the researcher in the interview, oral history is relegating its initial purpose, which was to place the voice of the subject centre-stage. Green and Troup also argue that oral historians may lose sight of the active agency of individuals with the current stress on 'unconscious cultural norms and imaginative complexes in structuring memories of the past'.[39] Of course, psychologists, sociologists, philosophers and historians approach oral history with different goals in mind. While psychologists may be more interested in using oral history to learn about memory, most historians are concerned with writing history, and in practice, combine both reconstructivist and interpretivist approaches, albeit giving priority to one or the other.

The study of immigration has been one of the key areas of research among oral historians. The interest of oral historians in migrant groups, reflects their concern to highlight the undocumented histories of marginalised or oppressed social groups. Thompson was of the opinion in the late 1970's that the history of immigrant groups was 'mainly documented only from outside as a social problem' and that an 'approach from the inside… is certain to become more important in Britain'.[40] The collection of life stories of immigrants in Bradford, undertaken in the 1980's was one of the first in-depth oral history studies of migrants in Britain. The range of papers presented at the 1998 Annual conference of the Oral History Society *Moving On: Testimonies of Migration* revealed the extent of use of oral history to study the migrant experience across a range of disciplines. Papers ranged from studies of Vietnamese refugees in the UK, to Greek-Cypriot women in the UK and London Transport's West Indian workforce. The popularity of the oral history method forms part of the current trend of the predominance of qualitative methods to study immigrant groups, among all disciplines. Sociological and psychological studies of immigration have moved away from positivist snapshots in time, which focused on the variables affecting the 'adjustment' or 'assimilation' of immigrants. Most studies of immigration now adopt qualitative approaches to understand the complexity of individual immigrant experiences and adopt a range of methods and approaches, including biographical and life history methods and post-colonial, post-modern and feminist approaches.

The popularity of oral history and the growth of interdisciplinarity engendered a wealth of historical studies about the lives and experiences of immigrants in Britain. Previously concerned primarily with the actual migration movement itself, or the mechanics of immigration policy, immigration historians now examine a range of subjects, including the social and cultural experiences of immigrants. Popular areas for consideration in recent years are the realms of identity and cultural adaptation.

Oral history has not only enabled shifts in the areas of investigation, it has also brought neglected nationalities to the fore, including Britain's East European nationalities. Other developments have also highlighted the presence of East Europeans in Britain. First, the collapse of the Soviet Union in 1990-91 has 'revived and strengthened nationalist aspirations in that part of the world and rekindled interest in Britain in the fate and existence of those "East European" refugees who came to Britain in the aftermath of war'.[41] Another factor which highlighted the presence of East Europeans in Britain, was the introduction of the War Crimes Act in 1991, which allowed 'for prosecution for murders in German-occupied territories before 1945 even if the accused were not British citizens at the time of the alleged offences'.[42] As Kay and Miles suggest, 'despite having been politically screened, the EVW recruitment scheme was one route through which possible was criminals could have entered Britain'.[43] Some of the EVWs in Britain, including Latvians, Lithuanians and Estonians were recruited into the German military during the Second World War[44], and although most of the recruits were front line troops, it has been argued that a small percentage of Latvians, Lithuanians and Estonians may have been involved in the murder of Jews.[45] Furthermore, it has been claimed that a few such war criminals may have slipped through the British Government's recruiting procedures for the EVW schemes and found their way into Britain. These arguments have been outlined by David Cesarani and Tom Bower.[46] Having previously discharged themselves of any obligations vis-à-vis the surrender or deportation of suspected war criminal, the 1991 Act marked an about turn in government policy. Lists of suspected war criminals were drawn up, and several attempts to bring sentence drew widespread media attention. In 1999, the first full trial of a suspected war criminal took place, and 78 year old Anthony Sawoniuk was found guilty of murdering Jews while serving as a police officer in Nazi-occupied Belarus. He was given a life sentence. It is now unlikely that any further trials will be held, due to insufficient supporting evidence, but the damage to Britain's EVW communities has already been done. Despite the fact that it has been conclusively shown that only a handful of war criminals are likely to be resident in Britain, the War Crimes Act has brought unwarranted and negative attention to Britain's EVW communities. In December 1999, the issue resurfaced when Konrad Kalejs, a suspected war criminal and Australian citizen was found to be living in Britain, after being deported from America and Canada. Jewish groups called for charges to be brought against Kalejs, who was alleged to have been a member of the Arajs Kommando, which carried out atrocities during the Second World War. News bulletins showed Kalejs staying at the Latvian retirement home, Catthorpe Manor, which a news story in *The Times* described as having 'a reputation for receiving its countrymen with open arms'. According to *The Times*, 'Konrad Kalejs was no exception'.[47] The attention given to the Kalejs story by the media showed the extent to which the war crimes issue remains alive among the public and media in Britain, Jewish groups globally and other western societies who received DPs at the end of the war.

Another recent trend within the field of immigration studies, which has influenced this project, has been the growth of interest in the related concepts of diaspora, globalization and transnationalism.[48] Within the social sciences, the diverse changes to the immigrant experience brought about by globalisation have promoted research into the arguably modern phenomenon of transnationalism, and the concept of diaspora has also recently received renewed attention. These issues have been particularly pertinent in the case of East Europeans abroad, who since the collapse of the Soviet Union, have been able to return to and travel to the homeland without any restrictions. Freedom to return to the homeland has in many cases brought questions such *as Where is home?* to the forefront. These issues apply to diverse nationalities such as Poles, Bosnians and Ukrainians, as well as Latvians, Lithuanians and Estonians.

Since this research was completed in the late 1990s, several key works relating to the history of Latvians, Lithuanians and Estonians in Britain have been published, most notably books by Thomas Lane and Linda McDowell.[49] I also wrote a journal article outlining the findings of some of this research published in 2006.[50] This book will contribute to this growing body of work. It is unique in that it uses a life history approach to track the transformation of identities and cultures through the journeys of migration and settlement, and from the inter-war period of Baltic independence, through the Soviet period, and right up until the re-declarations of independence in 1991 and beyond.

TEMINOLOGY AND THEORETICAL QUESTIONS

The research question: 'To what extent did Latvians, Lithuanians and Estonians in Britain assimilate?' appears outdated in the context of contemporary terminology. Indeed, the term 'assimilation' has become largely extinct among immigration specialists today. However, it formed a central part of immigration discourse among British Government officials in the 1940's, particularly in relation to the EVW schemes, so it is fitting to examine whether or not the Government's aims were achieved. An important aspect of this book will therefore be to assess the evolution of the Baltic communities in Britain from the British Government's perspective of assimilation in the 1940's. However, in assessing the extent to which the Baltic EVWs 'became British', the book will also analyse the development of the Baltic communities in the context of more recent immigration discourses favoured by both the British Government and immigration specialists, since it was not long before the government and academics became aware of the flaws and limitations of the assimilation concept as it stood in the 1940's. Thus, the question of whether or not the Balts assimilated will be supplemented by discussion of their development in relation to discourses about integration and multiculturalism. Other theories of immigrant adaptation will also be adopted to aid an understanding of the development of cultures and identities among the Baltic communities in Britain.

As the reader will be aware, theories and terminology's relating to the immigrant's encounter with the receiving society are voluminous and complex. As Van Hear noted, 'Problems of terminology are immediately encountered...'[51] In 1978, Holmes warned historians, 'Contemporary social science has, of course, produced a plethora of concepts in the field of immigrant and minority studies which reflect a variety of ideological viewpoints. But abundance can spell danger and the historian who wishes to consider these findings needs a discriminating eye…'[52] Since then however, the need for vigilance has remained. John Rex stressed that such problems are particularly great for those who engage in empirical work using these terms. Rex stated that, 'Those, like the present author, who actually do empirical work on questions of ethnicity and nationalism find that many of the concepts which are used here, very unclear, even though irritatingly close to those which they themselves must use, and also that the highly general conclusions to which they lead are at odds with empirical reality'.[53] One of the main problems is that while some writers insist 'on the strict definition of some term, and yet…other writers…are happy to let the term indicate a broad semantic range'.[54] Historians in particular have been criticised for their frequent use of terms without proper definition or thought.[55]

When this study first began, it was a study of ethnic identity among the Baltic communities in Britain. The original ESRC application read: *Ethnic Identity among Balts in Britain since 1945*. However, it soon became clear that the problems relating to the use of the term ethnic identity were immense, and that its use was hampering the research, and restricting what was intended as a primarily inductive study. Although I had a research question to answer, rather than test a hypothesis, the assumptions relating to the term ethnic identity meant that by using it, I was from the outset accepting various presuppositions about the evolution of immigrant communities. There have been many criticisms of the term ethnic identity. For example, post-colonial theorists suggest that the use of the term ethnic identity reflects the writing of the immigration histories by dominant nationalities, and as a result the term is used to focus primarily on the immigrant/receiving society relationship, to the neglect of immigrant/homeland relations. The latter relationship has been one of the areas of investigation of the emerging field of diaspora studies, which flourished over the course of this research project[56]. As this research project progressed, I became interested in the potential of the term diasporic identity, as a term which, I believed, could aid an understanding of the identities of exiled groups such as Latvians Lithuanians and Estonians. However, again it became obvious that the adoption of this term was leading to a study which was in effect testing a theory using empirical evidence, rather than allowing theories to develop from the empirical evidence at a later stage. At a fairly late stage in the research process, I decided to abandon these terms and opt for a broader inductive study of the Baltic communities, from which theories or terms could later be tested, if appropriate.

This type of manoeuvring is fairly typical in a qualitative research project, one of the characteristics of which is a non-linear path.

The stages of research design, fieldwork, analysis and writing-up are blurred and inform each other during the course of the project. Neuman described this as a 'cyclical research path', which 'makes successive passes through steps, sometimes moving backward and sideways before moving on'.[57]

Although the rejection of ethnic identity and diasporic identity as terms to guide the research led to an inductive study, relatively free from loaded and disputed terminology, the complete abandonment of terms has not been possible. I found that in discussing the settlement experiences of Latvians, Lithuanians and Estonians in Britain, terms were needed in order to describe these experiences. For example, even the use of the term 'adaptation' carries many meanings and is associated with certain discourses. Likewise 'adjustment', 'integration', or 'identity'. So it is necessary to describe how I have used these terms, and to provide definitions where appropriate here, although a full glossary of all the terms used in the book is provided at the back of the book.

The use of the term 'assimilation' in this study refers primarily to the British Government's understanding of the term in the 1940's. At that time, assimilation referred to the straight-line process whereby one ethnic group (usually a minority group) merges into another (usually the dominant group). Milda Danys noted that: 'Assimilation is a complex affair; one may assimilate economically or psychologically or culturally'.[58] In discussing assimilation, the British Government was referring primarily to the merging of cultures and identities; their aim was that the Baltic EVWs would eventually, not only act like the British, they would ultimately also feel British. Assimilation encompassed every sphere, including work, relations with the British public and private life. This book will address the question of whether or not the Baltic refugees assimilated culturally and whether or not they came to feel and/or became British, i.e. in the sense of their identities, cultures and nationalities. The questions will be assessed from the perspectives of the refugees themselves, the British Government and the British population. From the 1950's onwards, Britain's growing experience of immigration on a large-scale, primarily migrants from the Indian Sub-Continent, Africa and the Caribbean, led to an increasing sophistication in assimilation theories, as the complexity of the immigrant experience became clear. Whereas previously, the process of assimilation was viewed as primarily one-way, with the task of adaptation falling largely on the immigrant's shoulders, during the 1960's, assimilation became increasingly regarded as a two-way process. In 1968, Patterson wrote that: 'There is still no general agreement on the definition of the term assimilation'. However, her definition of the term reflected current thinking:

> Here it [assimilation] is used to denote complete adaptation by the incoming individual or groups and complete acceptance by the receiving society. The process is a reciprocal one, in that the receiving society may move some way towards the newcomers, but the main effort of adaptation falls on the latter, particularly in such a relatively homogenous and stable society as Britain.[59]

'Absorption' was a related term adopted by the British Government which in its general sense, referred to the overall absorption of immigrants in the wider society. The government viewed absorption as the process through which assimilation would be reached. However, it was also an end product. Like assimilation, the term absorption came to define a two-way process. For example, Sheila Patterson used the term 'industrial absorption' (one aspect of the wider absorption process) in 1968 to refer to the process of adaptation by the immigrant and acceptance by industry.[60]

I have used the term 'adjustment' in a broad sense, to refer to the response of the immigrant upon meeting with the receiving society, and how he or she 'adjusts' to the new country of residence. In the post-war years, the term adjustment generally meant adjustment towards assimilation into the 'host' society, although in later years it was used to refer to the process towards integration. Like assimilation, adjustment occurred in many spheres – for example, psychological or cultural. Adaptation has similarities with the term 'adjustment', and denotes the process through which the immigrant changes his or her way of living and culture as a result of living in a new country.[61]

The use of the terms 'acculturation', and 'integration' have been drawn from a theoretical study of refugee adaptation by Berry: 'Acculturation and Adaptation in a New Society' (*International Migration*, 1992)[62], which Van Hear has described as 'a useful framework for considering the encounter between minority groups (including migrants) and a larger society'.[63] Berry defines acculturation as 'culture change that results from continuous, first-hand contact between two distinct cultural groups'. Further 'while changes to both groups are implied in the definition, most changes in fact occur in the non-dominant (society of settlement) group'.[64] In this book it is the changes to the non-dominant groups – the Latvians, Lithuanians and Estonians that I will focus upon. While acculturation can be seen as a process, integration, along with the other potential results of acculturation – assimilation, marginalisation and separation – is an end result. Using Berry's definition, integration implies both entering into British society and adopting traits of British culture, while at the same time, maintaining elements of the homeland culture and ethnic distinctiveness.[65]

While Berry's definition of integration reflects contemporary thinking, integration first superseded assimilation as the British Government's favoured goal in the mid-1960's, influenced by increasing evidence of racial discrimination towards Britain's black and Asian communities, and a rejection of assimilation by these communities, who felt that it left little room for cultural maintenance and expression. There was also a heightened awareness that Britain was not a homogenous society and that there were variations in British culture and national identity, if indeed, a British national identity existed at all. This led to the question of what immigrants were supposed to be assimilating into. In a frequently quoted speech delivered in 1966, Roy Jenkins, the then Home Secretary argued against the homogenising notion of assimilation, in favour of integration. In Jenkins' view, the latter should be regarded, not as a 'flattening process of assimilation but as equal opportunity, accompanied by cultural diversity, in an atmosphere of mutual trust'.[66] Like assimilation, the use of the term integration has undergone many metamorphoses over the years, and has been subjected to detailed debate and analysis among academics.

Since the 1970's, multiculturalism[67] has emerged as a term increasingly called upon in government debates and the media. Multiculturalism currently has many meanings and conveys a picture of society as a mosaic of diverse ethnic communities, each free to express their cultures and identities, and sharing equal opportunities with the dominant ethnic community. Although multiculturalism has not replaced the goal of integration, it has supplemented it, and has perhaps become a more popular term to describe the goal which purportedly underlines contemporary government policies towards Britain's diverse ethnic communities.

Although I have not adopted the term ethnic identity to guide the study, I have used the term in some instances, where I have believed that it will aid understanding. I have defined ethnic identity as identification as a member of an ethnic group, ethnic group being defined as a group with shared descent and culture. National identity is defined differently to ethnic identity, in that it refers not to identification as a member of an ethnic group, but identification as a member of a nation state or other form of national unit, as well as identification with national culture. Ethnic and national identity can be the same or different. For example, a French man or woman may have a French ethnic and national identity. However, a Chinese man or woman in

Britain, may have a Chinese ethnic identity, but a British national identity. National identity is often linked to citizenship and nationality[68]. National and ethnic identity are discussed in more detail in the Glossary of Terms at the end of the book.

Other terms used in this book include: culture, diaspora, diasporic identity, exile identity, ethnicity, racialization, receiving society and transnationalism, all of which are defined in the *Glossary of Terms* at the end of the book, and in many cases, explanations of these terms appear where they are used in the main body of the book.

HOW THE STUDY WAS CARRIED OUT: METHODS AND APPROACHES

The research questions have determined the approaches and methods adopted to carry out the study. The research is a qualitative, mixed method study, which focuses on explanation and process, over a period of time, in this case throughout the life course of the individual immigrant, and immigrant communities. The research draws upon historical and sociological methods and approaches, and has benefited from the growing interdisciplinary approaches in immigration research. Although this study seeks to present the diversity of experience, it does not aim to provide either a wholly representative account or cover the full range of life histories.

Although I have approached this study from a historian's perspective, the book is deeply rooted within the qualitative approach often associated exclusively within the social sciences, but which also embraces the work of many historians. Qualitative research is grounded in a philosophical tradition that is broadly interpretive, in that it is concerned with how the social world is interpreted, understood, experienced or produced. Qualitative research seeks to understand the complexity and diversity of human experience, from a subject-centred approach. The focus of qualitative research on explanation and process influences the methods adopted by qualitative researchers, who tend to use non-representative sampling techniques, such as theoretical or snowballing sampling, and a variety of subject-centred methods, including the semi-structured or unstructured interview, open-ended questionnaires, participant observation or ethnographic fieldwork. The historian who uses these methods, usually supplements them with documentary and other primary source materials where available.

The research has been informed by several philosophical approaches associated with qualitative research, and in particular immigration related research. These include postmodernism, postcolonialism and oral history related approaches. The study cannot be characterised by the use of any one particular philosophical perspective. Rather, several approaches have guided and influenced the methods adopted in the study, and the analysis of the sources. For example, post-modernism and oral history have influenced an awareness of the subjectivity of memory, while post-colonial theories have highlighted the racialization of immigration-related discourses. Oral history related approaches have also been utilised, for example, consideration of the role of the interviewer and the social context in shaping the interview, and of how in personal testimonies, the present, shapes interpretations of the past. These perspectives have supplemented those connected with more conventional historical research, for example, approaches relating to textual and documentary analysis.

The research has been carried out using mixed methods, including interviews, questionnaires, participant observation as well as the more traditional documentary and secondary source research, favoured by conventional historians.

The core method adopted for this project was the in-depth oral history interview, combining the life history and semi-structured thematic interview approach. There are several reasons for giving pre-eminence to the oral history method. The first is a practical motivation. A dearth of English language sources relating to the migration and settlement experiences of Latvians, Lithuanians and Estonians in Britain has prompted the need to *create* sources. The oral history interview is the most suitable method to produce sources, which investigate the settlement experiences of Baltic refugees in Britain. First, it highlights individual experience, the value of which is explained by Benmayor and Skotnes:

> Knowing something of the utter uniqueness of particular individual migrant experiences certainly enhances our generalizations about the group experience, but it also elicits humility about the adequacy of these generalizations and a realization that few actual lives fully conform to the master narratives.
>
> ...the individual experience is always richer, more contradictory, more paradoxical than that which we represent as the experience of the group.[69]

Postmodernist theories have rejected the validity of master narratives in history, and with subjectivity at its very core, the oral history interview is the perfect tool for exposing the complexity and fluidity of individual migrants' lives, which are impossible to model or homogenise. In addition to providing richly textured, often subjective, explanation and interpretation, the oral history interview can also supply factual biographical data and description. The data provided by the oral history interviews in this study have been subjected to both reconstructive and interpretive analyses. Although the aims of the study have required that pre-eminence be given to the former approach, the latter has not been neglected. The use of interpretive oral history approaches are particularly important in considering the testimonies of exile communities, like the Latvians, Lithuanian and Estonian communities in Britain, due to the tendency of these groups, to glorify and idealise the past. Interpretive approaches draw attention to how present interpretations of a childhood in the homeland have been shaped by subsequent experiences and the distortion of memory, and do not necessarily provide an accurate reconstruction of the past. Biographical data and interpretation are woven together within the book, as are reconstructive and interpretive analyses.

A particularly important aspect in the lives of migrants revealed by the oral history interview, is how 'social forces impact and shape individuals, and how individuals, in turn, respond, act, and produce change in the larger social arena'.[70] In particular, an oral history interview can explore and reveal how individuals make decisions, for example, the decision to migrate to Britain.

An oral history interview enables the subject to become centre stage and to focus on their areas of concern, rather than the researcher's agenda. Of course, the interviewee's responses are shaped by the interview questions, the relationship between the interviewer and respondent, and the context of the interview. However, many of these difficulties can be overcome by awareness, reflexivity and scrutiny, attributes which are vital for historical research utilising any type of source. More so than any other approach, the oral history interview enables interaction with, and the questioning of, the witness. Lummis explained: 'One precise advantage of oral evidence is that it is interactive and one is not left alone, as with documentary evidence, to divine its significance; the 'source' can reflect upon the content and offer interpretation as well as facts'.[71]

The life history approach considers the refugees' whole life, not just experiences since settlement. The use of the life history approach in this study has led to an equal weighting of pre and post-settlement experiences, including an examination of the childhood of the young refugees in the homeland. By giving weight to pre-migration experiences, this study is at variance with most histories of the immigrant experience, which pay scant attention to this period in the refugees' life. The study also differs from the type of sociological investigations of the immigrant experience, which slice through history at a particular point in time, and use primarily sociological variables as measuring and explanatory tools.

Finally, sometimes regarded as a hindrance to the creation of objective data, one of the benefits of the oral history interview is to reveal how the present shapes interpretations of the past. The oral history interview can also show how individuals continually 'construct and reconstruct understandings of themselves and their larger social circumstances'.[72] While the retrospective nature of the oral history interview can pose problems of analysis, there is considerable evidence to suggest that testimonies provided near the end of a life are more reliable and honest than those provided by younger respondents, or testimonies taken either during or shortly after the event or process, which is being researched. Yow noted that: 'Near the end of a life, there is a need to look at things as honestly as possible to make sense of experiences over a lifetime...'[73] Research also indicates that while memory is selective and sometimes faulty, the reminiscence process beginning in ones 40's and continuing throughout the rest of one's life, means that: 'Memories of childhood, adolescence, and early adulthood may be more easily recalled than those from middle and late years. If the event or situation was significant to the individual, it will likely be remembered in some detail, especially its associated feelings'.[74] However, as Yow stresses, 'the interpretation may reflect current circumstances and needs'.[75] Thompson agrees that the problem of memory loss is not 'nearly as serious as is often believed', and that: 'Memory loss is in fact concentrated during and immediately after the perception of an event'.[76] In his view: 'There are numerous old people who retain a remarkably full and accurate memory of their earlier years'.[77] Many oral historians have also suggested that retrospective evidence of the type used by conventional historians, such as newspaper articles, court hearings or published biographies, do not present any intrinsically different problems to oral history. Many of the problems associated with oral history and other sources can be overcome by awareness of their limitations and potential bias, and by using other sources wherever possible to achieve the greatest validity and reliability. In this study, many different sources have been used to supplement and act as a check on interview material. While it is impossible to verify the facts of individual life histories, taken together, the thirty interviews and supplementary sources can lead to an approximate understanding of what happened, and at the very least present an interpretation of what happened. As Yow suggests,

...there is never absolute certainty about any event, about any fact, no matter what sources are used. No single source or combination of them can ever give a picture of the total complexity of reality. We cannot reconstruct a past or present event in its entirety because the evidence is always fragmentary.[78]

The criticisms about oral history sources closely relate to debates about the objectivity or subjectivity of history, discussion of which is beyond the scope of this book. It is important to note, however, that it is not simply the methods, which separate oral historians and conventional historians, but more importantly their approaches to history.

GAINING PARTICIPANTS FOR THE STUDY

Approximately 30 Latvians, Lithuanians and Estonians were interviewed for this project[79]. Most of the interviewees resided in Northern regions of England, primarily Yorkshire, Lancashire, Nottinghamshire, Derbyshire and Leicestershire. Although most of the respondents lived in areas of high Baltic settlement, for example, Leeds, Bradford, Manchester and Nottingham, about half a dozen were chosen from areas of negligible or nil Baltic settlement. All of the respondents were first generation immigrants, apart from three second generation participants, and one who came to Britain as an EVW child dependant. The youngest first generation interview participant was born in 1933, and the eldest in 1910. It is important to note that the participants composed the younger section of the original population, since many of the older refugees have died.

Interviews were semi-structured and lasted between two and three hours. They were then transcribed and manually coded. Rather than presenting the full life histories of individuals, I have extrapolated themes, and provided biographical context where it would aid understanding. Although this approach has produced fragmented individual histories, this was the most suitable way to present the interview material in a way, which fulfilled the goal of this study, which was to provide an introductory overview. This research will act as a springboard for future studies, which could include, for example, the analysis of individual case histories.

Various methods were used to gain participants for the study. The most effective approach was to contact, and visit, the various Latvian, Lithuanian and Estonian clubs in Britain, where I met members of the three communities and handed out information packs about the project. In addition to securing the participation of many regular club attendees, a snowball effect occurred, where members passed on information to other Latvians, Lithuanians and Estonians in Britain, including some who were not active community participants. Another method by which several participants were recruited was through my own personal contacts. For example, one participant who was not an active member of the community was gained through a neighbour in Sheffield. Another method involved writing to people with common Latvian, Lithuanian and Estonian names, who were listed in the telephone directory in areas of high Baltic settlement. I also advertised in the Lithuanian newsletter, *LYNES*.

I distributed an information pack to all potential participants, which contained a short questionnaire and a question asking whether they were willing to participate in the study. I sent an additional questionnaire to all those who wished to participate, in which they provided more information about themselves, including questions about community participation, visits to the homeland, marital status and whether they were married to a member of the community. The questionnaire also asked questions about cultural maintenance and identity. Approximately 40 people returned the questionnaires and indicated a willingness to participate, from which I chose about 25 to interview[80]. In selecting interview participants, I did not employ any statistical sampling techniques since these would have been unsuitable for a small-scale study of this nature. Instead, I adopted a theoretical sampling frame, where I chose a range of participants, according to nationality, gender, age, area of residence, marital status, nationality of marital partner, level of community participation, cultural maintenance and responses to questions about identities. I was particularly keen to interview as many Latvians, Lithuanians and Estonians as possible who were not active community members, people who may have been isolated from communities, and those who did not maintain cultural traditions or strong Latvian, Lithuanian or Estonian homeland identities. I was aware that most other similar studies of East Europeans in Britain, recruited primarily active community participants, who represent only a small section of the overall population. In addition, practical factors were also taken into consideration, particularly the constraints of time and money. A limited travel budget meant that most of the participants resided in the North of England. This also meant that I could travel to the participant, interview them and return within the same day.

The two-part questionnaire distributed to potential participants, as a way of securing and choosing participants was also used to provide a demographic framework for the study, and background for the interviews. In addition to providing an overview of individuals within the communities, the questionnaires of interview participants were analysed in conjunction with interview transcripts, and responses to similar questions, asked in the questionnaire and the interview were compared. The questionnaires were also useful for providing an overview of the contemporary state of Baltic DPs in Britain, including for example, the number of return visits to the homeland, frequency of club participation, English language skills and the maintenance of cultural traditions.

Another research technique, which was also used in several ways, was participant observation. This was utilised not only as a means of gaining participants, but also to gain an insight into the communities in Britain. Attendance at clubs and community events was invaluable and provided many unforeseen benefits. I was able to talk to first, second and third generation community members, and to build up relationships with members of the communities. This approach was vital not only to secure participants, but also to gain their trust so that individuals felt able to talk freely with me about their experiences. Several in-depth interviews were carried out within clubs and other community establishments, but were not tape-recorded, as they were often spur of the moment. I attended several clubs frequently, since I believed it was more rewarding to build up relationships in a small number of clubs, rather than try to cover all the clubs in Britain. I attended the Latvian club in Leeds, the Estonian club in Bradford, and to a lesser extent the Lithuanian club in Manchester, on many occasions, as well as several other clubs once only, or on an irregular basis. In addition to the clubs, I also visited one of the Latvian retirement villages at Straumèni in Leicestershire, the Lithuanian Marian Fathers chapel in Nottingham, and the Lithuanian Church in London. Aspects of the participant observation process included attending a St John's night celebration at the Estonian club in Bradford and the commemoration of Deportation Day at the Manchester Lithuanian club, sampling the cuisine and alcoholic beverages of the homelands in many different contexts, taking Christmas presents from a Latvian in Britain to his brother in Riga, being shown old photographs, school reports and stamp collections, being escorted on a sightseeing tour of Riga by a Latvian from Leeds and seeing dance and choir groups perform. Through community participation, I gained a deep insight into community life.

Participant observation at the Lithuanian Club in Manchester

DOCUMENTARY SOURCES

Documentary sources also provided a key source of evidence for this project, particularly vis-à-vis government policy in relation to the EVW schemes. British Government files in the Public Record Office in London were a particularly importance source of material relating to British Government policy towards Baltic DPs in Europe and the EVW schemes, contained principally in Foreign Office and Ministry of Labour files. Altogether, 125 separate files were consulted. These also provided useful sources written by representatives of the Baltic refugee communities. Often, these were in the form of appeals, requesting the British Government to ameliorate the situation of DPs in the Camps, and to improve conditions for EVWs. Soviet propaganda material and evidence of Britain's shifting foreign relations and policy towards the Baltic States were also found in FO files. In addition, information about the first years of settlement within Britain, the development of community structures, government assimilation strategies and the reported progress of the EVWs were also found in PRO files. Other government documents consulted included Hansard and the 1988 report of the All-Party Parliamentary War Crimes Group.

The sources of the Baltic communities were also extremely important in this study. A range of community documents were used, including newspapers, newsletters, pamphlets, books, and private documents. A detailed personal memoir written an Estonian in Britain, provided a useful English language account of a childhood on Saaremaa island in Estonia.[81] Although most of the publications of the Baltic communities are written in the homeland language, there are some notable exceptions and a number of books have English summaries. The newsletter, *LYNES*, intended for second and third generation Lithuanians and written mainly in English was a key source of information about the Lithuanian community, particularly in relation to younger generations. I received many of these publications from individual members of the communities. The publications of the world-wide Baltic diaspora were also useful, including publications written in the DP Camps, and various community journals. I was able to carry out research in the Latvian library at Straumēni in Leicestershire, where I consulted a variety of rare and useful publications.

A range of secondary sources were consulted. In addition to those already mentioned earlier in the introduction, general British immigration histories, theories of immigration and refugee settlement, studies of the Baltic diasporas in other countries, novels about Baltic migrants and works examining aspects of the history of the Baltic States were utilised. Various unpublished theses and dissertations were consulted, and several important publications were purchased during fieldwork trips to the Baltic states, many of which are difficult to acquire elsewhere.

Several interviews carried out by Bradford Heritage Recording Unit with Latvians, Lithuanians and Estonians in the 1980's were another useful source of material, and provided a useful pre-independence perspective on the communities.[82]

Finally, I interviewed several returnees in the Baltic States in the summer of 1997, as part of a fieldwork visit to all three homelands. The principal aim of the visit was to collate information about returnees, and diaspora visiting the homeland. In addition, I believed that it was impossible to research the Baltic communities in Britain without visiting the homeland, and during the course of the research project I made three trips to Latvia, Lithuania and Estonia, spending in total, 10 weeks in these countries. I was particularly interested to research life and culture during the inter-war period, to gain a fuller understanding of the present-day Baltic States and the changes which occurred during the Soviet period. During these visits I interviewed returnees, arranged meetings with Latvians, Lithuanians and Estonians from Britain who were on visits to the homeland, met locals and academics, carried out research in museums, and travelled to many areas of the Baltic States, in both winter and summer. Latvian friends in Riga also provided useful insights into contemporary life in independent Latvia.

Throughout the research process, various ethical and legal issues were considered, centring primarily around issues of consent, confidentiality and anonymity. Interview participants signed a consent form, and where the respondent requested that their name was not given, I have used pseudonyms, or simply the phrase: 'A Latvian man', for example. I have also used other methods to protect confidentiality where this was requested such as changing the town of residence or using different names for quotes from the same person. In some instances and where consent has been given the respondents real name has been used although not in all cases.

I decided to examine Latvians, Lithuanians and Estonians together for several reasons. The first is that the British Government homogenised Latvians, Lithuanians and Estonians together under the single category 'Balts' in discourses relating to the EVW schemes. Under this label, Latvians, Lithuanians and Estonians were jointly prioritised under both Balt Cygnet and Westward Ho!, and were regarded to be of equally high assimilation potential. The term 'Balts' actually refers to the ancient tribes from whom Latvians and Lithuanians descended. In contrast, Estonians were descendants from Finno-Ugric peoples. In part, the government's tendency to homogenise these nationalities demonstrated a lack of understanding of the extent of cultural and historical differences. It also reflected a common Foreign Policy towards these three states. Some Latvians, Lithuanians *and* Estonians do refer to themselves in a collective sense as 'Balts', although this appears to be rare.[83] More common self-designated, collective tags are the 'Baltic peoples' or the 'Baltic nationalities'. A second motivation for studying Latvians, Lithuanians and Estonians together is that they have shared a common history in the twentieth century, and particularly as post-war diaspora. All three nations underwent similar patterns of change during this century. Following the collapse of the Tsarist Empire, all three nations declared independence. The period of independence lasted only twenty years, before all three suffered Russian invasions, followed by a German occupation, and finally a second Russian onslaught, which led to the imposition of Soviet rule and incorporation into the USSR for almost half a century. All three countries regained independence in 1990-91. Due to common histories during the Second World War, the diasporas also share common experiences of displacement and resettlement, although there were some quite significant differences which will be discussed in this book. For example, very few Lithuanian men participated in the German military machine during the Second World War, in comparison to Latvians and Estonians, while Estonian men were the most likely of all three nations to be conscripted into the Russian army. It must be stressed that the tendency to group together these three nationalities is a twentieth century phenomenon. Vardys noted that: 'The experiences of the three Baltic nations converged only in our century, primarily after 1918... Prior to 1918, their individual courses of development had differed considerable despite the fact that all three had been parts of the Tsarist empire'.[84] Milosz also pointed out that the concept of 'Baltic States' arose only in the 1920's 'after the formation of the three small independent states, which looked so alike on the map'.[85] Indeed, Latvia and Estonia only came into existence as independent nations in 1920, while Lithuania had enjoyed independent statehood in the middle ages. By examining the three nationalities together, this study will draw out the commonalties and the differences, particularly in relation to settlement experiences and adaptation to life in Britain, given the variations in culture and origins. Detailed discussion of the different histories and cultures of Latvia, Lithuania and Estonia will be provided in Chapter Two: *The Homeland*. A final consideration in the joint study of Latvians, Lithuanians and Estonians in Britain, is the absence of histories of these nationalities. Given the elderly age of the communities and their decreasing number, it made sense to research the histories of the three communities before it was too late. This research was also intended as a springboard for future research, possibly individual studies of Latvians, Lithuanians and Estonians. Inevitably, the study of three nationalities rather than one has meant that some areas have been examined in less depth than may otherwise have been.

PLAN OF THE BOOK

Chapter One provides an introductory overview of the history of Latvians, Lithuanians and Estonians in Great Britain prior to 1945. Thereafter, the format of the book reflects the life history approach to the study of the Baltic communities in Britain, and follows a chronological path outlining the major periods within the lives of Latvians, Lithuanians and Estonians in Britain. Each chapter corresponds to a phase in the life history of the refugees, and is split into thematic sections. Chapters Two to Five deal with the period prior to settlement while Chapters Six to Nine relate to post-settlement life.

Chapter Two: *The Homeland*, describes the refugees' childhood's in the homeland and the countries in which they grew up, focusing particularly on cultures and national identities. Chapter Three: *Displacement*, examines the uprooting of the refugees during the Second

World War, describing how and why the refugees were displaced. The years spent in the DP Camps in Europe will be analysed in Chapter Four: *The Displaced Persons' Camps*. It was in the camps that the diasporas were formed and where exile cultures and identities were developed. The recruitment of Baltic DPs for labour in Britain will be discussed in Chapter Five: *Recruitment*, in which both government and refugee perspectives on recruitment will be presented. Chapter Six: *The First Years in Britain*, begins with the journey to Britain, and examines the refugees' early experiences in Britain, their reception by locals and the labour market and the refugees' responses. Chapter Seven: *The 1950's* begins with the lifting of the labour controls in 1951, which led to large numbers of the original EVW population re-emigrating to countries of the New World. This chapter will discuss the evolution of the post-emigration communities, and the development of working and family lives. Although the Baltic EVWs began to settle into life in Great Britain during the 1950's, from then on the communities began to root themselves firmly in Great Britain. This process is the subject of Chapter Eight: *Rooting*, which analyses the evolution of the communities from 1960 to the late-1980's. Chapter Nine: *The Restoration of Homeland Independence* analyses the meaning and significance of the restoration of homeland independence for the Baltic communities in Britain. The conclusion ties all the strands together and summarises the changing identities of Latvians, Lithuanians and Estonians in Britain since 1945. A brief postscript at the end of the book provides an introduction to the more recent immigration of Latvians, Lithuanians and Estonians to Britain since 2000, and summarises areas for further research and comparison.

CHAPTER 1

A Brief History of Latvians, Lithuanians and Estonians in Britain before 1946

ALTHOUGH THIS BOOK IS PRIMARILY CONCERNED with the history of the Latvian, Lithuanian and Estonian migration to Great Britain after the Second World War, this chapter will provide a brief overview of Baltic migration to Britain before this date. In the late-nineteenth and early twentieth century, significant numbers of Latvians, Lithuanians and Estonians migrated to Great Britain, sometimes for political refuge, and sometimes, for the purpose of economic gain or educational improvement. In addition, there was also some migration during the period of independence from 1918-1940, and during the Second World War. Between 1918 and 1946, diplomatic representations were established in London and community structures began to appear.

The most significant migration occurred during the late-Tsarist period, when all three present-day Baltic nations were constituent provinces of the Russian Empire. The late Imperial era was a period when living standards were under pressure, and particularly after the assassination of Alexander II in 1881, repression of political activists and intellectuals was widespread. In the late nineteenth century, Latvians, Lithuanians and Estonians set about constructing national identities in earnest, unifying and cementing national languages, and resurrecting ancient traditions. It was during this period when Russification policies were most vigorously pursued by the Tsarist State, and when Jews, of whom there were significant numbers in the Baltic provinces, particularly in Lithuania, were the main focus of repressive measures.

As a result, there were several types of migrants to Britain during this period: Latvians, Lithuanians and Estonians who migrated to gain a better standard of living; political refugees fleeing Tsarist oppression; and finally, Jewish refugees, who migrated to Britain in order to escape repression. These refugees and migrants did not enter Britain in one or two waves, nor was their migration at all organised. Rather a slow trickle of refugees entered Britain over the course of half a century until the First World War. Of the three nationalities, by far the largest numerically, were the Lithuanians, the reasons for which will be explained below.

The date of the arrival in Britain of the very first immigrant from Latvia, Lithuania or Estonia is not known. Indeed, very little is known about Latvian or Estonian immigration before 1918.[86] This contrasts with an ever-growing body of knowledge about Lithuanian migrants to Britain during the late-Tsarist period.

Latvian immigration to Britain during this period is not mentioned in any of the major histories of immigration to Britain.[87] *Latviešu Lielbritanijā*, a history of Latvians in Britain written by members of the British Latvian community, claims that the first sign of Latvians in Great Britain was the publication in London in 1899, of the first Latvian language monthly in Europe, *Latviešu Strādnieks* (The Latvian Worker).[88] It is likely that some Latvians migrated to Britain during the late nineteenth century, in order to seek better living conditions. Some intellectuals and political activists came to this country possibly to escape repression; certainly, following the 1905 Revolution in the Russian Empire, some Latvian revolutionaries, social democrats and nationalists sought refuge in Britain.[89] In the years up to the First World War, a number of Latvian sailors were also temporarily resident in British ports, particularly Cardiff and Liverpool. According to Jānis Andrups, the total number of all the above groups was never more than a few hundred.[90]

Even less is known about Estonians in Great Britain before 1918.[91] They were probably the least numerous of the three populations during this period, since many refugees and economic migrants were attracted to Scandinavian countries.

Immigration of Estonians to Britain up to the First World War 'appears to have consisted of individual merchant navy sailors and artisans in search of better working conditions'.[92] For example, one of Nigol Hindo's relations, a seaman in his youth, settled in Britain in 1850.[93] One of Heino Poopuu's neighbours from Saaremaa island in Estonia had an uncle, August Kreeps, a merchant navy sailor, who settled in Newcastle towards the end of the nineteenth century. Kreeps perished when his ship was torpedoed in 1917, but several of his descendants still live in the Newcastle area.[94]

According to Hindo, 12 Estonian tailors worked in London before the First World War, although none achieved 'any outstanding success in their craft.'[95] Hindo lists about 20 craftsmen in total, of different trades, who migrated to Britain before the First World War. [96] Hindo also notes two Estonians in London who achieved prominence during this period. One was Georg Hackenschmidt, a world class wrestler and weightlifter who settled in London in 1903. The other, a Mr Rogenhagen, a wealthy London businessman was born in Tallinn, and 'although he had lived in Britain for many years and became a naturalised British subject, still considered himself to be an Estonian'.[97]

Poopuu notes that 'Estonia…was severely affected by the 1905 revolution and its bloody aftermath, but there is no mention of it in Hindo's book'.[98] In *Estonia and the Estonians* (1987), Toivo Raun stated that, 'On December 10 [1905] martial law was declared in Tallinn and Harjumaa and much of the committee of the RSDWP as well as a large number of Estonian intellectuals were arrested. Others, Päts and Teemant fled to Finland and later to Western Europe.'[99] However, as Poopuu notes, 'whether any of the leaders of the reform movements, or some of the participants in the widespread uprising in the countryside that followed these arrests reached Britain, is not stated.'[100]

In comparison to the histories of Latvians and Estonians in Britain, the immigration of Lithuanians to Britain, particularly during the late Tsarist period has been documented to a far greater degree. This is partly due to the larger numbers of Lithuanians involved in the process, and also because of the relatively concentrated patterns of settlement.

According to a history of Lithuanians in Bradford written by members of the Bradford Lithuanian Club 'Vytis', 'The precise date of the arrival of the first Lithuanian immigrant in Great Britain….is not known.'[101] The first sizeable group of Lithuanians purported to have arrived on British shores, were POW's from the Crimean War, who settled in Britain in the 1860's[102] Other immigrants from Lithuania first began arriving in Britain shortly afterwards, probably some time after 1868, although here again, precise dates and figures are not known, and evidence verifying these accounts has yet to be found.[103] Recent research undertaken by a second generation Lithuanian in Britain, suggests that in Scotland, where many of the emigrants headed, 'although it is possible that an odd Lithuanian could have been in Scotland prior to 1881, the trickle that became a flood occurred during the following decade'.[104] The twenty-five year period from 1880 to 1914 witnessed the greatest number of arrivals to Britain. Census data makes the task of estimating numbers of Lithuanians in Britain extremely difficult as place of birth is noted as Poland, Russia or Russian Poland.[105] Statistical accounts of Lithuanians in Scotland show that Poles and Lithuanians were combined 'without giving any idea of the numbers or ratio of one to another, probably because the Lithuanians were all called and classed as Poles'.[106]

During the last three decades of the century, significant numbers of Lithuanians came to Britain searching for freedom and work.[107] The majority of these were on their way to the United States, stopping off temporarily in Britain to work and save money for the Atlantic crossing. Many ended up staying. These Lithuanians settled in different areas of Great Britain, with a large number in Scotland, particularly in Lanarkshire. Thanks to the work of J White, Murdoch Rodgers and Kenneth Lunn, there is now a significant reservoir of knowledge about Scottish Lithuanians, particularly in relation to employment patterns, trade union activity, the reaction of local communities and the response of Lithuanian immigrants to the Russian Revolution.[108] In 1998, the publication of *The Lithuanians in Scotland* written by a Scottish Lithuanian, and drawing upon extensive research and interviews, contributed to this growing knowledge.[109] Indeed, Lithuanian immigration to Scotland in this period is the most well-known aspect of Baltic migration to Britain, apart from the post-war wave. It has been estimated that as many as 7,000 Lithuanians may have resided in Scotland at the beginning of the twentieth century,[110] and Scotland quickly became the 'chief centre of Lithuanian cultural and intellectual life in Britain' during this period.[111] Lithuanians came to Scotland in particularly large numbers due to an attraction to the Scottish coalfield, which offered plentiful labour. A chain effect can also be discerned, where Lithuanians finding work reported back to their home village and relatives, who would then follow.

The Lithuanians who migrated to Scotland were Catholics who originated predominately from the peasant class in Lithuania, and soon became established members of the industrial working classes. Scottish Lithuanians set up political bodies, including a branch of the Lithuanian Social Democratic Party set up in 1903, and the Lithuanian Working Women's Association.[112]

In his article, 'Reactions to Lithuanian and Polish Immigrants in the Lanarkshire Coalfield', Kenneth Lunn explored the often hostile reactions of fellow workers in the coalfields to the Lithuanians.[113] Lunn

44

stressed the significance of the Lithuanian's peasant background. The emancipation of the serfs in 1865 had created a large landless proletariat. Many of those who migrated to Scotland were peasants or agricultural labourers, and most had never seen a mine before. Many came to the coalmines via labouring work in iron and steel. For example, at Glengarnock in Ayrshire, Lithuanians began work as 'spare furnacemen', and some then went into the mining industry in the area.[114] In many cases, the reactions of fellow workers were initially negative. In the first place, Lithuanians were regarded as a threat to employment and wage levels. They were also viewed as a danger to their fellow workers, since they were unskilled, and without fluency in English, and as a consequence, it was feared that the Lithuanians might not be able to communicate or respond in a situation of danger. However, as Lunn noted, much of the reaction from locals was merely of a curious nature, and once initial difficulties had been overcome in the workplace, Lithuanians were generally quickly accepted by the trade unions.[115]

Rodgers also researched the Scottish Lithuanian community in some depth, focusing particularly on the influence of Lithuanian political émigrés on the community and political developments.[116] Rodgers stressed the initial local hostility to the Lithuanians. In 1887, the Ayrshire Miner's Union demanded their removal on the grounds that 'their presence is a menace to the health and morality of the place and is, besides, being used to reduce the already too low wages earned by workmen'.[117] Local newspapers carried reports of the Lithuanians' 'reckless, drunken behaviour'.[118] *The Bellshill Speaker* reported in a long article on 20 July 1900 that the Lithuanians were a 'most barbarous people and [in this district] we seem to have the very scum of their nation'.[119]

Rodgers outlined the different newspapers and political organisations of the community. *Vaidelytė*(Vestal) was the first Lithuanian newspaper to be published in Britain, appearing in Glasgow in 1899.[120] Although the newspaper folded after five issues, a second paper *Laikas* (Time) was published in Scotland in 1905.[121]

After outlining the success of various Lithuanian political organisations in Scotland, Rodgers discussed the events of 1917, which brought about 'the end of a generation-long period when politics was never far from the centre of community life'.[122] The full and active part played by Lithuanians in both trade unions and socialist organisations was brought to an end by the Anglo-Russian Military Convention signed on 16 July 1917. Under the terms of the convention, all Russian males between 18 and 41 years in Britain were faced with either deportation for military service in Russia or conscription into the British army. The convention split the community and the effect was as Rodgers states to wipe 'out the wide variety of political and social organisations that were such a feature of community life'.[123] The majority opted to return to Russia. The dependants of those who chose this option were regarded as Bolshevik sympathisers and as a permanent financial liability and were repatriated in February and March 1920. In total about 600 women and children were sent back.[124]

Far less is known about Lithuanians in other parts of Britain during this period. However, it has been estimated that there were approximately fourteen Lithuanian families in Bradford before the First World War.[125] Buàys stated that these Lithuanians settled in Bradford and its outskirts in 1908. Most of them worked as tailors. Among Bradford's Lithuanians were the prolific tailors, J. Vaičiulaitis and J. Lobikis. There were also significant numbers of Lithuanians living in the Manchester area.[126] Substantial numbers also resided in London.[127] It has been estimated that by 1914, there were approximately 1,000 Lithuanians in London, and 4,000 in England as a whole.[128]

As Bučys noted, however, numbers of Lithuanians also dwindled as a result of re-emigration to the United States.[129] The proportion remaining and those emigrating is not known.

As Rodgers stressed, these Lithuanian immigrants can be distinguished from the separate wave of immigration during the same period of Lithuanian Jewish refugees.[130] According to Rodgers the two groups had virtually no contact with each other.[131] Some of these Lithuanian Jews came from the south-western corner of contemporary Lithuania, then part of Russian Poland, and the Pale of Settlement. Jews from Russian Poland began arriving in Britain from 1880 onwards, with numbers steadily increasing year on year. There are several explanations for the migration of Jews from Russian Poland to the West.[132] The first was an economic motivation. Jews did not achieve emancipation until 1917 and in the late nineteenth century, the majority remained confined to the Pale of Settlement, an area stretching from the Baltic to the Black Sea. While the 'Jewish population grew rapidly in the nineteenth century…the economy of the Pale did not grow vigorously enough to provide adequately for its inhabitants. In these circumstances labour was transferred from Eastern Europe towards the more advanced economies of the West'.[133] The second explanation was the persecution of the Jews by the Tsarist state, 'which was a major influence behind the movement of Jews to Britain….'[134] A third explanation is the change in the Jews' legal status 'spurred by the economic requirements of post-emancipation Russia', particularly the failure of a new law on resettlement.[135] Although a law on residence introduced in 1865 had potentially opened the door for large numbers of Jews (approximately one-fifth of those resident in the Pale[136]) to live outside the Pale of Settlement and be given empire-wide residence, as Klier has shown, the ambiguity of their new legal status left re-settlers 'at the mercy of numerous external forces'.[137] Faced with a choice between confinement to the Pale, harassment as a result of resettlement, or emigration, many of those able (generally those with the necessary resources) opted for emigration. The Jews thus came to Britain sometimes as refugees, sometimes as immigrants, the decision to leave based on 'a compound of emotions, calculations and individual circumstances'.[138] The numbers of Jews from present-day Lithuania who came to Britain during this period is not known.[139]

During the period of Latvian, Estonian and Lithuanian independence, from 1918 to 1940, there was a trickle of migrants to Britain and diplomatic representations were established in London.

From 1921, the new Latvian independent state was granted *de jure* recognition by the British Government, which enabled the formal establishment of diplomatic representation in London. A Latvian Legation had been established in London as early as 1918, and became the centre of Latvian diplomatic and political activity throughout the independence period, as well as both during and after the Second World War.[140] One of the key figures in Latvian diplomatic activity throughout and after the war years was Karlis Zariņš, also known as Charles Zarine, who arrived in London in 1933 to take up the post of Envoy Extraordinary and Minister Plenipotentiary and became one of the key figures in the establishment of a Latvian community in Britain. He promoted economic links between Britain and Latvia, as well as stimulating Latvian culture in Britain.[141] Significantly, Zariņš encouraged dialogue between the Latvian Lutheran Church and the Church of England shortly after his arrival in London. This led to the acceptance of intercommunion with the Lutheran Church of Latvia by the Church of England in 1939. As Andrups notes, 'This recognition had unforeseen benefits for the Latvian Church, when exiled Latvians, including clergymen arrived in Britain after World War Two.'[142] Zariņš continued his activities during the Second World War and after 1945, thereby cementing his reputation as a key figure in the Latvian minority in Britain.

The diplomatic representation of the Estonian Republic in London dates back to April 1918, when Prof. A Piip arrived there with a delegation. Crucially, Prof. Piip received important financial support and considerable moral boost from the ethnic Estonian officers serving in the Russian merchant navy, in his task of setting up the legation of the new Republic. In this goal he succeeded and several months later his representation was recognised by the Foreign Office as the Estonian Provisional Legation. [143]

A few months previously, on 16 February 1918, an organisation, *Londoni eesti Ilma Parteita Sotsiaal Gruppe. Eesthonien sotcial group*' was founded, with a loosely stated aim of promoting social life among its members. Although it floundered within a year for lack of support, the impetus gained from the founding of the Legation 'was not lost on the London Estonian community. On 7 July 1921, another organisation, *Londoni Eesti Selts* (London Estonian Society) held its founding meeting. This organisation set its aims wider, comprising social, cultural-recreational and educational functions. It was the only Estonian social-cultural organisation in Britain until the arrival of the refugees in 1947. It is still active today.'[144]

During the period of Estonian independence, Britain was regarded as a desirable place to come to learn and practise English. At this time, London offered a large variety of language courses, at beginners' and advanced levels. An intergovernmental agreement enabled foreign students to live with local families and earn their upkeep by doing a certain amount of housework. This arrangement eased financial costs.[145]

There were also entrants to the educational institutions specialising in catering, tailoring, commerce and economics. Some students were supported by grants from the Estonian government and by stipends from the British Council.[146]

Men and women who came to Britain at this time found it difficult to achieve a tolerable standard of living. The agreement described above had obviously been designed for young women. Probably as a result of this arrangement, in London, the number of Estonian women outnumbered men by a large margin. According to Hindo, by 1941, *Londoni Eesti Selts* had 81 members, including some sailors and people living outside the capital.[147] The proportion of the Estonian community in Britain who actually joined this organisation is not known.

Like Latvia and Estonia, the Lithuanian Republic gained diplomatic representation in London during the inter-war period. Unlike Latvia and Estonia, who gained *de jure* recognition from the

British Government in 1921, Lithuanian failed to achieve *de jure* status until 1922, primarily due to the problems surrounding Poland and Lithuania's impasse over the Vilnius region. In the academic literature, there is scant additional information about Lithuanians in Britain during the inter-war period, apart from the above-mentioned deportation of some Lithuanians and their dependants, and the concurrent weakening of cultural and social life in Scotland.[148]

During the Second World War, the new Soviet occupation authorities in Latvia, Lithuania and Estonia relieved the diplomatic representatives in London of their positions. The British Government was under increasing pressure to remove the diplomatic status of Latvian, Lithuanian and Estonian Ministers, but since it did not recognise *de jure*, the incorporation of the Baltic States into the Soviet Union, as a compromise, merely delegated the ministers to the end of the Diplomatic List. However, although the Ministers did not enjoy the same rights and privileges as previously, they were able to maintain contact with some Foreign Office officials and thus continued to exert pressure on the government. This situation continued throughout the German occupation and the post-war period.

During the Second World War, sailors increased the numbers of Baltic newcomers in Britain. Andrups notes that at the beginning of the war, there were approximately 50 Latvians living in London. This number gradually increased during the war years, 'due to the presence of Latvian sailors, who were employed either on British ships or were on Latvian ships that had been in the West at the outbreak of war and now formed part of the British and American merchant navvies.'[149]

Among Latvians, a Latvian association was founded in London for the first time during the Second World War, to bring the Latvians together and to campaign for Latvia's independence. The Society of Latvians in Great Britain (*Latvju biedrība Lielbritanijā*) was founded on 18 November 1941, Latvian National Day, at a meeting held at the Latvian Legation in London.[150] A monthly newspaper *Londonas Avīze*, later to become a weekly was published by the Society in 1942.[151]

The Latvian, Lithuanian and Estonian Legations in London undertook important work during the Second World War, pressuring the British Government to help find solutions to the refugee problem, and highlighting the injustice of the Russian occupation. The establishment of the Legations, organisations such as the Latvian Society, and newspapers provided foundations upon which the post-war refugees from the Baltic States could build.

Thus, there were discernible, albeit relatively small numbers of Latvians, Lithuanians and Estonians living in Great Britain prior to the post-war wave of refugees. By the time of the arrival of the first Baltic European Volunteer Workers (EVWs) in Britain in October 1946, significant steps had already been taken to establish political and social structures for Latvians, Lithuanians and Estonians in Britain. All three nations had diplomatic representations during the inter-war period, and although these ran into difficulties under the German and Russian occupations, they remained a solid support structure and organisational base for the refugees.

CHAPTER 2

The Homeland

> I suppose that initial growing up period were the formative
> years, well, that…sort of instils it into you…you see I had this
> farming background and the Estonian childhood, growing up in
> the country…it was very different to anything [in Britain].

(First Generation Estonian now living in Britain, born 1926[152])

ALTHOUGH THERE HAD BEEN SOME BALTIC MIGRATION
to Britain prior to 1946, the entry of 26,500 Baltic Refugees into Great
Britain was unprecedented. But what were the backgrounds of these
refugees: what sort of lives did they have before becoming refugees and
what were their homelands like? This chapter will discuss the first stages
of the refugees' lives – their childhoods and early adult lives growing up
in the inter-war republics of Latvia, Lithuania and Estonia, newly
independent countries with distinctive cultures.[153] A majority of the
recruits for labour in Great Britain were born during the 1920's, the first
decade of independence.[154] The homeland way of life was in marked
contrast to that which the Latvians, Lithuanians and Estonians would
later experience in Great Britain.

Although many studies of immigrant settlement pay only scant
attention to countries and cultures of origin[155], an understanding of
homeland life is extremely important in reaching any comprehension of
post-settlement experience and adaptation. An awareness of the
everyday life and cultures of the homeland will shed light on the extent
of the cultural change the refugees experienced in Britain, and the degree
to which they had to adapt. Furthermore, an assessment of the nature
and extent of national identity development among Latvians,
Lithuanians and Estonians during the inter-war period, will provide a

basis upon which to judge the extent of identity change during migration and settlement. This aspect is particularly interesting because the new states were themselves in a nascent and ongoing process of nation-building and national identity construction.

Rather than provide a rather predictable historical sketch of this period, which can be found elsewhere[156], I will briefly discuss eight factors, which summarise the key features of the refugees' childhood in the three homelands, relating to everyday life, culture and national identities.[157] They are: demographic and geographical overview; newly independent states and nascent national identities; a rural way of life; urbanisation and industrialisation; regional differences; religion; multi-ethnic societies; national days. These elements have been chosen to best exemplify life in Latvia, Lithuania and Estonia in the period 1918 to 1940, and were highlighted by the participants in this study when asked to discuss their experiences of growing up in the homelands. Discussion of these eight aspects will reveal both the similarities and the differences between Latvia, Lithuania and Estonia. I will end the chapter with a brief analysis of the nature of the exiles' recollections of the homeland and the implications of these memories for the development of exile identities in settlement.

HOMELAND REALITIES

- *A Demographic and Geographical Overview*

Latvia, Lithuania and Estonia are three small countries in north-east Europe, which lie on the south eastern shores of the Baltic Sea. Sandwiched between Russia and the rest of Eastern Europe, their unenviable geographical position has determined the course of their history for centuries. During the inter-war period, having pulled free from the control of the Russian Empire, they bordered the USSR, Poland and East Prussia. Between the two world wars, the geographical boundaries of Estonia, Latvia and Lithuania were slightly different from the present-day. One of the most significant differences was that the contemporary capital of Lithuania – Vilnius, was then part of Poland, having been captured by the Polish leader Pilsudski in 1920, during the wars of independence. As a result, Kaunas became the capital of inter-war Lithuania. Kaunas lay in the eastern interior of Lithuania while the capitals of Latvia and Estonia were ports on the Baltic Sea (Riga and Tallinn respectively). Inter-war Latvia, Lithuania and Estonia had small populations. In 1934, Estonia had a populace numbering just over 1.1 million, while Latvia had a more sizeable population of 1.95 million.[158]

Lithuania had the largest number of inhabitants - just under 2.4 million in 1937.[159] Lithuania was also the largest country in terms of area, although the fact that the distance from the northernmost point of Estonia to the southern tip of Lithuania is less than the length of England[160] gives some impression of the size of the three countries. Despite their small geographical area, the populations were fairly widely dispersed, although growing urbanisation and industrialisation was leading to a concentration of people in a small number of urban areas. As newly industrialising nations, communications and transport links were rudimentary. The landscape of the three countries composed a mixture of large swathes of forest and farmland, gently rolling countryside and stretches of coastline. Estonia, occupying the northernmost position of the three countries has a long stretch of coastline, on both its western and northern sides, as well as a number of small islands.

- ### *Newly Independent States and Nascent National Identities*

One of the most interesting characteristics of the Baltic refugees who came to Britain as EVWs, was that they grew up in newly independent countries. Latvia, Lithuania and Estonia only came into being as independent states in 1918, following centuries of rule by various foreign powers, most latterly by the Russian Empire. Prior to 1918, Latvia and Estonia had never existed as independent states in the form we know them today[161], and Lithuania had enjoyed only a brief spell of statehood prior to its submergence into the Polish-Lithuanian Commonwealth in 1387[162]. Indeed the word 'Estonian' entered the vocabulary only in 1860.[163]

Inter-war Latvia, Lithuania and Estonia were culturally distinct from each other, the result of unique paths of historical development and different foreign influences. Until the thirteenth century, all three contemporary Baltic States were a collection of independent kingdoms, inhabited by an array of diverse nationalities. The predecessors of contemporary Latvians, Lithuanians and Estonians populated various regions in the area alongside other nationalities, many of whom have died out over the course of history.[164] While Latvians and Lithuanians are descended from Baltic tribes in the region, Estonians are descendants of Finno-Ugric peoples, who were thought to have inhabited the region from the third millennium BC.[165] Indo-Europeans were believed to have settled in the areas of contemporary Latvia and Lithuania around the same period, and intermingled with the local populations to form the basis of the Baltic tribes. These complex beginnings explain the development of languages in the area. While

Lithuanian and Latvian are both Baltic languages, part of the Indo-European family, Estonian forms part of the Finno-Ugric group and is similar to both Finnish and Hungarian.

Between the thirteenth and eighteenth century, the Baltic region was invaded by several Western nations. The regions now composing Latvia and Estonia both succumbed to a German-led invasion, which resulted in to the imposition of Lutheran Christianity and the enserfment of the peasant populations. During subsequent centuries, different areas of present-day Latvia and Estonia were annexed by various foreign powers. In 1561, southern Estonia (Livonia) was integrated into the Polish-Lithuanian commonwealth, while the rest of the region was brought under Swedish rule.[166] Foreign regimes in charge of different parts of present-day Latvia during this period included the Vatican, Denmark, Prussia, Poland-Lithuania, Sweden and Russia.[167] Following the establishment of the Livonian State by the German Teutonic Knights in the thirteenth century,[168] in the fifteenth century, Livonia was partitioned and south-western Latvia became the Duchy of Kurland under the suzerainty of the Polish monarchy. The rest of Livonia became a dependency of the Polish-Lithuanian commonwealth, and from 1629 to 1721 was annexed by Sweden.[169] Swedish rule lasted until the start of the Great Northern War in the early eighteenth century.

The area of contemporary Lithuania was able to resist the German crusading onslaught, and in 1231, Grand Duke Mindaugas united Lithuanian tribes in the region into a nation, leading to a brief period of Lithuanian statehood. Under the leadership of his successors, notably Gediminas[170], Algirdas and Vytautas, the Lithuanian state expanded from the Baltic to the Black Sea.[171] In 1387, Lithuanian Grand Duke Jogaila accepted the crown of Poland and established the Polish-Lithuanian Commonwealth. This led to the permanent introduction of Latin Christianity into Lithuania[172] between 1387 and 1413. The union with Poland became institutionalised over a number of years, and in 1569[173], Lithuania was 'merged into a single state albeit with autonomy, which in time reduced ethnic Lithuania to a provincial status'.[174] The result was extensive Polonisation among nobles and gentry, who accepted the Polish language and customs in an attempt to improve and maintain their own status in the Commonwealth. The Polish influence on Lithuania's history has been one of the key defining characteristics of Lithuania's past, the influence of which lasts until today, most obviously through the status of Catholicism as the national religion.

During the eighteenth century, the territories comprising contemporary Latvia, Lithuania and Estonia became subjugated to the Russian Empire[175], a rule which lasted until 1918. Russian annexation transformed the different regions of contemporary Latvia, Lithuania and Estonia into constituent provinces of the Russian Empire. Until emancipation in the nineteenth century, the indigenous peasantry were ruled both by the German land-owning nobility (in Latvia and Estonia), the Polish nobles (in Lithuania), and the Russian State, which sought to Russify the local populations. Mirroring developments in the rest of Europe, Latvia, Lithuania and Estonia experienced national awakenings in the latter half of the nineteenth century, which led to the development of the concepts of national cultures and identities. Initially movements for greater cultural autonomy, and spearheaded by the German nobles and clergy in Latvia and Estonia, and by the Polish nobles and clergy in Lithuania, they soon developed into movements for greater political autonomy. Supported by the liberal intelligentsia and the new literate working classes, the latter having developed as a result of emancipation and industrialisation, these national movements demanded autonomy in the 1905 revolution. However, it was not until the collapse of Empire in both Russia and Germany that the opportunity was presented to successfully assert independence in 1918.[176] Independent statehood was finally secured in all three countries in 1920, following the wars of independence.[177]

The fact that the refugees spent their childhood in young countries had significance for their lives in the homeland for two main reasons. Firstly, they grew up during a period of intensive nation-building and transformation in many spheres of life. Secondly, the populations of these newly independent countries had under-developed national identities, and national cultures were still in the process of consolidation.

Nation-building sought to completely overhaul the political, social, and economic life of the three countries, as well as to strengthen national cultures and identities and thereby, produce a loyal citizenship. Political, social and economic reforms were far-reaching, and aimed to remove all vestiges of Russian control, including the powers of the German and Polish land-owning nobility. Politically, all three countries became constitutional democracies, in sharp contrast to the earlier experience of Tsarist autocracy. Democratic systems based on proportional representation were introduced which promoted a proliferation of small parties. However, the democratic experience was short-lived, brought to an end by increasing economic problems and the political instability caused by the large number of political parties.

Authoritarianism was established earliest in Lithuania, where in 1926, Antanas Smetona was brought to power by a military coup, overthrowing the democratic state and establishing an authoritarian regime.[178] Smetona's regime lasted until 1938, when foreign policy failures forced the establishment of a coalition government and gradual democratisation.[179] In Latvia, Karlis Ulmanis dissolved Parliament in 1934 and established an authoritarian regime, called the 'Government of National Unity' which he headed as President. In Estonia, from 1934 to 1938, President Konstantin Päts ruled by Presidential Decree partly in an attempt to pre-empt a far-rightist coup. A constitutional regime was re-established in Estonia in 1938.

Economically, one of the most significant developments in the inter-war period, was land reform, which was most extensive in Latvia and Estonia. Here, by redistributing land from the oppressive German land-owning nobility into the hands of the indigenous peasant population, land reforms constituted one of the key measures of nation building. Agricultural production formed the basis of the all three states' economies, and was energetically promoted. Other economic reforms attempted to re-organise and develop the industrial sphere, and new trading partners were sought, due to the closure of the Russian market. Economically, the inter-war states had both successes and failures. Lithuania started the inter-war years the most backward of the three countries and experienced the greatest economic growth. Agricultural production doubled during the inter-war period and by 1940[180], industrial output was 260 per cent of the 1913 output[181]. The Latvian economy was not so successful. Its economy failed to flourish and according to Soviet statistics, by 1940, Latvian industrial production recovered only to a level approximating pre-war output.[182] Vardys suggests that Estonia was perhaps more successful than Latvia in rebuilding its economy. By 1940, the 1913 output level had grown by 30 per cent.[183]

Despite mixed economic fortunes, social reform during this period was significant. Reforms led to the expansion of schooling and education system and the introduction of basic social welfare systems. Overall, there was a rise in living standards and wage levels in all three countries during the inter-war period.[184]

The second strategy of nation-building was the energetic promotion of national cultures and identities. How successful were the new states in instilling strong national identities and cultures among the Baltic populations during this period, and what did they consist of?

The concepts of national identity and national culture were embryonic, having been developed less than a century earlier, during the national awakenings in the late nineteenth century.[185]   Prior to the national awakenings there was little sense of national identities in the three provinces: different regions had distinctive identities, partly due to fragmented nature of the region under foreign rule and continuing under Russian rule.   Class and religious identities were also pronounced. During the national awakenings, movements developed to promote Estonian, Latvian and Lithuanian as the languages of instruction in schools, and folklore and national literature were promoted.   The national awakenings linked certain aspects of culture to national identities, so that Latvian, Lithuanian and Estonian identities became defined by certain cultural attributes.   The most important aspects of culture which came to define Latvian, Lithuanian and Estonian identities included language, literature and folklore, religion (in Lithuania), and the peasant and the rural way of life (see section on Rural Way of Life below).   Song Festivals also became an important aspect of national cultural identity in Latvia and Estonia. During the national awakenings, as Lieven stresses, part of the process of the growth of national self-awareness among the three nationalities involved defining themselves from others – 'a ceaseless repetition of the features making up 'national character' and distinguishing it from that of neighbours and rulers'.[186] Thus, it was those aspects of culture, which distinguished the indigenous population from their oppressive rulers, which formed the basis of national identities.

Despite the energetic promotion of national identities and cultures during this period, it is uncertain what the extent the national awakenings had instilled national identities into the populations by the date of independence, or whether indeed, the establishment of independent statehood reflected nationalism among the masses. Hobsbawm contends that the 1918 declarations of independence did not illustrate a strong sense of national identity among the masses. Rather, he asserts that there was 'no noticeable national demand' for independence among the Baltic populations in 1917.[187]

Whether or not Hobsbawm is correct, there is no doubt that national identities and the concept of a national culture, were still in the process of evolution by 1920.   Leaders of the newly independent states sought to solidify national identities and national cultures.   As in the national awakenings, language played a vital role as a means to solidify and unify the nation.   One of the earliest reforms was the recognition of Latvian, Lithuanian and Estonian as the official language of the state. Latvian, Lithuanian and Estonian language schools were organised, and national literature was promoted. In addition, arts, education and other cultural endeavours were promoted. Folk traditions, national literature, music, theatre and dance were vigorously supported by the State. The new states were embellished with a variety of symbols and motifs, denoting national identities and imprinting on the mind of every citizen, a series of identifiable national images. Flags, coats of arms and national anthems were introduced as symbols of the independent nations. The construction of national monuments, buildings and the establishment and modification of exhibits in national museums served to express independent nationhood further. In Latvia, it was during the independence period that the Monument of Freedom in Riga was first erected as a symbol of liberty.[188] The Ethnographic Open-Air Museum of Latvia was opened in Riga in 1924, to depict the life of the Latvian peasant.[189] Vieda Skultans notes how in the twentieth century, the farmstead became 'a symbol of Latvian ethnic identity'. The significance of the farmstead for Latvian national identity was reflected in the Open-Air museum which 'further elevated the farmstead from a real entity to a timeless mythical construct'.[190]

Monument of Freedom, Riga

National identity was also promoted in schools. The newly independent nations introduced curricula educating pupils about the history and culture of their nation. National literature and histories read both inside and outside schools was a key component of national identity construction. Nineteenth century Latvian, Lithuanian and Estonian poems and novels were read and new authors gained prestige. According to Skultans, 'the assimilation of cultural texts was not some mysterious and historically unspecifiable encounter. It took place in classrooms as children learnt to read from textbooks which recounted an ancestral past and instructed them in who they were now'.[191] As the school system was expanded, the classroom became one of the key forums for the consolidation of national identities. Folk songs were printed in school textbooks, which in Latvia were standardised throughout the country from the 1920's onwards.[192] History textbooks linked the child's own life with that of his or her predecessors, and constructed an identity, which was deeply rooted in the countryside: 'school texts aimed to create a sense of belonging and connection with the past in their young country readers'.[193] The different parts of the country were linked together in textbooks, to promote a sense of national unity. The young Latvians, Lithuanians and Estonians were not only taught about their own nation, but also about other countries in the world, including their previous oppressors and more respected nations, including Great Britain and Sweden. The Latvian, Lithuanian and Estonian states were clearly situated in the world, with charts and statistics comparing their nation's progress with that of other nations.

Another aspect of national identity construction was the reinterpretation of cultural origins and the rewriting of history. Even though many aspects of the emergent national cultures originated from foreign invaders or non-Latvian, Lithuanian and Estonian tribes in the region, the significance of these cultural elements to national identity was stressed by a reinterpretation of cultural origins; in other words, the manufacture of myths of the nation. Elements of pagan culture were woven into contemporary culture, and the richness of Baltic cultures before the cultural demolition of the foreign occupiers was stressed. According to Lieven, the proliferation of pagan elements and motifs in Baltic cultures has 'strong organic roots in Baltic peasant cultures as these continued and evolved from the pre-Christian period, though of course they became thoroughly mixed with Christian elements'.[194] During the inter-war period, the Baltic national states and nationalists attempted 'to reshape these traditions to their own purposes'.[195] In Latvia, President Ulmanis made extensive use of neo-pagan 'ethnic-religious' motifs during the 1930's. [196] History was also reconstructed to justify and give legitimacy to independent Baltic Republics. In Lithuania, the independent republic harked back to the glorious days of the Lithuanian Commonwealth (note not the *Polish*-Lithuanian commonwealth). All three states stressed the early histories of ethnic-Latvians, Lithuanians and Estonians and their predecessors, going as far back in time as the pre-historic era. In the conditions of independence, it was even more necessary to stress the distinctive culture and history of these nations before the era of foreign occupation, to justify separation. Anthony Smith stresses the special place of myths of descent in many of the worlds' nations. He states that: 'Ultimately it is the myths of origins and descent that links the modern nation to its ethnic basis, and defines it in relation to its destiny. Such myths are a defining characteristic of *ethnie*, and in more elaborate form and often with changed meanings and contents, they form one of the basic elements of nations'.[197]

During the inter-war period, national identities and national cultures were based upon the indigenous peasantry, in other words, they were the cultures and identities of the dominant ethnic group. As A D Smith notes, small nations are mostly defined by 'ethnic' features and their self-image is largely ethnic. After all, a distinctive culture and history is 'the raison d'être for their separate existence'.[198] However, at the start of the independence period, the construction of national identities appeared to embrace pluralism, rather than be merely synonymous with ethnic identities. One of the earliest measures of the new states was the granting of cultural autonomy to the largest ethnic minorities. For example, in Estonia, a decree guaranteeing cultural autonomy to minority groups comprised of at least 3,000 was passed. This law has since been regarded as a model for cultural pluralism.[199] However, during the 1930's, and even earlier in Lithuania, a drift towards an ethnically based national identity occurred, seen most explicitly during the rise to authoritarianism in all three states. Increasing economic and political problems promoted scapegoating, and the idea of the main enemies of the new states as Russia and the Polish and German nobility developed into a paranoia about multiple enemies, both within and outside the state. Some of Latvia, Lithuania's and Estonia's minority groups became scapegoats during the latter half of the inter-war period. In relatively homogenous Lithuania, the Polish minority encountered the greatest discrimination at the hands of the state, due partly to the history of Polish domination and the Polish ownership of Vilnius during the inter-war period, but also because of their economic power in the new state. Like Poles in Lithuania, Jewish and German groups in all three countries became viewed as a hindrance to the growth of an ethnic nation, and as enemies of the new states. One of the main reasons was that Germans and Jews and Poles initially enjoyed substantial economic power in urban, commercial and professional sectors of the economies. In this way, ethnicity ran sharply down class lines. In contrast to the above nationalities, Latvians, Lithuanians and Estonians were overwhelmingly peasants. The class basis of ethnic identities heightened animosity towards certain minorities as they were held to blame for economic problems. During the 1930's, nationalism assumed a distinctly class/ethnic basis. The withdrawal of minority cultural rights revealed discrimination at the level of the State; among some elements of the population animosity at grassroots level was far greater. In Latvia in particular, anti-minority sentiment was fuelled by government policy. Rothschild noted how Latvia's president, Ulmanis 'appealed to nationalistic emotions, which were always somewhat cruder and more chauvinist here than in Estonia, by pursuing anti-minority (especially anti-German and anti-Jewish) educational and economic policies and by pressing the "Latvianization" of Latgale'.[200]

Evidence suggest that attitudes towards Russian inhabitants during the inter-war period were negative, but that they were regarded as less of a threat than other groups, such as Jews or Germans, primarily because they had less economic power. Furthermore, the enemy had been and was still regarded as the Russian State and its dominant political doctrine - communism, not the Russian inhabitants, although many Russians were assumed to be communist. Although not perceived as such a threat to the economy as some other groups, they were certainly looked down upon, and regarded as uneducated and slovenly. The comments of a Lithuanian woman in Britain reveal the negative attitudes towards Russia in independent Lithuania:

> The attitude in the inter-war period towards Russia was "If you're Russian you're a communist and that was it. Russia was bad. Russia was not clever. If you're a Russian you're poor, you're uneducated. Russian was aligned with communism. Communism was bad and that was it. If you were a communist that was the…worst thing you could be, a communist and that was that.[201]

However, the extent of antipathy towards minority groups must not be exaggerated. There is some evidence that despite the growing idea of a state being based on the dominant ethnic group and culture, toleration and respect for other nationalities was present among a majority of the population even during the authoritarian phase. Juris Veidemanis' analysis of value systems in inter-war Latvia found that there was a common consensus supporting the value of 'Freedoms for minorities organisationally, religiously, educationally, politically and culturally'.[202] Only a few minority groups were singled out in a negative way, and others were accorded great respect and toleration, for example, the Norwegians and Swedes in Estonia, although their numbers were tiny in comparison to Russian, Jewish and German groups.

How far were the leaders successful in instilling national identities among the populations? Among participants there have been mixed viewpoints. A Lithuanian woman drew attention to the outpouring of patriotism during the independence period:

> The national identity in the inter-war period was very much a patriotic [national identity] you know, for the country...remember, became independent after 100 odd years of Russian rule and it ...was like a euphoria – "We go forward. We do that. We do this". Overall the country was progressive and...there was an expectancy of what the country would do. There was reasonable solidarity as well.

> It was a young country very quickly recovering from... Russian dominance and surging forward.

> Lithuanian patriotism was in its element really in those years, moving forward very much so.[203]

However, the testimonies of participants in this study suggest that rural, class based identities were more significant during this period than national identities. Religious and regional identities also persisted, hindering the development of national identities. Furthermore, despite attempts to develop distinctive and unified national cultures and identities, remnants of previous occupants pervaded every sphere of life. Inter-war Latvia, Lithuania and Estonia were multi-ethnic countries, with diverse cultures and wide regional differences all relics of their vibrant and multifaceted pasts. The cultural diversity of the Baltic States was emphasised by Heino Poopuu, who noted that even in a relatively isolated community on Saaremaa Island, reminders of Estonia's past were evident. Due to 'a continuous intermingling among the populations of several nations', Poopuu stated that:

> In such circumstances Saaremaa Estonians could hardly have developed and retained an absolute ethnic or cultural uniqueness. And as one might expect, many traces of close associations in the past with the Germans, Swedes and the Russians could be felt in many ways on the island. Most

obvious of these were the place names, disused manor houses, religions and many German family names.[204]

Age may have been a factor in the degree of national identity formation: the older the individual, partly as a result of education and the development of identities with age, the more likely that a sense of national identity had developed. Those who lived through the years of war, revolution, and the declarations of independence, may have developed a stronger sense of national identity, than those who were born later. On the other hand, a sense of national identity and culture was instilled into refugees who attended school during the independence period.

Some commentators have suggested that the political experiences and experiments of the three Baltic States during the inter-war period reflected the new cultural identities of the three states[205], and that although national identities were still nascent among the population, the experience of independence entrenched among the Baltic peoples a strong sense that national identities could 'only be exercised and preserved through maintenance of an independent state entity'.[206] This contrasted to the limited support for independence in 1918. Hope argues that 'the available evidence suggests that a new cultural identity born politically in the 1860's, and the new political democracy of 1920-2, continued to shape the political beliefs and actions of Estonians, Latvians and Lithuanians in a way undreamt of in Germany after 1933. This accounts in part for the egalitarian and stubborn defence of their separate identities in and since 1940'. [207] However, it could be argued that the evidence for this is somewhat patchy, and that it is likely that it was not until the loss of freedom in 1940, that political nationalism and robust national identities were forged, superseding regional, class and rural identities.

- *A Rural way of life*

The rural upbringing of the refugees was the most significant aspect of their childhood as they recall it in their testimonies. Historically, the Baltic States were farming nations, and despite growing urbanisation, the rural/urban ratio of the population remained high. In inter-war Latvia, only 36 per cent of the population lived in towns and cities, the remainder living in the countryside.[208] In Estonia a similar percentage resided in urban areas (33 per cent), but in Lithuania the urban population was far less (15 per cent), due to the relative sluggishness of Lithuania's industrialisation.[209] These percentages were reflected in the urban/rural backgrounds of the refugees who came to Britain, of whom an overwhelming majority came from rural areas, although a significant minority of Latvians and Estonians in this study lived in towns and cities.[210]

One of the most interesting features of the national movements in the nineteenth century had been the redefinition of the peasant and the reconstruction of peasant identity, particularly in Latvia and Estonia.[211] Prior to the awakenings, the peasant had been portrayed in an unflattering and uncomfortable way, as an immoral, lazy, wretched oppressed creature. Because Latvian and Estonian identity had previously been linked inextricably to peasant identity, the peasant stereotype meant that to be a Latvian or Estonian was to be an uneducated peasant. If one was educated, one would be assimilated to the Baltic German classes. A peasant could not be educated and remain a Latvian or Estonian. The national movements set out to redefine what it meant to be 'Latvian' or 'Estonian', to make it possible to be both educated and remain Latvian or Estonian. As a result of the national movements, the peasant was turned into a positive symbol of Latvian and Estonian nationhood. The Latvian and Estonian peasant was deemed to be hard-working, moral and competent, a mainstay of the nation. The redefined peasant was portrayed in the literature and folk-songs of the national movement.

The idea of the peasant as the mainstay of national economic survival was strengthened during the inter-war period.[212] Farming was still considered to be the most well respected occupation, and was thought to constitute the key means for the survival of the nation.[213] The farmstead became one of the most important symbols of independent Latvian, Lithuanian and Estonian nations.

During the 1920's and 1930's, most of the refugees in this study were children growing up on the farm, going to school and also helping out with work on the farm, and in the home. Among those who grew up in the countryside, the refugees who came to Britain derived from a wide variety of farming backgrounds[214]; some grew up in small self-sufficient farmsteads which grew barely enough to feed the family, while others lived on larger, profit-making farms. One Latvian in Britain, born in 1926, grew up on a large farmstead, which had 300 acres of farmland and 100 acres of forest.[215] Many of the farms undertook mixed farming, while others concentrated on one or two crops. Others undertook fishing as an important component of the farm's functions.

Life on the farmstead was described by most interview participants as a happy time. However, some of the interviewees stressed that despite being a happy time, there were many hardships. Life in the countryside was a fairly isolated, parochial existence. Some of the Latvians who came to Britain told me that they had only been to Riga once or twice as children and could not even remember it. A Latvian man, now living in Leeds described how as a child he saw Riga only three times:

> I haven't seen Latvia…when I left home I was 16. I was 16 when I left and at that time well, I was going to school, I was living in country. I've even been a couple of time in Riga, that's all, about three times, including the one when I was a right little one.[216]

Some of the participants stressed that life in the country was a hard, ascetic life. As young children they had few toys or luxuries, and had to work hard on the farm. One Lithuanian woman who was only a young child during the 1930's described life on the farm as a 'hard life'. Since her mother died in 1932, she had lived with her aunt and grandmother, and described how 'from early morning till…night they were working. I remember they [were] working really hard you know, my aunty, my grandmother and…well I had to help, like I said early mornings and night. Way of life.'[217] When I asked her if she remembers her childhood as a happy time, she replied: 'In a way I was happy. We had nothing like you know. You had nothing, but that was the way you know in Lithuania'.[218] She described how as children they played with sticks and 'whatever we could find, not many toys like.'[219]

For one Latvian man who grew up on a farm in Latvia, the relationship with nature gained from growing up on the farm was perhaps the most important aspect of his childhood in Latvia. The close relationship to the land gave him a firm sense of belonging in Latvia, and increased his bond to the country. He left his homeland at the age of sixteen. He commented:

> I was with it all the time. I was picking mushrooms and watching birds and all the time I was with nature you know…swimming in river and so on you know. I learnt to swim…I was very close to the earth. I did all the work what there was – ploughing and mowing and everything, you know. Of course I did it with horses…there weren't many tractors then. But I could do it and I did it. And I worked with the earth, with it. And that's where it came from, from the earth, that's where everywhere came from, the food and everything.[220]

Similar sentiments can be found in other testimonies. Heino Poopuu also described in an interview, how the childhood on the farm gave him a strong rural identity, which later formed a significant component of his Estonian identity. He commented on the huge differences between his Estonian childhood and his later life in Britain:

> I suppose that initial growing up period were the formative years, well, that…sort of instils it into you.

> …you see I had this farming background and the Estonian childhood, growing up in the country…it was very different to anything [in Britain]. Apart from the language differences and religion, the whole erm, the whole gist of life is quite different…that very basics you can't – much the same as your accent, you can't do much about it, even if you wanted to, it's still there, so, so perhaps I'm still a countryman to some extent.[221]

Heino noted the other differences between Britain and the homeland:

> …there's no open spaces here and no sea. Our home was…along one side of the farm, land was facing the sea, so all these things are…you see, our whole rhythm or routine was very different…[222]

The characteristics of family life in Latvia, Lithuania and Estonia originated from the rural way of life, and there were many similarities with traditional peasant families of other pre-industrial nations. Despite industrialisation, family life in towns and cities was still largely based on the rural family structure. The family was a very strong, close knit unit, often with a large extended family living close by, in the same village or region. Typically in Estonia and Latvia[223], a married couple had three or four children, in Lithuania, about four or five. Traditional gender relations persisted.

The cuisine of the inter-war Baltic States was another aspect of culture with roots firmly in the countryside. Since most farms were largely self-sufficient, cuisine reflected seasonal growing patterns. In addition to arable land growing a variety of crops including rye, barley, buckwheat and oats, a typical farmstead included a threshing barn, pigsty, orchard, granary, kitchen garden, potato bunker and smokehouse. Most farms kept at least one cow, several pigs and some poultry. A wide variety of fruits and vegetables were grown, including potatoes, cabbage, beetroot, onions, carrots, cucumbers, apples and various fruit bushes, including cranberries, blackberries and raspberries. Eggs were produced and a variety of milk products were made including sour cream, curd and cottage cheese. Some farms had beehives and produced large supplies of honey. The farmstead also made use of the surrounding landscape. Fishing in the sea, lakes and rivers was commonplace and berries and mushrooms were collected in wooded areas.

In urban areas, the cuisine was similar to that in the countryside – it still reflected the seasons, since much of the food was produced locally, but was a little more sophisticated and contained an increasing amount of imported foodstuffs. Urban diets also reflected the greater degree of foreign influences in the towns and cities and the multi-ethnic composition of urban populations.

In both towns and the countryside, 'workaday menus' were plain, simple, one-course affairs. The diet relied heavily on 'thick meat- or less frequently, fish soups or broths with permutations of added lentils, vegetables or cereals. These soups, eaten with rye bread, constituted the main meal of the day. Common main meals without meat or fish included 'porridge with butter and flour enriched mashed potatoes with bacon dripping'.[224] Bacon dripping was used in many recipes in all three Baltic Republics, to add flavour and nourishment. In Latvia for example, grey peas with bacon dripping was (and still is) a national favourite.[225] Puddings and desserts were usually eaten only on special occasions. A Latvian in Britain also noted that during the inter-war period: '…we didn't have…such things as sweets and chocolates and things.'[226] Each nation had its own national specialities, for example, one of the Lithuania's national dishes - potato pancakes – used two of the nations most popular foods together.

As in Britain, there was a great tradition of beer drinking among men in all three countries. All beer was home-brewed, and enjoyed on social and special occasions. Heino Poopuu discussed the significance of beer among the communities on Saaremaa:

> There is no doubt that our home-brew was a vital ingredient of what might be termed our culture or the way of life we led, for it wasn't only the completion of certain essential jobs at the farm that depended on its availability, but more important – our social life without beer would have been very dull and arid indeed. To say that some of our men would have been absolutely lost without it would not be an exaggeration.[227]

- *Urbanisation and Industrialisation*

During the inter-war period, the dual processes of urbanisation and industrialisation begun under Russian rule continued. Approximately one-third of the population of Latvia and Estonia lived in urban areas, and about one-seventh of Lithuania's inhabitants.[228] Urban living contrasted sharply with life in the countryside, although the differences during the inter-war period were less marked than during later decades due to the embryonic rise of urbanisation and industrialisation. A majority of the urban population had migrated to the town less than two generations before, and thus had brought with then many traditions and values from the rural life.

The most striking difference was that life in towns and cities was more cosmopolitan and culturally diverse than rural life. In the capital cities, architecture expressed a wide variety of foreign styles and influences, from Riga's art nouveau architecture to Tallinn's Swedish and Danish buildings. Many aspects of culture and everyday life in the cities were reminders of an occupied past and a multi-ethnic present, from the very name of Tallinn itself (meaning 'Danish castle'), to Riga's synagogues. Riga during the inter-war period was sometimes described as a 'small Paris'. A Latvian woman now in Britain, but who grew up in Riga, described the city in the inter-war period in the following terms:

> ...it was a lovely city. ...it was a really western city, nice shops and nice cinemas and being capital of Latvia, we had opera house there. We had three theatres, and no end of cinemas and everything happened there, exhibitions... It was, very, very nice there.

The new capital of Lithuania during the inter-war period - Kaunas was not as cosmopolitan or culturally diverse as Riga. Tallinn fell somewhere between the two, with some minority groups, and an array of cultural influences visible, particularly in its architecture, from Denmark, Sweden and Germany. As a seaport, and incredibly close to Helsinki, Tallinn like Riga enjoyed a wide variety of foreign influences from abroad.

Latvia and Estonia in particular, had significant minority groups, many of whom lived in the capital cities[229]. George Kennan wrote that during the inter-war period:

> Riga had the advantages of a variegated and highly cosmopolitan cultural life: newspapers and theatres in the Lettish, German, Russian and Yiddish tongues and vigorous

Lutheran, Roman Catholic, Russian Orthodox and Jewish religious communities.[230]

- ### *Regional differences*

It is important to stress that due to the varied historical pasts of different regions in the inter-war Baltic States, there were wide cultural differences between areas. The Latgale region, in eastern Latvia, which had been part of the Polish-Lithuanian Commonwealth, was perhaps the most extreme example of this. Unlike the rest of Latvia, which was mainly Lutheran, Latgale had a significant Catholic population even among the local Latvian majority. Commentators noted other differences beyond religion, which distinguished Latgale from other areas of Latvia. Most of Latvia's ethnic minorities lived in Latgale, and a 'distinctive dialect was spoken' even among the Latvian majority who according to Rothschild 'nursed a somewhat aggrieved sense of regional particularism'.[231] A Latvian in Britain described the different history, religion and identity in Latgale. He then described the religious heterogeneity in Latvia:

> There are some Catholics, but only the, mostly the Eastern part of Latvia. You see times back…when the eastern part was under Polish rule and the rest was under the Swedes and Danes you see. Now you see those were all Lutherans then you see, whereas Polish are Catholics you see… There was a lot of difference in a lot of things between the eastern part – the Latgale and between the other side, the other part of Latvia you see. ….of course they had more children. They weren't as educated you know… There are some Catholics in Kurzeme as well, in some parts – small pockets of Catholics you know. But mainly Catholics were in Eastern Latvia. But most [Latvians]…were Lutherans. There were some Orthodox, Russian Orthodox, you know from the Russian days when the Tsar and all that but there weren't many of them.[232]

Under the Russian Empire, Latgale had been administered separately from the rest of Latvia and only here did the collective village or *mir* take root. During the inter-war period, 'Latgale duplicated and complicated the general Latvian party system with a regional one of its own and was socio-economically the country's most underdeveloped region'.[233]

Other regions also had distinctive cultures and traditions, and varying degrees of regional identity were present in many areas. For example, Kurzeme[234] in Latvia and the island of Saaremaa in Estonia both had regional identities.

The Baltic refugees who came to Britain lived all over the geographical areas that constitute present-day Latvia, Lithuania and Estonia. Interestingly, although some Lithuanians grew up in the Vilnius region, which formed part of Poland during the inter-war period, they still regard themselves as Lithuanians from Lithuania.[235] A significant number of refugees came from Vilnius and its environs partly due to its location in the south of Lithuania, an area relatively easy to escape from.[236] The majority of the EVWs originated from the western areas of Latvia, Lithuania and Estonia, from where they could escape the advancing Russian armies with greater ease, and from where the German army recruited first. Those who lived in the east had less success in escaping the Russian occupiers. There were thus few refugees from the Latgale region in Latvia, compared to central and western areas, since this region fell to the Russians swiftly. Likewise there were fewer refugees from the north-eastern areas of Lithuania, in comparison with southern and western areas. Many of the refugees came from capital cities or large towns, from where it was easy to board a train west. The capitals of Latvia and Estonia, Riga and Tallinn are on the western side of the countries, and both were on the Baltic Sea, from where boats could be boarded.

- *Religion*

There was a revival of religion during the inter-war period, after decades of suppression by the Russian State. Latvia and Estonia were primarily Lutheran countries, due to the German introduction of Lutheran Christianity in the Middle Ages (although Latgale in Latvia was Catholic) and Lithuania was overwhelmingly Catholic, as a result of the introduction of Latin Christianity by the Polish-Lithuanian Commonwealth. Prior to the introduction of Christianity, paganism had been the dominant belief system among the local populations. As part of its Russification policies, Russia had sought to convert the local populations to Russian Orthodoxy. However, as already discussed, the battle to stop religious suppression became a focus of the national awakenings in the nineteenth century, particularly in Lithuania, where the struggle to gain religious freedoms turned into a fight to save the nation.

As newly independent countries, the revival of religion became part of the nation-building process, particularly in Lithuania, where religiosity was greatest, and the religio-national link strongest. In Lithuania, the overwhelming majority of the population was Roman Catholic. Catholics made up a majority of the ethnic Lithuanian nationality, which composed some 80 per cent of the population and the numbers were increased by the significant Polish Catholic minority in Lithuania. In 1939, 85.5 per cent of the population were Catholic, 4.5 per cent were Protestant, 7 per cent Jewish, 2.5 per cent Orthodox and 0.5 per cent other religions.[237] The numbers of active believers were significantly higher than among the Lutheran population in either Estonia or Latvia, and Catholicism formed an important component of everyday life. After the declaration of independence, the Catholic Church gained full freedoms and privileges.[238] The Catholic Church also played an important role in the politics, culture and education system of the new independent Lithuanian State.

Jānis Sapiets estimates that in Latvia, Lutheranism embraced over 55 per cent of believers.[239] Latvia had a significant Catholic population in its eastern Latgale province.[240] In 1936, approximately 25 per cent of all believers in Latvia were Catholics.[241] Of the remainder, 9 per cent were Orthodox believers, 5 per cent Old Believers, 5 per cent Jews, and the rest composed mainly Moravian Brethren, Baptists and Adventists.[242]

In Estonia, a greater percentage of believers were Lutherans, due partly to the higher homogeneity of the population, and there was a sizeable Orthodox minority in the eastern part of the country. According to the 1934 plebiscite, 78 per cent of the population were Lutherans, 19 per cent were Greek Orthodox[243], 0.2 per cent Roman Catholic, 0.4 per cent Jews and 2.4 per cent other denominations.[244]

The Hill of Crosses in Lithuania

The overwhelming majority of Estonians and Latvians who came to Britain were Lutheran, although a few Latvians were Catholics from the Latgale region of Latvia. Most of the Lutheran Latvians in Britain stressed to me that religion was important mainly for social reasons and that Lutheranism was not a particularly significant component of Latvian national identity during the inter-war period. This was partly due to the religious heterogeneity in Latvia, and also because of its link with the oppressive Baltic German nobility.[245] In Latvia, dissatisfaction with Lutheranism as a national religion resulted in attempts to establish a religion specifically linked to Latvia's national identity. The result was the organisation of *Dievturi*[246], a neo-pagan religion, which attempted to recreate the religious beliefs of the ancient Latvians who worshipped deities.[247] *Dievturi* (or 'God Keeping') was derived from Latvian folk songs, and although it was quite successful in inter-war Latvia, it only added to the heterogeneity of religious belief in Latvia, and weakened attempts by Latvian Lutherans to create a national religion.[248]

I asked a Latvian woman, now living in Britain who was born in 1923, and grew up on a farm if she was religious as a child, and if she went to church. She replied:

> Erm, not terribly religious no. Yes, I suppose more than I am now. I was at school and I used to have a prayer in the morning and we used to go to church. I was never really overly religious, no, never really devoted. Never really religious really.[249]

An Estonian man in Britain drew a comparison between the levels of attendance at Lutheran churches in the inter-war period and the Church of England today. He stated that among the English, 'most people get married in church and baptised perhaps, and that's about it, and occasionally they have to go to church. Well, that was much the same there, although Lutheran Church was a bit more formal in areas.'[250]

- ### *Multi-ethnic societies*

One of the key features of Latvia, Lithuania and Estonia was that they all had significant ethnic groups, due to the different countries who had ruled the region. Most of the ethnic groups lived in the capital cities, or in the case of Latvia, in eastern areas from where few refugees escaped. The proportions of the total populations belonging to ethnic minorities were approximately one-tenth in Estonia, one-fifth in Lithuania and one-quarter in Latvia.[251] Russians formed the largest minority in Estonia and Latvia (eight and ten per cent of the total population in 1934)[252], and Jews were the largest minority group in Lithuania (seven per cent in 1923).[253] Jews and Germans were also sizeable groups in Latvia and Estonia, and significant Polish and German communities existed in Lithuania. Since most of the refugees who came to Britain grew up in the countryside, they had little contact with ethnic minorities during the inter-war period.

A series of festivals, celebrations and religious days punctuated the routine in both town and country and formed a significant component of the culture and annual cycle of life in each nation. These included days marking events in the farming calendar, weddings, births, funerals, national days and name days. Some of these had been marked for centuries, some were new days introduced during independence, and others were old traditions now celebrated freely, having been repressed during the Tsarist years.

Some of the national festivals in the three Baltic States were based on the countries' ancient pagan past, when celebrations were held marking important dates in the farming calendar. One of the most important of the old traditions which was celebrated freely and with renewed vigour in the independence period was St. John's Day, an important fertility festival held at midsummer. St. John's Day was celebrated in all three Baltic countries, but was perhaps most important in Latvia. Jānis, a Latvian man, now living in Leeds described the celebrations in Latvia:

> St John's Day – that was the most…important thing for everybody in the countryside. Nobody went to sleep that night, until sunrise of course. That's allowed. That's allowed by the Latvian tradition. Well of course, where [there] was somebody called name Jānis…they had to stay at home and wait for somebody to call to, you know, they used to come singing in the neighbourhood. And then when that was done they spend about half an hour or so eating and drinking and what have you, and playing music and dancing or whatever and then you go to the next house where there is John…..where there is a John in the family, they're just waiting. They have to provide the beer and the eating and so on. [254]

New days of national significance were introduced during the inter-war period, and some which had been previously repressed, were restored. The celebration of these days was intended to bring the nation together and instil national pride. One of the most important of the new days was Independence Day, celebrating the new independence gained in 1918. Latvian Independence Day was celebrated on 18 November, Estonian Independence Day on 24 February and Lithuanian Independence Day on 16 February. However, the significance of these days was initially muted. Heino Poopuu described the celebration of the new National Independence Day in Estonia:

February the 24th was declared an annual public holiday to commemorate the Declaration of Estonian National Independence in 1918. This event lacked tradition and had some way to go before being accepted as a proper by the older generation in our community.[255]

However, in later correspondence he stressed that while 'older generations in my village certainly did not attend any of the annual Independence Day official ceremonies on 24 February but as a pupil of our local school I was expected to and did take part in these on several occasions.'[256] He attributed the lack of enthusiasm to the immaturity of independence and the 'conservatism of the country folk'.[257] Only later, during the Soviet Period and in exile, did the National Independence Days attain major significance as symbols of national identity.

In Estonia, St. John's Day assumed a dual significance in the new independent Republic. Heino Poopuu explained:

> …St John's Day, the traditional mid-summer celebration with dancing by the bonfires at night. This shortest night of the year was imbued with magical connotations of eternal youth and purity in Estonian folklore. The young Republic had adopted this festival for the purpose of commemorating a decisive battle in the War of Independence against the Germans and renamed it Victory Day. So, in addition to a pagan and Christian tradition, it had become an important patriotic occasion too, with brass band-led processions and rather lengthy speeches.[258]

According to Heino Poopuu, Victory Day which commemorated 'a victorious battle in the war of independence against a Baltic German force on 23 June 1920, celebrated on the eve of St. John's Day with procession and bonfires, was quite popular'.[259]

In Lithuania, where the Tsarist attacks on religion had been viewed as direct attacks on the Lithuanian nation, the celebration of religious festivals began to attain significance during the independence period as representations of Lithuanian independence. Although the Tsarist government had not attempted to circumvent religious activity to the same degree as the later Soviet governments, celebration of religious festivals also became celebrations of nationhood. The celebration of religious days was also popular in Latvia and Estonia, although the link to national identity was far weaker than in Lithuania. Heino Poopuu described the lavish festivities associated with Christmas and New Year's Eve in Estonia, while Easter and Whitsuntide in contrast 'passed quietly as days of rest and relaxation.'[260] He also remarked that in Estonia, somewhat ironically, despite the Lutheranism of the population, Catholic Saints' name days were 'still very much part of traditions'.[261]

Another important 'national cultural event' in the new independent states was the Song Festival. In Estonia, the Song Festival was held in Tallinn at four-five yearly intervals during the inter-war period. Heino Poopuu noted that since many people in outlying regions could not afford to travel to Tallinn for these events, smaller scale versions of it were held in the regions. For example, on the island of Saaremaa a smaller version was held in Kuressaare.[262]

MEMORIES OF THE HOMELAND

How were these years in the homeland remembered by participants in this study? This is significant, not only because memories can colour and sometimes distort reality, but also because memories and interpretations of life in the homeland influenced attempts to recreate and restore aspects of the inter-war life in exile. Ethnic identities and cultures in exile were based in part, on a remembered and mythologised past.[263]

When assessing narratives relating life in the homeland, but told in the present, it is important to remember that they may have been reconstructed as a result of later experiences, for example, life in exile, recent return visits, and the reminiscence process associated with ageing. As with the narratives of many exiled groups, many testimonies represented childhood in the homeland as idyllic, carefree and happy. The rural upbringing of the refugees was perhaps the most important aspect in the remembering the past as idyllic. This is illustrated by the comments of a Latvian, now living in Rochdale:

> I just think about it [the homeland] only...when I was twenty...eighteen, nineteen...oh, there were beautiful fields, all everything's nice, all meadows, all flowers, everything's nice. Nice farms.[264]

I asked a Lithuanian woman in Manchester, whether she recalled her life in Lithuania as an idyllic time. She replied: 'Yes. I remember independence...yeah. That time I always remember, the life, because it was very good. Very good life. Everything we got'.[265] This particular woman came to England in 1948 accompanied by her young daughter, who was not yet ten years old. Although she spent only her first few years in Lithuania, the daughter described how the Lithuanian community remembered independence as an idyllic period, and how the younger generations were taught about the 'wonderful' life there. She stated:

> I was taught that it was a wonderful life there. I was brought up in this dream - wonderful life, wonderful country. Everything was absolutely terrific. I was brought up in that spirit. We all were in fact. Everyone reminisced.[266]

In collective memory, the period of inter-war independence was regarded as a golden age. Just as during the independence period, history was reinterpreted to legitimise independence, so too the histories written during the Soviet period by Latvian, Lithuanian and Estonian émigré and dissident historians stress the achievements of the inter-war republics. The participants in this project frequently voiced the opinion that without the Soviet and German occupations, the Baltic States would now be on a par economically, socially and politically with the countries of Western Europe. They stressed the economic successes, and the return to democracy just as the war in Europe was breaking out. According to many exiles, the drift to authoritarianism which occurred in Lithuania from 1926 onwards, and in Latvia and Estonia during the mid to late thirties, was only brief and caused primarily by the economic problems brought about by the world recession and the immaturity of the democratic political systems.

Participants and historians have also stressed the cultural vitality of the inter-war period. Vardys stated that: 'In part because of these pre-1940 achievements, popular memories of the independence period have not only survived in the Baltic Republics, but also have been glamorised and romanticised'.[267] This may have been particularly true among those refugees who were only children in the homeland, and never had to cope with adult life and maintain a living.

However, despite a collective memory of the homeland as idyllic and happy years, it would be a mistake to suggest that all individual memories of childhood were remembered as happy. A Latvian man, now living in Leeds, grew up in Liepaja in Latvia, and left his home aged sixteen. His mother died when he was five, and with ten children in the family, the children were separated. Some of his brothers and sisters were placed in orphanages.[268] He described his unhappy childhood:

> I was [a] tough kid. I was bullied...expelled three times, expelled from school for fighting'. 'I came from [a] town. I wasn't brought up you know, in country on a farm, so they took

the mickey out of you when you came from town, so [you had to] stand up and fight for yourself.[269]

Other individuals also drew attention to some of the unhappy and negative aspects of life in the homeland, although this was only a minority. A few individuals stressed a hard, ascetic existence, living without luxuries and having to work long hours on the farmstead.

Although collective memory also tends to highlight the positive aspects of the homeland, it does occasionally acknowledge some of the negative elements of the inter-war homelands, particularly in relation to the rise of authoritarianism. Clare Thomson, a second generation Estonian in Britain asked her grandmother if President Päts, the Estonian President who led the country during the drift to authoritarianism in the 1930's, was really loved at the time, after seeing photographs of him with 'heavy jowls and a glowering expression'.[270] Her grandmother replied: 'Well yes…we thought Päts was a good man; we liked him well enough'. Thomson continued however: 'Nostalgia is…by no means unqualified'. Thomson drew attention to scepticism in the Baltic States about the rise of authoritarianism and the response of the governments to the first Soviet occupation.[271] Whether or not nostalgia is greater among émigrés than among those who remained in the homeland is difficult to judge. From my interviews with the Baltic communities in Britain, there is evidence of scepticism about the necessity of authoritarian rule for so many years. Referring to the authoritarian rule of Konstantin Päts, Heino Poopuu voiced the opinion that 'a return to freer democratic practices of the twenties…ought to have been quicker than it actually was'.[272] However, having now living though half a century of liberal democracy in Britain, the degree to which émigrés current opinions of the homeland, reflect attitudes contemporary to the period, is uncertain.

In interviews, memories of childhood and of the homeland were described as very fresh in the memory. Many of the participants in this study voiced the same opinion as one Latvian man who stated that: 'I remember everything from childhood more than I remember what happened yesterday'.[273] As a natural process of time and the ageing process, the clarity of homeland memories may have been intensified by the diasporic experience.[274]

THE HOMELAND - CONCLUDING REMARKS

The fact that the refugees spent their childhood in newly independent countries is significant. The inter-war period was an era of change. An important area of transformation was the ongoing process of modification and consolidation of national identities and national cultures. As the drift from pluralism to an ethnic nationalism suggests, national identity construction was ongoing. During this period, the idea of national cultures and national identities is somewhat illusory. Regional differences remained highly significant, as did religious and class-based identities. Many of those who lived in the countryside rarely visited other areas of their homeland, and knowledge of national developments was patchy. Although school was an important forum for the transmission of national identities in the countryside, it is doubtful that strong national identities or national cultures had formed among the refugees as children and young adults, by 1939. It is significant that many aspects of exile identities and cultures did not exactly replicate those present in the inter-war period. Exile cultures and identities were based partly on memories of the homeland (which as we have seen were not always indicative of reality) and perhaps more importantly, they developed further as a result of subsequent experiences of war, displacement and settlement. As this book will show, these events led to further modification of these cultures and identities. The fact that the Baltic refugees came from newly independent states with under-developed and rather malleable identities and cultures facilitated this process.

CHAPTER 3

Displacement

> We didn't really have a lot of things, but my father said that if
> you were a refugee, if you try to carry too much with you, you'd
> in the end lose everything, so take essentials... It's as if you get
> somewhere where you can live, you either get back or...start
> somewhere else. If you're alive and working you'll acquire
> things again and if you don't, you won't need them. Well if
> you're dead, you don't need them. So material goods you can
> lose, but you can rebuild again given a chance, but if you try to
> cart around so much that you can't cope with then you're going
> to be left behind somewhere and there's no point in running
> away from home, to be overtook by the army from which
> you're escaping somewhere else. So we had only a couple of
> suitcases each.
>
> (First Generation Latvian woman in Britain)[275]

IN 1939, MOST LATVIANS, LITHUANIANS AND ESTONIANS
who became refugees in the Second World War, were still children or
young adults living in their homelands, attending school, higher
education or starting their first jobs. Only seven years later, they were
refugees living in Displaced Persons Camps, about to go to Britain to
start a new life. It was during these intervening years that independence
came to an abrupt end and tens of thousands of Baltic citizens were
uprooted from their homelands. In 1940-41, the Baltic States endured
the first Soviet occupation, rapidly followed by a German occupation
from 1941-44. In the autumn of 1944, a second Russian offensive
began.

This chapter will discuss the four main ways that Latvians,
Lithuanians and Estonians in Britain became displaced from their

homelands during these years, and the stimuli to the uprooting – the Russian and German occupations. The four routes of displacement were: (1) Recruitment into the Russian army during the first Soviet occupation; (2) Recruitment for labour in Germany during the German occupation; (3) Recruitment for the German military; (4) Displacement in advance of the second Russian occupation.[276] The chapter will also assess the effects of these years on the refugees, particularly in relation to their newly developing national identities. Since the events of these years have been amply covered elsewhere, personal accounts, which reflect the diversity of wartime experience will form the centrepiece of this discussion.[277]

THE FIRST SOVIET OCCUPATION

The developments leading to the first Russian occupation of the Baltic States are infamous. On 23 August 1939, German and Russian Foreign Ministers, Joachim von Ribbentrop and Vyacheslav Mikhaylovich Molotov signed the so-called 'Nazi-Soviet Pact', a non-aggression pact, within which a 'secret protocol' assigned Latvia and Estonia to the Soviet sphere of influence and Lithuania to the German sphere. On 23 September, following the fall of Poland to Germany, a second secret protocol amended the pact, allocating Lithuania to the Soviet Union in return for German concessions in Poland.[278] These protocols laid the way open for Soviet occupation of the Baltic States, bringing to an end their independence which had been gained for the first time, only 21 years earlier in 1918.

Some population displacement took place shortly after the Nazi-Soviet Pact had been signed, when Hitler carried out the mass resettlement of Baltic Germans from Latvia and Estonia to Polish territories incorporated into the Reich.[279] The secret German-Soviet agreement in September 1939 had made provision for German nationals and ethnic Germans to migrate from areas under Soviet jurisdiction to those under German jurisdiction.[280] As a result, 13,700 Germans were evacuated from Estonia and 52,583 from Latvia.[281] They were to be employed to assist in the correction of Germany's wartime labour shortage; in short, Baltic labourers helped to provide the economic and technical basis for the German armies.[282]

Soviet designs on the Baltic States were achieved during the following nine months. As one Latvian stated, 'there was no war'.[283] 'The Russians just came in...they just occupied, without any war'.[284] On 23 September 1939, Estonia received an ultimatum, conceded on 2 October, leading to the establishment of Russian military bases on her soil. Similar developments took place in Latvia and Lithuania. In mid-

June 1940, all three Baltic States received ultimatums from Moscow demanding full military occupation and reconstruction of Baltic governments under Soviet supervision. Rigged elections were held in all three Baltic States in which candidates were chosen by the USSR, producing 'People's Assemblies', which 'requested' annexation to the Soviet Union in July 1940.[285] According to a Latvian woman in Great Britain, the Soviet regime claimed that, 'the Latvians had voted that they wanted the Soviet System.'[286] She described the rigged elections:

> Well of course we voted because they were already in, with the army and all your passport was stamped, whether you went to vote or not and there's only one thing to vote on…no choice, just the one. The passport was stamped so you could see who didn't go to vote. It was stamped and then as soon as this government was elected they went to Moscow and asked to join. So it was all a put-up job. On paper it looks all right. Yes the people voted, they wanted to join.[287]

The first Soviet occupation from June 1940 to June 1941 brought major changes to the lives of the inhabitants of the Baltic States. Experiences during these years account for the mass emigration in advance of the second Russian occupation, and the attitude towards the German occupation in 1941. Anatol Lieven, author of *The Baltic Revolution*, describes what happened during the early months of the occupation:

> The sessions of the 'People's Assemblies'…also passed measures nationalising industry and the banks. Many managers were sacked and replaced by local communists brought in from Russia, or even ordinary workers. The result was a steep fall in productivity. By the time of the German invasion of June 1941, 90 per cent of shops had also been expropriated.
>
> There was neither the time nor the structures to establish full control over local culture. Similarly, full collectivisation of agriculture did not follow annexation. However, all farms over 30 hectares (75 acres) were confiscated and distributed to smaller farmers. This led to a sharp reduction in production. Early in 1941 high requisition quotas were set up, partly to compensate for this fall, and partly to put pressure on farmers to join the collectives. The new rulers announced salary increases for poorer workers, but these were soon negated by price rises, and by demands for longer hours and harder work, backed by ferocious sanctions. When, in late 1940, the independent currencies were abolished and replaced by the rouble, the exchange rate was confiscatory and had the effect of destroying Baltic savings.[288]

Transformations of the political elite also took place, including the expansion and consolidation of the tiny local communist parties, through local support and Russian cadres, and the expulsion of non-communist left-wingers unwilling to convert to communism. Many members of the political elite from the independence period were deported, including Latvian President Karlis Ulmanis, who was deported to Russia, dying in prison there two years later.[289] President Konstantin Päts of Estonia was also deported and later died in an NKVD 'psychiatric clinic' in 1956.[290] By the end of 1940, arrests and deportations were at the rate of 200-300 a month.[291] Deportations culminated on the terrible night of 13-14 June 1941, when an estimated 100, 000 Latvian, Lithuanian and Estonian men, women and children, including many civil servants and professionals, were deported to Siberia in cattle trucks.[292] Those selected for deportation included the twenty-three categories of 'enemies of the people' and their families. These categories included government officials, businessmen, trade unionists and clergymen.[293] Milosz states that almost one per cent of the total population of the Baltic States was deported during this one night.[294] A substantial proportion spent the rest of their lives in Siberia, unable to return to Soviet-occupied homelands.

In 1955, Plensers described the deportations in Latvia when:

Over 15,000 Latvians, regardless of sex or age were dragged from their sleep to lorries and transported to railway "loading stations", where the male heads of families were separated from their wives and children. The deportees were crammed into freight cars. For sanitary purposes, the cars had holes cut into the floor, which also served as the only opening for air. Thus the victims were subjected to unbearable physical and mental torture in the stifling cars, scorched by the summer heat, without food and water. Their journey which ultimately took them to slave labour camps in remote districts of Arctic Russia and Siberia, lasted for several weeks.[295]

The night of 13-14 June became a symbol of the barbarism of Russia for the Baltic States, and also for the diaspora. Every year on the night of the 13-14 June, or as close to that date as possible, special remembrance gatherings are held in Latvian, Lithuanian and Estonian clubs across Great Britain, commemorating the deportations. Almost every Latvian, Lithuanian and Estonian knew a relative, friend or neighbour who was deported on that night. Deportations brought home to even the youngest Latvians, Lithuanians and Estonians the brutality of the Russian occupation. The experiences of a Latvian woman now living in Nottingham are not untypical:

My grandmother died in Siberia. My cousins grew up in Siberia. My auntie was there and my mother's cousin was there with his family.[296]

Another Latvian woman also lost her aunt, uncle and grandmother in the deportations. She describes what happened to those who were deported to Siberia:

I think it may not be true to say that every family had a family member deported but at least every family…at least knew someone either a friend or whatever, but a lot of people lost relatives and that was in '41, just before German army came in, 2 weeks before…it was war. They had little to eat in Russia and of course they wouldn't save any for people like this, I mean they were split off immediately…went to labour camps. The women, children were sent out to Kolkhoz. They didn't really want them…but whatever the women managed to…get from begging I suppose they'd give to children, and then…within a year they were all dead because of malnutrition and the children were picked up and put in homes.[297]

Many of the Baltic refugees in Britain, who are still alive today, were just teenagers, when the Russians first occupied the Baltic States in 1940-41. A Latvian woman from Riga who now lives in Nottingham described her experiences of the first occupation:

Well, of course they robbed the country, everything…everything was sent to [the] Soviet Union, and…you couldn't get anything in the shops anymore, and…what I can remember they had a lot of what they call the 'Demonstrations and Manifestations'. On certain days, you had to walk in these demonstrations…and you had to carry the placards, and…. 'Long live the Soviet Union', 'Long live the October Revolution', and all that. And, all I can remember, that year in my memory, is sort of very drab, very grey. I can remember, especially in the autumn and winter, it seemed the skies were grey, and you weren't happy at all, and….just the red flags everywhere.[298]

She was just 14 when the Soviets first occupied Latvia, and was still at school. She describes how the Soviet occupation affected her schooling:

…we were learning Middle Ages. Well, that was all right, but also we were still on the History of Latvia…that was cancelled, but instead of that you had to learn the Party, the Short Course of the Communist Party. That was the first thing you learnt at school.

Of course, mathematics they were the same. Grammar was the

same. The Latvian language that was the same, but the emphasis was put on those writers who...had tendencies to be on the left side of the communists...[299]

I asked her if it was the Latvian authors, rather than Russian authors whom they studied. She replied:

> Yes, we were only under the Soviet occupation for one year, so they couldn't get everything done in a year. [Laughs] Luckily![300]

While the Soviet regime was able to undertake some Sovietization of culture, including changes in school syllabi, restrictions on religious worship and the disbanding of community organisations, it was unable to achieve complete cultural assimilation, due to the relatively short period of occupation. However, significant changes did take place rapidly, leaving populations in no doubt about the Soviet regime's long term goals. In all three nations, all non-Communist-controlled public activity was proscribed. Political, social, religious and ideological groups which could not be assimilated within Communist fronts were disbanded.[301] The curricula saw drastic revisions, including the deletion of some writers in the native literary tradition. Many native writers had to undergo 'selective presentation'.[302] For example, Vincas Kudirka, author of Lithuania's national anthem was 'demonstrably excised from plans of study'.[303] Press control was introduced early. Printing houses and shops were taken over and lists of banned books and brochures were issued.[304]

In Lithuania, the Soviet regime began implementing its goals for the annihilation of Catholicism, although as Bourdeaux points out 'during the first Soviet occupation the persecution of the Church could not be carried through to its logical conclusion'.[305] Nevertheless, significant repressive measures did take place. Soviet law had always proclaimed that religious practice should be confined to worship within the four walls of a church.[306] Thus, all Catholic societies and organisations were annihilated, including the confiscation of their assets and all specialised activities were abolished, including chaplaincy work in hospitals and schools. Priests were forced to sign an oath of loyalty to the Soviet Union and all monastic and seminary land was confiscated. Wayside crosses and shrines were desecrated and demolished and several religious holidays were abolished. Intimidation of priests and believers brought fear to many Lithuanian Catholics, who composed over 85 per cent of the population in 1939.[307] These actions convinced Lithuanians of the Soviet regime's plans for the Catholic Church, an integral pillar of national life and identity.

Similar developments also took place in Latvia and Estonia, where the Lutheran Church was targeted in the Soviet regime's drive towards atheism. In Estonia, for example, church property was nationalised, the theology faculty of Tartu University was closed, and church publishing and chaplaincy work with children and youth were banned. Only Sunday church services and the celebration of key religious events, such as funerals were tolerated.[308]

Many of the participants in this study from all three Baltic States described the fear engendered by the Soviet occupation and how they were forced to live from day to day, able to make few plans for the future. It could be argued that the fear created by Soviet rule affected the populations more severely than the economic downturn. Despite growing shortages in foodstuffs[309] and the loss of savings, many families who lived on the farmstead were reasonably self-sufficient and were less affected than those living in towns. One Latvian woman who was just a teenager during the first Russian occupation and lived on a farmstead in the Latvian countryside remembers not missing much in the way of food, since the farm was almost completely self-sufficient.[310] The most important shortage as she recalls, was sugar.[311] Most importantly she felt scared to talk to anyone about the Russians for fear of reprisals.[312] Another Latvian from Leeds also described the fear engendered by the Russian occupation:

> I'm sorry to say, unless you've been occupied you can't…understand what it's like to be occupied by a foreign power. It's impossible to explain, so the people in Britain don't know except maybe the people in Guernsey and Jersey, they might be the only people that might understand what it means to be occupied, when you can't speak, when you…have three of four people and you can't have a discussion, because you don't know who's listening or maybe the third or the fourth person might be a collaborator or…whatever…you're living in fear all the time.[313]

The Russian occupation of the Baltic States between 1940-41 produced widespread hatred towards the Soviet regime among the Baltic populations. In Latvia, the year 1940-41 is known as the 'Year of Horrors' (*Balgais Gads*).[314] It served as the only personal experience of Soviet rule for all the refugees who came to Britain, and became etched in their memories throughout exile. Estimates for the numbers killed or deported during the first Soviet occupation are 34,250 in Latvia, almost 60,000 in Estonia and 75,000 in Lithuania.[315] The negative attitudes towards Russia, which existed during the inter-war period in all three countries, intensified as a result of the occupation. The Soviet regime was now deemed to be the primary enemy of the Latvian, Lithuanian and Estonian nations, and a virulent anti-Russian enmity quickly became an ingrained aspect of shifting national identities.

A Latvian who was only about ten years old when the Russian occupation began described his attitude towards the Russians:

> Well, as I say the Russians were very, very, very evil. They didn't…respect anybody or anybody's privileges or privacy or anything. They used to go around you know, robbing, raping and all the rest of it…[316]

An Estonian man in Britain drew attention to the more potent anti-Russian element in the Estonian identity as a result of the Russian occupation, which became more significant than the traditional anti-German feeling:

> Traditionally, Estonians [and Russians] are…historically, they were enemies. I don't know in what order, but probably Germans first, greatest, greatest [enemy]. To my grandfather…of course Germans were the enemy number one then, then Russians, Poles, Swedes, Danes and so on, but up to this Russian – the Communist period, the Germans were considered to be enemy number one. Estonians on the whole didn't like Germans. They respected them, but they didn't like them. The Russians, they didn't like them either very much, but they didn't particularly hate them, they tended to sort of look down on them a little bit, but communism changed all that, so enemy number one is Russia now and Russians.[317]

It was not only the oppressive measures unleashed by the Soviet regime, which engendered opposition to it. Most importantly perhaps, it was the loss of a hard-fought for independence, which solidified the previously embryonic national identities. Having previously been concerned about little other than the farmstead, the village, family and friends, the survival of the nation was now in threat. While outward displays of patriotism risked life and limb, the Russian occupation and, particularly, the deportations, instilled a deep sense of nationhood and patriotism into the young Latvians, Lithuanians and Estonians. The deportations linked the fate of the nation directly to the fate of loved ones, for the first time since the fall of the Tsarist Empire. During the Russian occupation, the threat to the nation through Sovietization was felt on a daily basis - in school, church, in shops, and even on the farmstead through the pressure to collectivise and the loss of savings. During this period, the home became the main arena for cultural expressions of national identity, where Latvian, Lithuanian and Estonian authors were read, national foods prepared and the fate of the homeland discussed in earnest. Those aspects of Latvian, Lithuanian and Estonian culture which differentiated Latvians, Lithuanians and Estonians from

Russians became increasingly linked to national identities.

Displacement 1: Recruitment into the Russian army

As well as engendering shifts in national identities, the first Russian occupation led to the first displacement of some Latvians, Lithuanians and Estonians, who later migrated to Great Britain – through recruitment into the Russian army, and subsequent displacement in Europe. This was the route only of a small minority of men who came to Britain, mainly Estonians.

Recruitment was most extensive among the Estonian population, due to the length of time taken by Germany to invade and occupy Estonia, during their summer offensive of the Baltic countries in 1941. According to Milosz, while the German attack swept through Lithuania and Latvia very quickly (within two weeks), Estonia took much longer (two months and longer for the islands) 'because the Germans had to stop to re-organise their supply lines, giving the Soviet army an opportunity to regroup at the approaches to Leningrad'.[318] As a result, Estonia suffered considerably more destruction and casualties. It also enabled mobilisation into the Soviet army, leading about 10,000 young Estonian men to deaths in Russian lumber camps.[319]

Some of the recruits were captured by the Germans during the war, and held as POW's in Germany. A small minority were able to escape when the Western front advanced, and later found their way to DP camps in Western occupation zones. The story of an Estonian man, now living in Britain illustrates one such displacement route. He recounted his experiences:

> ...the war started, Russia started mobilising people you know, men from Estonia to take to Russia and I was waiting with the first mobilisation from Tallinn, our capital...I was called up on 2 June 1941. So I was the first lot, but they had more after that.
>
> ...first of all they sent us all in the labour camps, and [at] that time there were terrible conditions - lack of food, cold...
>
> And in 1942, early on anyway, February I think...they started forming the national units, Estonian first, which consisted eventually of two divisions, called Estonian Riflecorps, and first time after training and all that, first time I were in battle of Velikie Luki, which ...started back end of '42, which were encircled by Russians before, and Germans were still encircled and Estonian units were put in to fight the Germans in that circle. Only one unit went to open front.
>
> I was in battle 6 January. We set off from Siberia just 23

December and we arrived just the night before the Velikie Luki by train, and then the following morning we were sent to battle. And [laughs] I was squadron leader and they all just vanished. We were made to storm a strong building and the Germans were in them...we didn't have anybody left. I got wounded and I, well I fell down in an old crater....

I was long enough in that crater. It was snow covered and well I didn't know what to do. I got wounded in the back with a splinter. I could feel blood running and I didn't know how bad it was....[320]

He managed eventually to get out of the crater and find help for his wound. He was sent back to battle at Velikie Luki a fortnight later, where he managed to survive another battle when, by his estimates, about 2250 men out of a regiment of 3000 were killed. After attempting to cross Lake Peipsi, which divides Estonia from Russia, he was captured by the Germans and held as a prisoner-of war. He was taken to a POW camp in Germany, near Essen where he describes the conditions:

We were woken up at five o'clock in the morning, and then we stood in the yard till eight o'clock.

Dinner was sort of bits of potatoes and like a pig swill with blood and....[we] had a pint of that in the evenings.

I was only there three months and I only weighed 48 kilos. I'm 80 now....[321]

When the Western front began to advance, the Germans took their POWs back behind the lines and he managed to escape to the Allied side, where he worked in a German village for a year. He then moved into a DP camp, before being recruited for work in a textile mill near Halifax. After six years of war and displacement, the young man finally landed in the port of Harwich, England, on 7 September 1947.[322]

Although like all the EVW stories, this man's experiences are unique, they give an impression of some of the ordeals endured by those recruited by the Russians and the hazardous journey from the homeland to Britain. Very few recruits to the Russian army found safety, and indeed the Estonian man interviewed above, informed me that he was the only member of the active Estonian community in his locality in Britain, who had fought on the Russian side.

THE GERMAN OCCUPATION 1941-1944

The German occupation of the Baltic States began just one week after the Russian deportations on 22 June 1941. Within days the Wehrmacht had cut a swathe into the Baltic and the Red Army fled westwards.

Promising to liberate the Latvians, Lithuanians and Estonians from Russian tyranny and arbitrary rule, the Germans were initially welcomed. As one commentator suggested, Latvians, like Lithuanians and Estonians 'had lived through a year so horrible that they bedecked their age-old enemies, the advancing Germans with flowers'.[323] A Latvian woman in Nottingham explained that before the mass deportations, Latvians 'hated the Germans as well because they were the rulers of Latvians for 700 years. But in this instance we were really pleased that they came'. [324]

The welcome was not wholehearted however: most Latvians, Lithuanians and Estonians regarded the Germans merely as the lesser of two evils. Andrejs Plakans stated that many Latvians 'believed that, under the circumstances, this "traditional enemy"(Germans) would be an improvement over the "traditional enemy"(Russians) whose brief rule had just been concluded'.[325] A Latvian woman stressed that the Latvians would have 'welcomed Ghenghis Khan if he had saved us from Russians'[326], and a Latvian man noted that while the Germans did liberate Latvia, 'of course the Germans weren't any friends really. We knew that they were occupiers just like the Russians were, but they were not as nasty as Russians were'.[327]

However, the welcoming of the German occupation, initially tinged with cynicism, soon turned to disillusionment, when German promises of autonomy came to naught. A Latvian woman described the feelings of disappointment. Initially, 'there was all Latvian flags out…but, they soon ordered them to be taken down you know. They (the Latvians) felt very much disappointed. Well, it was sort of get rid of one devil, and another one comes in'.[328] As German rule was consolidated, feelings of bitterness increased. *The Daily Telegraph* reported on 14 August 1941 that:

> Some Lithuanian "patriots" are now bitterly regretting the help they gave the Germans at the outset of the attack on Russia. They realise that the Nazi's have exploited them and flouted their national aspirations, which were encouraged as a prelude to war.[329]

Some of the interviewees were more positive about their experience of German rule, claiming that there was a return to a normality of sorts and that they were left alone by the Germans to get along with daily life. One Latvian woman, now living in Nottingham talked about how life returned to some sort of normality under the Germans:

We enjoyed the German films, and as I went to school again, we had dances, we could go to theatres. At least we, you know, we were free, from my opinion, because I was only a youngster then, we were free to do what we liked, but under the Russians you know, you couldn't. You were told you had to do this and you had to do that. Now you are going here...[330]

Another woman agreed that German rule was preferable to rule by Russia:

Well, maybe they [the Germans] were a bit better than Russians, but no, not that good. [They] still occupied the nation, but to me, Germans were better than Russians.[331]

One of the reasons why German rule was initially perceived as being more tolerable than Soviet rule was that Germanization was less of an urgent priority to the Germans, than Sovietization had been to the Soviets. Misiunas and Taagapera explain:

On the whole, cultural life was the area of national existence least affected by the German occupation. Although cultural and religious affairs were strictly supervised, the Nazis, unlike the Soviets, did not act on a perceived need to infuse them immediately with a particular ideology. The requirements of waging war obviously took precedence over those of eventual Germanization, and so these concerns were left largely in the hand of the local authorities.[332]

According to Misiunas and Taagapera, the motivation for neglecting cultural life was that:

In the short run, the Germans considered Baltic territory as an occupied region open to maximum exploitation of its resources for the general pursuit of the war effort, and the Baltic peoples were viewed primarily as providers of agricultural products and labor.[333]

Some changes relating to cultural life did take place, for example, censorship, and the Nazification of history and biology curricula in schools. However, the Germans offered some concessions in terms of the toleration of national culture. Organised religion was largely left alone and the performing arts, such as theatre and opera continued to function. In Latvia, the Latvian flag and national anthem were permitted and in 1943 a Song Festival was held.[334]

However, whilst successful in appeasing the Baltic populations initially, cultural concessions were insufficient to stem opposition to German rule in the longer term. In the economic sphere, the Germans sought to utilise Baltic territory as an exploitative resource to aid the war effort. Although some token restoration of private property took place in 1943, initial promises of full re-privatisation did not materialise.[335] The currency was re-valued, leaving the Baltic peoples, already fleeced by Soviet fiscal re-evaluations, virtually penniless.[336] Rationing in towns and cities continued to leave the self-sufficient farmers in a better position than urban dwellers, and, as under the first Soviet occupation, the black market flourished. Harsh economic policies fuelled the rising tide of resentment towards German rule during 1943. Other policies, which furthered opposition to German rule, were the enforced recruitment for labour in Germany and conscription into the German military forces, which also led to the second and third displacement routes of Latvians, Lithuanians and Estonians in Britain.

Displacement 2: Recruitment for labour in Germany

The second route of displacement for Latvians, Lithuanians and Estonians in Britain was conscription for labour in Germany, and subsequent dislocation in Germany at the end of the war. Only a minority of Latvians, Lithuanians and Estonians in Britain were uprooted via this route. The use of Baltic labour for manpower began almost immediately, and continued throughout the German occupation. Men and women from all three countries were recruited for labour. Approximately three per cent of the Lithuanian population was recruited for labour, two per cent of the Estonian population and one per cent of Latvians.

Recruitment for labour began in earnest from the end of 1941, when Germany began to requisition tens of thousands of Baltic workers for its factories. On 19 December 1941, Rosenberg decreed a general work obligation for those aged 18-45.[337] Failure to register was to be punished by three months' imprisonment and a 1,000 mark fine.[338] In 1942, university students were required to first serve a year in the German youth labour force (*Reicharbeitsdienst*).[339] Labour decrees continued throughout the German occupation. The Baltic populations were relatively successful in evading labour obligations, using a variety of avoidance tactics. Some fled to the woods, while for others, methods such as bribery of local officials were often enough to avoid labour conscription. However, as resistance increased, conscription methods grew harsher.[340] A Rosenberg[341] memo to Himmler on 20 July 1944 suggested that a total of 126, 000 Baltic workers had been sent to Germany, including 75,000 Lithuanians, 35,000 from Latvia and 15,000 from Estonia.[342] Baltic workers were employed in a wide variety of areas of labour. Some were engaged in military construction work or for work in the militarised industries, including women by the thousands.[343]

A Latvian woman in Britain who was selected for forced labour described very little about her experiences and despite her experiences felt that the Germans did not treat the Latvians as badly as had the Russians:

> I was sent to Germany to work. We probably would have tried to go anyway because I was absolutely terrified of the Russians. I would have thought I wouldn't have wanted to stay there no way and when you're young…it was quite heartbreaking really. It wasn't a happy time for us.[344]

A Lithuanian man in Bolton was also recruited for labour in Germany. He faced the choice of labour in Germany or digging trenches on the Eastern Front:

> I left Lithuania in 1943. I was 18 years of age. The war was going on in the east, and the Germans wanted workers and I had no choice. Actually, no, I had a choice. They said you want to go and dig trenches in the Eastern Front or you want to go to Germany and work in Germany? There at least there will be no lice. So I went to Germany and I worked. I worked on an airfield, and that's why I always have a great respect to the Royal Air Force because we used to…they used to bomb the flaming place and we used to fill the holes up you see [laughs]. And [they] used to come and bomb us while we were still there. Can you imagine on an airfield, flat as a pancake, nowhere to hide, no? So that was the experience. That was how I got to Germany.[345]

Displacement 3: Recruitment for the German military

Recruitment rapidly extended to the military sphere. Thousands of Latvian, Lithuanian and Estonian men were recruited into the German war machine from 1941 to 1943, later becoming captured by the Allies as POW's. Many were able, subsequently, to acquire DP status and migrate to Britain.

The recruitment of Latvians, Lithuanians and Estonians into the German military during this period is extremely controversial, and has brought negative media attention to Britain's Baltic communities. The major foci of controversy is whether some Latvians, Lithuanians and Estonians in Britain committed war crimes, particularly those who served in the Estonian and Latvian Legions - national armies created by the Germans, but led by Estonians and Latvians.[346] The fact that the Estonian and Latvian Legions were called the Estonian and Latvian 'Waffen SS' Legions has associated them with the activities of the

German Waffen SS units, which participated in the mass massacres of Eastern Europe's Jewish populations.

There is also controversy as to whether or not the members of the Legions volunteered and could therefore be described as collaborators with the Nazi regime, or whether they were conscripted. These issues have been raised because some historians claim that the British Government's screening of DPs prior to their recruitment as EVWs, was inadequate, and enabled war criminals and collaborators to enter Britain.[347]

In Great Britain, the War Crimes Act passed in 1991, allowed 'prosecution for murders in German-occupied territories before 1945 even if the accused were not British citizens at the time of the alleged offences'.[348] The Act marked an about-turn in government policy towards suspected East European war criminals in Britain. As late as 1983, in response to Soviet requests to extradite a suspected Estonian war criminal to the USSR for trial, Baroness Young, then Minister of State at the Foreign and Commonwealth Office had informed Patrick Ground, MP, that:

> In December 1950, the Government notified allied Governments represented on the United nations War Crimes Commission that we considered we had discharged our obligations with regard to the surrender of alleged war criminals. The Government also informed the War Crimes Commission that we no longer regarded ourselves under an obligation to deport such persons…We have at no time recognised *de jure* the incorporation of the territory of Estonia with the U.S.S.R.[349]

Until 1999, the Act had failed to bring sentence to any war criminals in Britain, due to lack of evidence, the elderly age and ill health of potential defendants.[350] However, in 1999 the first full trial of a suspected war criminal took place, when 78 year old Anthony Sawoniuk was found guilty of murdering Jews while serving as a police officer in Nazi-occupied Belarus, and was given a life sentence. It is unlikely that any more suspects will be brought to trial under the Act.[351]

Nevertheless, the issue remained very much alive, and was highlighted by the media coverage in December 1999, of Konrad Kalejs, a suspected Latvian war criminal and Australian citizen, who was found to be living in Britain, after being deported from America and Canada.[352] The evidence relating to war criminals entering Britain is extremely complex and contested[353], and as the matter is of limited relevance to this study[354], will not be discussed in depth here. Further information can be found elsewhere.[355] There is however a general consensus[356] in the evidence presented by the British government and Baltic representatives in the late–1940's[357], and among several eminent historians today, which is worth mentioning.[358] This consensus holds that the Latvian and Estonian Legions were largely front-line troops, and cannot be compared in any way to German Waffen-SS units. This point was stressed by a Latvian in Britain, who stated:

> You see there were quite a lot of SS and in the west they think that all SS is the same. Well [Latvian] Waffen SS were just units that were fighting in the front. That's all. We were SS units in the front.

> We were fighting Russians on the front along with anybody else...but because Latvians had this SS on they were war-mongers and god knows what, they were Nazis...[359]

Juris Sinka, author of *Latvia and Latvians* also stressed the point that the Latvian Legion was distinct from the German Waffen SS units:

> In the light of recent slanderous allegations, circulating in the west and originating largely from the Soviet Union, about the role of the Latvian and Estonian forces in the Second World War, it must be stated that these forces – whatever the label, and the label was not of the Baltic people's choosing - were ordinary conscript armed forces which received ordinary training and were used exclusively for fighting against Soviet armed forces. They had nothing whatever to do with the political SS units which received special training in German SS schools and carried out special assignments. The only special assignments the men of the Latvian Legion were ever required to carry out were concerned with military operations in particularly difficult sectors of the front line...[360]

These facts were later used by Baltic representatives in the case made to Allied governments to transfer former Legionaries into DP camps. In November 1944, the Latvian Legion gained permission to remove the SS initials from the uniforms of the Legion and substitute the former National Army emblem – the sun in the 15th Division and the National Fire Cross (reversed swastika) in the 19th division.[361] In 1950, the Displaced Persons Commission reversed the classification of the Legions as 'Waffen SS'.[362]

There is also a consensus that although some were volunteers (an unknown quantity), probably a majority of recruits to Latvian and Estonian Legions were forcibly conscripted. There is also recognition that some war criminals almost certainly did enter these countries, as testified by the trial of Anthony Sawoniuk. Those suspected include several members of the Byelorussian, Ukrainian, Polish and Baltic communities in Great Britain.[363] However, they composed a small percentage of the total labour recruit populations in these countries.

War crimes were most likely to have been carried out in several contexts, but not as part of the activities of the Baltic Legions. For example, they may have been carried out during the sporadic pogroms, which accompanied the German *Einsatzgruppen* killing units, which swept into the Baltic States, during the early phases of the German occupation. Thousand of Jews were also killed by the Latvian, Lithuanian and Estonian SD[364] units, which formed part of the German Secret Police. It is well-established that these units were killing squads, intimately involved in the murder of thousands of Jews. Perhaps the most notorious was a Latvian SD unit, the Arājs Commando, which carried out most of the Nazi atrocities in Latvia.[365] While Soviet organs have since 1945 attempted to elide the difference between the Latvian Legion and the Arājs Commando, these were separate units, with distinct activities.[366] Ezergailis stresses that the last major killing operation of Jews in Latvia occurred in March 1942, one year prior to the founding of the Legion: 'There was thus one year's hiatus between the call up of Latvians in the Legion and the atrocities'.[367] The main controversy relating to the Arājs Commando and the Legion, is that approximately half of Latvian SD members (Ezergailis estimates 600 out of a total of 1200) were transferred to the Latvian Legion in late 1944 after Germany lost most of its eastern territories.[368] As a result of the transfer, these SD men ended their criminal activities. However, the transfer created complications and embarrassment for the Latvian Legion when attempting to claim that its members had merely been front-line troops. Many SD members used the Legion as an alibi, which made the allied search for war criminals confusing. Ezergailis outlined the problem:

> The transfer of SD men into the Legion gave them an opportunity to mask their past, and, ultimately, on the basis of the DP quota, for some of the Latvian war criminals the chance to enter the United States and other Allied countries. The blood-type tattoo in the left armpit of the Legionaries was a red-herring to the allied officials. They took the tattoo as a sign of SS status. The problem was that the Latvian SD-men were never tattooed and thus, in effect, in the eyes of allied officials, they were untainted by Nazism.[369]

The possible role of Latvians, Lithuanians and Estonians in anti-Semitic activity during the war is a controversial issue, which will not be discussed here in any depth, except to state that most historians agree that anti-Semitism was whipped up by the Germans, and according to

Milosz, 'fanned by the erroneous impression that Jews suffered less than others from Soviet repression and by the unfortunately correct impression that Jews were relatively over-represented among the few pro-Soviet quislings'.[370] According to Hiden and Salmon:

> The record of Baltic collaboration in the murder of their Jewish fellow citizens is a shameful one. Yet there is little in their previous record to suggest that it would have taken place without German instigation. All three Baltic governments had a good record for their treatment of Jews between the wars.[371]

> There was no significant tradition of anti-Semitism in the Baltic countries. If there was resentment, it was generally directed against traditional ruling groups: German, Russian or Polish. Undoubtedly the period of Soviet rule between 1940 and 1941 brought about a change in this respect.[372]

The recruitment of the Baltic populations for German military purposes began as early as 1941, and over the next three years a variety of military and para-military groups were established in the Baltic States. The first recruitment was for Police Battalions[373]. After failing to secure the voluntary use of anti-Soviet resistance groups for its own military ends, Germany began to create Police Battalions in all three Baltic States. In Lithuania, they recruited from prisoners captured and held in POW camps, many of whom believed that they would be joining units of a reborn Lithuanian army.[374] Others were presented with the choice of recruitment or POW Camp.[375] Police Battalions were also created in Latvia and Estonia, largely staffed by volunteers. In Latvia, approximately 15,000 men participated in the Battalions.[376] Misiunas and Taagapera have cited several motivations for joining:

> A few were genuinely pro-Nazi, while others sought revenge against Bolshevism for the deportations or murders of dear ones and the indignities inflicted on their homelands. Some tried to cover up their earlier collaboration with the Soviets or to escape false accusations to that effect.[377]

In addition to the Police Battalions and the SD units already mentioned, Balts were also recruited for Wehrmacht auxiliaries(HiWi[378]), which recruited about 12,000 men from Latvia.[379] A variety of other units were also organised. For example, in Latvia, eight Border Guard battalions were formed, and large numbers of men 'were assigned to special units, such as motorised, transport, anti-aircraft, constructions, etc.'[380] Estonians and Latvians were also recruited for the Estonian and Latvian 'Voluntary' Waffen-SS Legions, which will be discussed below.

> Milosz estimates that 6,7 and 2 per cent of the total populations

of Estonia, Latvia and Lithuania respectively were recruited into German military forces by July 1944.[381] The greatest recruitment occurred in Latvia, where according to some calculations, a total of approximately 140,000 men served the Germans in 1944.[382] According to Misiunas and Taagapera, during the whole period of the German occupation, at least 70,000 Estonians joined the German army, and more than 10,000 may have died in action.[383] Far fewer numbers were recruited in Lithuania, where the Germans met with the stiffest opposition and resistance.

An overwhelming majority of Latvian and Estonian men who were displaced after being recruited into the German military, and who later migrated to Britain, fought in the Latvian and Estonian Legions. Far fewer Lithuanian men who came to Britain were displaced via recruitment into the German military, primarily as there was no Lithuanian equivalent of the Latvian and Estonian Legions. Some Latvians, Lithuanians and Estonians in Britain were displaced from their homelands as participants of different German military units, such as the Wehrmacht auxiliaries.

Recruitment for the Estonian and Latvian Legions began in early 1943. They were essentially a 'post-Stalingrad creation'.[384] After the collapse of the German summer offensive against Russia in 1942 and the landing of the Western Allies in North Africa, Germany decided to increase its use of Baltic manpower for military purposes. Silgailis states that by then it had became obvious that Germany would not be victorious and that sooner or later, the German army would have to withdraw from the territories occupied in Eastern Europe.[385] It was then that the Germans had the idea of raising national armies in the Baltic States, to prevent a second occupation by Russia. As a result, in early 1943 on the basis of Hitler's orders of 10 February, German authorities attempted to raise Baltic Legions of Waffen SS in all three states. They were successful only in Latvia and Estonia. In Lithuania, the German authorities plans for a national SS unit met with stiff resistance, and on 17 March 1943, induction was halted and the Lithuanians were declared unworthy of joining the SS.[386] A subsequent attempt to raise forces also failed – initially, the plan for a Territorial Force of 10,000 men to be commanded by Lithuanian Officers, under the command of General Plechavičius to fight Soviet partisans on Lithuanian territory, proved to be hugely successful.[387] The Lithuanian resistance saw an opportunity to establish a nucleus national army and supported the general. Recruitment was a huge success and volunteers exceeded the quota. However, in May, the Germans demanded the transfer of the newly recruited troops to the direct command of the SS.

The general refused, however, and his troops followed suit. The general was arrested and sent to the Salaspils concentration camp near Riga. A number of the resisting troops were executed, the SS was disarmed and about 3500 men were arrested and sent to the Luftwaffe in Germany. The remainder escaped capture and fled to the forests.[388]

In Latvia and Estonia, the plans to establish Legions were successful. Although part of the German army, the Legions were nominally under local command. Some sections of the population supported the idea of national units, believing that they would be fighting for the freedom of their country. However, Sinka argues that they were in effect offered a 'Hobson's Choice', either conscription and dispersal among the German forces, or enlistment in "voluntary" units officered by Latvians and Estonians. [389] A Latvian in Britain noted the motivations for choosing the latter option:

> Well, you see we didn't want to be…integrated into the German army at all. We wanted to stay Latvians separately, because we wanted to be Latvians. We're not Germans. We just didn't want the Germans as we didn't want the Russians. So what we wanted – we wanted a Latvian unit and it was called Latvian Voluntary SS [Legion]…they were all Latvians you see and there were Latvian Officers and everything you see, because we didn't want to be Germans. That's why we were a different unit separately you see…'[390]

The Germans conceded to one point upon which the Latvians and Estonians insisted – that they would not fight against the Western Allies, only against the Soviet forces on the Eastern Front.[391]

Recruitment was initially theoretically voluntary, but rapidly became enforced, even though the units continued to bear the name - Latvian and Estonian 'Voluntary' Waffen-SS Legions to give legitimacy to their formation. Ezergailis noted that in Latvia, although a call for volunteers went out, during the same month (February 1943), 'the Germans also organised a draft'.[392] Misiunas and Taagapera claim that in both Latvia and Estonia, while initially 'in theory, individuals had a choice, but the widely-known poor conditions in the Labour Battalions, combined with various pressures exerted by local recruitment officers, induced over half the "volunteers" to choose Legion service.'[393] The basis of the subsequent drafts was Rosenberg's[394] labour law of 19 December 1941.[395] Although the Hague Convention prohibited the induction of men and women in occupied territories for military purposes, it allowed their use for labour. Thus, the Nazis twisted the Rosenberg law, in order to conscript Baltic citizens for military purposes. Thus, the 'voluntary' tag was a way of bypassing international law. This point was stressed by a Latvian in Britain: 'They were wrong to call them in the army you see, so what they did…they called it a voluntary unit… I remember it clearly in papers. They set the call up dates and everything to report to join the Latvian Voluntary SS Legion…'[396]

The first draft of February 1943, called up men born between 1919 and 1924. Following the initial conscription, a new draft was called in Latvia and Estonia in October-November 1943.[397] Sinka points out that: 'The enlistment started in 1943 and those who did not respond to the mobilisation orders were arrested and sent to concentration camps'.[398] In the end, the call up years for the Latvian Legion were 1906 to 1926.[399] On 10 October 1944, men born between 1900 and 1905 were even called into service, although for digging fortifications.[400]

At its peak, the Estonian Legion was one division numbering 11,000 men.[401] The Latvian Legion composed two divisions: the 19th Division and the 15th Division, which according to Ezergailis initially numbered 12,298 and 14,446 men respectively.[402] Gradually other units, for example, construction and border-guard battalions were added to it. Members of the Legions engaged in front-line battles on the Eastern Front. The 15th Division was engaged in battles initially in the Volkhov swamps near St. Petersburg.[403] It undertook most of its fighting in 1944 covering the German retreat in the Northern sector of the Russian front and later, within Latvia.[404] In late-1944, the 15th Division was transferred to Pomerania, North Germany to convalesce, reorganise and replenish its ranks.[405] It then covered the retreat from Pomerania in the winter and spring of 1945. Most of the men in the 15th Division were captured by British and American forces in northern Germany, and held as Prisoners-of-War. The 19th Division was organised after the 15th Division, in January 1944. The 19th Division undertook most of its activity in Kurzeme, Latvia, holding the line against the Red Army in late-1944 and early-1945.[406] The 19th Division was one of the last military units in the Second World War to lay down its arms. Its members became Russian POWs and most were deported to Siberia.

Most Latvians and Estonians in Britain stressed that while most recruits were conscripted, some did volunteer. Others pointed out that in effect, they had little choice but to volunteer. A Latvian man in Britain, described the consequences if he had not joined the Legion: 'if I hadn't gone to Latvian Legion, they would have either…maybe not shot [me], but concentration camp definitely.[407]

An Estonian man who fought in the Russian army gave me his opinion about his fellow Estonians who were recruited into the German army:

Germans mobilised some Estonians, but some went voluntarily. They say they fought for Estonia. I don't believe them. I didn't volunteer. I was forced. I had no choice. But they volunteered for it. Some, not all. Some. Later on Germans mobilised, but there were some [who] went voluntarily. I'm not supposed to tell you that.[408]

One Latvian who volunteered for the German forces was well aware that the Latvians were in a no-win situation: 'If Germany won, we would have maybe ended up same as the rest of them, ended up in concentration camps or something like that. Because they will always find something to accuse you of and that's it'.[409] Another Latvian stated that while he saw the Germans as Latvia's liberators, 'afterwards we don't know what would have happened if Germany had won the war, we don't know that. Nobody knows, and going back to…Hitler's ideas because he wanted a pure German nation, so I don't see how we would have fitted into that. So perhaps we would have been as badly off under the Russian occupation I dare say. I don't know. Nobody knows that'.[410]

When in the spring of 1945, the Soviet Union extended the military front and occupation into the heart of Germany, Latvian, Lithuanian and Estonian members of various German military units were among those who attempted to avoid falling into the hands of the Soviet Union at this time, and made their way to the Allied lines, where they were made prisoners-of-war. POW's were placed in a variety of camps in Western Europe. Many former legionaries were housed in a large POW camp in Belgium.[411] Those in larger camps were able to establish contact with exile leaders, who pleaded their cases at Allied headquarters. This process led eventually to a reversal of the classification of the legionnaires as Waffen-SS.[412]

It was on 28 December 1945, while members of the Latvian Legion were in a Prisoner-of-War Camp in Belgium that the organisation *Daugavas Vanagi* was formed. *Daugavas Vanagi*, began as a welfare organisation for disabled servicemen and their families, war widows and orphans, but it soon became a national body 'concerned with the material and spiritual welfare of all Latvians in the West.'[413] Translated, *Daugavas Vanagi* means Falcons of the Daugava. The Daugava is the main river in Latvia flowing through Riga into the Baltic Sea. According to Rullis, the organisation 'was mainly for the ex-servicemen themselves, a welfare Fund, but it grew, it included women later on…and young people who wanted to join and so on after the years, you know.'[414] *Daugavas Vanagi* was established in all the major destination countries of Latvian émigrés, including Germany, Sweden,

Canada, America, Australia, France, Belgium, Brazil, New Zealand and Venezuela.

Displacement 4: Fleeing in advance of the second Russian occupation

While many young Baltic men were fighting on the German front or employed as labourers in Germany, other Latvians, Lithuanians and Estonians were still living under the German occupation, hoping for an end to the war. Some younger men had been lucky and missed the German drafts due to their age. As the Germans began to suffer heavy defeats during 1944, and their position in the Baltic's weakened, the threat of a second Russian invasion loomed. When rumours spread that an invasion was imminent, many Baltic citizens decided to flee. Having lived through the horrors of the first occupation, those who left their homeland during this period were not prepared to stay and risk deportation or murder. Large numbers of educated and professional people left in this wave of emigration. These types of people had figured disproportionately in the 1941 deportations, having been categorised as enemies of the people by the Soviet regime. Those fleeing included large numbers of academics, clergymen, actors, musicians, writers and artists. For example, 145 of the 241 Lutheran Ministers who still had congregations in Latvia in 1944 fled during this period.[415] A large percentage of Latvians, Lithuanians and Estonians in Britain were displaced in this manner, especially women, children, older refugees and Lithuanian men.

A Lithuanian woman fled Lithuania on 9 October 1944, as the Russian army had already made significant incursions into Lithuanian territory.[416] Her parents had been deported to Siberia during the first Russian occupation and as she and her husband were civil servants, they decided to leave. She was accompanied by her family, including her daughter, who explained what happened and why her parents decided to flee:

> We flew from Lithuania because we saw the saw the Russians taking away…all the intelligentsia [in 1941]. When the Russians came, my mother had information given to her that her parents were…deported to Siberia. They saw what was happening when the Russians came. They were arresting people. They actually saw all this around them…and they were afraid…because my mother worked for the local government and my father had been in the police force…and he was also employed by the local authority. They were civil servants. That is why they were afraid for themselves and they saw what was

happening to people around them. Because of their position and what they saw, they decided to leave.[417]

They saw people that had been murdered by Russians, drowned, murdered, hung. They actually saw that. Life was nothing then. Life meant for nothing.[418]

Because they [the Russians] came the second time, they didn't want to stay anymore. They didn't want to stay any more.[419]

The Russian army began to regain territory in Latvia, during the summer and autumn of 1944 and Riga fell on 13 October.[420] One Latvian woman from Riga explains why her family decided to leave their homeland:

The Museum of the Occupation of Latvia in Riga

We had Germans stationed in our cottage in the country as well for a short while and they were very friendly from Rhineland, and this one chap, I couldn't speak much German but my parents could and my auntie could and he said, "Well, be prepared because well, we can't defend any longer your country, and we will be withdrawing, so get ready to move out if you don't want to stay", so we knew that was it.[421]

We left on 27 September and the Russians occupied Riga on 13

October [1944].[422]

Another Latvian woman decided to leave Latvia when she heard the news about the advancing Russians. Several members of her family had been deported in 1941, and she was not willing to risk staying. Her mother was dithering about leaving. Her mother's sister had been one of the deportees along with her three children:

> My mother was dithering whether to leave or not, because her sister had three children…Anyway they got deported from the farm and my mum was dithering. She said, 'Well, supposing the children get back or whatever, because there won't be any family left'. The news was getting through that practically all the grown-ups had died and the children, they kind of put them in children's homes to grow up as proper Soviet Citizens you see, so she was sort of dithering whether to leave or not, and I said I wasn't going to stay: 'They got my aunt, but they're not going to get me', and then I went and Riga fell and I was already in that part of Latvia that never surrendered, and we'd agreed…we'd meet up in Liepaja and I went there and they…had left Riga so we met up in Liepaja again. 'Cos my dad was, it was '44, he was born '87, so he'd be what about 57 and it's not easy to leave everything and face an uncertain future, but then again I'd gone so they thought they'd come out.[423]

As the Russian armies overran parts of Eastern Latvia, many Latvian refugees settled initially in Kurzeme, in the west of Latvia, which remained under German control for some months. People made their way to Kurzeme 'in slow processions down country roads, with belongings piled high in horse-drawn wagons, with cattle and livestock driven alongside. Others fled by truck, car or bicycle, hand pulled wagon or simply walked along, leaving all material possessions behind'.[424] Even the journey from their homes to Kurzeme was hazardous. One Latvian reported that:

> When we were refugees in 1944, before we reached the docks of a place called Liepaja, which is on the Baltic coast…the Russian planes came over at treetop heights, and they shot indiscriminately at the people, horses whatever, because they knew that we were refugees…
>
> …maybe hundreds and women and children, men, who didn't escape, didn't get under the wagons or in the ditches deep enough.[425]

The German surrender in the spring of 1945 was unexpectedly sudden for the refugees in Kurzeme and they were forced to flee to Germany.

Another Latvian woman had fled to Kurzeme with her family in 1944, before being obliged to leave Latvia altogether by the German surrender. She described her journey:

> We went through Latvia, to Liepaja, to that port and it was getting so congested with refugees...but the [Latvian] army was still fighting in that corner of Latvia. They never lost. They had to surrender, when the armistice was signed, and they said, "You can't stay here. You've got to move to Germany". It was getting you know, too full, what with the military and everything. So people were loaded onto boats and then they went to one of the two Polish ports...I think the Germans call them Danzig and Gottenhaven, and the Poles call them Gdansk and Gdynia. And from then on you got put on trains and you got pulled back and pulled round Germany...and then we ended up in Mecklenburg and then the Germans retreated, the Russians came in there as well, because they came into Germany. Eventually we ended back in Schleswig and that stayed British.[426]

As Veidemanis points out, given that anti-German sentiment persisted among the refugees, the decision to go to Germany was extremely difficult. However, 'with the alternative being the choice of life under the Soviet regime, most did not hesitate long'.[427] Germany, interested in the Baltic peoples as workers, 'opened her doors and provided transportation for the fleeing refugees'.[428]

Estimates of the numbers fleeing their homelands during the autumn of 1944 and early 1945 vary. Milosz estimates that approximately 50,000 Lithuanians fled to Germany, 60,000 Estonians to Germany and Sweden and 100,000 Latvians to Germany during this period.[429] Plakans cites the figure for Latvians higher, at 120,000-150,000.[430] Likewise, Roos claims that 80,000 Estonians fled during this period to Sweden or Germany.[431] Evacuation to Germany was possible from Latvia for a longer time than Estonia or Lithuania because the Germans were entrenched in Western Latvia(Courland[432]) until the end of the war in May 1945.[433] Estonians fled to Sweden in large numbers across the Baltic Sea, partly because it was neutral during the war, and relatively near to Estonia compared to Germany. Roos claims that more Estonians would have fled Estonia 'had there been means of escape. People crowded onto anything that would float and an unknown number of boats sank in rough seas.'[434] For Latvians, emigration to Sweden was particularly hazardous due to the Soviet blockade of the eastern end of the Baltic Sea, and many escaping vessels vanished in transit, destroyed by mines or Soviet torpedoes.[435] Although they were hampered by an insufficient number of ships, a majority of Latvians were able to enter Germany through East-Prussian harbours.[436] A few entered overland by train. Lithuanians also fled by boat to East Prussia, and considerable numbers travelled overland to Germany.

Those fleeing included men, women, children of all ages. Plakans states that the majority who left Latvia were aged between 30 and 50.[437] Individual experiences of displacement varied enormously. Some fled as a family unit, others with neighbours or friends. Photographs of the refugees in museums in the Baltic States depict long lines of refugees with horses and carts and sacks of belongings. The journey from homeland to DP Camp was long and treacherous and often took many months, sometimes even one or two years. The refugees stopped at many places along the way to find temporary work or shelter. During this period they did not know where they were heading; the main concern was to avoid danger. The refugees experienced a great sense of disorientation - many felt that they were deserting their homelands and had no idea what their fate would be: 'Few were prepared for such flight, and even those who carefully packed belongings faced the bitter shock of having to leave everything behind'.[438] Many families were separated as a result of this dislocation. Some family members refused to leave their homeland and were left behind. Others had to leave so quickly that there was no hope of finding family members first. Bronė, a Lithuanian woman, was forced to flee Lithuania with her cousin, but without the rest of her family. She was living and working in a town, about twenty kilometres from the family home, and was unable to return, 'because [the] Russians were already there'.[439] She never heard what had happened to her family and did not write to them until she had retired at the age of sixty, for fear of the consequences for her family.[440] Experiences once in Germany were mixed. Some of the refugees who entered Germany prior to the end of the war, were placed in a variety of jobs, for example in German industry. Others worked on German farms. Some of the refugees also faced the necessity of a second escape, when in the spring of 1945, the Soviet Union extended the military front and occupation into the heart of Germany. While most of the respondents recall the years in German as an unhappy, uncertain time, one Latvian who was just 17 when she left Latvia describes it as 'an adventure'. She stated that although she liked Germany, 'It was rather strange to me, leaving Latvia. I was sorry. I think I cried for a few months every night because you know I missed it...But I liked Germany as well. It was like, sort of an adventure for me. It wasn't 'Oh you've left Latvia and that's it now", but of course at that time we hoped we would get back soon'.[441]

INTO THE DISPLACED PERSONS' CAMPS

After the German armistice was signed in May 1945, the Allies began to liberate concentration camp survivors, prisoners of war and forced labourers. The thousands of Baltic refugees who had flooded Europe during the last months of the war, were joined by liberated Baltic POW's, labourers and camp survivors. Estimates of the numbers of displaced Latvians, Lithuanians and Estonians in Germany and other countries in Europe vary. Numbers rose rapidly during 1945 and 1946. Kulischer estimates over 200,000 non-returning Balts in Europe at the end of the war[442], while Vernant states that by 1947 there were approximately 190,000 Baltic refugee in Germany alone.[443]

Initially at the close of war, the position of the Baltic refugees in Europe was precarious. Their political status was unclear due to the incorporation of the Baltic States into the Soviet Union, and many feared forcible repatriation, particularly those who had fought in the Germany army. The refugees were adamant that they would not return home until the Soviet regime had been ousted. Numbers who chose to repatriate were tiny. Approximately two per cent of the estimated 160-190,000 Balts in Germany applied for repatriation.[444] The British Government continued to withhold *de jure* recognition of the incorporation of the Baltic States into the Soviet Union, but stalled on its long-term stand on the issue. At this stage, the refugees viewed entering DP Camps as a risk, since from there they could easily be repatriated. As Krisciunas stresses, the refugees' fears were not unfounded.[445] In the first months after Germany's surrender, in fulfilment of their agreement at Yalta in February 1945, with the Russians, the Western Allies repatriated thousands of Ukrainians and Russians against their will. Under the terms of Yalta, Balts and other nationals whose countries had been absorbed into the USSR after 1 September 1939 were not forcibly repatriated to their homelands. However, the Foreign Office at this time lacked a clear policy on the ultimate fate of these refugees. In the course of 1945, the fears of the Baltic refugees were assuaged to a degree by official British and American pronouncements signalling the continued witholding of *de jure* recognition, and promising not to repatriate them. By the end of 1945, the Allies had gained sufficient trust among the refugees that they began moving in far greater numbers to the DP Camps. Krisciunas notes that Lithuanian publications, previously cautious on the subject, were now advising their countrymen to take advantage of the camp facilities since moving into them was no longer dangerous.[446]

The position of former recruits in the German forces was particularly complex and precarious at this time. While the status of civilian Baltic refugees became increasingly clear[447], that of former soldiers remained blurred. According to Cesarani, there were known to be around 50,00 Balts in the British zone of Germany in September 1945, of whom over 20,000 had served in the German armed forces.[448] Latvians constituted by far the largest contingent of former soldiers who had served in the German armed forces.[449] The situation of former Germany army recruits was exacerbated by rumours in the press of many of the Western Allied powers, charging former legionaries with collaboration with the Nazis.[450] Soviet propaganda fuelled these rumours, while the Soviet Union demanded the return of its Baltic 'citizens'. At this time, Germany and Austria were divided into four occupation zones: British, American, French and Soviet. Most of the Baltic refugees who had the misfortune to end up in the Soviet zone were forcibly repatriated; many of those who had served the German military forces suffered terrible fates under the Soviet regime. In western occupation zones, responsibility for refugees and DPs was divided between the military authorities and UNRRA[451]. Thus, in the British zone, responsibility for DP Camps was divided between the British military authorities[452] and UNRRA. Each had different policies towards refugees and DPs which gave rise to considerable confusion.[453] Furthermore, although UNRRA clarified its policies towards DP status from an early stage, the British authorities, who took charge of a significant share of the DP camps in the British zone, had ill-defined policies towards former legionaries throughout 1945. UNRRA's policies towards former soldiers were outlined in UNRRA Council's resolution No. 71 of February 1946, which specified that all those who could be qualified as 'war criminals, collaborators, quislings and traitors' must be excluded from DP status.[454] Also excluded were ex-Wehrmacht (German Army) personnel who were of non-German nationality or stateless, although non-German ex-Wehrmacht were able to secure aid either if they could show discharge papers and passed a military screening to show if they had been collaborators, war criminals, volunteers or if they were actually Volksdeutsche.[455] UNRRA eligibility screening began in early 1946. Some former soldiers refrained from registering with UNRRA in fear of repatriation and settled in the German countryside. While Britain continued to stall on the fate of Baltic POWs and refugees, ex-soldiers in the US zone suffered from an initially harsh American policy, which required them to produce a draft certificate proving that they were neither war criminals nor were collaborators with the Nazis.[456] Most of the men were unable to any certificate.

Almost as soon as the war came to a close, Latvian, Lithuanian and Estonian exile organisations and diplomatic representatives began pressuring the Allied authorities to reconsider the status of former soldiers and submitted evidence to show that they had not been involved in any criminal or treacherous activities.[457] The Baltic representatives emphasised that the Legions were forcibly conscripted by the German military and 'labelled "voluntary" only in order to circumvent international law which forbids the recruiting of soldiers from occupied populations'.[458] Representatives further argued that the legionaries were front-line troops and committed no war crimes. Appeals focused on legionaries as victims of the war and not the perpetrators or collaborators of Nazi violence. The Baltic nationalities were described by their representatives not only as anti-Soviet, but also as anti-Nazi; according to the Baltic representatives, the Baltic populations regarded Germany only as the lesser of two evils.

Throughout 1945, the British government continued to stall on the question of the status of former legionaries and many potential DPs were initially screened out. However, the Allied forces were in principle, loath to refuse DP status to Baltic citizens, since by doing so they exposed them to the threat of repatriation. The British Government was alarmed by rumours in July 1945 that the French were repatriating Baltic refugees, and stressed that a definitive policy on Baltic Nationals must be formulated in order to protect them from repatriation.[459] Arrangements were made to transfer surrendered Balts from French hands into British and American zones.[460] Although the French denied any such rumours, the incident had prompted the British authorities to treat the problem as an urgent issue, in need of early resolution. Policy was gradually worked out as a result of appeals from Baltic representatives, discussions in Parliament and information received by the Foreign Office.[461] The main area of concern was distinguishing those who had volunteered for service from those who had been forcibly conscripted, a task which Thomas Brimelow[462] of the Foreign Office described in October 1945 as 'impossible'.[463] A question mark also hung over the ultimate fate of the Baltic refugees, given that they could not be repatriated. Various options were discussed throughout 1945, including dispersal within Germany and their use as repatriation labour within Britain. None of the suggested policies received a great deal of support and the question of their ultimate disposal remained. In part, policy uncertainty towards Baltic refugees during 1945 reflected shifting relations with Russia. As Krisciunas stresses, this was 'a period of transition, from a time when the Eastern and Western powers were allies to a time when they were becoming adversaries'.[464]

However, British policy was clarified after December 1945, when the Russians demanded that Baltic citizens either be returned to their homelands or disbanded and discharged immediately. According to the findings of the All-Party Parliamentary War Crimes Group, this demand led to a swift change in the direction of British policy and the decision to discharge former legionaries into British administered DP Camps, together with the necessary screening procedures to filter out war criminals.[465] In reply to the proposal in Argus 256[466], Sugra 291 stated that 'we agree that racial Balts may be discharged and held in DP camps'.[467] The Foreign Office stressed however, that DP status may not be given to 'German Balts who acquired German citizenship by emigration in 1939'.[468] The military authorities clarified their position in correspondence from A G Street, Permanent Secretary of COGA to the Deputy Military Governor, British zone, Germany on 1 February 1946. Street distinguished between three classes of 'Balts'.[469] The first category were German Balts who were viewed by the Foreign Office as 'Germans' and not entitled to DP status.[470] The second category were: 'Balts, who, while not of German origin actually fought in the Wehrmacht'.[471] Street outlined policy in relation to this category:

> They are ex-enemies whose disposal is complicated by the fact that it would be incompatible with our general policy to send them home against their wish. Should they be treated as displaced persons and, as such, get better treatment than the ordinary German population? There are arguments against this but Marshal Zhukov's insistence on the disbandment of all enemy troops created a new situation and we therefore dispatched Sugra 292 authorising you to discharge these Balts and hold them in DP camps. There is the point which has been recently raised with you in Foreign Office telegram No. 105 whether it would not be possible, while nominally classing these people as DP's to see that they did not receive privileged treatment in the matter of food and accommodation.[472]

BAOR notified the British military authorities in January 1946 that there were some 16,484 'Baltic nationals ex-Wehrmacht' in the British zone in addition to 350 shortly to be arriving from Denmark.[473]

> The third category of Baltic refugees were:

> Balts who were displaced by the Germans, as slave labourers or were in Germany, say, as travellers overtaken by the war. Those in this class are genuine displaced persons and, in accordance with our general policy none should be repatriated against his will.[474]

Street concluded:

The Balts in categories (2) and (3) must accordingly be regarded as displaced persons and, under our general policy, none should be repatriated against his will. Thus, it would be against our general policy if they were given until 1st April, 1946 (or any other date) to make up their minds to go home, failing which they would lose their DP status. The problem of their final resettlement remains a matter for agreement between Governments. We hope that the Australian, Canadian and other Governments will shortly send exploratory missions to the British Zone with a view to the resettlement of some of these Balts.[475]

While this is not the place to present a lengthy discussion of British screening procedures, it is important to note that the evidence suggests rather rudimentary screening of refugees in comparison to UNRRA DP screening procedures. British screening tended to focus on proof of nationality as opposed to the question of collaboration.[476] Inadequate screening has been one of the key elements in the argument that the British Government failed to use sufficient procedures to screen out war criminals, and thereby allowed war criminals to enter Britain between 1946 and 1950.[477] According to the All-Party War Crimes Group: 'British policy towards the Balts was less stringent than that of the US or UNRRA.'[478] While 'UNRRA insisted that they prove their collaboration with Germany before being allowed to acquire DP status', British authorities on the other hand, 'assigned Balts this privileged category unless the authorities themselves had possession of evidence as to why they ought not do so.[479] Hence, according to the 'Report on the Entry of Nazi War Criminals and Collaborators into the UK, 1945-1950', in the British zone, Balts could acquire DP status as long as '(a) they were not Volksdeutsche Balts; (b) there was no evidence that they had volunteered for service with the German army and (c) that there was no evidence that they went of their own accord to Germany before 1 September 1939'.[480] However, Foreign Office files are also evidence of the fact that any Latvians, Lithuanians or Estonians who were suspected of war crimes based on information received by the Foreign Office, were subjected to extra scrutiny.[481] Foreign Office policy made it clear that while they could not 'regard Baltic nationals as war criminals or traitors when the only charge against them is that they fought against the Soviet armed forces', they had 'no wish to withhold them from justice if they are war criminals in the accepted sense'.[482] For suspected war criminals in each case, 'the production of satisfactory *prima facie* evidence that the person concerned has been guilty of a war crime in the ordinary sense' was required.[483] The approach of the British authorities towards war criminals and collaborators, which considered that a person be regarded as innocent until proved guilty, contrasted with that of the UNRRA, which decreed that a person must prove their innocence in order to acquire DP status. This point was actually raised by the Latvian refugee population who stated that UNRRA policy was 'analagous to the practices of totalitarian regimes' since the Screening Boards' approach was 'contrary to free world principles that a person be considered innocent until he can be proven guilty'.[484] Due to the relatively stringent screening procedures of UNRRA and the US, many former soldiers attempted to enter British DP Camps. Some former soldiers were able to enter camps in the US zone and those administered by UNRRA, as they were able to prove their enforced recruitment. Civilian refugees and forced labourers also entered a variety of camps in the American, French and British zones of Germany and Austria.

As they entered the DP Camps, the majority of Baltic refugees held high hopes for an imminent return to the homeland. That the Western powers refused to recognise the incorporation of the Baltic States into the homeland gave them hope that the Soviet Union would soon be ousted. While the first half of 1946 can be described as a period of hope among Baltic refugees, there were contradictory messages coming from Western Governments about their ultimate fate. On the one hand, indecision on the part of the Western Allies concerning policy towards Baltic refugees combined with a dearth of accurate news, to produce wild rumours in the DP Camps about the imminent return of the refugees. At this stage, the refugees hoped that the Western Powers would help them and that the Allies would decide the fate of the Baltic States. However, the enforced repatriation of 146 Balts (150 Latvians, 10 Lithuanians and 7 Estonians) by the Swedish Government in January 1946 concerned Baltic refugees in the British zone, since they felt they could not trust assurances from the British Government that they would not be repatriated. Nevertheless, as Krisčiunas notes, except for the first few months of uncertainty and the forcible repatriation of the Baltic internees from Sweden, late 1945 and early 1946 'can be represented as a period when the refugee position stabilised'.[485]

CONCLUDING COMMENTS

As a result of the war and the German and Russian occupations, from the late autumn of 1939 until the end of 1945, Estonia lost 25 per cent of its pre-war population, Latvia lost 30 per cent[486] and Lithuania lost 15 per cent, through death, deportation and migration.[487] War and occupation deaths during the same period were 8 per cent in Estonia and 9 per cent in Latvia and Lithuania.[488] By the close of the war, the

Soviet Union had consolidated its hold over Latvia, Lithuania and Estonia, bringing the final death throes to these small nations as independent states. Among the refugees in Germany about to enter the DP camps, many of whom had lost family and friends, and above all, their homeland, a sense of disorientation and anger set in. In six years, the young Latvians, Lithuanians and Estonians who we discussed in the previous chapter, many of whom were just teenagers going to school and helping on the farmstead, grew up rapidly. Some fought in armies, others trekked across Europe, while a smaller number worked as labourers in Germany. Many of the refugees were still in their late-teens at the time of displacement. For many, the ramifications of individual ordeals during this period were to be felt for a lifetime.

The period of war and displacement marked a turning point in the lives of the young refugees. Every individual experienced undreamt of, and 'as importantly, unplanned for, horrors and losses'.[489] The refugees experienced what David Mandelbaum has termed a 'turning', 'a break in the scenario of their life course'.[490] As Carpenter suggests: 'Such turnings mandate new roles, the establishing of fresh relations with a new set of people; they prompt and exact a redirection of thought and explicit attention to action, identity and purpose'.[491] Ordinary lives were interrupted: people lost careers, family, friends and homes. The upheavals of the Second World War upended the refugees' familiar world: 'Identity and role expectations, the very image of the future mutated rapidly'.[492] In addition to the loss of family, friends and homes, the Baltic refugees who gathered in Europe at the end of the war also experienced the loss of homeland. The dream of a return to the homeland, 'to a familiar and comfortable life'[493] which became a hallmark of the communities in exile, began in displacement.

By appropriating the homelands, the Russian and German occupations strengthened the national identities of Latvians, Lithuanians and Estonians. Anger and resentment fuelled nationalism during this period, yet it was unable to express itself fully until the nationalities came together and gained brief respite in the DP camps. Public displays of patriotism were too risky and the situation was not amenable to cultural expressions of identity. Although as one Lithuanian woman reported that Lithuanian national identity was 'strengthened' as a result of the years of war and occupation[494], it was in many ways a veiled patriotism, unable to exhibit itself, until neutral ground had been reached.

I asked an Estonian in Britain if the war strengthened his national identity and that of the Estonian nation. He stated that:

> ...to be quite honest I think that in the war, in the situation that the Estonians were in, it's a matter of survival you know. You

try to…keep your head down and hide yourself away…[495]

He agreed that life and death were more important concerns than national identity, although he stated that people still maintained their Estonian identity in a 'cultural sense'.[496] Although there were 'feelings of patriotism', as he suggests, in Estonia as in the other Baltic States, 'any public outpouring of patriotism would have been suicidal for a nation of one million squeezed between Stalinist Russia and Hitler's Germany'.[497]

CHAPTER 4

The Displaced Persons' Camps

> ...the DPs were a people in exile who still yearned for the tales, songs and prayers of their native lands. Many were convinced in addition that they, in exile, represented the heart, the living soul, of their people. *They* were now the sovereign nation – they in the crowded camps, far from the hills, the coasts, the fields of home.[498]

DURING 1945, TENS OF THOUSANDS OF LATVIAN, LITHUANIAN and Estonian refugees entered Displaced Persons' Camps in Germany and Austria. By 30 September 1945, over 178,904 Baltic refugees had gained DP status, of whom over fifty thousand were in camps in the British zone of Germany.[499] Numbers rose over subsequent months, reaching a peak in the summer of 1946. The DP Camps were inhabited by men, women and children of all ages and many different nationalities, including Poles, Yugoslavs, Hungarians, Ukrainians, Byelorussians – all victims of Soviet Russia's and Nazi Germany's war aims. Here, undernourished and living in frequently overcrowded conditions, the Baltic refugees spent up to five years of their lives. It was in the relatively safe haven of the camps that the uprooted Latvians, Lithuanians and Estonians began to assess their situation and when hopes for an imminent return to the homeland gradually faded. It was also in the DP Camps that exile identities and cultures began to take shape.

Life in the DP camps in Germany and Austria has been covered in several publications, most thoroughly in Mark Wyman's *DP: Europe's Displaced Persons, 1945-1951*.[500] However, this book deals with DPs of all nationalities, predominately in the American Zone of Germany. The experiences of Baltic refugees in the DP camps is discussed in several publications, although again, none deal specifically with Baltic DPs in the British Zone.[501] Most of the Baltic DPs who were recruited for labour in Britain were in camps in the British Zone of Germany, although some were in American or French zonal areas, because the British Government began recruiting from these DP camps, once the supply in the British zone began to dry up. A far smaller number of recruits came from DP camps in Austria. The focus of this chapter therefore, will be on the experiences of Baltic DPs in the British zones of Germany and Austria, with a stress on the personal experiences of Latvians, Lithuanians and Estonians who later came to Britain. The chapter will concentrate on the development of exile cultures and identities in the camps, with some introductory discussion of everyday life and material conditions.

THE ORGANISATION OF THE DP CAMPS, 1945-50

In July 1945, following the termination of SHAEF[502], the body previously jointly responsible with UNRRA (United Nations Relief and Rehabilitation Administration) for DPs and refugees in Germany during the war, Western Germany was 'divided under the command of three military zonal authorities, and each zone was free to make independent decisions regarding its displaced persons'.[503] Western Germany was thus divided into British, French and American zones, while Eastern Germany remained under Soviet command. The British military authorities controlled five regions in their zone (North Rhine, Westphalia, Hanover, Hansestadt Hamburg and Schleswig Holstein[504]), with headquarters at Lemgo. The British authorities also controlled part of western Austria, which was divided into French, British, American and Soviet zones, and organised under similar lines to Germany. New agreements negotiated at the end of 1945 and the beginning of 1946 specified that UNRRA[505] was to remain subordinate to the military authorities who were to exercise sovereign authority in western Germany.[506] Different responsibilities were allocated to UNRRA and the military authorities in the DP camps. Although, in theory the British military authorities had ultimate sovereignty, the British agreement specified that 'nothing in this Agreement shall be interpreted as derogating or detracting from or limiting the powers of the Commander-in-Chief' of UNRRA.[507] The military authorities also agreed not to impose 'obligations inconsistent with the resolutions of the UNRRA Council'.[508]

The military authorities had responsibility for: laws controlling the conduct of DPs; the procurement, storage and distribution of food, clothing and medicine; final permission for voluntary relief agencies to operate; transportation facilities; conditions of employment for DPs;

distribution of radio and newspapers, with the rights to censorship; the co-ordination of all resettlement movements. The UNRRA was responsible among other matters for: the maintenance of Central Headquarters for Germany together with the appropriate zonal and other subordinate headquarters to supervise the UNRRA operations; the procurement and operation of surplus military vehicles; the procurement of amenity supplies such as tobacco, razors, cigarettes, recreational and educational equipment; and finally, the operation of a Central Tracing Bureau to locate missing DPs.[509]

By the autumn of 1945, the mass repatriation period had come to an end and it had become increasingly clear that a new international agency would be required to oversee the resettlement of those refugees, who for one reason or another, were unable or unwilling to return to their homelands.[510] The joint operations of UNRRA and the military authorities had only been envisaged as a short-term solution, and a long term organisation was required. Thus, a new international agency, IRO (International Refugee Organisation), was established, with the specific task of resettling non-repatriable refugees. The IRO constitution was approved on 15 December 1946, and from 1 July 1947, acquired full responsibility 'for the care and maintenance of 712,675 refugees and displaced persons.'[511] By doing so, IRO replaced UNRRA in the task of care and maintenance of DPs after July 1947.

LIVING CONDITIONS AND DAILY LIFE IN THE DP CAMPS

Awareness of the living conditions and daily life in the camps facilitates an understanding of the DPs positive response to the recruitment requests of Western nations. However, despite poor conditions and the 'temporary' character of life, entering the DP Camps was a huge relief after years of war and displacement.

As the war ended and refugees from all over war-ravaged Europe began to flood the camps, the immense task faced by the UNRRA and the military authorities became clear. By 30 September 1945, there were a total of 648,784 DPs in the British zone of Germany, including Poles, Ukrainians, Byelorussians, Hungarians, Yugoslavs, Bulgarians and Romanians.[512] The number also included 50, 572 Balts.[513] There were a total of 178,904 Baltic DPs in Europe at this time.[514] Numbers rose over the following months. In September 1945 there were 21,453 Estonian, 64,979 Latvian and 47,269 Lithuanian DPs in Western Germany.[515] By June 1946, the numbers were 32,000 Estonians, 80,000 Latvians and 59,000 Lithuanians.[516] There were far fewer Baltic DPs in western zones of Austria. On 30 September 1945, there were 5,130 Baltic DPs in the US, French and British zones of Austria combined, including only 979 in the British zone.[517]

To cater for the needs of the vast number of DPs, suitable living accommodation had to be found. The DPs were accommodated in a wide variety of locations and dwellings all over West Germany and Austria, ranging from former munitions factories, to bombed out army barracks and even castles. These buildings were revamped and prepared to fit the needs of the DPs. Proudfoot explained:

> Extensive repairs were made to damaged buildings to make them fit for winter. Thousands of sheet-metal stoves were installed in rooms, with connecting stove pipes, more often than not, inserted through the windows. Central heating units were put in working order. Indoor toilets and wash rooms were repaired or installed. Thousands of double-decked bunks were replaced by cots, and many straw ticks were discarded for cotton felt mattresses. Many large rooms were partitioned to provide for desirable segregation. Indoor recreation halls and chapels were improvised.[518]

The conditions of the camps varied widely, from the extremely squalid to the reasonably clean and comfortable. The range of nationalities within the camps was also variable. While some of the camps contained several different nationalities, others were single-nationality camps. Although some of the refugees were relatively lucky in that they stayed in the same camp until their recruitment for labour in Britain, others moved from one location to another, often several times, generally from the smaller camps to larger ones. As the post-war organisation of the refugees gained momentum, and as refugees were either repatriated or recruited by western nations for labour, the system was re-ordered and re-organised. As soon as was possible, the smaller and less comfortable camps were closed and the refugees moved to larger, more habitable bases. A re-ordering towards single nationality camps also took place.

There were enormous differences in the individual experiences of Baltic DPs not only because of varying living conditions, but also due to the mechanics of displacement. While some Baltic refugees, including all those recruited during the war, came to the DP camps without their families, others arrived as family units or with at least one family member or spouse. While most of the Baltic men were without family, some of the women were lucky enough to have members of their family with them. Some of those who later came to Britain were still teenagers, and a few were accompanied by their parents. However, a majority of the Baltic DPs were aged 18-30 and without family.

A Latvian woman, now living in Nottingham fled from Riga with her parents in 1944, and eventually entered Spakenburg, a large DP camp at Geesthacht. Spakenburg accommodated about 3000 Latvians and a much smaller number of Lithuanians and Estonians. She described the conditions as follows:

> Oh we were lucky. It…used to be a munitions factory before and during the war, and they had the worker's houses, and we were housed in these sort of family houses and we had a room each which was very good, we had a room and we had a kitchen. There were three rooms upstairs. It was like…there was a room and the kitchen downstairs and three rooms upstairs, and there was probably just one person in a room, or…you were in a larger room, if you were brothers. We had two brothers above us and then two single persons in the other two rooms. And we were downstairs, three of us and the kitchen was…it was a communal kitchen, but I think the others, they must have had an electrical stove or something. They didn't come into the kitchen at all, so we had two rooms really.[519]

There was another camp in Geestacht called Saule, which accommodated an estimated 3-4000 Latvians. But there the conditions were not so good. The same witness described the conditions in Spakenburg as luxurious, 'because in the other camp [Saule] they were in barracks and there were about 14 people in a room or something like that. They were separated just with curtains or blankets even. They hung up an old blanket so you didn't see the other person's bed. But we were really well off'.[520]

Some of the larger camps, which housed up to as many as 10,000 DPs 'essentially were complete communities, with their own police and fire departments, schools and churches, entertainment and sports centres, print media and medical facilities'.[521] Several of these larger, well-organised camps formed a stark contrast with some of the smaller ones where facilities and conditions proved to be spartan.

Size was not always an indicator of conditions, however. In October 1946, Rev. Dr. Joseph B. Kučius, President of the United Lithuanian Relief Fund of America wrote a lengthy report on the condition of Lithuanian DPs, after visiting camps in all three zones of West Germany. The report was subsequently circulated to the British Government. He described the different types of accommodation in which DPs were housed:

> Turning to the purely material aspect of the present situation of the Lithuanian DPs, a distinction must be made between those

who are accommodated in larger camps in former military barracks, and those who are lodged in segregated blocks of houses, adapted to family life. The first group lives as if they were members of a depressed caste, under conditions reminiscent more of a hard labour prison or concentration camp, than of the life of free human beings. I had the opportunity of convincing myself personally of the innumerable hardships of such an existence in vast barracks, in which persons of both sexes and of various ages have been packed indiscriminately, enjoying only that measure of privacy which can be afforded by improvised curtains partitioning off the scant living space allotted. The disintegrating effect on tempers and nerves of life in perpetual turmoil, without a moment's peace, cannot be denied by an objective observer. The demoralisation which ensues, especially in the ranks of the youthful population of these "purgatories on earth" is incalculable. Often very much is made of the amenities of DP life, though, in reality, they are subjected to privations almost beyond human endurance. The bleakness and desolation which are the hallmarks of such camps on the inside, characterise them from the outside as well.[522]

For some DPs, living conditions were very poor. Many were crammed in small spaces with their families. A Latvian woman now in West Yorkshire fled Riga in January 1945, and reached the safety of Braunau-on-the-Inn DP camp in Austria in 1946. Here she stayed for two years until she came to England in 1948. The camp was housed in former army barracks, and initially everyone had to live together. Only later were families separated. The conditions were not so good - there was no social life, the food was poor, and the barracks were 'full of bugs'.[523]

DP camps in Austria were rumoured to be less comfortable than those in Germany, and the DPs themselves in a worse condition. Charles Zarine from the Latvian Legation in London, wrote to Mr. Hankey[524] in the Foreign Office in July 1946 stating that '…from the point of view of material welfare…[Austria] is the worst region for Baltic refugees.'[525]

Some of the Baltic DPs who came to Britain lived in the same camp. For example, I have encountered several Latvians who stayed at Gottorb castle DP camp in Schleswig, Northern Germany, where the conditions were reported to be good. Here, at one point, 800-1000 Latvians were housed. Two Latvians now living in Leeds, stayed in Gottorb castle DP camp. One of them described the camp as 'a lovely modern castle', with 'lovely water round', where:

...from smaller camps from other towns, the Latvians were all brought together to this castle and...because we had a school there as well – there were two, an ordinary school and a secondary school, so the lot of them who were coming for the school, they came over as well, so there was a lot of Latvians there.[526]

I might be exaggerating but I think there was nearly 1000 [Latvians there]...

The castle was four storeys high, and 'then there were some stables you know and all them were full as well.'[527] The other Latvian talked about how, 'as a big castle there were plenty of rooms. Some of them were divided of course, provisionally. Ours were. No, it was fairly, fairly good.'[528]

The food in the camps was generally meagre and of poor quality, because provisions in Germany both during and after the war were scarce. Generally, there was just enough to live on, but no more, and the necessary calorie requirements to maintain a stable weight were often not met. Initially, the DPs were well fed. During the summer of 1945, food supplies for DPs in western Germany ranged from 2300 to 2600 calories per day.[529] However during the autumn and winter food supplies dwindled. Rations in the British zone were cut to 2170 calories and then to 1850 by March 1946.[530] In July, the ration was decreased further to 1550 calories.[531] Again, the volume of provisions varied from camp to camp. A Latvian in Britain described the food in her camp:

We had it handed out. In some camps you had a kitchen, and you had soups and you had bread. You were given the bread and something to put on. But...even the bread – the bread was maize bread. I know that...I went to school and I was in a different camp for about three months, and that was winter '45-'46, right after the war, and we had this very coarse black bread and at one time we got some, we were given a little lard as well, and some onions and I know, all I had to eat, I didn't like soups very much and they weren't nice soups either and I had this black bread, a little bit of lard and onion on it. And I know one Christmas Eve, when I went home, my parents were in the camp, and all we had on that Christmas Eve - because I think they saved the nicer things for Christmas Day – we had boiled swede and sort of fresh herrings cooked in water. We didn't even have fat. I will always remember that. But then on Christmas Day, I'm sure we had something much nicer. Not enough, no.[532]

Most of the DPs talked about the insufficient food rations. Even basic foods became luxury items. A Lithuanian woman now living in Nottingham was a child at the time she stayed in Meerbeck DP camp. She recalled that, '…in Meerbeck, Father Christmas would bring us an orange. Now for me an orange…was fantastic. It was absolutely fantastic.'[533]

In most of the camps a black market operated where belongings such as jewellery would be sold for food or other items, such as cigarettes. A Latvian in Leeds explained the system:

> …you probably heard there used to be a lot of black market…selling…if you had a bit of money… Well, we were lucky. We had some of the Latvian money. Well of course the price of silver alone, the people in black market, they take it in exchange for whatever we wanted…so that eased things…[534]

Milda Danys reported the story of a Lithuanian woman in Oldenburg camp in the British zone, who traded her knitting for more food.[535] Although wool was practically unobtainable, it was possible to unravel old socks or sweaters. As Danys noted: 'Anyone who could sew or who could repair shoes could earn cigarettes, especially since the clothing handed out by the Red Cross and other charitable organisations rarely fitted properly.'[536]

Despite the poor conditions in many of the camps, the refugees felt that the DP camps were an enormous relief after months or years of war and displacement. An Estonian now in West Yorkshire spent two years in Oldenburg DP camp from 1945 to 1947, after a period spent fighting in the war on the German side. He described how, to have been through the war and then to have one's own bed, bedroom, three meals a day and pocket money, was 'marvellous'.[537] Oldenburg DP Camp was a lively camp with singing, dancing and sports for the young. He met people from many different nationalities and had some casual girlfriends in the camp. Describing the experience this Estonian stated that, at the time: 'We were in heaven'.[538]

Many of the young and single refugees formed relationships in the camps. There were many thousands of young single men and women with time on their hands, and with a rich social calendar in many of the camps, it was inevitable that many DPs formed close friendships and relationships with each other. Some DPs even got married in the camps. An Estonian man from Halifax was married in Stolzenau DP camp by a German Burgermeister in 1947, just months before coming to England with his new wife in September 1947.[539]

There were opportunities in the DP camps for those interested, to learn different trades, such as motor mechanics, tailoring or shoemaking.[540] Some of the DPs taught English or worked in the canteen or Post Office. Creative types wrote or painted. Children and teenagers were able to continue their studies in DP schools. However, despite these opportunities and the many cultural and sporting activities available, many DPs emphasised the day-to-day boredom in the camps, of long hours chatting about current events in the homeland and their future, of playing cards and feelings of impatience and frustration.

A Latvian witness, living in West Yorkshire, described how the refugees did not just sit back and wait for events to impact on them, but made a concerted effort to make the best of their present situation. From her experiences in Feldburg DP camp in Western Germany, which accommodated only Latvians, she made the following observations:

> ...well Latvians have got some bad, well how to say, characteristics, but there's one thing about Latvians we make things do...I mean we're active. We actually try to help ourselves. We don't expect help from other people and first of all we try. In this camp, we sort of did it up a bit, you know and try to make the most of things, you know. We weren't just sitting down and just waiting for someone to do something for us. We tried to improve things shall we say. That's one thing – we're sort of active. We're not really passive and waiting for things to happen. We do something. Oh we managed, yeah.[541]

Some of the DPs worked for UNRRA, and earned a wage while in the camps. From the outset it had been 'military policy to provide employment for displaced persons, and to encourage able-bodied men and women among them to volunteer for useful work'.[542] A majority were employed in an administrative capacity, although there was a variety of work, both in and outside the camps. In December 1946, it was calculated that 60 per cent of all employable males of the registered population in UNRRA administered centres in the British zone were working.[543] A Latvian man now in Leeds worked for UNRRA in a DP Camp in Germany, as a motor mechanic,[544] and a Latvian woman now living in Derby became an interpreter typist for UNRRA in an office in Schleswig DP camp.[545]

An Estonian DP from Lübbecke DP camp wrote a letter to *The Manchester Guardian* on 27 June 1946 stressing the self-reliance and high employment levels of Estonian DPs. He stated that:

> ...80 per cent of Estonians accommodated in DP camps in the British zone of Germany have voluntarily taken up employment

– not excepting those disabled, enfeebled by age, and mothers with small children – and in the camps themselves, as far as the shortcomings of recent times permitted, everything conceivable is being done by self-initiative to improve our life, education, sanitary and welfare conditions.[546]

Some of the DPs who later came to Britain were only children or teenagers when they first entered the camps. One Latvian DP was only twelve years old when he fled Latvia in the summer of 1944 with his parents. After fleeing across Germany, they eventually entered a DP camp in Hannover, and were subsequently transferred to a DP base in Greven. He explained how he had to stay in the camp until he became 18 in 1950, and was old enough to be accepted on the Westward Ho! recruitment scheme:

> ...it must have been from '47 to '50 that we stopped in Greven...and then we got transferred to Munster...but I couldn't...leave there until 1950, because...I were too young to work...so when I became of age that I could sign this relevant document, we came to England in 1950.[547]

A Lithuanian woman who I interviewed in the Midlands, was only a child when she came to the DP camps with her parents. Her family fled Lithuania on 9 October 1944, and during the next four years, stayed in a variety of dwellings and DP camps. From August 1945 to May 1948, the family was able to settle in Meerbeck DP camp, where they were given a private house in which to live. She recalls this period as a happy time. The camp accommodated mostly Lithuanian DPs, and a variety of Lithuanian associations were set up there. Comparing her experiences growing up in England after the war, with the years in Meerbeck, she stated that:

> I recall the childhood being more pleasant after wartime Germany, where we lived in Meerbeck, those years. Now there...I have pleasant childhood memories.[548]

Nevertheless, DP children were particularly susceptible to many of the common illnesses in the DP camps, for example, TB, which was common among DPs living in the confined, communal quarters of military barracks and similar dwellings. As with many other diseases, TB was exacerbated by the poor food rations. Two of the most common diseases caused by malnutrition were rickets and anaemia. Adults too, suffered from a wide variety of complaints, again exacerbated by decreasing food rations. To offset the spread of diseases, UNRRA organised a fairly extensive medical programme among the DPs, with at least one medical officer and several nurses present in each camp. Infirmaries were also established in the DP Camps and immunisation programmes were implemented. Those at risk were given vitamin supplements, and a dental service was provided in a majority of camps. The result of effective organisation was to prevent a real crisis or epidemic developing among the DP population.

The diplomatic representatives of Estonia, Latvia and Lithuania wrote frequent letters to Ministers within the British Government stressing the plight of the DPs, both prior to, and during the labour recruitment process. The Foreign Office files in London, are full of letters and appeals from Latvian, Lithuanian and Estonian representatives in London, and the various Baltic welfare committees. These appeals stressed the problems faced by the Baltic refugees and DPs in Europe, and sought to pressure governments and international organisations to ameliorate their situation.

The living conditions in the Camps began to improve only after the end of 1946, when DP numbers began to steadily decrease as a result of recruitment schemes organised by Western nations. The food situation in Germany also began to improve, and some of the worst camps were closed. Nevertheless, remaining DPs were frequently moved from camp to camp as the DP Camp system was re-ordered, and their health suffered from the length of time spent in the camps.

CULTURES AND IDENTIES

In DP Camps, after years of displacement and upheaval, the Baltic nationalities were able to come together, men, women and children, for the first time in months or even years. It was here that the Latvian, Lithuanian and Estonian diaspora began to form, and when identities as refugees and exiles began to take shape. Camps became communities, and national identities strengthened.

Particularly in the single nationality camps, the Estonian, Latvian and Lithuanian refugees began to create their own 'mini' Estonia's, Latvia's and Lithuania's. One Estonian DP stated that, 'The DP camps were like little states in the middle of somebody's country'.[549] Attempts to recreate the homeland in the confines of the camps was partly a way of remembering home, but also because the refugees felt an increasing responsibility now that they had reached the safe haven of the camps, to act as the guardians of the homeland. They believed that because those in the homeland were now unable to maintain national cultures and identities as a result of Soviet repression, that they had a responsibility as exiles to maintain cultures and identities on behalf of the homeland. Andrejs Eglitis, a Latvian DP poet summed up the huge responsibility felt by the DPs in the poem 'God, Thy Earth is Aflame', which contained the line: 'We are the hope and blossom of our native land!'[550]

Feelings of duty and responsibility to keep the Baltic cultures and identities alive on behalf of the homeland manifested themselves in a rich cultural scene and the reconstruction of national identities to fit the needs of DP life. The responsibilities of exile combined with boredom, nationalism and disorientation to fuel vibrant Latvian, Lithuanian and Estonian 'cultures in exile', both to restore the spirit of the homeland and its peoples, and to pass the time. Participation in cultural events and organisations embraced all DPs, many of whom had commemorated certain cultural traditions to only a minimal extent when they were living in the homeland prior to the war.

The celebration of homeland festivals and national holidays became important annual rituals in the DP camps, a new medium through which to express ethnic loyalties. Often, the celebration of these festivals, particularly those marking the hard fought for Latvian, Lithuanian and Estonian independence in 1918, were sad, sombre events. One Latvian DP stated that 'In the camps', the commemoration of Latvian Independence Day on 18 November, 'was a sorrowful day'.[551] Lithuanians celebrated 'Nation's Day' on 8 September, and marked Independence Day on 16 February. Estonian Independence Day was 24 February. The commemoration of some of the other important national days, marked annually in exile, first began in the DP camps. The most significant of these was Deportation Day on 14 June. This day marking the night in 1941 when thousands of Baltic citizens were deported to Siberia became one of the most important commemorative events among Baltic refugees in exile, including those in Great Britain. It is still recalled in Britain, and other Baltic exile communities around the world today.

While honouring the past 'through national celebrations in the camps was one way to retain a culture', another was, as Wyman explains:

> ...through artistic representations of that culture. DP camps soon became showcases for a wide variety of cultural activities – in literature, art, music, the theatre – that stressed the underlying theme of national uniqueness. These efforts were helped by the fact that large numbers of creative persons had fled to the West. (A Latvian scholar has estimated that 70 per cent of his country's writers, artists, musicians, and actors made it to western zones in 1945.[552]

Milda Danys drew a comparison with the importance of culture in the DP camps and its significance in 1918. She referred specifically to

Lithuanians, although her comments can also be applied to Latvians and Estonians. She stated that in the DP camps:

> Culture acquired a conscious political significance, as it had in the heroic phase of the fight for Lithuanian independence when poets wrote both patriotic poems and political manifestos.[553]

Choir groups, folk dance and singing groups, schools and sports groups were organised in the camps. A Baltic University was even set up to further the education of the homeland through its guardians abroad. Efforts were made to recreate as much as possible the life of the homeland. Although it was difficult to cook national dishes, except perhaps on special occasions like Christmas or St. John's Day, it was possible to replicate other traditions, for example, the building of traditional saunas in some of the camps.[554] Karl Aun described the centrality of culture in the lives of the DPs: 'In Germany, in the refugee camps, promotion of ethnic culture among refugees was not only an activity to pass the time but for many became a way of life'.[555]

Dr. Kučius described how folk dances and other shows put on by the DPs in the camps helped to bring vibrancy to an otherwise dreary existence in the drab surrounds of the camps:

> The shows put on by the DPs, featuring their beautiful songs and national dances, with the performers, both men and girls, dressed in their picturesque and ancient national costumes, to the accompaniment of native instruments, dispel somewhat the dreary impression created by the ordinary run of camps...[556]

Theatre became a particularly important avenue through which to dramatise the plight of the DPs, and to recall a past, already remembered as idyllic and happy. Folk plays were particularly common in Lithuanian DP theatre productions. Theatre had been extremely popular in the inter-war period in all three Baltic States, as it remains so today. It was thus inevitable that the theatre re-established its popularity in the DP camps, particularly given that it was a medium, which could work with as few or as many props and materials as were available. Many professional actors had fled from the Baltic States along with other creative professionals, such as writers, artists and musicians. The Estonian National Theatre was re-established at Oldenburg, and a Latvian theatre was set up at Meerbeck DP Camp.[557]

In addition to theatre, opera and ballet were also performed. The entire Latvian ballet had escaped to the west, and had re-established at Lübeck.[558] At Oldenburg DP camp, a Latvian opera was launched.[559] At Blomberg a vibrant community of artists, musicians, theatre and film directors was established.[560] This included prominent Estonian musical artists and Latvian artists and soloists.[561] A Lithuanian Opera Artists' Centre of the British zone was established at Blomberg[562], as were a Lithuanian Choir Assemble and the Lithuanian National Dancer Group[563], and the Riga Film Company began producing films and newsreels there.[564] At Meerbeck, a Latvian choir was established.[565]

These groups put on a variety of performances in the camps. In 1947, the Lithuanian Opera Artist's Centre at Blomberg succeeded in putting on a performance of Rossini's Opera, 'The Barber of Seville' under difficult DP conditions with self-made costumes and decorations.[566] This opera had previously been shown in DP camps of the British and American zones fourteen times.[567] Some of the groups were able to tour the DP camps, despite the difficulties entailed. The 'Foreign Estonians' Male Choir': "Estonia" toured many of the DP camps in the British zone, including Oldenburg DP camp on 10 July 1947.[568]

UNNRA assisted with activities in the camps, including cultural, sporting and recreational events. A wide variety of activities were set up for DP children, including summer camps, and scouts and guides organisations. In August 1948, the 'World's YMCA/YWCA Camp for Scouts and Guides "Baden-Powell"' was held at "Havenoth", Timmendorfer Strand. 570 Lithuanian, 600 Estonian and 1000 Latvian DP children between 10 and 16 years were sent to the camp, along with many other nationalities.[569]

A Latvian interviewed in Nottingham described the cultural activities at Spakenburg Camp. She was then still at school age, and lived there with her parents:

> There were choirs, theatres and there was the church as well, of course. There were dancers and my father he liked to do woodwork, so they had a workshop there, and there were about ten people who did all sorts of woodwork, and there were silversmiths and…well, I went to school still, so I was busy, …there were all sorts of people, teachers, professors, they were all there. Oh and in Germany we even had a Baltic University – Pinneburg, yes.[570]

The subjects taught at the different schools in the camps were wide ranging, particularly in the larger camps, where there were a greater number of highly educated refugees resident. In Spakenburg, the school offered all the traditional school subjects taught in Latvia, including botany, physics, maths, Latvian and foreign languages.[571] Some of the refugees who came to Britain were also taught English in the camps, although the standard of teaching was variable.

UNRRA was assisted by voluntary relief agencies in the establishment of educational facilities for DPs of all ages, from nursery school and kindergarten to professional training in universities and technical colleges.

Many of the university lecturers and professors from Baltic universities had fled their homelands in 1944. The Foreign Office made lists of the locations of these academics and the Baltic nations' most eminent scientists, in Germany. Many of them were in various DP camps in the British zone, including the DP Study Centre at Pinneburg, Hannover DP Camp, Göttingen DP camp, Blomberg DP camp and Geesthacht DP camp.[572]

A list of opportunities for 'Occupational Training and Professional Re-education' circulated by the Control Commission in September 1946, showed the range of institutions offering educational and training opportunities for DPs in the British zone.[573] The choices open to Baltic DPs included: Hamburg D.P Study Centre (formerly Baltic DP University); German Universities Scheme; Latvian Agricultural Training School; Estonian Agricultural Training School; Farm work; Home making schools; Art and Music school at Kabel; Baltic Technical School at Geestacht.[574] Flensburg Navigation School, sponsored by UNRRA was opened on 1 September 1946, with 150 students attending the first course. A variety of maritime related subjects were taught at the school, which was run for the benefit of DPs only. All the students at the school were Baltic DPs.[575]

The Baltic DPs in the British zone founded their own university, initially called the 'Baltic DP University', later the 'DP University Study Centre' at Hamburg, which opened its doors on 14 March 1946.[576] DP scholars from Latvia, Lithuania and Estonia founded eight faculties: medicine, chemistry, construction engineering, agronomy, mechanical engineering, natural sciences, mathematics, philology and law.[577] The 'Nominal Roll of Professors' of January 1946, listed 84 staff members, including distinguished Professors, PhD's and MA's from many different DP camps.[578] After much disagreement with the DP scholars, the authorities decided that the university was to be temporary, used mainly for 'early university career work, preparing students to transfer to established institutions'.[579] The change in the name of the establishment from 'University' to 'Study Centre' reflected these objectives. Enrolment soon topped one thousand.[580] In December 1946, the enrolment was 1,100, of which two-thirds were Lithuanians and the remaining one-third composed half of Latvians, and half of Estonians.[581] The same proportions applied to the teaching staff.[582] By December, there were 155 instructors and a number of administrative officers and clerical staff.[583]   The university faced difficulties and an unstable future right from the start. In early 1947, the British authorities moved the Study Centre to Pinneburg, twenty kilometres away, and while the facilities and conditions were improved, the question regarding its ultimate fate was raised again. Although, the DP scholars requested the movement of the university to the American zone, where they felt education among the DPs was taken more seriously, the British authorities refused. The university closed on 30 September 1949.[584]

In addition to the Pinneburg Study Centre, Baltic DPs had the opportunity to study at German Universities. Occupation authorities demanded the reservation of ten per cent of the quota for German universities for DPs.   According to Wyman 'these quotas were apparently filled'.[585] A Lithuanian publication advised college-age DPs to exploit these opportunities. In late 1945, it noted that at Marburg 'application for admission to the Medical faculty' were already being accepted and that 'dormitories are already provided for Lithuanian students' at Erlangen.[586]   By May 1946, DP enrolment in German universities reached 600 in the British zone of Germany.[587]   The numbers were far lower than in the American zone, which had achieved 4,000 university enrolments by the same date.[588]

In addition to the voluntary relief agencies working under agreement with UNRRA (e.g. the British Red Cross, the International Red Cross, the YMCA/YWCA), national and welfare committees were also established by the Baltic DPs. These organisations had both nationalist and welfare objectives, and aimed not only to restore independence, but also to ensure adequate care for DPs. One of the main tactics favoured to achieve both these goals was by appealing to western governments. Each nationality had its own national committee, for example, the Latvian Central Committee, as well as its own Red Cross organisation, which worked in close association with the central National Committee - for example, the Lithuanian Red Cross. [589]

Van Reenan suggests that the establishment of voluntary committees and organisations was a way for the DPs to become more independent and assert their national identity. He recalled the remarks of an observer, who had stated that, 'Being foreigners in a strange place made Lithuanians even more aware of their Lithuanianism', a comment which can be applied to all the Baltic nationalities.[590] 'A heightened sense of being different, a strong moral sense of duty to their homeland', combined with lack of any meaningful dialogue with either the Germans or the military authorities, 'contributed to their desire to be masters of their own fate in the diaspora.   The community's psychological independence found an outlet through voluntary committees and organisations.'[591]

Newspapers were circulated among the DP camps to keep the refugees up-to-date on the situation in the homeland, and the options regarding their future. Some DP centres produced their own newspapers or typed news-sheets. Throughout 1945 and 1946, the military authorities tolerated the circulation of a variety of newspapers among the DPs, some of which were printed in Germany, others in Sweden. For example, in Lübbecke, the following newspapers were published: *Libekas Vestnesis*, a Latvian newspaper; *Laisues Varpas*, a Lithuanian newspaper; *Sonumid*, an Estonian newspaper.[592] The Foreign Office noted that the following Latvian papers published were in the British Zone in March 1946: *Latvieshu Ziniu Dienesta Biletene*, published in Detmold, and *Latviu Sports* in Lübeck, Halle.[593] Regarding the circulation of ethnic language newspapers, H. C. Ruddell voiced the opinion in December 1945 that; 'The English who have allowed the Welsh to preserve their language should not do less for the Balts. There is to my mind, considerable similarity between the Celts and the Balts – small races with a civilisation older and probably truer then that of other nations who tend to swamp them'.[594]

Some of the newspapers authorised by UNRRA contained English phrases to learn, and articles about England and the English way of life. For example, a 1945 edition of the Latvian newspaper *Tevzeme* contained an article about the English school system.[595] A common section in the newspapers was a list of DP deaths. Newspapers also updated the DPs on international news, for example the Nuremburg trials. Radio broadcasts and news films also provided news updates.

DPs also had the opportunity to read national literature in the camps. Latvian, Lithuanian and Estonian publishing houses were established in Germany and Sweden to cater for the emergent diaspora. Literature was also published in magazines and literary reviews. Between 1945 and 1950, 1,179 Latvian books were produced by DPs in Sweden, Denmark and Germany, including new exile literature and Latvian classics, for example, works by Blaumanis, Poruks and Niedra.[596] By 1950, there were 16 Lithuanian publishing houses in Germany.[597] Many of the works published and reprinted were 'geared to preserve national identity and point an accusing finger at the Nazi or Soviet defiler'.[598] These initial years of exile witnessed the birth of a vibrant exile literature, a genre that continued throughout the entire Soviet period. Not all of the exile literature harked back to the past, or was sombre about the present. Some of it had positive themes, for example, the idea of beginning afresh.[599]

Through literature, song, theatre, ethnic language schooling and newspapers, the DPs sought to preserve the homeland language in displacement, a duty which the exiles regarded as paramount. Religion was also an important aspect of the homeland culture pinpointed for fervent maintenance, particularly among Lithuanians whose Catholicism was a significant component of their national identity. The large number of Lithuanian DP priests, who had fled from the approaching atheist armies of Soviet Russia in 1944, contributed to the recreation of the religious life of the homeland. An estimated 227 Lithuanian priests were in DP camps in Germany, one quarter of the pre-war number of priests in Lithuania.[600]   Large numbers of seminarians were also accommodated in the camps, some of whom were able to continue their studies at Eichstatt.[601]   Estonians and Latvians had their religious requirements catered for by Lutheran ministers in the camps. Although religion among these nationalities was not in most cases, inextricably linked to national identity in the way that Lithuanian-ness and Catholicism were, Lutheranism became increasingly important in exile. Religious ceremonies such as marriage and funerals were held in the camps, and became important events through which to express and perform ethnic customs and traditions.

Although the British Government was wary of nationalism fermenting in the DP Camps, it was initially fairly liberal regarding the cultural life of the refugees. At first, few restrictions were placed on the circulation of newspapers, and the cultural activities and welfare organisations of the Baltic DPs. Many of the Baltic refugees regarded the British zone as a model in this respect, and those in American and French DP camps were reported as wishing to transfer to camps under British control, since the cultural life there was deemed to be the most free and full.

Relations between the Baltic DPs and the British Military Authorities began to sour, however, as the months went on. During early 1946, the British military authorities began to implement changes in some of the camps, in relation to circulation of newspapers, cultural activities and welfare organisations. The change in the name of the Baltic University to 'Study Centre' was symptomatic of the changes. In early 1946, the welfare and national committees, which had been organised by the DPs, were disbanded. All National Committees in the British zone were closed and their funds withdrawn, including the Red Cross, although the British authorities recommended 'that the Red Cross workers should continue their duties under British control'.[602]   The British Government was concerned about the underlying nationalist objectives of some of these organisations. The military authorities were also worried about Soviet recriminations, and the growth of Soviet propaganda suggesting that the British Government was aiding and abetting fascist elements within these organisations. In January 1946, the Northern Department reported the reasons for its decision to suppress the committees:

> We have not banned the Baltic Committees merely because we have refused to recognise the Ukrainian Red Cross. We are against both for the same reason: viz., that welfare organisations of this nature would, and in the case of the Ukrainian Red Cross did, provide cover for political organisation and activity.[603]

In their place, the military authorities facilitated the establishment of the 'Baltic Welfare, Education and Employment Organisation' in March 1946, which would enable close monitoring, by both the military authorities and UNRRA. The military authorities outlined the functions of the new organisation in July 1946:

> In order to advise Control Commission for Germany (BE) and UNRRA on matters of Welfare, Education and employment among Balt Displaced Persons and other matters affecting the well-being of Balt Displaced Persons, an organisation to be called the Baltic Welfare, education and Employment Organisation has been established.[604]

There was substantial opposition from some quarters of the Baltic DP population regarding the suppression of national and welfare committees. Many DPs felt that the individual committees carried out valuable work, and that the needs of each nationality might be overlooked as a result of the establishment of the Baltic Welfare, Education and Employment Committee. Some of the organisations continued to operate clandestinely, but without financial injections, they found themselves largely immobile. Monsieur Torma, the former Estonian Ambassador, head of the Estonian Legation in London, wrote to the Foreign Office concerning the abolition of the 'freely elected committees', including the Estonian, Latvian and Lithuanian welfare committees.[605] As a result of pressure from the Baltic DPs the government made several concessions, including unblocking funds of the Latvian Red Cross, with the money to be shared out through the Baltic Welfare Committees to Estonians and Lithuanians.[606]

Newspapers published by the DPs in their own language were also closed and there was the threatened prohibition of Latvian, Lithuanian and Estonian newspapers from abroad, purportedly 'due to the tendency of such papers to contain anti-Soviet propaganda', although the publication of translations of British factual news reports was allowed.[607]

Monsieur Torma, head of the Estonian Legation in London, wrote to the Foreign Office in June 1946 stating his opposition to the fact that 'the publication of *Sönumid*, the largest Estonian paper printed in the British zone, has had to be discontinued by order of the military government'.[608] A. F. Lambert wrote to I. T. M. Pink at the Control Commission on 31 August 1948 stating that the Foreign Office had 'no objection to the publication in Latvian of factual news bulletins translated from the English'.[609] He noted in relation to Baltic newspapers from abroad that, 'unless such newspapers from abroad are free from anti-Soviet propaganda, they should not be permitted.'[610]

During 1946, Charles Zarine from the Latvian Legation in London sent numerous letters to members of the British Government requesting greater cultural freedoms in the camps. In July he wrote to Mr Hankey at the Foreign Office about the effects of the restrictive measures on the DPs:

> ...the recent change in the attitude change in the attitude of the authorities has had a very bad effect. It is interpreted that they are considered to be a nuisance of whom the authorities want to get rid, and all the recent reverses...are felt to be an indirect pressure to return home – to the Russians.[611]

The restrictions on cultural life and associations in the camps served to intensify the national identities of the refugees, and feelings of anger and disorientation. As a result of the pleas by the Baltic DPs and their representatives, however, some of the restrictions and implemented changes, were rescinded, although particularly in regard to newspapers, the government policy tended to change frequently. In September 1946, a new order permitted the circulation of camp news-sheets in the language of the camp inhabitants, and it was agreed that the publication of a Baltic weekly newspaper for the whole zone should be allowed.[612] Earlier in May 1946, J.M. Bullock of PW/DP Division had stated that 'although orders have been issued forbidding distribution of DP newspapers, it is acknowledged that their distribution cannot be stopped completely'.[613] As late as 1948 it was reported that Latvians, Lithuanians and Estonians each had their own weekly newspaper in the camps, as well as camp news-sheets.[614] The officially sponsored Latvian newspaper was called *Nedelas Apskats* (Weekly Review).[615] However, the newspapers were withdrawn after 3 January 1948, due to worries about anti-Soviet content and lack of paper.[616] The military authorities were again worried that the Soviet repatriation mission would have grounds for believing that the DPs camps acted as havens for anti-Soviet rhetoric. The rapidity of changes and uncertainty about policy in regard to DP newspapers and other cultural activities can partly be explained by the speed of change and hesitancy about relations with Russia during this period. The uncertainty spread to all areas of policy concerned with the Baltic refugees. I. T. M. Pink of the Control Commission, Berlin wrote to Cecil E King at Lübbecke about the lack of a clearly defined policy:

> I wish the Northern Department would make up their minds about the policy they wish us to follow in dealing with Balts...and would stop blowing hot one month and cold the next.[617]

Some members of the British Government felt that the restrictions on cultural activities in the DP camps were too harsh. J. H. Moore of the Refugee Department stated in May 1948 that:

> The Latvian Minister in London complained some time ago that the Latvian National Anthem, which the Latvians at Oldenburg wanted to sing on their National Day (18th November), had been censored by our authorities and that another national song had been banned altogether. PWDP Division have informed us that the ban was in fact imposed by Intelligence Division, who wished to ensure that nothing could possibly be construed as hostile or offensive to the Russians. We feel that we need perhaps not be so conscientious, regarding such matters, and that this censorship of national hymns and songs should be relaxed completely. If the DPs wish to hold memorial services of this nature they should be allowed to do so without interference.[618]

During their first months in the DP camps, the refugees' belief that they would soon be returning home, that the Allies would declare war on Russia and oust her from the Baltics furthered their identities as merely 'temporary' refugees. However, some of the younger refugees were already pessimistic about their future and reluctantly accepted that they would be absent from the homeland for a lengthy period. I asked a Latvian woman in Leeds if during the time that she was in the DP camp whether she hoped all the time that the war would end and that she would go back to Latvia. She replied, summing up the attitude of other young Latvians too:

> Yes, yes, at first yes we did, but we soon realised that that couldn't, that, that wasn't going to happen because the Russians were still there. Yeah, so we came to the realisation that that would be it.[619]

The DPs desire to return to a free, unoccupied homeland was intense. As they recovered from their experiences in the war and as refugees wandering from place to place, the initial relief of finding refuge in the DP camps turned into a desperate wish to return to a free homeland, to see families once more, and to restore their old lives. In his tour of the DP camps, Dr. Kučius asked the DPs about their wishes for the future. He summed up the common reply:

> We do not want anything, we do not need anything, create for us only the necessary conditions for returning home. We will travel hundreds of kilometres on foot, we will carry our children, we will surrender to you our last possessions, only restore in freedom to us the country of our birth.

> There is only one subject in the literature and poetry written in exile – homesickness for their war ravaged country, for its fields and skies.[620]

However, the Baltic refugees were unwilling to return to an occupied homeland under any circumstances. In the DP camps, the constant fear of repatriation heightened the ethnic solidarity of the refugees and increased resistance to Russian rule in the Baltics. Although the DPs felt far safer in the DP camps than out, their fears, sometimes well founded, other times irrational, increased their desire to find safe haven as far away from the Russian repatriation officers as possible. Russian repatriation officers were able to enter the camps initially, and attempted to lure the DPs back to the homeland. There were several incidents in the camps when Russian officers and Baltic DPs clashed. A few did accept repatriation offers, but the vast majority refused to return to a Soviet occupied homeland. Rumours about the fate of repatriates spread like wildfire through the camps. DPs heard about cases where repatriates were sent to Siberia or suffered a horrific fate in their homeland. One Estonian DP stated that: 'We have indisputable evidence that repatriates were destined for Siberia instead of for their native country or that they did not get farther than the prisons of the Soviet zone.'[621]

Secret voting about the issue of repatriation was held in some DP camps, organised by the British military authorities. Although it was held to ascertain numbers wanting to repatriate, the DPs feared that the voting was a preliminary to an enforced mass repatriation. Charles Zarine of the Latvian Legation wrote to Mr Hankey voicing the DPs concerns about repatriation:

> …it seems that some of the Military Government and UNRRA authorities are exercising indirect pressure on the DPs to be repatriated. Among other things continual enquiries are being made, questionnaires circulated and 'plebiscites' held in the camps. These repeated questionings about returning home

irritate and depress the DPs as they have declared quite plainly from the start that they have made up their minds that they cannot and will not return home as long as the Russians are there.[622]

Soviet propaganda was distributed in the camps, outlining the positive experiences of Baltic repatriates, and the undemocratic measures taken by western governments regarding DPs. Although Soviet propaganda was banned during the Berlin blockade of 1948, for the rest of the time the military authorities fell short of an official ban. Worries that such a ban would feed the Soviet propaganda machine, the Deputy High Commissioner also had another reason for the policy. He stated in 1950 that:

> We have always been in favour of imposing a ban on the importation of Soviet literature and its distribution in DP camps in the British zone, but that the Foreign Office have not shared our views on this subject, on the grounds that HMG's obligations under the IRO Constitution made it difficult to impose such a ban.[623]

Soviet pamphlets and newsletters distributed in the camps drew attention to fascist elements within the DP camps, and stressed that 'emigration could only be advantageous to those States who regard refugees and DPs as cheap labour.'[624] Soviet propaganda aimed was to increase repatriation among Balts and to turn them against western nations; the effort was however, largely unsuccessful. Only a tiny minority of Latvians, Lithuanians and Estonians from the British zone voluntarily repatriated to the Latvian, Lithuanian and Estonian Soviet Socialist Republics. It has been estimated that of an approximate total of 160,000 to 190,000 Latvians, Lithuanians and Estonians in Germany after the war, including those living outside the DP camps, only about two per cent applied for repatriation.[625]

This description of life in the DP camps, and the changes, which occurred as the months went on, provides the context for the acceptance of recruitment offers by western nations. The worsening of the situation for the DPs and the growing uncertainty regarding their future prompted members of Latvian, Lithuanian and Estonian associations and the representatives in London, to propose radical solutions. In September 1946, Prof. Mykolas Krupaviàius of the Supreme Lithuanian Committee of Liberation appealed to both the British Government and the United Nations Organisation about the present situation of the Lithuanian DPs and the possible solutions for their future.[626] First, he outlined the position of the DPs in September 1946:

Under the present circumstances, the displaced Lithuanians will be able to stand only one more winter in the Allied zones of Austria and Germany, not only because they are an onerous charge to the local occupation authorities and are often treated with ill-will by the local German administration, which has too readily forgotten who bears the true responsibility for the presence of Baltic Displaced Persons in such numbers in Germany, but also because life in such crowded conditions, often with several families living in a single room, without regular work and employment, without prospects of a better future, has a demoralising effect on them. The time has come for the definite settlement of the European Displaced Persons problem.[627]

Prof. Krupaviàius discussed the four options open to the military authorities: Repatriation; Absorption; Emigration Overseas; Provisional Resettlement in Europe.

Concerning the first option, repatriation, he noted that the DPs, 'refuse to return on any other terms than those of absolute freedom from alien domination and complete guarantee of their fundamental rights and liberties. Those who rashly ventured to return to their Soviet-occupied homes would simply risk death or torture and deportation to the desolate wastes of Siberia, which would be but a protracted form of death. This solution is, in the present political circumstances, wholly out of the question.[628] The option of absorption was also rejected:

Absorption in the population of those countries in which they are now settled is another solution of the Baltic Displaced Persons problem. But anyone cognisant of the present situation in those parts of Germany and Austria under the occupation of the Western Allies and of the temper prevailing there, will readily acquiesce in our view that at the present day such a solution is impracticable and, in our conviction, cannot even bear consideration.[629]

The third option considered was emigration overseas. Concerning this proposal Krupevičius stated:

Emigration to tropical and similar overseas countries, even if the appropriate states were to admit larger numbers of Baltic Displaced Persons, would entail their dispersal and eventual annihilation. The ranks of Baltic Displaced Persons include a very small percentage of labourers and farmers, the bulk of them consisting of intellectuals and of women and children. Without extraneous aid, they would not be able to settle in the novel and strange conditions of their new life, and even substantial grants would fail to make a success of such a venture. Of overseas countries the United States of America and Canada would be best suited for Baltic emigration. Over twenty-five per cent of the Lithuanian people is already established there, and it would be a relatively easy matter for Displaced Lithuanians to find a temporary haven there, pending their ultimate return to their homeland…[630]

The Baltic Displaced Persons were particularly keen that any possible solution would enable Baltic cultures and identities to survive, so that future transplantation in the homeland after independence had been restored, would be possible. They were opposed to any ideas, which might lead to the assimilation or annihilation of the Baltic identities. These concerns formed the rationale behind the fourth solution, favoured by Prof. Krupaviàius. It must be noted that not all DPs shared his views. Prof. Krupaviàius stated that:

The solution which would be best suited and most acceptable to Displaced Lithuanians in the present political circumstances would be their provisional resettlement in Europe. That would mean that Displaced Lithuanians (as well as Latvians and Estonians) would be settled in compact mass in some area of western Germany (e.g. the Rhineland), which would entail the transfer of the German population elsewhere. The area would be administered by the United Nations Organisation, or the organs set up by it for the care of refugees. Displaced Lithuanians could lead, more or less, the life of normal citizens, engage in farming, trade and industry, have an administration and a police of their own, schools and other cultural institutions.[631]

Only one of the above options - emigration overseas, was selected by western governments as a viable large-scale solution to the DP problem (although some absorption of Baltic DPs into the German economy did take place). Great Britain was the first country to recruit Baltic DPs on a mass scale, and in October 1946 began recruiting single Baltic women for the 'Balt Cygnet' scheme. 'Westward Ho!' was implemented in the spring of 1947, to include men and women from many different nationalities. Other western nations followed suit, and the emigration of Baltic DPs was transformed from a trickle to a flood. As more and more recruits left the camps for Great Britain and other recruiting western nations, those left in the camps became acutely aware of the reality of their situation. The DP community was fragmenting throughout the world, and return became an ever more distant prospect. Those who remained in the camps endured frequent moves from camp to camp, as the DP system was reordered and reorganised. The composition of the DPs in the camps changed as the years passed. As fit and healthy refugees were recruited, the majority of DPs remaining were the old, infirm and families with children. In 1950, the remaining DPs were handed over to the German authorities for absorption into the German economy.

CONCLUDING REMARKS

In anticipation of the emigration of the DPs to Great Britain and other western nations, the representative body of Latvian DPs in Germany published and circulated a statement entitled, 'The Latvian Stance in Alien Lands'. As Carpenter suggests, it was intended as 'a kind of send-off message'.[632] It stated: 'As exiles, we have a moral obligation to preserve our language and culture, and to raise future generations of Latvians who will be committed to our struggle for the restoration of Latvia's independence'.[633] Carpenter writes: 'This statement certified and codified what had transpired during the years in the DP camps: exile had become the new life script'.[634]

The union of thousands of Estonians, Latvians and Lithuanians in the DP camps after months or years of displacement was the first step in the formation of the diaspora, and of an identity as exiles. It was in the DP camps that the refugees first gained experience in the organisation of their countrymen abroad. In effect the DPs were *practising exile*. The construction of an exile identity in the DP camps entailed the reconstruction of Latvian, Lithuanian and Estonian national identities to fit the requirements of exile. For many DPs, particularly the younger refugees, national identities were formed for the very first time in the DP camps.

Joshua Fishman coined the term 'diaspora consciousness', 'to describe individuals who view themselves as the only ones at liberty to preserve and perpetuate the "true culture" during a period of "foreign occupation" of the homeland'.[635] The following statement by Carpenter can be applied to all three Baltic DP nationalities: 'Latvian diaspora consciousness was first fostered, shaped, and elaborated in the refugee camps'.[636]

The formation of a new diasporic or exile identity was an ironic and unintended consequence of the DP camps, which were initially established to facilitate repatriation after the conclusion of the war. Camp refugees had abundant free time, and 'although Allied authorities proscribed political associations, they encouraged cultural activities and organisations'.[637] In retrospect, the DPs view this period in the refugee camps 'as a time of intense cultural activism, a crucial training ground that laid the foundation for a subsequently viable exile society'.[638] Life in the DP camps was thus the first step in 'creating exile'.[639] The DP camps provided preliminary training for the exiles' future life in Britain. The camps imparted experience of life as diaspora, of life in a foreign country, and practice in the organisation of the refugees abroad. These were experiences which the DPs would take with them to Great Britain, where the diasporas and their new identities would undergo further consolidation and modification.

CHAPTER 5

Recruitment of Latvians, Lithuanians and Estonians for labour schemes in Britain

I realised we won't be able to return to Latvia so we had to go somewhere else and more or less this was nearer. It was in Europe. It was a bit nearer Latvia and there was an opportunity to work in [a] hospital so I came like that.' '...we knew there was no chance to go back to Latvia. There were Communists, Russians. We didn't want to go back there...and when you are young you are probably a bit more adventurous and why not do something about it, you know sort it out?

(First Generation Latvian woman)[640]

BETWEEN OCTOBER 1946 AND DECEMBER 1950, 26,000 Baltic DP's were recruited for labour as part of the British Government's European Volunteer Worker (EVW) schemes - Balt Cygnet and Westward Ho! In total, over 80,000 DP's of different nationalities participated in the schemes. Although the numbers recruited represented a small percentage of DPs in Europe, the EVW schemes were a milestone in British immigration history. The EVW schemes were by no means the first immigration schemes[641]; neither was this the first time Latvians, Lithuanians and Estonians had migrated to Britain, nor indeed the Poles, Yugoslavs and other Eastern Europeans who accompanied them. However, because of their size, organisation and contract basis, these schemes were a novelty in British immigration history. These characteristics allied to the intervention of the state and the 'fact that the original objective of the government was to double the size of the foreign labour force in Britain' meant that according to Kay and Miles, the schemes 'represented a minor revolution'.[642] Interestingly however, few similar schemes were ever implemented again, and although the contract labour scheme became a key feature of capitalist development in other European countries in the 1950's, it did not become popular in Britain.[643] The colonial immigrants who followed the EVWs onto Britain's shores migrated under a very different set of immigration rules and procedures. However, some aspects of the EVW schemes, particularly resettlement strategies, were employed in later immigration cases, for example, the Ugandan Asians in 1972 and the Hungarian refugees in 1956.[644]

The mechanics and details of the EVW schemes have been discussed in detail in several publications, most thoroughly in Diana Kay and Robert Miles's, *Refugees or Migrant Workers?: European Volunteer Worker's in Britain, 1946-51*, which built upon the research carried out by J A Tannahill several decades earlier, in *European Volunteer Workers in Britain*[645]. Recent works have discussed the importance of the EVW schemes in British immigration history, and shown how these schemes not only revealed ideas about assimilation, but also the presence within Government thinking, of a racialised hierarchy of labour in the post-1945 Labour Government[646]. According to Diana Kay and Robert Miles, Baltic refugees, who were the first recruits to the EVW schemes, were placed at the top of the racialised hierarchy, since they were deemed to be 'of good human stock'.[647] This contrasted to groups lower down the scale, for example, Byelorussians and Yugoslavs, who were not thought to be of such high quality material for the purposes of assimilation. The Balts were expected to assimilate easily into British society, and a series of measures designed to speed up the process were incorporated into plans for the labour schemes.

This chapter will discuss two main aspects of the EVW schemes: (1) the process of recruitment, including the motivations for the prioritisation of the Baltic nationalities and the details of the schemes, particularly strategies of assimilation; (2) the motivations of the refugees in participating on the EVW schemes.

BACKGROUND TO THE RECUITMENT OF 'BALTS' FOR LABOUR: DEBATES AND CONTEXT

Historians have begun to analyse the factors leading to the recruitment of some 80,000 EVWs for labour in Britain between 1946 and 1950.[648] Although historians have stressed that the EVW schemes must be viewed in the context both of post-war Europe and the domestic situation in Britain, there has, as yet, been only fragmentary analysis of Foreign Office motivations and files. A leading historian of the EVW schemes, Diana Kay has acknowledged that a full understanding of DP resettlement 'cannot be gained by considering the local circumstances of receiving countries alone'.[649] Yet to date, most of the discussion has centred on the motivations of the Ministry of Labour, and evidence from its files has been exhaustively examined. However, it is Foreign Office files which hold the key to understanding how Foreign Policy considerations, and the refugee situation in Europe impinged upon the decision making processes of the post-war Labour Government. This section will analyse the mechanics and processes leading to the implementation of the EVW schemes, from the perspectives of both the Ministry of Labour and the Foreign Office. Discussion will centre on the recruitment of Latvians, Lithuanians and Estonians.

In Europe, a few months after the end of the Second World War, immense political and economic difficulties were created for the British Government, by the hundreds of thousands of refugees stranded in DP Camps in the British zones of Germany and Austria. Meanwhile, at home in Britain, severe shortages of manpower, one of the results of the economic conditions created by the Second World War, was producing critical problems in the health service, agriculture, and industries such as textiles and coal. The EVW schemes can be seen as an attempt to ameliorate both international and internal difficulties: in short, both to lessen the DP crisis in Europe *and* to fill manpower gaps in Britain. As the internal and international situation altered, so too were the EVW schemes modified to suit changing circumstances at home and in Europe. The schemes were shaped not only by changing patterns of manpower shortage, but also by shifting Anglo-Soviet relations in the immediate post-war period.

The internal and international situation at the end of the Second World War planted the seeds for the introduction of the DP labour recruitment schemes. Several months after the close of war, the DP situation in Europe was already critical. In the British zone of Germany alone, by September 1945, there were already an estimated 650,000 DPs, and a further 60,000 in the British zone of Austria.[650] This was under half of the estimated 1.8 million DPs stranded in Europe.[651]   In September 1945, a total of 78,904 Baltic refugees had gained DP status in Europe.[652] In the British zone of Germany, Baltic DPs numbered 50,572 at this time, and in the British zone of Austria, 1000.[653] However, many more were still finding their way through Europe to the safety of the DP camps, and the numbers of DPs rose steadily over the coming months, reaching a peak in mid-1946. By June 1946, among the Baltic nationalities alone, there were 32,000 Estonians, 80,000 Latvians and 59,000 Lithuanians in the British zone of Germany.[654]

The DPs in the camps composed many different European nationalities, including Poles, Ukrainians, Czechoslovaks, Hungarians, Bulgarians, Yugoslavs, Romanians, Jews, Italians, Greeks and those nationalities referred to as Soviet nationals. Like Latvians, Lithuanians and Estonians, some of these nationalities, for example, Ukrainians and Poles, refused repatriation and were unwilling to return to Soviet-occupied homelands. Those who served in the German forces were particularly fearful of reprisals, and for most of the Baltic DPs, their experiences of Russian rule in 1940-41 had left them adamant that they would return home only when, and if, their countries were freed from communist tyranny. Lack of cultural, particularly religious, freedoms and the power of the secret police were among the specific motivations for refusing repatriation. Among the Baltic nationalities, only a tiny fraction applied for repatriation – an estimated two per cent of Latvians, Lithuanians and Estonians in Germany (including those living outside DP Camps).[655] The problem of repatriation was compounded by the presence of Soviet Repatriation Missions who toured some of the DP camps and demanded the return of all Soviet citizens. The Soviet Union and Great Britain clashed over the definition of a Soviet Citizen, which began to destabilise the precarious wartime alliance with Russia. The Soviet regime regarded all Balts as Soviet Citizens and demanded their speedy return to the Baltic States. Although the British Government still had to clearly define its policy towards Balts, it made it clear during 1945 that it would not forcibly repatriate Latvians, Lithuanians or Estonians, since they were not regarded as Soviet citizens. Foreign Office policy at the end of 1945, stated that, 'Persons from Estonia, Latvia and Lithuanian who wish to return home will be enabled to do so'. 'Persons from these countries who do not wish to return home will not be compelled to do so and the British authorities will provide for the maintenance of all such persons in the British zone'.[656] Thus, in addition to being faced with the question of what to do about the hundreds of thousands of DPs in its zone, the British Government also risked worsening relations with Russia over the issue of repatriation.

As the number of DPs grew and conditions deteriorated, humanitarian concerns grew. The United Nations called on Western nations to shoulder a share of the responsibility for these refugees and pressure increased on Great Britain, and other western nations to plan solutions.

A further problem was the growing financial burden of the DP camps. The British Government faced immense bills for post-war reconstruction at home and could ill-afford the financial costs of the DP camps. It was estimated that by 1947, the cost of the British zone of Germany to the British public was approximately 80 million pounds.[657]

Faced with the DP problem abroad, within Great Britain, the new Labour Government was formed in July 1945, to begin the post-war reconstruction process at home. One problem which became immediately apparent was the shortage of manpower at the end of the war. As a result, there was also a maldistribution of labour, which had led to an under-manning of some essential industries, while other less 'essential' industries were able to recruit labour more successfully. Key industries, particularly coal, textiles and agriculture were facing the greatest difficulties, as their failure to attract labour became increasingly apparent. There were also critical shortages in hospitals. The Economic Survey published in June 1946 noted the crisis in the coal industry. The additional manpower required to maintain the domestic fuel ration and exports at their current level and to keep industry fully supplied with coal was put at 40,000, while an increasing rate of wastage and falling rate of recruitment might bring about a reduction in manpower of 40,000 over the year to March 1947.[658] The overall manpower shortage was estimated at 230,000, a gap which rose to 630,000 in the Third Economic Survey of December 1946.[659] Manpower shortages threatened not only to promote wage inflation, but also to destabilise the entire economy.

At the end of the war therefore, the British Government faced severe problems both internally and externally. The economic problems of the government culminated in the coal crisis of 1947, partly caused by under-manning[660], while relations with Russia began to sour as early as 1946. This was due to several factors, including the Sovietisation of Eastern Europe and Soviet discontent over Britain's handling of DPs. However, in 1945 the British Government was still keen to foster amicable relations with Russia. The Labour Government, with Ernest Bevin as Foreign Minister, was unwilling to abandon the wartime alliance with Russia, although Bevin continued Churchill's policy of scepticism towards the USSR.[661]

The options for solving the problem of labour shortages were discussed within the government as early as the autumn of 1945. Tannahill claims that the first suggestion of using DPs to fill labour gaps in Britain was made at an inter-departmental meeting to discuss the supply of nurses and domestics in hospitals held on 17 September between the Ministries of Health and Labour. The shortage of hospital domestics had been acute during the war, and at the close of war, a 'near-crisis' had developed, especially in sanatoria.[662] The idea of recruiting DPs for labour was dismissed initially, but discussions continued during November 1945. Although the benefits to be gained were acknowledged by the Ministry of Labour, the associated difficulties had not yet been overcome.[663] At this stage, the potential for such a scheme to ameliorate the DP crisis had not yet been discussed, and the Foreign Office had yet to be involved in plans for the scheme.

One of the potential problems foreseen by the Ministry of Labour was that once recruited, DPs would not stay in the jobs allotted to them and that there was no way that they could be forced to stay. In November 1945, P. Goldberg, an official at the Ministry of Labour, discussed the potential problems of the recruitment of DPs:

> Most of the available women were said to be Poles and Balts. Among the latter, the keenest applicants for the jobs would be well-educated women who at the time of the German occupation of their countries had been studying for the learned professions. Such women would no doubt delude themselves into thinking that they would be willing to do domestic work in hospitals in order to get the opportunity of leaving the DP camps, but:
>
> (1) they would prima facie not be the most suitable persons to bring over for rough domestic work.
>
> (2) After a few weeks at the hospitals they would no doubt find very good reasons for changing their minds, and in this event there was no obvious way in which the Ministry could compel them to remain in hospital employment.[664]

As this correspondence suggests, Balts were cited early on as possible nationalities to recruit, although education was specified initially as a reason for not employing them.

Despite the potential problems associated with its introduction, the Ministry of Labour faced pressure to reconsider the recruitment of DPs from various quarters, including a leading chest physician, and according to Tannahill, it also seems likely that the Baltic Legations 'were making semi-official soundings about the possibility of assisting their refugees in Germany'.[665] Discussions continued throughout the winter of 1945 to 1946.[666] A further obstacle to the recruitment of DPs as hospital domestics, emerged when Mr. Goldberg at the Ministry of Labour, reported on 1 January 1946, that proposals to recruit hospital domestics from among Displaced Persons would have to be suspended until after the announcement by the newly-constituted National Joint Council of revised rates of pay for hospital domestics.[667] By March, however, the Council had agreed on fresh national rates, although local agreements had not yet been confirmed. Nevertheless, the agreement eased the way for the formulation of a labour scheme which was worked out, submitted to, and agreed, by the Foreign Labour Committee in April 1946. The scheme contained various labour restrictions, to overcome the problem of wastage.

The introduction of Balt Cygnet must be viewed in the context of British immigration policy before 1946. Although as the first large-scale contract labour scheme, Balt Cygnet had many novel aspects, it built upon immigration policy since the 1905 Aliens Act, which established a framework based on a legal distinction between 'British subject' and 'alien', the latter becoming subjected to newly established procedures of immigration control.[668] The Aliens Act was introduced in response to the thousands of newcomers from the Russian Empire, including ethnic Latvians, Lithuanians and Estonians and Jews.[669] A new Aliens Order of 1920 in force until 1953, furthered the 1905 Act and 'established a procedure to permit the entry into Britain of aliens seeking employment'.[670] Such aliens were required to enter Britain at an approved port and register with the police. An alien also had to produce a permit issued to his employer by the Ministry of Labour at the port of entry. This provision allowed for the recruitment of aliens for labour in Britain for a specified period of time, at the completion of which they were required to leave the country. During the Second World War, the Aliens Order of 1920 was adjusted to give the Home Office powers to issue visas to permit the employment of foreigners resident in Britain.[671]

In seeking manpower to fill undermanned industries in the immediate post-war period, the British Government did not limit itself to DPs. In March 1946, the 1920 Aliens Order was amended to restore to the Ministry of Labour and National Service (MLNS) powers to issue individual work permits.[672] At the end of the war, in addition to the employment of aliens on an individual basis, German and Italian POW's resident in Britain and the newly formed Polish Resettlement Corps were also used as sources of European foreign labour, and although their recruitment was not in the form of contract labour schemes, there were 'elements of compulsion and direction'.[673] However, neither the work permit scheme nor the employment of POW's and Poles was sufficient in relation to the demand for labour. In July 1945, the MLNS reached agreement with the Belgian Government for the recruitment of Belgian women for domestic work in hospitals, on a six-month renewable contract basis. About 900 women were recruited on this scheme in 1945 and 1946.[674]

BALT CYGNET

Balt Cygnet was formulated initially to recruit Baltic DP women for domestic work in hospitals and TB Sanatoria, an area of employment particularly unattractive to British workers, and for which the ongoing recruitment of Belgian women was regarded as insufficient. A draft of a Memorandum on a DP scheme, by the Ministry of Labour and National Service in May 1946, outlined the shortage of domestic staff in sanatoria:

> The need of the sanatoria for domestic workers is particularly acute for these institutions are often situated in remote country districts, and for this reason alone - i.e. apart from the widespread fear that inexperienced workers have of contracting TB if they are sent to work in institutions of this type - they have always been difficult to staff up with British women.[675]

Balt Cygnet was intended as a small-scale, trial scheme, which would be extended only if successful. Balt Cygnet built upon existing immigration policy and experience, but also contained some novel aspects. The instructions for Balt Cygnet were outlined in the Control Commission for Germany's (British Element), Technical Instruction no. 8, 'Recruitment of Displaced Persons for employment in British Sanatoria : Operation 'BALT CYGNET', issued on 26 August 1946.[676] Initially, Balt Cygnet was designed to recruit 1000 female DPs of Latvian, Lithuanian and Estonian nationality for employment in British Sanatoria. The conditions of service specified that: 'Women will be recruited in the first place for work in sanatoria as kitchen hands, general hands, ward maids, cleaners and laundry workers'. 'Women should be between the ages of 21 and 40, physically fit and willing to undertake domestic work of this character'.[677] Women were not allowed to change their employment in the first 12 months without the consent of the Ministry of Labour, and as aliens they were required to register with the police. No dependants were to be admitted, so the scheme was intended primarily for single women. Medical examinations screened out those with diseases such as TB, and pregnant DPs.

The first party of 100 Baltic women departed from Lübbecke on 16 October 1946, and travelled by ferry from Cuxhaven to Tilbury. Thereafter approximately 100 women travelled to Britain every week. The eleventh party of women sailed on 5 January 1947, completing phase 1 of Balt Cygnet.[678]

Throughout 1946, even before the implementation of the Phase 1 of the Balt Cygnet scheme, discussions were held regarding its extension beyond the planned 1000 recruits. Although Balt Cygnet was initially a Ministry of Labour devised project to attend to the urgent needs of British industry, the Foreign Office became increasingly involved with the plans for the labour scheme. The Foreign Office became aware of the potential of labour recruitment schemes to ameliorate the DP problem. Meanwhile, labour shortages were worsening. Both the Ministry of Labour and the Foreign Office regarded the initial plan for 1000 women as merely a start, and believed that if substantial solutions to both internal and external problems were to be found, further plans would have to be made.

On 17 September 1946, a memorandum by the Parliamentary Secretary to the MLNS on the 'Recruitment of Displaced persons from Germany for work in British hospitals' outlined the potential of an extension to the Balt Cygnet scheme, and noted reasons for choosing Baltic women recruits:

> At its third meeting the [Foreign Labour] Committee approved the scheme put forward in FLC (46) 6, for the recruitment, on an experimental basis, of up to 1000 women from DP camps in Germany for employment as domestic workers in our TB Sanatoria.
>
> One of our officers who recently visited a number of the Camps in the British Zone in connection with the scheme, reports that the women from the Baltic provinces, from whom volunteers are being sought, are of a very good type, and that it should be possible to recruit from among them suitable persons for employment in this country in numbers considerably in excess of the limit of 1,000 already agreed by the Committee'. 'Indeed, out of a total of employable women of Baltic origin estimated by the Authorities in the British Zone at about 20,000, it is thought that there may be no difficulty in selecting

as many as 5000 very suitable volunteers for work in this country.

They are generally of good appearance and habits and have been well looked after in the Camps. The general standard of education is good; most of them speak German as well as their own language, while many already speak English quite well, especially the younger ones.

Careful selection, combined with strict medical examination of the type which is being undertaken under the supervision of the Medical Director of UNRRA, should produce a substantial number of women of useful qualifications and of good health who would form a valuable addition to our manpower and a not undesirable element in our population.[679]

Mary Appleby at the Control Office in London, informed Mr. Crawford at the Foreign Office, in early September 1946 that:

Mr Goldberg was so impressed with the possibilities of the scheme and with the response which it is now meeting that he is asking the Minister of Labour to put a paper to the Cabinet suggesting that the scheme should be extended to allow 5000 instead of 1000 women to benefit. He also hopes to extend the categories of candidates from domestic servants in Sanatoria to domestic servants in General Hospitals and to nurses. He is very seriously considering advising the Minister of Labour that a further effort should be made to secure some of these DPs for General Domestic Service. He also told me that he was going to take up the possibility of bringing male DP labour to this country for agricultural and other purposes.[680]

The response to the scheme was lukewarm at first because many women, 'thought they were going to be sent to do unpleasant jobs in what amounted to Plague Centres in this country which no British woman would touch'.[681] However, tours by Ministry of Labour officials dispelled doubts, and promoted a huge response rate. Nevertheless, the Government was concerned that women may have waited for the new scheme in preference to accepting work in Sanatoria, and kept the details of a new scheme quiet.

The formulation of Phase 2 of Balt Cygnet was consolidated in December 1946. Phase 2 opened up recruitment for domestic work in General Hospitals, and not for sanatoria, unless, 'a woman specifically volunteers for this type of institution'.[682] Women had the option of being considered for nursing training or midwifery training, if suitable after the expiry of three months. Recruitment was still limited to women of Latvian, Estonian and Lithuanian origin.[683] Women between 40 and 50 were to be considered for this scheme, 'if they appear to be very suitable for this type of work and are physically fit'.[684]

The first party of women on the extended scheme, the twelfth party on Balt Cygnet left Cuxhaven on 11 January 1947. By the beginning of 1947, the scheme was proving such a success, that the numbers recruited were substantially increased. From 25 January, the number of recruits were increased to a target of 200 women each week. On 20 February 1947, Control Office informed Lemgo that, 'Ministers have decided that stage now reached when substantial acceleration of Balt-Cygnet weekly arrivals absolutely essential'.[685] On 21 February SUGRA 853 reported that 'the immediate target for Balt Cygnet is to be three to four hundred per week from 10 March, with expansion to five hundred as soon as possible thereafter.'[686]

In the planning and implementation of the labour recruitment schemes, the Ministry of Labour and the Foreign Office had different goals in mind. Whereas the Ministry of Labour viewed Balt Cygnet as a way to ameliorate labour shortages, the FO was also interested in the potential of labour schemes to ease the DP problem. Other departments - the Home Office and the Cabinet, also became actively involved in the planning and implementation of the schemes. In discussing the motivations for the prioritisation of Balts, one has to bear in mind the different priorities of the Ministry of Labour and the Foreign Office. Why did the Ministry of Labour devise a labour scheme initially intended only for Baltic nationalities? The name - Balt Cygnet in itself suggested the nationality exclusivity of the scheme. As discussions got under way between the Foreign Office and the Ministry of Labour to extend the scheme, why did the Balts continue to be prioritised?

From the Ministry of Labour's viewpoint, the sheer number of suitable Baltic DPs undoubtedly played a role in their prioritisation. At the same time, the number of Baltic DPs also posed a problem for the Foreign Office. Baltic DPs were among the largest of the DP nationality groups, along with Ukrainians and Poles. There were sizeable numbers of women and men aged between 18 and 50, and importantly for the Balt Cygnet scheme, there were large numbers of suitable female DPs. In September 1946, there was a total of over 63,000 Baltic women DPs, 18 years of age or older. There were also over 77,000 Baltic men, who were receiving UNRRA Assistance in Germany, the vast majority who were in DP camps. In total, there were over 180,000 Balts in Germany in September 1946.[687] On 27 November 1946, it was reported that in the British Zone of Germany alone, there were a total of 13,309 Estonians, 45,413 Latvians and 23,882 Lithuanians both inside and outside Displaced Persons camps. Of these, 35 per cent were assumed to be women between the ages of 18 and 50.[688]

According to Kay and Miles, racialisation played a major role in the prioritisation of the Baltic nationalities from the very beginning. Kay and Miles discussed the existence of a racialised hierarchy of labour, which they described as follows:

> The EVWs were not conceptualised as a single, homogenous category, but were minimally dichotomised. Nevertheless, they were all racialised: the discourse of 'race' was implicit (as in references to 'blood' and 'stock') and explicit in the drawing of conclusions about the 'suitability' of EVWs, but in combination with evaluations of their social and cultural attributes. And where racialisation was accompanied by negative evaluations of the EVWs, or of the presumed consequences of their presence, one can speak of racism as being a component part of official discourse.

> …the DPs became internally differentiated along a North-South divide. Those from the northern part of Eastern Europe (mainly the Baltic States) were regarded as eminently 'assimilable'. They were seen to be superior 'types', organised in strong and stable family groups, sharing in the Protestant work ethic and a more advanced industrial culture. By contrast, the going images of those from South Eastern Europe more closely approximated stereotypes of contemporary Third World Refugees. They were often depicted as 'simple peasant types', as being unversed in the ways of a complex industrial society and as being more 'racially' distinct, forming part of an ill-defined but alien 'Slav race'. As was the case with other countries recruiting from the DP camps, British officials exhibited an in-built, partially racialised bias towards the nationals from the Baltic States.[689]

Government discourse highlighted the positive attributes of the Balts throughout the planning of the Balt Cygnet scheme. As Kay and Miles suggest, the Baltic nationalities were regarded as excellent material for labour. In the memorandum by the Parliamentary Secretary to the MLNS on the 'Recruitment of Displaced persons from Germany for work in British hospitals' of 17 September 1946, the attributes of Baltic DPs were described. They were: 'of a very good type'; 'suitable persons for employment'; 'of good appearance and habits'; their standard of education was 'good'; and finally, they were 'of useful qualifications and of good health who would form a valuable addition to our manpower and a not undesirable element in our population'.[690]

Thus, not only were Balts regarded as hardworking, industrious workers, they were also perceived to have high potential for assimilation. Their level of education was now regarded as an asset, particularly their English language skills. In addition, their appearance, manners and behaviour also contributed to an assessment of Balts as 'good human stock'.[691]

One aspect of the racialisation of Latvians, Lithuanians and Estonians was the way they were homogenised under the name of 'Balts'[692] by the British Government. The British Government referred to ethnic Latvians, Lithuanians and Estonians collectively as 'Balts' throughout the lifetime of the labour schemes. The use of the term 'Balts'[693] partly reflected misunderstandings about the very different cultures of Latvians, Lithuanians and Estonians, but also suggested that the three nationalities were regarded equally, in terms of their assimilation and recruitment potential. When recruiting 'Balts', the government only accepted ethnic Latvians, Lithuanians and Estonians from the inter-war Baltic States, although some DPs disguised their nationality in order to enter Britain. Some Lithuanians from the Vilnius region, which was part of Poland in the inter-war period and some Jewish DPs fell into this category, for example. The fact that very few DPs had identification or nationality papers made it almost impossible for officials to prove the nationality of DPs.

It was not only officials from within the Ministry of Labour who pointed out the attributes of Baltic DPs. Foreign Office officials also described Baltic DPs very positively. Their views were influenced not only by pre-conceived racialised ideas, but also from reports of good behaviour in the DP camps. So to a degree, the Balts earned their good reputations. Ivor Pink informed Lambert in the Northern Department on 17 August 1946, that:

> Baltic DPs in the British Zone are, on the whole, better off than other DPs, not only because they have known how to organise themselves but also because their good behaviour has earned them the confidence and sympathy of the numerous authorities who look after them.[694]

Praise for the Baltic DPs was almost unanimous. In November 1946, N. C. D. Brownjohn also highlighted the assets of the Baltic DPs:

> The Baltic Displaced Persons are by far the best we have got containing a number of professional and better educated people. They give much less trouble and behave better than any of the other categories.[695]

J. B. Hynd wrote to Hector McNeill at the Foreign Office on 21 January 1947 that, 'Among the most orderly and capable DPs are the Balts and there is general agreement that they would make very good settlers, wherever openings can be found for them'.[696] Hector McNeill agreed, replying that he thought that the 'Balts are among the best' of the displaced persons.[697]

Kanty Cooper, who worked among DPs in Germany discussed the reasons for the prioritisation of Balts in her autobiographical work, *The Uprooted*. She stated:

> The Estonians, Latvians and Lithuanians were in a different category from the rest of the DPs. The majority had not come to Germany as forced labour like the Poles, Yugoslavs, Republican Spaniards and Greeks. They had come as refugees fleeing from the Russians who had occupied their lands between June and August 1940 while the German-Soviet Non-Aggression pact was still in force. They were enemies of our ally Russia and collaborators of our enemy Germany. Some of their men had joined the German army. But because they were cultivated, clean and reliable people they were usually the first asked for on emigration schemes. They belonged chiefly to the middle classes and many of them spoke excellent English. Most of the women would look more at home in the drawing room than in the kitchen, yet they were all prepared to work as scullery or ward maids for the first three months of their stay in England.[698]

Another important reason for the prioritisation of the Balts was that as one of the largest non-repatriable groups in Europe, their existence in DP camps was causing increasing friction in Anglo-Soviet relations. In 1946, the FO identified three main options for the disposal of DPs - repatriation, resettlement or emigration. The government undertook to find solutions for the DPs in that order. However, as Kay and Miles suggest, of the different DP nationalities, the Balts were perceived to be the least likely to agree to repatriation, and the question of what to do with them became particularly pressing. The repatriation of Baltic refugees to the Soviet Union by the Swedish government in January 1946 had caused an international outcry, and the government was keen that the Balts in the British Zone did not befall a similar fate.

The Duchess of Atholl highlighted the situation of the Baltic nationalities in *The Times* in May 1946. She described the fears of the Baltic DPs and stressed the inadequacies of the government's repatriation policies: The Duchess wrote:

> The terror caused by the possibility of enforced repatriation is such that many displaced persons from the Baltic States are hiding today outside the camps rather than take advantage of the food and shelter they provide. This is reported from both Italy and Austria. From the camps in the latter it is said that not less than 60% have fled to live a hand-to-mouth existence outside them, rather than risk being claimed by zealous repatriation officers.

> These people men especially are said to be in rags.....There is first hand evidence that His Majesty's Government's policy of refusing to allow any enforced repatriation has not always been fully implemented on the spot.[699]

To some extent, public exposure, such as the Duchess of Atholl's letter, increased pressure on the government to act to help the Balts.

Policy towards the disposal of the Balts remained unclear throughout 1946, despite ongoing preparation for the Balt Cygnet initiative. On 12 August 1946, I T M Pink, Political Division, HQ, CCG, Berlin wrote to Cecil E King, Political Division, Lübbecke, stating that:

> I wish the Northern Department would make up their minds about the policy they wish us to follow in dealing with the Balts and Ukrainians and would stop blowing hot one month and cold the next.[700]

In a Memorandum on Findings during a Tour of Displaced Persons Camps in Military Zones in Germany and Austria, the Foreign Office was informed that:

> The plight of the Baltic DPs is in many ways worse and their ultimate disposal may prove more difficult than in the case of other nationalities because they have no desire to resettle permanently overseas. It will also be impossible to persuade them to return home. They hold to the hope that somehow or

another and perhaps with our help, the Russians will be displaced from their countries and they can then, but not until then return home.[701]

The British Government's policy on repatriation was a source of conflict between Britain and the Soviet Union. The following statement by Political Division, CCG (BE) in December 1946, reflected the different status given to the Balts by Britain and the Soviet Union:

> The Soviet Government regards [the Balts] as Soviet Citizens while His Majesty's Government considers no person a Soviet citizen who was not a citizen of the Soviet Union and resident within its borders, as they were, on 1st September 1939.[702]

Thus, for Britain, repatriation of the Balts was not an option. During early 1946, the government recognised the incorporation of the Baltic States into the Soviet Union, *de facto*, but not *de jure*. This reflected the government's desire to tread a fine line between neither antagonising nor appeasing the Soviet Union. Government policy remained rather contradictory. For example, although the government refused the enforced repatriation of Balts, at the same time it allowed free access of the Soviet Repatriation Mission to all DP camps in the British Zone, and earlier had allowed the enforced repatriation of Cossacks in 1945, whose status as Soviet Citizens was also questionable. During 1946, while tension between the Soviet Union and Great Britain steadily increased, intensified by the Soviet Union's tightening of control over Eastern Europe, the government had not yet abandoned the idea of co-operation.

Since the Balts would not accept repatriation the options of resettlement or emigration were left. The main options discussed were absorption into the German economy or emigration overseas. The Baltic DPs themselves also regarded provisional resettlement in Europe, before returning to the homeland once independence had been re-established as a fourth option. At this stage, Balt Cygnet was not regarded as a way of substantially reducing DP numbers, primarily due to its small-scale. However, as early as late 1946 and January/February of 1947, the Foreign Office and officials from the Control Commission in Germany became interested in the potential role of a larger scheme in reducing DP numbers. In October 1946, following the implementation of Phase 1 of Balt Cygnet, N C D Brownjohn, Major General of the Control Commission in Germany wrote that:

> I consider...the time has now come to invite plans for the two further schemes for employment of Balts in the UK. The first

of these will involve the selection and movement of approximately 2,000 Balt women for employment as domestic servants; the second envisages the move of between 4,000 to 5,000 Balts for employment in Agriculture.[703]

However as Brownjohn acknowledged, 'no action to put these schemes into effect has been taken'[704], and it was some months before plans for a larger scheme were developed, although Phase 2 of Balt Cygnet got under way in January 1947.

During late 1946, discussion about the disposal of Baltic DPs focused on their possible absorption in the German economy or their resettlement in the British Dominions. The options were discussed in a letter by G. B. Vaughan-Hughes from the Foreign Office, to the Major-General, Deputy Chief of Staff for the Control Commission for Germany (British Element), in November 1946. About 500 Baltic women had already travelled to Britain under Phase 1 of Balt Cygnet:

> Control Office is anxious to consider the possibility of ultimately absorbing Baltic Displaced Persons in the British Zone of Germany into the German economy.
>
> We do not think that there can be any question of doing this whilst the Soviet Repatriation Mission remains in the British Zone. This Mission claims that all Balts are Soviet Citizens. If they were dispersed throughout the British Zone of Germany it would give the Soviet Mission unlimited opportunity to indulge in every variety of unpleasant activity.
>
> The Balts are otherwise the best of our Displaced Persons. They contain a large proportion of professional classes and give less trouble than other classes of Displaced Person. We do not think it is right to discriminate between different classes of Displaced persons and especially the Balts who are the best of them'. 'We also think that they are the most promising field for resettlement in the Dominions and if there is any intention of doing this it would be a pity to scatter them about the British Zone of Germany.[705]

N C D Brownjohn agreed with Vaughan-Hughes stating on 30 November 1946, that:

> If there is ever any possibility of overseas settlement in the British Dominions, the Balts would be the best and most useful class to take and might be a real asset to the country of their adoption.

None of these Balts are ever likely to accept repatriation. They have no government to protect them and in that respect their absorption into the German economy would cause less trouble than for example, similar action against the Poles.[706]

Increasingly however, recruitment of Baltic DPs for labour in Britain, became viewed as a possible way of decreasing numbers in the DP Camps. It was perceived that Balts would accept recruitment offers in large numbers, since they had no homeland to which they could return. Nevertheless, it was not until the formulation of plans for Westward Ho! that the labour schemes were perceived as large-scale projects, which would have any significant impact on DP numbers.

Towards the end of the Balt Cygnet scheme, recruitment was extended beyond Baltic DPs in the British zone of Germany. As early as February 1947, it was reported that the numbers of suitable Baltic women were beginning to dry up. On 24 February, the Control Commission sent a telegram to the Control Office, reporting that, 'Saturation point Balts will be reached end March unless consideration can be given to employment in England of males with dependants which would produce large response'.[707] ' On the same day, Control Office informed Lübbecke that, 'We now have authority to recruit single women, not only from among the Balts but also from among the Ukrainians'.[708]

Lübbecke reported on 15 March that:

Balt Cygnet has been going for some time and we have already shipped 1840 girls to the UK. It started off at the rate of 100 a week because the UK could not accept a greater number, this rate was stepped up to 200 a week last month. We have about 400 girls recruited and waiting to be shipped to the UK and the Ministry of Labour have increased their selection terms to cope with the wider nationality field, with the inclusion of Ukrainian girls, we hope this will result in increased recruitment. Shipping is at present a bottle neck as we have only been allotted 750 passages during the month of March and 900 during the month of April.[709]

During March 1947, the recruitment of Baltic nationalities was also extended to the US zone.

With the recruitment of Ukrainian DPs, the exclusivity of Balt Cygnet was ended. The Foreign Office was keen to recruit Ukrainians for many of the same reasons as the Balts: they were non-repatriable and therefore a potential source of conflict between Britain and Russia, and there were large numbers of suitable DPs for labour. However, the Ministry of Labour had its doubts towards their suitability for labour in Britain, describing them as uneducated peasant types, who were not perceived to be as hard working as the Balts, although the initial success of Ukrainian recruitment quelled these fears to some degree. The extension of recruitment of Baltic nationalities beyond the British zone suggested that despite small-scale Ukrainian recruitment, the Balts were still being prioritised. It also suggested that the Ministry of Labour's aim of decreasing manpower shortages was prioritised over the goal of decreasing DPs in the British zone of Germany.

The last party of 52 women was despatched on 2 May 1947, the 23rd party. In total, fewer than 2500 women were received in the UK as part of the Balt Cygnet scheme.[710]

WESTWARD HO!

Plans for Westward Ho! were being formulated as early as January 1947, by which time the success of Balt Cygnet had become apparent. From the start, Westward Ho! was intended as a large-scale scheme, encompassing a wider range of DPs, who it was envisaged would fill a variety of jobs in areas of manpower shortage. Importantly, men would be included on this scheme. Although Balts were initially prioritised on this scheme, recruitment quickly spread to other nationalities.

The proposal for a larger scheme was discussed at a meeting of the Cabinet on 30 January 1947. The Cabinet Minutes reported the discussion:

> The general view of the Cabinet was that there should be a much larger recruitment of suitable displaced persons in order to meet the needs of undermanned industries, and that the present arrangement under which recruitment was virtually limited to female labour for domestic service in hospitals and similar institutions should be abandoned. Recruitment should not be limited to women, and skilled men who could undertake useful work in this country should also be admitted.

According to the Minutes, the Cabinet:

> Invited the Foreign Labour Committee to work out as a matter of urgency a scheme for recruiting suitable labour for undermanned industries and services from among displaced persons in Europe, and agreed that the existing limitation

whereby recruitment was limited to women for domestic service in hospitals and similar institutions should be abandoned.[711]

On 21 February, SUGRA 853 stated that:

> It was agreed at a meeting held today in the Control Office with representatives of the Ministry of Labour that they should send representatives to Germany and Austria to arrange details for opening up importation of DPs into this country on a large scale as soon as possible.

> ...DPs will be moved to the United Kingdom from both zones at a total rate of 15,000 per month commencing end of March.[712]

On 26 February, W B Lyon from the Home Office wrote to Mrs Potter at the MLNS, discussing the potential effects of the introduction of a large-scale scheme on British immigration policy:

> In normal circumstances I doubt if the United Kingdom could properly be described as a country "concerned with migratory movements".

> However, it may well be that the position has been radically changed by present labour shortages...[713]

Miss Yates elaborated:

> Since the allocation to work here of the first thousand of these displaced persons was completed in 1946, Cabinet Policy has decreed that this Department should extend and accelerate the recruitment of many more displaced persons for the long term manpower shortages in British productive industry. The Department must therefore assume that in 1947 and thereafter this country will be recruiting permanent migratory groups for settlement[714]

The details of the Westward Ho! scheme were outlined in the Control Commission for Germany (British Element), Zonal Executive Instruction, no.9 (Provisional) : Employment of Displaced Persons in Great Britain - Operation "Westward Ho" of 3 April 1947.[715] Westward Ho! was open to both men and women from the British Zones of Germany and Austria for a wide range of occupations in Great Britain, including work in textiles, coal mining, agriculture, brick works and domestic work in hospitals. Recruits were to be aged 18-50, fit and healthy and required to pass security screenings[716] and medical checks. Recruits to Westward Ho! had to remain in specified employment for one year and thereafter could change their employment only with the approval of the Ministry of Labour. They were to receive 'the same wages, draw the same rations, make the same unemployment and health insurance contributions and pay the same taxes as British work people'.[717] An estimated 60, 000 to 100, 000 DPs were to be recruited under this scheme. The government aimed to bring in DPs as early as possible and build up to a rate of 15,000 per month.

Publicly, there was to be no distinction along the lines of nationality. The instruction stated that:

> There will be no distinction in recruitment on the grounds of nationality as this is primarily an industrial scheme, but it is the intention to give first priority to the stepping-up of recruitment of Baltic women for work in sanatoria and as domestic servants in Great Britain under the existing scheme known as "Balt Cygnet"; and thereafter that of Baltic and Ukrainian men. Initially Poles will have low recruitment priority until all those eligible for the Resettlement Corps in Great Britain have been "drawn off".[718]

The Press Notice issued on 19 April 1947, by the Ministry of Labour and National Service outlined the Westward Ho! scheme:

> Volunteering will be made open to all persons in the British Zones of Occupation who fall within the Displaced Person's category. The scheme is primarily an industrial one to meet labour shortages and selection is made on the basis of suitability for work in the undermanned industries. Unlike the existing scheme for the recruitment of Balt women for employment as domestics in hospitals and sanatoria the new scheme covers both men and women, although some of the latter will continue to go into essential domestic employment.[719]

As the Press Notice and the Zonal Executive Instruction suggested, Westward Ho! had clear gendered dimensions to recruitment. Women would be employed as domestics in hospitals and sanatoria, while men would be selected for undermanned industries and agriculture. However, there were some areas of employment which admitted both men and women. The largest employer of both men and women DPs was the textile industry, although even within textiles, certain types of work reserved for women, and others for men.

The instruction for Westward Ho! further stated that:

> HMG's policy is that priorities should remain as follows:

(a) Repatriation.

(b) Resettlement.

(c) Local Employment.

In general, except for the Poles, the possibilities of (a) have now been exhausted in the British Zone. Polish men, with the exception of miners will not be accepted for employment under this scheme until it is clear that no further repatriation of Poles is possible; nor will leaflets be distributed in Polish Camps.[720]

Under Westward Ho!, dependants were eligible to emigrate to Great Britain. However, it was emphasised that they would not be moved to Great Britain until the main flow of workers had gone.[721]

Importantly, the instruction also outlined plans for some of the DPs remaining in Germany. Point 28 of the instruction outlined the possibility of employing ex-Yugoslav officers who are not eligible for the Civil Mixed Watchmen's Service, in an administrative capacity and as interpreters in DP holding camps in Great Britain.[722]

The Civil Mixed Watchmen's Service, together with the Civil Mixed Labour Organisation were employed to undertake labour in Germany for the DP camps and other military government facilities. Some DPs were also working for the North German Timber Corporation. The instruction stated that members of these services would be allowed to volunteer for the scheme, only after it had been in place for some time, and if suitable volunteers could be found to take their place. It stated that there, 'would ultimately remain in Germany a "hard core" of DPs who will opt neither for repatriation or resettlement. It is from these that the final recruitment for CMWS and the CMLO should be made'.[723]

Thus unlike Balt Cygnet, Westward Ho! can be regarded as a package of measures designed not only to recruit for labour in Great Britain, but also to solve the problems of DPs in Germany.

Although publicly, there was to be little distinction between nationalities, privately, an unofficial hierarchy was continuing. Communications between various government officials reveal the various motivations behind the hierarchy. Basil Boothby from the FO, wrote the following to Miss Appleby on 22 April 1947:

We have always regretted the Foreign Labour Committee's decision not to allocate priorities to particular nationalities on political grounds, although we appreciate that it would be awkward if we were to make any public announcement of such a policy. However, I believe that in practice, the recruitment missions are bearing in mind such factors as the undesirability of recruiting Poles and the desirability of recruiting Balts.

He continued:

> You may be interested to know that for political reasons we consider that where possible priority should be given to Balts, Ukrainians, Yugoslavs and Soviet citizens (including White Russians).[724]

Clearly, the initial phase of Westward Ho! continued to prioritise Balts, and to some extent Ukrainians. During May, June and July recruitment was limited to Baltic and Ukrainian men.

The same reasons for prioritising Balts for Balt Cygnet underlay their initial prioritisation in the early stages of Westward Ho! The racialisation discourse among officials, apparent in discussions about the Balts suitability for Balt Cygnet was extended in deliberations for Westward Ho! Westward Ho! required men and women for labour in a variety of employment spheres. The minutes of the Third meeting of the Foreign Labour Committee, held on 14 May 1947, to discuss the scheme so far, suggested that the Balts were still deemed to be the best recruiting nationalities for all sectors of the economy. Not only were they regarded as the most suitable groups for domestic work and industry, they were also deemed to be the best agricultural workers. The meeting reported that:

> There was no reason to suppose that placing [EVWs in employment] would be difficult, particularly in agriculture, where the Balts should prove excellent material.[725]

In 1947, Boothby and Rouse had noted on a visit to an EVW holding camp in Britain that:

> The Balts have been found to be the most intelligent and the most suitable for skilled mechanical trades and the Ukrainians who are mostly of peasant or yeoman stock for agriculture.[726]

In discussions about the employment of Baltic DPs in industry, officials stressed their potential for integration within British labour. They were regarded as peaceable, and unlike Jewish DPs were not perceived to have communist sympathies, an important factor for relations with trade unions and the British public. In Britain at the end of the war, despite the events of the world conflict, public fear of the Communist spectre remained greater than the revulsion for fascism. A Foreign Office

Memorandum of March 1947 had noted that recruited '...DPs must be acceptable to public opinion in Britain and notably to the workers and trade unions'.[727]

In addition, the success of the Balt Cygnet scheme influenced the Ministry's continued prioritisation of Balts. The Latvian Minister wrote to M Hankey[728] at the FO, on 20 March 1947, that:

> The settling of Latvian women into work at British hospitals is going smoothly and there are already about 800 of them here. With very few exceptions the girls are extremely satisfied, and the Ministry of Labour and Welfare Officers are also praising them, so there is satisfaction to all concerned.[729]

The first recruits under Westward Ho! arrived at the end of April 1947. In just one week, over 1000 recruits were brought in, via two ports, Tilbury, for women only, and Hull, for men and women.[730] The third meeting of the Foreign Labour Committee reported that by 13 May, 4200 workers had been brought to the UK under Westward Ho!, and a further 4500 were due to arrive by the end of May. Of the total recruited by 13 May, about 42 per cent were women.[731]

During 1947, the Foreign Office became increasingly keen to resettle as many Balts as possible, since they were rapidly becoming the focus of weakening Anglo-Soviet relations. Politically, the existence of large numbers of Balts in the British Zone was becoming a growing embarrassment to Britain, due to the British Government's refusal to repatriate them. The British Government's policy on repatriation was only one source of conflict among many growing problems between Britain and the Soviet Union. Nevertheless, the government was still making efforts not to unnecessarily antagonise the USSR. A speech by Thomas Brimelow[732] of the Northern Department, in early 1947 described the difficulties caused by the issue of repatriation. He stated that the Soviet Government:

> ...is doing its' utmost to secure the return to the USSR of all Soviet citizens now living as Displaced Persons or Surrendered Enemy Personnel abroad. It remembers how easily the Germans obtained the services of dissident Soviet Citizens during the Second World War, and is determined not to allow them to be used against the Soviet Union a second time.[733]

He concluded that British policy was one of 'determination to avoid both appeasement and unnecessary provocation in dealings with the Soviet Union'.[734]

Despite Churchill's infamous Iron Curtain speech in March 1946, it was not until late 1947, that Britain's policy of seeking to revive co-operation with the Soviet Union was abandoned. The effects of this were rapid. Brimelow swiftly urged the closing down of the Soviet Repatriation Mission in the British Zone on the grounds that it might be a source of 'mischief' in a future West German state, although it was not fully shut down until 1950.[735] British policy contrasted with French policy at the time, which cautiously avoided confrontation with the USSR. Unlike Britain, France refused to recruit Balts, primarily because of the influence of communists within post-war governments and support for communism within the public at large. France was not keen to antagonise Russia and aimed to remain uninvolved in labour recruitment schemes, which might destabilise its fragile relationship with Russia. The British Consulate General in Baden-Baden noted that a British UNRRA official had reported to the Consulate early in 1947 that:

> ...while France was importing thousands of Italian workers, they would not encourage the migration to France of Balts and Poles living as displaced persons in their zone of Germany because by doing so they would give offence to the USSR.[736]

According to the Consulate, the official had attributed this attitude to, 'communist influence in the French Government'. The UNRRA official also 'spoke highly of the Balts, saying that they are a much better type than the Poles, more intelligent, honest and reliable, with a higher standard of education'.[737]

Because of France's reluctance to recruit Baltic DPs, the possibility that the British Government might recruit Latvians, Lithuanians and Estonians from the French zone of Germany arose. The British Consulate General wrote to the Refugee Department in the Foreign Office, in March 1947, stating that:

> The scheme for importing Balts into the United Kingdom only seems to be operating in the British Zone and as UNRRA would not appear to have a representative in London who could approach the competent authorities in London with such a request, we venture to make the suggestion that Balts in this zone be included in any scheme for recruiting labour for the UK as they obviously have little to hope for from their French patrons.[738]

The Refugee Department replied on 14 April 1947, that the Consulate General's letter about Displaced Persons in the French Zone of Germany:

...confirms what we have already heard about the unwillingness of the French Government to recruit Balts, Poles and other politically-embarrassing elements for work in France.

The French Government have recently proposed that we should pool our respective displaced persons labour resources in order to enlarge the scope of our respective recruitment activities. This proposal is very welcome to us since we are anxious to recruit Balts (but not Poles) while the French are apparently anxious to recruit persons of German ethnic origin. The qualities of the Balts are greatly appreciated here, and they rank high on our list of priorities.[739]

The prioritisation of Balts in the first months of Westward Ho! must therefore be viewed not only in the light of continuing labour shortages at home, but also the changing international situation, particularly shifting Anglo-Soviet relations.

However, over the course of Westward Ho!, the recruitment of Balts was limited by several factors. Their prioritisation did not mean unlimited immigration. Apart from being selective towards the health, fitness, suitability and background of the recruits, the government was concerned not to admit huge numbers of any particular nationality, in order to avoid the creation of nationalist ghettoes, and to encourage assimilation. Thus, although the Balts were positively racialised, they were still, first and foremost, 'immigrants'. Their recruitment reflected ideas about immigration within the post-war labour government, particularly notions regarding the assimilation of immigrants. In order to encourage assimilation, the government aimed to scatter the new minorities around the country, thus, when proposals to bring whole DP camps over to Britain were discussed, the idea was quickly abandoned. In June 1947, the Foreign Office explored the suggestion of 'bringing over whole camps of DPs who could form self-supporting communities'. The initial suggestion was the transferral of a DP camp to 'a site in Scotland' which was 'mentioned as a possible location for such a community which might number some 400 persons, preferably Balts'.[740] Specific DP camps proposed for transference included 'Rendsberg' Camp or DP camp 'Eutin', near Neustadt.[741] The proposals were discussed at a meeting in the Foreign Office on 30 June 1947. However, in addition to potential economic impracticalities of the scheme, the Home Office representative compared the proposal to the case of the Polish armed Forces and their dependants when, 'Ministers and parliament have recently reaffirmed the traditional British policy that immigrants should be spread over and absorbed into the native community'. He stated that 'Group Settlement' was, 'bad in principle and previous experiments have been unsuccessful'. In a Memoranda on the proposals, the Foreign Office noted that:

> The proposal to bring a DP community en bloc to this country would involve rather a new attitude to the settlement of foreigners here. While in undeveloped countries it has not been unusual for special communities to be established ranging from those on a national basis , e.g. Lithuanians in western Canada, to those on a religious basis, e.g. Mormons in Salt Lake City, it is not an idea which would go down easily in a somewhat overcrowded country like Great Britain. Hitherto the general policy has been to absorb foreigners into English life as much and as quickly as possible.[742]

A similar response was given to proposals for the transferral of the entire Baltic University at Pinneburg DP camp, the only university established in the DP camps. Mr Hankey told Mr Ball at the MLNS in August 1947, that if the Baltic University were to be established in this country:

> ...it would almost certainly become an emigrant centre of Baltic culture and Baltic nationalism. We are inclined to the view that what is really needed is some means of educating the Balts in English and in the background knowledge necessary to fit then for life in this country.[743]

Subsequently, A W Peterson at the Foreign Office, informed D M Nenk the following month that the government was against the establishment of a Baltic University in Great Britain for fear of, 'encouraging the formation of a compact Baltic colony in the United Kingdom'.[744]

The limits to post-war British immigration policy were summed up in the 1949 Royal Commission on Population :

> Immigration on a on a large scale into a fully established society like ours could only be welcomed without reserve if the immigrants were of good human stock and were not prevented by their religion or race from intermarrying with the host population and becoming merged with it. These conditions were fulfilled by intermittent large scale immigration in the past, notably by the Flemish and French Protestant refugees who settled in Great Britain at different times... All these considerations point to the conclusion that continuous large scale immigration would probably be impracticable and would

certainly be undesirable, and the possibility - it can be regarded as no more than a possibility - that the circumstances might compel us to consider it is among the undesirable consequences of the maintenance of family size below replacement level.[745]

Another limit to Baltic DP recruitment, was that as early as April 1947, it had become clear that Westward Ho! would have to begin recruiting other nationalities, since the pool of suitable Balts would run dry. While recruitment of Ukrainian women for Balt Cygnet had been a success and therefore continued under Westward Ho!, policy towards some of the other nationalities was still unclear, particularly those who were regarded as Soviet citizens. Discussions about Soviet Citizens among officials often reflected personal viewpoints towards Russia, and revealed the diversity of attitudes with the Foreign Office towards the deterioration of Anglo/Soviet Relations, and how to deal with this development. On 22 April 1947, Basil Boothby from the Foreign Office wrote to Miss Appleby:

> You may be interested to know that for political reasons we consider that where possible priority should be given to Balts, Ukrainians, Yugoslavs and Soviet citizens (including White Russians).

However, only a week later, T J Winterton wrote to Lord Pakenham regarding the pressures of recruitment in Austria, where there was very few Baltic DPs. In Winterton's view, because of this, instead of a priority system:

> ...it seems much more simple and effective to recruit from the whole body of Displaced Persons without regard to nationality except that we should exclude...persons whom we acknowledge to be Soviet citizens because of the certainty of trouble with the Soviet Union if we recruit such people.[746]

Thus by the end of April 1947, despite deteriorating Anglo-Soviet relations, the government remained keen to avoid antagonism with the Soviet Union and decided to avoid recruiting DPs whom the British government acknowledged to be Soviet citizens, specifically citizens of the Soviet Union territories as of September 1939. This did not include Balts, or Poles or Ukrainians from Galicia (Eastern Poland before 1939) and Capartho-Ukraine (Eastern Czechoslovakia before the outbreak of war). Acknowledged Soviet Citizens included Great Russians, Ukrainians from pre-1939 Ukrainian borders, and Byelorussians. However, the definition of who was, and who was not, a Soviet citizen was problematic and caused huge problems. Many Ukrainians claimed they were from former non-Soviet areas, and due to the widespread loss of identity papers it was difficult to prove otherwise.

In addition to Soviet citizens, other nationalities were knocked off the recruitment list during the early months of Westwards Ho!, at least for the time being. Specifically these included Jews and Poles. Winterton had written to Lord Pakenham on 30 April 1947, that recruitment from Austria where there were very few Baltic DPs, should be opened up to the:

> ...whole body of Displaced Persons without regard to nationality except that we should exclude Jews and Polish men because of the opposition from public opinion at home.

Winterton continued:

> The one criterion which we should like to follow in selection is the suitability of the individual Displaced Person as a worker and as a potential citizen of Britain. I understand that the Foreign Office and Home Office share our view that no discrimination is necessary on nationality grounds.[747]

Tony Kushner estimated that while Jews made up one quarter of the population of Displaced Persons camps in Europe, 'the percentage of Jews coming under the British schemes was probably less than one per cent'.[748] The reasons for the exclusion of Jews under the EVW schemes are complex, with much of the important source material on the subject being withheld under the Public Records Act. Various explanations have been put forward, including negative racialisation, anti-Semitism among the British public, and the perceived link between Jews and Communism during the Second World War. According to Kushner, negative racialisation played a key role: while the Balts were regarded as 'good human stock', hard workers, the Jews in contrast were considered 'poor workers, parasitical and of poor stock - unlikely and unwilling to integrate into British society'.[749] A Foreign Office Memorandum of March 1947, entitled, 'Recruitment of Displaced Persons for Great Britain', suggests that anti-Semitism among the British public also played a key role in dissuading policy-makers from recruiting Jews:

> The selection of DPs must be highly discriminatory... There is...one main objection to including all DPs within the field, i.e. the proviso that the DPs must be acceptable to public opinion in Britain and notably to the workers and trade unions. For example, the situation in Palestine, and anti-semitics [sic], clearly prevent the recruitment of Jews.[750]

Finally, the British Government was concerned that the link between Jews and Communism might lead to the creation of centres of communist unrest. As Tony Kushner points out, in contrast, others in the DP camps who were viciously anti-Communist, for example, many Balts were:

> ...perceived as much better investments. That their anti-Communism might have slipped into murderous pro-Nazism in the war was not generally seen as problematic. For a tiny minority who were actively recruited, as Tom Bower has shown, it was positively advantageous in terms of their use in intelligence networks and scientific programmes.[751]

Here, Kushner is referring to the involvement of some Balts in the German forces during the Second World War, and the alleged war crimes carried out by a tiny minority. Tom Bower argued in *The Red Web*[752] that some Baltic EVWs were recruited by the British Government to engage in spying activities in the Baltic States. In Bower and Cesarani's[753] view, the opportunity to recruit Balts, with strong anti-communist sympathies for spying activities was one of the reasons for their prioritisation. The participants in this study have confirmed that some Baltic EVWs were recruited for spying activities. However, the small numbers used as intelligence suggest that this was undoubtedly a secondary motivation for the recruitment of Baltic DPs for labour.

Unlike the Jews, the Poles were not ruled out altogether, but they were relegated to the bottom of the list during 1946 and 1947, particularly Polish men. The Zonal Executive Instruction for Westward-Ho! stated the following:

> Initially Poles will have low recruitment priority until all those eligible for the Resettlement Corps in Great Britain have been "drawn off".[754]

Poles were to be excluded initially because of the large numbers of ex-Polish servicemen already in Britain, and the government's policy to limit the influx of any one particular nationality. Kay and Miles also suggested experience with the demobilised Polish troops, led the government to conclude that as a group they raised 'very considerable political and social difficulties', they constituted labour of a 'poor quality' and were a 'particularly difficult people to assimilate'.[755]

With the omission of Jews and Soviet Citizens, and the demotion of Poles from recruitment in the short-term, the field of available nationalities was drastically reduced. Nevertheless, from mid-

1947 onwards, Westward Ho! was gradually widened to cover many different nationalities and recruitment from American and French zones. The fourth progress report by the MLNS on the recruitment of EVWs for Westward Ho!, reported on 31 July, that a 'wide nationality field [is] now open'.[756] This was the result of various recruitment considerations from mid-to-late 1947. The severity of the economic crisis at home and the refugee crisis in Germany were both intensifying, while relations with Russia were swiftly deteriorating. Furthermore, the field of Baltic and Ukrainian recruits was dwindling. The numbers of fit and healthy Balts between the ages of 18 and 35 in Europe was decreasing, although there were still sizeable numbers. By 16 June 1947, there were a reported 32,248 Baltic men and 21, 672 Baltic women in the British Zone.[757] In the British Zone of Austria, in early July there were an estimated 500 male and 1100 female Balts.[758]

Concern was also expressed during 1947 at the decline in numbers of suitable women DPs available for recruitment. Rouse from the Ministry of Labour and National Service wrote to Miss Appleby in May 1947 claiming that there was not enough Baltic and Ukrainian women in the British zone.[759] Women were required for various fields of employment, including textiles and domestic work. Insufficient numbers of Baltic and Ukrainian women led the government to open up the field of recruitment for women to different nationalities. At the same time, recruitment was limited to Baltic and Ukrainian men, because they were still in plentiful supply. The Control Commission informed the Foreign Office on 9 July 1947, that, 'Operation "Westward Ho!"...is open to all nationalities but priorities reached at present include males of Baltic and Ukrainian origin only and females of all nationalities'.[760]

Because of the gender imbalance, Rouse discussed the possibilities of extending the field of recruitment to other zones of occupation to Austria, and to the French and German Zones of Germany.[761] In late summer 1947, recruitment was extended to the French Zone of Germany in August, in order to increase female recruits. The Anglo-French agreement provided for the recruitment of volunteers for 'Westward Ho!' from the French Zone. As a result of this initiative, 2000 single unattached women were to be recruited from 25 August 1947.[762]

Negotiations were also begun with the US zone authorities. A report in August 1947, estimated that there were over 80,000 Balts in the US zone in July 1947.[763] A F Rouse (MLNS) informed L Dow from P.C.I.R.O. in September that, 'Our intention in the immediate future is to use the American Zone of Germany solely for the purpose of recruiting single, unattached women'. He estimated about 20,000 women would be recruited.[764] By September, the Ministry of Labour was being given, 'free access to all the camps in the US Zone of Germany'.[765]

The statistics for Westward Ho! revealed the gender imbalance in the first few months of the scheme. While there were 5253 men shipped to the UK, there were only 1485 women.[766] In May 1947, the first full month of Westward Ho!, the nationalities of the women shipped from Cuxhaven to Hull were as follows; 205 Estonians, 466 Latvians, 235 Lithuanians and 579 Ukrainians.[767] Ukrainians also accounted for the second largest number of men, behind the Latvians.[768] By December 1947, over 14,000 Baltic men were shipped to the UK under Westward Ho!, compared to just over 3, 500 women.[769]

Practical difficulties influenced the gender of recruits. For example, in July 1947, accommodation difficulties in England led to a temporary suspension of all recruitment, except for single, unattached women.[770]

By October 1947, the nationality composition of EVWs coming to Britain had widened, to include Yugoslavs and other Europeans, although Balts were still the favoured nationalities. On a visit to an EVW holding camp at Market Harborough, England, Mr Boothby and Mr Rouse noted the following:

> The present proportions are a microcosm of the total which has passed through the camp; that is to say an important majority of nationals of the former Baltic States, a minority of Ukrainians, and a sprinkling of Yugoslavs and other Europeans.[771]

In November, pressure was placed on countries like Britain to continue to work towards the solution of the refugee problem. The General Assembly of the UN Draft Resolution on Refugees of 11 November 1947 recommended the following:

> ...that each member of the UN adopt urgent measures for the early return of the repatriable refugees and displaced persons to their countries of origin having regard to General Assembly resolution of 12 February 1946, and for settling a fair share of non-repatriable refugees and displaced persons in its country.[772]

By November 1947, some 30,000 EVWs had come to Great Britain.[773] Although the instructions for Westward Ho! contained provision for the admittance of dependants, the original zonal instruction stated that, 'It is HMG's policy that the bulk of accepted dependants should not be moved to Great Britain till the main flow of workers has gone'.[774] However, officials began to voice the opinion that the postponement of the movement of dependants was acting to deter potential recruits, particularly those with families. The first movement of dependants thus began at the end of 1947. Priority was given to dependants of EVW s who were brought over in the initial stages of Westward Ho!, which in practice meant Balts or Ukrainians.

During 1948, the field of recruitment was widened even further. The principal reason for the expansion was the need to increase the number of female recruits to cope with demand for female labour at home. The demand was so great and the need to clear the DP camps so pressing, that the government opened up recruitment to those nationalities which it had previously objected. Early in 1948, the recruitment of former enemy nationals - Hungarians, Romanians and Bulgarians began.[775]   In total, an estimated 800 Romanians, 91 Bulgarians and 2539 Hungarians were recruited over the lifetime of the scheme.[776] The decision to recruit these groups who were comparatively small in number is indicative of the government's desire to clear the camps, and fill labour shortages at home, but perhaps more importantly, it reflected the change in the government's attitude towards Germany and Russia by 1948. By now, the Cold War had become an inescapable reality, while attitudes towards Germany and Axis satellite countries had noticeably softened. Further evidence of the latter trend, was the recruitment of Volksdeutsche from 1948, despite the fact that they were considered enemy nationals and there had been a previous policy against their recruitment. The existence of large numbers of Volksdeutsche women was attractive to the government, which remained desperate for female recruits. Over the next 2 years 1,257 were recruited.[777] In 1948, the government also extended recruitment to DPs from Czechoslovakia, who had escaped the *coup d'etat* and across the borders into Germany as political refugees.[778] After May 1949, 1319 Sudeten women who had been driven from Czechoslovakia into Bavaria in the US Zone of Germany were recruited.[779]

Tannahill states that during 1948 and 1949: 'There was a tendency for quality as well as numbers to fall not only because standards of age and physical fitness were lowered but because some of the later arrivals were the less desirables'.[780]

The last recruits arrived during 1950. On 4 May the '2000' scheme for the admission of refugees into the UK was announced. This was an extension of the Distressed Relatives Scheme, first introduced in 1948. The extension allowed for the admittance of 2,000 DPs 'for whom accommodation and maintenance would be provided by relatives, private persons or voluntary organisations, who were prepared to take continuing responsibility for them'.[781]

By December 1950, the number of Latvians, Lithuanians and Estonians recruited as part of the EVW schemes was as follows: 12,919 Latvians, with 1322 dependants; 6186 Lithuanians and 741 dependants; 5154 Estonians, with 504 dependants.[782]

THE RECRUITS

In October 1948, Logan Gray wrote to F B A Rundall at the Refugee Department, with his ideas about why the Baltic DPs wished to come to Britain:

> The majority of these Baltic Displaced persons…belong to the peasant class and we feel that living and working conditions in the United Kingdom must compare favourably with those to which the people were accustomed in pre-war times in their own countries.[783]

This was one government official's analysis of the Baltic DPs motivations for coming to Britain. However, what of the viewpoints of the labour scheme participants themselves? I asked all the interviewees in this project, all of whom passed medical and security screenings successfully, why they decided to accept the recruitment offers of the British Government. Each individual had a different set of motivations for coming to Britain. Several reasons were cited, the most important being the desire to leave the poor material conditions of the DP camps and Germany. The DPs could see no prospects or future for themselves in Germany, and the younger DPs in particular were eager to work, to start afresh and begin to make a living.

A Latvian woman who came to Britain in May 1947 described the recruitment schemes:

> It's fifty years ago this May, so one begins to forget, but I think…it was a case of people between 18 and 50 and you had to be fit. They weren't taking invalids…because it was meant to be mainly physical work. For men, it was mines and agricultural work and brick factories in Bedford and things like that, and women, they were mainly textiles, 'cos there's some big textile companies around Bradford. Most of them are in Yorkshire…[784]

She explained her motivations for migration to Britain:

> Well, Germany wasn't really a place for settling in, because after the war it was pretty devastated, and there wasn't really a chance to start again, so I thought I'd come.[785]

A fear of repatriation also played a role in the DPs desire to leave Germany; the refugees were keen to get as far away from the Soviet repatriation officers as possible. The Soviet Repatriation Officers continued their work in the British zone until 19 April 1950.[786] A dread of repatriation was particularly strong among those who had served with the German army, since they knew their ultimate fate if they returned to the homeland. Although the screening processes for recruitment were fairly stringent, Britain showed a greater willingness to accept DPs who had served in the German army than some of the other recruiting nations, for example, the United States. Among former army recruits therefore, the options of resettlement were limited.

So while the DPs had decided that they wanted to leave Germany, what were the reasons for coming specifically to Great Britain? Various motivations were cited.

Some DPs were attracted by the type of work offered by the British authorities. Agricultural labour was popular among men who had been brought up on farms, and hospital work appealed to some of the women. Most of the recruits however, viewed the labour schemes simply as a short-term solution. Long term career aspirations were rarely considered when accepting labour, and indeed, many of the DPs who accepted the recruitment offers cared little about the type of work available. They were simply eager to work, to earn money, and to buy enough food to eat. An interviewer for the *News Chronicle* interviewed the first batch of 87 women recruited for the Balt Cygnet scheme on 22 October 1946. The reporter stated that:

> Everyone I spoke to and they ranged from the eldest, over 40, to a 20 year old medical student, said that had volunteered because they wanted to work and earn money".[787]

Kanty Cooper was present in the DP camps during the implementation of the recruitment schemes. She recounted the statement of one woman who had been recruited:

> You have to be realistic…I can't go back to my home. I can't live independently without money. I have no profession but I am strong, not afraid of work and, I hope, moderately

intelligent. To clean a room or peel potatoes can't be hard to learn. I shall do whatever I am asked to do, however dirty.[788]

However, the type of jobs available also dissuaded many of the DPs from coming to Britain, particularly those who were educated, and eager to return to their professions. The stringent work restrictions were unappealing to DPs who wished to resume their studies or professions as quickly as possible. Some professional and educated DPs did accept the recruitment offers, however, although many of these later emigrated to the United States, Australia or Canada, where they could pursue their careers with vigour. Among professionals and educated DPs, recruitment for labour in Britain was simply a stopgap solution, which gave them some money and an opportunity to re-emigrate later.

For some DPs, the fact that Britain was the first country to offer a large-scale recruitment scheme was the most important factor. They were desperate to leave, and simply took the first opportunity which arose. A Latvian DP stated quite plainly the reason why he and other Latvians came to Britain:

Because that was first opportunity – to come to Britain, because we wanted to leave Germany and that was the first opportunity.[789]

Another Latvian agreed:

Well, Britain was the first to offer. Ah no, first was actually Belgium, but [they] wanted coalminers only. They wanted somebody that had actually done coalmining first of all and Latvians didn't have any coalmining to speak of, so that ruled us out. You see, nobody really wanted to know what the coalmining was going to be like and so on.[790]

Perhaps the most important reason cited for coming to Great Britain was that it was nearer to home than the USA or Canada. For some this was important because Britain and the Baltic States were all in Europe, therefore it meant that culturally, there would be more similarities than with countries farther afield. For others, Britain's proximity was important because it meant that it was nearer to the homeland in the event of return.

There was a discernible divide between the recruits, in the sense that for some, recruitment to Britain signified a realisation that they would not be returning to their homelands in the near future. Migration to Britain represented a belief that they would be exiled for many years, if not forever. This attitude was discernible particularly among the younger recruits, who viewed migration to Britain as the start of a new life. The younger recruits had not yet established their lives in the homeland when the war began. Many did not yet have families, nor had they begun their career paths. Others, however, accepted the British offers of labour, precisely because Britain was nearer to home than the USA or Canada, and therefore it would be relatively easy to return. Recruitment was symptomatic of their firm belief in an imminent return. This motivation for coming to Britain was present in a majority of the older recruits, who felt too old to start again – they simply wanted to return to the lives they had created for themselves before the war in the homeland.

An Estonian man accepted a recruitment offer for Westward Ho!, and following screenings and medical tests came to England in November 1947 to work as an agricultural labourer. Clinging to a belief of return, he cited the main reason for coming specifically to England was that it was nearer to home than Canada, Australia and the US, where he also had the opportunity to go. Another motivation was that since the English are Europeans like the Estonians, the two nations must be fairly similar.[791]

A Latvian man explained why many Latvians chose Britain:

> Now I don't know if you've heard this before from somebody else, but that's been my idea, and also I suppose, a lot of other people's as well, that we always hoped, well, in an awful kind of way…I don't know how to express it, that there would be another war…and the Russians get kicked out, get kicked back where they belong. That's what we all hoped. Obviously there would have been deaths and…destruction. But that never happened. So that's why we came to England, a lot of us.[792]

A Latvian woman also stated her reasons:

> I realised we won't be able to return to Latvia so we had to go somewhere else and more or less this was nearer. It was in Europe. It was a bit nearer Latvia and there was an opportunity to work in [a] hospital so I came like that.' '…we knew there was no chance to go back to Latvia. There were Communists, Russians. We didn't want to go back there…and when you are young you are probably a bit more adventurous and why not do something about it, you know sort it out?[793]

The opportunities to join family members already recruited as EVWs and/or to bring dependants to Britain were also cited as motivations for participation in the labour schemes. Some of the recruits wanted to join spouses or other relations or friends who had already been recruited on the British schemes. Some couples applied for recruitment at the same time, although they were accepted only on an individual basis, not as a couple. Balt Cygnet recruited only single women without dependants, and for most of these women, family considerations were not an issue. However, Westward Ho! opened up recruitment to both men and women, and allowed the transfer of dependants at a later stage. This initiative presented DP families and couples with the opportunity to recreate family life in Great Britain.

Among most of the DPs, a variety of motivating factors influenced their decision, each based on a different individual set of circumstances. This is illustrated by the case of a first generation Latvian woman, now living in Nottingham, was recruited for domestic work in hospitals as part of the Westward Ho! Scheme in October 1947. She stated the main reason for accepting recruitment was a desire to leave the terrible material conditions that existed in the camps in Germany. She was single at the time, but lived with her parents in a DP camp in the British zone. She was then aged twenty and claims that her parents made most of the arrangements concerning her application for recruitment. The decision to come to Britain was made primarily by her parents. She stated:

> Oh, it was so bad. The conditions were so bad. We wanted to get away. The food, oh it was…[sighs]…as I told you, it was so little and so, so bad, that you know, you were thinking about food most of the time. And the conditions in Germany, well you didn't sort of…you realised that you weren't going back to Latvia…not straight away, and so you had to go somewhere where you could find a job.[794]

Family considerations were also important for this woman. Her parents were allowed to enter Britain a year later as dependants, and together they were able to recreate family life in Britain. Another motivation was the type of work offered. She had already been thinking about hospital work, and so when the opportunity arose, she took it.[795]

A Lithuanian woman who came to Britain also described the different reasons for her decision. The main reason was its proximity to home: 'because England is nearer Lithuania'.[796] She also explained that she and other Lithuanians felt that they had to leave Germany because there was not enough food, and because so many of them were young, they were impatient to work.[797]

Another factor behind the arrival of the Balts in Britain can be related to government policy. The government attempted to lure the DPs to participate in the schemes using a variety of methods. As well as posting notices on boards, the recruitment officers gave speeches and distributed leaflets outlining the attractions of the schemes. Leaflets advertising the schemes showed pictures of the recruits at work in British factories, and were often printed in several languages, including Estonian, Latvian and Lithuanian. One leaflet aimed at different nationalities was entitled: 'She's Making Her Future In The British Rayon Industry'.[798] It was printed in both English and German, and had photographs of happy recruits hard at work. Captions were printed under the photographs. For example:

> Smiling Adele greets her friends who are still in Germany. Adele came to England early in 1947 and is engaged on the pleasant work of wrapping a protective covering round the delicate "cakes" of rayon yarn.[799]

Another photo showing a slightly older man hard at work read:

> How fit and well this man looks! He is earning a good wage at a large modern rayon factory where working conditions are excellent. Here he is "washing" cakes of rayon yarn which will later be made into lovely fabrics or used for tyre cord.[800]

A picture of a young women read:

> 21 year old Genowefa is now an expert at handling this British-made high speed knitting machine which is the most efficient of its kind in the world. She makes lovely pastel coloured fabrics - a joy for any girl to look at.[801]

The government's job was made easier as the recruitment schemes got into full swing, and as positive reports from Baltic DPs already in Great Britain filtered back to the camps. Recruits were even invited to revisit the camps to tell their stories. It was reported in November 1947 that:

> One of the most successful means of inducing people to volunteer has been the visiting of DP camps by Baltic girls who came to U.K. to work under the original Balt-Cygnet scheme some months ago and who have been able to give a first hand account of their good treatment and happy lives in this country.[802]

Extracts from letters from recruits already in Britain were displayed in Information Centres in DP camps to induce recruitment. Here are two extracts from recruits from coalmining, which were displayed in an attempt to increase recruitment into the coalmines, one of the key shortage areas:

1. <u>V.P. Age 23, Latvian, Arrived in England 14.11.47</u>

    I am settled in England and in the Coalmining Industry. I am now on Grade I pay which is as much earned as by the fully skilled English coalface worker. In my leisure time I play Table Tennis and billiards in the Hostel, also I like to watch football matches. I like to go out in the country and visit English Inns. I read and have my own English books. The Hostel food and accommodation is good and I would recommend other EVWs to England.[803]

2. <u>J.K. Age 39, Latvian, Arrived in England 1.11.47</u>

    I have been coalmining for four months and I am now settled to Coalmining and the English way of living. I have had no worries or troubles since I arrived in England. The Hostel food and accommodation is very good. I spend some of my leisure in reading English books and on Sundays I have one and a half hours tuition in the English language. I also like to go to the Cinema and walk in the country. I have friends at Horsforth, Nr. Leeds whom I visit fairly frequently. I would recommend other EVWs to coalmining because I get on very well with the English people.[804]

Such positive stories filtering back from recruits into the DP camps may have influenced the decisions of some other DPs, thereby producing a chain effect.

CONCLUDING REMARKS

The recruitment of Latvians, Lithuanians and Estonians for labour represented the first large-scale organised movement of these nationalities to Great Britain. Indeed, the EVW schemes were the first systematic immigration schemes on such a grand scale, ever implemented by a British Government. Although it has been shown that there were many different considerations involved in recruiting different nationalities, an important motivation was the racialisation of nationalities among policy makers. In the government's racialised hierarchy, the Baltic nationalities were at the top of the list. The racialised hierarchy of different nationalities related very closely to ideas about assimilation, within the post-war government. The recruitment of Latvians, Lithuanians and Estonians, and other prioritised nationalities, was based partly on a belief that these nationalities would assimilate into British society. As Kathleen Paul noted, 'Expecting them to fill gaps in the labour force in the short term, policy makers clearly also expected these aliens to become British subjects in both form and substance in the long term'.[805] Becoming British in substance, was to be achieved not only through the design of the labour schemes, but also through a series of measures prepared for the DPs arrival in Britain, which together, aimed to promote assimilation. Elements of the labour schemes' design intended to facilitate assimilation included limiting the admittance of any one nationality, the scattering of DPs within workplaces and the country, and the prioritisation of single refugees. Other measures after arrival included English lessons, social evenings promoting the mixing of EVWs with the British public, and lack of support for the maintenance of Latvian, Lithuanian and Estonian cultures and identities. Becoming British in form was facilitated through provisions for EVWs to apply for British citizenship after five years. A Circular from the FO to all H M Embassies and Legations, in December 1947, stated that, 'After the statutory period of residence in the United Kingdom (viz. 5 years) EVWs will have the same right as any other alien to apply for British nationality'.[806]

However, to what extent would the Baltic EVWs become British in form and substance, given that the national identities of these three culturally distinctive groups had strengthened as a result of their wartime and displacement experiences, and the fact that an overwhelming majority regarded their stay in Britain as merely temporary?

CHAPTER 6

'What on Earth Am I Doing Here?':
The first few years in Britain

'…we were the first strangers apart from the Poles, but we were strangers, and…I think our culture…was so different from the culture here, it was probably…difficult to assimilate or to get close together. For starters, people did not speak the language anyway, speak English…' (Lithuanian child dependant[807])

AFTER BEING ACCEPTED AS EUROPEAN VOLUNTEER WORKERS (EVWs), the Latvian, Lithuanian and Estonian DPs began their journey westwards to start their new lives in Great Britain. Despite believing at the time that their stay would only be temporary, the vast majority of the refugees never again resided in their homelands. The Baltic EVWs remained refugees or exiles until the declaration of Latvian, Lithuanian and Estonian independence in 1991. For a majority of the Baltic refugees, the years of exile were also the years of adulthood[808]; the young refugees in this study spent their twenties, thirties, forties and fifties in Britain, while the homeland remained under the firm grip of the Soviet Union. During their first years in Britain, how did the EVWs adjust and settle in? *Did* they settle in? What were the different responses to resettlement? What measures did the British Government introduce to encourage assimilation, and how did the EVWs reconcile British and homeland cultures? Finally, what were the responses of local communities and British labour? This chapter examines the initial period of resettlement until the end of labour controls in 1951, but will begin with the EVWs journey from the DP Camps to Great Britain.

THE JOURNEY TO GREAT BRITAIN

The first stage in the journey was the transfer of the refugees from the DP camps to a Regional Collecting Centre[809] and then to the Embarkation Transit Camp[810] at Münster, in North-west Germany, where they stayed for several days, before taking a train to either Cuxhaven in Germany, or the Hook of Holland. Here the refugees boarded ships sailing either to Tilbury or Harwich, on England's southern coast or Hull, in the east. The boat trip was usually overnight, and after embarkation in the morning, most of the Latvian, Lithuanian and Estonian men and women travelled by train to holding camps[811], where they stayed for a short period, sometimes as little as 24 hours, until onward accommodation was found. From the holding camps the refugees usually travelled to a hostel or other temporary accommodation and from there they were recruited by employers for labour.[812] Those refugees arriving in England via the port of Harwich or Tilbury, and heading north, boarded a train to London, where they spent a night in a hotel,[813] before continuing their journey to the holding camps or hostels. One EVW woman recalls that in the hotel, 'we were given cutlery, soap and towel, and were able to have a bath again'.[814] Doctors were also on hand when the recruits first arrived, to check that the workers were fit and healthy, and to test women for pregnancy.

The recruits took only limited belongings with them on the journey, often only one small suitcase, or some clothes wrapped in a blanket. The refugees had few possessions left after years of displacement and accumulated scarcely any items in the DP camps. Tannahill felt that:

> ...it was pitiful to see them arrive with their few belongings wrapped in a blanket. These were often a miscellaneous collection of rubbish, hoarded with the miserly care of the homeless, but sometimes included what was obviously loot, such as the two sewing machines brought by one girl.[815]

Tannahill also noted that 'Clothing...was always scarce. Many girls arrived at the textile mills with no underclothes and few outer garments'.[816] The *News Chronicle* reported the arrival of 87 EVW women in 1946, to undertake domestic work in hospitals in Lancashire and Cheshire: 'Some carried all their belongings in a grey army blanket; others wore fur coats and smart hats'.[817] Efforts had been made by the military authorities to hand out clothes in transit[818]; however, these were often insufficient. Nevertheless, at the very least, it was ensured that if they did not have one already, the refugees were provided with warm coats for the journey across the North Sea.

On arrival at the English ports, the refugees were given some pocket money. One EVW recalled that she was given one pound (£1) on disembarkation at Harwich.[819] A Latvian arriving two years later was given 30 shillings on arrival.[820] The EVWs were met by WVS (Women's Voluntary Service) volunteers, who accompanied them to either a hotel, hostel or other temporary lodgings. Many of the participants in this study noted how friendly the WVS workers were. A leaflet issued by the WVS described some of its functions:

> WVS work in close contact with the Ministry of Labour Welfare Department through all the operations affecting the EVWs once they land here. We meet the boats at Harwich and act as escorts and interpreters on the journey to the Reception Centre in London. Next day our escorts accompany the party to one of the Holding Hostels.[821]

Their work did not stop there however:

> WVS also help with the first shopping trip expedition, a visit to the church, or the cinema, they start right away teaching English and collecting papers and magazines for them; they arrange hospitality and try to set up concerts or social evenings in local clubs.[822]

Kristine, a Latvian woman, now in Nottingham accepted work as a nursing orderly on the Balt Cygnet scheme, which meant leaving her parents behind in the DP Camp in Germany. She described the journey:

> I enjoyed the journey. I was with friends. There were lots of young…ones from the school [in the DP Camp] as well. First, we went to a transit camp, which wasn't very far away from our camp, and then we were moved to Münster… That was the big transit camp. And from there we were put on the train, and we went to the Hook of Holland and during the night we went on a ferry and came to Harwich, and I think most of the night I stayed on the deck, and I was looking at the stars, because I love sea, and I hadn't been near the sea for a long time. It was very nice.[823]

She continued:

> …by train we came from Harwich to Liverpool Street Station, and oh…it was a dull day and so it wasn't very impressive.[824]

From the ports in the south of England, most of the refugees travelled to London in the early morning. Kristine stated that when she travelled on the train from Harwich to London, it was:

> …sometime in the morning, because we travelled during the night and we stayed in a church building. I think it was Hans Place in London, and apparently we were taken by double-decker bus from the Liverpool Street Station to this building in Hans Place, and my friend tells me that we went upstairs and I found a ten shilling note on the bus…but I can't remember about it. Well, if she said I must have done. I don't know what I did with it either. I just don't know. And after that we were…after one night, we were sent to this transit camp. It's called Wigsley near Lincoln.[825]

In most cases, the refugees' first impressions of Britain as they passed through industrialised war-recovering cities were unforgettable, although hardly positive. The adjectives used in the descriptions of Britain on the journey from the ports to the holding camps are telling: they are of a dull, grey, drab, foggy, smoky and smoggy, 1940's Britain. The refugees' depiction of Britain reflected the huge contrast between this 'never seen before' landscape, and the newly industrialising, green, rural and picturesque vista that was the homeland. It seemed that even experiences of war ravaged Germany had not prepared the refugees for the industrialised urban sprawl of many of Britain's towns and cities.

The book *Latvieši Lielbritanijā* described the first impressions of a group of Latvians arriving in England on 17 October 1947:

> Travelling by train, their first impressions were pleasant and reminded them of Latvia. On reaching the outskirts of London, the impact of poverty, dirt, huge factories and run-down urban housing areas was overwhelming. After the train, the experience of travelling by double-decker bus from the station to their hotel felt very strange. Registration, medical examination and an evening meal ended the first day in England. After a typical English breakfast they were taken to work. On their journey through the centre of London they marvelled at the well-dressed people in the streets and the crowded shop windows. They felt happy to have escaped the ruins of Germany, but sad for their homeland so far away. Words from a newspaper reminded them: "England has been reached, but not yet Latvia".[826] .

Vida, a Lithuanian woman came to England with her mother in 1948. She was aged nine. Her father had been recruited as a European Volunteer Worker, and Vida, her brother and mother travelled to England as dependants, to go and live with him. Vida described the journey:

> We were driven to London. We came to London. We stayed overnight in London, don't ask me where…some sort of dark place to me, and then sat on a train. We were in a train and we travelled to Nottingham and my first recollection of England were…chimneys! I'd never seen chimneys like it and I'd never seen houses so close together and dark. It was very different, very, very different. We arrived in May. I remember it was springtime in May. It was an overcast day and the WVS woman I recall was extremely pleasant and nice and so on…[827]

Like many of the refugee stories, Vida's recollections of her initial impressions are vivid. She continued:

> …and I recall we were taken to this terraced house – I didn't know it was terraced at the time type of thing, up these narrow stairs and there was my father…and that's where we started our lives in Britain'.[828]

Local and national newspapers reported the arrival of the Baltic DPs all over Britain. *The Western Morning News* of Plymouth reported on 21 November 1946 that: 'DPs Arrive in Devon For Domestic Work: Six to be Employed in Sanatoria'.[829] The article wrote that:

> Six of the 54 displaced persons from the British Zone of Germany who landed at Tilbury on Monday, including Estonians, Latvians and Lithuanians arrived in Devon yesterday to take up domestic work at Hawksmoor (Bovey Tracy) and at Didsworthy (South Brent).
>
> A welcome surprise for Ministry of Labour Officials and representatives of the Women's Voluntary Service who met the women was that several spoke sufficient English to make themselves understood despite the fact that they commenced the study of the language only recently.[830]

INITIAL EXPERIENCES

Accommodation

Following their arrival in Great Britain, almost all of the Baltic men and a smaller majority of the Baltic women EVWs, spent their first few months in hostels and camps dotted around Great Britain, including Devon, Yorkshire, Lancashire, Lincolnshire, the Midlands, Wales and Scotland.[831] Men and women remained in the hostels and camps until they were assigned work, and in some cases continued to reside there during their initial employment contract. Depending upon the type of work allocated during the recruitment interview, the refugees were sent to hostels or camps either run by their employers or near to the places of work. Hostels and camps were run by different bodies including the National Service Hostels Corporation, the County Agricultural Executive Committees, the YMCA, and some private firms, for example, mill hostels.

Hostel and camp life offered the refugees a measure of emotional security when they first arrived in Britain, and were a manageable stepping stone from the DP camps in Europe. Not only were they cheap, but they also provided the opportunity to be with fellow countrymen. Tannahill stated that for 'some of the older men who had left wives and families behind in Europe, it is perhaps the most satisfactory form of accommodation'.[832] Older inhabitants were less keen than younger refugees to enter the outside world and enjoyed the companionship and close-knit character of hostel life. However, it was also an existence of communal feeding and dormitory accommodation, housing between eight to twelve men, 'an unnatural life', which many of the refugees had tired of in the DP Camps.[833] Hostels were usually segregated, dividing men, women and families and there were restrictions on. Most of the agricultural hostels were extremely isolated, often miles from the nearest town or village. One Latvian woman who initially stayed at Wigsley camp in Lincolnshire described the isolation of the camp. I had asked her what her first impressions of Britain were. She replied:

> Well, in the first place we didn't see an awful lot of it, because living in the camp, you didn't see the life as such much at all, because the camp was on the site of a wartime airfield which was pretty much in the middle of nowhere, so the first impressions were...you went to Lincoln shopping with what bit of money you had, which again was very little and the shops were pretty empty after the war as well. But no, we thought you

know, it's quite nice, but…the beginning was quite limited contact with local people because in the camp, the people who were in charge of various sections of the camp, they were British, and then from then downwards, it was all the DPs that had come in.[834]

Conditions in the hostels and camps were extremely variable. Initially, recreational facilities were frequently inadequate, although these did improve.[835] By 1949, it was reported that: 'Cinema shows, billiards, table tennis, football, volley-ball and dances are provided in most hostels'.[836] However, even the government acceded that light entertainment often did 'not satisfy the desire of many foreigners for creative activity, and there is considerable scope for hobbies and recreational pursuits of all kinds to be developed'.[837] As they had done previously in the DP Camps, the different nationalities organised their own cultural activities, both to fill their time and to provide a home from home for the refugees. Opportunities for learning English while living in the camps and hostels were limited, although English classes and lectures were held in some of the hostels. The difficulty of learning English in the hostel environment was furthered by the fact that inhabitants were generally not regarded as members of the local community.[838] This also increased the need for organising a full schedule of activities in the camps and hostels.[839] One Latvian described the situation in agricultural workers' camps in Sussex:

> There was virtually no socialising between locals and camp inhabitants, partly due to the inability to communicate in English and partly because the English farmers rarely invited anyone inside their homes, preferring to conduct business on their doorstep. Thus isolated, the Latvian EVWs organised their own churches and congregations, social activities, choirs and dance groups. There were also English classes, lectures and dances. Local branches of the Latvian organisations (e.g. the Society of Latvians in Britain, the Latvian Welfare Fund and the Latvian National Council) were established.[840]

Even in camps where adequate facilities and activities were organised, it was common that as one Latvian noted, 'many still felt depressed by their uncertain future and the endless years of camp life'.[841] Many of the hostel inhabitants, particularly the younger men and women hankered for more freedom, privacy and better living conditions.

The government viewed the camps and hostels as temporary accommodation and aimed to house the refugees in private billets as soon as possible. Hostels were perceived to hinder assimilation into the local community; yet in many areas they were the only option, since housing shortages in Britain after the war had put private accommodation at a premium. Tannahill noted that the accommodation problem 'was difficult from the start'.[842] Women were prioritised in the accommodation sphere, with attempts made to house them as soon as suitable private accommodation became available. The first batch of female refugees recruited for labour on the Balt Cygnet scheme usually received housing in large boarding houses, often with three or four women to a room. Women who were initially sent to a hostel were often moved into lodgings within months. As more and more women entered Great Britain under the Westward Ho! scheme, it became difficult to provide private accommodation for all the women. Many textile firms, large employers of EVW women began providing mill hostels for their female recruits.

An additional problem with hostel accommodation was that relations between hostel inhabitants of different nationalities were reportedly far from amicable. Most of the hostels accommodated mixed nationalities, and Latvians, Lithuanians and Estonians often shared with Ukrainians, Poles, Yugoslavs and Belorussians. Women who were housed in hostels were also frequently expected to share with other nationalities, although Balt Cygnet women initially shared only with their own or another of the Baltic nationalities. A government report undertaken in the spring of 1949 described the problem:

> Among the foreign workers there are nationals of all the countries now under Soviet influence, a dozen or more nationalities. Between some of them there is a definite animosity, and it is only in hostels where there is a wise and friendly warden or manager (and often his wife) that the different races mix freely. As a rule they prefer to remain within their own little national groups.[843]

The participants in this study have reported mixed experiences, with some stating that inter-ethnic relations in the camps were relatively harmonious. One Latvian woman, stated that in Wigsley hostel, where there 'were quite a lot of Balts, Estonians and...but it wasn't just one nationality, it was whatever'[844], relations between the various nationality groups were 'quite reasonable. We used to play volleyball and things every night, so it was quite all right and the British officers were very nice'.[845]

Accommodation facilities in both the hostels and private houses were extremely basic. Even women lucky enough to be housed by the authorities in boarding houses women faced poor conditions. Many of the refugees who began their lives in hostels and camps were soon eager to move into private accommodation. This was especially difficult in the mining and rural areas where private accommodation was sparse, as compared to the larger industrial towns.[846] Private accommodation was often virtually uninhabitable, particularly in urban localities. In textile areas, many houses lacked sanitation and bathrooms.[847] Large numbers of Baltic women left textile work quickly, primarily because the accommodation in these areas was so appalling. Most of the EVWs who lived in private accommodation had to share rooms and the conditions were cramped. It was not unusual for up to four single men or women to share one bedroom. One Estonian who had recently married and was working in textiles in Halifax found the living conditions for himself and his wife to be unbearable. He described the situation as follows:

> It were a house where we lived, like a room and a kitchen sort of thing. It weren't very old, but it was very small, two bedrooms and [the] bedroom was so small…we couldn't get dressed together. We had to wait our turn. And well, we were fed up really, absolutely fed up because we got our dinners from factory and…where we lived… We had recently got married and we tried to get somewhere of our own.[848]

After help from the factory management eventually they found a flat of their own to rent:

> It was a pound a week. Two rooms…first and second floor…and we had a small bathroom and like a kitchen and eventually my sister came to live with us… We came to work back end of September. That were in following March.[849]

A minority of Baltic refugees chose to remain in the hostels, while a few were required to stay temporarily in hostels against their choice, due to the dearth of private accommodation. The hostel population in January 1949 was still high at 50,000 (all EVW nationalities).[850] This compared to an approximate total of 80,000 EVW nationalities employed in Britain by the spring of 1949.[851] Although a majority of EVWs remained in hostels in January 1949, it is probable that as the first to enter Britain, Baltic refugees were also among the first group to leave the hostels. It is clear that the trend towards private accommodation had already begun by 1949, even while EVWs were still being admitted into the country. A report held by the Ministry of Labour suggested that the hostel situation had improved so much by 1949 that the EVWs 'have no wish to take advantage of the occasional opportunities of being housed in private billets'.[852] This claim is not supported by interview evidence, which suggests that perhaps a majority of Baltic refugees had already left voluntarily or were planning to leave the communal life of the hostels to make a living in the industrial towns of Britain.

Initial Employment Experiences

The Baltic refugees were usually assigned their first jobs within several weeks of their arrival. The initial work assignments of Baltic refugees varied, although all were in areas of manpower shortage. The 2500 Balt Cygnet women undertook work as kitchen hands, general ward maids, cleaners, laundry workers, nurses and midwives in tuberculosis sanatoria and hospitals. The areas of labour initially undertaken by Baltic refugees engaged on 'Westward Ho!' included: agricultural labour; textile work; domestic service in hospitals and other institutions; nursing; working in the steelworks; coalmining; forestry; working in the building materials industry, for example brickworks; various jobs in the Hostels including administration; and finally, other miscellaneous jobs approved by the Ministry of Labour, for example, work in ammunitions depots.[853]

The geographical distribution of the Baltic communities in the early years reflected the areas where these industries and jobs were located. The largest numbers were assigned to industrial areas of the North of England (particularly the textile towns of West Yorkshire and Lancashire) and the Midlands, although communities were also established in Wales and Scotland and diverse regions of England. Among Latvians the most sizeable communities developed in Bradford, Leeds, Manchester, Nottingham, Mansfield, Chesterfield, Coventry, Leicester, Birmingham, Wolverhampton, Corby, Bedford and Peterborough. Smaller Latvian communities also developed in Scotland and Wales. The geographical development of Lithuanian and Estonian communities followed a similar pattern, although due to their smaller numbers, particularly the Estonians, sizeable communities were formed in fewer areas. Estonian, Latvian and Lithuanian women arrived in Scotland primarily to undertake work in hospitals, joining men working in agriculture, coalmining and forestry. In Wales, relatively small numbers of Latvian, Lithuanian and Estonian EVWs worked primarily in TB hospitals, brickworks, coalmining and tin-mines. Agricultural workers were distributed all over Great Britain, as far north as Scotland,

and as far south as Devon. Forestry recruits were sent primarily to Scotland, while a popular destination for EVWs employed in the brickworks industry was Bedford. Recruits for nursing and domestic service were distributed in many different regions of Britain and coalminers were assigned mainly to Yorkshire and Scotland.

The refugees' early experiences of employment were variable. While some of the refugees enjoyed the work first assigned to them and remained in the same job even after a year, others were dissatisfied and changed their employment as soon as possible. There are instances of some Baltic refugees moving to half a dozen different camp or hostels and undertaking many different jobs by 1950.[854] Some even transferred from the job they had first been assigned, to another area of labour shortage almost as soon as they arrived. One Latvian, who came to Britain to engage in agricultural work in 1947, aged 20, stated that he quickly changed his mind after seeing the dilapidated, cranky equipment, which was quite unlike the well-maintained machinery he had operated on the farmstead in Latvia. He described his experiences:

> Well, first of all when we came, we came to Full Sutton from Hull, landed in Hull and then Full Sutton. We had a camp there.

> ...after two months, a firm from Leeds came to see who wanted to work in [the] textile industry. And I had a look around. I didn't like the agriculture because I didn't like the rusty machinery all the farmers had left outside'. 'It was so rusty and that was never my idea of farming, so...I didn't want to go in coalmining. Some of them did but not myself, so I thought well we'll try textiles, see what it is like. So I joined the firm of W E Yates in Bramley and I spent there until 1964, working for them. First of all in the wool mixing department. It was very mucky, up to the eyes.[855]

Occasionally, work could not be found for the refugees immediately. This was particularly the case for refugees in agricultural hostels in the winter months, although also at other times of the year, and was especially frustrating for the younger refugees who were keen to start work and earn money. One Latvian man, who stayed in Full Sutton camp in Humberside detailed in a diary the 'boredom and lack of purpose felt by those who were eager to work, but who were kept waiting for months'.[856] Some of the men adopted an active approach to their problem and actually went out and found work for themselves, when the employers failed to come to them. One Estonian man arrived in England on the 'Westward Ho!' scheme in May 1947, and was sent to Priory Road Camp near Hull. After being there for some time without being offered any employment, he and some of the other refugees in the camp decided to go round local farms and find work. He described the situation:

> We landed in Hull – Priory Road Camp that was the first one. …but…nothing moved so [a] few of us, I can't remember, six or seven of us, we went round in farms in the summer and the farmers took us on. We went hay-making and corn-stacking and you know, did some work.[857]

Beginning life as an agricultural worker was very common among Baltic men. Heino, an young Estonian man, was one of thousands of young Baltic men who undertook this kind work initially. Like many of the Estonian refugees, he was familiar with agricultural work, although there were differences in practices and the scale of operations. According to Heino, some of the agricultural camps accommodating the EVWs had previously been used by the Land Army during the Second World War. He described his experiences:

> We were simply taking the place of wartime seasonal workers…living in the hostels and so that's what we did. We lived there and then the farmers, when they…needed some hands, working hands…they informed the proper authorities and then we were put on the truck, and taken there and brought back in the evening…that was the first summer and then after, the second year I was taken on as a member of the staff of one of those camps and then the third, it was 1949 I think and they closed those camps and so they told us then, 'Well, that's it. We're closing the camp and you have to find your own way round', and so we went on our own. We still had to register with the police, being aliens and…we couldn't take any job that was not approved by the Ministry of Labour.[858]

After finishing agricultural work, he then carried out a succession of jobs, including working in the Navy, before gaining a permanent position in nursing, where he remained until he retired. He described his first experiences of work following the closure of the agricultural camp in 1949:

> First year, I went to Derby as a Christmas rush postman, yeah. Quite a pleasant introduction. Played music while you worked and while we were sorting out the [mail]. Tended to get lost in Derby a little bit and then one of those textile factories just

outside Derby, that was the first job and then that didn't last. It didn't suit me very well.[859]

Like Heino, most EVWs only undertook agricultural work for a short period, before moving to other areas of employment, most popularly textile work. The range of jobs undertaken by EVWs within textiles was enormous and included various types of work in cotton spinning and doubling, woollens and worsteds, hosiery, rayon and silk manufacture, flax manufacture, textile bleaching, dyeing and finishing, and machine work in wholesale clothing.[860] EVWs employed as textile workers had to work long hours and the tasks were usually very heavy, noisy and dirty. The hours of one Latvian woman who worked in a cotton mill in Rochdale from seven in the morning to five at night, with a lunch break[861], were fairly typical, but despite the long hours she reportedly 'enjoyed' the work.[862] A young Latvian man, now living in Leeds, began working the night shift at Yates's Ltd. in Bramley, but could get little sleep in the hostel where he lived during the day and became exhausted.[863] He quickly transferred to a daytime job in another mill. Frequent switching of jobs and firms was common among those working in the textile mills, since it was an area of severe labour shortage and there were always jobs available if the initial post was unsuitable.

A significant minority of Latvian, Lithuanian and Estonian men were engaged as coalminers during their first years in Great Britain in different areas of Britain, including Scotland, the Midlands and the North of England.[864] Coalmining recruits received intensive training and English language instruction for safety reasons.[865] As with the other areas of employment, reported experiences of coalmining were variable. One Latvian felt that coalmining offered reasonable employment: work was in eight hour shifts, and the food and living conditions were good.[866] However, at Hardwick Camp near Chesterfield, Latvian mining recruits lived 16 to each brick-built barrack, the food was poor and the accommodation was reportedly 'very cold'.[867] Reports from Baltic refugees in other areas of work, such as forestry, brickworks, steelworks and domestic service were also variable.[868] The refugees tended to describe both the positive and negative aspects of their work: for example, one Latvian woman noted that her work as a domestic was 'boring and humiliating, but not hard'.[869] Another Latvian who worked in the building materials industry noted that the work 'was not easy, but the weekly wages of £4 10 shillings to £8 12 shillings, were considerably more than farm hands received, and less than six months after arrival everyone had acquired suits'.[870]

Some of the refugees who had good English were able to work as interpreters or administrators in the holding camps and hostels. A Lithuanian man worked as an interpreter in an agricultural worker's camp in Penrith. He described his experiences:

> [I] landed in Hull and [I] was in Transit Camp for about oh, maybe a couple of months, and then [I] came to Penrith in western Cumbria and it was [an] agricultural workers camp and...I became an interpreter. So I never worked on the farm. I just sorted, tried to sort everybody's else's problems you know. That's what I did in England when I first came...[871]

During the first few years of settlement, the patterns of employment shifts among EVWs brought about substantial migration from rural to urban areas. This was due mainly to the increasing unpopularity of agricultural work and the allure of the towns and cities. Frequently the move coincided with the transfer from hostel to private accommodation and the refugees' desire to improve their living and working conditions. Young male refugees who had spent a year or more in a men only hostel were keen to meet young women from their own nationality. One Estonian man who came to Britain aged 22 was first employed as a kitchen porter in an agricultural workers' hostel near Kinross in northern Scotland, before later moving to Bradford, a growing centre of the Baltic communities, where he settled permanently.[872] Tannahill summed the motivations for the rural/urban migration:

> 'Higher wages, better housing prospects and greater opportunities for meeting their fellow countrymen were the chief attractions'.[873]

EVWs who wished to migrate from rural to urban areas were able to exploit the opportunities offered by the completion of the initial labour contract, which stipulated that the refugees had to work in the specified post for one year, and were thereafter able to change their employment, as long as it was approved by the Ministry of Labour. Generally, this meant the field of employment was limited to areas of manpower shortage. There was a degree of misunderstanding among EVWs about the labour requirements, which had arisen from language difficulties and lack of clarity in EVW recruitment literature. According to Tannahill, some of the EVWs were under the impression that they were required to work in a Ministry of Labour approved post for only one year, and thereafter were free to choose their employment. Tannahill noted that Ministry of Labour controls were 'humanely exercised', and some of the EVWs were allowed to take up employment outside the approved field, once they had completed the initial year of service.[874] This is illustrated by the experiences of a young Latvian woman, who had initially been employed as a caterer's clerk for the National Service Hostels Corporation Camps in Wigsley. She married her husband in Wigsley camp, and when her husband secured a post working in offices in a large textile firm, she was also offered a position. Both she and her husband spoke good English. Her husband had been an interpreter for the Ministry of Labour, during which time he had become acquainted with the personnel manager of one of the large textile firms, who invited both Latvians to work in offices at the firm. According to the Latvian woman, the Ministry of Labour 'released me because there again you see they knew my husband, but the Hostels Corporation didn't want me to go. They said, "You can't go. I mean you came over on that engagement and you have to stay", but I went to [the] Ministry of Labour in Lincoln, they said, "Yes. Yes. We'll give you a paper…" So it proves it's who you know'.[875]

A majority of the refugees reported that they adjusted to different working practices successfully, and those who had never been employed previously, quickly became proficient in their jobs. Adjustment was often easier for the younger refugees, who had not yet embarked upon their careers. The younger EVWs were generally more open-minded about the work available and in a sense, had fewer expectations, having no benchmark against which to base their aspirations. If the refugees found their initial job unsuitable, they were usually able to find a satisfactory alternative within the Ministry of Labour's designated manpower shortage areas. One Latvian girl who worked in a hospital in Britain, having previously been at school when the war broke out in Latvia, found it easy to adapt. She stated that:

> The hospital, it was, I don't know. It was something new, but it didn't worry me, because I wasn't worried about working, you know. I could do the jobs.[876]

The opportunities to restart careers or education were limited during the first years in Britain. A few of the Baltic refugees were able to continue their education[877], although this was certainly not the experience of the overwhelming majority. In December 1949, the British Government decided that EVWs who had been awarded open scholarships to Universities and who had worked well for eighteen months could be released from employment to undertake a full-time course lasting two years or longer.[878] The course had to be approved by the Ministry of Labour and the applicant was required prove that he or she could be self-supporting, while studying.[879] By 1950, the numbers able to enter universities was small.[880]

A few professionals were also able to continue their careers, although again this was also rare. Latvian dentists were allowed to practice in Great Britain from the start,[881] however, the majority of Baltic refugees who remained in Britain had to settle for fewer educational and professional opportunities than would have been open to them in the homeland.

After the completion of the initial labour contract, small numbers of Baltic EVWs[882] returned to Germany.[883] Some had taken up labour in Great Britain on the assumption that it was only a temporary contract and returned to Germany after a year. Others proved to be unfit for work in England, while some went back to Germany to re-emigrate to Canada with their families.[884] In addition, the evidence suggests that a few of the Baltic refugees returned to their homeland, although the numbers are impossible to quantify. Tannahill cited the case of an Estonian woman who returned to Estonia, although this was probably an isolated case.[885]

Family Life: The early years in Britain

The speed at which the refugees were able to restore some semblance of a family life in Britain varied enormously. Whilst the majority of Baltic EVWs remained single and without family during the early years in Britain, a minority were able to recreate family life. This was achieved in three ways: through dependants being admitted into Britain; spouses or other family members also participating in the EVV schemes; marriage in Britain.

The rapidity with which some Baltic refugees recreated family life through marriage in Britain is illustrated by the following two cases. A Latvian woman was married less than a year after arriving in Britain age 26, to a Latvian man.[886] She was married at Keighley parish Church in West Yorkshire, and was able to recreate many of the characteristics of a traditional Latvian wedding. The service was performed in Latvian by a Lutheran minister and the bride wore a white dress with a myrtle head-dress.[887] This woman gave birth to her first child in 1950. Another Latvian woman was married in 1949 at the age of 23 to a Latvian man.[888] She became pregnant and stopped working at the textile mill where she had been employed in Lancashire. She gave birth to a son in 1950. Shortly afterwards she and her husband moved to Bradford, by then the centre of a vibrant Latvian community.

Marriage offered a way for the young refugees without family in Britain, to create stability in their lives. It was hardly surprising that long-term relationships were formed quickly, due to the large numbers of single men and women employed as EVWs in Britain. Some of the young couples who married in Britain, had met in the DP Camps, while others met in the hostels and community centres in Britain. Many of the young women who married during this period were in their mid-twenties, and were eager to settle down and start families. Marriages which took place during the first few years in Britain consisted mainly of same nationality marriages. Due to the high male/female ratio among all three Baltic nationalities[889], women were able to choose from among large numbers of eligible single men of their own nationality. Men on the other hand had fewer opportunities to marry women from their own nationality and were obliged to look beyond their own nationality group for potential marriage partners. Consequently many men did not get married until the 1950's or later, after they had left the hostels and began to mix with members of other communities.

Some refugees were able to create a kind of surrogate family by sharing houses with other members of their own community. Although the conditions were often cramped, these arrangements provided security and support for the refugees during the difficult first years.

The need to recreate something resembling family life during the early years in Britain was furthered by the continuing lack of contact with family in the homeland. Until Stalin's death in 1953, many of the Baltic refugees in Great Britain were too frightened to attempt to make contact with their relatives in the homeland, concerned both for their own safety and that of their friends and relatives. The Stalin regime in the Baltic States disseminated propaganda deriding the exiles as 'deserters'. The exiles felt that if family members were exposed as relations of 'deserters', the Soviet regime would take its revenge. On the other hand, the exiles were however keen to let their relatives know their whereabouts and that they were safe. Complicated methods of communication were therefore devised, including the use of third parties to communicate information, and the development of sophisticated coding techniques.[890]

RESPONSES TOWARDS THE REFUGEES

The Response from British Labour

If a majority of the Baltic refugees can be said to have adjusted to new working practices relatively quickly, how were they received by British labour - by fellow British employees, employers and trade unions?

The response towards the EVWs from British labour has been analysed in several studies[891], and therefore will not be discussed in any great depth here. Perhaps the most important point to make is that for the most part, Ministry of Labour policies had been carefully formulated to facilitate the entry of the EVWs into the British labour market, and to mitigate negative responses from British labour. Agreements between the Ministry of Labour and the unions of those industries which were singled out for EVW employment, were 'negotiated at a national level and were aimed at establishing a general formula for the avoidance of problems in the placement of the new workforce'.[892] Most of the agreements stipulated 'full union rates of pay, union membership and a clause which stated that foreigners would only be employed in the absence of suitable British labour'.[893] The employment of the EVWs in undermanned areas reduced hostile responses; workers had little ground for accusing the EVWs of stealing jobs from British men, although a few such accusations inevitably surfaced. Ensuring that wage levels of EVWs were kept at the same rate as British employees also reduced charges of cheap or slave labour. The involvement of EVWs in trade unions also helped the process of successful integration into the British labour market. Although xenophobia and racism did occur on the part of British workers, and hostile responses can be traced from some employers and trade unions, these were often overcome by the experience of working with the EVWs.

However, such generalities tend to mask disparate experiences. It is clear that the variety of responses from British labour differed from one locality and specific situation to another. From his discussion of labour responses in the Scottish coalfields, Kenneth Lunn noted that both positive and negative stereotypes of the 'foreigners' existed, and that, 'hostile views were not, except in a few cases, fixed or permanent'.[894] Negative attitudes arose from several factors, including the perceived threats to jobs and accommodation, and from cultural and political clashes, particularly the alleged fascist tendencies of the newcomers and their hostility to Britain's wartime ally, Russia. Positive images came primarily from everyday contact with the EVWs and from an awareness that the refugees were helping in the post-war reconstruction of Britain. Differences in responses towards the EVWs also arose as agreements negotiated by the Ministry of Labour and the trade unions at a national level sometimes ran into difficulties at a local level. The specific factory or workplace, the branch of industry, the characteristics of the local economy, local and EVW attitudes, as well as the national economy and political climate all contributed to the range and diversity of responses and experiences.[895]

Very few of the participants in this study reported instances of discrimination or hostility towards them, from either fellow workers or employers. Most of the refugees described amicable relations with their British work-mates during the first few years of settlement. The fact that in many work places, especially in towns, there were usually very few workers from their own nationality employed in the same factory or institution, necessitated getting to know British workers. Even in large textile companies, it was likely that only a handful of any one nationality were working in a particular factory.

There were some difficulties with communication, which led occasionally to misunderstandings and hindered the formation of friendships between the locals and the refugees. That English language ability was an important factor which eased relations with the locals was noted in the 'Report of an Enquiry by one of H. M. Inspectors of School's during January, February and April, 1949 into the teaching of English to foreign workers':

> Industrial tensions become exaggerated when the foreigner and our own workers cannot talk things over, and the foreigner's impression that he is "slave labour", or is being victimised in some way, is deepened, while some of our own people are inclined to forget that a man who cannot speak English has the same flesh, blood, nerves and affections as himself, and is inclined sometimes to dismiss him as "one of those foreigners".[896]

Many of the respondents in the study stated that they worked harder than many of the local employees and were thus viewed as excellent workers by employers. However, this characteristic also occasionally made them unpopular with fellow workers. The same report from the H M Inspector of Schools in 1949 noted that:

> Nearly all the foreigner workers are industrious and thrifty. Employers of all kinds are in general very satisfied with them, and as a result some of the workers have become unpopular

with our own people working beside them because they do not fully understand restrictive practices.[897]

Nevertheless, Tannahill stressed that:

> The anxiety of the EVWs to earn money quickly was sometimes criticised, but they soon learnt that to arrive early in the morning and start their machines or to work through the lunch break was unpopular with their workmates and was forbidden on safety grounds by the management.[898]

A Latvian woman described the differences between English and Latvian approaches to work in the following terms:

> I think the Latvians used to work a different way than the locals because we were told: 'Take it easy. Slow down.' I remember that because I think in Latvia you see, if there was a job you get it done, and then you have a rest, but apparently here you couldn't. You had to spread the job out. You were supposed to be doing something all the time. You couldn't, you know, just finish the job and then stand on one side. No that wasn't the thing at that time anyway.[899]

She recalled that, because she and another Latvian employee were such hard workers: 'I think there might have been a bit of jealousy at times, I don't know, but I think we were a happy crowd.' During these initial years, she socialised with both new English friends and other Latvians. The English girls 'used to ask us to their homes for tea. No, it was a happy time. Oh and there was a Latvian men's camp, an agricultural camp too, and we used to meet the boys there as well'.[900] One Latvian woman claimed that there was discrimination from employers in one of the factories where she worked, although she had a more positive experience when she changed factory.[901]

Suspicion and opposition to the EVWs from English workers certainly existed and promoted discord and friction, as evidenced by newspapers and journal articles from the period.[902] Nevertheless, as conflicts are more newsworthy than lack of conflict, for every reported incident, it is likely that there were many more trouble-free and amicable working relationships.[903] Evidence from the interviews supports this claim, and it appears that although cases of racism and discrimination existed, they were relatively isolated, and that in general, relations both between the Baltic workers and fellow British workers and employers were harmonious.[904]

The response of local populations

What about the attitudes towards the Baltic EVWs of local residents, as the refugees began to move out of the hostels into private accommodation, often in areas of a predominately English, Scottish or Welsh population? Tannahill summed up the attitude of local British populations towards the EVW community initially, as one of 'tolerance, tinged with some suspicion, which is mainly economic but is partly…political'.[905] The British public received the refugees 'with their customary lack of effusion. Sometimes there was opposition; sometimes (and this too could be hurtful) there was indifference. But many of the EVWs speak with gratitude of widespread tolerance, helpfulness and patience'.[906] Indeed, the variety of local responses mirrored that of British labour, and was based on a number of variables including the specific locality, the individual EVW, local and national attitudes, political viewpoints and accommodation in the area, to name just a few. As Bülbring noted: 'The reception of the refugees by the British population varies a great deal from hostility and indifference at one extreme to interest and friendliness at the other'.[907]

An important factor affecting the temperature of the Balts' reception in Britain, as they moved out of camps and hostels into private accommodation, was the availability of accommodation in the area. Just as some locals charged the EVWs with stealing their jobs, some residents also accused Baltic refugees of taking much needed accommodation, which in many areas was at a premium during the early post-war years. Experiences varied in different localities, but in some, signs were put up in boarding houses stating that East Europeans were not welcome. If the EVWs were seen to be enjoying a higher standard of living than locals in the area, this also caused acrimony. Discussing the reception of EVWs, Bülbring stated in 1954 that:

> On the whole it can be said that their reception is better the more similar their living conditions are to those of the local population. In return the attitude of the refugees becomes more social and less shy and exclusive towards the local population.[908]

Baltic refugees received similar treatment to other East Europeans; in general, the British population was unable to distinguish between the different East European nationalities. Latvians, Lithuanians and Estonians were frequently called 'Poles', due to the large numbers of Polish ex-servicemen who had been based in Britain during the war and who were demobilised in 1946 and subsequently transferred into the

Polish Resettlement Corps (PRC).[909] A Lithuanian woman explained the mistaken identities of Baltic refugees in Britain as a result of the Polish resettlement:

> Oh when we coming you know in England, here well, they only know Polish, Polish – "Are you a Pole?", you know. First thing they ask you, as soon as you open your mouth, "Are you Polish?". Yeah, because they must know Polish people here, there's so many people. "Are you Polish?" "No, I'm not – Lithuanian". "Where is that?"[910]

A Latvian man reported that: 'Pole they used to call me. We wasn't Latvian we were Poles'. His wife agreed: 'Oh yes, to start with, because nobody knew we were Latvian. If you didn't speak English then you were Polish'.[911] This point was re-iterated by Bülbring: 'No distinction between nationalities was made by the local people, and many of them speak of any refugee as a Pole!'[912]

Experiences of local attitudes among participants in this study were mixed. A majority claimed that they themselves suffered little hostility, but felt that this may not have been the experience of others. One Latvian woman reported that: 'I must say that I think I have been very, very lucky, because…in all these years I can't say that I met people who had been nasty to me because I'm not English'.[913]

A significant minority had different experiences; they reported examples of abuse and a hostile reaction among locals: one woman reported that: 'By the locals you were to put it bluntly a bloody foreigner'. She repeated this point later on in the same interview: 'We were Displaced Persons, foreigners even. There were no two ways about it. We were foreigners. We were very much told so, quite often'.[914]

The degree of animosity felt by the refugees from the local community sometimes depended on different interpretations of a certain situation. For example, while one Latvian man reacted badly to being called a Pole, his wife did not feel that this was abusive.[915]

An Estonian man pointed out that British people were suspicious of the Baltic refugees, because initially, prior to the start of the Cold War, the British and the Baltic refugees had very different attitudes towards Russia, Britain's ally in the war:

> …Russia and England were Allies and most of Estonians, they were sort of, well we didn't like Russians and [the] English

couldn't understand why we didn't like Russia because Russia was their ally.[916]

Referring to local attitudes towards the EVWs, Lunn raised a related point:

> In political terms, there were tensions based on the alleged "fascist" tendencies of the newcomers. There had been well-publicised incidents of anti-Semitism among the Polish forces in Scotland during the war years and sometimes vehement anti-Soviet views expressed by Poles and other East Europeans were taken as indicators of fascist sympathies.[917]

One Lithuanian woman who entered Britain as a child dependant felt that the refugees were accepted only because they were 'orphans of the war'. She described how the differences in culture and language made it difficult to become friendly with British people:

> ...we were the first strangers apart from the Poles, but we were strangers, and...I think our culture...was so different from the culture here, it was probably...difficult to assimilate or to get close together. For starters, people did not speak the language anyway, speak English...[918]

As we have seen, although some of the Baltic EVWs became friendly with English work-mates, the opportunities to meet British people during the first few years were limited, particularly among those still living in hostels. Even among those accommodated in private billets, many of the refugees did not easily make friends with the locals during the first few years, due to several factors. These included unwillingness on either part, poor English, lack of opportunity, local hostility (real or perceived), cultural differences or even shyness. Again, the factors involved varied greatly from individual to individual.

GOVERNMENT POLICIES OF ASSIMILATION

As already discussed in Chapter Five, government rhetoric contained in Ministry of Labour and Foreign Office files suggests that the British government aimed to assimilate, to 'merge' the Baltic and other East European EVW populations into the British community as rapidly as possible. While discourses of assimilation are now out-dated, they are extremely useful in that they reflect ideas about assimilation contemporary to the period. In brief, in the late 1940's, assimilation was regarded as a straight-line process, where one culture (generally the minority culture) merged into another culture (the dominant culture, that of the majority), until ultimately no traces of the former were visible. The aim therefore was that Latvian, Lithuanian and Estonian cultures and identities would eventually merge into the British culture and identity, and that at the end of this process, no remnants of the original homeland culture and identity would be discernible.

Some commentators have noted that while the British Government clearly articulated its aims and objectives regarding the assimilation of the EVWs, the means by which to achieve these goals were not adequately thought out in advance of the refugees' arrival. Many of the policies were formulated only as a result of the implementation of the Balt Cygnet and Westward Ho! schemes, when it quickly became apparent that assimilation would be a long-term process. Several policies were enacted as part of the schemes, for example, the dispersal of the communities nationally, locally and in the workplace. Others were implemented after the EVWs arrival, but with only a measure of success, for example, the attempt to move the communities into private accommodation as quickly as possible. Other recommendations were discussed as the schemes got under way. These included: providing English language lessons; educating the Balts about British society; establishing mixed Baltic/British social groups and activities. Allied to these approaches was a lack of support for Baltic cultures and identities. Apart from a handful of local authorities providing space for weekend schools for children, national and local authorities provided few facilities for the maintenance of Baltic cultures and communities. One Lithuanian woman described the situation as follows:

> Once we were here there were no concessions given to us whatsoever about anything. Neither the language...the whole idea was immediately that we would assimilate as quickly as possible...there was no assistance whatsoever.

> You were given no assistance to retain your identity at the beginning, whatsoever, simply because that was the Iron Curtain [and] there would be no return. [919]

Government reports and recommendations in the years during the implementation of the EVW schemes, reveal government thinking in relation to policies which it believed would hasten the assimilation process. The British government regarded the fact that by 1949, significant numbers of Baltic EVWs, particularly men, were still living in hostels, as one of the most serious obstacles to achieving assimilation, and believed that much of the reluctance to move out of the hostels and settle elsewhere was due to the tenacity of the return myth. J.G. Stewart at the Ministry of Labour and National Service, informed H. H. Sellar, in May 1949, that, 'particularly in the more isolated areas, it seems that they are continuing to exist in somewhat isolated communities and are not taking any real roots in this country'.[920] Stewart advised Sellar that:

> ...what is most needed is to get the EVWs into clubs and societies of all kinds which will enable them to meet British people in an informal way, encourage them to learn more English than they need simply for the purpose of their job and for simple types of shopping, and enable them to form individual friendships with British people.[921]

Regional Welfare Officers were employed by the National Service Hostels' Corporation to take charge of the welfare of EVWs in each region, and to implement strategies to encourage assimilation. J. G. Stewart wrote to the Regional Controller of All Regions on 16 August 1949, recommending a series of measures to facilitate the assimilation of EVWs into British life.[922] These included teaching EVWs English, securing accommodation in private lodgings, and the organisation of social events, where EVWs mixed with the British population. Stewart concluded that:

> It is generally agreed that EVWs living in private lodgings have a greater opportunity and incentive to become assimilated into the community than those living in hostels'. Every effort should therefore be made to 'encourage and assist EVWs to find private lodging accommodation.

He also noted that Social Clubs which attempt to mix EVWs with the local population were very successful. He stated that:

> In a number of Regions, the Women's Voluntary Services and other voluntary organisations and groups of interested people have started clubs to which both British persons and foreign workers are encouraged to belong, so that the assimilation of the latter may be encouraged through joint social activities.
>
> It is impossible to over-estimate the importance of activities of this kind: informal social activities leading to individual friendships between EVWs and British people provide the most effective means of assimilation.

Stewart also emphasised the importance of learning English:

An individual worker with an elementary knowledge of the language stands a much greater chance of successfully fitting himself into the life of the community and of participating fully in its activities.

Furthermore, Stewart recommended the encouragement of schemes enabling EVWs to take time off work to learn English.[923]

In addition to language classes, and the organisation of social events where EVWs mixed with local British people, other measures were implemented to aid assimilation. A booklet was prepared for EVWs by the Central Office of Information called *'To Help You Settle in Britain'*.[924] Another booklet entitled *'Contemporary Life in Britain'* aimed to familiarise the refugees with the British way of life.[925]

REFUGEE ATTITUDES TOWARDS SETTLEMENT

While the British Government was keen to hasten assimilation, the refugees' first few years in Britain were characterised by resistance to the idea of permanent resettlement. The Baltic refugees were at first under the impression that their period of labour was short-term and that they would shortly return to the homeland, following liberation by the Allies. The so-called 'myth of return' was promoted by community organisations, representatives and publications. One government report described the EVW as a 'bird of passage', to describe how the refugees saw themselves.[926] This term had similarities with the Lithuanian interpretation of DP – *Diėvo Paukšteliai*, which translated means 'God's Little Birds'.[927] This meaning of the abbreviation DP is revealing of the refugees' belief that someday they would return. Exile writers and poets also used the metaphor of birds, to describe the refugees' situation.[928] The comparison suggested that Britain was but a temporary resting place and that when the metaphoric seasons turned, the refugees, like migrating birds would return to their homelands.

The time-scale of the envisaged return shifted considerably during the early years in Britain. During the first months or years, the refugees believed that they would be able to go back to the homeland shortly, but as time passed, the possibility of being able to return seemed an increasingly distant prospect. Individuals held their own beliefs about when the communities would be able to return. One Latvian interviewee, now living in Leeds stated that:

'…we realised straight away we wouldn't go back as long as there was a communist government. We wouldn't go back. No way…'[929]

Her comments (which have almost certainly been influenced by hindsight) contrast with the testimonies of other individuals, who talked about how they believed in an imminent return throughout their early years in Britain.

The tenacity of the return myth transcended developments in the homeland from 1946 to 1950, which even during these early years of incorporation into the USSR, pointed towards lengthy Soviet rule over the Baltic Republics. News reaching the Baltic communities was fragmentary, and often misleading, due to the difficulties of receiving accurate information throughout the Stalin era. Nevertheless, Baltic exile communities across the world linked up and exchanged information, through newsletters, radio programmes, reports and newspapers. Community newspapers in Great Britain printed information received from these sources, from the western media and any information coming out of the homeland, for example from relatives.

During the early years in Britain, the three communities heard about disturbing events in the homelands. Intensive Stalinization of the Baltic republics was followed by a second wave of deportations in 1949, when thousands of ethnic Latvians, Lithuanians and Estonians, mainly farmers and their families, were forcibly resettled in central Russia and the Asian republics to work on collective and state farms. In Latvia alone, an estimated 70,000 Latvians were deported from 24 to 27 March 1949.[930] Deportations continued until 1952 and precipitated the total collectivisation of agriculture in all three Baltic republics. As a result of the Soviet annexation of the Baltic States, several boundary adjustments were made, which reduced the territories of Latvia and Estonia.[931] Repression of religion had begun in earnest and the Sovietization of industry was already leading to the influx of Russian migrants into the Baltic States as manpower.[932]

In the early years of settlement, homeland developments had two main effects on the Baltic communities in Britain. Firstly, they did little to weaken the return myth, which the communities continued to propagate. The communities clung to the hope that guerrilla activities in the homelands and efforts to establish governments-in-exile would be successful. The diaspora joined together in the political campaigns for independence. Second, events in the homeland heightened the exile's sense of duty towards the homeland and contributed to the development of exile identities and cultures. Not only were the Baltic states now subjugated nations, but their whole way of life, culture and national identities were perceived to be in jeopardy.

There is no doubt that a belief in return hindered the resettlement process in the first few years.

H B M Murphy defined resettlement as follows:

> Resettlement begins when the refugee ceases to regard his state of life as a purely temporary one and begins to plan for a future based on his present environment. The planning need not have been very conscious – some individuals never consciously make plans – and ideas of a change of life later, by repatriation for instance, under a new regime need not have been abandoned; but some mental gesture of acceptance of current conditions must have been made. Where this is not done, as happens with those people whose minds remain wholly in the past, or with those who live an asocial life from day to day, then resettlement cannot be said ever to have taken place.[933]

According to Murphy, the resettlement process 'implies a pushing out of new roots, and an acceptance and nourishing of these roots by the new environment'.[934] Clearly, while some of the younger refugees did enter the resettlement phase before 1950, possibly an overwhelming majority did not begin to glimpse a future in Great Britain until the early 1950's. For many, this process took far longer.

John Brown summarised the two main reactions to their new lives in Britain, among Latvian refugees in Bedford. These approaches were also to be found among Lithuanian and Estonian communities. According to Brown, the first group:

> ...turned inwards towards their own people, their own kind, seeking security against past, present and future: brutal memories of war and personal loss, crowded conditions of communal living, the demands of coping in an alien land among people of an alien tongue.[935]

This reaction to life in Britain occurred among refugees of all ages and from all walks of life, but was more common among the older refugees, for whom displacement had disrupted a settled family life, and halted careers. For refugees in their thirties and older, starting afresh would prove to be more difficult than for younger refugees. For the former group, migration to Britain was accompanied by disorientation, disillusionment and despair, which deepened as the return myth weakened. The realisation that they may never see family and friends in the homeland again and would probably be unable to restart their careers and education began to sink in.

The disorientation and disillusionment of many of the refugees combined with the effects of experiences of war and displacement to produce a relatively high incidence of mental illness among Baltic refugees. According to a study carried out by H B M Murphy in 1952, the incidence of mental illness and suicide among the three Baltic nationalities, as with the other EVW communities since coming to Great Britain was far higher than the resident population.[936] The most common diagnoses among European refugees in 1949 included schizophrenia and depression.[937]   H B M Murphy recorded suicide statistics among the Latvian population, which were he stated, 'remarkably high'. Indeed Murphy's figures of 14 suicides (12 men, 2 women) among the Latvian community between October 1949 and September 1951, equalling 6.09 males and 2.56 females per ten thousand of the population 'merit the mournful claim to be the highest for any published data on a representative community'.[938]

In seeking to understand the higher rate of suicides and mental illness among the EVW populations, Murphy pointed to the characteristics of the DP population, which differentiated it even from other immigrant groups:

> The chief factor in refugee status which is responsible for an increased susceptibility to mental disorder cannot yet be said to have been defined, but there seem strong theoretical grounds for inculpating four interlocking factors, namely: (a) loss of homeland, where a feeling of homeland had previously existed; (b) experience of persecution, including physical injury and starvation; (c) cultural difficulty in adjusting to new conditions; (d) general social isolation.[939]

Murphy noted that the loss of family in resettlement for a majority of the EVWs was one of the most important factors in promoting mental health problems. Bülbring stated that it was not surprising that mental illness and especially, neurotic complaints, were more common among the refugees than in the English population, 'considering the hardships many of them have undergone, as a result of war, deportation, forced labour, P.O.W camps D.P. camps, separation from home, families and friends, uncertainty about their fate and long periods of more or less severe malnutrition. In addition, the insecurity of not having really settled, their homesickness and hope for return to their homeland, their anxiety about the future all aggravate mental strain'.[940]

Physical ailments were also common during the early years among many of the refugees, their health having been weakened by the long years of war and displacement. Bülbring noted a high incidence of tuberculosis among the EVW population.[941] A Latvian man in this study reported suffering from 'Galloping' TB[942] in 1949, and was obliged to spend a prolonged period in hospital.[943] Commentators of the period also reported an inclination to heavy drinking, particularly among older, single male EVWs.[944]

While many of the refugees suffered mental and physical problems during the first years of settlement, others had more positive experiences. Often this was due to an optimistic approach to settlement. This characteristic marked out the second group of Latvians, distinguished by Brown in his study of Bedford:

> Others looked outwards, impatient of the hostels and their ways, eager to explore the possibilities of the new country, to make their own way. These stronger spirits turned their minds to learning English, to seeking lodgings in town. Here, their task was long and painful, as it had been for the Poles.[945]

Younger refugees were more likely to adopt a positive approach to life in Britain. Most of them had still been in school or had just embarked on higher education or a career, and did not yet have families of their own. They had lost some of the most important years of their adult lives during the years of war and displacement and were keen to make up for lost time. In spite of difficulties such as ignorance of the English language and the shortage of accommodation, they were pleased at last to have found somewhere to settle, if only temporarily, so that they could begin to carve out new lives for themselves. Those who were able to send for dependants to join them also felt positive about the migration to Britain. For this group, arrival in Britain represented an 'opportunity to resume something resembling a normal life'.[946] A positive attitude towards settlement had a cumulative effect so that those refugees who adopted an optimistic outlook found it easier to adapt to life in Britain.

Brown's separation of Latvians into two groups is helpful, although it over-simplifies the heterogeneity of attitudes and experiences during the early years of settlement. Even young refugees who felt positive about resettlement reported difficulties settling in at first. They too, sought the security of the ethnic community, and at times, shied from taking constructive steps towards adaptation. The testimonies of Latvians, Lithuanians and Estonians who entered Britain, whilst in their early twenties is evidence of fluctuations in attitudes and feelings. Despite being pleased to come to Britain, one young Latvian reported feeling 'sick' during the early days of settlement,[947] while a young Estonian man noted that Estonian refugees were 'disorientated for quite a long time...'[948]:

> ...we felt rather traumatised... Most people felt you could write what three, four, five years off their lives. In fact, they were so cross with losing all your families and background...[949]

One of the factors which was of the utmost importance in shaping attitudes towards settlement was the relationship with the local population. The experiences of one young Lithuanian dependant shows how local attitudes, which she described as both unfriendly and ignorant, increased feelings of being a foreigner, and thereby heightened a sense of alienation.[950] She also explained the pressures to assimilate in the early years:

> By the locals you were to put it bluntly a bloody foreigner...so...you tried to make yourselves as English as possible, as quickly as possible. You were given no assistance to retain your identity at the beginning, whatsoever, simply because that was the Iron Curtain [and] there would be no return. Nobody knew any more about Lithuania as time went on... Nobody. Even [in] the schools the maps were Soviet Union full stop, you know and that was it.[951]

> ... you grew up [with] almost a kind of, almost a deep down hate inside you for...being alienated at the beginning.[952]

For this woman, feeling like a foreigner motivated her to make herself more English. For other refugees the opposite was true. Alienation made them feel ever more isolated and promoted withdrawal into the refugee community. For these refugees, feelings of alienation promoted resistance to integration, and heightened national identities and the desire to maintain ethnic cultures.

Although a large percentage of the refugees felt like foreigners and outsiders at the beginning, among many of the younger refugees, this feeling quickly dissipated as they settled in at work and within the local community. I asked one Latvian woman if she has ever felt like an outsider in Britain. She replied, 'Maybe at the beginning, but not really'.[953] Others, like the Lithuanian woman described above, did feel like 'foreigners', throughout their early years in Britain. The requirement that EVWs had to register with the police whenever they moved to a different locality certainly reinforced the fact that their formal status was as aliens. For some, this heightened their sense of being outsiders, often for many years, long after they had begun to feel at home in Great Britain. Registration also induced fear among some of the refugees that the information given may be used for repatriation purposes.

LATVIAN, LITHUANIAN AND ESTONIAN COMMUNITY STRUCTURES AND ACTIVITIES

During the first years in Britain, the new communities began to assess the spiritual, practical, financial and cultural needs of the new DPs. Latvian, Lithuanian and Estonian community structures developed rapidly, despite the continuing belief in return. Initially they were intended mainly for the purpose of helping the refugees through a temporary stay in Britain, to campaign for the restoration of independence and to provide support for DP populations in Germany who were unable to re-emigrate. As the years passed and return seemed an ever more elusive goal, more solid structures emerged, with long-term aims and objectives.

On 21 December 1947, Latvian refugees in Britain renewed the work of *Daugavas Vanagi (DVF)*, the Latvian Welfare organisation which had been established in a Belgium Prisoner-of-War Camp in 1945, calling it in English, the Latvian Welfare Fund. In 1950, the DVF purchased a property in London, 72. Queensborough Terrace, to be the British branch headquarters and the social centre for Latvians in the London area.[954] *Latvians in Great Britain*, a publication produced by 'The Latvian National Council in Great Britain' described the initial functions of the DVF:

> In the early years, a particular concern of the DVF was the plight of those of their countrymen in Germany and Austria who because of physical disability or old age or having large families were unable to emigrate. Support in the form of food, clothing and money was provided. Those with tuberculosis were sent medical supplies.[955]

In November 1949, 'The Latvian National Council in Great Britain' (*Latviešu nacionālā padome Lielbritanijā*), was established at the Latvian Legation in London as a representative body for Latvians in Great

Britain.[956]   The statutes of the Council accepted in November 1949 laid down the aims of the organisation: to represent the Latvians living in Great Britain, to care for their cultural and material well-being, and to work for the re-establishment of an independent state of Latvia.[957]   The work of the executive committee was divided into the following sections: administrative and financial, information, education, cultural, youth, legal and welfare.   The work undertaken and relative importance of each of these sections changed over the years to come.   Initially, the legal and welfare section were important, 'when Latvian immigrants had language difficulties, when they frequently had to deal with various British institutions and when the elderly and invalids often had serious financial problems'.[958]   The cultural, youth and education sections organised various social, educational and cultural activities during the first few years of the Council's existence, while the information section collated and passed on information to the British press and politicians about conditions in Latvia.[959]

The Association of Estonians in Great Britain (*Inglismaa Eeestlaste Ühing*) was founded in 1947 'to serve the interests in this country, both those resident from before the Second World War and those displaced by the war'.[960]

The Lithuanian Association in Great Britain (DBLS - *Didžiosios Britanijos Lietuvių Sajunga*) was also founded in 1947, on 2 July.[961]   The first DBLS AGM took place on 22/23 November at Great Cumberland Hall, near Marble Arch in London.[962]   During this meeting, the DBLS statutes 'accepted the World Lithuanian Charter and proclaimed this to be the Great Britain Lithuanians' declaration.[963]   At the second DBLS AGM in 1948, it was agreed that shares would be issued in order to buy necessary central premises in London, to act as a base for the Lithuanian community in Great Britain.   It was envisaged that central premises would house an office, library, club, newspaper editing and flats for employees and visitors to London.[964]   Lithuanian House Limited was formed in July 1950 by the central committee of DBLS to handle the community's financial affairs, and central premises were bought in October 1950 in Holland Park, London.[965]

Local branches of the Latvian, Lithuanian and Estonian organisations were established fairly rapidly in areas of Latvian, Lithuanian and Estonian communities.   The publication *Lithuanians in Bradford* noted that the Bradford branch of the 'Lithuanian Association in Great Britain' was founded in 1947.[966]   Other branches were quickly established in areas of Lithuanian community.   The DVF and the Association of Estonians in Britain also set up local groups in diverse areas of Britain during the early years. In addition to clubs in many areas of England, branches of the DVF were also set up at Armadale and Edinburgh in Scotland, and at Swansea in South Wales. In the early years, local branches of Latvian, Lithuanian and Estonian organisations were established not only in towns and cities, but also in hostels and camps, for example in agricultural or mining areas. Occupational groups and organisations were also established; for example, in 1950, the Group of Latvian Foresters in Great Britain was founded and the Doncaster Latvians' Coalminers Group was set up on 18 September 1948.[967] However, due to the wide geographical dispersion of Latvians, Lithuanians and Estonians in Great Britain, groups and clubs could not be established in all areas, and some Baltic refugees had to get by without the support of community structures, or cultural and social activities. For example, writing about Latvian community life in Scotland in 1948, one Latvian noted that only Latvians 'who lived and worked in Edinburgh and the surrounding area participated in the Latvian community life'.[968] Nevertheless, until the re-emigration of thousands of Latvians, Lithuanians and Estonians to the New World in the 1950's, large numbers of Baltic refugees were still housed in hostels and camps, where there were other members from their own nationality. In most cases, this prevented isolation in the absence of formal community structures.

The post-war Baltic refugees established community structures largely separate from pre-war Baltic communities in Britain, even in Scotland, where there were still significant communities of Lithuanians, who had migrated at the end of the nineteenth, and early twentieth century.[969] The pre and post-war communities were starkly different in many ways, and in some areas, conflicts arose. For example, the bulk of the members of pre-war communities had emigrated from the Russian Empire, not from independent Baltic States and apart from intellectuals and political émigrés, a majority had underdeveloped national identities. Many spoke Russian. Writing about the different waves of Lithuanian migration to Britain in the last century and a half, one Lithuanian discussed the relations between the post-war Lithuanian community and the pre-war Lithuanian communities:

> The end of the Second World War brought yet another wave of Lithuanians into the wider world, displaced persons (DPs) who were welcomed as labour. But when this group met with the established locals, there were many conflicts. Language for one, outlook for another and money too; they were all from the same nation but different. In some places there was acceptance and they lived happily. In other the conflict was too strong and

divergence increased. Eventually, as the older earlier generation died, the DPs took over and ran everything.[970]

The diplomatic representations of the three Baltic nations in London, which had been set up during the inter-war period of independence, continued to play a large role in supporting the Baltic exile communities in Britain and in Europe.[971] Even after the arrival of the first Baltic refugees in Britain, they continued to wield pressure on Allied governments, requesting greater support for Baltic DPs in Germany. The diplomatic representations campaigned vigorously in the first years after the war for the restoration of homeland independence, and letters were written to the Ministry of Labour requesting improvements in various aspects of the refugees' living and working conditions in Britain. [972] The aims of the refugees vis-à-vis the homelands were also fostered by the Baltic Council, established in 1947, to undertake campaigning work and promote political, social, economic and cultural ties between the Baltic countries and Britain.[973]

Newspapers were also published as voice-pieces of the Latvian, Lithuanian and Estonian communities in Great Britain. Community newspapers informed the diaspora not only of developments with the communities in Britain, but also of changes within the world-wide diaspora and perhaps most importantly of all, of events in the homelands.

The establishment of solid community structures and organisations provided stability and security for the refugees. A Latvian woman from Leeds described the importance of the Latvian community in the early years:

> It was a very strong community and at first it was really good for us because it was somewhere to go, somewhere to meet people… I missed Latvia very much when I first came here, very much for quite a long time and just to meet somebody Latvian, it was like sort of meeting a close relative really right at first, the first years and so it was nice to go, to meet to do something and to take part in something, various activities. That was quite important to start with.[974]

> It was sort of a little home from home, you know. Yes, there were people with similar feelings and you know, we were together and erm, sort of various activities, it helped a lot in those early years really. It was really good for me anyway…[975]

To a degree, solid community structures and organisations also partially fulfilled the gap left by loss of family, providing support and close friendship. One Latvian described the Latvian organisations as a 'big family', helping keep the Latvians together.[976]

Barry Stein noted the importance of the ethnic community among refugee populations, during the initial period of settlement:

> The ethnic community eases the shock of adjustment and transition for the refugee. It lessens the danger of social and personality disorganization, and it provides a group identity and a network of relationships, associations and institutions.[977]

Thus, the ethnic community allows the refugee to 'function' while at the same time, adjusting and adapting to a new life and culture. In this way, the ethnic community may in some respects aid adaptation, a fact which the British Government appeared to underestimate.

In addition to social functions, the activities of the organised community contributed to the fulfilment of the political and cultural responsibilities of exile. Initially, the Latvian, Lithuanian and Estonian communities in Great Britain were able to continue the cultural vibrancy displayed in the DP Camps, despite members working long hours in new jobs. Various social and cultural activities were organised in hostels, the camps and in the centres of Baltic community, aimed at keeping the identity and culture of the homeland alive, as well as helping the communities through difficult times. In some of the camps and hostels, insufficient recreational facilities and lack of communications with the locals prompted Baltic EVWs to organise their own cultural events, often in the same vein as those previously established in the DP Camps. It was in the Latvian, Lithuanian and Estonian clubs and associations that the exile culture and identity was further consolidated and enacted. The exile cultures of the DP camps were modified to suit the circumstances of life in Britain, and as news of the threats to Latvian, Lithuanian and Estonian cultures and identities in the homeland reached the diaspora, exile cultures and identities were adjusted to provided the greatest defence against the annihilation of the Baltic nations.

The communities organised most of the cultural and social events by themselves and felt that they were given no help or support at the beginning by the authorities in relation to cultural maintenance. One Lithuanian living in Nottingham reported that:

> Once we were here...there was no assistance whatsoever. At the beginning I only recall ...we were allowed to use school

halls for our concerts for a number of years and then the Saturday school for a while, and then I don't recall that any more, probably because people…did emigrate and numbers decreased.[978]

From a very early stage, among all three Baltic communities, song and dance formed an important part of cultures in exile, as they had earlier in the DP Camps. According to the publication *Latvians in Great Britain*:

> …in exile, song along with dance proves [proved] to be the strongest means of maintaining language and tradition and of instilling in both performer and listener alike an acute awareness of national identity.[979]

The publication continued:

> After arrival in Britain, Latvians immediately established choirs. Men far outnumbered women, and those living in agricultural hostels and other close communities soon formed male voice ensembles. A programme of a major Latvian event in 1949 shows the participation of five mixed choirs and seventeen male voice choirs and ensembles.[980]

Social and cultural activities were organised all over Britain in the first few years – in the camps, hostels and community association branches, for community members of all ages, including the youth. The organisation of sports activities was particularly popular. Activities had both social and cultural functions. For example, Lithuanian scouting[981], which was begun in Britain in 1947, combined a mixture of social and cultural activities for Lithuanian children.[982] Other cultural activities included a thriving book trade among the Latvian community and weekend language schools for children, for the purpose of teaching basic Latvian, Lithuanian and Estonian education and language to the younger generation. The maintenance of language among the first generation and its transmission to younger generations was seen as a vital defence against Russification in the homeland and assimilation in Britain.

Annual national days and festivals were celebrated and commemorated, including the new days begun in exile, for example Deportation Day. In exile in Great Britain, the anniversaries of Latvian, Lithuanian and Estonian independence became particularly important, a trend which had begun in the DP camps of Germany.[983] While the commemoration of this day had been purely a celebratory event in the independent homelands, in exile, these occasions were tinged with anger and sadness. Speeches were given in hostels, camps and centres of Baltic community up and down Britain. For example, thirty years after the establishment of Latvia's independence in 1918, on 18 November 1948, a speech was given by Adolfs Perkons at an agricultural camp in Wainhouse Corner in Devon.[984] The speech stressed the significance of 18 November when thoughts turned 'to the years spent working and building their home country', but in 1948, 'only God' knew when they would be able to return. Perkons then gave a short overview of the history of Latvia and its people and the maintenance of Latvian culture - their folk songs, folklore and applied arts - despite aggression by neighbouring powers. He concluded by stating that Latvians in Great Britain were lucky to be able to celebrate this thirtieth anniversary in a free country, and that the Latvian nation trusted that stand of the Western Powers, who did 'not recognise the annexation of the Baltic States'.[985] Speeches in camps, hostels and clubs all over Britain mirrored these themes, as did commemorations of Lithuanian and Estonian independence.

During the first few years, the cultural and social life of the Baltic communities was particularly rich. Although some of the refugees were keen to save as much money as possible and therefore restricted their social activities, many of the refugees had a full social life in the early years, despite working long hours. One Estonian reported that he went out every night; others socialised at weekends. Solid community structures and vibrant cultural and social activities also meant that the communities were able to operate in a kind of 'cell'[986] outside work, precluding the need for socialising within the British community. Nevertheless, we have shown already that some of the refugees, particularly younger, single EVWs also socialised with English people and other nationalities.[987]

As in the DP Camps, religion played an important role among the exile communities. In a rare example of the British government supporting the EVWs cultural needs, the EVW schemes contained provisions for the spiritual welfare of the refugees. The zonal instruction for Westward Ho! specified that arrangements would be made 'with the National Hostels Corporation to safeguard the spiritual welfare of D.P.'s in Great Britain by sending D.P. pastors and priests to British camps'.[988] With this arrangement, priests and pastors representing the different religious denominations of the three nationalities were able to come from the DP Camps to Great Britain, to care for the spiritual needs of the refugees. For example, on 28 April 1948, the IRO reported that a Latvian Archbishop who was a DP left the British Zone of Germany to come to Great Britain in order 'to care for the spiritual welfare of the EVWs employed in Great Britain'.[989] Due to the dispersion of the EVWs in Britain, church representatives usually served a large area, covering different parishes and camps. Even before the implementation of these arrangements, Lutheran clergyman Roberts Slokenbergs, had been one of the very first post-war Latvian refugees to enter Britain, and became pastor of the London Latvian Evangelical Lutheran Church congregation, founded in October 1945.[990] In 1949, Latvian Lutherans held their first annual synod, and Latvian services started to take place all over Britain.[991] For example, in Edinburgh, the Latvian Evangelical Lutheran Church held services from July 1948. Catholic leaders also travelled to Britain to care for Lithuanian and Latvian Catholics, and Estonian Lutheran communities were also provided for. The Lithuanian community in Great Britain was granted permission to hold Lithuanian church services in Catholic churches in many parts of Britain. In 1948, the Lithuanian community in Bradford appealed to Leeds Bishop John Poskitt to allow church services in Lithuanian.[992] Permission was granted and the first Lithuanian Roman Catholic service in St. Ann's Church, Bradford was conducted on 14 March 1948 by a Lithuanian priest Jonas Kuzmickis.[993]

During the early years of exile, religion served many functions. Church representatives and services provided the refugees not only with spiritual guidance, but also practical support. Latvian, Lithuanian and Estonian church services recreated an element of life in the homeland and enabled members of the communities to offer mutual support to one another in difficult times. Church services provided another place, in addition to the clubs and associations, where the communities could meet and socialise. For Lithuanian communities, Catholicism had composed an important element of Lithuanian national identities throughout the national independence period and before. The significance of Catholicism in relation to national identity grew further during the Soviet period, not only in the homeland where it was undergoing severe repression by the Soviet State, but also among exiles. Although the religio-national link had never been particularly strong in Latvia and Estonia, Lutheranism also grew significantly in importance among exiled Estonian and Latvian communities, and among homeland populations during the Soviet period. For all three communities, religion demarcated the communities not only from the British population, but also from the Soviet atheist State. In this way, religion acted as a marker of nationality and of identity. In exile, religion provided an opportunity for the use of the national language and for the continuation of national ceremonies and traditions. Religions in exile were vehicles for the maintenance of the transmission of national values and beliefs.   Church services also provided a forum for the commemoration of the loss of independence and for the expressions of hope for the restoration of independence.   Prayers were spoken for loved ones exiled in Germany, and for those who remained in the homelands, for liberation and also for the safe return home of all the refugees.

CONCLUDING COMMENTS: TOWARDS ASSIMILATION?

Levels of adjustment and adaptation by 1951

By 1951, adaptation to life in Britain remained sluggish for several reasons, including the large hostel population even by 1949 and the continued uncertainty of a long-term stay in Britain.   Adaptation only began to take place at a steady pace once the refugees had secured private accommodation and began to fend for themselves, for example, shopping, using public transport and generally looking after themselves, all of which necessitated learning English and conversing with the locals. Not surprisingly, adjustment was quickest among those refugees who were keen to leave the hostels and camps and make their own way in Britain. These were usually the refugees who adopted a positive outlook and wanted to make the most of the opportunities offered to them. This approach was most prevalent among the younger, single refugees.

The 'Regional Reports on Progress of the Assimilation of the European Volunteer Workers' revealed the authorities' assessment of the state of the East European EVW communities by February 1950, and the degree of assimilation already achieved.[994]   The North-western Region stated the following:

> Assimilation of EVWs proceeding slowly but surely.   Many EVWs however regard their present stay as a temporary expedient until they can return home or emigrate. The peasant class tend to keep to themselves and display no eagerness to learn English.

The report from the Northern Region also highlighted how the myth of return was perceived to be hindering 'absorption': 'Some EVWs are uncertain as to their future and this has a detrimental effect on their absorption into the British community'. According to the report from the East and West Riding: 'Assimilation will clearly be a long term process', while the Southern Region noted that:

Foreign Workers in private lodgings settle down most satisfactorily. Those in hostels where EVWs predominate tend to cling to their own national groups. A large proportion do not want to become assimilated as they look on their stay here as being temporary.

Areas where EVWs have been given entertainment or exhibitions on nationalistic lines and where there have been British audiences show the best results in assimilation. Success depends on local British residents who will take an interest and assist in a practical way and on EVWs who will co-operate.

The report from Scotland also suggested that: 'the settling down process is speediest where workers are dispersed as individuals'. The view that dispersal into private lodgings promoted quicker integration was echoed by the report from Wales:

Gradual but steady drift from hostels to private lodgings where there is a much greater opportunity and incentive to become assimilated, but provision of houses in which foreign workers can live with their own families will be a factor even more conducive to their integration.

Finally, the Midlands region stressed the link between age and the potential for integration:

Younger workers are much more likely to become integrated into the British community than older people who tend to remain aloof.[995]

One of the most important factors cited by the government as responsible for retarding adjustment, was the sluggish rate at which the refugees learnt English. When they first came to Britain, most of the Baltic refugees did not know the English language, and by 1950, progress remained slow. 'Not a word' was the reported knowledge of English of one Lithuanian woman when she first arrived in Britain, and although some of the refugees had undertaken lessons in the DP Camps, and knew some basic words and phrases, they formed a minority. [996] Opportunities for developing the language were limited among those living in hostels or in Baltic households. Even at work, learning English was not always easy. One woman who worked in a textile factory stated that despite the fact that there were only a few other Lithuanians working there, there were few possibilities to learn English with the 'machines going'[997], making it almost impossible to communicate above the noise. Regional accents also presented difficulties for EVWs struggling to learn English. One Estonian reported that he 'couldn't understand a word they were saying in Yorkshire'.[998] During the first few years, the Baltic refugees continued to use their homeland language in most spheres of life. The maintenance of a large hostel population even by 1949 meant that few needed to learn English. Even at the workplace, many found they could get by with only pigeon English.

The 'Report on an enquiry made by one of H.M. Inspectors of School during January, February and April 1949 into the teaching of English to foreign workers' commented on the acquisition of language skills in the spring of 1949:[999]

> Thousands of them [EVWs] know little or no English, and thousands more know only sufficient to do a little shopping, in spite of the fact that many have been eighteen months in this country. The European Voluntary workers[1000] were dispersed into employment after only a few days in holding camps, and although valiant efforts were made to teach them a little English before they took up employment, the time was much too short.[1001]

The report continued:

> It is difficult to organise English classes for foreigners who vary enormously in intelligence, educational background, age, and knowledge of English, and it is even more difficult to get them to attend the classes which are provided.[1002]

The report acknowledged that many of the refugees survived quite easily without English, particularly those residing in hostels:

> Most of them get along quite comfortably without much knowledge of English. They are provided with interpreters in most hostels, they are paid the same whether they speak English or not, on the whole people are very helpful in shops and on journeys, all the notices in the hostels that concern them are printed in their own language, they read their national newspapers in their own tongue, and they have usually a few compatriots in the hostel with whom they may converse.[1003]

As recommended by the Ministry of Labour, local authorities and various voluntary bodies had begun English classes. However, as Tannahill and the above report notes, they were neither very successful, nor well attended.[1004] There were various reasons for this response by the refugees. The first was that after a hard day's work at the factory or in the fields, most of the workers were simply too tired to attend a language class. Second, many of the teachers were not particularly skilled, and taught rather dull classes, often directly from a textbook. This was not a particularly suitable approach for exhausted workers. Third, and perhaps most importantly, the continuing belief in a temporary stay in Britain did not provide motivation to learn English. This last view was echoed in the report by the H M Inspector of Schools, which stated that:

> The vast majority [of EVWs] are quite convinced that a war with Russia is imminent and that when Russia has been duly vanquished they will be able to return to their own countries. A number of the women workers want to marry and settle here, but very few of the men envisage staying here permanently. Those who do not think they will be able to return to their own countries would like to emigrate again to America or Canada, S. Africa or Australia, where they could escape from the Control of Engagements Order and their own conditions of employment. This certainty that they will not be here for many years encourages them to look upon the learning of English as unimportant.[1005]

Thus, from the British Government's perspective, by 1951, the effects of the policy of assimilation were unclear. In some instances, assimilation policies had the unintended consequence of sparking resentment among the refugees. A Lithuanian woman, now living in Nottingham, recalls being asked by a priest to attend an English ladies group, but she ignored his request.[1006] Pressures to assimilate presented the refugees with a dual threat to national identities and cultures, both from Sovietization in the homeland and from the British government. This provided even greater motivation to maintain homeland cultures and identities. Stadulis noted that:

> The refugees themselves resent conspicuous efforts to assimilate them *en masse*, but once they feel that they are accepted for their individual (often synonymous with "national") qualities, they seem ready to give their best to the new community.[1007]

Tannahill summed up the difficulties facing the government, stating that the 'official policy of assimilation was placed to some extent, on the horns of a dilemma', since the desire for assimilation would develop only slowly, and without a desire, official encouragement 'was bound to fall on deaf ears'.[1008]

The lack of desire to assimilate or even to settle in Britain was instrumental in slowing the processes of adjustment and adaptation, among a majority of the refugee population. That half of the Baltic EVWs did not even want to remain in Britain, let alone adapt to the British way of life is evidenced by the large-scale emigration of the 1950's. Among the remainder, the heterogeneity of responses and attitudes towards settlement began to shape diverse, complex communities which varied significantly within different localities, clubs and from one individual to another.

As time passed, the complexity of refugee settlement patterns and processes became clearer, particularly with the immigration of colonial newcomers in the 1950's. In the late-1940's, the British Government's ideas about assimilation had been conceived in a country with no previous experience of a large-scale, organised immigration scheme of this kind. Experiences during the subsequent decades not only in Britain, but also in other countries, were to reveal the flaws in straight-line assimilation theories, and to change governmental and academic discourse about assimilation and the adaptation of refugees.

CHAPTER 7

Settling in? : The 1950's

The lifting of labour controls on 1 January 1951 marked a watershed for the Latvian community. The EVWs now had more choice in finding work and the small communities in hostels and camps began to break up. Furthermore, many thousands who were dissatisfied with their prospects in Britain and realised that there could be no early return home to Latvia, further emigrated in the early 1950's, principally to Canada. Of the 14,000 or so Latvian EVWs and their dependants who had arrived in Britain after the war, perhaps about 9000 remained.

(Jānis Andrups, 'A History of Latvians in Great Britain'[1009])

THE 1950'S MARKED THE EMERGENCE of a greater sense of permanency among Latvian, Lithuanian and Estonian communities in Great Britain. There were a number of important developments during this decade which transformed the communities. The lifting of labour controls in 1951 gave the refugees the freedom to take up employment of their own choice and to re-emigrate. Nearly half the members of the post-war Baltic refugee population in Great Britain chose to emigrate to the countries of the New World. Although the early 1950's were marked by continued disorientation and uncertainty about whether or not to settle in Britain, from the mid-fifties onwards, post re-emigration communities began to settle down to their new life in Britain. In general, the Baltic EVWs started to feel more at ease with their new home, and began to plan for the future. Many of the younger Baltic refugees formed relationships and married. They also started to have children, and by 1960, the second generation of Latvian, Lithuanian and Estonian children had become a sizeable group. Working lives were cemented and future careers were forged. As in the first few years, there were a wide variety of experiences among individuals, reflecting the heterogeneity of backgrounds of the original refugee population.

During the 1950's, homeland developments were pivotal to the evolution of the communities. Not only was the increasing intractability of Soviet rule over the homelands a stimuli to mass re-emigration to the New World, it also promoted the settling in of the communities in Britain. Furthermore, strategies of Soviet repression of Baltic cultures and identities influenced the character of cultures and identities in exile, to provide the greatest defence against annihilation.

Although Stalin's death in 1953 and the accession of Khrushchev to power brought some hope that the Soviet Union's grip on the Baltic nations would ease, events soon conspired to quash any optimism. Among Lithuanians the end of the Forest Brother's campaign to free Lithuania in 1954 was a turning point, while for all East European nationalities in Britain, the brutal crushing of the Hungarian Revolution in 1956 emphasised the brutality and tenacity of the Soviet regime.

During the 1950's, developments in the homelands not only threatened the Latvian, Lithuanian and Estonian nations, identities and cultures, they also transformed the economy and environment of the three Soviet republics. The influx of Russian immigrant labour to fulfil the manpower requirements of rapid industrial development led to decreases in the indigenous share of the population, most severely in Latvia and Estonian. In Latvia for example, the combination of Russian immigrant labour and the decrease in population as a result of war, displacement and deportations, brought the ethnic Latvian share of the population from 75.5 per cent in 1935, to 60 per cent in 1953.[1010] The impact of Soviet industrial expansion on the environment was enormous. Huge Soviet style industrial complexes and towering apartment blocks housing immigrant newcomers were constructed, shadowing clapboard cottages and largely European designed architecture, built on a human scale. These large-scale imposing structures were metaphors for the Soviet Union's hegemony over the

Baltic nations, and formed part of the homogenisation of the Soviet Republics.

In the area of culture, attempts to Russify Baltic cultures were uneven and varied across the three countries. Some areas of culture were left relatively untouched, while others were selected for severe repression. For example, a contrast can be drawn between religion, which was pinpointed for severe repression, and the Latvian, Lithuanian and Estonian languages, which retained official status. Other areas of suppression, included literature and the visual arts which were searched for any deviation from the official line of Soviet realism, and dissenting writers deported to labour camps, some to die in captivity. A measure of cultural liberalisation was introduced after 1956/57 as a result of Khrushchev's 'Thaw', and continued during the 1960's. However, liberalisation was measured in relation to the harsh Stalin years, and led to only incremental change. For example, A further example was that although Latvian texts reappeared in the late 1950's following fairly indiscriminate censorship and the almost wholesale destruction of Latvian literature under Stalin, they came with forewards, which gave advice and cautions on their reading.[1011]

It is unclear to what extent the refugees in Britain received accurate information about the level of repression of homeland culture. Academics in the West were unable to reflect upon the extent of the Russification of culture until the late 1980's and beyond, due to the inaccurate and patchy information received prior to the Gorbachev period. Comments from Baltic refugees who have visited the homeland since independence that they were surprised that so much Baltic culture had survived Sovietization, suggests that they were under the impression that Russification of culture was more extensive than it actually was in reality.

Importantly, it was the perceived risks to homeland cultures and identities which influenced their maintenance in exile. Myth or reality, news of developments in the homeland had far-reaching consequences for the diaspora. John Brown, for example, noted the effects of Soviet consolidation in Eastern Europe on the Latvian exiles of Bedford:

> As EVWs, Latvians had to work three years as indentured labourers before they were 'freed'. By this time, the early fifties, political relationships between East and West had deteriorated to a seemingly implacable condition of cold war. Soviet control of Eastern Europe had tightened and for the people of the Baltic States, integral parts of the Soviet Union, hopes for

freedom and independence had become hopelessly remote. It was time for the Latvians of Bedford to take stock, to face the bitter realisation that there was no way back, at lest not for a very long time. They would have to dig in where they were, carry on as best they could, or seek opportunities elsewhere, perhaps even further away from their own country.[1012]

THE LIFTING OF LABOUR CONTROLS

Employment restrictions were lifted in the early 1950's, enabling Latvians, Lithuanians and Estonians in Great Britain to seek employment of their own choice. Many of the refugees had already changed jobs from their original placement to another area approved by the Ministry of Labour. For example, many men had already moved from agricultural labour to work in textiles. A large number continued within these areas for several years; some have even remained in textiles throughout their whole lives. Others chose new career paths.

Some of the areas of work initially taken up by the EVWs proved to be more popular in the long term than others. In Tannahill's survey of the EVW communities in the mid 1950's, he noted the types of employment which they had left in particularly large numbers following the lifting of labour controls, and those original 'undermanned industries' which remained popular at least until the date of his study (1956).[1013] Tannahill observed that the most striking fact was the extent of the flight from agriculture, the beginnings of which had already begun to take place before 1950, as we have already seen.[1014] Large numbers also left coalmining, forestry, brickmaking and allied industries, hospitals and private domestic service.[1015] However, although coalmining experienced heavy wastage in the first two years until 1949, thereafter it was much less. Tannahill stated that on 30 June 1956, 'there were still 3,806 EVWs in the industry. High wages and the availability of colliery houses are obviously important'.[1016] The only original undermanned industry, which had experienced a rise in EVW employment by 1950 - the textile industry, also encountered a drop during the 1950's, but it was relatively small compared with any of the other original undermanned industries.[1017] Tannahill also noted that his sample survey suggested that the iron and steel industry 'probably still employs about as many as were first placed there'.[1018]

The drop in numbers can be accounted for partly by emigration, but also by a desire among the remaining EVWs to take up employment of their choice, usually posts with better prospects or higher wages. A small number, particularly the younger refugees began to take college courses or university degrees to improve their employment opportunities during the 1950's. For those starting families this was more difficult. One Latvian woman was able to study pharmacy at university with the help of her parents who had come to Britain as dependants. After first working as a nursing orderly, then in a hosiery firm, followed by a lace firm, as a result of her new qualifications, she was able to gain employment in a Boots pharmacy in Nottingham. This gave her career stability and good prospects. She worked in Boots for 37 years until she retired.[1019]

The scope of jobs taken up by Latvians, Lithuanians and Estonians in Britain during the 1950's was wide ranging. Jobs undertaken among Baltic refugees outside the original fields of employment, unearthed in the course of the present study included: bus driver; postman; the Merchant Navy; porter for a furniture shop; pharmacist; shop manager; hospital porter; salesman; kiln operator; cabinet maker; glassworks worker.[1020] A significant minority of the participants continued to work in various jobs in textiles for several years; some remained in this field for a substantial proportion or all of their working lives.[1021] A few of the refugees became self-employed as a route to social or economic betterment.[1022] Tannahill noted one or two cases of EVWs in partnership buying a small farm, and in towns some EVWs were able to open small foodstuffs shops to supply the needs of their fellow nationals.[1023] One young Latvian in Manchester opened a bookshop, which he combined with a selling agency for leather or wood 'objets d'art' made by other Latvians.[1024] One of the Latvians I interviewed earned a living by buying and renovating houses and selling them.[1025]

The choice of employment was often influenced by changes in individual circumstances during the 1950's, for example, getting married, moving to a new locality, buying a house, starting a family or having to care for elderly relatives. The decision to return to education, to take up a new career, or resume an old line of work from the days of the homeland, reflected the new sense of greater permanency among the post-emigration Baltic communities in Britain.

What is striking about the Baltic exiles in Britain, is that unlike those who emigrated to the USA or Canada, relatively few became professionals, such as lawyers, doctors, dentists, teachers or accountants. Some of the refugees did enter professional careers, for example, several Latvian refugees became university academics, and there are numerous other examples of Baltic refugees entering high-status white-collar jobs.

However, in comparison to Baltic exiles in the countries of the New World, the numbers were small; an overwhelming majority were engaged in manual or relatively low-paid white-collar jobs. The disparity in terms of class and occupation between Britain and countries of the New World partly originates in the DPs decision to come to Britain, or wait for the opportunity to go to America, Canada or Australia. Some DPs were unhappy with the opportunities offered by Britain and perceived that greater educational and career prospects existed elsewhere. Among those who did decide to migrate to Britain, the restrictions of the initial labour contract hampered the fulfilment of education and training opportunities among younger refugees. Once the initial labour contract had ended it was much more difficult to start new careers. By this time, many had family and financial responsibilities, and possibly felt that it was too late to begin afresh.

RE-EMIGRATION TO THE NEW WORLD

A third reason for the smaller number of professionals in Britain, was that most of the educated and possibly, more enterprising EVWs in Britain re-emigrated to countries of the New World, following the lifting of labour controls in 1951. A higher proportion of Lithuanians re-emigrated to the USA or Canada, since many had connections with the earlier wave of immigrants who had left the homeland in the late nineteenth and early twentieth century.[1026] But, as just emphasised many of the Latvian, Lithuanian and Estonian men and women who re-emigrated were professionals and educated people who were frustrated with the lack of opportunities to further their careers in Great Britain. According to one Latvian I interviewed, large-scale migration to Canada took place among Latvians 'because Britain wasn't interested in the intellectual, just the muscle power', and 'because the laws were different'[1027], enabling young Latvians to pursue educational and career opportunities of their choice. Re-emigration left many centres of Latvian, Lithuanian and Estonian community depleted which affected cultural and social organisations. For example, the publication *Latvians in Great Britain* noted that re-emigration forced many of the smaller Latvian choirs and ensembles out of existence.[1028] A Latvian echoed this, stating that Latvian 'society would have been much richer, if we hadn't lost that many'.[1029] The post-war Lithuanian community in Manchester was apparently halved by re-emigration.[1030] A member of the Manchester Lithuanian community explained: 'Again it's the standard of living. People used to say that there were more opportunities over there'.[1031] Australia became an increasingly popular destination because at that time 'it was Assisted Passages even. You could go for ten pounds'.[1032] While larger areas of Latvian, Lithuanian and Estonian community, such as Bradford, Leeds or Manchester survived re-emigration and retained vitality, smaller areas of Baltic population were weakened. In particular, the smaller communities in Scotland and Wales were hit particularly severely by re-emigration, although community structures in and around the capital cities, Edinburgh and Swansea survived. Re-emigration coincided with the closure of many hostels, and left some of the Baltic refugees isolated.

The precise numbers re-emigrating are not known. According to Kay and Miles, a quarter of the total number of EVWs recruited, left Britain during the 1950's, although they do not provide a reference for their information. [1033] The communities themselves are equally vague. Latvians in Great Britain state that 'several thousand Latvians re-emigrated' during the early fifties[1034], and Latvia and Latvians state that 'a large number went on to other countries, mainly Canada and Australia'.[1035] In Tannahill's sample, 48 per cent of Lithuanians emigrated, 44 per cent of Estonians and 23 per cent of Latvians.[1036] The larger number of Lithuanians emigrating was accounted for by the large Lithuanian populations already residing in America and Canada.

Another reason for emigration to the New World was that in the early days it was perceived that unlike in Britain, in the New World 'various substantial communities could continue to exist within the State (enjoying facilities such as the provision of books in their own language in the public libraries), and the immigrant could soon forget that he was a "foreigner"'[1037] The EVWs experiences during their first years in Britain had made them very aware of their status as aliens, and as foreigners. Stories about the immense possibilities for career advancement and the cultural vibrancy of minority groups, emanating from immigrants already in the New World, reinforced images of the freedoms and riches to be enjoyed in these lands. Undoubtedly, the British government's zeal for assimilation was also a factor in the re-emigration of thousands of Baltic EVWs to the New World. Nevertheless, as communities began to settle and feel more comfortable in Britain, and as the government plans for assimilation of the EVWs were put on a back-burner due to the increasing numbers of colonial immigrants, the numbers emigrating dropped off.

Among the emigrants, re-emigration signalled an acknowledgement that return to the homeland would not be imminent. Many of the Baltic refugees had come to Britain because it was nearer home; re-emigration to the New World meant that return would be even more difficult. Re-emigration undoubtedly had a psychological effect on the communities left in Great Britain; the fact that so many of their countrymen had given up hope for imminent return inevitably influenced their outlook. However, one can also argue that those who remained in Britain did so because they maintained a belief in return; again, there was a wide variety of attitudes among individuals.

ADAPTING TO LIFE IN BRITAIN[1038]

During the 1950's, a gradual adjustment to life in Britain took place among a majority of the refugees. Among those who remained in Britain, the large-scale move into private accommodation and the lifting of employment restrictions were followed by the beginnings of widespread adaptation to life in Britain. The speed and extent of this process varied among individuals, and was dependent upon many factors. Resistance to putting down roots, apparent during the first few years decreased, as the refugees realised they were not returning imminently. Adaptation did not mean the abandonment of homeland cultures and identities however. For most refugees, gradual adjustment to British culture and society occurred alongside the continued and often vigorous, maintenance of homeland cultures and identities.

How were the very different cultures of the homeland and Great Britain reconciled during the early years?

Vida, a Lithuanian child dependant described adaptation to British culture among her family. She had come to Britain with her mother and brother to join her father, an EVW, in 1948. The family was thus an all Lithuanian family unit:

> I would say it has taken us near enough to gradually adopt English customs, near enough to about, after about five years…[1039]

She cited the example of food as an illustration:

> I recall various foods that we used to have as a child and the strange thing is, I remember those food very well, when erm, because we stopped after a five year gap, you know, you sort of take in the foods of the country you live in. We had some Lithuanian youngsters at our camp last year and they were still eating the same sort of soups that I recall we used to eat years and years ago, when we first came to England, sort of…white carrot soups, milky carrot soups…and also things made with

flour, just simply little dumplings things and so on that we used to have a lot of. I recall all that type of food which we gradually now keep on just special occasions maybe festive occasions.[1040]

The example of food, as an element of the homeland culture, reveals the difficulty of maintaining the homeland culture in the different circumstances of life in Britain, especially during the rationing years, immediately after the end of the war. Study of food or cuisine also shows how cultural elements were adapted and acquired a different significance in exile.

Although it was considerably easier to maintain the homeland cuisine in Britain than it had been in the DP camps (which provided barely enough calories for the refugees, let alone the opportunity to cook traditional recipes, except on the rarest occasion), nevertheless, in the post-war conditions of Britain, many of the ingredients required to cook traditional cuisine were difficult to obtain in many areas, and as importantly, often expensive. However, because a large percentage of the Latvian, Lithuanian and Estonian diets in the homeland were based on staple foodstuffs such as potatoes, grains and dairy products, many of the refugees were able to cook modified versions of daily homeland recipes, once they had moved into private accommodation. As with some of the other aspects of Baltic homeland cultures, food attained significance in exile in Britain, previously absent in the homeland. This was partly due to the many years of war and displacement, and even in the hostels in Britain, when the refugees had lived largely without homeland cuisine. Although national cuisine was threatened by British culture, it was not an aspect of Baltic cultures perceived as being particularly endangered by Sovietization, unlike religion, language and folk traditions. Furthermore, food had never been an important aspect of national revivals in the late-nineteenth century. Thus, the significance of cuisine as an element of national identity and culture became most marked when consumed at a religious or national celebration. For example, among Lithuanians, the twelve-course meal eaten on Christmas Eve, called *Kučios* had symbolism beyond its purely religious meaning. On occasions such as this, food became an integral part of expressions of national identity, in a way that had not attained the same symbolic meaning in the independent homelands.

While the refugees tried to improve their English, they also maintained the language of the homeland. The significance of language as arguably the most important marker of identity was consolidated during the 1950's, as the refugees perceived it to be threatened by the increasing teaching of Russian language in schools in the homeland.

Literature, folk songs, dance and folk arts and crafts were also vital elements of language maintenance. Among both the diaspora and in the homeland, the symbolic significance of national literature was heightened as repression of national writers got under way. Religion also continued to play an important role in Baltic exile cultures, particularly among Lithuanians. Here again, Soviet oppression of Catholicism in the homeland served to strengthen the religio-national bond.

As the example of religion suggests, as Soviet repression of culture selected particular elements of culture for eradication and weakening in the homeland, exile cultures were modified and certain elements highlighted in order to provide the greatest defence against the homogenising effects of Sovietization. The possibility of assimilation into British culture was not perceived as a comparable threat for several reasons. First, relative cultural freedom meant that resistance to 'becoming British', did not meet with the same response from the authorities, as did resistance to accepting certain traits of 'Soviet man' (*Homo Sovieticus*), for example, through continued religious observance. Second, assimilation of Baltic refugees in Britain, did not pose the same threat to the nation as did Sovietization. It became increasingly accepted among the communities that while maintenance of homeland cultures and identities remained a duty of exile, this did not preclude adaptation to life in Britain. As early as 1949, the Lithuanian Charter had stipulated that: 'A Lithuanian is loyal to his country of residence'.[1041] Thus, the idea of government officials in the 1940's and 1950's, that the strength of community structures and activities was a significant factor hindering plans for the integration and assimilation of the EVWs, was not necessarily true for all the refugees. For many refugees, the community provided security and a forum for the expression of national identity, while at the same time, they continued to adapt to British life outside the community.[1042] Some of the refugees used the community only temporarily to ease transition, while others maintained active participation throughout the 1950's, despite busy family and personal lives.

A Soviet building in Riga built in the 1950's and traditional Latvian buildings in front.

Of course, for some refugees, immersion in the homeland community was a way to avoid adjustment, and they continued to resist adaptation to life in Britain. This was particularly common among older refugees, although disorientation remained evident among some of the younger refugees particularly during the first half of the decade. The problems suffered by some of the EVWs when they first arrived in Britain, including health problems and feelings of isolation persisted. One Estonian noted that the refugees were 'disorientated for quite a long time', until the economic struggle and the building of family life took over from the mid-fifties onwards.[1043] John Brown noted that for some of the older Latvian refugees in Bedford, the burden of realisation of the consequences for them, of the Soviet Union's tightening grip on the homeland in the early fifties, was 'too great': 'Several committed suicide. Others were broken in mind or retreated permanently from reality'. 'Some became alcoholics'.[1044]

HOUSE BUYING IN THE 1950's

After working for several years, the Baltic refugees were able to save enough money to buy houses, a symbolic act, revealing the refugees' acceptance of a long term stay in Britain. Saving up for a house was one of the primary goals of the young refugees and they lived frugally for years in order to be able to purchase their own properties. In the homelands, renting had been virtually unknown, and the overwhelming majority of adult residents were house-owners. Often, young families had lived with elderly relatives on the farmstead, and took over the running of the farm when their parents became elderly. When the parents died, the property was then passed down, usually to the eldest son. Ownership of a house was thus regarded as a necessary first step towards creating a stable life in Britain. One Lithuanian woman joked that another reason the Lithuanian families had to buy houses was because, living two or three families together in rented accommodation, they were 'falling out'.[1045] Overtime and part-time jobs, combined with thrift were the means by which Baltic refugees saved money for house-purchase.[1046] Few were able to buy their own houses individually by this stage however. During the 1950's, couples or groups of young men bought houses together. Many couples were keen to work hard to buy a house before planning for a family. The comparatively low prices and plentiful supply of houses in the textile towns of the north proved to be particularly popular to Baltic refugees.[1047] Tannahill wrote that:

> The buying started in the North where the houses were cheaper. Sometimes a group bought one of the large old-fashioned houses; more often, a married couple selected a small terraced house, which might even be scheduled for demolition in a few years. But before long houses were being bought in the Midlands and in London too.[1048]

By the mid-1950's, some EVWs began to qualify for Council Houses or N.C.B. houses.[1049] Some of the EVWs moved to New Towns, particularly Corby, where Development Corporation houses were relatively easy to acquire and employment was plentiful.[1050] Different local authorities had varying rules regarding the allocation of Council housing: while some required at least an application for naturalisation, others such as Bradford did not.[1051] By 1956, a majority of the married and many of the single EVWs owned their own house.[1052]

Some of the EVWs chose to stay in the remaining hostels, although many had closed their doors by the mid-1950's. Tannahill notes that by mid-1956 the EVW hostel population of 50,000 in January 1949 (includes all EVW nationalities), had been reduced to about 3,000.[1053] Most of the remaining EVW hostel residents were over 40, and were either single or had left behind families in the homeland.[1054] Some EVWs left the hostels for life in the towns but later returned. Tannahill noted that, '...many of the residents are happy enough, but inevitably their lives must lack something, and this is reflected in the tendency to excessive drinking, particularly by those who have lost all contact with their families'.[1055]

FAMILY LIFE IN THE 1950's

The creation and consolidation of family life was another way that the Baltic refugees began to settle in Britain. By 1960, a sizeable second generation of Latvians, Lithuanians and Estonians had formed. Many same nationality marriages took place during the 1950's, and men who were forced to look beyond their own nationality for a marriage partner also began marrying during this decade. According to statistics cited by Tannahill, in the Bradford area from 1951-55, British wives headed the table of brides for Lithuanian men and took second place to the 'home nationality' for Latvians and Estonians.[1056] A Lithuanian woman reported that in Manchester, the most popular nationalities of brides among Lithuanian men were Italians, British and Germans.[1057] The popularity of Italian women among Lithuanian men may be partly due to a shared Catholic religion. Few Latvian and Estonian men married Italian women. Most of the men and women whom I interviewed could state numerous cases of Latvian, Lithuanian or Estonian men marrying outside their nationality, but few could cite any Baltic women marrying outside their nationality.[1058] Due to the disparity in numbers of men and women who came to Britain, most Baltic women were able to marry within their nationality.

Marriage within the same nationality offered refugees the opportunity to recreate family/household traditions from the homeland, as far as possible in the conditions of Britain. These traditions included national cuisine, birth, wedding and funeral customs, the transmission of values through the generations and gender relations within the family. Maintenance of culture within intermarriages was more difficult. Tannahill cited clashing cultures as one reason for the failure of marriages between Baltic men and British women. He noted that cultural and class differences were often to blame, particularly differing gender roles among British and Baltic women. A Latvian interviewed by

Tannahill placed the blame for failure on the British side on two grounds.[1059] First, 'British girls were too independent to accept the husband as master of the house'.[1060] Second, the 'British girls met by EVWs at dances and elsewhere were sometimes of rather poor upbringing who had little sympathy with the different backgrounds of their husbands'.[1061] A Lithuanian apportioned the blame equally, citing three pitfalls of mixed marriages: a tendency for the British wife to pay insufficient attention to cooking; a tendency for the EVW man to drink excessively; finally, the difficulties of different religions.[1062]

Large numbers of Baltic men did not marry at all, and remained single. Tannahill noted that the failure of some unions with British girls tended to make some of the remaining single men wary of contracting such a union hastily.[1063] Other men may have felt too old to marry and start families. Other men had left wives in the homeland or had lost them during the years of war, occupation and displacement. While carrying out this study, there have been incidental remarks about men and women who were married more than once, having left behind a spouse in the homeland. Unable to contact, and often not even knowing if they were alive, some of the refugees decided to remarry once in Britain.

During the 1950's, communication with relatives in the homeland improved slightly. After Stalin's death, some refugees began writing to relatives and friends for the first time, although they were still cautious.[1064] Furthermore, the Krushchev 'Thaw' starting from 1956/57 led to some concessions regarding the granting of exit visas enabling relatives to join family members abroad. As a result of talks between the British Foreign Secretary and Khrushchev and Gromyko[1065], followed up by the application of pressure throughout 1959, Khrushchev agreed that a number of relatives from the Baltic States and other Eastern European countries would be able to join families in Britain. Foreign Office files contain lists of all those who submitted the necessary applications 'to the appropriate Soviet authorities for permission to leave the Soviet Union for temporary or permanent residence with relatives in the UK, Australia, New Zealand and South Africa'. All told, 133 applications were made to come to the UK, of which 64 were residents of the Baltic States. On 13 May 1959, Soviet exit visas were granted to a number of Baltic residents, mainly the elderly to join their relatives in the UK.[1066]

THE DEVELOPMENT OF THE BALTIC COMMUNITIES IN THE 1950'S

During the 1950's, Baltic community structures and organisations continued to develop, despite the severe depletion of numbers by emigration. The communities were now financially more prosperous, and able to start buying properties for Latvian, Lithuanian and Estonian clubs and headquarters. Clubs and properties were purchased in the centres of Baltic community. In 1955, the Lithuanian Association in Great Britain purchased Headley Park, known as *Sodyba*, as a holiday/retirement home for the Lithuanian community, near Bordon in Hampshire.[1067] Headley Park was first named *Prieglauda – Vasarvietė*, a fairly literal translation of its functions, broadly meaning retirement home and health resort, but in 1956, its name was changed to *Sodyba*, translated as 'farmstead'. The new metaphoric name reflected the intended character of Headley Park, which aimed to recreate aspects of the Lithuanian farmstead, in effect to reconstruct home both for retired Lithuanians and Lithuanian holidaymakers. *Sodyba* quickly earned its name, growing typical farmstead produce and rearing animals found on the farmstead. Sodyba also ran a fishing club and a rifle club. It not only provided a home for elderly Lithuanian refugees, but was also a centre where various annual youth and cultural events took place.

New premises were also bought for Lithuanian House Limited. In 1953, the Latvian National Council began to lease Nieuport House in Almeley, Herefordshire 'for use as an old people's home and as a venue for children's summer camps'.[1068] During the same year, the London Latvian Evangelical Lutheran Church started to lease Rowfant House, near Crawley in Sussex for similar reasons. Both properties were later purchased by the lessees.[1069]

Throughout the 1950's, the differing size of the three communities was apparent in the number of branch organisations, clubs, and community facilities. While the Latvian community was able to acquire many sizeable properties to cater for its exiles, the far smaller Estonian community purchased far fewer properties. The number of properties owned by the Lithuanian community also reflected its position as the middle in size of the three communities.

Compared with later years, the local branches of the Latvians, Lithuanian and Estonian community organisations were reasonably active in the 1950's, and a relatively large percentage of the community participated. However, there was some decline in participation over the course of the decade.

The vitality of community organisation was affected by two main trends in the internal migration of Baltic refugees during the 1950's. The first was a continuation of the move towards centres of Baltic community, so that to some extent, the community life in these areas renewed some of their pre-re-emigration vitality. The second trend was less prevalent; a general dispersal throughout the country of Latvians, Lithuanians and Estonians. This was primarily the result of intermarriage among men and the exploitation of employment opportunities outside areas of Baltic concentration.

Other developments within the communities also took place during the 1950's, which threatened the long-term future of many branches. The most important trend was the shift of focus of many of the refugees towards family life. In some ways the clubs benefited with this concentration on family life, since it meant the birth of a new generation of Latvians, Lithuanians and Estonians, which promoted some revitalisation of the communities. However, men were also marrying non-Baltic women in large numbers, and others were concentrating on work to build a good standard of living for their new and growing families. Thus, even by the mid-1950's, despite the continued development of community structures and organisations, the combination of re-emigration and the focus on family life meant that the levels of membership and attendance had already decreased substantially from 1950 levels. The *Lithuanian Youth News Sheet (LYNES)* noted the effects of re-emigration and the focus on family life on choirs, dance and sports groups: 'During 1947-1949 there were a large number of choirs, national dance, drama and sports groups. These groups formed and disintegrated and reformed again. In these first years it would not have been possible to ignore the problems of these groups'.[1070] 'Shortly after that period, emigration to distant lands drastically reduced the numbers. The remaining "activists" became active in pursuing outside interests, consequently distancing themselves from organised Lithuanian activity'. These trends also took place among most of the other EVW communities. Writing in 1954, Bülbring noted that, 'the membership of many local branches of the national organisations has gradually declined, partly because some members have re-emigrated, but there has also been a slow shift of interest among the refugees towards the new country. This is specially true where the refugees live in private accommodation in the midst of the local population'.[1071]

During the 1950's, political activities continued to focus upon attempts to restore Latvian, Lithuanian and Estonian independence, especially after Stalin's death when hopes were briefly revitalised. Links between the diaspora of different nations were strengthened in an attempt to increase pressure on western nations to restore independence. Links between the three Baltic communities and with other East European diaspora both within Britain and across the world were also forged. One result of this was the establishment of the Assembly of Captive European Nations (ACEN), in New York on 20 September 1954 by representatives of nine 'captive' countries – Albania, Bulgaria, Czechoslovakia, Estonia, Hungary, Latvia, Lithuania, Poland and Romania.[1072] This organisation sought to heighten pressure on western governments by joining forces with one another. The communities supported the attempts made by Baltic diasporas across the world to bring about the re-establishment of independence, for example, the formation of governments in exile. For example, BBC Monitor reported on 23 January 1953 that the Estonian Exile Government had been formed in Oslo.[1073] The communities in Britain kept up-to-date with homeland related news, primarily through community newspapers published in Britain, but also various newsletters, newspapers and reports, published abroad and by the diaspora and various organisations across the world. For example the 'Newsletter from Behind the Iron Curtain', published in Stockholm by the Estonian Information Centre, provided reports on communist activities in Eastern Europe.[1074] The libraries and clubs of the Latvian, Lithuanian and Estonian associations in Britain usually held copies of newspapers, newsletters and reports for the communities to read. Few publications came directly from the homeland and these were primarily propaganda, sometimes subtly disguised, although usually quite blatantly so. The three Baltic communities used all the channels at their disposal to urge the British government to take up their cause. In addition to pressure from diplomatic channels, the communities organised street protests and demonstrations and gave speeches within their community. Representatives from the Latvian, Lithuanian and Estonian associations in Britain also wrote letters to government officials. The Chairman of the Lithuanian Association in Great Britain, M. Bajorinas wrote to Prime Minister, Churchill on 4 November 1953. His letter contained the following message:

> It is the fervent hope of all Lithuanians that this great nation, following its centuries old traditions of freedom and defence against aggression, will in no circumstances recognise the annexation of Lithuania and other Baltic States by Soviet Russia,

and will not leave these unfortunate peoples in the clutches of the eternal enemy of humanity – Soviet Communism.

We all pray to the Almighty to grant you indomitable strength and continuous robust health in guiding this great nation into [a] brighter future.[1075]

Diplomatic pressure also continued. In 1954, the Latvian, Lithuanian and Estonian Ministers in England made appeals to the British Government to bring up the question of the Baltic States in the forthcoming conference of Foreign Ministers of Great Britain, France, the USA and the USSR in Berlin, on 25 January. Charles Zarine of the Latvian Legation wrote to Anthony Eden, Secretary of State, stressing that, 'all Latvians, wherever now living, are looking for the day when their country shall again be independent and free...'[1076]

Appeals were also stepped up prior to the visit of Marshal Bulganin[1077] and Nikita Khrushchev to the United Kingdom in 1956, to pressurise the British government to raise the issue of the Baltic States during their visit.[1078]

Cultural activities in the clubs continued in the same vein as had been begun in the late-1940's and included choir and dance groups, the celebration and commemoration of national and religious festivals, weekend language schools for second generation children, crafts and the preparation of the homeland cuisine.

CHANGING ATTITUDES OF BRITISH SOCIETY IN THE 1950's

Although when the EVWs entered Great Britain in the late-1940's, they were the largest organised group of labour migrants in Britain's history, trends in the 1950's served to conceal their prominence within Britain. One important factor leading to a growing acceptance of EVWs as members of British society was changing immigration trends during the 1950's. Beginning with the docking of Empire Windrush at Tilbury Docks, near London, in June 1948, thousands of immigrants from the Caribbean and Indian Sub-Continent began arriving in Britain over the next decade. The majority of colonial immigrants during the 1950's were from the British West Indies, and they settled in many of the industrial cities where Baltic and other East European populations resided, for example, Bradford and Leeds. The numbers of colonial immigrants rose year on year, reaching a peak in the 1950's of 46,000 in 1956.[1079] Numbers only significantly dropped temporarily in 1958 and

1959.[1080] As these new immigrants tried to find employment and accommodation, the focus of British society's attention shifted away from the East European groups, who were becoming increasingly invisible, towards the more numerous and visible colonial migrants. Greater public toleration of the Baltic refugees also increased by the deepening of the Cold War, which tended to heighten sympathy for their plight.

CONCLUDING COMMENTS

It was during the1950's that H B M Murphy's definition of 'resettlement' can be said to have taken place among the majority of the Baltic refugees.[1081] The communities of 1960 contrasted markedly with those in 1950, not only in terms of physical volume and composition, but also in relation to attitudes towards settlement and the sense of permanency felt among the refugees. The diminution of hopes for independence brought about by the failure of Krushchev's rule to bring any significant change to the political status of the Baltic States within the Soviet Union, was vital in producing acceptance of a long-term stay. During the 1950's, the Baltic communities in Britain began to focus on family and working lives, and already by 1960, a weakening of community activity could be discerned, despite the growth of a second generation. House buying and marriage outside the community meant that it became increasingly difficult for the refugees to return home at a moment's notice, in the event of independence. Re-emigration overseas also drew the refugees further away from their homeland.

One Estonian summed up the process of change among the Estonian community in Great Britain during the 1950's, trends which were also experienced by the Latvian and Lithuanian communities:

> Initially…in the fifties, early fifties, I think we tended to regard this as a very short term thing being in exile…

> In fact [we] got disorientated for quite a long time, but then gradually the economic struggle took over. You had to create your homes and support families…but initially political activity in the fifties, early fifties was quite active. Demonstrations and…petitions…

> But then from the mid-fifties onwards then there was mostly this rebuilding of the life abroad that took over.

So [during a] certain period, family and careers took over. Well, except [among] those near the Estonian houses they continued throughout where they had more Estonians congregated, so that's Bradford and Leicester, also London.

They continued in a pretty…sort of stereotype fashion.[1082]

The fairly dramatic changes to the Baltic communities during the 1950's laid the foundations of the communities for the subsequent three decades, when the rooting process begun in the fifties continued apace.

CHAPTER 8

Rooting: 1960-1985

Since the war I do not hear anything of my family. Now I feel like English. But when I go to social evenings with Latvians, I feel like Latvian again. My wife is Irish. My children are English. They all like it here. I would be very happy to go back to Latvia, just for holiday…but you would not get visa. You frightened to go. And sometimes I see people begin to think of home, they do not know where they are. I try to put it out of my mind.

Sometimes I think of myself, with big beard, walking in my own country. And no one recognises me, not even my own brother. Stranger in my own country… You don't hear of many people going back.[1083]

THESE ARE THE WORDS OF A LATVIAN MAN interviewed in Bedford in 1969 by John Brown. They reveal the huge changes undergone among many of the refugees in just two decades. Fifteen years later in 1984, a Latvian refugee interviewed by Bradford Heritage Recording Unit stated that she felt quite English, and that if Latvia became independent she would not return, because she felt too old to start again.[1084] She felt that maintenance of the Latvian language was really only for sentimental reasons and that the Latvian community in Great Britain would 'die out'. An Estonian man interviewed in the same year stated that although his nationality was Estonian, his loyalties were with England.[1085] These comments contrast sharply with notions surrounding the myth of return in the 1950's, and the responsibilities of exile.

Between 1960 and 1985, the Latvian, Lithuanian and Estonian populations in Great Britain rooted in Britain. Although the views of the Latvians and Estonians above are not necessarily representative of their communities, they do reflect the fact that by 1985, integration[1086] had occurred to a large extent among many individuals, and among the communities at large. This chapter will focus on five areas to illustrate the processes of rooting and integration: Family life; Working Lives; Citizenship; the Second and Third Generations; the Organised Community.

FAMILY LIFE 1960-1985

The continuation of Soviet control of the homeland stimulated the consolidation of family life in Britain between 1960 and 1985. In the 1960's, the youngest of the married refugees were in their thirties and forties and busy bringing up growing children. Family life was facilitated by the growing financial prosperity of the refugees, and the fact that almost all had bought their own houses. Some had even purchased their own cars. A few, primarily younger men, married for the first time during the 1960's, and began to have families, although large numbers also remained single.

Although there are few available statistics on the demography or marital patterns of Baltic refugees in Britain during this period, John Brown noted the family and age structure of Latvian refugees in Bedford, as of 1 June 1969. The population of 176 native-born Latvians (151 men and 25 women) in Bedford were all over the age of 40.[1087] Eighty-nine of them were single, including 4 women. The remaining 87 were married. Of these, 21 were married to Latvians (amounting to 84 per cent of Latvian women but only 14 per cent of Latvian men in Bedford) and 45 to other nationalities. Of the wives, 27 were English. Brown also noted the number of second generation Latvians in Bedford. The children of the first generation numbered 80; of whom 23 were of Latvian parentage and 57 of mixed marriages. All the children were under 20. Twenty-three of the families were childless, including 9 Latvian and 14 mixed marriages.[1088]

Some aspects of the situation in Bedford were fairly representative of the general Latvian community in Britain, most obviously the age of the first and second generation and the large number of mixed marriages and single men. As in Bedford, this study has also found that a significant minority of married couples remained childless. The Latvian community in Bedford was slightly different from some of the other areas of Latvian community however, primarily in the disproportionately high percentage of Latvian men to women. Although there was a significantly higher proportion of Latvian men to women among the community as a whole[1089], this characteristic was even more acute in Bedford due to the male-dominated brick industries in the town, which were the principal employers of EVWs in Bedford. Brown noted that in 1948, 98 per cent of the 300 Latvian EVWs in Bedford were employed in the brick industry.[1090] The very low population of Latvian woman in Bedford compared to some of the other areas of Latvian population may mean that the proportion of all-Latvian marriages as a percentage of the Bedford Latvian population was less than in other areas. The low number of women was also partly responsible for the particularly high number of single men in Bedford.

Similar observations could also be made in coalmining or steelworking towns and regions, which also employed large numbers of EVW men, for example Derby or Sheffield. In comparison, in textile areas, such as Rochdale, Bradford and Leeds, where large numbers of women were employed in textile factories, there existed a more equitable ratio (although still disproportionate) of men to women. These gender distributions and inequalities also existed among Lithuanian and Estonian refugees. The very low number of the latter in particular meant that there were only several areas (notably London, Leicester and Bradford), where both Estonian men and women existed in significant quantities to lead to a sizeable proportion of same nationality marriages. Of course, marriages to refugees of the same nationality outside one's own locality did occur.

Family life influenced the integration process in several ways. In his study of Latvians in Bedford, Brown found that homeland cultures and identities were most successfully maintained among same-nationality couples and that intermarriage had a detrimental effect on homeland cultural maintenance. Same nationality couples spoke the homeland language at home, cooked homeland cuisine regularly, and were more likely to maintain some of the norms, values and traditions of the homeland. In contrast, those who had married outside their nationality usually spoke English in the home, and rapidly embraced English culture, although this effect was dissipated if the man had married a woman of non-British background. This dichotomy, nevertheless, is overly simplistic. One inter-married Latvian, now living in Leeds, noted that being married to an English woman 'didn't really affect' his Latvian culture and identity, which he described as strong. He noted that his wife's encouragement was an important factor in this maintenance: 'My wife is very supportive'.[1091]

According to theories of refugee adaptation, single refugees who never married were less likely to integrate within the receiving society, and were more likely to suffer feelings of alienation, resulting in the separation or marginalization of the refugee. Single refugees, of whom almost all within the Baltic communities were men, found it more difficult to gain fluency in English due to the lack of English influences within the home. They also lacked the more general integrative influences of marriage to a non-Latvian, Lithuanian or Estonian, or from children. While separation means the maintenance of the homeland culture and immersion in the diasporic community to the exclusion of fully engaging with British society and culture, marginalization leads to exclusion and alienation from both the receiving society and the diasporic community. According to Berry, single refugees were particularly vulnerable to marginalization, which is accompanied by a good deal of individual confusion and stress: 'It is characterised by striking out against the larger society and by feelings of alienation, loss of identity....'[1092] Marginalized exiles lose 'cultural and psychological contact with both their traditional culture and the larger society'.[1093] Marginalization may have been most common among single men who did not participate in the diasporic community, often through geographical isolation.[1094] While carrying out the research for this study, I found little evidence of large numbers of marginalized refugees, other than one or two cases cited by a Social Worker in West Yorkshire.[1095] Some marginalized refugees may have had more specific problems, such as the one of mental illnesses described by H B M Murphy in Chapter Six. I would have found it difficult to encounter many marginalized refugees during my research, since by losing contact with both the homeland community and the receiving society, they also become extremely difficult for the researcher to find; thus, the numbers of marginalized refugees remain an enigma. Furthermore, as regards separation, although I came across a number of single refugees, who had become immersed in the homeland community, to the exclusion of fully engaging in British society, because of the small size of the communities, it was impossible for the refugees to avoid completely participation in British society. Few Baltic refugees in Britain thus became separated from British society in this way.

While families were growing in Britain, contact with family in the homeland remained minimal. Continued censorship meant that even among those who were not too scared to write, relatives on both sides had very little sense of what was really happening in the lives of loved ones. A Latvian man discussed the correspondence he had with his brother in Latvia: '...he was very cautious what he wrote. I were writing fairly, fairly openly, but then again I knew that if I wrote far too openly or gave any information away then....my brother would suffer...'[1096] Although a few refugees met relatives during homeland visits with *Intourist*[1097], many lived through the entire exile period not daring to attempt to contact lost relatives and not knowing whether they were dead or alive. To some extent, refugees with families of their own in Britain were able to turn their attention and thoughts to their own family, but single refugees had to find other ways of coping, perhaps by focusing on friends, hobbies, work or the organised community.

From the end of the 1970's onwards, the refugees began to approach retirement and grown-up children began to leave home, to pursue careers and to start families of their own. During the 1980's, a growing third generation transformed some of the original refugees into grandparents. By 1985, many of the refugees had small extended families, and were beginning to enjoy a financially secure retirement.

WORKING LIVES 1960-1985

The years 1960 to 1985 covered a large span of the refugees' working lives in Britain. By the 1960's, most of the refugees had become settled in their employment, having found a job, which suited them. Many refugees climbed the ladder of their chosen line of work, and were satisfied with their jobs. In the 1960's a sizeable minority remained in the original undermanned areas of employment, such as textiles. Brown noted that of the 176 Latvians who remained in Bedford in 1969, 62 still worked in the brickyards, five were self-employed, five working in trades they had before the war, but many had learnt new skills in 'several spheres of life'.[1098] According to Brown: 'In great part, their skills are practical, and no Latvians are employed in commercial enterprises'.[1099] Some of the refugees who continued to work in the original undermanned industries became the victims of structural change in the economic sphere, particularly the shrinking of Britain's manufacturing base.[1100] For example, some of those employed in textiles were required to find work elsewhere, when the textile industry suffered a downturn from the late-1960's onwards.[1101] Another discernible trend during this period was that as the refugees became more prosperous and confident, the numbers who became self-employed increased, although this route remained confined to a tiny minority. Although many of the creative

DPs who had come to Britain were unable to earn a living in their field, for example, artists, musicians and intellectuals, many were able to further pursuits in their spare time as a result of the increased stability in their lives.

Work was a major factor facilitating the integration of the refugees during the 1960's and 1970's. Not only did these employment experiences promote fluency in English and broaden the refugees' social sphere, British labour became increasingly tolerant towards the refugees. The influx of colonial immigrants in the 1960's, many of whom entered manual employment made the EVWs increasingly invisible. Levels of integration at work were such that many of the refugees reported 'feeling British' at work, and some even blamed their employment for weakening homeland language skills.

Retirement, a process beginning in the 1970's, had mixed consequences for the acculturation process. On the one hand, it provided the opportunity to reengage with the community and with one's past. Retired members of the communities had more time to participate in the community, and many reported an increase in their participation in community activities as a result of retirement. Some also talked about reminiscing about the homeland more regularly since retirement, which an Estonian participant attributed to old age rather than exile. When I asked him if he reminisced more following his retirement, he replied:

> Yes. That is so yes. I think, well I was thinking why it is so. I think it is to do with age. It's nothing to do with politics or being abroad, I don't think, or being in a foreign country. It's just that I think that's what old people do. They...withdraw, I think.

He agreed that he remembered his childhood in an idyllic, 'storybook' way, that 'You forget the nasty bits', and that 'this is part of the ageing process'.[1102] Not all the refugees reported an increase in reminiscence, however. I asked one Latvian woman if she reminisced more about Latvia as she got older. She replied: 'No, no. Not really. Not really. I've forgotten most of it now'.[1103]

On the other hand, for some of the ageing exiles, retirement also brought with it deterioration of health and particularly for some single men and widowed refugees, who were not very actively involved in the homeland community, feelings of isolation. For others who had failed to integrate fully into British society, retirement sometimes heralded even greater separation from British life and further weakening of the English language.

THE SECOND AND THIRD GENERATIONS

Although this study is primarily an examination of first generation Latvians, Lithuanians and Estonians, analysis of the development of the second and third generations can illuminate the processes of rooting and integration among the first generation.

The way in which first generation refugees decided to bring up their children (as Latvians, Lithuanians, Estonians, as British, or as half and half), reflected their belief in the permanency of exile, and the importance of their role as guardians of the homeland. Language, the cornerstone of Latvian, Lithuanian and Estonian identities was regarded by many exiles, as the most important element in the transmission of culture through the generations. The Lithuanian Charter, a set of guiding principles for the Lithuanian exile communities, adopted by DBLS and DBLJS, stressed its importance: 'The strongest bond of any national community is language. To a Lithuanian the Lithuanian language is his national pride'. The Charter also noted that: 'The family is the lifeblood of a nation.' 'A Lithuanian passes on to future generations the existence of the Lithuanian Nation that his parents preserved, so that we may live for ever-more.'[1104]

Many refugees were torn between their sense of duty as exiles and a firm belief that Britain was to be theirs and their children's permanent home. The dilemma about how to bring up one's children had emerged in the 1950's, but became particularly pressing as the children reached school age. Many parents felt that it was more of a priority that their children learn and understand English, so that they were not at a disadvantage at school, made friends easily and felt a sense of belonging in Britain. Some refugees did not even teach their children the homeland language because they feared 'it might prove a handicap to learning or getting on. Names were changed for the same reason'[1105] A Latvian woman, now living in Leeds, explained her dilemma about whether or not to bring up her children as Latvians. I asked her how she and her Latvian husband raised their two sons, and whether she taught them Latvian. She replied:

> Well...yes, to start with. When they were babies I did speak Latvian. That came naturally, that's how I felt, I could talk to them in Latvian. Then when they came to school age I

knew...they had to learn English. Besides they were mixing with English children...and somehow they picked up the [English] language.[1106]

When her children showed no interest in attending the Latvian weekend school, she did not force them to attend:

> I tried to take them to [the] Latvian [school]. There was Latvian Sunday school, Saturday school, they didn't like it and I thought, well why should I force them to do it if they don't like it? No they didn't really like it. I don't think it [Latvia] interests them.[1107]

She explained her motivation for not imposing the Latvian language on her children, and encouraging them to learn English:

> I mean they're living here and they should feel a home. They shouldn't be sort of half and half which is really...I don't think that's very good really, if you're, if you feel like that. I don't agree with it really.

Her decision not to force the Latvian culture upon her children, was based partly on a recognition that they would not be returning 'as long as there was a communist government', and reflected her belief that settlement in Britain would be permanent: 'I wanted them to feel a home here since we weren't going back I was going to help them to feel them to belong here, to belong somewhere. They have to have a home somewhere. And of course that did change my attitude as well...'[1108]

Some parents were keen for their children to learn the homeland language however, and went to great lengths to achieve this. Even among this group of parents, however, there was an acknowledgement that their children had to learn English, and they were aware of the difficult task of bringing their children up as Latvians, Lithuanians or Estonians within British society.

A Latvian man, now living in Leeds wanted his son to be brought up as a Latvian, but found that external influences made this feat almost impossible. I asked him whether he and his Latvian wife brought up their son, an only child, as Latvian or English. He replied:

> Oh, as a Latvian of course, yeah, yeah, but you know that parents' influence is not very much. They go to school. When they leave that high school, go to university. They are away in English society. Not much influence at all. Of course he is

speaking both languages yes. But that's all…I wanted him to go back to Latvia to live there but no, he thinks different.[1109]

Children from single nationality households were more likely than those from intermarried households to be raised as Latvians, Lithuanians or Estonians. That single nationality households usually spoke the homeland language at home aided this process. However, as the above comments show, external influences were great, and hindered many parents' wishes that their children maintain the Latvian, Lithuanian or Estonian culture and identity. Even though most pre-school children of single nationality parentage, learned the homeland language as their first language, when they reached school age, they became fluent in English fairly quickly, and homeland language skills weakened. By the time, the second generation left school, many had poor homeland language ability. The sons of the Latvian woman first mentioned in this section, lost most of their Latvian. One has 'sort of forgotten nearly completely', although the other still 'understands Latvian quite well'.[1110] Both are now married to English wives, speak English within the home and very rarely speak Latvian. Interestingly, the development of the second generation was an enormous influence on the integration of the first generation. For all-Latvian, Lithuanian or Estonian families, children introduced British influences into the household, and their fluency in English even aided English language skills among the first generation.

Even though many individuals were uncertain about how to bring up their children, there was initially no question about the duty of the organised community to transmit the homeland culture and identity to the second generation, a central part of the responsibility of exile. Transmission of the homeland identity and culture to the young was regarded as the only way that the diaspora, and thereby the best interests of the homeland, would survive. There were various ways that the organised communities attempted to do this. The transmission of the homeland language was catered for by weekend language schools, first set up in the 'fifties to provide lessons in the homeland language to children in areas of high Latvian, Lithuanian or Estonian concentration. An array of cultural activities was also organised, including folk dance groups, choirs and summer youth camps.

Despite the best efforts of the organised community, the influence of British society on the second generation became apparent from an early stage. The task of maintaining homeland culture and identity among the second generation was going to be a much more difficult task than maintenance among the first generation. In addition to weak language skills, many children took only a limited interest in homeland culture and participation in the community. Their interest waned further as they grew up.

Although until the 1960's, Latvian, Lithuanian or Estonian was the language used in community publications, speeches, events and AGM's, it was becoming apparent that if this were to continue without changes, many members of the second generation would in effect be excluded from the communities. However, despite the urgent need for change, the first generation retained what were regarded by the second generation as rather traditional views towards the organisation of activities, which did not address the differences between the first and second generation. As the children grew into teenagers many became alienated from the community. They found that the endless historical debates and political orientation of many of the clubs had little relevance for them and the stress on tradition tedious. But many activities in the sixties continued to require the use of the homeland language, despite the fact that only a small percentage of youngsters were fluent or even competent in Latvian, Lithuanian or Estonian. There were some efforts to address the needs of the second generation. For example, the Lithuanian community organised youth rallies, efforts were made to set up a language centre and a youth organisation, but these were largely unsuccessful.

The unwillingness of the first generation to address the needs of the second generation reflected the initially fixed and inflexible nature of exile cultures and identities, which remained virtually unchanged from the DP Camps. There was a conflict between the belief held by some of the first generation, that they were the authentic exiles who knew best how to carry forward homeland cultures and identities in settlement, and the growing acknowledgement that compromises would have to be made if the diaspora were to survive.

The failure of the first generation to retain the support and interest of the second generation into adulthood became increasingly evident during the 1970's when the majority left school and started employment, which often entailed a move away from the city or town they grew up. There was upward mobility among the second generation, with a significant percentage undertaking further and higher education courses, and later establishing professional careers. Some of those who moved to new cities became involved in the Latvian, Lithuanian or Estonian community there, but this occurred to any significant degree in London only, and even then among a minority. These developments contributed to the decline of the organised communities.

It was only when the second generation and some of those who had come to Britain as child dependants took matters in hand that positive steps towards meeting the needs of youth were taken. Furthermore, according to *LYNES*, the first generation agreed eventually that 'Lithuanian youth should organise its own activities, rather than being led by the older generation'.[1111] Beginning in the early 'seventies, Latvian, Lithuanian and Estonian youth (often in their twenties and thirties, but regarded by the older generation as 'youth'), began to develop youth groups, activities and publications, which aimed to lure second generation members back into community participation, and were designed to enable those with poor language skills to participate. Lithuanian youth were the most innovative and organised, inspired by the success of youth programmes and organisations in the USA and Canada. In January 1978, a newsletter for Lithuanian youth was published, first as the 'Lithuanian Youth News-Sheet' (later as *Saulė* and then *LYNES*), as a supplement to *Europas Lietuvis*, the newspaper of the British Lithuanian community. The first news-sheet was a small two-page edition. The newsletter was written both in English and Lithuanian, and intended to unify Lithuanian youth, to provide information about the community, stimulate interest and participation and to reach all members of the community, including isolated youth who did not live in an area of Lithuanian community.

As early as 1979, *LYNES* began to call for the establishment of a Lithuanian Youth Association in Great Britain and in 1981, the DBLJS (*Didžiosios Britanijos Lietuvių Jaunimo Sąjunga* - Lithuanian Youth Association in Great Britain) was established. The Constitution of the Lithuanian Youth Association in Great Britain accepted at the DBLJS General Meeting in January 1981, defined the purposes and aims of the organisation as; to promote and co-ordinate youth activities, arranging aid where necessary; to form groups to carry out the work of DBLJS; and to inform and influence the opinions of people of other nationalities about Lithuania and the Lithuanian nation.[1112] The Constitution further specified that: 'The languages of the DBLJS are Lithuanian and English', and that: 'The members of the DBLJS are young Lithuanian descendants, people of other nationalities who have married Lithuanian descendants, and those who closely involve themselves with Lithuanians'.[1113] The rules of the constitution reflected the need both to introduce English as a language of communication and to have relaxed membership criteria, in order to ensure the survival of Lithuanian associations beyond the first generation.

Among the Latvian and Estonian communities youth organisations and activities were also established. In 1973, *Tulevik* (meaning 'The Future') was founded 'with the aim of promoting Estonian youth's involvement in the Estonian social-cultural activities in this country and abroad'.[1114]   In addition to organising choirs and ensembles, the main event in the *Tulevik* calendar was the organisation of an annual summer camp. Among the Latvian community, there was a branch of 'The Association of Latvian Youth in Europe', and 'The Latvian National Council in Great Britain' also had a youth section, both of which organised a variety of social, cultural and educational activities.[1115]

One of the difficulties presented to the communities in the 1970's and early 1980's, was the wide range in age of the second generation, and the growing need to cater for an emergent third generation. In 1981, *LYNES* noted that the ages of the second generation range from 20 to 60.[1116] The need to put limits on the age range in order to establish a viable and focused organisation led the DBLJS to impose an age range on membership of between 16 and 35.[1117]

The new youth organisations co-ordinated a range of activities in Britain involving the second and emergent third generation, complementing those arranged by the first generation. Activities which were organised included various social events, sports, summer camps, and language classes. Some of the activities were new, while others were those previously organised by the first generation, and were taken over and run, often slightly differently, by the younger generations. For example, among the Lithuanian community, the Lithuanian scouts' movement which had been originally established during the early years of settlement, was particularly popular, and like many of the other organisations and activities, leadership passed gradually to the younger generations.

Other activities also proved successful among the younger generations. *Vakaronės*, a traditional social gathering of Lithuanians, described by *LYNES* as "a sit-in, a talk-in, and a drink-in"[1118], usually at a volunteer's house, often with a special cultural theme, for example, Lithuanian folk customs and mythology, became especially popular among second generation Lithuanians in London and Nottingham. *LYNES* noted in 1986 that *Vakaronės* were held every six weeks or so in London and that the Nottingham-based Lithuanians were planning their own *Vakaronės* season in 1987.[1119]   The December 1986 edition of *LYNES* noted that the theme of the next *Vakaronės* in January 1987 was 'the traditional Lithuanian folk wedding, its customs and traditions'.[1120]

London proved to be the centre of youth activity among all three communities. In 1985, *LYNES* noted the regional variations in Lithuanian youth activity:

> The Midlands may well contain the greatest potential number of young Didž-Brits, Lanarkshire may boast of the oldest legacy of UK based, Lithuanian activity and the North-west reminisce over its (comparatively) recent heydays - but it is London that has by far the greatest range of activity and resources available today.[1121]

Indeed, London was the centre of second generation activity among all three communities (to a lesser extent among Estonians), which maintained activity throughout and benefited from the in-migration of young professionals and those embarking on new careers. *LYNES* outlined the activities of Lithuanian youth in London in 1985.[1122] There was a football team called 'Lithuania Victoria FC', composed of about twenty members all from the Lithuanian Sports and Social Club in Victoria Park Road, London, E9. The team played in Lithuanian national colours. The dance group '*Lietuva*' originally formed in 1969 was still going strong, performing in Britain and in Lithuanian Folk Dance Festivals abroad.

Events and activities were also organised with other East European youth, for example at a special Baltic Evening in Swansea in 1983, dance groups of the Latvian, Lithuanian, Estonian and Ukrainian youth in Britain performed. *LYNES* reported that, 'strong links have now been formed with the youth of Estonia and Latvia in England. None of our communities is large and perhaps survival and the way forward for us lies in unity and support for each other'.[1123]

The second generation linked up with youth in other parts of the world for the purposes of Youth Congresses, Rallies and Festivals. At these events the younger generations were able to learn or improve their knowledge of the homeland language, learn about its history and culture and participate in various cultural activities. The youth organisations among the Lithuanian diaspora were particularly well-organised both in Britain and on an international level, partly due to the size of the diaspora in the countries of the New World. The international organisation of Lithuanian youth (DBLJS) organised a World Youth Congress, every 4-5 years, to 'bring together youth from all over the West'[1124], for example, in 1983 the fifth Lithuanian World Youth Congress was held in Chicago,[1125] and in the winter of 1987/88 the *VI Kongresas* was held in Australia.[1126] In many ways, the links with the global diaspora were more open among the second generation, than they had been with the first, due to the expansion of low cost travel.

The effects of growing up within British society manifested itself in the ethnic identities of the second generation, of whom a majority regarded themselves as British or half-and-half, with only a handful describing themselves as Latvians, Lithuanians or Estonians. In 1981, *LYNES* discussed the identities of second generation Lithuanians, and explained why the vast majority thought of themselves as British, even those born of all-Lithuanian parentage:

> Second generation Lithuanians are either born or have spent a large part of their childhood here in Britain and have been subject to the influences of this country in their most formative years. While the home maintains Lithuanian influences to a large degree[1127], for children educated and articulate in English, these are often moderated by the English way of life. Also the range of activities offered by the British social scene is vast, and the second generation often has to decide between British and Lithuanian attitudes on certain issues.[1128]

Given the small number of second generation Latvians, Lithuanians and Estonians in any given area, the overwhelming majority married a non-Latvian, Lithuanian or Estonian nationality. According to the author of the article, intermarriage weakened the maintenance of Lithuanian traditions: 'Loyalty to the home and parents will ensure that certain rites are observed and maintained to please parents, but as people gradually intermarry with the indigenous group they lose the traditions of their parents, so to all intents and purposes these "Anglo-Lithuanians" pass for British and indeed are British, with British passports, qualifications and points of reference. Given then that second and especially third generation Lithuanians can at will be British, they have the choice whether or not to maintain the Lithuanian connection'.[1129] The author then contrasted the maintenance of the 'Lithuanian connection' for first and second generation Lithuanians. For the first generation the link is maintained 'because it fulfils a need for them, whereas their descendants can actually choose whether or not they maintain these links'.[1130] Not all those among the second and third generations, who chose to maintain links with the communities came from same nationality parentage. A young Lithuanian explained his motivations for maintaining the 'Lithuanian connection' in 1983:

> Being of mixed parentage I have not grown up a Lithuanian speaker and my interest in Lithuanian affairs were non-existent

until 1982. Since then, I have gone from strength to strength in terms of community involvement: participating in most DBLJS activities and joining the '*Lietuva* ' dance group. In this time I have endeavoured to learn Lithuanian and can now hold, albeit basic conversations in Lithuanian. My basic motives are political and I would like to see greater involvement by young Lithuanians in this sphere.[1131]

A majority of third generation of Latvian, Lithuanian and Estonian refugees in Britain were thoroughly assimilated. Born and growing up during the 1970's and 1980's, the overwhelming majority with only one Latvian, Lithuanian or Estonian parent, they usually had little or no interest in or significant knowledge of the land where their grandparent(s) grew up. This was not surprising given that many were born to intermarried parents, the Latvian, Lithuanian or Estonian parent(s) themselves having poor Latvian, Lithuanian or Estonian language skills.

Many activities organised for the third generation were run by the second generation who had a relatively open outlook regarding cultural transmission, and were generally aware of the interests and needs of their children. *Lithuania*, a thick pamphlet, published by Lithuanian Scouting in Great Britain during the 1980's, reflected the changes across the generations. The authors explained that *Lithuania* was written in English due to the difficulties of the third generation learning the language of their grandparent(s), 'so that young people of Lithuanian descent [can] obtain an introduction to Lithuania and to their own family roots and are reminded that they, too, are true Lithuanians'.[1132]

By the early 1980's, despite attempts to arouse interest, second and third generation, participation remained low. As with the first generation, only a small hard core of second generation Latvians, Lithuanians and Estonians maintained active involvement in the communities and sought to carve out a solid future for the second generation. This characteristic among the Lithuanian community was highlighted by *LYNES* in 1981: 'Certain people few in number carry the load for many others.'[1133] A few regained interest as they entered their twenties, but many more were disinterested, concentrating instead on their families and careers. In 1981, the DBLJS General Meeting estimated that there were about 1000 young Lithuanians in Great Britain 'and that each year some 10 % were lost to the community forever. Without drastic action the British Lithuanian Community could not hope to survive'.[1134] Other developments also reflected the declining interest. After an initial growth during the early 1980's, *LYNES* began to falter and in 1985, the editor reported having received only eight contributions in 9 months.[1135] Some of the dance and choir groups also ended, having insufficient numbers, although strategies such as drawing members from two generations or from among English spouses extended the life of a few groups.

As the second generation grew more vocal within the organised communities, wider differences of opinion emerged between them and the first generation concerning how the communities should be organised. Some members believed that the community was still not doing enough to fuel the interest of younger members, and unless they did so, extinction of the Baltic communities in Great Britain would occur. However, there remained resistance to change among the first generation, who felt that their aims and ideals must be preserved and that the inter-war cultures and identities should be maintained.

Differences of opinion about how the communities should be organised were voiced at AGM's, youth meetings and in community publications. *LYNES* reported a debate at a *Vakaroné* at Lithuanian House, London in 1985 where young Lithuanians argued that 'the elder Lithuanian community did not provide an adequate environment to nurture cultural development in the young'.[1136] The debate then discussed the reasons for the lack of second generation interest. It stated that because almost all the Lithuanians were of peasant stock, with few professionals among then, the 'development of Lithuanian schools and the arts were slow to evolve'. The high ratio of men to women resulting in high intermarriage rates and the small population due to re-emigration also contributed to the problem. Other reasons discussed included social prejudice resulting in Lithuanian youth denying their ancestry and an unorganised youth movement, which 'led to apathy and lack of awareness'. Finally, the generation gap: was emphasised: 'Lithuanian youth are full of ideas that probably sound outlandish to the older generation'.[1137]

It was clear by the 1980's that the communities had not succeeded in retaining the interest of significant numbers of Latvian, Lithuanian and Estonian youth, despite second generation innovations. Clubs continued to be run and attended largely by the original refugees. An overwhelming majority of the second and third generations had assimilated: apart from among the handful of young activists, primarily of all-Latvian, Lithuanian or Estonian parentage, maintenance of culture was largely symbolic beyond the first generation. Despite the continued participation of a handful of young members in several areas, the degree of involvement was insufficient to sustain the clubs beyond the first generation, without the injection of new participants.

THE ORGANISED COMMUNITIES 1960-1985

Between 1960 and 1985, developments in family and working lives, the rooting and integration process, and homeland stagnation had a knock-on effect upon the organised community. This period saw a gradual decline in participation and activity, and although a hard-core of community activists and regular members ensured that most of the clubs and local branches remained active, a small number were forced to close. Although there were some shifts in the functions of the organised community, primarily as a response to the ageing of the communities, in many ways, as for the homeland, this was a period of stagnation for the organised community. Although the organised communities remained vibrant during the early 1960's, it was the 1970's, which witnessed a drop in participation and a scaling down of activities. The lack of interest of the second generation was one reason for this decline, but is it possible to locate other factors?

Most participants in this project cited the focus on work and family life as the main reason for the decay of the organised community. Work and family life decreased time available to partake in community activities and often reduced dependence on the organised community. Referring to the Estonian community, an Estonian man, now living in Chesterfield, noted that notwithstanding the continuation of cultural, social and political activities: 'For all that, signs of decline in...interest in the Estonian national-cultural activity were unmistakable perhaps from [the] mid-seventies onwards...'[1138] He described how the 'rebuilding of the life' took over from the middle of the 1950's onwards: 'In fact I know this from my own experience. I tried to fit myself in, in various ways including [the] Merchant Navy for a while...but then I came back and went into nursing in 1956. And there were quite a few in this hospital, quite a few Estonians, but gradually I got absorbed in my career and my family here, and then early sixties [I] came to live in Chesterfield and practically lost touch with the majority of Estonian communities.'[1139] Another Estonian man interviewed in 1984, described how he let his participation in the nearby Estonian community 'lapse' after marrying an Irish girl and starting a family, and stated that he was not currently 'very deeply' involved. His job as a cook at Leeds Road Hospital in Bradford had left him little time for connecting with the community, and he noted that although he felt sad that he had drifted away, he also felt a little indifferent. He claimed that he had become 'carried away' with his wife and family.[1140] A Latvian man, now living in Leeds, also explained how his job working on the buses left him little time for community involvement. He stated that after about the middle of the 1950's, 'I didn't mix with Latvians because my work wouldn't allow me, and particularly when I went on the buses, well that wouldn't allow me at all, because to some extent it were me own fault for opening me big mouth that I could speak German and that, you know, so they…kept shuffling me here and there you know on the long distance ones as well you see.'[1141]

Another reason cited was the increasing geographical distance of many refugees from centres of Baltic community. From 1960 onwards, a continued trend of geographical dispersal both within cities and within Britain as a whole also impacted on community structures. Within cities and towns, as members of the communities became more financially prosperous, they began to move away from the areas of original Latvian, Lithuanian or Estonian community, towards more affluent areas of towns and cities, and particularly towards the suburbs. This followed the general trend towards suburban habitation within cities among the British population at large. Within Britain as a whole, members of the Baltic communities continued to move away from areas of Baltic settlement, as they became less reliant on the community and followed career openings. This trend was particularly marked among intermarried men, although even among this group, a majority remained within travelling distance of an area of Baltic community. Many were now able to make use of cars or improved public transport to maintain their links with the community.

The path of one Estonian man during the 1960's reflected the experiences of some of the intermarried Baltic refugees in Britain, who migrated away from an area of Baltic community, and the longer term effects.[1142] He married an English woman in Derby, where he was initially living and employed in nursing. He then moved to Scarborough on the coast of East Yorkshire in 1961, primarily so that his wife could live nearer to her family, but also with hopes of finding a better job. He started work as a kiln operator before obtaining work as a salesman. While Derby had been the centre of a relatively small, but reasonably active Estonian community, in Scarborough he found himself completely cut off from the Estonian community in Britain, although he remained in close contact with several Estonian friends in other parts of Britain. After moving to Scarborough his maintenance of Estonian culture was virtually nil. He stated that 'lots of English habits I've learnt from my wife's family'. Since moving to Scarborough he had attended the Latvian club in Bradford only a couple of times, 'they're all strangers…', and was informed about developments within the Estonian community in Britain primarily from one of his Estonian friends who lived in Chesterfield. He socialised with local English people and became immersed in family life. An analysis of the interview suggests that this Estonian has fully assimilated into British life in a cultural sense, although his identity remained Estonian. He stated that, 'I know I'm not British', but also stressed that if he had the citizenship he would probably call himself British. He felt that his home was in Britain, and said that 'I'm probably better British than most of Britain'. He described himself as 'isolated' from the Estonian community, and since his retirement and divorce from his wife six years ago, he has not significantly increased his participation in the Estonian community. Although geographical distance is not perhaps the main reason for his lack of attendance now, it was certainly one of the main reasons that he became so rooted in the British society, and alienated from the nearest Estonian community during the 1960's. Those refugees who lived nearer clubs were more able to maintain some links through the years of immersion in family and working lives, and found it easier to re-connect in the late-'eighties.

Although many intermarried men did migrate away from areas of Baltic settlement, large numbers remained frequent club participants, and it was not unusual for intermarried men to be accompanied by their non-Baltic spouse, of whom some were also regular attendees. For many intermarried men, community participation was the main way of maintaining links with the diaspora and thereby with the homeland culture and language. So the effects of intermarriage on community participation were not wholly negative.

To some extent, the high number of single men within the communities aided the survival of clubs and branches, because they tended to be the most habitual attendees. Many clubs were male-dominated, which had an impact on the nature of activities which took place. In the larger areas of Baltic community, women tended to prepare ethnic cuisine and undertook certain cultural activities, such as weaving or embroidery. Some men did lead dance and song groups, but they were more likely to organise political activities, or attend the clubs simply for the purposes of socialising and drinking.

The London Latvian Centre

Another of the reasons cited by some refugees for low participation, was stagnation in the homeland and the consequent feeling that the direction of one's energies towards vigorous community participation and homeland cultural maintenance was futile. On the other hand, continued homeland occupation provided motivation for sustained cultural and community activity, and from this perspective, aided the survival of the organised community. Cultural and social activities within the clubs continued in, what one Estonian described as 'a stereotype fashion'[1143], modelled almost exactly on those taking place in the DP Camps, reflecting the continuation of the belief in exile duty and responsibility. In particular, the important national days and festivals continued to be celebrated and commemorated with vigour.[1144] Folk traditions, and song and dance groups were also important features of cultural activity during the years 1960 to 1985, although as with all areas of cultural life, low community participation brought some waning of these pursuits. Language retained its significance as the most vigorously defended aspect of culture during this period, its importance strengthened by news of the increasing threat of Russification to the homeland language. Language was defended through literature, publications, song, and as the main language of communication among the first generation. The revival of the Song Festival among the Latvian and Estonian diaspora was a particularly important development during this period, with European and international song festival organised regularly, occasionally in Britain. Related to the defence of language was support for education, which again was perceived to be increasingly threatened by Russification. Education was regarded as an important medium for the transmission of national identity, and thus as a potentially lethal tool in the hands of the Soviet regime. The Lithuanian Charter noted the importance of education for the Lithuanian nation: 'The school is the home of the national spirit. The highest duty of any Lithuanian is to be the benefactor of a Lithuanian school'.[1145] Education was supported through voluntary donations to schools in the homeland[1146], and by maintaining Latvian, Lithuanian and Estonian weekend schools in Britain.

Whereas previously, the language used within the community had been solely that of the homeland, the 1960's onwards witnessed an increasing use of English within the community, primarily for the purposes of maintaining the participation of the second and third generations. The need to reach a wider audience in the west to highlight the plight of the Baltic States also motivated the community to use English either as the main or as an additional language in certain publications. Examples included dissident and campaign literature intended for the general public and western governments.

There was some subtle modification of organised cultural activity during the period 1960-1985, brought about by shifting patterns of cultural repression in the homeland, the influence of the dissident movement and changes within British society.

One particularly notable aspect of invigorated cultural activity during this period was in the area of religion, brought about by the intensified Soviet campaign against religion, particularly in Lithuania. As the Lithuanian Catholic Church became increasingly oppressed and as a result, provided the focal point of the growing opposition movement in the homeland, the religio-national link among the diaspora also strengthened. Lithuanians in Britain supported the religious dissident movement in Lithuania - there was even an underground publishing and distribution centre in Britain. Among Latvians and Estonians it can be argued that the significance of freedom of religion as a national-cultural trait was firmly established during exile, with church services acting as an important arena for expressions of culture among the diaspora. Unlike in Lithuania, the link between any one religious institution and national identity was somewhat tenuous; rather Christianity in general was viewed as a key element distinguishing Latvians and Estonians from their atheist oppressors. As with all cultural activities, however, participation in church services was affected by the focus on family and working lives during this period. One Latvian man, now living in Leeds, noted that his participation in Latvian church services dwindled as his work life took over, in the same way that it had affected his participation in the local Latvian club. He told me that; '…to be honest with you Emily, in the thirty years that I were on the buses, I only went to Church…at Christmas…about six times, because I were working'.[1147]

As the example of religion shows, the activities of the organised communities were influenced by the expansion of the dissident movement from the 1960's onwards. The soaring publication and circulation of books and periodicals was one of the most obvious outcomes of dissident activity. In Britain, this stimulated exile publication and led to increased access to exile and dissident literature from all over the world. Clandestine sites for the distribution of dissident literature were established[1148] and publishing houses such as 'NIDA BOOK CLUB' (Nida Press) flourished. Nida Press produced Lithuanian 'literary books, memoirs and annual almanachs of belles lettres "*Pradalgés*" (The Swathes)', and published *LYNES* initially.[1149] Nida Press also published works from the other Baltic communities, including the well-known *Latvia and Latvians* by Juris Sinka.[1150]

Other changes globally and within British society affected the organised Baltic communities in Britain during the period 1960 to 1985, particularly the effects of globalisation. For example, increasing ease of international travel facilitated trans-diasporic links and growing availability of diverse foodstuffs eased the maintenance of homeland cuisine.

Political campaigning also continued during this period, although there is no doubt that continued stagnation in the homeland led to a decline in political activity compared to earlier years. The growing dissident movement from the 1960's onwards re-ignited the protest movement among the diaspora to some degree. Community publications urged the diaspora to partake in political campaigns and to support dissident activity. For example, *LYNES* called on second generation Lithuanians to participate in Lithuania's Underground Press and to help Lithuanian's persecuted believers. It asked young Lithuanians to acquaint themselves with the *Chronicle of the Catholic Church in Lithuania*, a *samizdat* journal aimed at highlighting the plight of the suppressed Lithuanian Catholic Church.[1151] Joint political campaigning in co-operation either with the global diaspora, the dissident movement, or with other Baltic and East European communities was regarded as the most effective method of protest during this period, given the small size of the communities in Britain. Particularly significant during this period was the Captive Nations' Committee, an association of so-called captive nations including Latvia, Lithuania and Estonia and other oppressed East European nations.[1152] This organisation was established in 1963, to highlight the plight of these nations to western governments and the general public, and to carry out political campaigning on behalf of the homeland. The national and international Latvian, Lithuanian and Estonian organisations also continued important campaigning work, as did diplomatic representatives in Britain.

Nevertheless, according to Mōckunas, previously supported governments-in-exile, suffered a major decline in popularity during this period.[1153] Furthermore, many of the interviewees reported only a marginal personal involvement in political campaigning and organisations during these years, although some did take part in particularly large anti-Soviet demonstrations. More popular were the politically-orientated commemorations, particularly Deportations Day[1154] and Independence Day[1155], which usually combined a cultural (for example, folk dancing and singing) and political programme. Political speeches had a nationalist agenda, highlighting both glorious and tragic elements of the nation's past and calling for future independence of the homeland. Some of the refugees who gained citizenship during this period[1156] used their political leverage to write letters to their local MP informing them of the plight of their homeland and requesting them to raise the issue in Parliament. In the absence of political leverage in the homeland, the maintenance of pressure on western governments and highlighting the plight of the Baltic States to the western public, were tactics favoured by the diaspora. This was after all, a period when school atlases submerged the Baltic States into the Soviet Union, and when the average member of the general public confused the Baltic and the Balkans (many still do!). Cultural programmes and exhibitions were one way for the community to present the homeland culture to a non-Baltic audience. An example of one of these types of events was the large exhibition of Lithuanian art was held in Bradford Central Library in 1975.[1157] An important part of the Baltic refugees' political campaigning was to highlight the plight of political prisoners in the homeland, and to campaign on their behalf. This role was furthered from the 1960's onwards as Brezhnev's oppressive regime placed dissenting individuals into prisons, labour camps and psychiatric prison hospitals in large numbers and as links with the dissident movement grew. Other methods of support were also organised; for example, in 1983 *LYNES* called upon its readers to send birthday cards to Lithuanian prisoners-of-conscience.[1158] Another important element of providing support to the homeland was voluntary donations to homeland residents. Most clubs and societies organised a variety of collections, some intended for individuals, others to support schools or other institutions.

The most obvious change to the activities of the organised communities, which took place from the 1970's onwards, was the need to address the requirements of a growing retired and elderly population. In 1978, *Latvians in Great Britain*, revealed this new area of concern as one of three major spheres of activity.[1159] The publication noted that while the ultimate aim of Latvian organisations in the West was 'the renewal of an independent democratic state', uncertainty as to when this might occur meant that 'in the meantime' there were 'several major areas' in which Latvian organisations were active. First, was the task 'of drawing the attention of Western political leaders and public opinion to the fact that Latvia is an occupied country, subject to Soviet colonisation and russification....'[1160] The second goal was to maintain and crucially *develop* the Latvian cultural tradition. Strategies included the publication of books and periodicals and providing opportunities for the works of Latvian composers and play-rights to be performed. The transmission of culture to the second generation and encouraging their participation in the community was also a key activity in the goal of maintaining culture. The welfare of the elderly was cited as the third key area of activity.

The welfare of the communities' elderly refugees became a key concern for community organisations, particularly since their needs were not met by an inadequate social services system. Social services placed members of smaller minority groups such as the three Baltic populations within old people's homes, which did not cater for different nationality groups. Many refugees wanted to spend their last years within the homeland community. The largest of the three communities, the Latvians faced the most acute problem numerically and the community felt that significant provision was needed. The solution was to acquire properties, which could serve multiple functions. In 1988, a report written by the British Refugee Council 'Age in Exile: A report on elderly exiles in the United Kingdom' noted that there were 'four residential for retired people run by various Latvian organisations'. According to the report, one feature common to them all is that they 'provide residential care mixed with holiday accommodation and also are used for conferences, meetings, concerts, seminars, and children's holiday camps'.[1161] Through the establishment of retirement homes, ethnic distinctiveness was maintained into elderly age, and showed that assimilation had not yet taken place.

The first property Rowfant House in West Sussex was leased in 1953, and purchased entirely by voluntary contributions in 1961, becoming the property of the London Latvian Evangelical Lutheran Church. Voluntary workers restored the neglected property and garden, within the twenty acres of park land. In 1988 it had 30 residents. Accommodation for weekend guests was available and it also housed a licensed social club. Residents took part in all activities held there, including concerts, lectures, church services and the traditional Jânis Day celebrations. Although there was no nursing care, a local doctor visited regularly.[1162]

Musmajas, at Wolston, near Coventry owned by *Daugavas Vanagi's* Coventry Branch, began as a licensed social club, and was used for weekend schools, meetings and various cultural activities. Standing in 15 acres of parkland, *Musmajas* was adjusted to house up to 14 permanent residents, and had spare rooms for weekend guests. The 1988 report noted that it also had residential nursing staff.[1163]

Nieuport House in Almeley, Herefordshire, was run by the Latvian National Council and had been rented from the Hereford Local Authority since 1953. The 1988 report noted that the property could house up to 50 residents and also accommodate weekend guests. Nieuport House, hosted annual summer camps for children, youth conferences, seminars, fancy dress parties and Jânis Day celebrations. It housed a library and social club for residents only.[1164]

Finally, the increasing need for further retirement accommodation led in the purchase of Catthorpe Manor in Leicestershire, called *Straumeni* in 1975, to cater primarily for retired members of the community, but also as a meeting and cultural centre for Latvians of all ages. In 1988, *Straumeni* was able to house 58 residents. *Straumeni* was bought by *Daugavas Vanagi*, entirely from voluntary contributions. The manor provided and continues to offer retirement accommodation and medical facilities, as well as operating as a general centre for the holding of community events. In the 1980's, new bungalows were built to provide independent accommodation for retired Latvians.[1165] I visited *Straumeni* in March 1997, and was struck to find what can only be described as a kind of Latvian village tucked away deep in the Leicestershire countryside. Catthorpe Manor stands in acres of grounds, with bluebell woods, pagan structures and a small lake. The complex houses Latvian newspaper publishing facilities, a bar/cafe, halls for the holding of special events, independent retirement accommodation within the Manor, catering facilities, guest rooms, a sick bay, a library, retirement bungalows, landscaped gardens and a chapel. *Straumeni* has been one of the main locations for the celebration of St. John's Day, and also acts as the location for *Daugavas Vanagi* AGM's.

A 1988 report on elderly exiles in the United Kingdom noted that Latvians also had access to the British Refugee Council residential home, Agnew House.[1166] Neither the Lithuanian nor the Estonian community had such extensive facilities. As regards provision from central and local government, or from voluntary agencies, Estonians and Lithuanians received no provision other than housing assistance from the British Refugee Council.[1167] The Lithuanian community continued to make full use of *Sodyba* (Headley Park) as a retirement home and centre for cultural activities and youth camps. *LYNES* noted in 1980 that unlike the Latvian community which had four *Sodyba's*, the Lithuanian community had only one.[1168] In August 1980, Sodyba had 13 retired residents.[1169] Although the Latvian community had four homes, and Lithuanians one, these were insufficient, and members from both groups also used local authority rest homes. The Estonian community had no separate provision for retired Estonians and no comparable residencies. This meant that elderly refugees who were unable to look after themselves were obliged to use local authority provisions. The communities catered for the ageing exiles in other ways. For example, the Latvian Welfare Fund provided talking Books for ageing Latvians with fading vision.[1170] In some areas, the communities also organised visiting schemes to the elderly.

Since the 1980's, various reports from the British Refugee Council, refugee projects and Social Workers have highlighted the particular problems faced by elderly Baltic refugees, and the need for greater provision by local and central government. They have drawn attention to several particular difficulties. One was that some elderly refugees were unable to attend clubs and community events due to disabilities, illness or frailty. As a result, they often became isolated, despite many having previously been active members. For some, language had become a problem, in the sense that in retirement, they reverted back to using the homeland language as their primary language, and lost fluency in English.

The retirement and ageing of the refugees from the 1970's onwards had two very different effects on the organised communities. On the one hand, retirement provided greater time and opportunity to take part once again in the life of the organised community, whilst on the other, illness and death reduced participation. An Estonian who retired in 1984 after working as a psychiatric nurse explained the difference retirement made.[1171] He moved to Chesterfield in the early 'sixties, where there were very few other Estonians. He stated that he 'practically lost touch with the majority of Estonian communities', and became immersed in his working and family life. He noted the effects as follows: 'I have [had] one or two [Estonian] friends, continuously but I practically lost the use of the Estonian language'. During his retirement, he became actively involved in the Estonian Association in Great Britain, and was elevated to the position of Club Secretary. I asked him how retirement had changed his life as an Estonian, and if it had given him more time to be an Estonian. He replied:

> Certainly yeah. Yes, while you're nursing…it's a lot of training. It's four and a half years training. I was at Open University for five years, so while those things were going on, you couldn't think of sitting and being Estonian. [laughs] You just had to get on with whatever is….whatever you're at. You could not…have been doing…all this clerical work. I couldn't have done that, anything like that, and as I say, Estonian language, well I almost forgot it…Yes, I think it's since retirement [that] I've again…got a bit gradually more interested in things Estonian and…I don't know whether I feel more Estonian because of that. [1172]

Another feature of the development of the organised community during the period 1960 to 1985, was the implementation of various strategies to revive community activities and participation. Financial necessity also prompted changes. Many clubs and community facilities opened their doors to the general public in many different ways, primarily to help community finances. For example, *Sodyba*, the Lithuanian retirement and holiday home established a Rifle Club in the 1960's, with members drawn from both the Lithuanian and local communities.[1173] Rowfant House, a Latvian residential home, leased and later owned by the London Latvian Evangelical Lutheran Church, opened its licensed social club to locals from the surrounding districts. The proceeds from the club helped to run the entire property.[1174] Other clubs welcomed the local populations to drink at the bar.[1175] *Bradfordo Lietuvių Veikla*

Didžiojoje Britanijoje (Lithuanians in Bradford), welcomed the local population of Bradford to the club.[1176] In these ways, the communities became more open, and less cell-like, as compared with the late 1940's and 1950's.

Latvian, Lithuanian and Estonian communities continued to share facilities with each other and other East European nationalities as a way of mitigating poor or non-existent facilities. For example, in Bradford, the Latvian and Estonian clubs were in the same road, and here members even drank at each other's bar. *LYNES* reported in 1980 that Lithuanians danced at the Polish Catholic Club in Wolverhampton and that Lithuanians held get-togethers at the Ukrainian club in Nottingham.[1177] Many more examples of sharing facilities occurred all over the country, especially in areas where the population was insufficient for the existence of a clubhouse. Often halls would be borrowed to hold dances and other celebrations. All developments enabled the refugees to mix both with locals and other East European nationalities, and reflected the ease felt by the Baltic refugees with other communities.

Despite attempts to bring about a reversal of waning community participation, decline continued, becoming most evident initially in the smaller local Latvian, Lithuanian and Estonian communities, where low participation made clubs and branches financially non-viable. Areas of high Latvian, Lithuanian or Estonian concentration with popular clubs, found that although members' involvement fell, the large numbers living in the area meant that clubs remained vibrant for many years. As the largest of the three communities, with arguably the strongest organisational structure - *Daugavas Vanagi*, Latvians suffered the least decline in the period 1960 to 1985, in terms of the survival of clubs and also the levels of participation. *Daugavas Vanagi* benefited not only from a large membership, but also from its central national structure, which formed part of a larger international organisation. This gave it financial clout, and the ability to partially address local weaknesses and problems with centralised funds and support if necessary. In 1978, *Latvians in Great Britain* noted that the DVF retained 32 local branches with 2100 members.[1178] The Latvian National Council in Great Britain was also a solid organisation, serving the interests of Latvians in Great Britain and extending the work done by the DVF in social, cultural and political fields.

The main Lithuanian organisation, the DBLS, was also fairly steadfast, and benefited from a centralised structure and individual membership. However, membership levels were far lower than achieved by *Daugavas Vanagi*, due to the smaller original number of migrants, and several branches closed during the early 1980's. In 1981, the Lithuanian Association of Great Britain's AGM noted there were currently 20 local branches of the Lithuanian Association. These were Birmingham, Bradford, Bolton, Central Branch, Coventry, Derby, Gloucester-Strand, Headley Park, Kettering-Corby, Leicester, Leigh, London, Maidenhead, Manchester, Nottingham, Preston, Rochdale, Scotland, Stoke-on-Trent, Wolverhampton. There was also the 'Lithuanian Engineers and Architects'.[1179] Over the next few years however, several of these branches suffered irreversible decline and extinction. An example was the decline of the Leicester branch of the Lithuanian Association in Great Britain. In the initial years, the Leicester branch was purportedly 'the most progressive', with social events drawing many Lithuanians from other towns. Cultural and sports groups and a Saturday school were organised during the 1950's and 1960's. However, according to *LYNES*: 'Regrettably as numbers declined so did the activity. Attempts were made at revival with little success. Despite continued cultural activity, the DBLS branch was officially closed in 1982.[1180] However, decline was not wholesale during this period. For example, Lithuanians in Scotland acquired a new club in Mossend, Lanarkshire, and an extension was later built in 1983.[1181]

In contrast to the DVF and the DBLS, the Estonian community structure – the 'Association of Estonians in Great Britain' (*Inglismaa Eestlaste Ühing*) was a fairly loose society, which did not have individual membership, but 'acted as a co-ordinating body' and as a collector and disseminator of information.[1182] Various organisations were affiliated to I.E.U, including the clubs in London, Leicester and Bradford, societies in other areas and those representing ex-servicemen and the younger generations. Due to the small size of the Estonian community, only a few clubhouses and societies were maintained. In comparison to the DVF which was able to purchase over 12 large properties in Britain during the period of exile, Estonians bought only 3 such properties.

Decline in community participation did not only affect clubs and branches, it also contributed to the extinction of some community publications, which suffered growing financial difficulties. Examples were the London Lithuanian paper, which became integrated into *Europas Lietuvis*, a weekly paper for Lithuanians in Britain, and the London Latvian paper - *Londonas Avize*, formed in 1942 became integrated in 1971 into a European-wide paper for Latvians printed in Germany - *Briva Latvija*.[1183]

CITIZENSHIP

The acquisition of British citizenship illustrates one aspect of the integration process, specifically, how some Baltic refugees 'became British' in terms of nationality. Large, although non-quantifiable, numbers of Latvians, Lithuanians and Estonians claimed British nationality. This acquisition provided the refugees, formerly legally designated as aliens, the same privileges as British citizens, including the right to a British passport and the ability to vote in elections. In a sense this represented the formal integration into British society, enabling the refugees not only to take part in the political process of the country in which they lived, but also to gain access to certain social and economic institutions previously denied to them.

British citizenship could be acquired through naturalisation by two methods. Baltic women who married British subjects could apply for British nationality. Second, as aliens, the refugees were eligible to apply for naturalisation under the Second Schedule of the British Nationality Act of 1948. Under the provisions of the Act the refugees were eligible after living in Great Britain for a period of eight years.[1184] Thus, the process of acquiring citizenship began from the mid-fifties onwards. Tannahill reported that by 1958, the extent of naturalisation among non-emigrating refugees was 'still very small'.[1185] Excluding the women who married British subjects (a very small number among Latvians, Lithuanians and Estonians, due to the far greater number of male Baltic EVWs), Tannahill noted that the proportion of those naturalised probably did not exceed 5 per cent. However, he estimated that the proportion would rise over subsequent years since it was only three or four years since most EVWs qualified to apply for citizenship. Within the groups of 128 EVWs interviewed by Tannahill in 1958, nearly one third said they 'had it in mind'.[1186] Bruno Rullis, a Latvian, was one of a small number of refugees who took up citizenship in the 1950's. [1187] He had applied for citizenship in 1955 as soon as he was eligible, primarily in order to apply for his mother to come and live in England. Bruno described this early period of Khrushchev's rule as a 'slack' time, when a number of exit visas were granted to enable relatives to join EVWs in Great Britain and Australia.

Aside from financial considerations (naturalisation cost £20 in 1958, a large amount in those days), there was division among the communities and individuals about whether or not to take up British citizenship. Many were initially undecided and waited several years, before taking the final plunge. The refugees in this study cite different motivations for their decision. Many of the reasons given by respondents in my study were identical to those found by Tannahill in his interviews. Motivations were usually based on practical and identity considerations, and were not necessarily reflective of integration or identity change, although it depended upon the date of naturalisation. Those who took up citizenship in the 1960's often did so for very different reasons from those who applied in the 1980's. In the 1960's, some regarded British citizenship as a betrayal of one's identity and homeland, and felt that it might prejudice their chances of returning. Others viewed naturalisation as a practical measure, to gain the same rights and privileges as the native British. It would also enable them to travel to the homeland without fear. There may have been irrational fears among a few refugees that they still might be forcibly repatriated. Tannahill noted that some refugees applied for citizenship 'for the sake of their children', or if they took up particular types of jobs, where British nationality was an advantage or necessity, for example, sea-captain.[1188] One of the reasons for not taking up citizenship was a feeling among many of the refugees that naturalisation would not make a great deal of difference to their lives, and as Tannahill states, some felt that even with citizenship, they would still be regarded as foreigners. This was the feeling of a Latvian man I interviewed who never applied for citizenship. He stated his reason: 'Well among English, we're still foreigners whether we have citizenship or not'.[1189] Finally, inertia also played its part in failing to apply for citizenship. Some of the respondents in my study said that they always meant to get around to it, but never quite managed to apply. Often when they did eventually try to secure citizenship, the cost or length of the application dissuaded them.

A Latvian woman from Leeds who married another Latvian took up British citizenship during the early 1960's at a cost of £25-00. She felt that it was important to take up British citizenship because 'it sort of made you belong more. You could sort of go to the library and borrow a book, otherwise you had to…sort of guarantee that you live here…'[1190]

A Latvian woman in Derby who also took up citizenship in the early 1960's described her reasons for doing so:

> Some people objected to doing it. They were Latvians. They would stay Latvian. My dad said you can change a citizenship. You can't change what you're born, you know the nationality you 're born with is yours. But if you live in a country and you work there and you're a citizen of that country then it's right and then again you've got a voice. See if you're British citizen, then you've got an MP who you can appeal [to] on your behalf.

If you're not, you're a non-entity. You're nothing. And if you travel abroad, you've got nothing behind you if you're not anybody's citizen, you see. There is a travel document people could get for travelling, but they needed visas and things, more than you did with a British Passport. So we thought it over and decided that it was the right thing to do, because if you live in a country, and you work for it, you're sort of loyal to that country.[1191]

This woman then, distinguished nationality from citizenship. For her, British citizenship was not a betrayal of ones' ethnic identity. As she stated '…if you're a Scot you're a Scot. You're British, but you're a Scot, like if you're a Welshman, you don't really lose that, because what you have is British. You can't become English or can't become Scotch. It's really what you're born, you know by blood you belong to something, but you can be British and have a voice in the life of the country in which you live'.[1192]

Another Latvian man who married a Latvian woman, and who maintained a very strong Latvian identity and active participation in the local Latvian community still felt that it was important to take up citizenship. He cited the main reason as being too fearful to visit his homeland without a British passport. I asked him if he felt that it was important to take up British citizenship? He replied: 'Oh yes, first you see, you are not very safe. Very, very afraid of what …may happen. You see when …[those] Bolsheviks [were] in the country you are never sure what may happen. And so I visited my country with British passport – that is safer'.[1193]

In the 1970's and 1980's, the main reason for taking up citizenship was to enable the refugees to travel to the homeland, which became easier and more popular during this period. As time passed, considerations related to the changed conception of where home was also became important. By the 1970's and 1980's many refugees felt that Britain was now their home and since they were unlikely to be returning to the Baltic States, citizenship could provide them with a greater sense of belonging. Generally, however, practical motivations were the main impetus, particularly as the cost of citizenship continued to rise.

In summary therefore, the acquisition of citizenship changed the nationalities of Latvians, Lithuanians and Estonians in Britain, and transformed them from aliens into citizens. While citizenship does not appear to have altered their ethnic identities, it appears to have brought about a shift in their national identities, i.e. their identification as members of a nation state. As long as the homeland was part of the Soviet Union, they did not feel that it was home; for many, although certainly not all, Britain was becoming home. Particularly for those who became British citizens, the growing feeling that Britain was their home, meant that increasingly they felt British, not only in terms of nationality, but also in terms of their national identities. Although some refugees did not wish to take up British nationality because they felt that it was a betrayal of ones homeland to do so, others felt that one could be both British and Latvian, Lithuanian or Estonian, and that ethnic identities and loyalties to the homeland were not weakened by a change in nationality, or even, national identity.

CONCLUDING REMARKS 1960-1985

If by claiming British nationality, the Baltic refugees can be said, to some extent, to have become British in form, what can be summarised from the evidence presented in this chapter thus far, in relation to their becoming British in substance?

So far five areas (Family Life, Working Lives, the Second and Third Generations, the Organised Community, Citizenship) have illustrated the rooting process which occurred among the Baltic refugees in Britain from 1960 to 1985. Examination of these five areas has suggested that by 1985, substantial integration of Baltic exiles in Britain had taken place. Recapping on Berry's definition of integration, it 'implies some maintenance of the cultural integrity of the group (that is some reaction or resistance to change as well as the movement to become an integral part of a larger societal framework (that is some adjustment)'.[1194] Integration therefore involves both the retention of cultural identity and the move to join the dominant society. Of course, not all individuals integrated: small numbers assimilated, or became marginalized or separated, the other three outcomes of the acculturation process as outlined by Berry.[1195] However, an overwhelming majority of individuals, and therefore the communities as a whole, integrated during this period. A similar process of integration took place among all three communities.

The evidence provided by John Brown's study of Latvians in Bedford in 1969, and the interviews carried out by Bradford Heritage recording Unit in 1984 are worth summarising here, since they illustrate the extent, nature and time-scale of integration, as well as the heterogeneity of individual experience.[1196]

John Brown's study of Latvians in Bedford suggests that by 1969, although many of the refugees had adjusted successfully to life in Britain, and embraced elements of British culture, homeland cultural maintenance was still fairly high by this date.[1197] Brown's interviews with Latvians in Bedford revealed several interesting characteristics of the acculturation process.

One Latvian man interviewed by Brown, noted that he felt 'like English. But when I go to social evenings with Latvians, I feel like Latvian again'.[1198] This comment suggested the emergence of Paden first termed 'situational ethnicity' in 1967, a concept furthered by Okamura in 1981.[1199] 'Situational ethnicity' refers to the juxtaposition of ethnicity and social situation, in simple terms, the idea that one is able to choose the identities expressed in any particular social situation. For example, one could be Latvian in the Latvian club, but British in the workplace. Situational ethnicity is evidence of integration, since to be able to choose which identities to express in any particular social situation requires a certain degree of English language fluency and other cultural attributes.

The same Latvian also talked about how he sometimes imagined himself in Latvia: 'And no-one recognises me, not even my own brother. Stranger in my own country....' He also mentioned that he 'would be very happy to go back to Latvia', 'but just for [a] holiday'.[1200] His comments suggest that as early as 1969, Latvians in Britain had begun to feel different to Latvians in the homeland. Some exiles believed that they had changed to such an extent, that they would feel like foreigners in their own homelands. Another Latvian interviewed by Brown raised a similar point: 'There is no question now of going back. In any case, there is now in Latvia a completely new generation. There, I would be a complete stranger, far more a stranger than I am here'.[1201] Brown glossed the Latvian man's comment with the following statement: 'Here is his place now, where his family is. Here he belongs'.[1202] These Latvian's comments also suggest the abandonment of the idea of return. Most refugees felt that their stay in Britain would be permanent, and even if the homeland became independent again, they were not certain if they would return. Brown noted the effects of the recognition of permanency among the Latvians of Bedford: 'Latvians are not people to delude themselves. Most recognise that, as time passes, as they themselves grow older, roots in Bedford grow deeper, their children's needs develop, and the dream of freedom and independence for their won country continues to lie cold, so their will to preserve their identity also inevitably weakens'.[1203]

Brown also illustrated the different degrees of Latvian cultural maintenance among Latvians in Bedford. One Latvian man, who was married to a Latvian maintained the homeland culture within the household to a large degree: the family spoke Latvian at home; the children attended Latvian social evenings and one daughter engaged in traditional dancing. Another Latvian was married to an English woman, and although his children were interested in Latvia and Latvian culture, they did not speak Latvian and he did 'not force their interest'. Although the Bedford Latvian community was quite small (176 native-born Latvians in 1969), Latvian club meetings and Lutheran Church services were held regularly, a Latvian library contained 13000 books, and dance and language classes were organised for children.[1204]

Although Brown's account suggests that integration was already beginning to occur by 1969, he inferred that some of the older Latvians had not integrated; indeed, his comments suggest that a small number became marginalised or separated. Brown cited the comments of a pub licensee he had interviewed, whose pub was frequented by a group of Latvians: 'The Latvians are the saddest of all. Despairing drinkers. They'll drink for days on end. All heavy drinking'.[1205] 'Some of them, I think died really in the war. They saw too much. And they know they cannot go back. They have accepted that they will die here. In that state, some people turn to religion, some turn to drink…. Those Latvians are the most lost of all'. The pub licensee noted one particular Latvian man who was deaf and dumb: 'he doesn't want a hearing aid, he doesn't want to know anything any more. He just cut himself off. And now he has drunk himself out. He is waiting to die'. Brown also noted the case of a Latvian woman of 76 years, who 'wants only to return to Latvia'. 'Here, she has nothing in common with anyone outside her family. She speaks no English, has no friends, and hates the climate'.[1206]

Three interviews carried out by the Bradford Heritage Recording Unit in 1984 (two with Latvian women and one with an Estonian man), illustrate how far the process of integration had developed since 1969, and highlight some key features of this progression. They also reveal heterogeneity among integrated Baltic refugees in Britain.

The interviews demonstrate the integration process in several areas: social life, including participation in the homeland community; identities and orientation to the homeland; and cultural maintenance (including the raising of children).

The three refugees had different social lives and degrees of participation in the homeland community, although none could be described as active or regular attendees. Sylvia[1207], a first generation Latvian woman, who lived in Bradford, the centre of a vibrant Latvian community, stated that she had a 'few' Latvian friends and went to the Latvian club in Bradford 'occasionally'. However, she also spoke about her English friends, with whom she enjoyed good relationships. Lennart[1208], a first generation Estonian man, who lived in Bradford, described how he had let his involvement in the local Estonian community in Bradford 'lapse' after marrying an Irish girl and starting a family, and that he was not currently 'very deeply' involved, although he expressed a desire to reconnect with the community. The third interviewee, Laura[1209], a first generation Latvian woman, who lived in Bingley, stated that she continued to participate in the Latvian club in Leeds, and went to the Lutheran Church services held once a month in Leeds. However, although she used to have many Latvian friends, she felt isolated from the community in Bingley. She also had many English friends.

The comments of the three interviewees in relation to identities and orientation to the homeland also suggested integration. Sylvia noted that: 'I know I'm a foreigner, but I don't feel like one'. When the interviewer asked her if she felt 'quite English', she replied 'Yes'. She also talked about how some Latvians in Britain made the following comment: 'If Latvia was free, I would just walk over'. However, she noted that she felt too old to start again.[1210] When Lennart was asked what nationality he felt himself to be, he replied that he was Estonian. However, he noted that his loyalties were to England. He used the metaphor of the football match, stating that he would cheer for England, as that is where his sympathies lay. Lennart noted that he had not faced any discrimination or problems with being Estonian. He had not acquired British citizenship, and because he did not have a vote, was disinterested in British politics. He stated that he would go back to Estonia if he knew it was 100 per cent safe to do so. However, Lennart stressed that the homeland would not be the same as it was when he lived there, and he also believed that he would feel more foreign there, than he did in Britain.[1211] Laura noted that although her three daughters had visited Latvia to visit, she had not, although she did express a wish to visit. Although she maintained many elements of Latvian culture within Britain, there was nothing that she missed about Latvia.[1212]

In relation to culture, the three accounts suggest that retention of homeland culture was extremely variable, and that in many cases, maintenance could not be described as vigorous. Of the three interviewees, Laura maintained the most aspects of the homeland culture. She attended the Lutheran Church services on a monthly basis, read Latvian newspapers, attended some of the celebrations at the Latvian club, and continued to cook Latvian food. However, she stressed that she cooked a mixture of Latvian, French, Italian and English food, and particularly loved fish and chips and meat pie.[1213] Sylvia stated that she did not think that, apart from food, there were many differences between the English and the Latvian way of life, and she said that personally, she was 'not bothered' about Latvian food.[1214] Lennart described how he found it difficult to speak Estonian at times, and sometimes spoke English and Estonian at the same time, reflecting some weakening of homeland language skills even among the first generation.[1215]

Differences also emerged in the raising of children, although again, the testimonies suggest that integration had occurred. Sylvia had initially sent her son to a weekly Latvian school, but because he was finding it hard to learn English language, she soon decided to end this arrangement. Her view that: 'Really the Latvian language is only for sentimental reasons', suggests some weakening of the notion of exile responsibility.[1216] Lennart shared a similar attitude. He had also tried to teach his children Latvian when were very young, but did not sustain this. His rationale was as follows: 'What good would it have done them to be good little Estonians? English is the language where your bread comes from'.[1217] Laura also taught her three children Latvian when they were very young. They spoke Latvian at home and were sent to a Latvian Saturday school. They also did traditional Latvian dancing. Laura felt that it was important to teach her daughters about Latvian culture and customs. However, she described them as being a little bit of Latvian and English.[1218]

In seeking to understand why integration occurred during the period 1960 to 1985, the influences of the homeland, British society, and the diaspora itself must be considered. Of these three factors, the influence of the homeland was decisive.

During the years 1960 to 1985, continued Soviet control of the homelands shaped the evolution of the diasporic communities. Soviet occupation was the reason they became, and continued to be, exiles. The political stagnation and prolonged degradation of the Baltic republics, and continued isolation from the homelands, had two major effects on the diaspora. On the one hand, political stagnation promoted the rooting and integration process in Britain, and led to some weakening of the link between the diaspora and the homeland. The entrenchment of Soviet power contributed to the fading of the myth of return, and prompted the refugees to settle into a long stay in Britain, which looked increasingly permanent as the years passed. The Baltic EVWs concentrated on family and working lives, which sometimes led to reduced participation in the homeland community. While some were simply too busy to partake in community activities, others felt that vigorous campaigning and cultural maintenance was pointless, given the intractability of Soviet rule. The latter view led to some weakening of exile identities, and reduction in participation in the diasporic community. Many refugees simply wanted to try to forget about the homeland. One Latvian in Bedford, interviewed by Brown in 1969, stated that: '…sometimes I see people begin to think of home, they do not know where they are. I try to put it out of my mind'.[1219] A Latvian man, now living in Leeds, also described how he and other Latvians tried to forget about the homeland, because 'it were pointless': '…up to 1991, I think most of us tried to forget it. Now I'm sure I'm speaking for lots of Latvians, because it were pointless us thinking about it, I mean perhaps for those people that had relations you know, but in my case I had nobody, so it was just a memory, a country that's been suppressed by a foreign power and that's as far as it goes…'[1220] Even among Latvians, Lithuanians and Estonians who turned away from the organised community, a sense of duty as exile rarely disappeared completely, and most refugees continued to maintain their homeland culture to some degree. Some participants in this study who had let their involvement in the organised community slip reported feelings of guilt about not adequately fulfilling their roles as exiles.

The long term physical and mental separation from the homeland contributed to the growing orientation away from the homeland. This was noted by John Brown in 1970, who stated that the Latvian community in Bedford was 'losing ground'. He gave his explanations for the decline:

> Nothing can overcome the barrier of physical separation. The children, for the most part think of Latvia as a dreamland; some are not even sure where it is on the map. Without the sustenance of real, physical knowledge, it would be impossible for these children to conceive of their identity as other than English.[1221]

On the other hand, entrenchment of the Soviet Union kept exile identities and cultures alive. Many refugees refused to renounce the struggle to regain independence, and their belief in the necessity of maintaining cultures and identities in exile remained steadfast. Many of those in this category were active community participants and leaders. The influence of their attitude towards the continued duty of exile was reflected in the continuing propagation of a myth of return in community publications, albeit with a decreasing sense of certainty. The organised communities took a lead in keeping the duty of exile alive. The following statements in *LYNES*, the Lithuanian youth news-sheet in 1981 underlines how the responsibilities of exile were stressed by community publications:

> A country can survive while its culture lives. Keeping Lithuanians alive is another way of ensuring that Lithuania stays alive.

> Lithuania needs a voice outside the Soviet silence and we must be that voice so that should the dream of independence become a reality there would be people to pass on ideas and help with the struggle'. The responsibilities of exile were not just the preservation of cultures and identities; it also included political campaigning – 'to raise a case for the oppressed.[1222]

Throughout the years 1960 to 1985, the character of repression in the homelands influenced exile cultures and identities. The activities of the dissident movement in the Baltic republics were also a stimulus to the actions of the diaspora. In the homelands, dissident activities focused on preserving aspects of cultures and identities, which were most severely repressed, and those which made the Baltic peoples different from Russians, indeed 'everything that made them different from the system in which the Baltic republics had been enveloped.[1223]   Similarly, the diaspora in Britain also focused on maintaining these aspects of culture in Britain. The different character and effects of Sovietization in the three republics influenced the different character of the national movements in the three republics.   Thus, Lithuanians stressed Catholicism and Latvians and Estonians focused on their folk cultures. All three vigorously maintained the homeland language as the ultimate defence against Russification.

Throughout exile, the diaspora used similar strategies in an attempt to preserve cultures and identities for transplantation, focusing on language, folk cultures and particularly among Lithuanians, religion - all the aspects which they felt to be at the core of the homeland identity and culture, and which were perceived to be threatened by Soviet rule. These strategies were at the heart of the exile culture and identity, and were noted by the publication *Latvians in Great Britain*, which described one of the key aims of Latvian organisations in Britain as the maintenance and development of the Latvian cultural tradition '*especially in directions that are prohibited in Latvia*'.[1224]

Nevertheless, despite the continued calls of the organised community to the exiles to fulfil their responsibilities as guardians of the homeland, a gradual weakening of exile identity took place between 1960 and 1991, among both individuals, and to a lesser degree, at the level of the organised community. The length of homeland occupation led to changes in the goals and aims of the communities, which in turn influenced the cultures and identities of the exile communities. As it became increasingly clear that the homelands would not become independent for many years, attention was focused inward, on the diaspora in Britain and retaining its unique character and identity. The ageing of the communities and the development of the second generation were decisive in this development. Liūtas Mockūnas described the shift in the goals of the Lithuanian émigré community during this period. According to Mockūnas, after the mid-sixties, the emigration no longer regarded itself as a substitute for Lithuania and that its cultural, creative and political roles became viewed as 'auxiliary at best'.[1225]

CHAPTER 9

The restoration of homeland independence

Well, I am Lithuanian yes, but if somebody says, 'Do you want to go back and live there?', I should say straight away, 'No, no', because so many years gone. All the generation mostly die. The younger generation [in Lithuania] is brought up different way. It's not the way when I [was] brought up. And that make me feel that I couldn't be there happy. I am happy here. I am very, very happy here and yes, visit, yes, for one week, for a few days....but no more.

We thought we were the up-to-date original Lithuanians, and it was a shock to find that in fact, Lithuanians in Soviet times had moved on. There were patriotic undercurrents. They had moved on. Their...culture, their ways of approaching culture were if you like, more up to date. We had actually aged. Our attitudes in that direction had aged. We were living in the past.

(First Generation Lithuanian mother - top quote, and daughter - bottom quote)[1226]

AN ESTONIAN MAN IN BRITAIN stated that the restoration of homeland independence in 1991 represented the end of exile for the Baltic communities in Britain. His comment summed up the significance of liberation for the communities; they were no longer exiles or refugees, and were free to return to their homelands. Independence was the goal for which the communities had been striving, for half a century. However, when liberation came, the implications for the Baltic communities were not as straightforward as had previously been envisaged. On their arrival in Britain they had imagined the mass return of the diaspora to the homeland and the transplantation of cultures and identities. In 1991, the meaning of independence for the diaspora was uncertain.

Against this background the following questions are raised: How many returned to the homeland to visit or to live? What were their motivations in returning or staying in Britain? What were the effects on identities, and on the role of the organised communities, whose main goal had originally been to work tirelessly for independence? How did independence alter the relationship between the diaspora and Great Britain and between the diaspora and the homeland? How far did independence mark a second major turning point in the lives of the refugees? Finally, a further effect of homeland independence was to stimulate the migration of Latvians, Lithuanians and Estonians from the Baltic States to Britain during decade after independence. What has been the impact of these so-called *new* migrants on the established communities?

It must be noted that as this research was undertaken in the mid to late 1990's, the story covered in this chapter is to some extent a 'snapshot in time' and that the effects of independence would continue to be felt over subsequent years. One of the major effects of independence which occurred more recently, specifically in 2004, was that the Baltic States were able to join the European Union: this led to significant migration from these countries to the UK and to other European countries. This in turn, impacted on the Latvian, Lithuanian and Estonian communities in the UK and other countries. Although this is not covered in this book in any detail it will be dealt with briefly in a postscript at the end of the book.

THE ROAD TO INDEPENDENCE, 1985-1991

When Mikhail Gorbachev came to power as General Secretary of the Communist Party of the Soviet Union in 1985, there were few signs that his rule would bring about any shift in the fortunes of the three Baltic SSR's. However, changes did begin to occur, unexpectedly and rapidly, as a result of the introduction of the policies of *Glasnost* and *Perestroika* in 1986. Change took almost five decades to come, but when it did so, developments were brisk – from stagnation to liberation in just six years. As the road to independence in Latvia, Lithuania and Estonia has been covered elsewhere in detail, I will concentrate on the impact of developments on the Baltic diaspora in Britain.

The first effect of *Glasnost* on the diaspora was an increased flow of accurate news emanating from the homelands. Western journalists and television crew were allowed greater access than ever before, although controls were still exercised. Increased media coverage heightened public awareness of the Baltic republics. *LYNES* reported in August 1989 that the high coverage of events in the Baltic States has 'had a knock - on effect in the lives of people of Estonian, Latvian and Lithuanian descent living here in Britain', due to the greater awareness of the British public. *LYNES* addressed its audience of young Lithuanians:

> You must have experienced it. You are asked your name and after your reply, the usual question about its origin. The instead of the usual inane smile (as if to say "Mm, yes – I know where that is – near Rumania isn't it?", you are greeted with instant comprehension and, maybe, an intelligent comment, like, "Lithuania! Isn't that where Sajudis [Lithuanian Popular Front] recently had such a sweeping election victory?"[1227]

This was echoed by a Latvian woman who stated that nobody knew where Latvia was, 'Not until, when this *Perestroika* started. *Glasnost* and *Perestroika*. Then everybody said; "I know where Latvia is now"'.[1228]

Among Latvians, Lithuanians and Estonians in Britain, the movement towards independence brought about a significant upsurge in community activities and participation in Latvian, Lithuanian and Estonian clubs. Baltic refugees in Britain reported that members previously engrossed in work and family responsibilities reconnected with the communities. By the late-1980's, all had retired, and with children having grown up and left home, they had more time to devote to community activities. The revitalisation of the Baltic diaspora's globally was described by Solveiga Miezitis in 1990:

> We cannot overlook the fact that within the last decade, the Baltic communities abroad have been rapidly dwindling in size and activity level. However, during 1989 and 1990, the freer contacts with the homeland have infused our communities with renewed vigor and cultural activity. Many who had lost interest, and others who had become alienated or assimilated, have found a new raison d'être for participation in the ethnic community…[1229]

In the late-1980's, the communities set to work to highlight the plight of the Baltic States to the British public, to apply pressure on the British Government to support the push for independence, and to aid the nationalist movements in the homelands. Compared to diaspora in America or Canada, the Latvian diaspora in Britain played a lesser, primarily indirect role in aiding the nationalist movements, mainly due to the smaller numbers and fewer indirect links.[1230] Strategies designed to support the independence movements included the distribution of *samizdat* material, and linking up with exiles and dissidents globally. The Baltic Council was formed, with representative members from all three communities, with the aim of highlighting the plight of the Baltic States to the general public and to educate the public about the history and culture of the region. In 1987 and 1989, Baltic Focus was held in London, organised by the Baltic Council to publicise Latvia, Lithuania and Estonia to the British public.[1231] Baltic Focus included a full programme of folk singing, dancing, and mounted exhibitions relating to the culture and history of the region.

In the late-1980's, hope that homeland independence might be achieved was accompanied by unease, as the diaspora feared the Soviet regime's response. The author of an article in *The Sunday Telegraph* in November 1988 suggested that apprehension was justified, given that: 'Spring in the Soviet Union has traditionally been followed by winter'.[1232] Not only were the diaspora uneasy, they did not at first, expect any significant changes within their homelands. In 1988, in the introduction to *Latvia and Latvians*, Juris Sinka outlined the political and economic changes associated with *Glasnost* and *Perestroika* in the Soviet Union, before posing the following questions: 'And what about Latvia, Estonia, Lithuania and other captive non-Russian nations in the Soviet Union? Has their status altered in any way? Has life for their people changed in the direction of greater political freedom or even independence?' He answered: 'The bitter truth is that neither Gorbachev nor any other Kremlin leader has said or done anything to engender the hope that Latvia or any other captive nation would be allowed to secede from the Soviet Union and enjoy independent existence as a free and sovereign state.'[1233] Sinka stated that although some local inhabitants in the homelands were hopeful that the Gorbachev era would usher in some freedom for the homeland, in his view, the few concessions granted by the Soviet authorities were quite possibly 'a passing whim of the new Soviet leader'. Further, that Latvians may 'yet have to face a rude awakening'.[1234]

However, developments continued apace, and in 1991, less than three years on from Sinka's projections, Latvia, Lithuania and Estonia regained their independence. In Britain, celebrations took time to get under way, as the diaspora waited for the consolidation of independence, particularly recognition by the United Nations and the Soviet Union. A Lithuanian mother and daughter stated that when independence was declared there were no celebrations at the Manchester club: 'Not in our club'. London maybe yeah', 'but we were all glued to the telly'.[1235] Many Latvians, Lithuanians and Estonians felt rather cut-off from events in the homeland and it took time for the reality of independence to sink in. Many feared that it would not last. I asked a Latvian how he felt when Latvia became independent again. He replied: 'Oh, delighted, delighted, but [it] could be short-lived'.[1236] News that the Soviet Union had recognised the independence of the three Baltic States on 6 September 1991, and membership of the United Nations on 17 September provided some reassurance, although some members of the diaspora retain pessimism about the permanency of independence even today.

THE MEANING OF INDEPENDENCE FOR THE BALTIC COMMUNITIES IN BRITAIN

As independence finally became a reality, the diaspora began to wonder about the consequences for the homeland. The Baltic communities in Britain felt that while independence was a happy event, it was not so much independence in itself, but what it brought which was the most important thing. Views about the prospects for a successful transition from communism evolved over the years following independence. While most were optimistic about the future of their homeland, others felt concerned about the road ahead. One Latvian in Leeds stated bluntly: 'I don't think they will make anything out of it.'[1237] In 1992, Juris Sinka wrote in the introduction to the Australian edition of *Latvia and Latvians* that Latvia remained in a 'rather precarious situation', and that: 'Unfortunately, the freedom and independence for whose recovery the Latvians have fought, suffered and died are accompanied by problems which have considerably dampened the initial euphoria and must be solved if Latvia is to become viable as a State again.'[1238] Developments during subsequent years persuaded Sinka and the diaspora to become more optimistic about the future. Sinka wrote in 1996, that since the publication of the 1992 edition, 'Latvian has scored quite a few successes in many spheres', including the economy, the appearance of Riga and the progression of the younger generations, and that these 'positive aspects of life in Latvia may help to solve the problems in the social sector...'[1239]

As well as evaluating the consequences of independence for the homeland, the diaspora also began to assess the meaning for themselves, as individuals and as communities. One thing was clear - the aim of independence which they had been working towards for so long had now been achieved, and as a result Latvians, Lithuanians and Estonians in Britain were no longer exiles or refugees. They were now free to return to the homeland, and for the first time, they would be able to choose whether to live in Britain or the homeland. What were the consequences of this situation? The initial euphoria of achieving independence was quickly replaced by a more uncertain feeling of *Where do we go from here?* Initially, independence brought about a need for reassessment, both of the future goals and direction of the communities whose primary goal had now been achieved, and among individuals who had to assess the meaning and impact of independence on his or her life. A few were certain and had been at the start of the liberation process -- that they would return to their homelands to live. Most of the refugees however, spent some time considering the implications and their response to independence. Would they visit? Would they return? The vast majority decided fairly quickly that although they would be unable or did not wish to return to live there, they would visit as soon as they were able.

The opening of physical links between the diaspora and the homeland was the first and most visible consequence of independence for Latvians, Lithuanians and Estonians in Britain. Members of the diaspora were now not only able to visit and return to the homeland, but there was also greater cultural exchange and a heightened awareness of life in the Baltic States, due to the improved accuracy of news and information emanating from the homelands.

VISITING THE HOMELAND

The possibility of visiting and travelling freely around the homeland, meeting up with relatives and friends, and seeing the places where one grew up was in many ways the most obvious effect of independence on the lives of the diaspora. Shortly after independence, the diaspora were able to apply for Latvian, Lithuanian and Estonian passports from the new Embassies in London. Almost all of the participants in this study returned to their homeland to visit in the first few years following independence, an experience described by all respondents as highly emotional. For some, contact was made with long lost friends and relatives for the first time. Visiting experiences were mixed, but overall positive. A Latvian woman described her first visit to Riga in 1992 with her Latvian husband:

> ...it was very emotional. There were quite a few people [who] met us at the airport and they have this habit of going to meet you at the airport with flowers, and I ended up with lots of them, so I said, 'Can you park me at the Freedom Monument?[1240]' and they said, 'Well, if we can find a space' and I said 'Right we'll go there', and I took all the flowers and laid them at the Monument because that, that's what people did in those days and when I got back to where we were staying with my husband's nephew...she'd got all vases. She said 'I'm sure you've been given lots of flowers' and I said 'Yeah, but they're, they're all at the Monument'. 'Cos people used to do that you know. It's like, like re-addressing Riga again, sort of coming back and signing on again you know...[1241]

I asked a Lithuanian ma living in Manchester : 'How has the restoration of independence changed your life as a Lithuanian in Great Britain?' His reply was as follows:

> Change inside, it has changed very, very much. We were all pleased that Lithuania is free, and like I say you know I went for a holiday to see my family, and I felt free, going to anywhere I wanted, doing anything I wanted. When the Soviets were running the country I went twice, but then from the radius of the hotel [you could] only go [a] radius [of] ten kilometres, so we felt like prisoners in the camp.[1242]

Following independence, he travelled to Lithuania in 1992: 'I visited the place where I growing [grew up], and I visited my relations in different towns and where I lived...'[1243]

The importance of opened links to family was expressed by a Lithuanian woman who stated that independence affected the Lithuanian community in Britain, 'in a sense that there was almost like a sigh of relief. You could actually feel the sigh of relief, because it opened the doors to their families...'[1244] A Lithuanian women living in Nottingham described the importance of the freedom to travel freely without fear:

> You feel free, because I can speak on the road freely. I'm not frightened. Russia time if I met my relations...I [was] frightened.[1245]

Many of the refugees spoke about the shock they experienced upon seeing relatives for the first time in fifty years. Sisters, brothers, parents and cousins were now fifty years older, and many refugees could barely recognise them. Nor could their relations recognise the returning diaspora on many occasions. One Latvian man talked about his experiences upon return to the homeland in 1992:

> I went back, just spur of the moment I decided. There was a seat free – chartered plane. I went home and well, I didn't expect to meet anybody, any relations but as it happened I found some [had] been to Siberia, come back, broken mentally and physically by it. Died. Just last year, one died, two of them died. So. Sister still is okay. Shock when erm, seen her before the war and when I see her now. You...shock – like you know, like you can't overcome. Well, that's how it is.[1246]

Not all those who visited the homeland were shocked by what they found, particularly those who had visited with the Soviet travel agency, *Intourist* during the Soviet period, when despite the lack of freedom to travel were often able to invite relatives to meet them at the hotel they were staying in. Others who had communicated regularly may have sent photographs. A Latvian from Leeds, stated that: 'I didn't meet a great deal of people that I didn't know. I knew some of my neighbours, ex-neighbours and so on, and they were just the same as I remembered them then and with all my family I didn't have any difficulty whatever'.[1247]

One of the main changes experienced through visits was the dramatic change to the rural and urban landscape. Most felt that industrial and urban developments were detrimental. A Latvian man living in Leeds explained how his home village had changed:

> A lot of it is different now, I mean the village there used to be, well just like a little centre there. It's like a little town like, with streets now. There was no streets before, there were just roads going that way and that way and that's it you know.

However, even though the village had changed, the fact that it was still there and that he was there were the important things: 'But the place is there. The place is there. And that's what matters so much you know. That's why I said as soon as there was [a] chance to go, we went.'[1248] Bruno first revisited Latvia with his family in 1990, even before independence had been secured:

You see I said that as soon as I can go back where I like and see who I like in Latvia I'll go back, because it's, it's been so dear to me you know, everything, I've grown up there as a child you know it's in me. I'm part of all that. A lot of people don't want to go back because they think it will be all different. Of course, it will be different. I know when I went there I felt sad. Well you feel sad either way. But it's there. To be there. To feel it.[1249]

Although most participants talked about the deterioration of the urban and rural landscape, a few felt that the industrial and urban developments were on the whole positive. One Lithuanian returnee stated:

Well, I'm in a minority because when I came and when I saw...how Lithuania [had] changed since I saw it last I was very pleased. I noticed electrification. I noticed the road system. I noticed improvements...outside the towns, so many ships. We've now got a navy, with accepted war ships. The improvement in air travel...there was no air travel when I left. Cities [are] most probably not to my liking, because this is the pattern of the Soviet architecture...but again it fulfils its function. New communities are [being] built up, so it's quite nice, and there's quite desirable residential places, so I've found many changes. Most of them are favourable, I mean favoured.[1250]

Tallinn Main Square

Many of the participants described what they perceived as negative changes to Latvians, Lithuanians and Estonians in the homeland, particularly in terms of attitudes and character. Most of the diaspora blame the years of Soviet occupation for this. I asked a Latvian woman if she felt that the mentality of Latvians had changed since the inter-war period. She replied:

> Yes... To our opinion they are very...they don't care. I suppose they are improving now, but they didn't care very much about their surroundings...

> Well, I thought we were very, you know like, very tidy, very clean, and like the Europeans. Well, I can explain this, that when we came, first we came to Germany during the war and we didn't feel that we were a lower class or...when you go to a strange country, well we felt equal and that was the same when we came here...

> But now, when we had the visitors [from the homeland], to start with they said, 'Oh we're just poor people, we're just country people and we have...we don't have anything', and they sort of, they feel that they are [a] lower class than they used to be and I think it is because of the Russians...[1251]

A final aspect discussed by most of the interviewees, particularly Latvians and Estonians, was the presence of Russians, especially in the capital cities, and related to this, the lingering usage of Russian particularly during the early post-independence years, even among ethnic Latvians, Lithuanians and Estonians. One Latvian found that on his first visit to Latvia after independence, '…going into shops in Riga…there was hardly anybody [that] wanted to speak Latvian…and they were very obstinate…'[1252] Although more Russians spoke Latvian when he returned in 1995, 'apart from what they had to sell me or tell me in the shop…no further conversation was possible at all.'[1253]

Another Latvian explained how disappointed the diaspora was, when they saw how Latvians in the homeland had grown accustomed to having Russians around:

> …people are a bit disappointed here, because over the fifty years that they've been under the Soviet regime, they got used to having Russians around, and to us it's very… You go along and hear a Russian in Riga and it sends shivers down your spine, you know. You come back to your home country and all the people on the buses speaking Russian and you kind of…but they don't feel it so much, because they've been going to work and being on that bus and then they all speak Russian by now, so it doesn't jar, but if you go to what you consider your to be your country and you find people all round you talking a language you don't understand…and they've lost the feeling because in fifty years they've been discouraged to think of themselves as Latvians, sort of, you will be citizen of the Soviet Union sort of thing, everybody's equal, and they flooded the country with Russians and they've done it everywhere…[1254]

A Latvian woman compared Russians in Latvia, with Latvians in Britain:

> …it's different say if you compare us being in England and the Russians being in [Latvia] because the Russians were the conquerors, they were the upper class, while they lived in Latvia and of course there's quite a lot of resentment about that and I don't think it's easily overcome. They just don't like them full stop, you know and I always think like, 'When in Rome, you do as the Romans do', so if they want to stay in Latvia they should learn the language, like we did in England. I mean we wouldn't dream of asking you to speak Latvian or whatever, we should learn…[1255]

Although many members of the Latvian and Estonian diaspora regarded the presence of Russians in the homeland as a major obstacle in the rebuilding of their homelands, a view sometimes furthered by visits, not all had this view. I asked one Estonian how he felt about the Russians in Estonia. He replied:

> Well, a lot of Russians are born there. So I suppose, how do you feel about me being here, it's the same thing in a way. I've nothing against Russians. They're stubborn of course...[1256]

> Well, you see the Russians there, I don't think they're all in with the same cap they are sort of split.

> ...some Russians didn't like the system before and some don't like it now and some don't like any of it. Well, I've nothing against Russian people as such...But our people don't like a lot of them.[1257]

For some, visits modified previously bitter feelings towards the Russians in the homeland. This was the experience of one Latvian, who changed his attitudes towards Russians after a friendly gesture from a Russian. He explained:

> I had a very bitter feeling and not only me, but I think majority were speaking about bitter feelings about the Russians you know what I mean...but I'll tell you this much. Since I went...when me and Juris went to Riga in '95, we could see, practically see Juris' house, but we couldn't get to it, because of one-way systems. And I never forget as long as I live, there were this Russian chap.

> So, he...were crossing this road and I asked, called him over, so he came and stopped and I said, 'Can you tell us how we can get over there to that street over there?', and he were Russian and he could hardly speak Latvian, but I never, never forget as long as I live, he bent over backwards to try to explain. He went and picked up a stick, a branch and he tried to draw a map in the sand, and...I thought the Russians can be kind as well. And you know since then, I haven't condemned them as well. It might be just me, but I thought they're human as well.[1258]

Thus, through visits, the refugees not only re-established contact with friends and family, they were also able to experience present day life in the Baltic States and to understand the situation there more clearly. Upon return, they shared their experiences with other members of the community. Many Latvians, Lithuanians and Estonians in Britain returned to their homelands during the decade following independence on a regular basis, usually at least every other year, and the visits lasted on average about two to four weeks. Many claimed that they would visit more regularly if they were financially able, or in better health.

Unfortunately, some of those who wished to visit were unable due to poor health and a few chose not to. There were several reasons for this decision. Perhaps the most common was a desire to retain untainted the images of the homeland from a pre-war childhood. Some of those without family or friends felt there was little point in returning if there was nobody to visit. There was also the fear among some, that returning to the homeland would awaken painful memories. A Latvian woman living in Leeds explained her reasons for not returning to visit:

> ...I've never been back mostly because I haven't any relatives left, any close relatives left in Latvia. That was probably [the] main reason. And again I was happy while I was there and they always say you should never go back where you've been happy and it's been too many years and so I've never been back really now. That's it.[1259]

One Latvian woman also told me that she would not return to the homeland because she felt so angry towards the Russians there, and was afraid of what she might do to them if she visited Latvia.[1260]

EASTWARDS HOME? : RETURNING TO THE HOMELAND

In the decade following the restoration of independence, only a tiny minority of first generation Latvians, Lithuanians and Estonians from Great Britain returned to their homelands to live, some of whom I interviewed in the summer of 1997. At that time, all three communities gave very low estimates of the numbers of returnees. However, precise figures are elusive. A Lithuanian returnee based in Vilnius estimated about 10 Lithuanian returnees from the first generation, and while the Estonian community estimated a similar number of Estonian refugees, it appeared that there were greater numbers of Latvian returnees, most likely due to the greater size of the community in Britain.[1261]. Although a few first generation returnees opened up shops, businesses or engaged in politics, the vast majority returned simply to spend their retirement years and to die in their homeland. For example, Latvian returnees from Britain opened up a hotel (*Radi un Draugi*) and a restaurant (*Vincents*[1262]), to name just two enterprises, and among those retired, I even found returnees teaching English to earn some extra money. A non-quantifiable number of second generation Latvians, Lithuanians and Estonians also migrated to the Baltic States, most frequently on a temporary basis, for example, for educational or employment purposes. The increasing number of international firms establishing branches in the Baltic States, and universities running courses geared to foreign students stimulated this type of migration. I also met a second generation Latvian, who had taken on the running of his parents' former farmstead, and who at the time was heavily engaged in agricultural politics.

The low number of returnees from Britain contrasted with a higher flow of returning diaspora from America, Canada and other countries in the West, although the percentages were likely to have been broadly similar. Partly this was due to the larger overall numbers, but may also have been related to the higher number of professionals in these countries, as well as the greater capital required to venture into business. Latvians, Lithuanians and Estonians from America, Canada and Australia opened businesses and gained important positions within the economic and political spheres. For example, in the 1993 elections to the *Saiema*, members of the diaspora gained seats in the Latvian Parliament.[1263] Members of the Canadian and American diaspora respectively were voted in as Latvian and Lithuanian Presidents in the late 1990's.[1264] Indeed, the influence of returnees on the newly independent homelands has been immense, and warrants further research.

Among Latvians, Lithuanians and Estonians from Britain who decided to return, a number of considerations influenced their decision. Although identity based considerations, a desire to return to one's roots and come 'home' were usually the decisive factors, rarely were they been the only motivations in the decision to return. Other influences were also significant, particularly the existence of family in the homeland, work opportunities, the absence of family in Great Britain or the chance to reclaim family property.[1265] Dissatisfaction with life in England also played a part, combined with the knowledge that pensions go much further in Latvian than Britain.

A small number of Latvians, Lithuanians and Estonians from Britain returned to the homeland, simply because they wanted to die there. A Lithuanian woman explained: 'I think it's probably…because they started their lives in Lithuania, they want to finish their life in Lithuania'.[1266]

A Latvian returnee in Riga, whom I interviewed in 1997, summed up the main reason for his return: 'Well it's the roots. It's home you know.'[1267]   However, he also talked about other considerations in his decision to return to Latvia:

> Well they're all dying out the Latvians [in Britain]...and I was getting a bit lonely and not direct family, sisters, I don't have any left, but loads of cousins and...a nephew and...well they're all around here [Riga] and out in the country, further up, up north from here.[1268]

The fact that he was single with no children gave him the flexibility to return. Many of the returnees were single or widowed, and a few Latvian, Lithuanian and Estonian couples also returned. A spouse's lack of desire to live in the Baltic States was often a significant reason for not returning. However, one Lithuanian man I interviewed had returned to Vilnius to live, despite his wife's opposition. As editor of the Lithuanian newspaper *Europas Lietuvis* ('Europe's Lithuanians'), he saw an opportunity after independence had been declared, to take the paper to Lithuania and edit it from Vilnius. In doing so, he hoped to make the paper more profitable, after a period of financial difficulties, while it had been published in England. He returned to Vilnius in the autumn of 1992. He described why he had come:

> This was a sort of homecoming...because I always wanted to be in Lithuania...I saw in this a chance, not only to come, but to come as a working man.[1269]

However, his overwhelming desire to return meant that he did so despite the fact that this meant leaving his wife in England. He explained:

> ...family conflict became apparent, because my wife didn't want to come. Reasons? I don't know even today, but there was probably some apprehension, some, some...well there was something but she definitely stated that she did not want to come.[1270]

The author on a fieldwork trip to Lithuania

A few non-Baltic spouses did agree to live in the homeland although this was rare. In the only case I encountered, which involved a second generation Latvian man, this experiment was unsuccessful. He returned to Latvia, initially accompanied by his English wife and children, and his Latvian parents and grandparents, with the intention of reclaiming the family farm and transforming it into a working farm.[1271] He explained his reasons for returning:

> It was a very difficult decision. It was a decision based on many factors and it's difficult to put it down to one factor. An important factor was that...because both my parents were Latvian and I lived with my grandparents in England who were also Latvian from my mother's side, brought up in a Latvian community or very close to a Latvian community, I knew a lot about Latvia. There were a lot of hopes that...Latvia developed very quickly on its first declaration of independence after the First World War...it was looked upon as our hopes, opportunities to develop along with the country as one thing. For ourselves, the other thing was that we lived in a town in England...and I'd always had an interest in farming and it was not possible to do in England, yet I always wanted to do

farming, so I came to Latvian where I was able to have a farm.[1272]

Unfortunately, at the time of the interview, his wife had returned to England with one of the children, and it was uncertain what the future held. Like many returnees, this Latvian faced a variety of challenges after the move to the homeland, including hostility from locals and burglary of farm machinery. However, he persisted and as a result of joining a large farmers association, began to integrate successfully into Latvian society. Like many members of the second generation, he has a dual identity, and when I asked him where he belonged, he jokingly replied: 'On the Moon', a statement that nevertheless reflected the feeling that he did not fully belong either in England or in Latvia. The first generation Latvian returnee introduced earlier also had a dual sense of belonging. Living in Latvia did not mean that he shed all links with Britain. At the time of the interview he was debating whether or not to spend six months of every year in Latvia and six months in Britain. Subsequently he decided to live indefinitely in Latvia, but to visit Britain and the Latvian community there regularly. An Estonian in Britain told me about the story of an Estonian woman who returned to her homeland, having spent years looking out of her window in Sheffield and longing for the homeland. Now in the homeland, she looks out of her window and longs for Sheffield.

Even for the small minority of returnees from Britain who felt certain that the homeland was their home, bonds to Britain remained. Returnees brought with them values and culture influenced by fifty years of life in Britain, and had to adapt to a very different country from that which they left half a century earlier. A Lithuanian returnee explained:

> I have no complaints, no regrets, and once or twice I went back to England, I went like a visitor, and after about a week or two weeks I wanted to go home.

> I don't miss it [England] at all. Well, it's nice to be in London...[1273]

However, he also stated that:

> ...if for instance Britain was in some sort of danger or some sort, needed some sort of support, of course I'll be first there. It was, it gave me [a] second home, it still is a home of my family, my former family, my...son and daughter. They have their own family...

That's [Britain] where…I appreciate the civil order, for instance the model I will always…recommend to adopt similar model over here…at the municipal level.

There's a variety of what they've achieved in England, Great Britain I most probably would [recommend]. Well, I don't know anything else. This is it. And most probably the way I think, just like I …accused people of thinking like socialists, I most probably think like British. And this unfortunately I cannot [change]. Many times it was remarked, 'Oh you behave like a British', although I'm not. But this, this is all ingrained…socialisation.[1274]

Returnees were initially treated rather cautiously, but gradually became accepted back into society and as the countries re-orientated themselves towards Europe, the views and opinions of returnees became respected to the extent that many gained important positions in the political and economic spheres.

NON-RETURNEES – THE DECISION TO REMAIN IN BRITAIN

The vast majority of first generation refugees did not return to their homelands to live. While some were unable to return, due to poor health or financial reasons, and therefore had no choice, the majority decided not to return, citing a mixture of practical and identity based considerations.

Among the practical reasons mentioned, perhaps the most important explanation provided was age, the fact that they were too old to start again. One Latvian stated simply: '[I'm] too old to go back'.[1275] Age was also the main reason cited by a Latvian lady in Derbyshire, who I asked if she had ever considered returning. She replied:

Not really because I think if I were younger I might do because…there's a lot of demand for people with English you see. You could work for a British firm or something because you'd have use of both languages…but I mean at my age there's not much point. To start moving…I mean it was enough from Chaddesden to Spondon, and…it's very difficult to get flats and things in Riga. It's very crowded. You'd have to find somewhere to live and all the palaver… I think when you're in your seventies it's a bit much.[1276]

She also described some of the other practical problems associated with return:

> ...it would be rather difficult. I wouldn't like to drive in Riga for instance, they drive on the other side, with all the trams running in the middle of the road. You'd have to start from scratch a lot of things and it's difficult to get someone to do something.

> In Riga, I think they're a bit disorganised yet and you don't know who to trust and who not to trust, because there's a lot of like cowboy firms and things, and they know the ones that live there, but I mean if you went in from abroad, you'd probably get ripped off because they think you're a fool...that's again something the Russians have brought in. This paying under the table and we're no good at it...[1277]

Some of the respondents felt that they would return if they were single, including men from both intermarriages and same nationality marriages. However, after spending fifty years - the largest part of their life in Britain they were too rooted to move - they had family, houses and a life in England. An elderly Latvian from Leeds described the rooting process and the role of family in the decision to stay:

> We hoped to go back to live from the beginning, but now you see we get old, we get settled here slowly. Many people married here, get children here. Our cemetery is full. Some people whose husband or wife has died don't like to leave [they] just want to stay where they are. So there it is. Some people went [have gone] back now, because you know it, from '91 it's independent again.

> I personally wanted to go back and I went several times, but my son is not going back and my wife wants to stay where the son is. How can I do it? [I am] 86 years? What will I do there? And there is no very close relatives to us, and of course if they were there, I would go back at once. Not for a better life, no, but just because that is my country and there is my people. That is only reason.[1278]

An Estonian man also cited family as one of the main reasons for not returning.

> I never considered it [returning] seriously because of the family and I can't, it's not open, it's not an option that is open to me, but I felt that I probably could. I still feel that I probably

[could] because being…as long as I get income from here, then I will be reasonably all right, but I could not live say with their means. If I had to exist on the pension that they are receiving, I could not.[1279]

Another Latvian man from Leeds also felt that he would return if he was on his own: 'If I was on my own I would [return], I would yeah. Because the cultural ties are stronger for me there, if I was on my own, if I didn't have a family.'[1280]   He even pointed out the benefits of returning to Latvia: 'Besides, just imagine even as a pensioner I get [a] pension about 8 times more than they do. So you can imagine how well off you are.'[1281]

Another Latvian pointed out that it costs only £2000-00 to buy a house in Latvia.[1282]   One woman from Sheffield was reported to have had a new house built from scratch in Latvia, able to afford it due to the low prices of building materials and labour.[1283]   Although the low cost of living in the homeland was cited as a benefit of returning, other factors tended to dissuade the diaspora.   These included the complexities of bureaucracy, instability of banks, and poor healthcare, the latter factor particularly important given the fact that the original refugees are now all in their late-sixties and beyond.

Being rooted in Britain also had identity-based aspects. Although age and practical considerations were often been the most important factors in the decision to stay, factors relating to identity and conceptions of home and belonging were also significant. This was summed up by the comments of a Lithuanian woman in Britain;

> Well, I am Lithuanian yes, but if somebody says, 'Do you want to go back and live there?', I should say straight away, 'No, no', because so many years gone.   All the generation mostly die. The younger generation [in Lithuania] is brought up different way.   It's not that way when I [was] brought up.   And that make me feeling that I couldn't be there happy.   I am happy here.   I am very, very happy here, and yes, visit, yes, for one week, for a few days…but no more.[1284]

As the next section suggests, identities and conceptions of home not only contributed to the decision to stay in Britain, they were also transformed by this decision.

CHANGING IDENTITIES IN BRITAIN POST-INDEPENDENCE

The fact that the Baltic diaspora in Britain were no longer exiles, free to return to live in the homeland, but choosing in most cases, to remain in Britain, impacted upon their conceptions of home and belonging, and in many cases, confused their identities as Latvians, Lithuanians and Estonians. In short, the bonds to Britain and the homeland shifted.

Following independence, the diaspora consisted of three segments: first, those for whom independence reaffirmed their bond to the homeland and enabled them to return to live in the place they regarded as home - the homeland. Members of this group also included those who wish to return to the homeland, but who were unable due to family commitments or health. For the second segment, independence highlighted and strengthened the bond to Britain, which was now regarded as home. For many in this group, their bond to the homeland was still in a process of evolution, having been confused by return visits. Many felt that they no longer belonged in the homeland: they felt different to the locals there, even feeling like foreigners in their own homeland. For some Latvians, Lithuanians and Estonians, this feeling decreased as they visited the homeland more regularly, and as the re-opening of the links between the individual and the homeland meant that the Latvian, Lithuanian or Estonian aspect of their identities could be expressed more freely and more fully. Ultimately, however, this group wished to remain in Britain. Finally, there were those for whom independence highlighted the confused nature of their identities, which they were yet to resolve; they felt split between Britain and the homeland, and while some felt that they belong in both places, others felt that they belonged in neither. They had no clear sense that Britain was home or where they belonged.

The evidence suggests that at the time this research was undertaken in the mid to late 1990s, the second group was currently the most numerous. Visits to the homeland engendered shifts in their identities as Latvians, Lithuanians and Estonians and the bond to the homeland. Latvians, Lithuanians and Estonians in Britain experienced feelings of alienation and of being foreigners in their own homeland. Feelings of difference were exacerbated by the fact that local inhabitants in the homeland often regarded and treated the émigrés as foreigners.

The different accents of the visiting diaspora, and for some, a loss of fluency in the homeland language identified them to the locals as returning diaspora. Loss of fluency was particularly common among intermarried diaspora. An Estonian man talked about his lack of fluency in Estonian:

> ...it does come back in a certain fashion, but you find you can't...say it correct way, you know, you kind of say things upside-down and you're kind of looking for some word, [but] you can't...get that word out, and there's certain words you just don't know...some of the trees, things like that...you just can't think of the Estonian word for it at all...until you look it up in the dictionary then it comes to you.[1285]

> ...you see they definitely all noticed that I had some kind of accent and you can't find the words, certain words, you have to find some other word that means the same thing

> ...when I go to Estonia and I listen to people, I can understand almost everything I feel like I'm Estonian, but when it comes to me to talk, to explain or to do things I find it quite difficult.[1286]

Many of the refugees had picked up slight regional accents. For example, I could discern traces of Yorkshire or Lancashire in some of their accents. A Latvian man stated that when he visited Latvia he felt different from the local population there. He explained why: 'Even if I speak to them they look...You speak Latvian but it's not Latvian accent. You speak foreign accent.'[1287] Young children in Liepaja even laughed at him when he spoke: 'Yeah, they called me bloody foreigner. I spoke then in my own language like, you know in Latvian...'[1288] A Lithuanian woman had a similar experience:

> Yeah, they [called] me foreigner in Lithuania now. They say, 'You look foreigner'... If I speak in Lithuanian, 'Your accent is foreigner'. I speak in Lithuanian. I am born in Lithuania. I went to high school, everything, and they [call] me foreigner still. It's upsetting you know upsetting.[1289]

It was not only language or accent, which distinguished the visiting diaspora. A Latvian woman from Nottingham explained how the locals could tell them apart straight away: '...the Latvians in Latvia, they say they can tell us straight away because of our behaviour, how we look and how we smile, and how we talk...we have the confidence and they don't...they could tell straight away if someone was from abroad.'[1290]

Visits also quashed romantic visions of pre-war homelands, which were replaced by the sometimes, harsh realities of the Baltic States in the 1990s. Greater knowledge about standards of living, the perceived lack of security and poor health care prompted many individuals to feel a greater sense of gratitude for their lives in Britain. One Latvian woman described her visits to the homeland:

> Well, the first time it was very pleasant, because we met all the relatives after so many years. But the second time, you can see behind all the scenes then. You can see what the country has become and more of their nature and I was very upset because the country was very neglected, and we travelled quite a lot, and then you realise how the people talk then as well, what their opinions are, which are quite different from ours.[1291]

The idea that the inhabitants of the Baltic States had in some way been *Sovietised*, and had a different way of thinking from members of the diaspora was a very common theme in the interviews. There was also an acknowledgement of how far the diaspora's own attitudes and values had changed as a result of living in Britain. The result was an increase in feelings of difference between the local and émigré populations. Not only did many members of the diaspora hardly know their relatives when they first returned, they also realised that even relatives saw the world differently. Both these factors contributed to feelings of not belonging. One Estonian man explained:

> I certainly didn't feel as if I belonged in the first...couple of weeks, you didn't know the people you know, they are relatives of mine – it was just a couple of weeks short of 40 years that I saw my brothers and sister.
>
> I felt that I could live there, but that's probably deceptive, if you go as a tourist that's one thing and then you start living there is another thing, so I...I'm not taken as a local person by my relatives, although we are, we feel like brothers and sisters and all that, but there are differences as well. My thinking is a bit different to theirs.
>
> They're more sort of...I think they're more sort of [pause], more practical...well more concerned with things...you can touch and see...more...materialistic. Ideas, they seem to be less concerned with.
>
> ...as a pensioner now I feel pretty - in comparison to them I feel quite erm, quite sort of erm, well off. But there, there is quite a struggle to make ends meet. They have to work a lot, a lot harder, so I suppose that's conditions...to see things in a different way.[1292]

Some members of the Latvian, Lithuanian and Estonian communities in Britain were even dissuaded from visiting the homeland through a fear of feeling and being regarded as foreigners, if they did so. A Latvian woman from Leeds who had never returned to visit, primarily because she had no family left there, felt that she would not belong in Latvia if she returned. She linked not belonging to the fact that she felt that her Latvian identity had weakened. I asked her whether she had a stronger or weaker sense of Latvian identity than she did when she first came to Britain. She replied:

> Weaker, weaker, much weaker now, yes. Oh yes, I think I would probably feel an outsider if I went back to Latvia. Would feel an outsider there definitely.
>
> I don't think I would fit in anymore. No way. I've been over 50 years now in England, in Yorkshire, longer than anywhere else [laughs].[1293]

For some Latvians, Lithuanians and Estonians in Britain, visits further confused already contested identities. One Latvian talked about how after visiting Latvia, he felt as if he did not belong there, but nor did he feel that he belonged in Britain: 'When I came [went] to Latvia…it's all different. I not fit in. We don't fit in you know. We are foreigners over there. Same as we're foreigners here. It's a tragedy in one way.'[1294] Another Latvian man talked about how he still felt like an 'outsider' in Britain, yet even though he felt that his identity was 'just the same' then as when he first came to Britain, he also 'felt different' when he visited Latvia.[1295]

Some Latvians, Lithuanians and Estonian felt that they belonged in both the homeland and Britain, a feeling reinforced by visits to the homeland, and were yet to reconcile the dual nature of their identities. This characteristic was described by an Estonian man living in Chesterfield, who I asked whether or not he felt like a foreigner when he travelled to Estonia. He replied:

> No, I don't feel like a foreigner, but, but I don't err, I don't particularly feel like erm [pause] as if I belong there. That's an odd thing. I've heard of other people, well in Leicester, an educated person she said, she said it herself, and also comparing notes with Swedish Estonians, if they are in Sweden or in this country they feel like Estonians, but if they go to Estonia they feel either British or Swedes, I think that is…if I'm in Estonia I think I'm more of a Briton than a…I think…if I think of my home, it's here, it's here. It's a very odd thing, a very odd thing.

And whereas if I'm here, then I think I'm more of an Estonian than anything else.[1296]

A Latvian woman expressed similar views. I asked her the following question: 'So when you go over there [Latvia], would you say that you identify more with British people than with the Latvians in Latvia today, or do you think you can't compare it?' She gave the following reply:

> It's rather difficult you know. You identify with the Latvian people there because you are a Latvian, but you also belong here, because you've spent, I mean I've only spent 19, hardly 19, I was just turned 19 when I left Latvia so I spent 18 years there, and I've spent 50 here, so you certainly have a sense of belonging here as well. I mean you've got, you know, your home and whatever you've got, you've got it here. I should say one's split sort of halfway as it were. In a way you go there and then you talk, 'Oh you must go home', and at the same time, you go home and as I say, you suddenly start reckoning well, if I don't buy this and if I don't do that, then next spring I can go again, so…the pull is both ways.[1297]

For this woman, the presence of Russians in the homeland was one of the most important factors contributing to a feeling that she had difficulty identifying with the country in which she grew up. She explained: '…it's just that when you go there [Latvia], the country to which you belong doesn't quite feel the same anymore, but you still feel Latvian, it's just that you think the country's gone wrong'.[1298] She continued:

> …the country isn't quite what we left…I mean we left a country that was Latvian and you go back to Riga now and it's still Russian and a lot of the way they do things they've been made to do them the way Russians do, which we didn't do before.[1299]

This woman hints at what many Latvians, Lithuanians and Estonians in Britain felt - they were from pre-war Latvia, Lithuania and Estonia and did not fit into the new post-independent States. Many were however, beginning to accept that while they no longer belonged in the homeland, they could still enjoy what it has to offer, and maintain contact with family and friends. For a majority of the diaspora, independence enabled them to embrace their ethnic culture and identity in the homeland, and at the same time, led to a greater appreciation of life in Britain. In this sense, independence brought about the complete integration of the diaspora in Britain; they were now free to, and did, enjoy both worlds. During visits to Latvia, visiting diaspora spoke their homeland language, ate homeland cuisine, and immersed themselves in the life there. Some had the opportunity to take part in important festivals and celebrations, for example Song Festivals and the celebrations of independence. Back in Britain, they returned to a way of life that was part British, part Latvian. They voted in elections in Britain, they met English friends and attended Latvian clubs.

Thus, although the diaspora returned to the homeland on visits and in this way, re-engaged with the homeland, they also felt a greater sense of permanency in Britain, as well, as a heightened sense that Britain was home. Britain was where they belonged. This feeling was expressed by a Lithuanian woman:

> Lithuania – my homeland. I love Lithuania you know…I love Lithuania, but my life [is] here you know.[1300]

An Estonian man echoed this sentiment, stating the following, in reply to the question: 'Where do you think that you belong?':

> Well, I belong here, I'm sure of it, because of the family, I can't live anywhere else. And…I don't feel at home when I go to Estonia. I got family [there], I got my brother and I've got pretty well used to them. We get along, but as a guest, but not as a local person.[1301]

The sense of permanency was undoubtedly strengthened by the fact that the diaspora could no longer be regarded as refugees or exiles, and had therefore chosen to remain in Britain. Their changed status was acknowledged by comments such as: 'I'm not any more [a] refugee…'[1302]

THE EFFECTS OF INDEPENDENCE ON THE ORGANISED COMMUNITIES

Inevitably, the opening up of links between the diaspora and the homeland engendered a shift in the goals and activities of the organised communities. The achievement of independence, the main aim of the organised community throughout exile, freed the communities up to concentrate on other tasks. Independence brought the communities into a new phase of existence and led to a reassessment of their aims.

The intended role of the diaspora following independence - to replant Latvian, Lithuanian and Estonian cultures and identities in the homeland, was largely defunct as a result of independence. Although the diaspora felt that the culture in the homeland was not as rich as it had been in the inter-war period, they were surprised that it had survived and had, in fact, moved on. This awareness, since independence, contributed to a belief that the residents of the homeland were quite capable of looking after themselves, and that it was their responsibility to take cultures and identities forward in a way that suited them. This acknowledgement led to a reduced role for the diaspora. A Lithuanian stated that one of the effects of independence was that in part 'it closed the doors to cultural activity here. It was felt that there was no need to continue because it was already there much better and so on'.[1303] A Latvian woman expressed the post-independence realisation of the extent of the changes:

> ...there are changes [in the homeland] definitely, but then there are changes in England in fifty years...I mean there would have been changes in fifty years anywhere, because people look at things differently, but it's not quite what we left and I think it is wrong in a way to go back fifty years later and expect to find what you left isn't it?[1304]

A Lithuanian woman also described the effect of a new awareness of culture in the homeland since independence on the communities:

> We thought we were the up-to-date original Lithuanians, and it was a shock to find that in fact, Lithuanians in Soviet times had moved on. There were patriotic undercurrents. They had moved on. Their...culture, their ways of approaching culture were if you like, more up to date. We had actually aged. Our attitudes in that direction had aged. We were living in the past. Really that summarises it.[1305]

According to Marian Rubchak, the tendency to underestimate the fact that the homelands have moved on in their absence is characteristic of diasporic groups. She states that: '...external exiles are likely to underestimate the inexorable fact that the people they left behind continue to develop culturally, politically, and economically in response to their own changing circumstances, and without the exiles' participation'.[1306].

Latvian, Lithuanian and Estonian cultural activities in Britain continued after homeland independence was declared, although the orientation of many of these events shifted. For example, commemorations of independence became happy, relaxed, celebrations compared to their previous sombre, nationalist-militaristic orientation. These events became strictly for the community in Britain, rather than a way of maintaining culture on the homeland's behalf. One change from the Soviet years was increased cultural exchange between Britain and the homeland. In particular, dance groups, musicians and singers were invited to Britain on a regular basis to perform concerts to the diaspora and the British public. Many Latvians, Lithuanians and Estonians also attended cultural events in the homeland during visits, for example, Song Festivals. One Latvian noted that cultural activity in Britain had waned due to the popularity of such events. Speaking about the celebration of St John's Day in Britain, he noted the following:

> ...of course there's too many old men now and the young ones are not taking part. It would have been different I think if Latvia wasn't free because everything is sort of thrown into...the goings on in Latvia. They go to – next year there's a Latvian Song Festival in Riga'.[1307]

Although the idea of the transplantation of cultures and identities back into the homeland became regarded as somewhat inappropriate, the communities did feel that they still had some role in helping to re-build their homeland. As well as individuals helping their families financially in various ways, the communities also undertook important charitable work on behalf of schools and communities in the homeland, and also played a minor role in the politics, economy and culture of the homeland. The communities also increased charitable donations on behalf of the homeland, primarily since the passage of goods became far easier. For example, the Latvian club in Leeds regularly sent parcels of clothes, shoes and other goods to Latvia. A Latvian woman talked about the sometimes, overwhelming desire to help relatives and locals in the homeland:

> ...we think a lot about the people in Latvia. You sort of, you want to help them. At first we used to send parcels and clothes, although we've been sending parcels all these years, but not very [often] you know, approximately twice a year because they used to be big parcels. They used to be about 44 pounds.

> And the first few years we were really...you know you thought yes, we'll do this and we'll do that and now we realise they are not quite the same people as we thought they were. And I also read somewhere that you can have a nervous complex and one of the reasons is that you want to do too much good, because when we were going out we thought, oh, we could buy this for that girl and this for that girl and that was all we thought and we could take that with us or we could send that, and I thought, oh now, this is going to the extremes, and since I read about it, no

I have to pull myself together and we do get things when we go, but we've certainly calmed down'[1308]

One way of helping relatives post-independence was to hand over to them, or allow them to live in, properties reclaimed by the diaspora. Many Latvians, Lithuanians and Estonians in Britain were unable or unwilling to restore and live in the properties themselves. A Latvian woman from Nottingham described how she and her Latvian husband helped out relatives in Latvia. She began by talking about the reclamation of her husband's father's house:

> ...[he] has got his father's house, where his brother and the family, where his brother and the family who stayed in Latvia lived, but he didn't want to claim half of it, so he gave it to his sister-in-law. We still have to help out. They need a new roof....but we are helping because...you feel sorry for them as well because...well, you probably heard about this bank. Well, it's the same as in Albania, the pyramid banking and she had some money, a little money in the bank and she lost that and now she's a pensioner, so she can't save any money, and our god-daughter who is the niece, she's our god-daughter and she's got a job locally but it doesn't pay much, so we have to help.[1309]

Another aspect of the communities' new relationship with the homeland was the ability, for all those with Latvian, Lithuanian or Estonian citizenship to vote in elections in the homeland, and thus to influence the life of the country. There was a tendency in the early post-independence years, for the diaspora to vote for rightist, nationalist orientated parties, which favoured tough citizenship policies, excluding large sections of the post-war Russian diaspora. For example, for the elections to the Latvian *Saiema*[1310] in June 1993, Marija, a Latvian woman, told me that *Fatherland and Freedom* and the *LNNK* (Latvian National Independence Movement) were the most popular parties among Latvian diaspora in Britain.[1311] Both parties aimed to exclude post-war Russian speaking immigrants from gaining Latvian citizenship, and even desired to repatriate them to their countries of origin. According to Marija, the main reason for these parties' popularity was the diaspora's attitude towards Russians in the homeland - the belief that Russians should not be given citizenship due to the long term effects on the ethnic composition of Latvia: 'so people go for the sort of nationalistic' parties.[1312] Another popular party among the diaspora was *Latvia's Way*, a centrist party which had actually been organised by the western Latvian diaspora. Marija estimated that in the Nottingham and Derby area, about two-thirds of the number eligible to vote did so, despite complicated procedures.[1313] Although total numbers voting in Britain were small, the combined vote of the global Latvian diaspora was significant, enough to influence the politics in the homeland albeit in a small way, even while remaining abroad.

Although the majority of Latvians in Britain who voted in elections, supported parties with similar policies towards the Russian population, not all Latvians agreed about the direction in which Latvia should go in the future and the means to achieving it. This was symptomatic of the fact that views among the Latvian, Lithuanian and Estonian diaspora's were constantly evolving, as the economic and political situation in the homeland transformed. The differing political perspectives of the diaspora suggested that although prior to independence, the diaspora were united in the common goal of independence, post-liberation, the communities were divided not only in their response to independence, but also in their attitudes towards the rebuilding of the homeland.

Unlike during the Soviet period, when the diaspora was unable to influence politics in the homeland, they felt that they could play a small role in influencing the political life of the homeland. Some members of the Baltic communities felt that having lived in a successful democracy and market economy, that they could use their knowledge and expertise for the good of the homeland. One Latvian man even felt that he had a better understanding of the politics and economy of the homeland, than the locals. He explained why:

> When I go to Latvia, even with the politicians I could speak with some authority with them, because in the communist regime they were starved of proper information. The books that they read, they were specially cooked for the purpose to mislead Latvians.[1314]

As organisations which campaigned for political independence, such as 'The Captive Nations Committee' came to an end, other groups and associations came into being to prepare and disseminate information about the Baltic States in the Western World, as well as to discuss the various options for the Baltic States' political future. Examples included 'The British-Baltic Association', linked with the University of Bradford, and 'The Baltic Committee' in Bradford.[1315] The Baltic Council continued to play a role in highlighting the political situation in the Baltic States (as well as fostering cultural exchange), and the organised communities and diplomatic representatives also campaigned on behalf of the Baltic States, for example, pressuring western governments to speed up the process of EU and Nato membership.

As the communities continued to age, another area given greater attention during the 1990s was the care of the elderly, although many of the structures established to meet their needs had already been set up prior to independence. Finally, the clubs also focused their attention to the future of the communities to a greater extent than before, although this was more related to the ageing of the population than the effects of independence. The decline of the first generation population highlighted the increasing need to revive second and third generation interest, and also to attract new members to the communities. During the years since independence, the second generation increasingly took on responsibilities for running community structures and organisations. The implications of this transfer of power were wide reaching, and included shifting criteria for membership to the ethnic community, and changes in the goals and aims of the communities.

BALTIC MIGRATION TO BRITAIN 1991-2000

Independence not only stimulated visits and migration from Britain to the homeland, it also led to migration from the homeland to Britain. This migration consisted of three main types: firstly, those who came to Britain for the purposes of educational or cultural exchange, an intentionally temporary migration; second, those who could be described as economic migrants, who travelled to Britain in search of better jobs and a higher standard of living; thirdly, there were those who have made the passage to Britain as political refugees, and who sought asylum. The latter category was been particularly numerous in the mid to late 1990s. These newcomers headed mainly for London and other large cities in Britain, and many approached the established communities for support. The addition of these new migrants into the established communities brought about some revitalisation, particularly in London, just as the entry of post-Second World War migrants into areas inhabited by late nineteenth and early twentieth century Baltic migrants led to a revival in these areas. However, tensions also emerged. The largest numbers of new migrants came from Lithuania, which according to the Home Office was one of 'the top 35 asylum producing countries in the United Kingdom' in 1999.[1316] It was partly due to their large number that the impact of these so-called 'New migrants' on the established communities was most significant among the Lithuanian community, and serious divisions arose.

According to UNHCR statistics, the monthly average of Lithuanians applying for asylum in Britain was 100 in 1998.[1317] In the first 11 months of 1998, '1170 Lithuanian asylum seekers arrived in Britain', 'second only to Turkey and the former Yugoslavia'.[1318] Numbers of Lithuanian asylum applicants dropped in 1999. In January 1999, applications for asylum numbered 86, and in February 1999, only 25.[1319] The decline has been attributed to the implementation by the Lithuanian authorities of new measures requested by the British government at a meeting in London between the Lithuanian Minister for the Interior and the Secretary of the British Home Office on 19 January 1999.[1320] New measures included passengers on flights from Lithuania to London providing more detailed information about their travel, and their personal information being recorded by officers of the national migration service at Vilnius Airport. Border checks on buses leaving Lithuania were also stepped up.[1321]

During the first half of 1999, *LYNES* and *Europas Lietuvis* discussed the tensions arising between the so-called 'New Lithuanians' and the 'British Lithuanians'. *LYNES* stressed the term 'British Lithuanians' to highlight their distinctiveness and differences from the 'New Lithuanians'. In February 1999, it reported that 'New Lithuanians' in London had already established a new branch *Lietuvių Namų* at Lithuanian House, Freeland Road in London, with a membership of 100 and rising.[1322] The editor asked: 'Is this a take-over by the new Liths?'. His concerns were that:

> ...many are political asylum seekers having only a temporary license to reside in this country. They are not keen to include the British Liths in their circle of activities. Where do. we British Liths stand in this encroaching foray on our community assets? There were 800 DBLS members in Gt. Britain last year. If a new branch registers with over 400 members, its representatives have the power to nominate and elect their own directors to control the British Lithuanian assets in this country. In other words a complete takeover.[1323]

These comments expressed the fear that because 'New Lithuanians' considerably outnumber 'British Lithuanians' they had the potential to take over the Lithuanian organisation DBLS. The British Government's policy of dispersal of asylum seekers also raised fears that new Lithuanians might predominate in local branches, and eventually take over the small regional associations. Concern was also expressed in *LYNES* that they were choosing not to join established DBLS groups and instead had set up a new branch of their own. According to *LYNES*, due to the actions of New Lithuanians: 'In one swoop we have an "us" and "them" culture'. One focus of the debate was the 'New Lithuanians' eligibility for membership of the DBLS. Particularly important in this respect was the condition of membership in Article 4 of the DBLS Constitution, which stated that 'no person shall be admitted as a member of the Association unless (a) he is *resident in Great Britain...*'.[1324] The debate centred around whether asylum seekers, who composed a large percentage of the New Lithuanians, could be regarded as 'resident ' in Great. The question, 'What should be the standpoint of DBLS with regard to Lithuanian citizens arriving into UK and seeking political asylum?', was discussed at a meeting of the DBLS directors on 23 February 1999, at the Lithuanian Embassy in London, in which even the Leader of the Lithuanian Parliament, Vytautas Landsbergis was involved.[1325]

Various actions by 'New Lithuanians' were of particular concern to the established Lithuanian community. The headline of the March 1999 edition of *LYNES* 'DBLS Members Beware', revealed the extent of this unease. The headline story discussed the proposal by a New Lithuanian 'to ban English in all DBLS meetings and, further, to bar any non-Lithuanian speaking member from seeking a Directorship in either DBLS or Lithuanian House Ltd.'[1326] As *LYNES* noted , this would, if implemented 'serve to disenfranchise the spouses of mixed marriages along with a substantial portion of children and grandchildren. As many of these members of the Association speak little or no Lithuanian, they could not (would not) attend meetings as these would be carried out only in Lithuanian. More than 50% of DBLS would become disenfranchised. Over time they (our children and grandchildren) would disappear from the Lithuanian scene and culture'.[1327]

Many British Lithuanians were aware that the community did need 'new blood' but did not want the new Lithuanians to become the dominant force in the community. In previous years, the input of new blood was regarded as a positive development. The editor of *LYNES* had noted to me in an interview in 1997, that although there had been a decline in cultural activities since independence 'we're beginning to liven up a little the activity with the help of the...new Lithuanians that are living in this country and we...have I think we have a firm belief now that some sort of identity will still remain here...because of the new arrivals'.[1328] However, she did note the differences between the new Lithuanians and the established communities:

Although the new arrivals' culture is still so very different now from ours – we are Anglified anyway, but...steps are being taken now through various ways...to link closer together. They're being done and I have a feeling that there will be some form of identity left, although the new Lithuanians are at the moment more concerned with earning their bread and butter and work all hours God sends and have little time, but that we feel will ease.[1329]

She also stated that the new Lithuanians 'stand out because they're young energetic...they sort of give a little boost to the older community'.[1330]

The approach of the 1999 AGM's of the British Lithuanian Association in Great Britain and Lithuanian House Limited showed that the aim to link closer together was a long way off. Candidates from both the British Lithuanian community and the new Lithuanians stood for positions in the Central Committee of the DBLS and other sections of both organisations. Campaigning among British Lithuanians grew, and knives were reportedly 'drawn'.[1331] The elections held on 24 and 25 April 1999 produced a resounding victory for British Lithuanians, with many younger Lithuanians gaining important positions.[1332] The new Chairman, a younger Lithuanian, quickly stated that the DBLS aimed to 'to encompass the old and new Lithuanians within Great Britain' and 'to clear the misunderstandings arisen amongst the old and new wave Lithuanians'.[1333] The Chairman even went as far as to propose the following: 'It is obvious that we shall require to alter our Memorandum and Articles to take account of new wave Lithuanians living temporarily on these shores. To this end we shall select a Working Group which will prepare a draft constitution to be ratified at the AGM next year'.[1334]

In July 1999, the Chairman of the DBLS Advisory Council, another young Lithuanian agreed that 'we have to re-open dialogue with the "new Lithuanians" and reassure them that we DO see them playing an important role in the life of our Community'. He stressed that: '...we all need to understand very clearly that unless the Association looks to the future, believes that there can be a future and attempts to shape that future the Lithuanian Community in Great Britain will soon cease to exist as a coherent entity that we can recognise'.[1335]

At the time that this research was completed in 2000, the debate surrounding membership was continuing and it appeared likely that there would be further changes and developments within the DBLS throughout 2000 and into the new millenium.

The conflict between the 'New Lithuanians' and 'British Lithuanians' is significant in several ways. Most importantly, it revealed the shifting membership of the ethnic community over time. For example, debates suggest that the elderly generation felt that non-Lithuanian spouses and second and third generation Lithuanians had more right to membership than Lithuanian newcomers, although the younger generation were moving towards the inclusion of new Lithuanians. Second, it reveals the extent of difference between British Lithuanians and New Lithuanians. This can be compared to the differences experienced by visiting diaspora in the homeland between themselves and the locals. Third, the conflict reveals the generation gap and the significance of the transfer of the power balance between first and second generation Lithuanians. Finally, the conflict highlighted the future of the British Baltic communities, with the younger generations stressing the point that without new blood, and possibly modifications to the makeup of the community, it had little chance of survival.

CONCLUDING REMARKS: INDEPENDENCE – A SECOND TURNING POINT FOR LATVIANS, LITHUANIANS AND ESTONIANS IN BRITAIN

I asked one Latvian couple whether independence had made a big change to their lives. Their reply was: 'No, not really no. We still live here I mean we don't think [of] going back, not to live, not to stay, I mean yeah for visiting. It's nice to go visiting'.[1336] A Latvian woman from Nottingham gave the following answer in reply to the question: 'How has independence changed your life as a Latvian in Great Britain? How did you feel?':

> I don't know how it has changed. At first I was very happy and people used to come from Latvia to visit and it was erm, sort of nice to know that they are free, they've got their independence now. Well, then I realised it's not for me anymore because I didn't have anybody there any more. They were all dead. I've got a brother, but he's in England and my husband's mother died. He didn't have anybody. There was nobody there. There was nobody to go to really...and of course I had my children, my two sons here. They were both married -- [they] married English girls, so they couldn't go back. They wouldn't want that. So it was out of the questions and...by that time I wasn't really missing it any more. That was it. That was finished more or less then. But it was to know that...it's changed things.

Things have changed for them over there, but I still never really considered going back. Like I say it's too long. I've been away too long really.[1337]

Unsurprisingly, the restoration of independence did not lead to the large-scale return of the diaspora, as had been envisaged when the refugees first came to Britain. More interestingly, independence has changed the way Latvians, Lithuanians and Estonians in Britain regard themselves. As a result of liberation, individuals and communities have redefined themselves, their identities and roles as diaspora in Britain. Although a few refugees returned to their home – the homeland to live, for the vast majority, independence has strengthened their bond to Britain.

Independence has also engendered a shift in the role of the organised community vis-à-vis the homeland, with the diaspora now playing only a minor role in helping the revitalisation of ethnic culture and identity. Yet despite the demise of the diaspora's role and the strengthened bond to Britain, the opening of links to the homeland has brought about some revitalisation of the communities at home, and opened up transnational links. Independence has enabled the diaspora to embrace their ethnic cultures, and to revisit their pasts. Despite the extinction of the traditional diasporan myth of return, independence has not threatened their position as diaspora. If anything diasporic identities have been strengthened as a result of independence. Although the diaspora did not fulfil the return myth upon independence, this was only one aspect of the diasporic existence. Tölöyan stated that:

> ...it makes more sense to think of diasporan or diasporic existence as not necessarily involving a physical return but rather a re-turn, a repeated turning to the concept and/or reality of the homeland and other diasporan kin through memory, written and visual texts, travel, gifts and assistance, et cetera. The orientation towards the homeland can be symbolic, ritual, religious. It may manifest itself in philanthropic concern, in a desire to influence the development of politics and culture in the homeland, and - in the contemporary world - to influence the government of the hostland in favour of the homeland, or on behalf of one's needier kin in yet a third country, through lobbies and other forms of gift giving.[1338]

As a result of independence, the diaspora have re-orientated themselves in relation to the homeland and Great Britain, and their responsibilities towards the homeland and 'hostland' has altered. On the whole they have felt that the changes have been positive. The majority now feel that they have the best of both worlds: the opportunity to reconnect with the homeland and ethnic culture (which is seen less and less as a duty, although some do still feel a moral obligation to the homeland), while at the same time, enjoy the benefits of retirement in Britain. In this sense, integration has been achieved to its fullest extent, and has in fact been spurred on by independence. This integration was summed up by an Estonian man, who at the time of the interview, was Secretary of the Association of Estonians in Great Britain:

> ...my own family, local people [English neighbours], local environment, national politics and concerns that affect me are my real world. Being Estonian in the sense of being active organiser now that Estonia is an independent country is comparable to a pastime that I feel a moral duty to pursue. I would sum it up something like that: I feel I am an Estonian who has adapted to the British way of life to a sufficient degree that enables him to live in harmony with the local community, relatively free of inner feelings of conflict or a sense of cultural deprivation, but who nonetheless feels a need as well as an obligation to maintain loose ties with his Estonian roots through his family in Estonia and the Estonian community in the UK.[1339]

For further analysis of the effects of homeland independence on the Baltic communities in Britain see my journal articles in the Journal of Baltic Studies. Although this paper focuses on the Latvian community it contains comparative analysis on the Estonian and Lithuanian communities in Britain.[1340]

CHAPTER 10

Conclusion

People can't be loyal to two nations, any more than they can be loyal to two masters.

(Norman Tebbit, Speech at Tory Party Conference in Blackpool, 1997)

[I'm a] British citizen you know, swore allegiance to Queen you know. She's still my Queen, but as I said my...roots are here [in Latvia] you know, and that's why I came back here... Sometimes, I say I have one foot in Britain and one foot in Latvia, sort of split. Maybe it would be the best way you know, to spend six months there and six months here. (Latvian returnee)[1341]

If I'm in EstoniaI think I'm more of a Briton...whereas if I'm here, then I think I'm more of an Estonian than anything else. (First Generation Estonian)[1342]

AT THE CLOSE OF THIS RESEARCH IN 2000, THE POST-WAR LATVIAN, LITHUANIAN AND ESTONIAN communities in Britain were in severe decline. Although there were pockets of Latvian, Lithuanian and Estonian communities in major cities, the majority of people in Britain were probably completely unaware of their presence. The only surviving remnants of their presence on Britain's physical landscape consisted of a handful of club-houses in former industrial areas of towns and cities and several retirement homes in the English countryside. All were largely inconspicuous, often marked only by small plaques by the door. For example, a Latvian retirement village was tucked away in the Leicestershire countryside at Catthorpe Manor, and both a Latvian and Estonian club were hidden off the main road, Manningham Lane, in a small cul-de-sac in Bradford. Slightly more discernible was the Lithuanian club in Manchester, housed in a large Victorian mansion on Middleton Road, painted in the Lithuanian national colours. However, there was little to suggest that the unassuming Victorian house in a street of residential houses in Hound's Lane, Nottingham is home to the Catholic Order, the Lithuanian Marian Fathers, and in Soviet times, was the site of *samizdat* publication and distribution. In London, the presence of Latvian, Lithuanian and Estonian diaspora was rather more visible, particularly since some of the clubs are situated in well-heeled areas, for example, Daugavas Vanagi House, the social centre of the London Latvian community is located in Queensborough Terrace, Bayswater. However, it stood (and still stands today) rather unassumingly among a row of hotels, and a passer-by would be unaware of its presence. Nor is one likely to notice the small Lithuanian church at 21 The Oval off Hackney Road in London.

Although locals in cities such as Leeds, Bradford or Manchester, which had sizeable East European migration in the period after the Second World War, may have been more aware of the presence of Latvians, Lithuanians or Estonians in their city, in areas without clubs or significant Baltic populations, the diaspora were hidden from view. The extent of their integration was also a disguising factor: most first generation individuals had excellent English, although some still had slight accents and imperfect, or in a very few cases, poor, English. That they were white and European also acted as a mask. Their names continued to mark them out however, although some had Anglicised versions, which were adopted in certain contexts. Although in Soviet times, political demonstrations and cultural events brought the Baltic populations into the news, in the decade following Baltic independence these became events of the past, and in the more cheerful and less nationalist post-independence atmosphere, the diaspora largely kept themselves to themselves.

If outwardly, these groups were inconspicuous, what happened behind the scenes, in the clubs or at home? To what extent had individuals become British, in form and substance, as intended by the British Government in the late-1940's? As the first generation were dying out, what was the end-point of the acculturation process? While the last chapter described the effects of independence upon the Baltic communities in Britain, the conclusion will present a summary of their characteristics at the close of this research in 2000, as well as some thoughts about their future. I will then summarise the major findings of the study and the implications of the study for immigration theories and research.

THE SCENE IN 2000: A SNAPSHOT

Although this book has been primarily a historical analysis of Baltic DP's in Britain, it has also been a survey of the situation in the late 1990s - the period in which the research was undertaken. What were the main characteristics of the Baltic communities in Britain in the late 1990s, and what was the state of their cultures and identities at the end of the first generation's lives? Below is a brief sociological 'snapshot', a synchronic account which slices through the communities at one point in time at the end of the twentieth century.

In the late 1990s, as throughout their lives, great heterogeneity existed among Latvians, Lithuanians and Estonians regarding every aspect of their lives. Diversity existed not only in relation to levels of integration and ethnic/national identities, but also in terms of family life and standards of living, as well as social and private lives. Latvians, Lithuanians and Estonians in Britain maintained homeland cultures and identities, and adopted elements of British culture and national identity to different degrees, and they also lived their lives in Britain in heterogeneous ways. By using the life history approach this research has attempted to show the complexity and diversity of individuals' lives, which cannot be simplified or modelled. Each individual's unique life path resulted in a variety of life experiences and situations. Compare for example, two individuals in this study. First, an Estonian man whom I interviewed, who was divorced from his English wife and lived on his own in a village near Scarborough, distant from the nearest Estonian community. He maintained little contact with the Estonian community, and his social life revolved around English locals, for example, he was an active member of a local chess club, consisting mainly of English players. At the time of the interview, he had never returned to his homeland.[1343] His situation differed markedly from a Latvian man I interviewed who lived about 100 yards from the local Latvian club. He lived with his German-Latvian wife, some years his junior, and their children, one of whom was still a teenager. He attended the Latvian club regularly and had many Latvian friends living nearby. In addition to maintaining Latvian culture and visiting the homeland regularly, he had fully integrated into British society.[1344]

These case studies described the experiences of just two individuals, but what can be noted about the three communities as a whole? I will begin with demographics. At the end of the millennium, the Latvian, Lithuanian and Estonian post-Second World War diaspora in Britain were communities in decline. When I began this project in 1995, all three communities suggested that approximately half of the original refugee population were still alive. Over the course of the project, the numbers declined sharply, and although accurate demographic data was unavailable, it appeared that less than half of the original refugee population remained, excluding those who re-migrated in the 'fifties. If one includes those who re-emigrated during the early 'fifties, the number drops to approximately one-third to one-quarter, the percentage varying across the three communities. One Latvian in Nottingham estimated that while there were over 300 Latvians in the Nottingham area, when she first arrived in 1950, there were only 100 or 150 by the end of the 1990s.[1345] A leaflet produced by the Estonian Association in 1997, suggested that the Estonian community numbered 1000.[1346] This compares to an initial number of approximately 5000 Estonians migrating to Britain as part of the EVW schemes by December 1950.[1347] The original size disparities between the three nationalities remained: Latvians were the largest group, Lithuanians middle in size, and Estonians the smallest. Most of the original population were in their seventies and eighties when I undertook the research. The youngest of the original refugees was aged 67 in 1999[1348], although child dependants who accompanied their parents were younger. In my sample, the eldest interview participant was 87, and the youngest was 64, when I interviewed them in 1997. It is important to note, that those who were not still alive at the time of the research constituted the older section of the original population, and had a survey of the Baltic communities been undertaken ten years previously (for example, in the late 1980s), the sociological snapshot may have been quite different. It is likely for example, that the younger cohort were more integrated than older refugees, and there is a higher probability that they married, had families, and they were also more likely than older refugees to live away from an area of Baltic community.[1349]

This study has found that while most of the first generation were married at the time the research was undertaken, a significant minority were widowed, single or divorced. The number widowed was increasing as the older generation aged. Because some did not marry, these Latvians, Lithuanians and Estonians would not have had children and questionnaire and interview responses suggest that this was the case for approximately one-sixth of the original refugees (although the percentage may have been higher among older refugees). Most of the first generation had some surviving family members in the homeland, and those who did, were able to keep in contact, not only through letters but also through visits. A minority either had no close family members left in the homeland or had lost contact with them, and did not know who and how many in their family remained alive at that time.

At the date of the research in the late 1990s, a majority of the diaspora had close physical connections with the homeland. About half the Baltic diaspora visited Latvia, Lithuania or Estonia at least every other year. Among questionnaire participants, some 90 per cent had returned to visit. Of these, twenty-five per cent had returned once, fifteen per cent twice, and sixty per cent more than twice by 1997. In addition, many members of the diaspora regularly invited their relations from the homeland to visit Britain.

The majority of the diaspora continued to live in the original areas of settlement, although within towns and cities substantial migration to the suburbs in earlier years meant that most were scattered through outlying districts, usually a significant distance away from clubhouses. A few still lived within walking distance from the clubs, which were originally situated within areas of Latvian, Lithuanian and Estonian habitation. The level at which the community continued to live in the areas previously inhabited by Latvians, Lithuanians and Estonians varied in different cities and was dependent upon various factors, including the continued desirability of an area. In Manchester, for example, Lithuanians continued to live in the once popular areas around the club in Middleton road and in Eccles. These localities had remained very desirable residential quarters. However, in Leeds, the Latvian clubs in Bradford and Leeds were located in Manningham and Chapeltown respectively, areas which over the years, had become somewhat run-down and undesirable areas to live. Consequently the number of Latvians, Lithuanians and Estonians living there fell dramatically as they were able to afford to move to more desirable areas. Among those who participated in the questionnaire study, 20 per cent lived 1-2 miles from a club, 6 per cent 3-5 miles, 22 per cent 5-10 miles, 44 per cent 10-50 miles and 9 per cent over 50 miles.[1350] The fact that over half of these participants lived over 10 miles from a clubhouse is evidence not only of the small number of clubs, but also the wide distribution of the diaspora. The main areas of habitation in the late 1990s for all three communities included London, Yorkshire (especially Leeds and Bradford and to a lesser extent places like Doncaster, Halifax, Bingley, Chesterfield, Sheffield), Lancashire (particularly Manchester and Rochdale), Derbyshire, the Midlands (especially Birmingham),

Nottinghamshire (including Nottingham and Mansfield), London, Bedford, and some areas of Wales and Scotland. The diaspora continued to live in the regions where undermanned industries existed in the immediate post-war period, for example, coal mining, textiles, brick works, iron and steel. However, participants in this study also lived in diverse areas, for example, Irton, near Scarborough, Slough, Newcastle (Staffordshire) and Finchampstead (Berkshire). Furthermore, since the restoration of homeland independence, some members of the Baltic diaspora had returned to live in the homeland, although as this study has shown, they numbered only a handful.

At the time the research was undertaken in the late nineties after living in Britain for fifty years, most Latvians, Lithuanians and Estonians were financially stable, having worked for most of their lives. Almost all the first generation owned their own homes, had cars and lived comfortably. State pensions and employment pensions were supplemented for some of those who fought in units attached to the German forces, by pensions from the German government, administered through the Department of Social Security in Britain.[1351] Not all however, claimed their entitlement.

As we have seen, a significant, although non-quantifiable number had British nationality. Since independence, the three diaspora groups have also been able to claim citizenship of the newly independent homelands, and to have Latvian, Lithuanian or Estonian *and* British nationality. Although numbers are difficult to quantify, evidence from the small sample in this study suggests that about half currently had dual nationality at the time of the study. A sizeable minority had claimed the citizenship of the homeland since independence without having previously claimed British nationality.

What about the picture regarding the organised communities in the year 2000 – community structures and activities? What were current rates of participation?

Attendance at Latvian, Lithuanian and Estonian clubs and participation in community events and activities was relatively low compared to earlier years, yet continued to be the main way in which Latvians, Lithuanians and Estonians in Britain maintained homeland cultures and identities. The structure of the organised communities remained very similar to those established in the 1940's and 1950's. However, the size and composition of the membership had altered significantly, as had the leadership, goals and activities of the communities.

The Latvian community's two main organisations: *Daugavas Vanagi* and 'The Latvian National Council in Great Britain', remained very active. *Daugavas Vanagi* (DVF) remained the more important of the two organisations and is also currently still the most solid organisational structure among the three communities. Membership had fallen dramatically, but continued to encompass a large percentage of Latvians in Britain. Although some club branches had been wound up by the date of this research, the DVF was remarkably successful in maintaining clubhouses and branches in many areas. In 1978, there were 32 branches of the DVF in Britain[1352], and the overwhelming majority remained in 2000, including branches in South Wales, Wolverhampton, Catthorpe Manor branch, Carlisle, Leicester and Nottingham.[1353] In Yorkshire and Lancashire alone, six clubs with social clubs were listed by a Latvian in Leeds, in 1997, at Bolton, Bradford, Doncaster, Huddersfield, Halifax and Leeds.[1354] 'The Latvian National Council in Great Britain' continued its traditional function – to extend the work done by the DVF in social, cultural and political fields and serving the interests of the British Latvian community. In addition, the Latvian Lutheran Evangelical Church continued to fulfil the religious and spiritual needs of the Latvian Lutheran community. Ministers visited various Latvian communities regularly, giving services at local churches. The Church was also running a Latvian retirement home, Rowfant House in Sussex. At the close of my fieldwork, the three other retirement/holiday/cultural centres remained - *Straumeni* at Catthorpe Manor, *Musmajas* at Wolston near Coventry, and Nieuport House at Almeley in Herefordshire, although the future of Almeley was looking increasingly uncertain. (Almeley House was eventually sold in the late 1990s).

The main structure of the Lithuanian community, the DBLS (*Didÿiosios Britanijos Lietuviũ Sajunga*), remained active, and Lithuanian House Ltd. continued to manage the financial affairs of the Lithuanian community. Although several branches closed during the 1980's, clubhouses or Lithuanian centres were being maintained in London, Nottingham, Manchester, Bradford and Bellshill. According to LYNES, as of January 1999, there were 22 branches of the Lithuanian Association in Great Britain.[1355] In 1998 and 1999, the DBLS appeared to be expanding, with the opening of several new clubs, and the closure and re-opening of the Sodyba branch (re-named Sodas branch). Two branches, at Leicester and Northampton, re-opened after being wound up in the early 1980's.[1356] A new branch, Lithuanian House, Freeland Road in Ealing was opened, composed entirely of 'new' Lithuanian migrants.[1357] The opening of this branch revealed the role of recent immigrants in the revival of the community.[1358] *Sodyba*, a Lithuanian retirement home and holiday centre in Hampshire also continued to serve the Lithuanian community. The Lithuanian community also had its own church St Casimir's, at The Oval in London, which also acted as a base for the Lithuanian Church Club. In Nottingham the Lithuanian Marian Fathers had a chapel in Hounds Road. As for all Latvians and Estonians, Lithuanians living in other areas did not have their own church: instead, church services were held on a monthly basis in local churches. Apart from London and Nottingham, *LYNES* noted that Roman Catholic Church services were held regularly in Bradford, Eccles, Manchester, Derby, Sodyba, and Bellshill, Lanark (Scotland).[1359]

At the time that the research was undertaken there was less information available concerning the Estonian community, due to a dearth of English language publications. What was clear however, was that at the end of the twentieth century, the 'Association of Estonians in Great Britain' (*Inglismaa Eestlaste Ühing*) remained active and maintained three Estonian clubs, in London, Leicester and Bradford, and several societies in other areas, including those representing ex-servicemen and the younger generations.

The functions of these organisations differed from their activities in the pre-independence era, when the restoration of independence was the main goal of the communities. In the decase following independence, the clubs carried out primarily social, cultural and philanthropic functions relating to the diaspora in Britain, and the homeland. They also helped to care for the elderly diasporic populations in Britain, and to welcome and assist the settlement of post-independence migrants. Another aspect of the organisations' work was to co-ordinate various cultural events with the diaspora abroad, particularly youth activities, including international youth congresses and sporting, musical and dance events. Although political campaigning was greatly reduced compared to earlier years, the organisations continued to campaign on behalf of the homeland, for example, pressuring western governments to speed up the process of EU and Nato membership. One of the most important functions of these organisations was to maintain the running of Latvian, Lithuanian and Estonian social clubs and groups up and down the country. Apart from their social function - a meeting place for members of the community to get together, the clubs had various cultural, political and philanthropic roles. These included the organisation of cultural activities for the community, youth activities, the collection of charitable donations for individuals and organisations in the homeland, political work, including co-ordinating the collection of votes for homeland elections and campaigning work, as well as helping the elderly in the local community.

The information leaflet of the Association of Estonians in Great Britain outlined the purpose of the association in 1997: 'The objectives of the association are to spread knowledge about Estonian life and culture, and to work, with other organisations, for the preservation of an Estonian identity within a democratic state'.[1360] The latter objective suggested a further function of the associations in the post-independence era – to help preserve ethnic identities and cultures in the homelands. This aim would be achieved by fostering cultural exchange between the diaspora and the homeland, for example, helping to bring over musicians and cultural groups from the homeland to Britain, and also by supporting various cultural, educational and political groups, which were seen as cultivating Latvian, Lithuanian and Estonian cultural traditions and identities. As this book has suggested, the role of the diaspora as defenders of homeland cultures and identities waned as a result of independence. Post-independence, the diaspora have considered their role as ancillary, primarily to aid and support work already been carried out in the homeland, and to inspire and facilitate the restoration of ethnic cultures and identities where possible.

At the time this research was undertaken, the leadership of these organisations was being increasingly passed to the second generation. Leadership patterns varied across the three communities and among different localities. Among the three communities, the Latvian organisation the DVF had the most difficulties passing leadership to younger generations, possibly because its original raison d'être - an organisation for ex-servicemen and their families – may have been less relevant for younger generations. In contrast, the Lithuanian community was relatively successful at transferring leadership to younger first and second generation members. Elections to the Lithuanian Youth Association in Great Britain, DBLJS in 1999 also saw younger members of the second generation taking seats, older third generation members and even 'new' Lithuanians being elected.[1361] It is not only the central sections of Latvian, Lithuanian and Estonian organisations which underwent change. The leadership of local branches also shifted, a trend led by the London branches which had a high degree of youth participation and recent migrants. However changes also took place in areas outside London, for example, among the Estonian community, a leadership shift took place at the Estonian club in Bradford, when a second generation Estonian was elected Chairman.[1362]

The percentage of the first generation population who were members of community organisations - who attended clubs and participated in community activities, at the time of the research was difficult to estimate. Questionnaires suggested that approximately 90 per cent attended clubs, although the figure was likely to be significantly lower given that over 90 per cent of the participants selected for this study had some connection with a club. The questionnaires suggested that of those who did attend, a majority did so several times a year only (56 per cent). Only 3 per cent attended more than twice a week, 10 per cent once or twice a week and 31 per cent visited the clubs several times a month. Those who frequented the clubs most regularly generally lived closer to the clubs than those who did not. Unless they lived nearby, most of the diaspora attended the clubs only for special events and occasions, such as National Independence Day. While some clubs succeeded in attracting second generation participation, other clubs failed. *LYNES* estimated in January 1999 that over 80 per cent of DBLS branch members were over seventy years.[1363] Some clubs also attracted the participation of post-independence migrants, although as we saw in the last chapter, this development initially caused friction among the Lithuanian community. Clubs which managed to retain and attract second generation members and newcomers included those in London, but others also succeeded, for example, the Estonian club in Bradford. Regular participants of many of the clubs, however, mainly consisted of first generation members, and numbers attending were often low. For example, at the Manchester Lithuanian Club, a medium-sized club, unless there was a special event, a Lithuanian regular attendee estimated that only about six or seven Lithuanians attended on Saturdays.[1364] Once a month, when a Lithuanian Church service were held at a local Catholic Church, St. Chad's, the numbers rose and people attended from different parts of Manchester and surrounding areas, including Rochdale. One Lithuanian woman estimated that about 30 participated in the Church service.[1365] Due to low attendance, almost all of the clubs, including some in London, were only open at weekends and possibly one day in the week at the time of the research. For example, the Lithuanian club in Manchester was open on Saturdays, Sundays and Mondays.[1366] The Lithuanian Sports and Social Club in Victoria Park Road in London was open on Fridays, Saturdays and Sundays.

Because the exiles tended to move away from the clubs as they became more prosperous, the majority lived some distance from them and as they became older and in some cases less mobile, this change made it more difficult for some to attend the clubs regularly. A Latvian woman explained why in addition to the declining population, the number of Latvians attending the Latvian club in Nottingham had decreased: '…a lot of them don't come now. But you can understand if you are old and you don't want to travel. We live so near, but we don't go very often'.[1367]

At the time of the research in the mid – late 1990s, low attendance figures were contributing to growing financial difficulties, particularly for smaller clubs. These were being met with a variety of responses, including installing fruit machines into bars to increase profits, continuing discussion about the financial viability of certain clubs and buildings, and decreasing opening hours. One of the challenges for the organisations and individual clubs that faced a declining first generation population was to maintain and increase the participation of second and third generation Latvians, Lithuanians and Estonians. Some clubs continued to organise activities for these groups, but others failed to retain their interest, particularly as these groups were busy with work and raising families. The post-independence migrants were also increasingly viewed as a potential source of membership, despite some initial friction between the 'new' and 'old' migrants.

The youth activities and youth sections of the communities were surviving, albeit with far reduced participation compared to earlier years. The so-called 'youth' organisations were composed of a then, not so youthful, second generation, and a few third generation members. The Lithuanian youth organisation, the DBLJS (*Didžiosios Britanijos Lietuvių Jaunimo Sąjunga* – Lithuanian Youth Association in Great Britain), which was intended initially for Lithuanians between 16 and 35 years, had many members in their thirties and forties, and few younger Lithuanians. Among the Latvian Association, youth were represented in the British branch of 'The Association of Latvian Youth in Europe' and a youth section of 'The Latvian National Council in Great Britain'. *Tulevik* (The Future) was the Estonian communities' youth association. All of these groups organised a range of events and activities, including language classes, youth camps and social evenings. In addition to the youth organisations, there were a variety of other groups for the younger generations, including Lithuanian scouts and various dance and choir ensembles. Weekend language schools also persisted in a few areas, for example on a trip the Latvian club in Leeds in 1995, I learnt that about 12 children attended Latvian language classes in the schoolroom on Saturday mornings.[1368] Language classes were one area where new migrants, many with young children were making a big difference to attendance figures, although the different levels of language proficiency among recent child migrants and third generation children posed a challenge for teachers. The problem of maintaining interest among younger generations can be seen by looking at the circulation figures of *LYNES*, the Lithuanian Youth Newsheet. In January 1999, the editor noted that '*LYNES* has a readership of 114'.[1369] *LYNES* also noted that 94 per cent of its readership were over 36 years, and half were over 51.[1370] In January 1999, the editor of LYNES noted that the DBLJS had only 25 members in 1998, but even so, described the association as 'reasonably active'.[1371]

The organisation of cultural activities continued in similar fashion to that evident during the Soviet era, albeit with a less nationalist character. The days of national remembrance or importance remained the most prominent events in the cultural calendar. The numbers attending such events were small in comparison to earlier years, and the tone no longer so sombre or militaristic: rather they were happy, celebratory, family events, and despite falling participation, commemorations of the National Independence Days and Deportations Day continued to attract a sizeable crowd, with members of three generations often attending. St. John's Day at midsummer also remained popular. A Latvian woman explained how Latvians in Nottingham celebrate National Independence Day on 18 November:

> Well, there's usually a talk and singing and well, these days we do it, we hold it at the club and there's usually refreshments. People sit at the table and in the club we can't have concerts really, but before we used to have a dance even. We used to have a concert in one of the big halls before and either a choir or a soloist, and we had records and dance afterwards.[1372]

I attended several days of national significance during my fieldwork. The commemoration of Deportations Day at the Manchester Lithuanian Club in 1998 was primarily a social, family occasion, when members of the communities met to enjoy themselves. Three generations of Lithuanians marked the day with a barbecue, a dance group performed and a third generation talent competition was held. There were no speeches and the melancholy of earlier years was absent. St. John's Day at the Estonian Club in Bradford in 1997 was also a family day, with three generations attending. There were various talks given by invited quests, including a speech about the progress of the Estonian independent state, there was a performance by an Estonian choir group, and bonfires were lit in the grounds of the club.

The Lithuanian Newsletter of the DBLJS showed how Lithuanian Independence Day on 16 February, marking the establishment of independence in 1918, was celebrated in 1999. On 14 February, the day was celebrated with High Mass at the Lithuanian Church of St. Casimir at The Oval in London. The *Gimtinė* folk ensemble also performed a selection of songs and music. Also in celebration of Lithuanian Independence Day, a commemorative concert was held at Lithuanian House in London on 13 February. The programme included pupils from the re-opened Saturday school *Maironis* and performances by the folk ensemble *Gimtinė*.

Although active members of the three communities continued to attend such events, many did not. Others were discriminatory about which events they attend. I asked a Latvian man in Leeds which Latvian traditions or festivals he participated in. He replied: 'Well, when it's concerts, like you if it's something like Remembrance Day, Church festivals or something like that, but otherwise no'. I also asked him if he celebrated St. John's Day: 'I used to, but I think it's faded now. It's not much. They go somewhere, I don't know where. I don't know – I don't take part in it. It's not really what it actually is, they just pretend'.[1373]

Among all three communities, a remaining few dance and song groups continued to exist and perform at days of national importance at home, and also travel abroad. Independence facilitated cultural exchange between the diaspora and the homeland. One of the features of some of the dance and song groups was the mix of generations within the group, due to insufficient participants from any one generation.

Each community continued to publish a range of newspapers, newsletters and journals to update the diaspora with news about activities in their locality, within Britain as a whole and globally. These publications also related news from the homeland, and other international news, which may affect the homeland or the diaspora, for example, events in Russia or Britain. The three diasporic communities in Britain also received publications from the global diaspora and the homeland. The Lithuanian community in Britain issued three publications at the time of the research: *LYNES*, the Lithuanian Youth Newsheet, written in both English and Lithuanian; *Europas Lietuvis*, a newspaper for Lithuanians in Europe presently published in Britain; and *Budekimė*, the Lithuanian scouts journal. The Latvian community issued several publications, including *Brīvā Latvija*, a European wide Latvian paper published weekly from Catthorpe Manor in Leicestershire. Latvians in different localities also published their own newsletters, for example the DVF branches in the East Midlands (Chesterfield, Derby, Leicester, Mansfield,

Nottingham) published a bi-monthly Information Bulletin: *'Mūsu Balss'* ('Our Voice'). Among the Estonian community, the main publication continued to be *Eesti Hääl*, which is a fortnightly Estonian language newspaper.

As a result of the declarations of independence, Latvian, Lithuanian and Estonian Ambassadors and Embassies were restored in London. In addition to the traditional functions of Embassies, these undertook important work with the diaspora, including supporting social, cultural and political activities. They have also carried out important campaigning work on behalf of the homelands, supporting applications for asylum in Britain and co-ordinating a variety of activities between the diaspora and groups and organisations in the homelands. In addition, the Baltic Council, which was established in 1947, to undertake joint campaigning, and to work towards closer political, economic, social and cultural ties between the Baltic States and Great Britain, continued, with representatives of the three Baltic communities as members. According to *LYNES*, in 1999, one of the main functions of the Baltic Council in the 1990s was to 'campaign for admission of the Baltic States into the European Union and Nato'.[1374] It also held regular commemorative services in London marking the June 1941 Deportations. According to *LYNES*: 'The role of the Baltic Council has changed today and has moved from a political [role] to social and cultural [roles]. Today the Council was [is] looking more towards co-operation of the three communities in this country'.[1375] *LYNES* detailed a meeting of the Baltic Council in October 1999, where members of the three communities discussed the future of the communities in Britain and strategies to overcome present difficulties relating to falling participation.[1376] Estonians asked the question: 'Do we really know the size of our communities? Sooner or later we will have to share premises'. Latvians made the following points: 'Community is ageing. We have to work together much more. There has been a reduction of activity and commitment. We must organise something together'. The Lithuanian members discussed the problems of the legality of residency of Lithuanian Asylum seekers, and their large number in the London area. They also discussed the fact that younger Lithuanians did not know the language. The Baltic Council represents one way in which Latvians, Lithuanians and Estonians in Britain have co-operated on various issues, because of their shared histories and experiences. As in the Soviet era, the three nationalities continued to share facilities both with each other, and with other East European diaspora, and also to organise joint activities.

- ### *Have Baltic DPs become 'British' in form and substance?*

Moving on to the question of how far have the original refugees become British in form and/or substance, i.e. did they assimilate?, this research has found that the majority of the first generation have integrated, but not assimilated into British society. Latvians, Lithuanians and Estonians integrated in that they maintained some cultural traditions from the homeland, while at the same time, entered into British society and adopted elements of British society. At a group level, the continued presence of clubs and associations in Britain has been evidence of the maintenance of cultural integrity of the group, implying that assimilation had not yet taken place. These findings are echoed in studies of first generation Baltic diaspora in other parts of the world. For example, in her study of Lithuanians in Canada, Milda Danys found that first generation Lithuanians did not assimilate, noting that 'few first generation immigrants really do'.[1377] The clubs and branches remained the most important sphere for cultural retention, although another important arena for the preservation of homeland culture outside of Britain - the homeland – was in the post-independence period, becoming increasingly significant. This book has discussed the variety of ways in which the first generation has integrated – the different levels and character of cultural retention, the varying degrees of adoption of British culture, and the different spheres in which cultural maintenance takes place.

Findings from interviews and community documents have been confirmed by questionnaire responses. One question presented ten alternative statements about levels of adaptation to the British way of life and the maintenance of Latvian, Lithuanian or Estonian culture and identity, from which the respondent had to choose the one most fitting to his/her own experiences (See the Interview Schedule at the back of the book). Of the responses, the largest number, some fifty per cent stated that the following phrase most accurately described their experiences of life in Britain: 'I have fully adapted to the British way of life and maintained strong (Latvian, Lithuanian, Estonian) cultural traditions and have a strong (Latvian.....) identity'. This is suggestive of full integration. The phrase 'I have partially adapted to the British way of life and have kept strong (Latvian.....) cultural traditions and a strong (Latvian.....) identity' summed up the experiences of approximately one-fifth of the participants, while one-eighth felt that the phrase: 'I have fully adapted to the British way of life and have lost many aspects of my (Latvian......) culture, but have maintained a strong (Latvian.....) identity', summed up their experiences the most accurately. The remained twenty per cent of participants were spread fairly evenly across the following two choices: 'I have partially adapted to the British way of life and have also lost some of my (Latvian.....) cultural traditions and identity' and 'I have partially adapted to the British way of life and have maintained a strong (Latvian.....) identity, although I have lost many (Latvian.....) cultural traditions'. None of the respondents opted for the three choices which began with 'I have not really adapted to the British way of life...' One Latvian man chose his own description which was full adaptation to the British way of life and maintenance of Latvian culture, with some loss of Latvian identity. Interestingly all those who felt that the phrase 'I have partially adapted to the British way of life, and have maintained a strong (Latvian....) identity and culture' were those who married within the same ethnic group, while a significant majority of intermarried men felt that they had maintained a strong homeland culture and identity and had fully adapted to the British way of life, suggesting that intermarriage does not necessarily lead to a weakening of ethnic cultures and identities among the first generation at least.

In which ways did the Baltic DP's in Britain enter into British society and adopt elements of British culture? The most obvious aspect of cultural adjustment was learning English. Most of the first generation who participated in this research were either fluent in English or had very good spoken English. Among questionnaire participants, for written English, just under two-fifths believed they were fluent, almost two-fifths stated that they had good written English and just under a quarter believed they have poor written English. Nearly half were fluent in their reading skills, about two-fifths good, and under one-tenth had poor English reading skills. About two-fifths had fluent spoken English, a higher number - almost half had good spoken English and over one-tenth had poor spoken English. These are self-descriptions and not necessarily accurate, for example, some of those who wrote that they only had 'good' spoken English and whom I later interviewed, I would describe as fluent, and likewise one or two who stated that they had poor spoken English, I would describe as having good spoken English. Some of the participants pointed out that both their English and their homeland language has deteriorated since retirement. Deterioration of English since retirement was particularly common among those married to another Latvian, Lithuanian or Estonian. However, visiting the homeland usually led to improvements in homeland language skills: however, a significant number were no longer fluent in the homeland language, particularly in their spoken language skills.

As this book has demonstrated, there have been many other ways in which the first generation adopted British culture, and entered into British society. At a very basic level their way of life in Britain, a post-industrial society, contrasted markedly from their pre-war rural lives in the homelands. Many have had British friends and cooked British cuisine. They read British newspapers and watched British television. They enjoyed equal rights of access to Britain's educational, health, financial and legal institutions. Now retired, they have made use of social services, claimed state pensions and used the National Health Service. Many became British citizens, and have had full voting rights. Not only have the first generation adapted to a culture, that is uniquely British, they have also adapted to a post-modern, global culture, which has formed an integral part of the British way of life. Consider for example, how shopping in Britain's American style supermarkets with the vast choice of produce from all over the globe, contrasts with the self-sufficient farmsteads of the homeland in the 1920's and 1930's.

This book has also discussed the ways in which homeland culture has been preserved and has been adapted or 'translated' in Britain.[1378] At a community level, culture retention remains largely unchanged in the post-independence period from that in the Soviet period. Conserved cultural traits have included language, folklore, religion, the commemoration of various national days, and to a lesser degree, cuisine.

Aspects of cultural maintenance among individuals has varied widely, for example, language and participation in the homeland community have been the most important ways some have preserved their homeland culture, while others have maintained culture, through cuisine, crafts or by reading literature and poetry by Latvian, Lithuanian or Estonian authors. The following comment by a Lithuanian woman suggests the variety of ways in which homeland culture has been maintained:

> Well, with my friends with my nationality you know, I talk, I talk or I cook or I go to mass with Lithuanians' 'I've got [Lithuanian] music on tapes, I have yeah. I have about 50 tapes you know, and sister's sending paper's every month, magazines [from Lithuania]...I won't do without. And I have Lithuanian books.[1379]

This book has shown how homeland independence brought about a shift in attitudes towards homeland cultural maintenance, compared to earlier years. The responsibilities of exile diminished and there was no longer such a deep sense of duty involved in the defence of culture. Some even began to regard homeland cultural maintenance as a kind of hobby. This attitude, particularly among younger generations provides another explanation for low community participation. I asked an Estonian man, who was relatively isolated from the Estonian community if he kept up Estonian traditions. He replied:

> ...the things is you see...well not really. There are some dates and what have you, this and that you see, but I mean it's too childish, you grew out of these things. Err, you know because these old customs they are traditionally carried out and...I mean these old customs you know that they were all, err, well not scientifically sound or what have you, it's just sort of a habit or a fairy, country tale or what have you. And what probably a story what somebody has told some time has carried or what have you and when you grow up and specially being isolated you see, you don't carry the flag sort of thing you know. I mean they're too silly to, yeah well...if you live among the community yeah, I suppose they bring it up, err, and then you probably have calendars too don't you, because I mean I know it's my fault, I haven't bought expensive calendar for ages, but these English calendars ...you're lucky of the Sunday's marked...You need an almanac or something...[1380]

However, some members of the first generation continued to feel a sense of obligation to retain homeland culture, and even if motive changed, among an overwhelming majority, it remained an integral part of private and social lives. One Lithuanian inferred that the main responsibility of the diaspora in the post-independence period was not towards the homeland, but towards maintaining the survival of clubs and cultural activities in Britain, and that this was one reason for continued participation in the organised community. Speaking about his motivations for attending the monthly church services in Manchester, he noted that he went 'because if I won't go, another won't go...if nobody will go, they will close it here, that's it. So going...sometimes, [even if it is] raining, everything, you have to go yeah'.[1381]

Integration for Latvians, Lithuanians and Estonians in Britain has meant that at the end of the twentieth century, they lived in two cultures: their homeland culture and British culture. Often, these worlds were not separate, but intermeshed. They spoke both English and the homeland language, cooked both British and the homeland cuisine, had both English or other nationality friends as well as friends from the homeland community; and they read literature and newspapers from both Britain and the homeland community. Some aspects of homeland culture were stripped and replaced by British culture, while others were maintained with different degrees of translation. Some cultural aspects, for example, cuisine, mixed homeland and British cultural traditions. This process of the stripping or modification of culture also occurred at the level of the organised community, although to a lesser degree.

Like culture, identities also underwent a process of translation since settlement in Britain. In earlier chapters, I argued that many members of the diaspora had dual loyalties and identities, and that one could distinguish between ethnic and national identities. It has been argued that although the nominal aspect of their ethnic identities has not changed – they are still Latvians, Lithuanians and Estonians, there has been a shift in the meaning, content and expression of ethnic identities, in their conceptions of home and belonging, and in their national identities. It has been suggested that the restoration of homeland independence emphasised their bond to Britain: many began to feel like foreigners in their own homelands, heightening their sense of belonging in Britain, and strengthening their sense of having a British or an English national identity. Not all of the refugees I interviewed considered that they were integrated, that they belonged in Britain or even that Britain was their home, but that they felt so rooted in Britain that return was not an option. This book has shown however, that many did consider that they belonged in Britain, even though they still regarded themselves as Latvian, Lithuanian or Estonian in terms of their ethnic identities. Crucially they became Latvians, Lithuanians and Estonians *in Britain*, and identified with both homeland and British or English culture. The study has shown that it is possible to be loyal to two nations, and to have one foot in Britain and another in the homeland.

The findings from the interviews were also rather crudely confirmed by questionnaire responses to a question about identity. The question did not specify whether identity meant ethnic or national identity. The question posed was: Which of the following best describes your identity? Six choices were provided: Latvian, Lithuanian, Estonian; Half Latvian, Lithuanian or Estonian and half British; Mostly (Latvian…..), but partly British; Mostly British, but partly (Latvian…..); Other. Of the respondents, half stated that their identity was best described as Latvian, Lithuanian or Estonian. One quarter stated that they regarded themselves as mostly Latvian, Lithuanian or Estonian, but partly British. Just under one-quarter felt that they were half British and half Latvian, Lithuanian or Estonian. Only one respondent, an Estonian man, stated that he considered himself to be mainly British. Thus, half the respondents felt that their identities consisted of a mix of both the homeland identity and British identity. Among the other half, although they identified themselves as Latvians, Lithuanians or Estonians, other questionnaire responses and interview comments suggest that they were integrated in Britain and felt a strong attachment to Britain.

The following comments by a Lithuanian woman in Manchester, who interestingly, opted for the 'Lithuanian' choice in the questionnaire, reveal these characteristics. I asked her to describe her identity in the interview:

Oh, fifty, fifty. But I'm still Lithuanian. I have a British passport.

It's my home there. It's lovely…it's my home. I been visiting with everybody…but like I said, I don't think so I move there.

Lithuania – my homeland. I love Lithuania you know…I love Lithuania, but my life [is] here you know'.[1382]

In addition to a sense of loyalty and belonging in Britain, many Latvians, Lithuanians and Estonians also had regional loyalties and identities. When asked to describe his identity, a Latvian man stated that: 'I am a Latvian from Lancashire'.[1383] A sense of identification with Yorkshire was also described by some Latvians in Leeds.[1384] Like ethnic identities, regional identities were not in conflict with national identities: they could be Latvians, British and identify themselves with Yorkshire at the same time.

While the first generation had divided and somewhat confused loyalties and identities, among the second and third generation, this book has shown that an overwhelming majority had primarily British cultures and identities, although a few did have split ethnicity. This book has discussed how among the Lithuanian community, the British aspect of their identities has been reflected in a growing trend towards the usage of the term 'British Lithuanians', particularly among the younger generations. By the year 2000 only a small minority of the second generation and an even lesser number of the third generation were participating in the organised community and taking part in cultural activities.

HISTORICAL SUMMARY

In this section I will limit myself to answering four questions:

1) How far were pre-settlement experiences significant in shaping settlement patterns?;

2) To what extent did the government's design of the EVW schemes, and assimilation policies affect the acculturation of the communities?;

3) How far were homeland developments significant in shaping the development of the communities?;

4) Finally, were there any other factors, which particularly influenced the integration process?

1) How far were pre-settlement experiences significant in shaping settlement patterns?

The assumption advanced at the start of the book that it is impossible to understand post-settlement experiences without examination of pre-settlement experiences, has certainly been borne out in this book. The study has shown how experiences during childhood, war, displacement, and in the DP Camps, contributed decisively to the specific character of the development of the communities and individuals in Britain.

Chapter Two: *The Homeland* examined the childhood, everyday lives and societies in which the refugees grew up, which are crucial to any understanding of post-settlement life. The book has suggested that the bases of Baltic cultures on the eve of the Second World War, centred around language, the farmstead and the farming calendar, folklore, and in the case of Lithuania, Catholicism. I suggested that national identities in the homeland were embryonic in 1939, on the eve of the first Russian occupation, and that the cultural bases of these identities were still in the process of formation. This book has shown how it was the very immaturity and malleability of identities in 1939 of these identities, which facilitated their future development and transformation in the stages of displacement and settlement. The youthfulness of pre-war identities in the homeland combined with the effects of Sovietisation in the homelands, and integration in Britain, meant that the diaspora and homeland inhabitants followed separate paths of identity and cultural development, so that when independence was restored, there was a huge divide between the two communities.

The circumstances of the refugees' displacement were significant in shaping the exile communities, and in strengthening the emotional attachment to the homeland throughout the years of settlement. The events which occurred during the German and Russian occupations became a vital part of future Baltic identities, both in the homelands and among the diaspora, and promoted the idealisation of pre-war life. The young age of the refugees upon displacement was also important for the flexibility of identities. It enabled the translation of identities in exile, while at the same time, the fact that most of the refugees had spent at least their childhood and teenage years in the homeland, meant that the emotional link to it remained strong throughout their lives in Britain.

Finally, the years in the DP Camps were extremely significant in the process of the development of exile cultures and identities. It was there that the greatest transformation of national identities took place - national identities were solidified, and exile identities and cultures formed. In these ways, pre-settlement experiences form the core of any explanation of life in Britain.

2) To what extent did the government's design of the EVW schemes, and assimilation policies affect the acculturation of the communities?

In other words, were government policies successful in bringing about the assimilation of the Baltic communities? Were government aims fulfilled?

Two key elements of the design of the EVW schemes were the small size and the dispersal of the three communities across Great Britain. In the planning of the EVW schemes, the British Government emphasised in correspondence the importance of avoiding the creation of nationalist ghettos and quickly dismissed the idea of importing whole DP communities *en masse*.[1385] Policies towards the recruitment of Poles showed further the government's unwillingness to recruit large numbers of any one nationality. The small size and dispersal of the three communities certainly obstructed the construction of any compact Baltic colonies. Instead, large numbers of smaller communities were formed and the diaspora lived among the British community. The result was high rates of intermarriage and rapid adjustment into British society, leading in the long term to integration.

Another aspect of the dispersal of the communities was diffusion in the workplace, which was motivated partly out of necessity, but was also a conscious plan to ease industrial absorption. In most factories, hospitals or coal-mines for example, the numbers of any one nationality were limited. Many interview participants reported only one or two other countrymen in their workplace. This dispersal meant that the refugees learnt English and made friends with others workers, thus facilitating their integration.

Another facet of the EVW scheme's design was the prioritisation of single men and women. Dependants and married couples were not encouraged. Married couples had to be recruited separately, and limited numbers of dependants were allowed to enter Britain only once Westward Ho! was well under way.[1386] This policy combined with the disproportionate numbers of men and women recruited, and the small size and dispersal of the communities, to promote high rates of intermarriage. Although the effects of intermarriage upon cultural maintenance and identities were limited in the first generation, there is no doubt that intermarriage was an important reason for the assimilation of younger generations.

Once the EVW's had arrived on Britain's shores, several policies were implemented, which were designed to encourage adaptation and eventually lead to assimilation. These included encouraging the EVW's to move into private accommodation as quickly as possible, the provision of English lessons, the organisation of mixed social evenings with locals, and the distribution of leaflets and other literature to help the EVW's settle in Britain. These measures were implemented sporadically and were frequently ill thought out. In many cases, overt pressure on the EVW's to encourage them to participate in some of the government's programmes backfired. This book has suggested that aside from encouraging the EVW's to move into private billets, these policies were of little success in encouraging adaptation, and that other factors such as dispersal in the workplace were more successful in facilitating integration.

Another important policy was the preparation of British Labour to receive the EVW's. Various measures were implemented in advance of the EVW's arrival, which facilitated their absorption into the labour market. These included equal rates of pay, dispersal within the workplace, and placement only where suitable local labour could not be found. Although there was some friction between the EVW's and fellow employees, on the whole, government policies promoted harmonious relations between EVW's and British labour, a factor which certainly promoted adjustment and later, integration.

Finally, although assimilation did not occur in the first generation, except among a minority of individuals, the process was begun in the second generation and completed in the third generation.[1387] The assimilation of younger generations has been aided by high intermarriage rates, geographical dispersal and the small size of the communities. The government was aware that assimilation would not occur automatically. Indeed, several government documents reveal a belief that assimilation would be a long-term process, although there was little to suggest whether or not the government thought that assimilation would occur among the first generation or in later generations.[1388] If one takes a multi-generational perspective, government policies can be seen to have been successful, even though assimilation did not occur among the first generation.

3) How far were homeland developments significant in shaping the development of the communities?

This research has revealed the decisive impact of historical events and processes in the homeland upon the evolution of the diaspora communities in Britain. Soviet occupation was the reason they became and continued to be exiles until 1991. The length of the Soviet occupation and stagnation within the Soviet Union promoted the rooting of the populations in Britain, and brought about a weakening of the return myth. Events within the homeland during the early years of settlement brought hope to the refugees, for example, the guerrilla activities until the early 1950's, Stalin's death and the thaw under Khrushchev. Such events served to lengthen the lifetime of the return myth and promoted some resistance to adaptation or integration in Britain. They also provided motivation to maintain ethnic cultures and identities on behalf of the homeland, an essential part of the responsibilities of exile. However, as the occupation of the homeland continued and the Soviet Union's grip over the homeland appeared steadfast, the refugees in Britain began to plan for their long-term future in Britain. They married, started families, bought houses and worked hard. While some refugees were determined to maintain their roles as guardians of the homeland despite the apparent intransigence of the situation, others began to feel that such efforts were futile and concentrated instead on their private lives and building their futures in Britain. Many were able to follow both paths, but significant numbers fell away from the communities and participation plummeted. It was during the long period of stagnation within the Soviet Union, during the 1960's and 1970's that the most serious decline occurred.

This book has also discussed the direct impact of the homeland upon the communities in the late 1980's and the effects of the restoration of independence. The advent of Glasnost and Perestroika and the growth of the national independence movements promoted a revival of interest and participation in clubs and branches. Independence ended the refugees' status as exiles, and led to significant changes in the identities and roles of the communities. In particular, independence brought about a reassessment of homeland identities and strengthened the bond to Britain. In short, independence completed the integration process. This is epitomised by the ability of Latvians, Lithuanians and Estonians in Britain to hold dual nationality; thus, they are fully integrated in both substance and form. A Latvian man in Britain noted this phenomena:

> I am a British and Latvian subject.

> I can go either way, yeah. I can go with a British passport or a Latvian passport. The only thing is, it's easier for me to show British people British passport and the Latvians, a Latvian passport.[1389]

The effects of independence on the Baltic communities in Britain have been echoed in other studies of the effects of independence on diaspora groups. For example, in a recent study of the Croatian diaspora in Canada, Daphne Winland concluded that independence has brought about shifts in Croatian diasporic identities and forced the diaspora to re-evaluate their identity vis-à-vis the homeland. She wrote that:

> Independence…has introduced new challenges for Croatians, the most important of which is how to (re)define themselves to each other and to the state in which they live. Rather than inspiring unity and a reinvigorated, resilient sense of Croatian identity and community, independence has forced many Croatians to re-evaluate and re-negotiate long-held sentiments and narratives, not only of the mother country but of their identity as Croatians and as Canadians.[1390]

The unique features of the Soviet occupation of the homeland were a direct influence upon the development of the Baltic diasporan communities in Britain. The nature of Soviet repression within the three homelands contributed to the character of the diasporic communities in Britain. In particular, the areas of culture targeted for repression by the Soviet Union were those most vigorously maintained in Britain. The sealed nature of the homelands, for example, restrictions on travel, vetting of all mail and tightly controlled news output, contributed to the physical re-orientation away from the homeland, although emotional links were retained. The Baltic diaspora knew very little about realities in the homeland during the Soviet period, which contributed to myths about the annihilation of cultures and identities. They themselves were misled by anti-Soviet propaganda: as one Latvian woman stated: 'I think we were really brainwashed about the communists ourselves because we just hated them'.[1391] When they returned to the homelands from the late 1980's onwards, they were surprised at the extent of cultural maintenance, and felt that their role as guardians of homeland culture was no longer necessary, a feeling which intensified after independence.

The significance of homeland developments in the evolution of the refugees in Britain is a characteristic phenomenon of diaspora communities, and can be traced in the histories of other diaspora groups in the world. In an essay entitled 'The Impact of Homelands upon Diasporas', Walker Connor illustrated the significance of the homeland developments upon diasporic communities, and the emotional significance of the homeland.[1392] He noted that:

> The ethnic homeland is far more than territory. As evidenced by the near universal use of such emotionally charged terms as the motherland, the fatherland, the native land, the ancestral land, land where my fathers died and, not least, the homeland, the territory so identified becomes imbued with an emotional, almost reverential dimension.[1393]

One of the principal distinguishing features which contributes to the evolution of diasporic communities is a continuing orientation towards the homeland, either physical or emotional. The emotional significance of the homeland among the Baltic diaspora is best revealed in Latvian, Lithuanian and Estonian exile literature and poetry from the Soviet period. Participants in this study also conveyed the emotional attachment to the homeland, which persisted despite integration. A Lithuanian woman expressed the continuing attachment to the homeland, despite stating that her home is 'here': 'Lithuania...my homeland. I love Lithuania you know...I love Lithuania, but my home is here you know'.[1394] A Latvian woman stated that her Latvian identity had not weakened since arrival in Britain, and explained the reason why: 'because I still consider, well it is my...how can I say...you see in

English language you haven't got the word. It's my mother's land isn't it, or what the Germans call Vaterland. It is. Wherever I go it will be that. I may settle down somewhere else but that is the land and I will still love it'. 'I don't think you can explain that to somebody who hasn't gone through that'.[1395] Others pointed to the importance of the circumstances of displacement in the retention of an emotional link to the homeland. A Latvian man stated that it is 'very difficult to explain unless, as I said you were born elsewhere, do you know what I mean?, and then you've been forced out of that particular…place or district or whatever, and you live somewhere else although you're happy where you're living, but somehow your tie are there [in the homeland] all the time, do you know what I'm trying to say? It's a bit difficult to explain. It's something that is internal isn't it? It's not something that you express outwardly do you know what I'm trying to say?'[1396]

4) Were there any other factors, which particularly influenced the integration process?

Among the wide range of other factors, which impacted upon the integration process, three are of particular interest: British Society; age and time spent in Britain; and the influence of younger generations.

The first factor - British Society, composes several elements, including: relations with British labour and local communities; cultural similarities; and shifting British cultures and identities. Not only were the refugees profoundly affected by developments within the homeland, they were also influenced by an evolving Britain.

British society was initially sceptical of the new arrivals in the late 1940's, and this response contributed to some feelings of alienation and unease among the Baltic communities at first. However, among local populations and British Labour, any hostility weakened with the arrival of newcomers from the Caribbean and Indian Sub-Continent from the 1950's onwards, and as the refugees themselves adjusted to British society, for example, by learning English. Weakening discrimination and growing acceptance decreased feelings of being a foreigner, and aided integration. The lack of pressure to assimilate after the first few years had the effect of weakening any attempts to defend Baltic cultures and identities against the homogenising effects of British society. The need to protect homeland cultures and identities from the Soviet Union was always greater than the perceived need to shield them from British culture. This experience differs from that of some other diaspora groups, who find themselves threatened not only by the new regime in the homeland, but also by the new receiving society. For such communities, marginalization from the new society may occur, as well as a greater defence of homeland cultures and identities.

Some participants have suggested that Baltic and British cultures were fairly similar, both being North European, and that this facilitated integration. Others pointed to the homogenising globalising influences during the second half of the twentieth century across the world, which has led to greater similarities in culture among different countries. One of the reasons that the Balts' were recruited in the first place was a belief that they would adjust easily into British society. Racialised stereotyping suggested that they shared Britain's North European Protestant work ethic, were educated and fairly sophisticated in various ways. Although there are many significant cultural differences between the homelands and Britain both when the refugees first arrived and by the end of twentieth century, some participants, most notably Latvians stressed the similarities. I asked the eldest participant in the study, a Latvian man, in his eighty-sixth year, about the differences between the Latvian and the British way of life. He stressed that there were many similarities between the Latvian and the British cultures: 'You see, we are all Christians, and the traditions are similar as the English, as in Latvia, because there is…our folk traditions is [are] different.....but we are celebrating Christmas like a religious feast so it is similar'. 'You see I would say.....there's not much difference between British and Latvian and European, every nation, except traditions…' He spoke about the globalisation of culture: 'I can't understand how some people is talking about national culture, no the culture is international'. 'Except [as] I said, traditions which come from centuries, centuries ago from past'. I asked him if he ate Latvian foods in Britain. (His wife is Latvian). He replied:

> Sometimes yes, but very, very seldom. Now you see, wife is going in that [those] big shops – like Asda, Sainsbury or these stores and buys the same as [the British], [there's] not much difference…and now you see our traditions slowly is [are] dying out because just, it's more convenient. She just goes out there and buys something. I think you can walk where you want, the same hotels is similar all over the world. All over I have been – in America, I've been in Thailand and in South Africa – the same hotels exactly. Similar. No difference. The culture is international mostly.[1397]

Another Latvian man stressed that many elements of Latvian cuisine were similar to the British or European diet. I asked him if he

356

retained Latvian culinary traditions at Christmas. He replied: 'Well, they're very similar to English. Very similar – turkey or goose or whatever. Christmas Tree, decorations, presents... You see we're not far away from England in lots of ways you know'.[1398] An Estonian man stated that: 'Estonian and English, I mean they're not all that much different really.'[1399] The similarities between British and Baltic cultures is another dimension to consider, when analysing the following refugees' comments that it was 'fairly easy' to integrate into British society,[1400] and it took about five years to 'gradually adopt British customs'.[1401]

This book has stressed throughout, that this study has specifically been an examination of the younger segment of the original refugee population, and that this characteristic has consequences for the findings. In particular, it has been suggested that younger refugees integrated more rapidly and to a greater degree, then older refugees, a finding borne out by the following participant's comments. I asked the oldest participant in the sample, a Latvian man, who had come to Britain age 37 years, the following question: 'Do you think that - if you had come to Britain when you were a bit younger, maybe at 20, do you think you would have integrated a bit more into British society?' He replied: 'Oh yes, definitely. The younger people integrated much more, for example, my friend has two daughters, they was just 3, 4 years old [when they came to Britain], so they are...the same as British'.[1402] Interestingly however, a Latvian woman who left Latvia with her parents at age 17 felt that she had been old enough, to ensure the maintenance of a strong emotional link: 'You see, somebody who is rather younger probably would forget about Latvia, but I was 17. I've spent my childhood and my youth there really, so it's much nearer to me. I'm more attached to it than somebody who was much, much younger. And you see my parents they were Latvians whatever happened. They wouldn't dream of becoming British'.[1403] In general, younger refugees spent the longest time in Britain, and this also contributed to integration. A Latvian woman stated that the following: 'I suppose I am integrated as much as is possible'. She noted that would feel an outsider if she returned to Latvia. Her explanation was related to time spent in Britain: 'I don't think I would fit in anymore. No way. I've been over 50 years now in England, in Yorkshire, longer than anywhere else'.[1404]

Finally, another influence upon the development of the first generation was the assimilation of younger generations. Children introduced British influences into the household, for example, through language, friends and youth culture.[1405] When I asked a Lithuanian woman how long it took her to adapt to life in Britain, she stated: 'Oh, twenty, twenty years. When kids here, children going to school... You feel more settled'.[1406] A Latvian woman noted how her efforts to make her children feel at home in Britain, including not forcing them to learn Latvian, changed her own approach towards settlement in Britain: 'I wanted them to feel a home here since we weren't going back…and of course that did change my attitude as well'.[1407] The influence of younger generations on original refugee or migrant communities is a potentially fruitful area of research, which deserves greater attention.

THE FUTURE OF THE BALTIC COMMUNITIES IN BRITAIN: (The perspective from the late - 1990s)

What are the implications of the findings of this research for the future of the Baltic communities in Britain? (It must be noted that this study was undertaken before the migration of significant numbers of Latvians, Lithuanians and Estonians after the Baltic States joined the European Union in 2004, and that the future of the Baltic communities now in 2013, looks quite different from the prospects as they stood in the late 1990s).

At the end of the 1990s, there was a mixture of pessimism and optimism among the communities about the future. In July 1999, a member of the Lithuanian community wrote starkly about the state of the Lithuanian community in Great Britain:

> The membership [of the Lithuanian Association in Great Britain] is principally of pensionable age. Few of these branches exist in other than name. Seemingly they have long since given up hope of attracting younger members. In many cases, only the parents or grandparents in a family belong to their local branch of the Association. There are no dance groups and not too many singing groups! Over the *years 'Europas Lietuvis'* has been sent to an ever-decreasing number of subscribers. This gloomy picture is well known to all of us.[1408]

However, the author noted some cause for optimism:

> But it need not be so. Sodas branch and the London 'First branch' have both demonstrated that it is quite easy to buck the trend of falling membership by actively seeking out members long lapsed, or by attracting new members from well-established Lithuanian families. The same could happen all over England.

The author noted, however, that the Lithuanian community needed to change its attitudes and approach:

> And we all need to understand very clearly that unless the Association looks to the future and attempts to shape that future, the Lithuanian Community in Great Britain will soon cease to exist as a coherent entity that we can recognise.

> We need to recognise that for far too long the Association has been wedded to the past... It is time...to move forward.[1409]

There is no doubt that independence led to some reinvigoration of the communities, and earlier predictions concerning the rate of the community's decline may have been overly pessimistic. For example, one Latvian woman interviewed by BHRU in 1984 was adamant that the Latvian community in Britain would die out.[1410] A decade later in 1994, the Latvian community remained active, although its decline was clearly visible. Most of those I interviewed for this study across all three communities felt that their community would remain active only in certain areas, particularly London, and one or two other cities. Significant numbers of participants predicted that their community would have a life span of only ten years. The major reason cited is the lack of interest of younger generations. I asked a Latvian woman what she thought would happen to the Latvian community in the future and whether the second generation will take over the running of the clubs. She replied:

> No, no, no. They are more assimilated into the English, into the local society. No.(sighs) That's a problem we are thinking about, about what will happen. I think it will last another 10-15 years...[1411]

At the time of the study, many of the Latvian, Lithuanian and Estonian clubs were suffering increasing financial problems, and although some were bolstered by central funds, the future looked increasingly bleak. As this book has suggested, in the majority of cases, the second and third generations had assimilated and cultural maintenance was largely symbolic. It looked unlikely that this phenomenon could be reversed, and that other solutions needed to be found. The three communities were dealing with the issue in different ways. The research has shown how the Lithuanian community in particular was very pro-active in seeking to solve its problems, and debates about the current state of the community were held among all three generations. An important factor was an acknowledgement of the realities facing the community since the 1970's, and adjustments to membership and community structures and activities to take account of factors, such as poor language skills of younger generations. Another factor may be the fact that the Lithuanian community has a longer history of settlement in Britain than the Latvian or Estonian groups, and may have learnt from the decline of the wave of Lithuanian immigrants who preceded them in the late-nineteenth century. They were also able to build upon that community, and in some instances, for example, in Scotland, work together. This experience was also being utilised in fostering amicable relations with recent Lithuanian migrants from the homeland. The Lithuanian community in Britain has also been strengthened by particularly strong links with other diaspora communities globally. Because of these characteristics, it appears at the time of the research that the Lithuanian community was relatively well prepared for the future and would be able to survive beyond the first generation, albeit with some eventual dissolution of some local branches.

The Latvian community had the advantage of larger numbers than either Lithuanians or Estonians, the support of the DVF, which had a strong central structure, both nationally and internationally, and the greater financial strength of the community. However, the Latvian community had severe difficulties maintaining the interest of the second and third generation. At the time of the research it looked as though the Latvian DVF branch in London, and possibly some clubs in Northern regions of England would endure, but that serious decline would occur over subsequent decades.

The Estonians community, by far the smallest of the communities faced the most difficulties at the time of the research, although as with the Lithuanian and Latvian community, the migration of newcomers to London was helping to reinvigorate some local branches and ensure the survival of larger branches, particularly the London branch. The smaller number of clubhouses meant that greater effort was concentrated on retaining them, and, consequently, it is looked likely that the clubs in Leicester and Bradford would survive for the foreseeable future.

At the time of the research it appeared likely that the immigration of newcomers since the restoration of independence would offset the decline, and this has since been borne out to be the case. Their arrival invigorated the communities and provided optimism for the future of the communities in Britain. This phenomenon was seen most strikingly among the Lithuanian community, which has opened four new clubs in 1998 and 1999. In October 1999, LYNES also noted that the Lithuanian Scouts Association 'had a growing number of new members from the new Lithuanians'.[1412] However, these developments could not mask the continuing decline in regions outside London, particularly in the North, where fewer 'new' immigrants lived. It was unclear at the time whether a policy decision by the Home Office to spread asylum seekers across Britain, and to move them out of London, where many boroughs were apparently unable to cope with the numbers, would aid the survival of the Baltic communities in other areas. Much depended upon the permanency of these migrants, and their interest in maintaining the community structures currently in existence, or whether they wish to build their own communities separate from the post-war diaspora. The communities themselves had an acute interest in the new migrants, and although they were aware of the potential benefits to membership, they were also concerned about the possibility of new migrants gaining dominance within certain clubs and localities, and changing the character of the communities. In a letter to the editor, in the December 1999 issue of *LYNES*, a Lithuanian in Manchester noted that:

> London and its outlying regions has 80% of asylum seekers of various nationalities and it is envisaged to transfer approximately 6,500 per month to the Northern regions of Great Britain. The organisers are stating that nationalities should remain together within their own ethnic groups. Lithuanians are long established both in Bradford and Manchester and both have club facilities. It could come to pass that the local authorities will take note of this when considering the transfer of Lithuanian asylum seekers. It is a fact that our community leaders are now well into pensionable age. If we should have an influx of new Lithuanians, who will co-ordinate activities, social events etc.? Both clubs currently have relatively small membership lists. How shall we deal with this influx, especially majority membership of both clubs? Both Manchester and Bradford clubs require [need] to give these matters serious thought.[1413]

Even at the time that this research was undertaken - in the mid – to – late 1990s, the character and composition of the Baltic communities in Britain was undergoing changes as a result of homeland independence and the new migrants to Britain from the Baltic States. The following decade would see further profound changes which would see community organisations and structures undergoing further transformation as tens of thousands of Latvians, Lithuanians and Estonians came to Britain as a result of the Baltic States entry into the

European Union and the right this gave their citizens to work in other countries of the EU. This phenomenon will be explored in further detail in the Postscript.

Postscript

Latvian, Lithuanian and Estonian Migration to Britain since 2000

Since 2000, when I completed this research project, there has been significant Latvian, Lithuanian and Estonian migration to the UK,[1414] principally as a result of these countries joining the European Union (EU) in 2004. As a result of joining the EU, Latvians, Lithuanians and Estonians have been able to travel freely to Great Britain to work, and many have done so. Although there was some migration from the Baltic States to Britain during the 1990s and the first few years of the new millennium, migration increased significantly as a result of the new freedoms engendered by joining the EU. This section provides a brief overview of the main characteristics of this migration, as well as pointers to sources of further information.

The extent to which migration from the Baltic States took place as a result of EU membership can be seen by some research by the Office for National Statistics, which analysed data from the Worker Registration Scheme (WRS) for the period May 2004-December 2006.[1415] Workers from the three Baltic States and the other five countries joining the EU in 2004 (Czech Republic, Hungary, Poland, Slovakia and Slovenia), a group collectively known as the A8, were required to register on the Worker Registration Scheme in order to take up employment in the UK. The data shows that while Poles constituted the largest number of migrants to the UK from all A8 countries, Lithuanians were the second greatest in number. During the 31 month period surveyed, they constituted 10.7% (54,529 people) of the A8 total, and headed to areas in London, the South East, the North East, Northern Ireland, Eastern England and parts of Cornwall and

Herefordshire.[1416] The geographical pattern of Latvians within the UK was similar and they made up 5.7% (28,810 people) of the A8 total migration to the UK. Particular concentrations of Latvians were also found to be in the Outer Hebrides of Scotland where they represented 40.9% of the A8 total and the East Riding of Yorkshire where they accounted for 37.7% of the A8 total. Estonians were smaller in number, numbering 5441 in this 31 month period, 1.1% of the A8 total, and they headed for London, as well as areas of the South East, Wales, South Lanarkshire and Northamptonshire.[1417]

According to the Office for National Statistics, the data from this survey suggests that 'there are networks pulling certain groups to particular areas'.[1418]   However, although some headed for traditional areas of Latvian, Lithuanian and Estonian concentration, others did not. Compared to the post-war migration, the new migrants have been more widely dispersed around the UK with significant numbers settling in areas with negligible previous Baltic migration for example, in Devon and Cornwall. A recent report by the Centre for Population Change in 2012, suggests that 'unlike many previous waves of immigration', the initial destinations of East and central European migrants 'have been remarkably geographically dispersed as opposed to being centred on major conurbations with an existing history of receiving immigrants'.[1419] This has had a major impact on local authorities which have had limited experience of immigration, and it also has implications on Latvian, Lithuanian and Estonian community structures as new groups and organisations have sprung up in some areas in response to the settlement of these migrants.[1420]

Unlike the post war migration, the recent migration from the Baltic States since 2000 has been primarily economic; it has been composed mainly of young single people in their twenties looking for work and people looking for a better quality life for their families. The WRS data is useful in that it also shows which industries the new migrants were concentrated in.[1421] Over one third went to work in the administration, management and business services sector, approximately 20% in hospitality and catering, one-tenth in agriculture, 5% in food processing, almost 5% in retail and related services, as well as in health and medical services and smaller percentages in transport, the computer services industry and financial services.[1422] The majority worked on a full-time basis, with the majority earning relatively low pay rates of between £4.50 and £5.99 an hour. However about one-fifth earned over £6 an hour with concentrations of these higher earners living mainly in the South East and relatively prosperous areas such as Oxfordshire.[1423]

Over the course of subsequent years, these migration patterns broadly continued, with Lithuanians forming the highest number of migrants to the UK of the three Baltic nationalities, and Estonians the smallest. Partly this reflected the differing population size of the three countries, with Lithuania having the highest population (approximately 3 million in 2012, and Estonia the smallest (an estimated 1.1 million in 2011), with Latvia falling between the two at 2.2 million in 2011. Another reason cited by Helen Pidd in an article in *The Guardian* newspaper in early 2013, is that Lithuanians suffered particularly badly from the effects of the global recession with public spending cuts of 30% across the board in 2009, which led to a spike in Lithuanian migration to Britain in 2010. [1424] In 2009, 15,815 Lithuanians left for the UK, while in 2010, 40,901 Lithuanians left for the UK.[1425] This number dropped to 26,935 in 2011 and dropped further from 2011-13.[1426]

Compared to the number of Poles migrating to Britain, the number of Lithuanians migrating to the UK has been relatively small: however it is still highly significant and considerably outnumbers those who migrated in the period following the Second World War.[1427] Census data from 2011 shows the extent of Lithuanian migration, recording a figure of 97,083 Lithuanians in England and Wales.[1428] The figure recorded by the Census was 39,817 Lithuanians in London, 0.5% of the total migrant population. The highest concentration of Lithuanians in London is in the London Borough of Newham, which according to the 2011 Census had 8348 Lithuanian residents, compared to a 2001 population of just 360.[1429] Official Census data is regarded as an underestimate by the Lithuanian community who estimate there are currently approximately 200,000 Lithuanians in the UK as a whole (including Scotland and Northern Ireland) with 100,000 of them in London. One Lithuanian website notes that Census figures underestimate true numbers as landlords put pressure on migrants not to complete Census forms, and because the Census recorded place of birth rather than ethnicity so it did not include Lithuanians born in England and Wales.[1430]

Second in terms of numbers of migrants to Britain were Latvians. Data from National Insurance registration shows how many Latvians migrated to the UK as a whole (Great Britain and Northern Ireland) in the years following EU enlargement. In 2004 after Latvia joined the EU, 3,700 Latvians registered for a UK National Insurance Number (NiNo), meaning they could work in the UK; this number rose to 13,500 in 2005.[1431] Figures rose in subsequent years. By March 2010, nearly 75,000 Latvians had acquired NINOs.[1432] However, as Straumanis points out in an article on the Latvians Online website, NiNo's do 'not necessarily track permanent immigrants, just people who are living in the UK', and some of these may have since returned to Latvia or moved onto another country.[1433]

Estonians came to the UK in fewer numbers for several reasons; firstly, as already stated, Estonia has a much smaller population than Latvia or Lithuania; secondly, Estonia has fared better economically principally due to its close ties with the Scandinavian countries; and thirdly, because of these close ties, many Estonians chose to migrate to these Scandinavian countries. The relatively small size of the Estonian community in the UK may also have been a factor. Figures from National Insurance number registrations (NiNo's) from 2011/12 show the difference between the number of Estonian migrants to the UK and those of Latvians and Estonians.[1434] In 2011/12, only 2,150 Estonians registered for a NiNo, a 10% decrease on the previous year 2010/11.[1435] This compares to figures in the same year (2011/12) of Latvians of 18,590 and Lithuanians of 33,190. The NiNo data is useful in tracking the number of Estonians who have migrated to the UK: it is important to point out that there is significantly less data and analysis available on Estonian migration to the UK compared to Lithuanians or Latvians as they came in far smaller numbers.

The document on NiNo's produced by the Department of Work and Pensions (DWP) is also useful as it lists unemployment data for the three Baltic countries which may have been one trigger for out-migration.[1436] In 2011 for example, while there was an unemployment rate of 15.4% in Lithuania and the same in Latvia, Estonia had an unemployment rate of 12.5%. While this is lower than Latvia and Lithuania, the difference is not so significant that it would on its own account for the significantly smaller level of Estonian migration to the UK. Therefore the factors suggested above including the ties with Scandinavia and the smaller size of the Estonian community in the UK may have played significant roles: in any migration flow, both 'push' and 'pull' factors play a role and it may well be that there simply has not been enough of a 'pull' towards the UK compared to Scandinavian or other European countries.

It is unclear how many of the new migrants will settle permanently in the UK, and how many will return to the Baltic States. Many are settling down and starting families with children settling at schools and growing up, but others may decide to return to Latvia, Lithuania and Estonia. In fact, sizeable numbers have already done so. According to the Lithuanian Embassy for example, in 2012, 6,000 people returned to Lithuania from Britain. The Embassy believes that more will return as the economic situation in Lithuania improves[1437]. All three Baltic States have seen quite a serious exodus from their countries and are currently implementing strategies to attempt to halt out-migration.

Further, recent data suggest that migration from the Baltic States to the UK is declining. For example, NiNo registrations from Latvia fell by 32% in 2011/12 compared to 2010/11, with 18,600 Latvians registering in 2011/12. The number of Lithuanians registering for NiNos fell by 19% in 2011/12 compared to the previous year with 33,200 Lithuanians registering in 2011/12.[1438]

As already stated although some of the new migrants have headed for jobs in areas of the UK which do not have large Latvian, Lithuanian or Estonian communities, many others have migrated to areas of established communities, for example, London and areas in the Midlands and Yorkshire. The effect of the recent migration on the established post-Second World War communities has been immense. Although there have been tensions in some areas, the new migrants have brought a new vitality and vigour to the established communities, and have also in some areas, set up their own community groups and organisations. For example, recent Lithuanian migrants set up the British Lithuanian Basketball League which is now flourishing with over 500 members and the Lithuanian City of London Club, set up for 'high-flying' Lithuanians working in the city and professional jobs in London.[1439] Latvian, Lithuanian and Estonian community websites show the vigour and vitality that many of the clubs and associations are now experiencing. Most of the community organisations that existed in 2000 continue, with some reporting significantly increased participation levels, and many of the language schools have also been revitalised as the new migrants want to ensure that their children learn Latvian, Lithuanian or Estonian.

One of the main differences with the newer migrants and the older established communities is the ability of the new migrants to move freely between Britain and the Baltic States both through travel and via social media. For example, many migrants use email or Facebook as a way of connecting with friends and relatives all over the world, and it would be interesting to assess the impact of this on identities and levels of belonging, compared to the post war migrants who struggled to keep in touch with their homelands during the years of Soviet occupation.

The arrival of the new migrants from the Baltic States has opened up many other interesting avenues of research, and a great deal of work is on-going assessing the experiences of the recent migrants.[1440] The migration of Latvians, Lithuanians and Estonians to the UK over the last decade raises many other interesting research questions in relation to the post war migrant communities, for example:

- To what extent have the new migrants settled in areas of post-war Baltic communities and what is the relationship between the new migrants and the post-war communities?
- How will the recent migration of Latvians, Lithuanians and Estonians to the UK affect identities, in terms of what it means to be a Latvian, Lithuanian or Estonian in the UK today?

- How does the British Government's policy towards migration from the Baltic States in recent years compare to policies and attitudes after the Second World War?
- How do public and media attitudes towards migrant workers from the Baltic States as compared to migrants from Southern East European States, for example, Romania and Bulgaria mirror attitudes in the post Second World War period?
- Finally, how will the new migrants influence and change the established communities' maintenance of cultures and identities as Latvians, Lithuanians and Estonians in Britain today?

ENDNOTES

[1] LAB 26/247, 'English for Foreign Workers', Report of an Enquiry made by one of HM Inspectors of Schools during January, February and April 1949 into the teaching of English to Foreign Workers, with special reference to the relevant social and labour problems involved.

[2] Lithuanian Charter, Adopted by the Supreme Committee for the Liberation of Lithuania, 14 June 1949. Reprinted in *LYNES* (Lithuanian Youth News-sheet), no 27, July 1982. Insert.

[3] Home Office files suggest that by 31 December 1950, a total of 26, 826 Baltic DPs including dependants had arrived in Britain by 31 December 1950. Of these 12,919 with 1322 dependants were Latvians, Lithuanians numbered 6186 and 741 dependants, and Estonians 5154, with 504 dependants. H0213/596, cited by Kay, D. and Miles, R. (1992) *Refugees or Migrant Workers?: European Volunteer Workers in Britain, 1946-51*, London: Routledge, p 43.

[4] In 1946, the Polish second corps which had served under British command during the war were allowed to enter Britain, later followed by dependants. The British Government identified this population as a potential source of labour, particularly in coal mining and agriculture in 1946. In May the Polish Resettlement Corps was founded, as a result of which 115,000 Poles chose to resettle in Britain. Other sources of labour drawn upon after the war included German and Italian POW's already resident in Britain. In 1946, the 1920 Aliens Act was amended to restore to the Ministry of Labour and National Service powers to issue individual work permits to aliens seeking employment in Britain. Further, the MLNS reached agreement with Belgian Government for the recruitment of Belgian women for work in hospitals in Britain on a six-month renewable contract basis. 900 were recruited in 1945-46. (Kay & Miles, *Refugees or Migrant Workers?*, pp 35-38).

[5] Kay, D. & Miles, R. (1992) *Refugees or Migrant Workers?: European Volunteer Workers in Britain, 1946-51*, London: Routledge.

[6] LAB8/90, 1945, Ministry of Health Proposal to bring Displaced Persons from camps to the UK for domestic work in Sanatoria, Memorandum by the parliamentary Secretary to MLNS, 'Recruitment of Displaced Persons from Germany for work in British Hospitals', 17/9/46.

[7] Paul, K. (1997) *Whitewashing Britain: Race and Citizenship in the post-war era*, Ithaca and London: Cornell University Press, p xiii.

[8] Tannahill, J. A. (1958) *European Volunteer Workers in Britain*, Manchester: Manchester University Press.

[9] Brown, J. (1970) *The Un-Melting Pot: An English Town and its Immigrants*, London and Basingstoke: Macmillan, Chapter 3: 'Latvia', pp 44-55.

[10] There is a large and still growing body of work on Poles in Britain. See: Mills, J. (1963) 'Britain's community of Poles', *New Society*, 18 July 1963; Nocon, A. (1996) 'A Reluctant Welcome?: Poles in Britain during the 1940's', *Oral History*, Spring 1996: 79-87; Patterson, S. (1977) 'The Poles: An Exile Community in Britain', in Watson, J. L (ed.) *Between Two Cultures: Immigrants and Minorities in Britain*, Oxford: Blackwell; Sword, K. (1993)'The Poles in London', in

Merriman, N. (ed.) *The Peopling of London: Fifteen Thousand Years from overseas*, London: Museum of London; Sword, K., Davies, N. & Ciechanowski, J. (1989) *The Formation of the Polish Community in Great Britain, 1939-50*, London: SEES; Temple, B. (1995) 'Telling Tales: Accounts and Selves in the Journey of British Poles', *Oral History*, Autumn 1995: 60-64; Winslow, M. (1999) 'Polish Migration to Britain: War , Exile and Mental Health', *Oral History*, Spring 1999: 57-64; Zubrzycki, J. (1956) *Polish Immigrants in Britain*, The Hague.

[11] In the 1980's the Bradford Heritage Recording Unit recorded interviews with Ukrainians in Bradford. This project was supplemented by a study carried out in the 1990's - see: Smith, T., Perks, R. and Smith, G. (1998) *Ukraine's Forbidden History*, Stockport: Dewi Lewis Publishing.

[12] Jeffcoate, R. & Mayor, B. (1982) *Bedford: Portrait of a Multi-Ethnic Town*, Milton Keynes: Open University Press; Anon. (1982) *Migration and Settlement*, Milton Keynes: Open University Press.

[13] Patterson, S. (1968) *Immigrants in Industry*, London: Oxford University Press. For a definition of absorption and industrial absorption, see Glossary of Terms.

[14] Merrimann, N. (ed.) (1993) *The Peopling of London: Fifteen Thousand Years of Settlement from Overseas*, London: The Museum of London; Kershen, A. J. (ed.) (1997) *London: the promised land?*, Aldershot & Brookfield: Avebury.

[15] Research into the Irish and Jewish populations in Great Britain has a long history, with significant works published long before the surge of interest in immigration history begun in the 1970's and 1980's. See for example: Jackson, J. A. (1963) *The Irish in Britain*, London: Routledge and Kegan Paul; Handley, J. E. (1947)*The Irish in Modern Scotland*, Cork: Cork University Press; Lipman, V. D. (1954) *Social History of the Jews in England, 1850-1950*, Watts; Gartner, L. P. (1960) *The Jewish Immigrant in England, 1870-1914*, Allen & Unwin, reprinted 1973.

[16] While there were some significant publications on the EVWs in the years immediately following the schemes, there has been a gap of some twenty or thirty years when there was virtually no research into the EVWs. This was largely due to the plethora of works on the immigrants from the Caribbean and Indian sub-continent, in the 1960's and 1970's, which focused attention away from smaller immigrant groups.

[17] On Germans see for example: Sherman, A. J. (1973) *Island Refuge : Britain and Refugees from the Third Reich*, 1933-1939, Paul Elek; Ashton, R. (1986) *Little Germany : Exile and Asylum in Victorian Britain*, Oxford; Panayi, P. (1988) *The Enemy in Our Midst : Germans in Britain during the First World War*, Oxford. On Italians see: Sponza, L. (1988) *Italian Immigrants in Nineteenth Century Britain : Realities and Images*, Leicester; Hughes, C. (1991) *Lime, Lemon and Sarsparilla: the Italian Community in South Wales, 1881-1945*, Bridgend.

[18] Research on the Lithuanian immigrants who came to Britain in the late-nineteenth and early twentieth century has been begun by Kenneth Lunn, Murdoch Rogers and J White. See Chapter 1 A Brief History of Latvians, Lithuanians and Estonians in Great Britain before 1946', for further details. Also see: Lunn, K. (1980) 'Reactions to Lithuanian and Polish Immigrants in the Lanarkshire Coalfield, 1880-1914', in Lunn, K. (ed.) *Hosts, Immigrants & Minorities : Historical Responses to British Society, 1870-1914*, Folkestone: Dawson;

Rodgers, M. (1982) 'The Anglo-Russian Military Convention and the Lithuanian Immigrant Community in Lanarkshire, Scotland, 1914-20', *Immigrants and Minorities*, 1; Rodgers, M. 91984) 'Political Developments in the Lithuanian Community in Scotland, c. 1890-1923' in Slatter, J. (ed.) *From the Other Shore : Russian Political Emigrants in Britain, 1880-1917*, London; Rodgers, M. (1985) 'The Lithuanians', *History Today*, July 1985: 15-20; White, J. D. (1975) 'Scottish Lithuanians and the Russian Revolution', *Journal of Baltic Studies*, 6(1). A recent book, written by a Scottish Lithuanian, John Millar (Lithuanian name – Jonas Stepšis) (1988) *The Lithuanians in Scotland: A Personal View*, Isle of Colonsay: House of Lochar, gives a detailed account of the Lithuanians in Scotland, and uses oral history interviews and documentary evidence. It is also critical of some of the above analyses. Research to date has concentrated on the more numerous Lithuanian populations in Scotland, to the neglect of Lithuanians in other parts of Great Britain, for example Manchester and London.

[19] Husband, C. (ed.) (1982) *Race in Britain: Continuity and Change*, London: Hutchinson.

[20] Rees, T. (1982) 'Immigration policies in the United Kingdom', in Husband, C. (ed.) *Race in Britain*, pp 75-96.

[21] Holmes, C. (1988) *John Bull's Island : Immigration and British Society, 1871-1971*, Basingstoke and London: Macmillan.

[22] Ibid., p 210.

[23] Panayi, P. (1994) *Immigration, ethnicity and racism in Britain, 1815-1945*, Manchester: Manchester University Press, p 1.

[24] Ibid., p 2.

[25] Banks, M. (1996) *Ethnicity: Anthropological Constructions*, London & New York: Routledge, p 89.

[26] There have been several works on the Latvian, Lithuanian and Estonian communities in Great Britain. These are mainly factual accounts of the communities, giving details of the different organisations and clubs in Great Britain, information on prominent individuals within the communities, the cultural and social activities of the communities, including dance groups, summer camps, weekend language schools, choirs, celebration of national days and commemorative events. The various campaigns for independence are also outlined in some of the books. Although most of the publications are written in the homeland language, some have summaries in English. Often, this is to enable members of the second generation, the majority of whom are not fluent in the homeland language, to learn about their community. On the Latvian community see: Auziņa-Smita, I. (1995) *Latvieši Lielbritanijā* (Latvians in Great Britain), vol 1, London: Latvian National Council in Great Britain and Daugavas Vanagi. The aim of the book is 'to help younger generations of Latvians and also people living in Latvia to understand and appreciate the experiences of Latvians who immigrated to Britain and how they struggled to establish themselves here, at the same time never forgetting Latvia and doing everything possible for its benefit from afar.' The book contains a history of the Latvians in Great Britain; individual memories of Latvians in Britain about their experiences of settlement and adaptation; the history of the Latvian gold

deposits in the Bank of England; extensive English summaries, and an extensive bibliography and list of archive sources. A booklet entitled *Latvians in Great Britain*, Latvian National Council in Great Britain, 1995, provides an introductory overview of the history of the post-war Latvian community in Great Britain in English. *Latvia and Latvians* by Juris Sinka (1988), 2nd Edn., London: Daugavas Vanagi, also has some information on Latvians in Great Britain, again written in English. On Lithuanians see: Barėnas, K. (1978) *Britanijos Lietuviai, 1947-1973* (Lithuanians in Britain, 1947-1973), London: Lithuanian Association in Great Britain. This comprehensive book covers the history of the post-war Lithuanian community in Great Britain in great detail, and includes sections on all the Lithuanian communities in Great Britain. Another volume covering the period since 1973 is being prepared. Unfortunately there are no English summaries. *Bradfordo Lietuvių Veikla Didžiojoje Britanijoje*, 1947-1995 (Lithuanians in Bradford, 1947-1995), edited by members from the Bradford Lithuanian Club 'Vytis', published in Vilnius, 1995, describes the history of the Lithuanian club in Bradford since 1947 and contains a brief English summary. On Estonians see: Hindo, N. (1968) *Eesti organisatsioonid Inglismal 1918-1968*. There are also various publications written by the London, Leicester and Bradford branches of the Estonian Association in Great Britain

[27] A notable exception is *Latvieši Lielbritanijā*, edited by Inese Auziņa-Smita, which contains discussion of Latvians' experiences of settlement in Britain and includes personal memories and input by members of the Latvian communities about their life in Britain.

[28] Panayi, *Immigration, ethnicity and racism in Britain*, p 2.

[29] Thompson, P. (1992) *The Edwardians: The remaking of British society*, Routledge, London and New York: Second Edition, p xviii.

[30] Thomas, W. I. and Znaniecki, F. (1918) *The Polish Peasant in Europe and America: Monograph of an Immigrant Group*, Chicago: University of Chicago Press.

[31] Green, A. & Troup, K. (1999) *The Houses of History: A Critical reader in twentieth-century history and theory*, Manchester: Manchester University Press, p 231.

[32] Green, A. & Troup, Ibid.

[33] Ibid., p 230.

[34] Roper, M. (1996) 'Oral History', in Brivati, B., Buxton, J. & Sheldon, A. (eds.) (1996) *The Contemporary History Handbook*, Manchester, p 346.

[35] Thompson, *The Edwardians*, p 17.

[36] Roper, 'Oral History', p 347.

[37] Green & Troup, *Houses of History*, p 233.

[38] Thompson, (1992) *The Edwardians*, Second Edition, p xviii.

[39] Green and Troup, *Houses of History*, p 237.

[40] Thomson, A. (1999) 'Moving Stories: Oral History and Migration Studies', *Oral History*, Spring 1999, p 26.

[41] Kay & Miles, *Refugees or Migrant Workers?*, p 2.

[42] Ward, S. (1995) 'War Crimes case thrown into chaos', *The Independent*, 27 September 1995, p 2.

[43] Kay & Miles, *Refugees or Migrant Workers?*, p 3.

[44] These issues will be explored in depth in Chapter 3: *Displacement*

[45] See: Cesarani, D. (1992) *Justice Delayed: How Britain became a refuge for Nazi War Criminals*, London: Heinemann and Bower,T. (1989) *The Red Web: M16 and the KGB Master Coup*, London: Aurum.

[46] See: Cesarani, Ibid. and Bower, Ibid.

[47] Johnstone, H. 'Country home offers luxury for Latvians', *The Times*, 30/12/99, p 4.

[48] Transnationalism and Diaspora are defined in the *Glossary of Terms* at the back of the book.

[49] Lane, T. (2004) *Victims of Stalin and Hitler: The Exodus of Poles and Balts to Britain*, Hampshire and New York, Palgrave Macmillan; McDowell. L., (2005) *Hard Labour: The Forgotten Voices of Latvian migrant 'Volunteer' Workers,* London, UCL.

[50] Gilbert, E. (2002) 'The Impact of Homeland Independence on the Latvian Community in Great Britain', *Journal of Baltic Studies*, 33(3): 280-306.

[51] Van Hear, N. (1998) *New Diasporas: The mass exodus, dispersal and regrouping of migrant communities*, Seattle: University of Washington Press, p 55.

[52] Holmes, C. (1978) 'Introduction: Immigrants and Minorities in Britain', *Immigrants and Minorities in British Society*, London: George Allen & Unwin, p 20.

[53] Rex, J. 'Ethnic Identity and the Nation State: the Political Sociology of Multi-cultural Societies', *Social Identities*, 1(1), p 22.

[54] Ibid.

[55] For example, Philip Gleason criticised historians for using the term 'identity' without proper thought or explanation. (Gleason, P. (1983) 'Identifying Identity: A Semantic History' in Sollors, W. (ed.) (1996) *Theories of Ethnicity: A Classical Reader*, London & Basingstoke: Macmillan, p 460).

[56] In 1997, the introduction to the new series of books on *Global Diasporas* edited by Robin Cohen stated that, 'The assumption that minorities and migrants will demonstrate an exclusive loyalty to the nation-state is now questionable. Scholars of nationalism, international migration and ethnic relations need new conceptual maps and fresh case studies to understand the growth of complex transnational identities. The old idea of 'diaspora' may provide this framework.' (Cohen, R. (ed.) (1997) *Global Diasporas: An Introduction*, London: UCL Press). Since the start of this study, the field of diaspora studies has grown enormously. A new journal *Diaspora* has been one of the results of the growth of diaspora studies, and has been a key forum for discussion of the concept of diaspora, and related concepts, including 'diasporic identity'.

[57] Neuman, W. L. (1994) *Social Research Methods: Qualitative and Quantitative Approaches*, Second Edition, Boston & London: Allyn & Bacon, p 319.

[58] Danys, M. (1986) *DP: Lithuanian Immigration to Canada after the Second World War*, Toronto: Multicultural History Society of Ontario, p 299.

[59] Patterson, S. (1968) *Immigrants in Industry*, London: Oxford University Press, London, p 7.

[60] Ibid.

[61] See the Glossary of Terms for more discussion of the use of the terms 'adjustment' and 'adaptation' in this book.

[62] Berry, J. W. (1992) 'Acculturation and Adaptation in a New Society', *International Migration*, 30.

[63] Van Hear, *New Diasporas*, p 55.

[64] Berry, 'Acculturation and Adaptation', pp 69-70.

[65] Ibid., pp 69-85.

[66] Brah, A. (1996) *Cartographies of Diaspora: Contesting identities*, London & New York: Routledge, p 25.

[67] Multiculturalism is defined in the Glossary of Terms.

[68] Nationality is defined in the Glossary of Terms at the back of the book.

[69] Benmayor, R. & Skotnes, A. (ed.) (1994) *Migration and Identity*, International Yearbook of Oral History and Life Stories, volume III, Oxford: OUP, pp 14-15.

[70] Ibid.

[71] Lummis, T. (1987) *Listening to History: The Authenticity of Oral Evidence*, London: Hutchinson, p 43.

[72] Ibid., p 14.

[73] Yow, V. R. (1994) *Recording Oral History: A Practical Guide for Social Scientists*, London & New Dehli: Sage, p 18.

[74] Ibid., p 21.

[75] Ibid.

[76] Thompson, *The Edwardians*, p xix.

[77] Ibid.

[78] Yow, *Recording Oral History*, p 22.

[79] This included tape-recorded interviews, lasting two to three hours, with 24 people (8 women, 16 men) and five shorter non-recorded interviews. In addition, I also utilised three interviews recorded by the Bradford Heritage Recording Unit (see page 25).

[80] The returnees I interviewed were not recruited via the questionnaire approach.

[81] Poopuu, H. (1985-86) *Remembering Pussa*, Unpublished personal memoir.

[82] These interviews can be found in Bradford Central Library.

[83] See the use of the term 'Balts' in: Lieven, A. (1993) *The Baltic Revolution: Estonia, Latvia and Lithuania and the Path to Independence*, New Haven and London: Yale University Press. The use of the term 'Balts' to refer to Latvians, Lithuanians and Estonians collectively can also be seen in Clare Thomson's (1992) *The Singing Revolution: A Journey through the Baltic States*, London: Michael Joseph. Clare Thomson is a second generation Estonian in Britain.

[84] Stanley Vardys, V. (1975) 'Modernization and Baltic Nationalism', *Problems of Communism*, 24(5), p 34.

[85] Milosz, C. (1984) 'Lithuania, Latvia and Estonia 1940-1980: Similarities and differences', *Baltic Forum*, 1(1), p 39.

[86] The dearth of information regarding Latvians, Lithuanians and Estonians in Britain before the post-war wave of immigration relates partly to the fact that until 1918 all three countries were part of the Russian Empire. It is unlikely

that the different nationalities of the Empire would have been recorded in any immigration records as such. Place of birth specified Russia or in the case of Lithuania, sometimes Poland or Russian Poland, because of course, Latvia, Lithuania and Estonia did not then exist. Diplomatic representation began only as the result of independence during the inter-war period. Much of the information in the sources which I have used, about Latvians, Lithuanians and Estonians in Britain in the inter-war period, has been gained from the archives of these diplomatic representations, for example, the Latvian Legation in London. It must be stressed that due to the lack of sources and information regarding Latvian, Lithuanian and Estonian immigration to Great Britain prior to the Second World War, the following brief account is necessarily tentative.

[87]   In comparison, the diplomatic representation of the Latvian Republic in London, during the inter-war period is well known.

[88]   Andrups, J. (1995) 'A History of Latvians in Great Britain', (English translation by Andris Abakuks), p 446 in Auziņa-Smita, I. (ed.), *Latvieši Lielbritanijā,* London: Latvian National Council in Great Britain.

[89]   Ibid.

[90] Ibid.

[91] The immigration of Estonians, like that of Latvians, and unlike Lithuanians, is not mentioned in any of the major works on immigration into Great Britain. There is no mention of any Estonian or Latvian immigration into Britain before the Second World War, for example in works like *John Bulls Island* (Colin Holmes, Macmillan, 1988). Apart from the fact that there was no significant 'wave' of immigration, there are also difficulties with finding any such evidence, particularly before 1918, when Estonia was part of the Russian Empire. It is unlikely that the different nationalities of the Russian Empire were noted as such in government immigration records. The diplomatic representation of Estonia in Britain during the inter-war period is well recorded, although immigration during this period is not. All of the following information was provided by an Estonian in Britain, Heino Poopuu, who translated from Estonian, the relevant sections from Nigol Hindo's book, *Eesti organisatsioonid Inglismaal 1918-1968* (Estonian Organisations in England, 1918-1968). As Poopuu notes, 'Its author regrets that in researching for this book, he had no access to the archival libraries in Estonia and that he was unable to examine the relevant Immigration Departments' Registers in this country. Another limitation is his emphasis on London'. Heino supplemented this with some additional information of his own.

[92] Heino Poopuu, translation and abridgement of Hindo, N. (1968) *Eesti organisatsioonid inglismaal, 1918-1968.*

[93] Ibid.

[94] Information provided by Heino Poopuu, an Estonian from Chesterfield.

[95] Nigol Hindo, Ibid.

[96] Ibid.

[97] Heino Poopuu, translation and abridgement of Nigol Hindo, ibid.

[98] Information provided by Heino Poopuu.

[99] Raun, T. (1987) *Estonia and the Estonians.*

[100] Information provided by Heino Poopuu.

[101] Bucys, A. (ed.) (1995) *Bradfordo Lietuviu Veikla didžojoje Britanijoje* (Lithuanians in Bradford, 1947-1995), Bradfordo Lietuvių Klubas 'Vytis', Vilnius: Lietuvos Literaturos Fondas: - 'Litfonda', p 116, (Abstract, English summary).

[102] Ibid.

[103] Ibid.

[104] Millar, J. (Jonas Stepšis) (1998) *The Lithuanians in Scotland: A Personal View*, Isle of Colonsay: House of Lochar, pp 10-11.

[105] As explained in Chapter Two, at the end of the nineteenth century Lithuania was divided between the Polish and Baltic (Kovno and Vilna) provinces of the Russian Empire.

[106] Millar, Lithuanians in Scotland, p 34.

[107] For discussion of the motivations for emigration see: Millar, *The Lithuanians in Scotland*, pp 16-20.

[108] Research on the Lithuanian immigrants who came to Britain in the late-nineteenth and early twentieth century has been begun by Kenneth Lunn, Murdoch Rodgers and J White. See : Lunn, K. (1980) 'Reactions to Lithuanian and Polish Immigrants in the Lanarkshire Coalfield, 1880-1914', in Lunn, K. (ed.), *Hosts, Immigrants & Minorities : Historical Responses to British Society, 1870-1914*, Folkestone: Dawson; Rodgers, M. (1982) 'The Anglo-Russian Military Convention and the Lithuanian Immigrant Community in Lanarkshire, Scotland, 1914-20', *Immigrants and Minorities*, 1; Rodgers, M. (1984) 'Political Developments in the Lithuanian Community in Scotland, c. 1890-1923' in Slatter, J. (ed.) *From the Other Shore : Russian Political Emigrants in Britain, 1880-1917*, London, pp 141-156; Rodgers, M. (1985) 'The Lithuanians', *History Today*, 35(July), pp 15-20; White, J. D. (1975) 'Scottish Lithuanians and the Russian Revolution', *Journal of Baltic Studies*, 6(1). However, the research to date is fragmented and concentrates on the more numerous Lithuanian populations in Scotland, to the neglect of Lithuanians in other parts of Great Britain. The research also fails to use any oral evidence, which could be profitably gained by talking with the children and grandchildren of the first generation, some of whom I have accidentally come into contact with in my own research. The post-war Lithuanian populations also have information about these earlier immigrants, since in many areas, for example Manchester, they came into close contact with them, particularly in the early years. The contact between these earlier immigrants and the post-war Lithuanians is another area of study, which has not yet been researched.

[109] Millar, J. (Jonas Stepšis) (1998) *The Lithuanians in Scotland: A Personal View*, Isle of Colonsay: House of Lochar.

[110] Rodgers, M. (1985) 'The Lithuanians', *History Today*, 35(July), p 15.

[111] White, J. D. (1975) 'Scottish Lithuanians and the Russian Revolution', *Journal of Baltic Studies*, 6(1), p 2, cited in Holmes, C. (1988) *John Bull's Island*, p 29.

[112] Panayi, 1994, p 97.

[113] Lunn, 1980.

[114] Ibid, p 310.

[115] Ibid, p 314 and p 333.

[116] Rodgers, 'Political Developments in the Lithuanian Community in Scotland, c. 1890-1923' , pp 141-156

[117] Ibid., p 141.

[118] Ibid.

[119] Ibid.

[120] Ibid., p 142.

[121] Ibid., p 143.

[122] Ibid., p 152.

[123] Ibid., p 149.

[124] Ibid., p 152.

[125] Buàys, A.   (ed.) (1995) *Bradfordo Lietuvių Veikla didžiojoje Britanijoje* (Lithuanians in Bradford, 1947-1995), Bradfordo LietuviųKlubas 'Vytis', Vilnius: Lietuvos Literaturos Fondas: - 'Litfonda', p 116, (Abstract, English summary).

[126] This has been borne out by my interviews with Lithuanians in Manchester.

[127] Buàys (ed.), *Bradfordo Lietuviu*, p 116.

[128] Holmes, *John Bull's Island*, 1988, p 29.

[129] Bučys (ed.), *Bradfordo Lietuviu*, p 116.

[130] Rodgers, 'The Lithuanians', p 15.

[131] Ibid.

[132] See: Holmes, *John's Bull's Island*, p 27.

[133] Ibid.

[134] Ibid.

[135] Klier, J. (1995) *Imperial Russia's Jewish Question, 1855-1881*, Cambridge, CUP, p 292.

[136] Ibid., p 293.

[137] Ibid., p 294.

[138] Rodgers, 'The Lithuanians', p 28.

[139] By 1911, there were 95,541 resident Russian Poles in England and Wales alone, and they constituted the largest European-born minority in Scotland. (Holmes, *John Bull's Island*, 1988, p 26) Due to the division of contemporary Lithuania (south-west Lithuania in Russian Poland, the rest in the Russian Empire), it is impossible to calculate the numbers of Lithuanian Jews who settled in Britain. Census data recorded place of birth as Russia, Russian Poland or Poland. Because of this the task of estimating the number of Lithuanians is virtually impossible, while the task of estimating the numbers of Lithuanian Jews is even more problematic.

[140] Andrups, J. (1995) 'A History of Latvians in Great Britain', (English translation by Andris Abakuks), in Auziða-Smita, I. (ed.), *Latvieši Lielbritanijā*, London: Latvian National Council in Great Britain. Ibid., p 447.

[141]   Ibid.

[142]   Ibid., p 448.

[143] Heino Poopuu, translation and abridgement of Nigol Hindo.

[144] Heino Poopuu, information from Hindo, ibid.

[145] Hindo, Ibid.

[146] Ibid.

[147] Ibid.

[148] There is further information in Lithuanian in some of the publications produced by the Lithuanian community. See for example: Barénas, K. (1978) *Britanijos Lietuviai*, 1947-1973 (Lithuanians in Britain, 1947-1973), London: Lithuanian Association in Great Britain, p 243 for information on the inter-war activities of Lithuanians in Manchester.

[149] Ibid., p 449.

[150] Ibid.

[151] Ibid.

[152] Playback No: 06, First Generation Latvian man.

[153] Some of the older refugees were born during the earlier period of Russian rule of the Baltic provinces prior to 1918 and of these, some were in their twenties and thirties during the two decades of independence. In this chapter as in the rest of the study, I will focus primarily on the experiences of the Latvians, Lithuanians and Estonians who participated in this study, who as already mentioned, form the younger section of the original refugee population. The oldest participant in my study was born in 1910. Experiences of older refugees who may have been in their thirties or older at the time of displacement can not be discussed in depth, since there are no oral testimonies available for these people. I will however, attempt to show where the experiences of the refugees in my sample were typical, and where the older refugees' experiences may have differed.

[154] Among the participants in my study, an overwhelming majority were born between 1920 and 1928.

[155] See for example: Danys, M. (1986) *DP: Lithuanian Immigration to Canada after the Second World War*, Toronto: Multicultural History Society of Ontario. This book is an analysis of the migration and settlement of Lithuanians in Canada. It begins with a chapter on 'Lithuania in World War Two', and discusses the culture of the inter-war years, the period in which the refugees grew up, only in fragments.

[156] For an introduction to the inter-war period, as well as an account of earlier history, see: Von Rauch, G. (1995) *The Baltic States: The Years of Independence, 1917-1940*, London: Hurst & Co.

[157] Most studies of the Baltic States during the inter-war period focus on political and economic developments, social reform programmes, and the laws on cultural autonomy of the minorities. Most pay scant attention to life at the grassroots, everyday level and provide little understanding of life for the average person. There are some exceptions, which I have utilised in this section in addition to interview transcripts. See: Veidemanis, J. (1982) *Social Change, Major Value Systems of Latvians at Home, as Refugees, and as Immigrants*, Occasional Publications in Anthropology, University of Northern Colorado, Colorado: Museum of Anthropology. An Estonian in Britain, Heino Poopuu also wrote a lengthy memoir about his life on a farm on Saaremaa island during the interwar period called *Remembering Pussa*, in 1985-6.

[158] Von Rauch, *The Baltic States*, p 82.

[159] Ibid., p 85.

[160] Noble, J. (1994) *Baltic States and Kaliningrad: a travel survival kit*, London: Lonely Planet, p 27.

[161] This is not the impression given by many nationalist histories which for example, refer to Estonia and Latvia in the thirteenth century, and talk about the loss of independence as a result of foreign invasion in the thirteenth century.

[162] Although Lithuania was independent during this time, what we know today as ethnic Lithuania was actually a tiny part of this state, and ethnic Lithuanians formed a minority of the population. Thus the 1918 declaration of an independent Lithuania marked the proclamation of an independent state in which ethnic Lithuanians for the first time enjoyed majority status.

[163] Hobsbawm, E. J. (1992) *Nations and Nationalism since 1780: Programme, Myth, Reality*, Second Edition, Cambridge: Cambridge University Press, p 48.

[164] The fact that other tribes in the region have died out has been one of the key elements in the nationalist campaigns in the three Baltic countries since the end of the nineteenth century, and particularly since the Soviet occupation. The idea of the 'survival' of the nation is still a concern today, and is reflected in citizenship policies in Estonia and Latvia. It is also noteworthy to mention here that tracing the lines of descent to ancient Baltic and Finno-Ugric tribes has been one of the key characteristics of national identity construction particularly during the twentieth century. Many histories written by Baltic scholars are keen to trace ethnic roots and cultures, in order to justify the legitimacy of independent states. This has been particularly necessary for Latvia and Estonia, where independent statehood had never existed until 1918.

[165] Kionka, R. (1990) 'Estonians', Smith, G. (ed.), *The Nationalities Question in the Soviet Union*, London & New York: Longman.

[166] Stanley Vardys, V. (1983) 'Polish Echoes in the Baltic', *Problems of Communism*, July-August, p 23.

[167] Dreifelds, J. (1996) *Latvia in Transition*, Cambridge: Cambridge University Press, p 22.

[168] Smith, 'Latvians', p 54.

[169] See: Smith, G. (1990) 'Latvians', in Smith, G. (ed.) *The Nationalities Question*, London & New York: Longman, pp 54-55.

[170] The different rulers of independent Lithuania during the thirteenth and fourteenth centuries have become symbols of Lithuanian nationhood. The resurrection of Lithuania's rulers from this period as national symbols is a process that has begun again during the post-1991 independence period. Gediminas for example, who founded Vilnius in 1323 has been restored as a symbol of independent Lithuania through the erection of a statue in Cathedral Square, Vilnius, right in the heart of the city. The statue was erected in September 1996.

[171] Stanley Vardys, 'Lithuanians', in Smith, G. (ed.) *The Nationalities Question*, London & New York: Longman, p 72. Lithuania during this period enjoyed independent statehood and was at one point (1430) the largest country in Europe. However, ethnic Lithuanians were actually a minority in this state.

[172] Jakub Karpinski clarifies the meaning of the term 'Lithuania' from the 14th to the 19th centuries since its territorial boundaries extended beyond those of today's meaning of the term. He stated that: 'Lithuania, as the term was understood in the 14th to 19th centuries, referred to territories inhabited by people of various ethnic, religious, and linguistic identities. Many of them were *Rusini* (Ruthenians) – ancestors of today's Belarusians and Ukrainians – and of Orthodox religion. Official documents of the Lithuanian Grand Duchy were often written in *Ruski* (Old Ruthenian), a predecessor of Belarusian. Lithuanian ethnic territory was only a small part of the Lithuanian Grand Duchy, which included today's Smolensk, Russia, not to mention today's Belarusian Minsk or Vitebsk'. (Karpinski, J. (1997) 'Poland and Lithuania Look Toward a Common Future', *Transition*, 3(6), pp 15-16).

[173] Known as the Union of Lublin.

[174] Stanley Vardys, 'Lithuanians', p 73.

[175] In 1721, the Treaty of Nystadt following the Great Northern War, imposed Russian rule over the territories constituting south and north Estonia and most of Latvia. In Latvia, the process of annexation was completed by the third annexation of Poland in 1795. Lithuania was annexed by Russia in one go, by the final partition of Poland in 1795.

[176] In Latvia, a resolution was passed demanding the establishment of an independent and neutral Latvia in October 1917, by the newly formed Riga Democratic Bloc. The Latvian People's Council declared independence on 18 November 1918. (Smith, 'Latvians', p 56) During the Russian civil war, and in the face of an impending German invasion, the Republic of Estonia was declared on 24 February 1918, by the Executive Committee of the Estonian National Council (Kionka, 'Estonians', pp 42-43). On 16 February 1918, a key date in Lithuania's history, Lithuania finally emerged from the ruins of the Tsarist Empire and the collapsed German Kaiserreich as an independent democratic republic. (Stanley Vardys, 'Lithuanians', p 73).

[177] The Estonian Republic survived a German invasion and an onslaught by Bolshevik troops, and after fifteen months of fighting the Republic of Estonia and Soviet Russia signed the Treaty of Tartu on 2 February 1920. According to the peace treaty, Russia renounced in perpetuity all rights to Estonia. (Kionka, 'Estonians', pp 42-43). Although a Red army invasion in 1919 briefly led to the establishment of a Latvian Soviet Republic, this was quickly overthrown by Latvian nationalist troops with the aid of the western allies. (Smith, 'Latvians', p 56) A Treaty was signed between Latvia and Soviet Russia on 11 August 1920, in which Russia recognised Latvia's independence and renounced all rights of the previous tsarist Russian government towards Latvia's territories. (Jõeste, M. (1991) *The Baltic States: A Reference Book*, Tallinn, Riga, Vilnius: Estonian Encyclopaedia Publishers, Latvian Encyclopaedia Publishers, Lithuanian Encyclopaedia Publishers, p 94).

[178] Commentators have put forward various explanations for the early rise of authoritarianism in Lithuania. Only of the most frequently cited causes is the effect of the loss of Vilnius on Lithuania's nation-building process. Vilnius was an important economic and spiritual centre for Lithuania, and the loss promoted a more fervent nationalism in Lithuania, than in either Latvia or Estonia, and one with markedly anti-Polish overtones. The relative homogeneity of the Lithuanian nation promoted the rise of an ethnic based nationalism more quickly than in either Latvia or Estonia. Combined with Lithuania's relative backwardness, the deprivation of Vilnius at the heart of the nation severely stunted the growth of a democratic nation-building process.

[179] Stanley Vardys, 'Lithuanians', p 74..

[180] Avizienis, R. & Hough, W. J. (1995) Guide to Lithuania, Bucks: Bradt Publications.

[181] Stanley Vardys, V. (1975) 'Modernization and Baltic Nationalism', *Problems of Communism*, 24(5), p 35.

[182] Ibid.

[183] Ibid.

[184] Ibid.

[185] Some historians argue that an embryonic Lithuanian culture and identity emerged during the earlier period of Lithuanian statehood.

[186] Lieven, *The Baltic Revolution*, p 17.

[187] Hobsbawm cites as evidence the voting figures for the Russian Constituent Assembly in November 1917, analysed by Radkey, O. (1989) *Russia Goes to the Polls*, London: Ithaca. (Hobsbawm, E. J. (1992) *Nations and Nationalism since 1780: Programme, Myth, Reality*, Second Edition, Cambridge: CUP.

[188] The Freedom Monument in Riga became one of the most important symbols of independence and the homeland among exile communities abroad during the Soviet period. One Latvian in Britain told me that the first time she returned to her homeland, she instructed her family who had met her at the airport and presented her with bouquets of flowers, to stop by the Freedom Monument on the way home. She stopped here and laid all the flowers at the foot of the Monument, as the first thing she did when she returned to Latvia.

[189] *Latvijas Muzeji* (Museums of Latvia), Latvian Museums Association, p 18.

[190] Skultans, *Testimony of Lives*, p 147.

[191] Ibid., p 142.

[192] Ibid., p 152.

[193] Ibid.

[194] Lieven, *Baltic Revolution*, p 114.

[195] Ibid., p 115.

[196] Ibid.

[197] Smith, A. D. (1988) 'The Myth of the 'Modern Nation' and the myths of nations', *Ethnic and Racial Studies*, 11(1), p 14.

[198] Ibid., p 12.

[199] Kionka, 'Estonians', p 43.

[200] Rothschild, *Europe between the Two World Wars*, p 377.

Playback No: 13, First Generation Lithuanian mother and daughter.

202 Veidemanis, *Social Change, Major Value Systems of Latvians, at Home, as Refugees and as Immigrants*, p 116.

203 Playback No: 13, First Generation Lithuanian mother and daughter.

204 Poopuu, *Remembering Pussa*, p 3.

205 Hope, N. 'Interwar Statehood: Symbol and Reality', Smith, G. (ed.) *The Baltic States*, p 64.

206 Misiunas, R. & Taagapera, R. (1993) *The Baltic States: Years of Dependence, 1940-1990*, 2nd Edn., London: Hurst & Co, pp 43-44.

207 Hope, 'Interwar Statehood: Symbol and Reality', p 64.

208 Rothschild, *Europe between the Two World Wars*, p 369. 'Urban' is defined here as a locality of over two thousand people.

209 Ibid.

210 The rural/urban background ratio of the refugees who came to Britain, broadly reflected the proportion of the population who were engaged in agriculture during the mid-1930's. These proportions were as follows: three-fifths (Estonia), two-thirds (Latvia), three-quarters (Lithuania). (Rothschild, *Europe between the Two World Wars*, p 369)

211 Skultans, V., 'A Positive Self-Image' in *The Testimony of Lives*, pp 143-147.

212 Rein Taagepera described the national obsession with farming among Estonians during the inter-war period as 'The Farm Mystique'. She stated that: 'Acquisition of land had been the main goal for most Estonians during the preceding century, and this land hunger was largely settled only with the land reform of the 1920's. Meanwhile city jobs continued to be seen as something alien. Farming was felt to be the only honourable activity, in principle, even by those numerous Estonians who had settled in the cities.' Taagapera, R. (1993) *Estonia: Return to Independence*, San Fransisco and Oxford: Westview Press, p 52. Taagapera's comments can also be applied to Latvia and Lithuania.

213 The prestige attached to the peasant was one of the main developments of the national awakenings, which attempted to redefine the peasant from being a wretched, oppressed immoral creature, to a highly respected, moral, hard-working individual.

214 As will be discussed in more depth later in the book, large numbers of intellectuals, artists, musicians and professionals were displaced as a result of the Russian and German occupations; however, most of these refugees migrated to the United States, Canada or Australia, where opportunities to continue their careers were greater than in Great Britain.

215 Playback No: 05, First Generation Latvian man.

216 Playback No: 06, First Generation Latvian man.

217 Playback No: 17, First Generation Lithuanian mother and daughter.

218 Ibid.

219 Ibid.

220 Playback No: 06, First Generation Latvian man.

221 Playback No: 16, First Generation Estonian man.

222 Ibid.

[223] According to Karnups, in inter-war Latvia the typical number of children was four (between three and six in rural areas and between two and five in urban areas). Ibid.

[224] Poopuu, *Remembering Pussa*, p 45.

[225] The Latvian name for this dish is: *Zirņi ar Speķi*.

[226] Playback No: 14, First Generation Latvian man.

[227] Poopuu, *Remembering Pussa.*, p 73.

[228] Rothschild, *Europe between the Two World Wars*, p 369. 'Urban' is defined here as a locality of over two thousand people.

[229] See section on 'Multi-ethnic societies' below.

[230] George Kennan quoted by Lieven, *The Baltic Revolution*, p 16.

[231] Rothschild, *Europe between the Two World Wars*, p 374.

[232] Playback No: 06, First Generation Latvian man.

[233] Rothschild, *Europe between the Two World Wars*, p 374.

[234] Kurzeme (Courland) was part of the Polish-Lithuanian Commonwealth, and here some Polish cultural influences lingered.

[235] Ethnic Lithuanians who came from the Vilnius region regard themselves as Lithuanians from Lithuania, because Vilnius was previously part of the Russian Baltic provinces. Poland only assumed ownership of Vilnius following the First World War. During the inter-war period Lithuanians still regarded Vilnius and its environs as Lithuanian.

[236] From the Vilnius region, most of the refugees fled through Poland and then Germany.

[237] Anon. (1985) 'The Church in Lithuania', *Pro Mundi Vita: Dossiers*, 3, p 4.

[238] Vardys, V. S. (1981) 'Freedom of Religion, Lithuania and the Chronicle: An Introduction', *Chronicle of the Catholic Church in Lithuania*, 1(1-9) Chicago: Loyola University Press and Society for the Publication of the Chronicle of the Catholic Church in Lithuania Inc., p xxix.

[239] Sapiets, J. (1984) 'Religion', Sīmanis, V. V. (ed.), *Latvia*, St Charles: The Book Latvia Inc., p 57.

[240] There were also significant numbers of Catholics in Kurzeme (Courland) in western Latvia, which had been part of the Polish-Lithuanian Commonwealth in the sixteenth and seventeenth centuries.

[241] Sapiets, J. (1984) 'Religion', Sìmanis, V. V. (ed.), *Latvia*, St Charles: The Book Latvia Inc., p 57.

[242] Ibid.

[243] Also known as the *Setukests*. (Rothschild, J. (1974) *Europe between the Two World Wars*, Seattle and London: University of Washington Press, p 370)

[244] Estonian Committee in Göttingen (1946) *Estonia: My Beautiful Land*, p 56.

[245] This will be explained later in the section on *National Identities*

[246] 'Dievs' means 'God' in Latvian.

[247] Lieven claims that *dievturi* was 'closely linked with Latvian fascist groups to the right of Ulmanis'. Since independence *Dievturiba* has been revived. (Lieven, *Baltic Revolution*, p 115).

[248] J Tupešu, 'Ancient Latvian Religion', in Vito Vitauts Sìmanis, *Latvia*, The Book Latvia Inc., St. Charles, 1984, p 72.

[249] Playback No: 03, First Generation Latvian woman.

[250] Playback No: 16, First Generation Estonian man.

[251] Rothschild, *Europe between the Two World Wars*, p 369.

[252] Smith, G. (1996) *The Baltic States: The National Self-Determination of Estonia, Latvia and Lithuania*, Basingstoke and London: Macmillan, p 52.

[253] Ibid.

[254] Playback No: 05, First Generation Latvian man.

[255] Poopuu, *Remembering Pussa*, p 70.

[256] Correspondence from Heino Poopuu.

[257] Ibid.

[258] Poopuu, *Remembering Pussa*, p 70.

[259] Correspondence from Heino Poopuu.

[260] Poopuu, *Remembering Pussa*, p 70.

[261] Correspondence from Heino Poopuu.

[262] Ibid.

[263] The significance of memory in exile will be an ongoing aspect of discussion throughout the book.

[264] Playback No: 12, First Generation Latvian man.

[265] Playback No: 13, First Generation Lithuanian mother and daughter.

[266] Ibid.

[267] Stanley Vardys, 'Modernization and Baltic Nationalism', p 36.

[268] Playback No: 07, First Generation Latvian man.

[269] Ibid.

[270] Thomson, C. (1992) *The Singing Revolution: A Journey Through the Baltic States*, London: Michael Joseph, p 82.

[271] Ibid.

[272] Correspondence from Heino Poopuu.

[273] Playback No: 05, First Generation Latvian man.

[274] The complexity of memory and the ageing process is beyond the scope of this book.

[275] Playback No: 08, First Generation Latvian woman.

[276] There were several other ways that the populations of the Baltic States were displaced during this period, which will also be briefly mentioned in this chapter. However, an overwhelming majority of Latvians, Lithuanians and Estonians in Britain were displaced via one of the four processes discussed in this chapter. For more information about population movements during this period, see: Kulischer, E. M. (1943) *The Displacement of Population in Europe*, Montreal, pp 62-64.

[277] Since this chapter is rather ambitious in the range of subject matter under discussion, much of the information relating to the history of the war in the Baltic States and the displacement of Latvians, Lithuanians and Estonians will be brief, since these subjects have been covered in histories elsewhere. For the Russian and German occupations see: Bilmanis, A. (1970) *A History of Latvia* (Part vi: 'Again the Predatory Powers'), Westport, Connecticut: Greenwood Press; Danys, M. (1986) *DP: Lithuanian Immigration to Canada after the Second World War* (ch 1: 'Lithuania in World War Two'); Hiden, J. & Salmon, P. (1991) *The*

Baltic Nations and Europe: Estonia, Latvia & Lithuania in the Twentieth Century, London & New York: Longman; Kirby, D. (1994) 'Incorporation: The Molotov-Ribbentrop Pact', in Smith, G. (ed.) *The Baltic States: The National Self-determination of Estonia, Latvia and Lithuania*, Basingstoke & London: Macmillan, pp 69-85; Lieven, A. (1993) *The Baltic Revolution: Estonia, Latvia, Lithuania and the Path to Independence*, New Haven & London: Yale University Press; Misiunas, R. & Taagapera, R. (1993) *The Baltic States: Years of Dependence, 1940-1990*, 2nd Edn., London: Hurst & Co; Plakans, A. (1995) *Latvia: A Short History*, Stanford University, California: Hoover University Press; Roos, A. (1985) *Estonia: A Nation Unconquered*, Baltimore: Estonian World Council; Vardys, V. S. & Misiunas, R. J. (eds.) *The Baltic States in Peace and War, 1917-45*, Pennsylvania and London: University Park; Vardys, V. S. & Sedaitis, J. B. (1997) *Lithuania: The Rebel Nation*, Boulder, Colorado: Westview. For the recruitment of Latvians into the German army see also: Cesarani, D. (1992) *Justice Delayed: How Britain became a Refuge for Nazi War Criminals*, Heinemann: London; Ezergailis, A. (ed.) (1997) *The Latvian Legion: Heroes, Nazis or Victims?: A Collection of Documents from OSS War-Crimes investigation files, 1945-50*, Riga: The Historical Institute of Latvia; Plensners, A. (1955) *A Small Nation's Struggle for Freedom: Latvian Soldiers in World War II*, Stockholm: Latvian National Foundation; Silgailis, A. (1986) *Latvian Legion*, San Jose, California: James Bender Publishing. For the displacement of Latvians, Lithuanians and Estonians during the period of the Second World War see: Danys, M. *DP* (ch 2: 'Lithuanians in Wartime Germany'); Kulischer, E. M. (1948) *Europe on the Move: War and Population Changes, 1917-1947*, New York: Columbia University Press; Kulischer, E. M. (1943) *The Displacement of Population in Europe*, Montreal; Proudfoot, M. J. (1957) *European Refugees: 1939-52, A Study in Forced Population Movement*, London: Faber & Faber. Also see bibliography for further sources relating to this period.

[278] The protocol recognised the 'interest of Lithuania in the Vilnius area' effectively handing Vilnius back to Lithuania from Poland. Hiden & Salmon , *The Baltic Nations and Europe*, p 105.

[279] The legal basis of the transfer of Baltic Germans to Germany was provided by treaties between Germany and Estonia (15/10/39), and Latvia (30/10/39). Kulischer, E. M. (1943) *The Displacement of Population in Europe*, Montreal: International Labour Office, p 12.

[280] Hiden & Salmon , *The Baltic Nations and Europe*, p 115.

[281] Ibid. It is known that a certain number of non-German Balts mingled among these Baltic German refugees, taking advantage of the opportunity to leave for Germany. According to Kulischer these voluntary emigrants were mainly members of wealthy families, businessmen etc., who fled for fear of the economic and social consequences of a possible Russian occupation. (Eugene M. Kulischer, *The Displacement of Population in Europe*, International Labour Office, Montreal, 1943, p 12) According to Vernant, the same thing occurred after the German-Soviet transfer agreements, signed on 10 January 1941, when numbers of German and non-German Balts decided to leave for Germany. Germany actually encouraged this movement and even granted some non-Germans, German nationality. (Vernant, J. (1953) *The Refugee in the Post-War*

World, London: George Allen & Unwin, pp 67-68). In the case of Latvian refugees who migrated to Germany in 1941, Kârlis Kalniðø pointed out however, that a majority retained their Latvian citizenship, returned home to Latvia during the German occupation and that their 'sojourn' to Germany must be regarded as an 'episode'. These arguments were used after the war in pleading DP status for these refugees who were later deported to Germany when the Germans began their retreat from Latvia. (Kârlis Kalniðø, 'Latvian Refugees of 1941', Part of document entitled 'Latvian Eligibility for DP Status', prepared on behalf of the Latvian Red Cross in Esslingen DP camp, US Zone, Germany, 1948, in Ezergailis, A. (ed.) (1997) *The Latvian Legion - Heroes, Nazis or Victims?: A collection of documents from OSS War-Crimes investigation files, 1945-50*, Riga: The Historical Institute of Latvia, p 34.) While most Latvian and Estonian Germans left in late 1939, 16,000 people left in 1941, bringing the total up to 80,000. This compares to a declared pre-war German population in Latvia and Estonia of 78,000. 50,167 people left Lithuania for Germany after Hitler's seizure of Klaipeda. This number compares to a declared German population of 35,000. (Misiunas, R. & Taagapera, R. (1993) *The Baltic States: Years of Dependence, 1940-1990*, 2nd Edn., London: Hurst & Co, p 40-41)

282 Kulischer, E. M. (1948) *Europe on the Move: War and Population Changes, 1917-47*, New York: Columbia University Press, p 264.

283 Playback No: 04, First Generation Latvian man.

284 Ibid.

285 Lieven, *The Baltic Revolution*, p 84.

286 Playback No: 08, First Generation Latvian woman.

287 Ibid.

288 Lieven, *The Baltic Revolution*, p 84.

289 Ibid., p 85.

290 Ibid.

291 Ibid., p 86.

292 Bower, *Red Web*, p 33.

293 Hiden & Salmon, *The Baltic Nations*, p 115.

294 Milosz, C. (1984) 'Lithuania, Latvia and Estonia, 1940-1980: Similarities and Differences', *Baltic Forum*, 1(1), p 41.

295 Plensners, A. (1955) *A Small Nation's Struggle for Freedom: Latvian Soldiers in World War II*, Stockholm: Latvian National Foundation, pp 7-8.

296 Playback No: 01, First Generation Latvian woman.

297 Playback No: 08, First Generation Latvian woman.

298 Playback No: 01, First Generation Latvian woman.

299 Ibid.

300 Ibid.

301 Misiunas & Taagapera, The Baltic States: Years of Dependence, p 24.

302 Ibid., p 37.

303 Ibid.

304 Ibid.

305 Bourdeaux, M. (1979) *Land of Crosses: The Struggle for Religious Freedom in Lithuania, 1939-1978*, Devon: Augustine Publishing Company, p 3.

306 Ibid., p 5.

307 Ibid., p 2.

308 Jõeste, M. et. al. (1991) *The Baltic States: A Reference Book*, Tallinn, Riga & Vilnius: Estonian, Latvian and Lithuanian Encyclopaedia Publishers, p 36.

309 One Lithuanian woman reported that: 'In a month all [the] shops were empty'. (Playback No: 17, First Generation Lithuanian woman).

310 B0060, First Generation Latvian woman, BHRU.

311 Ibid.

312 Ibid.

313 Playback No: 14, First Generation Latvian man.

314 Plakans, A. (1995) *The Latvians: A Short History*, Stanford: Hoover Institution Press, p 149.

315 Vizulis, I. J. (1985) *Nations under Duress: The Baltic States*, New York: Port Washington, pp 102-104.

316 Playback No: 14, First Generation Latvian man.

317 Playback No: 16, First Generation Estonian man.

318 Milosz, 'Lithuania, Latvia and Estonia, 1940-1980: Similarities and Differences', p 41.

319 Misiunas and Taagapera state that most of the Baltic Red Army recruits were considered unreliable and were thus sent to die in labour camps. They estimate that the peak number of ethnic Latvians, Lithuanians and Estonians in Red Army combat units may have been 18,000 Estonians (of whom 800 surrendered to the Germans at Velikie Luki in December 1942), 10,000 Latvians and 5,000 Lithuanians. (Misiunas & Taagapera, *The Baltic States: Years of Dependence,* p 70).

320 Playback No: 02, First Generation Estonian man.

321 Ibid.

322 Ibid.

323 Simanis, V. V. (ed.) (1984) *Latvia*, St Charles: The Book Latvia Inc., p 197.

324 Playback No: 01, First Generation Latvian woman.

325 Plakans, A. (1995) *The Latvians: A Short History*, Stanford University, Stanford: Hoover Institution Press, p 149.

326 Playback No: 03, First Generation Latvian woman.

327 Playback No: 05, First Generation Latvian man.

328 Playback No: 10, First Generation Latvian man.

329 'No Reward for Traitors "Lithuanian Dupes"', from Special Correspondent, *The Daily Telegraph*, 14 August 1941.

330 Playback No: 01, First Generation Latvian woman.

331 Playback No: 17, First Generation Lithuanian woman.

332 Misiunas & Taagapera, *The Baltic States: Years of Dependence*, p 54.

333 Ibid., p 53.

334 Sīmanis (ed.) *Latvia*, p 199.

335 Misiunas & Taagapera, *The Baltic States: Years of Dependence*, p 53.

336 Ibid.

337 Ibid., p 55.

338 Ibid.

339 Ibid.

[340] Ibid., p 56.

[341] Alfred Rosenberg was a leading Nazi ideologue, who was entrusted by Hitler in May 1941 with the task of planning the 'occupation of the European East'. Rosenberg was actually a Baltic German born in Tallinn and educated in Riga. (Hiden & Salmon, *Baltic Nations and Europe*, pp 94, 109 & 116).

[342] Misiunas & Taagapera, *The Baltic States: Years of Dependence*, p 56.

[343] 'Latvian Eligibility for DP Status', Report by Kārlis Kalniņš, Camp Elder of Latvian Centre Esslingen, Ex-Secretary General of Latvian Red Cross, Ezergailis(ed.) *The Latvian Legion*, p 32.

[344] Playback No: 03, First Generation Latvian woman.

[345] Playback No: 19, First Generation Lithuanian man.

[346] See: David Cesarani, *Justice Delayed: How Britain became a Refuge for Nazi War Criminals*, Heinemann, London, 1992; Ezergailis, A. (ed.) (1997) *The Latvian Legion: Heroes, Nazis or Victims?: A Collection of Documents from OSS War-Crimes investigation files, 1945-50*, Riga: The Historical Institute of Latvia; Silgailis, A. (1986) *Latvian Legion*, San Jose: California, James Bender Publishing; *'Report on the Entry of Nazi War Criminals and Collaborators into the UK, 1945-1950'*, The All-Party Parliamentary War Crimes Group, November 1988.

[347] See: David Cesarani, *Justice Delayed: How Britain became a Refuge for Nazi War Criminals*, Heinemann, London, 1992.

[348] Ward, S. (1995)'War Crimes case thrown into chaos', *The Independent*, 27 September 1995, p 2.

[349] The *'Report on the Entry of Nazi War Criminals and Collaborators into the UK'* outlined the case of Ain Erwin Mere, an Estonian who came to Britain in April 1947, who was accused of war crimes by the USSR. Great Britain did not investigate any of the accusations put forward by the USSR and denied the extradition request. Ain Erwin Mere died on 5 April 1969. (*'Report on the Entry of Nazi War Criminals and Collaborators into the UK, 1945-1950'*, The All-Party Parliamentary War Crimes Group, November 1988, pp 78-79).

[350] Several suspects have also died. One of the suspects was a Latvian, Harry Svikeris who died in 1995. Mr. Svikeris was allegedly the second strongest case on Scotland Yard's list in 1995. (Ward, S. (1995)'War Crimes case thrown into chaos', *The Independent*, 27 September 1995, p 2).

[351] Sawoniuk was the last suspect on the Home Office's list thought to have enough evidence against him to be brought to trial.

[352] Jewish groups called for charges to be brought against Kalejs, who was alleged to have been a member of the Arajs Commando, which carried out atrocities during the Second World War. Newspapers carried the story on front pages.

[353] The British government collected a significant body of evidence both during and after the Second World War, which is held primarily in Foreign Office files. Other Allied governments such as the United States also carried out in-depth investigations. These sources contain an array of documents, including among others: German mobilisation orders; letters and reports written by various Latvian, Lithuanian and Estonian representatives and organisations, for example, the Latvian Legation in London and the Latvian Red Cross;

intelligence reports; surveys and correspondence from the British and American military authorities; information and correspondence from refugee organisations; the results of screening procedures. Various historians have interpreted these primary documents, and in Great Britain, the 'Report on the Entry of Nazi War Criminals and Collaborators into the UK, 1945-1950' published in 1988, also carried out an in-depth analysis of these sources. To my knowledge, these are perhaps the most important sources available to date. International Refugee organisations also hold some materials, as do German and Russian archives, although records left by occupying forces in the Baltic States are scant. Other sources include memoirs of men involved in the actual events of the period, perhaps most notably, *Latvian Legion*, written by one of the Latvian Legion's founding officers, Arthur Silgailis. Baltic historians including émigré historians have also produced analyses of the issues. Finally, oral history studies, such as this one, also contain useful information.

[354] The debates are important in this study only in so far as they may heighten understanding of the different experiences of the refugees who came to Britain. Experiences in the German army may also have had implications for identity formation.

[355] See for example the following studies: Biezais, H. (1992) *Latvija Kāškrusta varā*: Sveši kungi, pašu ļaudis, Gauja; Bower, T. (1989) *The Red Web: MI6 and the KGB Master Coup*, London: Aurum; Cesarani, D. (1992) *Justice Delayed: How Britain became a Refuge for Nazi War Criminals*, London: Heinemann; Ezergailis, A. (1996) *The Holocaust in Latvia*, Riga: The Historical Institute of Latvia & Washington DC: The Holocaust Memorial Museum, Washington DC; Ezergailis, A. (ed) (1997) *The Latvian Legion: Heroes, Nazis or Victims?: A Collection of Documents from OSS War-Crimes investigation files, 1945-50*, Riga: The Historical Institute of Latvia; Freivalds, O. (ed.) *Latviešu karavīrs Otrā pasaules kara laikā: dokumentu un atmiņu krājums (The Latvian Soldiers in World War II)*, vol. I-VIII, Daugavas Vanagu izdevniecība, 1970—1984; Silgailis, A. (1986) *Latvian Legion*, San Jose, California: James Bender Publishing; 'Report on the Entry of Nazi War Criminals and Collaborators into the UK, 1945-1950', The All-Party Parliamentary War Crimes Group, November 1988. Also see general historical works on this period listed in the bibliography. All of these sources need to be analysed carefully, taking into account factors such as: Who wrote the documents? What were their motivations? Might the documents be biased? These were the difficulties faced by Western governments during the 1940's, when opportunities for thorough verification were limited.

[356] This consensus has been disputed by David Cesarani in his 1992 book *Justice Delayed*.

[357] The British Government's opinion has been modified slightly by the findings of the All-Party Parliamentary War Crimes Committee in 1988. However, despite conceding that some war criminals may have entered Great Britain, primarily through lax screening procedures, the general consensus still stands.

[358] See: Ezergailis, A. (ed.) (1997) *The Latvian Legion: Heroes, Nazis or Victims?: A Collection of Documents from OSS War-Crimes investigation files, 1945-50*, Riga: The Historical Institute of Latvia.

359 Ibid.

360 Sinka, *Latvia and Latvians*, p 30.

361 'Latvian Eligibility for DP Status', Report by Kārlis Kalniņš, Camp Elder of Latvian Centre Esslingen, Ex-Secretary General of Latvian Red Cross, Ezergailis(ed), *The Latvian Legion: Heroes, Nazis or Victims*, p 31.

362 In 1950, the UNRRA Commissioner Harry N. Rosenfield, informed the Latvian Ambassador to the US, J. Feldmanis the results of the Displaced Persons Commission, which finally removed the SS tag from the Baltic Legions. The Commission approved the following motion: 'That the Baltic Waffen SS. Units (Baltic Legions) are to be considered as separate and distinct in purpose, ideology, activities, and qualifications for membership from the German SS, and therefore the Commission holds them not to be a movement hostile to the Government of the United States under Section 13 of the Displaced Persons Act, as amended.' Rosenfield's Letter to Feldmanis, September 12, 1950 in Ezergailis, *The Latvian Legion – Heroes, Nazis or Victims?*, pp 93-94.

363 In 1995 the Scotland Yard War crimes Unit, in consultation with the Crown Prosecution Service was investigating about 14 suspects. Some of these have since been deemed to ill to stand trial or have died.

364 SD is short for *Sicherheitsdienst*.

365 Ezergailis (ed.), *Latvian Legion: Heroes, Nazis or Victims?*, p 12.

366 Ibid.

367 Ibid.

368 Ibid.

369 Ibid., p 12.

370 Milosz, 'Lithuania, Latvia and Estonia, 1940-1980: Similarities and Differences', p 44.

371 Hiden & Salmon, *Baltic Nations and Europe*, p 118-119.

372 Ibid., p 119.

373 None of the refugees whom I have interviewed stated that they had participated in the Police Battalions.

374 Vardys & Sedaitis, *Lithuania*, p 58.

375 Misiunas & Taagapera, *Baltic States: Years of Dependence*, p 57.

376 Ezergailis(ed), *The Latvian Legion: Heroes, Nazis or Victims?*, p 9.

377 Misiunas & Taagapera, *The Baltic States: Years of Dependence*, p 56.

378 Abbreviation of Hilfswillige der Wehrmacht.

379 '*Report on the Entry of Nazi War Criminals and Collaborators into the UK, 1945-1950*', The All-Party Parliamentary War Crimes Group, November 1988, pp 78-79. Plensners (who puts the figure of Latvian draftees much higher at 27,000 based on statistics from the Chief of the SS-Ersatzkommando) describes the situation of Latvian draftees into Wehrmacht auxiliaries: 'In small groups these unfortunate and unprotected Latvians were thrown from one place to another as the German units moved. They made persistent appeals to the Latvian authorities, especially to the Inspector General of the Legion, whose determined efforts later resulted in many transfers to Latvian units. A large number resorted to desertion but were frequently caught and court-martialled. Other deserters reported to the Legion hoping for protection, and it was

possible to arrange their unofficial transfer'. (Plensners, *A Small Nation's Struggle for Freedom*, pp 39-40).

[380] 'Latvian Eligibility for DP Status', Report by Kârlis Kalniðø, Camp Elder of Latvian Centre Esslingen, Ex-Secretary General of Latvian Red Cross, Ezergailis(ed), *The Latvian Legion: Heroes, Nazis or Victims?*, p 32.

[381] Milosz, 'Lithuania, Latvia and Estonia, 1940-1980: Similarities and Differences', p 43.

[382] Ezergailis(ed), *The Latvian Legion*, p 9. For numbers of Latvian men serving in the different German forces see: *Latvju Enciklopēdija*, Stockholm, 1955. The numbers of Latvians serving in the various German forces as listed below by Ezergailis have been challenged by Kārlis Kangeris (Centre of Baltic Studies, Stockholm University), although as of the publication of Ezergailis's edited volume he had not yet published these figures.

[383] Misiunas & Taagapera, *The Baltic States: Years of Dependence*, p 60.

[384] Ibid., p 10.

[385] Silgailis, *Latvian Legion*, p 5.

[386] Misiunas & Taagapera, *Baltic States: Years of Dependence*, p 58.

[387] Vardys & Sedaitis, *Lithuania: The Rebel Nation*, p 58.

[388] Ibid.

[389] Sinka, J. (1988) *Latvia and Latvians*, London: Daugavas Vanagi, 1988, p 30.

[390] Playback No: 06, First Generation Latvian man.

[391] Sinka, J. (1988) *Latvia and Latvians*, p 30.

[392] Ezergailis(ed), *The Latvian Legion: Heroes, Nazis or Victims?*, p 10.

[393] Misiunas & Taagapera, *Baltic States: Years of Dependence, 1940-1990*, p 58.

[394] Alfred Rosenberg was a leading Nazi ideologue, who was entrusted by Hitler in May 1941 with the task of planning the 'occupation of the European East'. Rosenberg was actually a Baltic German born in Tallinn and educated in Riga. (Hiden & Salmon, *Baltic Nations and Europe*, pp 94, 109 & 116).

[395] Ezergailis(ed), *The Latvian Legion: Heroes, Nazis or Victims?*, p 10.

[396] Playback No: 06, First Generation Latvian man.

[397] Ezergailis(ed), *The Latvian Legion: Heroes, Nazis or Victims?*, p 10.

[398] The validity of this claim is difficult to verify. (Sinka, *Latvia and Latvians*, p 30).

[399] Ezergailis(ed), *The Latvian Legion: Heroes, Nazis or Victims?*, p 10.

[400] Ibid.

[401] Misiunas & Taagapera, *Baltic States: Years of Dependence*, p 58.

[402] Ezergailis(ed), *The Latvian Legion: Heroes, Nazis or Victims*, p 9.

[403] Ibid., p 10.

[404] Ibid.

[405] Ibid.

[406] Ibid.

[407] Playback No: 10, First Generation Latvian man.

[408] Playback No: 02, First Generation Estonian man.

[409] Playback No: 07, First Generation Latvian man.

[410] Playback No: 14, First Generation Latvian man.

[411] Most former Latvian legionaries who formed the largest contingent of Baltic ex-army personnel were transferred to a camp in Zedelghen, Belgium at the end of September, 1945. (Cesarani, *Justice Delayed*, p 44).

[412] In 1950, the UNRRA Commissioner Harry N. Rosenfield, informed the Latvian Ambassador to the US, J. Feldmanis the results of the Displaced Persons Commission, which finally removed the SS tag from the Baltic Legions. The Commission approved the following motion: 'That the Baltic Waffen SS. Units (Baltic Legions) are to be considered as separate and distinct in purpose, ideology, activities, and qualifications for membership from the German SS, and therefore the Commission holds them not to be a movement hostile to the Government of the United States under Section 13 of the Displaced Persons Act, as amended.' Rosenfield's Letter to Feldmanis, September 12, 1950 in Ezergailis, *The Latvian Legion – Heroes, Nazis or Victims?*, pp 93-94. This decision followed earlier decisions by the British Government to regard the Baltic Legions as separate units from the German SS. Earlier American policy had barred thousands of legionaries from emigration to the US as part of labour schemes, while a more lenient British policy had enabled their migration to Great Britain as European Voluntary Workers.

[413] Sinka, *Latvia and Latvians*, p 53.

[414] Playback No: 06, First Generation Latvian man.

[415] Andrejs Plakans, *The Latvians: A Short History*, Hoover Institution Press, Stanford, 1995, p 152.

[416] The eastern border of Lithuania was crossed in early July. Vilnius fell on 13 July, while Kaunas was abandoned by the Wehrmacht on 1 August. The Soviet advance was temporarily halted by a German counterattack which secured German control over the Klaipėda area until January 1945. (Misiunas & Taagapera, *The Baltic States: Years of Dependence,* p 71).

[417] Playback No: 13, First Generation Lithuanian mother and daughter. In this passage the daughter is translating the words of her mother.

[418] Ibid.

[419] Ibid.

[420] The Red Army reached the Gulf of Riga in late July 1944, temporarily severing German land connections with Estonia. These were restored, which allowed a relatively orderly withdrawal in September. Riga fell on 13 October, while by late October only Courland (Kurzeme) remained in German hands. (Misiunas & Taagapera, *The Baltic States: Years of Dependence,* p 71).

[421] Playback No: 01, First Generation Latvian woman.

[422] Ibid.

[423] Playback No: 08, First Generation Latvian woman.

[424] Simanis (ed), *Latvia*, p 202.

[425] Playback No: 14, First Generation Latvian man.

[426] Playback No: 08, First Generation Latvian woman.

[427] Veidemanis, *Social Change, Major Value Systems of Latvians, at Home, as Refugees, and as Immigrants*, p 121.

[428] Ibid. Significant numbers of refugees were actually forcibly evacuated from their homelands by the German army at this time.

[429] Milosz, 'Lithuania, Latvia and Estonia, 1940-1980: Similarities and Differences', p 44.

[430] Plakans, *The Latvians: A Short History*, p 152.

[431] Roos, *A Nation Unconquered*, p 43.

[432] Another name for Kurzeme.

[433] Milosz, 'Lithuania, Latvia and Estonia, 1940-1980: Similarities and Differences', p 45

[434] Roos, *A Nation Unconquered*, p 43.

[435] Veidemanis, *Social Change, Major Value Systems of Latvians, at Home, as Refugees, and as Immigrants*, p 121.

[436] Ibid.

[437] Plakans, *The Latvians: A Short History*, p 152.

[438] Carpenter, 'A Detour through America', p 102.

[439] Playback No; 17, First Generation Lithuanian woman.

[440] Ibid. Fear of the consequences for the family in the homeland was common among the Baltic refugees in Britain. For some, the fear stopped them from writing at all, while others wrote cautiously, fully aware that both their letters and any reply would more than likely be censored by Soviet authorities.

[441] Playback No: 01, First Generation Latvian woman.

[442] Eugene M. Kulischer quoted by Elliott, M. (1982) *Pawns of Yalta: Soviet Refugees and America's Role in their Repatriation*, Urbana: University of Illinois Press, p 174.

[443] Vernant, *The Refugee in the Post-War World*, p 67.

[444] Ibid., p 68.

[445] Krisčiunas, R. G. 91983) 'The Emigrant Experience: The Decision of Lithuanian Refugees to Emigrate, 1945-1950', *Lituanus*, 29(2), p 31.

[446] Ibid., p 32.

[447] Latvians, Lithuanian and Estonian refugees who had not served in the German army were able to gain aid from UNRRA.

[448] Cesarani, *Justice Delayed*, p 44.

[449] 15,000 Latvians who had served the German armed forces went into captivity in May 1945. (Ibid.)

[450] Krisčiunas cites examples in the American Press, which presented the Baltic refugees to the American public as pro-Nazi collaborators who had fled their homelands because they feared retribution. However, as Krisčiunas notes, many papers contained contradictory opinions reflecting shifting attitudes towards Soviet Russia in the West. The New York Times for example, condemned the Balts in one issue and exonerated them in another. (Krisčiunas, 'The Emigrant Experience...', *Lituanus*, p 34).

[451] The United Nations Relief and Rehabilitation Administration (UNRRA) was joined by the Intergovernmental Committee on Refugees (ICGR) until 1947 in helping to carry out the relief work of the Allied Armies. ICGR concentrated its efforts on resettlement of non-repatriable DPs. UNRRA established a network of DP camps and in October 1945 took over responsibility for most of the camps run by the occupation authorities. See Chapter Seven for more

information on the division of responsibility and the various refugee organisations, such as UNRRA and IGCR.

452 The Control Commission for Germany (CCG) took charge of the British zone of Germany, while responsibility for Austria lay with the Allied Commission for Austria – British Element (ACA – BE). Overall control for non-military matters was exercised through the Control Office for Germany and Austria (COGA) until April 1947, thereafter by the Foreign Office. Responsibility for DPs and POWs with CCG and ACA-BE lay with the Prisoners of War and Displaced Persons Division (PW&DP).

453 The following discussion provides only a brief analysis of British and UNRRA policy towards Baltic refugees.

454 Veidemanis, *Social Change, Major Value Systems of Latvians, at Home, as Refugees, and as Immigrants*, p 125.

455 'Report on the Entry of Nazi War Criminals and Collaborators into the UK, 1945-1950', The All-Party Parliamentary War Crimes Group, November 1988, p 4.

456 Veidemanis, *Social Change, Major Value Systems of Latvians, at Home, as Refugees, and as Immigrants*, p 126.

457 For further discussion and examples of these petitions and memoranda see: FO371 files in the Public Record Office; '*Report on the Entry of Nazi War Criminals and Collaborators into the UK, 1945-1950*', The All-Party Parliamentary War Crimes Group, November 1988; Cesarani, *Justice Delayed*; Ezergailis, *The Latvian Legion – Heroes, Nazis or Victims?*

458 Veidemanis, *Social Change, Major Value Systems of Latvians, at Home, as Refugees, and as Immigran*ts, p 126.

459 Cesarani, *Justice Delayed*, p 45.

460 Ibid.

461 For a full analysis of policy maneuvering see: 'Report on the Entry of Nazi War Criminals and Collaborators into the UK, 1945-1950', The All-Party Parliamentary War Crimes Group, November 1988.

462 Thomas Brimelow had served at the Moscow Embassy in 1942-45 before moving to the Northern Department of the FO.

463 FO371/47052, Brimelow to C E King, HQ Political Division CCG, 31 October 1945.

464 Kriščiunas, 'The Emigrant Experience: The Decision of Lithuanian Refugees to Emigrate, 1945-1950', p 34.

465 'Report on the Entry of Nazi War Criminals and Collaborators into the UK, 1945-1950', The All-Party Parliamentary War Crimes Group, November 1988, p 10.

466 FO371/453, ARGUS 256, 21 December 1945.

467 FO1049/612, SUGRA 291, December 1945.

468 Ibid.

469 FO1049/526, A G Street, Permanent Secretary, Control Office for Germany and Austria to Deputy Military Governor, British zone, Germany, 1/2/46.

470 Ibid.

471 Ibid.

[472] Ibid.

[473] FO1049/612, 'Transference of Balts to DP Camps', BAOR to 1 Corps District, 8 Corps District, 30 Corps District, January 1946.

[474] Ibid.

[475] Ibid. See Chapter Three for a full discussion of Government maneuvering towards the final resettlement of Baltic refugees.

[476] A draft outline of screening procedures from July 1946 stated that claimants to Baltic Nationality were to be interrogated with seven questions. Five of these questions focused on nationality, for example: (v) Is the mother tongue of the claimant the language of the country whose nationality he claims? The final two questions asked: (vi) Are his documents authentic?, (vii) What are the salient points in his case history? (FO1049/613, R B Longe, Lt Colonel, for Chief PW & DP Division, CCG (BE) to HQ Mil Gov North Rhine Region, Wetfalen, Hansestadt Hamburg and 30 Corps District, July 1946). However, potential DPs also had to fill out a rather lengthy questionnaire detailing a year by year account of their activities during the war. The questionnaire also asked many questions about nationality and involvement in military organisations. (FO945/386, 13A, CCG (BE) and UNNRRA, 'Questionnaire for DP's', CCG (BE) and PW & DP Division, Technical Instruction No. 10, 'Eligibility for Displaced Persons Status'.

[477] This has been the argument of The All-Party Parliamentary War Crimes Group, whose report was published in 1988: 'Report on the Entry of Nazi War Criminals and Collaborators into the UK, 1945-1950'. The report found that 'the screening process applied to Baltic Displaced Persons (DPs) in the British zone of Germany was notably superficial'. (p 83) The findings of this report led to the presentation of War Crimes Bill to Parliament, and finally the passing of a War Crimes Act in 1991. The principal researcher of the All-Party Parliamentary War Crimes Group, David Cesarani, a scholar of Jewish origin, also argued that screening procedures were insufficient in his 1992 volume, *Justice Delayed: How Britain became a Refuge for Nazi War Criminals.*

[478] *'Report on the Entry of Nazi War Criminals and Collaborators into the UK, 1945-1950'*, The All-Party Parliamentary War Crimes Group, November 1988, p 14.

[479] Ibid.

[480] Ibid.

[481] Foreign Office files suggest that anyone suspected of any war crimes was subjected to stringent scrutiny; thus it was perhaps not as easy as the above quote suggests for any suspected war criminals to slip through the net. However, this is not the place for a full-scale discussion of the arguments, which require a separate research project which questions the analysis put forward by David Cesarani.

[482] FO371/55974, From FO to the Political Adviser to Commander-in-Chief Germany (Berlin), 4/2/46. These statements about who the FO regarded as a war criminal came after the Soviets demanded the return of named alleged Baltic war criminals held under British control in Denmark.

[483] Ibid.

484 Veidemanis, *Social Change, Major Value Systems of Latvians, at Home, as Refugees, and as Immigrants*, p 126.

485 Krisčiunas, 'The Emigrant Experience: The Decision of Lithuanian Refugees to Emigrate, 1945-1950', p 34.

486 By mid-1945, the population of Latvia had reduced from an estimated pre-war (1939) total of 2.0 million to about 1.4 million. In overall terms, the number of ethnic Latvians in Latvia at the end of the war was about 300,000 less than in 1939. (Plakans, *The Latvians: A Short History*, p 152.)

487 Lithuania lost only 15% because it regained territory around Klaipeda and east of Vilnius. These figures are cited by Milosz, 'Lithuania, Latvia and Estonia, 1940-1980: Similarities and Differences', p 45.

488 Ibid.

489 Carpenter, I. G. (1990) 'A Detour through America: The Latvian Émigré experience in Jānis' Jaunsudrabiņš' *Tā Mums Iet*', in Metuzāle-Kangere, B. & Rinholm, H. D. (eds.) *Symposium Balticum: A Festschrift to honour Professor Velta Rūķe-Draviņa*, Hamburg: Helmut Buske Verlag, p 102.

490 David Mandelbaum quoted by Carpenter, I. G. (1988) 'Exile as Life Career Model', in Hofer, T. & Niedermüller, P. *Life History as Cultural Construction/Performance*, Budapest: Ethnographic Institute, p 330.

491 Ibid.

492 Carpenter, 'Exile as Life Career Model', p 330.

493 Carpenter, 'A Detour through America', p 103.

494 Playback No: 17, First Generation Lithuanian woman.

495 Playback No: 16, First Generation Estonian man.

496 Correspondence from Heino Poopuu.

497 Ibid.

498 Wyman, M. (1989) *DP: Europe's Displaced Persons, 1945-1951*, London & Toronto: Associated University Presses, p 157.

499 Proudfoot, M. (1957) *European Refugees, 1939-52: A Study in Forced Population Movement*, London: Faber & Faber, p 238.

500 Ibid.

501 See: Danys, M. (1986) *DP: Lithuanian Immigration to Canada after the Second World War*, Toronto: Multicultural History Society of Ontario, (see particularly ch. 3: 'DP Camps: "A Temporary Life"'); Proudfoot, M. J. (1957) *European Refugees: 1939-52: A Study in Forced Population Movement*, London: Faber & Faber; Van Reenan, A. J. (1990) *Lithuanian Diaspora: Königsberg to Chicago*, New York: University Press of America; Veidemanis, J. (1982) *Social Change, Major Value Systems of Latvians at Home, as Refugees, and as Immigrants*, Occasional Publications in Anthropology, Ethnology Series, 38(1) Colorado: University of Northern Colorado, Museum of Anthropology.

502 SHAEF (Supreme Headquarters Allied Expeditionary Force)

503 Proudfoot, *European Refugees*, p 230.

504 Ibid., p 235.

505 UNRRA was formally established at the White House on 9 November 1943 as an international relief agency, to provide care and relief for the refugees of

the Second World War, and economic rehabilitation. (Proudfoot, *European Refugees*, pp 98-100)

[506] Ibid., p 230.

[507] Ibid.

[508] Ibid.

[509] Ibid., Table 13: The Division of Responsibility for Displaced Persons between the Military Authorities and UNRRA in Western Germany during the Period 1 October 1945 to 30 June 1947, pp 231-234.

[510] Ibid., p 399.

[511] Ibid., p 406.

[512] Ibid., p 238.

[513] Ibid.

[514] Ibid. The number included 54,844 Estonians; 72,922 Latvians; 51,138 Lithuanians.

[515] Ibid., p 291.

[516] Ibid.

[517] Ibid., Table 14: 'European Displaced Persons by Claimed Nationality and Location: 30 September 1945', pp 238-39.

[518] Ibid., pp 250-251.

[519] Playback No: 01, First Generation Latvian woman.

[520] Ibid.

[521] Carpenter, I. G. (1996) 'Baltic Peoples: Lithuanians, Latvians and Estonians', in Taylor Jr., R. M. & McBirney, C. A. (1996) *Peopling Indiana: The Ethnic Experience*, Indianapolis: Indiana Historical Society, p 60.

[522] FO371/5597, Memorandum on Lithuanian Displaced Persons by Rev. Dr. Joseph B. Kučius, President of the United Lithuanian Relief Fund of America, circulated by M. Balutis, Lithuanian Legation to the Foreign Office, 7/10/46.

[523] BHRU: BO122/1, First Generation Latvian woman.

[524] R M A Hankey was Head of the Northern Department of the Foreign Office from 1946-48.

[525] FO371/55976: Letter from Charles Zarine, Latvian Legation to Mr. Hankey, Foreign Office, 3 July 1946.

[526] Playback No: 06, First Generation Latvian man.

[527] Ibid.

[528] Playback No: 05, First Generation Latvian man.

[529] Proudfoot, *European Refugees*, p 251.

[530] Ibid., p 252.

[531] Ibid.

[532] Ibid.

[533] Playback No: 13, Lithuanian child dependant.

[534] Playback No: 14, First Generation Latvian man.

[535] Danys, *DP*, 1986, p 50.

[536] Ibid.

[537] BHRU: BO127/01, First Generation Estonian man.

[538] Ibid.

[539] Playback No: 02, First Generation Estonian man.

[540] Playback No: 07, First Generation Latvian man.

[541] Playback No: 03, First Generation Latvian woman.

[542] Proudfoot, *European Refugees*, p 254.

[543] Ibid., p 256.

[544] Playback No: 14, First Generation Latvian man.

[545] Playback No: 08, First Generation Latvian woman.

[546] FO 371/55977, 1946: Disposal of ex-Wehrmacht Balts: Treatment of Baltic DPs, 'UNRRA and Displaced Persons', Letter by Dr. Jaak Kask, Estonian DP, Lübeck, June 27 to the Editor of the *Manchester Guardian*, 5 July 1946.

[547] Playback No: 14, First Generation Latvian man.

[548] Playback No: 13, First Generation Lithuanian woman.

[549] BHRU: BO127/01, First Generation Estonian man.

[550] Wyman, *DP*, p 156.

[551] Ibid., p 158.

[552] Ibid., p 160.

[553] Danys, *DP*, p 275.

[554] Playback No: 07, First Generation Latvian man. According to this participant, there was a traditional sauna in Geesthacht DP camp.

[555] Aun, K. (1985) *The Political Refugees: A History of the Estonians in Canada*, Toronto: McClleland and Steward Ltd, p 40.

[556] FO371/5597, Memorandum on Lithuanian Displaced Persons by Rev. Dr. Joseph B. Kučius, President of the United Lithuanian Relief Fund of America, circulated by M. Balutis, Lithuanian Legation to the Foreign Office, 7/10/46.

[557] FO1052/445, 'DPs: Baltic Nationals', Ref: 260-1, 'Estonian National Theatre at Oldenburg', Ref: 256-7, 'Latvian Theatre at Meerbeck'.

[558] Wyman, *DP*, p163.

[559] Ibid., pp 163-164.

[560] Ibid., p 164.

[561] FO1052/445, 'DPs : Baltic Nationals', Ref: 262, 'Lists of Estonian musical artists at Baltic Artists Centre in Blomberg'.

[562] Ibid., Ref: 241-244, 'Lithuanian Opera Artists' Centre of the British zone at Blomberg-Augustdorf'.

[563] Ibid., Ref: 255, 'Lithuanian Choir Assemble & Lithuanian National Dancer Group at the Camp Blomberg DP Ass. Centre'.

[564] Wyman, *DP*, p 164.

[565] FO1052/445: 'DPs: Baltic Nationals', Ref: 258-9, 'Latvian choir at Meerbeck'.

[566] Ibid., Ref: 241, 'Lithuanian Opera Artist's Centre Blomberg-Augustdorf...'

[567] Ibid.

[568] Ibid., Ref: 246, Foreign Estonians' Male Choir 'Estonia'.

[569] FO1052/185, World's YMCA/YWCA to G. Lamont-Watt Esq., PW/DP Division, CCG Lemgo, 15/7/48.

[570] Playback No: 01, First Generation Latvian woman.

[571] Ibid.

[572] FO1052/445, Refs: 239-240, List of Latvian scientists and Academic Professors in the British Zone & 247-253, Teaching Staff of Lithuanian Universities in the British Zone.

[573] FO1032/2242, CCG to CCG & Austria, 11/9/46, Appendix 'A' to HQ/09222/Sec G, 'Educational and Occupational Training'.

[574] FO1032/2242, Appendix 'A' to HQ/09222/Sec G, 'Educational and Occupational Training, from CCG to CCG & Austria, 11/9/46.

[575] FO1052/445, Ref: 187.

[576] Wyman, *DP*, p 126.

[577] Ibid.

[578] FO371/55974, 'Baltic University Camp: Nominal Roll of Professors', Political Division Lübecke to Northern Dep't, 20/1/46.

[579] Mark Wyman, *DP*, p 127.

[580] Ibid.

[581] FO371/55977, Memorandum from A. Dickson, Secretariat, Zonal Executive Offices, Lubbecke, to CCG & A, 12/12/46.

[582] Ibid.

[583] Ibid.

[584] Wyman, *DP*, p 127.

[585] Ibid., p 122.

[586] Ibid.

[587] Ibid.

[588] Ibid.

[589] FO1049/612, GSI HQ 30 Corps District to CCG, 'Balt Activities in 30 Corps District'.

[590] Van Reenan, A. J. (1990) *Lithuanian Diaspora: Königsberg to Chicago*, New York: University Press of America, p 142.

[591] Ibid.

[592] FO1056/43, From Chief, PR/ISC Group, CCG(BE) to HQ Mil. Gov. – All Regions, 26/3/46. (Newspaper Titles Transliterated from the original by the Foreign Office)

[593] FO1056/43, From Major Cleaver to Hamburg GNSBZ, 16/3/46.

[594] FO1056/43, From H C Ruddell, Major, Information Control Unit to Info. Services Control Branch, CCG 14/12/45.

[595] FO1056/43, Ibid.

[596] Wyman, *DP*, p 161.

[597] Ibid.

[598] Ibid.

[599] Mark Wyman explains: 'For many writers the end of the war marked an escape, a new freedom. As the Lithuanian critic Rimvydas Øilbajoris argued, home and prison are similar – "they both surround a person with four walls, encouraging the illusion that the world ends where they do. The holocaust of war blew down the walls of home, making us both naked and free". It was tragic, he argued, but it opened "new horizons, new countries, new civilisations, new ways of perceiving and understanding things". Many DP writers thrived in

this setting and enlarged the vision of their literature. Later critics would find much outstanding writing produced in the period'. (Wyman, *DP*, p 162)

600 Danys, *DP*, 1986, p 289.

601 Ibid.

602 FO371/55976, A. H. Lambert, Foreign Office to Lieutenant Colonel V. M. Hammer, War Office, 24 July 1946.

603 FO1049/414, Northern Department, FO to Political Division, CCG, Berlin, 4/1/46.

604 FO1049/613, 'Baltic Welfare, Education and Employment Organisation', Appendix "X" to PWDP/58337/1 of 8 July 1946.

605 FO1049/415, Monsieur Torma, the Estonian ex-Minister, concerning the treatment of Estonians in Germany to F. A. Warner, 27/6/46.

606 FO371/55977, N15832/252/59: Funds of the Latvian Red Cross.

607 Ibid.

608 FO1049/415, Monsieur Torma, the Estonian ex-Minister, concerning the treatment of Estonians in Germany to F. A. Warner, 27/6/46.

609 FO1049/415, A. F. Lambert, F.O., to I. T. M. Pink, CCG, Berlin, 31/8/46.

610 Ibid.

611 Ibid.

612 FO1049/415, CCG(BE) Incoming Restricted Message from Concomb, to Confolk, 7/9/46.

613 FO1056/43, J M Bullock, PWDP Division to PR/ISC Group, CCG(BE), 9 May 1946.

614 FO371/72058, WR584/51/48, From R. O. Pulverman, PWDP Div. To F.O.

615 FO371/72058, Monsieur. Zarine, Latvian Legation to M. Hankey, 15/1/48.

616 FO371/72058, WR584/51/48, From R. O. Pulverman, PWDP Div. To F.O.

617 FO1049/415, I. T. M. Pink, Political Division, HQ, CCG, Berlin to Cecil E. King, Political Division, Lübbecke, 12/8/46.

618 FO371/72058, WR1319/51/48, J H Moore, Refugee Department to Political Division, 7/5/48.

619 Playback No: 03, First Generation Latvian woman.

620 FO371/5597, Memorandum on Lithuanian Displaced Persons by Rev. Dr. Joseph B. Kučius, President of the United Lithuanian Relief Fund of America, circulated by M. Balutis, Lithuanian Legation to the Foreign Office, 7/10/46.

621 FO371/55976: Letter from Dr. Jaak Kask, Estonian DP, Lübeck, June 27 to the Editor of the Manchester Guardian, published 5 July 1946.

622 FO371/55976: Letter from Charles Zarine, Latvian Legation to Mr. Hankey, Foreign Office, 3 July 1946.

623 FO1008/185, Deputy High Commissioner to Ralph Murray, FO, 19/8/50.

624 FO1052/360, PW/DP Branch, CCG, Regional Commissioner, Hannover to PW & DP Division, CCG Lemgo, 15/4/47. The subject of the letter was 'Anti-British and America Propaganda distributed by UNRRA', and contained extracts of a pamphlet distributed officially by UNRRA to Rotenburg camp by A. J. Vyschinski, entitled 'The International Organisation for Refugees'. The

pamphlet was a Soviet publication, supplied by the Soviet repatriation mission and distributed by UNRRA. There were two copies of the pamphlet, one in Russian, the other in Latvian.

[625] Carpenter, I. G. (1996) 'Baltic Peoples: Lithuanians, Latvians and Estonians', in Taylor, JR., R. M. & McBirney, R. A. *Peopling Indiana: The Ethnic Experience*, Indianapolis: Indiana Historical Society, p 60.

[626] FO371/55977, Memorandum on Lithuanian Displaced Persons by Prof. Mykolas Krupaviàius, 30 September 1946 distributed from Lithuanian Legation to the Foreign Office, 15/10/46. Also submitted to the forthcoming United Nations Assembly by the Supreme Lithuanian Committee of Liberation.

[627] Ibid., p 4.

[628] Ibid., pp 5-6.

[629] Ibid., p 6.

[630] Ibid.

[631] FO371/55977, Memorandum on Lithuanian Displaced Persons by Prof. Mykolas Krupaviàius, 30 September 1946 distributed from Lithuanian Legation to the Foreign Office, 15/10/46. Also submitted to the forthcoming United Nations Assembly by the Supreme Lithuanian Committee of Liberation, p 6.

[632] Carpenter, I. G. (1988) 'Exile as Life Career Model', in Hofer, T. & Niedermüller, P. (eds.) *Life History as Cultural Construction/Performance*, Budapest: Ethnographic Institute, p 331.

[633] Ibid.

[634] Ibid.

[635] Joshua Fishman cited by Carpenter, I. G. (1996) 'Festival as Reconciliation: Latvian Exile Homecoming in 1990', *Journal of Folklore Research*, 33(2), p 93.

[636] Carpenter, 'Festival as Reconciliation', p 93.

[637] Ibid.

[638] Ibid.

[639] Carpenter, I. G. (1988) *Being Latvian in Exile: Folklore as Ideology*, Unpublished PhD dissertation, Indiana Univerity.

[640] Playback No: 01, First Generation Latvian woman.

[641] Balt Cygnet was preceded by a scheme, which recruited Belgian women for domestic work in hospitals. (See: Kay & Miles, *Refugees or Migrant Workers?*, p 38). The Polish resettlement schemes which preceded the EVW schemes was also an important antecedent to the schemes, and there were also various work permit schemes which provided for the immigration of individual workers. These will be discussed further on in this chapter.

[642] Kay & Miles, *Refugees or Migrant Workers?*, p 161.

[643] Ibid., p 162.

[644] Husband, C. (ed.) (1992) *'Race' in Britain: Continuity and Change*, London: Hutchinson, p 80.

[645] Tannahill, J. A. (1957) *European Volunteer Workers in Britain*, Manchester: Manchester University Press.

[646] See: Paul, K. (1997) *Whitewashing Britain: Race and Citizenship in the Postwar Era*, Ithaca and London: Cornell University Press. Also see: Kay & Miles, *Refugees or Migrant Workers?*

[647] Kay & Miles, *Refugees or Migrant Workers?*

[648] See: Kay, D. & Miles, R. (1992) *Refugees or Migrant Workers?: European Volunteer Workers in Britain*, 1946-1951, London: Routledge. This is the first major work on EVWs in Britain since Tannahill, J.A. (1957) *European Volunteer Workers in Britain*, Manchester: Manchester University Press. Tannahill was a civil servant who worked on the EVW schemes, and although his work provides a useful introduction to the subject, there are no source references to enable a researcher to verify Tannahill's information. See also: Bülbring, M. (1954) 'Postwar Refugees in Great Britain', *Population Studies*, viii(2): 99-112; Kay, D. (1995) 'The Resettlement of Displaced Persons in Europe, 1946-1951', in Cohen, R. (ed.), *The Cambridge Survey of World Migration*, Cambridge: CUP; Paul, K. 91997) *Whitewashing Britain: Race and Citizenship in the Postwar Era*, Ithaca and London: Cornell University Press; Stadulis, E. (1952) 'The Resettlement of Displaced Persons in the UK', *Population Studies*, March 1952.

[649] Kay, D. (1995) 'The Resettlement of Displaced Persons in Europe, 1946-1951', in Cohen, R. (ed.), *The Cambridge Survey of World Migration*, Cambridge: CUP, p 156.

[650] Proudfoot, *European Refugees*, pp 238-239.

[651] Wyman, *DP*, p 37.

[652] Proudfoot, *European Refugees*, p 238.

[653] Ibid., pp 238-39.

[654] Ibid., p 291.

[655] Carpenter, I. G. (1996) 'Baltic Peoples: Lithuanians, Latvians and Estonians', in Taylor, JR., R. M. & McBirney, C. A. *Peopling Indiana: The Ethnic Experience*, Indianapolis: Indiana Historical Society, p 60.

[656] FO 1049/652, 1946, Ukrainian and Baltic Refugees: policy on treatment and repatriation, N137777/2977/59, Brimelow, FO to King, 31/10/45.

[657] Ibid.

[658] Cairncross, A. (1985) *Years of Recovery: British Economic Policy, 1945-51*, London: Methuen, p 358.

[659] Ibid., p 389.

[660] Brooke, S. (1995) *Reform and Reconstruction: Britain after the War, 1945-51*, Manchester: Manchester University Press, p 15.

[661661] Rothwell, V. (1982) *Britain and the Cold War*, London: Jonathon Cape, p 14; Morgan, K. O. (1984) *Labour in Power, 1945-1951*, Oxford: Clarendon Press, p 260.

[662] Tannahill, *European Volunteer Workers*, p 19.

[663] Ibid., pp 19-20.

[664] LAB 8/90, 1945, Ministry of Health Proposal to bring Displaced Persons from camps to the UK for Domestic Work in Sanatoria, P Goldberg to Mrs. Gulland, 21/11/45.

[665] Tannahill, *European Volunteer Workers*, p 19.

[666] Ibid., p 20.

[667] LAB 8/90, 1945, Ministry of Health Proposal to bring Displaced Persons from camps to the UK for Domestic Work in Sanatoria, P Goldberg to Milne, 1/1/46.

[668] Kay & Miles, *Refugees or Migrant Workers?*, p 36.

[669] See Chapter 1: 'A Brief History of Latvians, Lithuanians and Estonians in Britain before 1946'.

[670] Ibid.

[671] Ibid.

[672] Ibid.

[673] Ibid., p 35.

[674] Ibid., p 38.

[675] FO945/496, 1945-46, Operation 'Balt Cygnet': Scheme for reception of DP's for domestic and hospital service in the UK, 10B, Draft of Memorandum on DP Scheme, Ministry of Labour and National Service, 4/5/46.

[676] FO FO945/496, 1945-46, Operation 'Balt Cygnet': Scheme for reception of DP's for domestic and hospital service in the UK, 34A, CCG (BE), PW & DP Division, Technical Instruction No. 8, 'Recruitment of Displaced Persons for employment in British Sanatoria. Operation "Balt Cygnet".

[677] Ibid.

[678] FO945/496, 1946-47, Operation 'Balt Cygnet': Scheme for reception of DP's, vol 1, 89A-165A.

[679] LAB8/90, 1945, Ministry of Health Proposal to bring Displaced Persons from camps to the UK for domestic work in Sanatoria, Memorandum by the Parliamentary Secretary to MLNS, 'Recruitment of Displaced Persons from Germany for work in British Hospitals', 17/9/46.

[680] FO945/496, 1945-46, Operation 'Balt Cygnet': Scheme for Reception of DP's for Domestic and Hospital Service in UK, Mary Appleby to Mr Crawford, 4/9/46.

[681] Ibid.

[682] FO945/496, 1946-47, Operation 'Balt Cygnet': Scheme for reception of DP's, 145A, Letter from MLNS to Miss Appleby, CO for Germany and Austria, 5/12/46.

[683] FO945/496, Ibid., 145B, MLNS, 'Recruitment of Women and Girls from Displaced Persons Camps for Domestic Work in British Hospitals: Brief Outline of Scheme'.

[684] Ibid., 145B, Appendix: Conditions of Service of Displaced Persons to be Employed on Domestic Work at British Hospitals and Similar Institutions.

[685] FO945/497, 1947, Operation 'Balt Cygnet': Scheme for reception of DP's, vol ii, 50A, Telegram from Control Office to Lemgo, 20/2/47.

[686] FO945/499, Recruitment of DP labour for UK (Austria), vol 1, 50A, SUGRA 853, Transfer of DP's to UK, From Control Office to Berlin and Vienna, 21/2/47.

[687] FO371/66709, 1947, Recruitment of DP's for work in the UK, WR398/77/48, Displaced Persons receiving UNRRA assistance in Germany, September 1946, UNRRA.

[688] FO945/499, Recruitment of DP Labour for UK (Austria), vol 1, 14A, R S Crawford to M A Bevin, Minister of Labour, 18/12/46.

[689] Kay & Miles, *Refugees or Migrant Workers?*, pp 123-124.

690 LAB8/90, 1945, Ministry of Health Proposal to bring Displaced Persons from camps to the UK for domestic work in Sanatoria, Memorandum by the Parliamentary Secretary to MLNS, 'Recruitment of Displaced Persons from Germany for work in British Hospitals', 17/9/46.

691 Kay & Miles, *Refugees or Migrant Workers?*

692 I will occasionally use the term 'Balts' in the context of references to British Government policy.

693 The Balts were actually ancient tribes from which Latvians and Lithuanians descended. Estonians in contrast are descended from Finno-Ugric peoples. Some Latvians and Estonians do talk about themselves as Balts when referring to all the Baltic nationalities, but when referring to their nationality, they describe themselves as Latvians, Lithuanians or Estonians.

694 FO371/55977, 1946, Disposal of ex-Wehrmacht Balts: Treatment of Baltic DP's, N10919/252/59 : 'Situation of Estonians in British Zone in Germany', Letter from Ivor Pink to A E Lambert, Northern Department, Foreign Office, 17 August 1946.

695 FO1032/846, Treatment of Baltic Displaced Persons, 4A: Brownjohn, Major General, Deputy Chief of Staff (policy), CCG, Berlin, 30/11/46.

696 FO945/499, Recruitment of DP Labour for UK (Austria), vol 1, 29A: J B Hynd to Hector McNeil, Foreign Office, 21/1/47.

697 Ibid., 32A: McNeill to J B Hynd, 23/1/47.

698 Cooper, K. (1979) *The Uprooted: Agony and triumph among the debris of War*, London: Quartet Books, p 122.

699 Letter from the Duchess of Atholl, *The Times*, 25/5/46.

700 FO1049/415, Baltic Nationals, vol ii, Pink to King, 12/8/46.

701 FO371/55977, 1946, Disposal of ex-Wehrmacht Balts: treatment of Baltic DP's, N12842/252/59: 'Memorandum on Findings During a Tour of DP Camps in Military Zones in Germany and Austria', 15 October 1946.

702 FO1049/415, Baltic Nationals, vol ii, Political Division, CCG (BE), Berlin, to HQ Military Governor, Hannover Region, 27/11/46, amended by Political Division, CCG (BE) ,Berlin to Military Governor, Hannover Region, 6/12/46.

703 FO1052/445, 'Employment of Baltic Labour in UK', from N C D Brownjohn, Major-General, CCG to CCG & A, 28/10/46.

704 Ibid.

705 FO1032/846, Treatment of Baltic Displaced Persons, 3B, G B Vaughan-Hughes to Deputy Chief of Staff (policy), 30/11/46.

706 FO1032/846, Treatment of Baltic Displaced Persons, 4A, Brownjohn to Control Commission for Germany and Austria, 30/11/46.

707 FO371/66709, 1947, Recruitment of DP's for work in the UK, Wr 670/77/48, Operation Balt Cygnet, Telegram Lemgo to Control Office, 24/2/47.

708 FO945/497, 54A, Telegram from Control Office to Lübbecke, 24/2/47.

709 FO945/499, Recruitment of DP Labour for UK (Austria), vol 1, 99A, telegram from Lübbecke to Control Office, 15/3/47.

710 FO945/497, Ibid., Mary Appleby to Mr. Ivimy, 4/6/47.

711 CAB 14 (47), Cabinet Minutes, 30 January 1947, 'Foreign Labour', p 95.

712 FO945/499, Recruitment of DP Labour for UK (Austria), vol 1, 50A, SUGRA 853, From Control Office to Berlin & Vienna, 21/2/47: Transfer of DP's to UK.

713 LAB8/97, 1947, Foreign Labour Division replies to I.L.O Questionnaire on migrants, H.O. (Aliens Department), W B Lyon to Mrs Potter, MLNS, 26/2/47.

714 LAB8/97, 1947, Foreign Labour Division replies to I.L.O Questionnaire on migrants, 'I.L.O Questionnaire', Miss Yates, MLNS to Mrs Potter, 13/3/47.

715 FO371/66711, 1946-47, Recruitment of Displaced Persons for Work in the UK, WR 1369/77/48, Control Commission for Germany (British Element), Zonal Executive Instruction no 9 (Provisional), Employment of Displaced Persons in Great Britain – "Operation Westward Ho!", 3 April 1947.

716 Security screening of DP's has been a controversial issue among some historians and Jewish groups who have stated that it was due to lax screenings that war criminals were able to enter Britain. This is an extremely complex issue and is outside the scope of this book. In brief, the government changed its policy towards screening throughout the lifetime of the EVW schemes, but based policy on a view that the UNRRA security screenings carried out to assess nationality and eligibility for DP status were generally adequate, and that therefore only minimal screening was necessary to confirm eligibility for EVW status. UNRRA screenings carried out 3 types of screenings to establish: nationality; eligibility for assistance by UNRRA; identity of war criminal, traitors and collaborators. (See: FO 371/66714, WR3776/77/48, 'European Volunteer Workers', Mr Rouse (M/Lab) to Mr Boothby, 2/12/47; FO945/386, 1946-1947, Machinery for Screening DP's, 5A, Control Office for G & A to CCG, Berlin & Acabrit Vienna (Allied Commission for Austria); FO945/504, 1947, Recruitment of DP Labour in Austria and Germany for Employment of DP's, EBACA 572, Vienna to CO, 9/3/47. Also see: Cesarani, *Justice Delayed* & Kay and Miles, *Refugees or Migrant Workers?*).

717 FO371/72040, 1948, Recruitment of DP's for work in the UK, vol II, WR3353/18/48, Article on EVWs designed for publication in US by Miss. J Hodgson, 15/10/48, p 1.

718 Ibid.

719 FO37/66711, WR 1369/77/48, MLNS – Press Notice: Recruitment of Displaced Persons from the British Zones of Germany and Austria for Employment in Great Britain, no 8, 19/4/47.

720 FO371/66711, 1946-47, Recruitment of Displaced Persons for Work in the UK, WR 1369/77/48, Control Commission for Germany (British Element), Zonal Executive Instruction no 9 (Provisional), Employment of Displaced Persons in Great Britain – "Operation Westwards Ho!", 3 April 1947.

721 Ibid.

722 Ibid.

723 Ibid.

724 FO371/66710, 1947, Recruitment of Displaced Persons for Work in the UK, WR1217/77/48: Transfer of DP's to the UK, Boothby to Appleby, 22 April 1947.

725 FO371/66711, WR1885/77/48, Recruitment of European Volunteer Workers: Extract of minutes from third meeting of Foreign Labour Committee held on 14 May 1947, p 4.

726 FO371/66713, Recruitment of DP's for work in the UK, WR3373/77/48, Visit of Mr Boothby and Mr Rouse to an EVW Holding Camp, 6/10/47.

727 Quote from Kulischer in Kushner, 'Holocaust Survivors...', p 154.

728 R M A Hankey, employed in FO (1943-45), chargé at Warsaw (1945-46), Head of Northern Department (1946-48). Like Brimelow, Hankey was anti-Soviet by late 1946.

729 FO371/65760, 1947, Admission of Baltic DP's into the UK, M Zarine to M Hankey, 20/3/47.

730 FO371/66711, WR1369/77/48, MLNS Press Notice, no 8, Recruitment of Displaced persons from the British Zones of Germany and Austria for Employment in Great Britain, 19/4/47, p 2.

731 FO371/66711, WR1885/77/48, Recruitment of European Volunteer Workers: Extract of minutes from third meeting of Foreign Labour Committee held on 14 May 1947, p 4.

732 Thomas Brimelow, employed in Northern Department of the FO, with special responsibility for Soviet affairs, 1945-48. Previous at Moscow Embassy (1942-45). Brimelow was a key figure in the formulation of policy which resulted in the abandonment of co-operation with the Soviet Union in late 1947.

733 Rothwell, V. (1981) Britain and the Cold War, London: Jonathon Cape, p 19.

734 Ibid.

735 Ibid. & FO1008/185, 1950, 'Communist Propaganda in Camps for Displaced Persons'.

736 FO371/66710, 1947, Recruitment of Displaced Persons for Work in the UK, WR1284/77/48: Recruitment of Baltic Displaced Persons for Work in the UK, Refugee Department, Foreign Office to British Consulate General, Baden-Baden, 14 April 1947.

737 Ibid.

738 FO371/66710, 1947, Recruitment of Displaced Persons for Work in the UK, WR1284/77/48: Recruitment of Baltic Displaced Persons for Work in the UK, Refugee Department, Foreign Office to British Consulate General, Baden-Baden, 14 April 1947.

739 FO371/66710, 1947, Recruitment of Displaced Persons for Work in the UK, WR1284/77/48: Recruitment of Baltic Displaced Persons for Work in the UK, Refugee Department, Foreign Office to British Consulate General, Baden-Baden, 14 April 1947.

740 FO945/514, DP's: Block Settlement in the UK, Foreign Office (German Section) to PW/DP Division (Lemgo), 17 June 1947.

741 FO945/514, DP's: Block Settlement in the UK, 17A: 'Proposal to bring Wrangel Kaserne, Rendsberg Camp or DP camp, Eutin, Nr. Neustadt'.

742 FO945/514, 1947, DP's: Block Settlement in the UK, 10A: 'Proposal to move DP Communities en bloc to Great Britain' – a memoranda.

[743] FO371/65766, 1947, Welfare of Latvians in the UK, Mr Hankey to Mr Ball, 18/8/47.

[744] FO371/65766, 1947, Welfare of Latvians in the UK, N10486/6945/59: Establishment of a Baltic university in the UK, A W Peterson to D M Nenk, 6/9/47.

[745] Cmd 7695, *Royal Commission on Population*, London, June 1949.

[746] FO371/66711, 1947, Recruitment of Displaced Persons for Work in the UK, WR1887/77/48, T J Winterton, Austria to Lord Pakenham, FO, 30 April 1947.

[747] FO371/66711, 1947, Recruitment of Displaced Persons for Work in the UK, WR1887/77/48, T J Winterton, Austria to Lord Pakenham, FO, 30 April 1947.

[748] Kushner, T. (1995) 'Holocaust Survivors in Great Britain: An Overview and Research Agenda', *Journal of Holocaust Education*, 4(2), p 154.

[749] Kushner, 'Holcaust Survivors...', p 153.

[750] Quote from Kulischer in Kushner, 'Holocaust Survivors...', p 154.

[751] Kushner, 'Holocaust Survivors...', p 153.

[752] Bower, T. (1989) *The Red Web: M16 and the KGB Master Coup*, London: Aurum Press.

[753] See: Cesarani, D. (1992) *Justice Delayed: How Britain became a refuge for Nazi war criminals*, London: Mandarin.

[754] FO371/66711, 1046, Recruitment of Displaced Persons for Work in the UK, WR1369/77/48, Control Commission for Germany (British Element), Zonal Executive Instruction no 9 (Provisional), 'Employment of Displaced Persons in Great Britain – "Operation Westwards Ho!"', 3 April 1947.

[755] Kay & Miles, *Refugees or Migrant Workers?*, pp 123.   Source: CAB134/301, Cabinet Foreign Labour Committee, 23 May 1946.

[756] FO371/66713, 1947, Recruitment of DP's for work in the UK, WR2877/77/48, FLC, Fourth Progress Report by the MLNS: recruitment of EVWs (Westward Ho!), 31/7/47.

[757] FO1052/487, Westward Ho!: Policy, Lübbecke to FO, 9 July 1947.

[758] FO1052/487, Westward Ho!: Policy, FO to Berlin, 11 July 1947.

[759] FO945/516, 1947, Recruitment of DP Labour in Austria and Germany (American Zones) for UK, 26A, A F Rouse, Minister of Labour and National Service to L Dow, PCIRO.

[760] FO1052/487, Westward Ho!: Policy, Lübbecke to FO, 9/7/47.

[761] FO945/516, 1947, Recruitment of DP Labour in Austria and Germany (American Zones) for UK, 1A, Rouse, Minister of labour and National Service to Miss Appleby, FO, 21/5/47.

[762] FO1006/513, 1947-1948, Westward Ho!: Policy, vol i, 24, D Craig, PWDP Division, CCG, Lemgo to PWDP Branch, Land Niedersachsen etc., 11/8/47. Subject: Volunteer from the French Zone of Germany.

[763] FO945/516, 1947, Recruitment of DP Labour in Austria and Germany (American Zones) for UK, 13B, Extension of 'Westward Ho!' to the US Zone of Germany. Report on Negotiations with PCIRO Authorities in the US Zone, 11 August 1947.

[764] FO945/516, 1947, Recruitment of DP Labour in Austria and Germany (American Zones) for UK, 26 A, A F Rouse, MLNS to L Dow, PCIRO, 19/9/47.

[765] FO371/66713, 1947, Recruitment of DP's for work in the UK, WR3373/77/48, Agreement between HMG & PCIRO on the recruitment of DP's in the US Zone of Germany, 23/9/47.

[766] HO213/1794, 1947-1948, Operation "Westward Ho!" – Arrangements for employment of DP's, 1, Immigration Officers Report, Seedorf DP Camp, Westward Ho, Monthly Situation Report, 5/6/47.

[767] Ibid.

[768] Ibid.

[769] HO213/1794, 1947-1948, Operation "Westward Ho!" – Arrangements for employment of DP's, 5, Münster DP Transit Camp, Progress Report for December 1947, 3/1/48.

[770] FO1052/487, Westward Ho! Policy, no 6, FO to PWDP Lemgo no 720 Basic of 11 July 1947.

[771] FO371/66713, Recruitment of DP's for work in the UK, WR3373/77/48, Visit of Mr Boothby and Mr Rouse to an EVW Holding Camp, 6/10/47.

[772] FO371/66714, WR3679/77/48, Circular no. 0199, Resettlement of Displaced Persons, Annex A: General Assembly Draft Resolution on Refugees of 11 November 1947, p 3, point 6, FO 10/12/47.

[773] FO371/66714, WR3679/77/48, Circular no. 0199, Resettlement of Displaced Persons, Annex B: Westward Ho! The Resettlement of Displaced Persons in the UK, FO, 10/2/47.

[774] FO371/66711, 1946-47, Recruitment of Displaced Persons for Work in the UK, WR 1369/77/48, Control Commission for Germany (British Element), Zonal Executive Instruction no 9 (Provisional), Employment of Displaced Persons in Great Britain – "Operation Westwards Ho!", 3 April 1947.

[775] Tannahill, *European Volunteer Workers*, p 28.

[776] Ibid., p 30.

[777] Ibid., p 29.

[778] Ibid.

[779] Tannahill, European Volunteer Workers, p 29.

[780] Ibid., pp 29-30.

[781] Tannahill, *European Volunteer Workers*, pp 49-50.

[782] Kay and Miles, *Refugees or Migrant Workers?*, p 43.

[783] FO1049/1403, DP's: Employment in UK, Logan-Gray to F B A Randall, Refugee Department, Foreign Office, 11/10/48.

[784] Playback No: 08, First Generation Latvian woman.

[785] Ibid.

[786] FO1008/185, 1950, 'Communist Propaganda in Camps for Displaced Persons'.

[787] FO945/496, '87 D.P. Women Welcome Hard Work Here', *News Chronicle*, 22/10/46.

[788] Cooper, K. (1979) *The Uprooted: Agony and Triumph among the Debris of War*, London: Quartet Books, p 122.

[789] Playback No: 04, First Generation Latvian man.

[790] Playback No: 05, First Generation Latvian man.

[791] BO127/01, First Generation Estonian, born 1925, BHRU.

[792] Playback No: 14, First Generation Latvian man.

[793] Playback No: 03, First Generation Latvian woman.

[794] Playback No: 01, First Generation Latvian woman.

[795] Ibid.

[796] Playback No: 17, First Generation Lithuanian woman.

[797] Ibid.

[798] FO1006/513, 'In Der Britischen Rayon-Industrie Finden Sie Ihre Zukunft: She's Making Her Way in the British Rayon Industry'.

[799] Ibid.

[800] Ibid.

[801] Ibid.

[802] FO945/503, German Refugee Dep't, Memoranda, 'Westward Ho! – The Resettlement of DP's in the UK', 17/11/47.

[803] FO1006/514, 'Operation "Westward Ho!" – Letters from DP's who have become coalminers in GB, From PW & DP Division, Lemgo to PWDP Division Branches, 28 June 1948.

[804] Ibid.

[805] Paul, *Whitewashing Britain*, p xiii.

[806] FO371/66714, WR3679/77/48, Circular No. 0199, 'Resettlement of Displaced Persons', Annex B, 'Westward Ho! The Resettlement of Displaced Persons in the United Kingdom', FO to all H M Embassies and Legations, 10/12/47.

[807] Playback No: 13, Lithuanian child dependent.

[808] Although this chapter, like the rest of the book, focuses on first generation Latvians, Lithuanians and Estonians, there will also be some examination of the experiences of the second and third generation, and of dependants (old and young) who joined the EVWs from DP Camps in Europe.

[809] There were three Regional Collecting Centres (RCC), one in each of the three British zone regions of Germany (Schleswig-Holstein, North Rhine Westphalia, Land Niedersachsen). Each had a capacity of 1000. The actions taken in the RCC's, included Nominal Rolls, TB Screening, Intelligence, Exits and entries and Passport Control. (Source: FO1032/830, 32A, Appendix A to minutes of meeting held at PW & DP Division, Lemgo, 10/3/47).

[810] The Embarkation Camp had a capacity of 6000. A small reserve of clothing was held there. (Source: FO1032/830, 32A, Appendix A to minutes of meeting held at PW & DP Division, Lemgo, 10/3/47).

[811] Many of the holding camps were former Prisoner-of-War camps or army barracks.

[812] Occasionally, the refugees were able to travel directly to a hostel, without going to a holding camp.

[813] The hotel in London used for the temporary accommodation of EVWs was at Hans Place, SW1.

814 Appendix F: Letter from E.V.W.S, (1), Burnley, 26.9.1948, Tannahill, J. A. (1958) *European Volunteer Workers in Britain*, Manchester: Manchester University Press, p 130.

815 Tannahill, *European Volunteer Workers*, p 66.

816 Tannahill also noted that after their arrival in Britain, the Cotton Board sponsored an appeal to British workers for spare clothing for the refugees, and the response 'was considerable'. Tannahill, Ibid.

817 FO945/496, 103A, '87 D.P. Women Welcome Hard Work Here', by News Chronicle Reporter, *News Chronicle*, 22/10/46.

818 A small reserve of clothing was held at the Münster Embarkation Transit Camp, to provide basic items to those EVWs lacking the essentials. (Source: FO1032/830, 32A, Appendix A to minutes of meeting held at PW & DP Division, Lemgo, 10/3/47).

819 Appendix F: Letter from E.V.W.S, (1), Burnley, 26.9.1948, Tannahill, *European Volunteer Workers*, p 130.

820 Playback No: 14, First Generation Latvian man. This represents a 50 per cent increase in pocket money.

821 FO371/66713, WR3329/77/48, Leaflet Issued by WVS about their work with EVWs, September 1947, p 2.

822 Ibid.

823 Playback No: 1, First Generation Latvian woman.

824 Ibid.

825 Ibid.

826 This is an English summary of a contribution by the Latvian author Gunārs Priednieks. 'In the Mirror of the Past', English Summaries by Grunts, M. V. & Smith, I. A. (1995) *Latvieši Lielbritanijā*, Latvian National Council in Great Britain, p 455-56.

827 Playback No: 13, First Generation Lithuanian woman.

828 Ibid.

829 *The Western Morning News*, 21/11/46, 216a, Wiener Library.

830 Ibid.

831 Different holding camps and hostels were allocated to serve designated regions. For example, EVWs allocated to work in the East and West Ridings were allocated to Full Sutton Camp, Stamford Bridge, Nr. York or to Priory Road Camp, Priory Road, Hull. (Source: FO945/502, 86A, Allocation of Holding Camps to Regions).

832 Tannahill, *European Volunteer Workers*, p 85.

833 Ibid.

834 Playback No: 08, First Generation Latvian woman

835 Recreational facilities in the hostels were extremely variable. While one Latvian noted at Bearley camp, near Stratford-upon-Avon, there were 'diverse sports activities', another Latvian noted that in a different camp that although there were sports activities, 'socially it was rather quiet'. In another camp for agricultural workers in Hertfordshire, one Latvian reported that: 'Camp facilities were meagre', and 'gambling and drinking were the most popular pastimes at weekends'. These are English summaries of contributions by Latvians in

Britain, 'In the Mirror of the Past', English summaries by Grunts and Smith, *Latvieši Lielbritanijā*, p 457.

[836] LAB26/247, 'English for Foreign Workers': 'Report of an Enquiry by one of H. M. Inspectors of School's during January, February and April, 1949 into the teaching of English to foreign workers, with special reference to the relevant social and labour problems involved', p 6.

[837] LAB26/247, 'English for Foreign Workers', op cit., p 7.

[838] This was not always the case. There are many examples where EVWs were welcomed into local areas. One Latvian remembered how EVWs from a camp near Leighton Buzzard, Bedfordshire, housing EVWs employed in the building materials industry were 'welcome guests at the local pubs, because they were good spenders'. English summary of contribution by Arv. Zaķis, in 'In the Mirror of the Past', English Summaries by Grunts and Smith, *Latvieši Lielbritanijā*, p 460.

[839] Tannahill, *European Volunteer Workers*, p 85.

[840] English summary of a contribution by Imants Bērziņš, 'In the Mirror of the Past', English Summaries by Grunts and Smith, *Latvieši Lielbritanijā*, p 456.

[841] English summary of an article in *Londonas Avize* (5/3/48), 'In the Mirror of the Past', ibid., p 457.

[842] Tannahill, *European Volunteer Workers*, p 66.

[843] LAB26/247, 'English for Foreign Workers': 'Report of an Enquiry by one of H. M. Inspectors of School's during January, February and April, 1949 into the teaching of English to foreign workers, with special reference to the relevant social and labour problems involved', p 5.

[844] Playback No: 08, First Generation Latvian woman.

[845] Ibid.

[846] Tannahill, *European Volunteer Workers*, p 67.

[847] Ibid.

[848] Playback No: 02, First Generation Estonian man.

[849] Ibid.

[850] Ibid. p 85.

[851] LAB26/247, 'English for Foreign Workers', p 2.

[852] Ibid.

[853] Working in Ammunitions Depots was fairly rare among the EVWs, but illustrates the range of miscellaneous jobs undertaken by Baltic refugees. 'In the Mirror of the Past', English Summaries by Grunts and Smith, *Latvieši Lielbritanijā*, p 460, describes the case of one Latvian who was sent along with a group of other EVWs, to work at the Royal Army Central Ammunition Depot (CAD Bramley) near Basingstoke, where they worked for the Royal Engineers and Sappers, earning £3 10 s per week.

[854] See for example the life history of an Estonian man, BO 127/01, BHRU.

[855] Playback No: 05, First Generation Latvian man.

[856] English summary of extracts from the diary of Augusts Butka, 'In the Mirror of the Past', ibid., p 456.

[857] Playback No: 21, First Generation Estonian man.

[858] Playback No: 16, First Generation Estonian man.

859 Ibid.

860 Tannahill, *European Volunteer Workers*, p 38.

861 A Latvian woman reported that lunch breaks were usually half an hour or three-quarters of an hour. BO 060, First Generation Latvian woman, BHRU.

862 BO 122/01, First Generation Latvian woman, BHRU.

863 Playback No: 06, First Generation Latvian man.

864 None of those whom I interviewed had been employed in coalmining.

865 One Latvian EVW reports that some of the courses lasted over three months. (English summary of contribution by Arnold Muižinieks in 'In the Mirror of the Past', translated by Grunts and Smith, *Latvieši Lielbritanijā*, p 458.

866 Ibid.

867 English summary of contribution by A. Kazaks in 'In the Mirror of the Past', ibid., p 458.

868 See the contributions by Latvian EVWs collected in the chapter 'In the Mirror of the Past', Ibid., pp 453-465.

869 English summary of contribution by Jautrīte Svenne in 'In the Mirror of the Past', *Latvieši Lielbritanijā*, p 461.

870 English summary of contribution by Arv. Zaķis in 'In the Mirror of the Past', ibid., p 460.

871 Playback No: 19, First Generation Lithuanian man.

872 BO 127/01, First Generation Estonian man, BHRU.

873 Tannahill, *European Volunteer Workers*, p 72.

874 Ibid. (Tannahill notes that during 1949, almost 800 men and 300 women from the EVW population were placed in employment outside the 'approved field' of undermanned industries', Tannahill, *European Volunteer Workers*, p 53)

875 Playback No: 08, First Generation Latvian woman.

876 Ibid.

877 For further information, see Tannahill, *European Volunteer Workers*, p 73.

878 Ibid.

879 Ibid.

880 In the eighteen months following this ruling, 44 applications from among all EVW nationalities were received, the majority accepted. I do not have figures for the numbers of Baltic applicants, although from this figure it is likely to be no more than a handful. (Tannahill, ibid., p 73).

881 Tannahill, ibid., p 82.

882 The Control Commission noted on 21 April 1948 that it was mainly Balts who returned to Germany. (FO1006/513, no 167, CCG, Lübbecke to PWDP, Land Schleswig-Holstein, 21/4/48).

883 Initially, there was some confusion about the right of EVWs to re-enter the continent. A Tripartite Agreement covering the three western Allied zones of Europe was negotiated in early 1948, which gave individuals the right to return to Germany within 18 months of leaving. No formal instrument regulating return to Austria ever existed. Each case was dealt with on an individual basis, and eventually, authorities worked to the same rules as in Germany. (Tannahill, *European Volunteer Workers*, p 40).

884 The Control Commission states that one woman returned 'to join husband for emigration purposes'. Ibid.

885 Ibid., p 98.

886 BO 060, First Generation Latvian woman, BHRU.

887 Ibid.

888 BO 122/1, First Generation Latvian woman, BHRU.

889 Women formed approximately one-quarter of the Latvian and Lithuanian communities and two-fifths of the Estonian population. Approximations based on figures from HO213/596, cited in Kay and Miles, *Refugees or Migrant Workers?*, p 43.

890 I was told this by a Baltic refugee in Britain.

891 See: Maud Bülbring, 'Post-War Refugees in Great Britain', *Population Studies*, vol viii, part 2, November 1954, pp 99-112; Peter Jackson, 'The Racialisation of Labour in Post-war Bradford', *Journal of Historical Geography*, vol 18, no 2, 1992, pp 190-209; D Kay and R Miles, *Refugees or Migrant Workers?: European Volunteer Workers in Britain, 1946-1951*, Routledge, London, 1992; Kenneth Lunn, 'The Employment of Polish and European Volunteer Workers in the Scottish Coalfields, 1945 – 1950', in Klaus Tenfelde (ed), *Towards a Social History of Mining in the Nineteenth and Twentieth Centuries*, Munich, C. H. Beck, 1992, pp 582-592; Elizabeth Stadulis, 'The Resettlement of Displaced Persons in the United Kingdom', *Population Studies*, vol v, no 3, March 1952, pp 207-237; J A Tannahill, *European Volunteer Workers in Britain*, Manchester University Press, 1958, p 46.

892 Lunn, 'The Employment of Polish and European Volunteer Workers in the Scottish Coalfields, 1945 – 1950', p 585.

893 Ibid.

894 Ibid., p 590.

895 Ibid.

896 LAB26/247, 'English for Foreign Workers', p 3.

897 LAB26/247, Ibid., p 5.

898 Tannahill, *European Volunteer Workers*, p 70.

899 Playback No: 01, First Generation Latvian woman.

900 Ibid.

901 BO122/1, First Generation Latvian woman, BHRU.

902 Lunn notes reports from various newspapers in Scotland about the EVWs. The *Cowdenbeath Advertiser* reported that there was anger at the eviction of Scottish industrial workers from an NCB hostel to make room for DPs. *Cowdenbeath Advertiser*, 28 November, 5 December 1947, cited in Lunn, 'The Employment of Polish and European Volunteer Workers in the Scottish Coalfields, 1945 – 1950', in Klaus Tenfelde (ed), *Towards a Social History of Mining in the Nineteenth and Twentieth Centuries*, p 590.

903 Newspapers did sometimes print news stories reporting positive relations between the EVWs and the local population. For example, the *Dunfermline and West Fife Journal* reported that at the Townhill Miner's Hostel in Dunfermline, British, French, Africans, Poles and British Hondurans lived together with 'no

hint of any antagonism'. *Dunfermline and West Fife Journal*, 6 April 1947 cited in Lunn, ibid., p 590.

[904] Sheila Patterson carried out a study of EVWs and other immigrants in industry in the late 1950's examining the levels of industrial accommodation and absorption achieved. Her results will be mentioned in the next chapter. (Sheila Patterson, *Immigrants in Industry*, London, Oxford University Press, 1958.)

[905] Tannahill, *European Volunteer Workers*, p 100.

[906] Ibid., p 70.

[907] Bülbring, Post-War Refugees in Britain', p 105.

[908] Ibid.

[909] These men had been members of the Polish Free Forces and either did not wish to, or were debarred from a return to a Stalinised Poland. An estimated 100,000 men plus dependants were enrolled in the PRC, and a large number found employment in Britain during the first years after the war. This amounted to the first large-scale resettlement of East Europeans in Great Britain in such a short period of time. Lunn, 'The Employment of Polish and European Volunteer Workers in the Scottish Coalfields, 1945 – 1950', p 583.

[910] Playback No: 17, First Generation Lithuanian woman.

[911] Playback No: 01, First Generation Latvian woman.

[912] Bülbring, Post-War Refugees in Britain', p 105.

[913] Playback No: 01, First Generation Latvian woman.

[914] Playback No: 13, First Generation Lithuanian woman and daughter.

[915] Playback No: 01, First Generation Latvian woman.

[916] Playback No: 02, First Generation Estonian man.

[917] Lunn, 'The Employment of Polish and European Volunteer Workers in the Scottish Coalfields', p 585.

[918] Ibid.

[919] Playback No: 13, Lithuanian child dependant.

[920] FO1006/247, J.G. Stewart to H.H. Sellar, 31/5/49.

[921] Ibid.

[922] LAB26/247, J.G. Stewart, Ministry of Labour and National Service to the Regional Controller, All Regions, 16 August 1949.

[923] Ibid.

[924] Tannahill, *European Volunteer Workers*, p 68.

[925] Ibid., p 69.

[926] LAB26/247, 'English for Foreign Workers', p 3.

[927] This information was provided by a Lithuanian woman in Nottingham.

[928] For example, the story by Latvian writer, Knuts Lesins: *The Dove*. See: Brown, J. (1970) *The Un-Melting Pot: An English Town and its Immigrants*, Basingstoke & London: Macmillan, p 45.

[929] Playback No: 03, First Generation Latvian woman.

[930] Sinka, J. (1988) *Latvia and Latvians*, London: Daugavas Vanagi, p 31.

[931] The territory of Lithuania had been increased by the Soviet occupation in 1940, due to the agreement between Russia and Germany, which effectively handed Vilnius back to Lithuania in return for German concessions in Poland. Klaipeda was also returned to Lithuania. In contrast, Estonia and Latvia were

obliged to cede part of their territories to the Russian federal republic. According to Hiden and Salmon, Estonia lost five per cent of its prewar territory and 6 per cent of its pre-war population. Latvia lost approximately two percent of territory and population. (Hiden, J. & Salmon, P. (1991) *The Baltic Nations and Europe: Estonia, Latvia and Lithuania in the Twentieth Century*, London & New York: Longman, p 129-130).

[932] The Soviet Union initially used German POW's for labour in the Baltic States, but soon came to rely on immigrant Russian labour. (Hiden & Salmon, ibid., p 130).

[933] Murphy, H. B. M. (1955) 'The Conditions of Resettlement', in Murphy, H. B. M. (ed) *Flight and Resettlement*, Switzerland: UNESCO, p 91.

[934] Ibid.

[935] Brown, *The Un-melting Pot*, p 30.

[936] Murphy (ed.), *Flight and Resettlement*, 1955.

[937] Other diagnoses were Paranoia, Schizoid, Manic-Depressive Psychosis, Mania, Anxiety State, Anxiety Neurosis, Psychoneurosis, Primary Dementia and Delusional State. 'Table 2. Diagnoses', Ibid., p 180.

[938] Ibid., pp 182-183.

[939] Ibid., p 187.

[940] Bülbring, Post-War Refugees in Britain', p 108.

[941] Ibid.

[942] Galloping Tuberculosis is a particularly severe form of TB.

[943] Playback No: 07, First Generation Latvian man.

[944] This phenomenon was also mentioned to me in passing by several members of the Baltic communities.

[945] Brown, *The Un-melting Pot*, p 30.

[946] Anon. (1958) *Latvians in Great Britain*, London: The Latvian National Council in Great Britain, part 3: 'Arrival in Great Britain'.

[947] Playback No: 12, First Generation Latvian man.

[948] Ibid.

[949] Playback No: 16, First Generation Estonian man.

[950] This woman was aged eight when she came to Britain in 1948. Playback No: 13, First Generation Lithuanian woman and daughter.

[951] Playback No: 13, First Generation Lithuanian woman and daughter.

[952] Ibid.

[953] Playback No: 08, First Generation Latvian woman.

[954] Anon. (1978) *Latvians in Great Britain*, London: London: The Latvian National Council in Great Britain, part 6, 'The Latvian Welfare Fund'.

[955] Ibid.

[956] Twenty-five elected members were to form the Council, and the first elections were held in 1950, with the participation of some 7,000 voters . (Anon., *Latvians in Great Britain*, part 5, 'The Latvian National Council in Great Britain'.)

[957] Ibid.

[958] Ibid.

[959] Ibid.

960 The chairman of the association from 1947-49 was Dr. Jaak Taul, and from 1949-51 Kapten Bernhard Nelberg. *I.E.Ü* *ia Eesti Haal: 50a Inglismaal*, Association of Estonians in Great Britain, p 16.

961 'A little bit of DBLS history', Extracts taken from Britanijos Lietuviai (Britain's Lithuanians) 1947-1973 edited by Barėnas, K. in *LYNES (Lithuanian Youth Newsheet)*, Lithuanian Youth Association in Great Britain, 8(September 1996), p 1.

962 Ibid.

963 Ibid.

964 Ibid.

965 Ibid., p 2.

966 Lithuanians in Bradford, 1947-1995', (Abstract in English), *Bradfordo Lietuvių Veikla Didžiojoje Britanijoje (Lithuanians in Bradford)*, Lithuanian Club 'Vytis', Vilnius, 1995, p 117.

967 English summary of contributions by Voldemārs Blankenburgs and Alfons Freimanis in 'In the Mirror of the Past', translated by Grunts and Smith, *Latvieši Lielbritanijā*, pp 458-459.

968 English summary of contribution by Milda Brantevica in 'In the Mirror of the Past', ibid., p 462.

969 See Chapter 1: 'A Brief History of Latvians, Lithuanians and Estonians in Britain before 1946'.

970 Letters to the Editor, Podvoiskis, J. (1999) 'Community and integration: Are we as one or is it "us and them"?', *LYNES (Lithuanian Youth Newsheet)*, 36(February). In the letter, Podvoiskis compares the state of present-day relations between post-independence Lithuanian migrants in Britain and the established DP community, with the relations between the DP community and pre-war Lithuanian emigrants after 1945. In both cases there has been conflict.

971 During the Second World War, the new Soviet occupation authorities in Latvia, Lithuania and Estonia had relieved the diplomatic representatives in London of their positions. The British Government was under increasing pressure to remove the diplomatic status of Latvian, Lithuanian and Estonian Ministers, but since it did not recognise *de jure*, the incorporation of the Baltic States into the Soviet Union, but as a compromise, merely delegated the ministers to the end of the Diplomatic List. Thus, although the Ministers did not enjoy the same rights and privileges as previously, they were able to maintain contact with some Foreign Office officials and continued to exert pressure on the government. This situation continued throughout the Soviet period.

972 See the section on political activities for further information.

973 *LYNES*, 45 (November 1999), p 4.

974 Playback No: 03, First Generation Latvian woman.

975 Ibid.

976 BO 060, First Generation Latvian woman, BHRU.

977 Stein, B. N. (1981) 'The Refugee Experience: Defining the Parameters of a Field of Study', *International Migration Review*, 15(1), p 329.

978 Playback No: 13, First Generation Lithuanian mother and daughter.

[979] Anon., *Latvians in Great Britain*, part 8: 'Choirs and folk dance groups'.

[980] Ibid. The publication also noted that re-emigration and the closing down of hostels forced the smaller ensembles out of existence.

[981] The Lithuanian Scout movement had begun in Vilnius in 1918, and after the Second World War spread world-wide among the Lithuanian diaspora. (*LYNES*, 24(March 1998))

[982] Ibid.

[983] As discussed in Chapter Five, the character of this day changed after the end of independence.

[984] 'The 30th Anniversary of Latvia's independence', English summary of the text of a speech by Ādolfs Pērkons, in 'In the Mirror of the Past', translated by Grunts, M. V. & Smith, I. A. *Latvieši Lielbritanijā*, p 465.

[985] Ibid.

[986] This was the term used by a Lithuanian woman to describe how her family and the Lithuanian community operated within British society in the early years. Playback No: 13, Second Generation Lithuanian woman.

[987] See page 233.

[988] FO371/66711, Wr1929/77/48, Operation "Westward Ho!", Zonal Instruction: Operation "Westward Ho!", Allied Commission for Austria (British Element): Recruitment of DPs for Employment in Great Britain, 21/5/47.

[989] FO1006/513, no 185, CCG, From IRO, British Zone HQ to PWDP, CCG, 28/4/48.

[990] Andrups, J. 'A History of Latvians in Great Britain', English summary by Andris Abakus, *Latvieši Lielbritanijā*, p 450.

[991] Anon. (1978) *Latvians in Great Britain*, London: The Latvian National Council in Great Britain, part 7: 'Church Life'.

[992] 'Lithuanians in Bradford, 1947-1995', (Abstract in English), *Bradfordo Lietuvių Veikla Didžiojoje Britanijoje (Lithuanians in Bradford)*, Lithuanian Club 'Vytis', Vilnius, 1995, p 117.

[993] Ibid.

[994] LAB26/247, 'Regional Reports on the Progress of the Assimilation of the European Volunteer Workers, February 1950'.

[995] Ibid.

[996] Playback No: 17, First Generation Lithuanian woman.

[997] Ibid.

[998] Playback No: 21, First Generation Estonian man.

[999] LAB26/247, 'English for Foreign Workers': 'Report of an Enquiry by one of H. M. Inspectors of School's during January, February and April, 1949 into the teaching of English to foreign workers, with special reference to the relevant social and labour problems involved'.

[1000] As spelt in the original document.

[1001] Ibid., p 2.

[1002] Ibid., p 2.

[1003] Ibid., p 4.

[1004] Tannahill, *European Volunteer Workers*, p 68.

[1005] LAB26/247, 'English for Foreign Workers', pp 4-5.

[1006] Playback No: 13, First Generation Lithuanian woman.

[1007] Ibid., p 236.

[1008] LAB26/247, J.G. Stewart, Ministry of Labour and National Service to the Regional Controller, All Regions, 16 August 1949, p 69.

[1009] Andrups, J. (1995) 'A History of Latvians in Great Britain', English summary by Andris Abakuks, *Latviesi Lielbritanija*, Latvian National Council in Great Britain, p 451-452.

[1010] Skultans, V. (1998) *The Testimony of Lives: Memory and Narrative in post-Soviet Latvia*, London and New York: Routledge, p 176.

[1011] Skultans, *Testimony of Lives*, p 177.

[1012] Brown, *The Un-Melting Pot*, p 51.

[1013] Tannahill does not offer a breakdown of employment trends among different nationality groups, so it is impossible to estimate the numbers of Latvians, Lithuanians and Estonians leaving or remaining different fields of employment. Tannahill, *European Volunteer Workers*, pp 78-84.

[1014] Ibid., p 78.

[1015] Not surprisingly, numbers also dropped of those working for the National Service Hostels Corporation. There was also a drop in numbers of EVWs first employed by the War Office at Ordnance Depots. Ibid., pp 78-79.

[1016] Ibid., p 79.

[1017] Ibid., p 80.

[1018] The steel industry was one of the smaller employers of EVWs as compared with textiles or coal mining. Ibid., p 81.

[1019] Playback No: 01, First Generation Latvian woman.

[1020] Information from interviews carried out by the author.

[1021] Due to the large numbers of participants interviewed in the textile towns of Leeds, Bradford and Lancashire, the numbers continuing to work in textiles in my sample is not necessarily representative of the whole population, rather it reflects the areas where the participants live.

[1022] Tannahill, *European Volunteer Workers in Britain*, p 81.

[1023] Ibid., p 78 and pp 82-83. The nationalities of these EVWs are not cited. The opportunities to open a successful shop were probably more limited among the Baltic communities than among say the Polish community, whose numbers were far larger. Nevertheless, it is clear that some foodstuffs businesses were established by the Baltic communities. For example, I have been informed of an excellent Latvian bakery in Leeds, which sold rye bread and other foodstuffs at a market stall in Leeds. The bakery has since been sold.

[1024] Tannahill, *European Volunteer Workers*, pp 81-82.

[1025] Playback No: 04, First Generation Latvian man.

[1026] Tannahill, *European Volunteer Workers*, p 12. See Chapter Five for further information about Baltic emigration during the latter part of the nineteenth century.

[1027] Playback No: 05, First Generation Latvian man.

[1028] Anon. (1978) *Latvians in Great Britain*, The Latvian National Council in Great Britain, London, part 8: 'Choirs and folk dance groups'.

[1029] Playback No: 05, First Generation Latvian man.

1030 According to a Lithuanian woman in Manchester. Playback No: 017, First Generation Lithuanian mother and daughter.

1031 Ibid., Second Generation Lithuanian woman.

1032 Ibid.

1033 Kay and Miles, *Refugees or Migrant Workers?*, p 158.

1034 Anon., *Latvians in Great Britain*, part 3. 'Arrival in Great Britain'.

1035 Sinka, *Latvia and Latvians*, p 51.

1036 Tannahill's sample composed only a minute percentage of the populations. His sample composed 27 Lithuanians, 65 Latvians, 41 Estonians. These figures are not large enough to make accurate generalising statements. (See: Appendix L, Tannahill, *European Volunteer Workers*, pp 139-140).

1037 Tannahill, *European Volunteer Workers*, p 69.

1038 The use of the terms adaptation and adjustment in this book have been discussed in the introduction to the book, and are more fully defined in the *Glossary of Terms* at the back of the book.

1039 Playback No: 13, First Generation Lithuanian woman and dependent daughter.

1040 Ibid.

1041 Lithuanian Charter, copy inserted in *LYNES*, 27 (July 1982).

1042 See Chapter Six for more discussion of the role of the ethnic community in aiding transition and adaptation among refugees. Also see: Stein, B.N. (1981) 'The Refugee Experience: Defining the Parameters of a Field of Study', *International Migration Review*, 15(1), p 329.

1043 Playback No: 16, First Generation Estonian man.

1044 Brown, J. (1970) *The Un-Melting Pot: An English Town and its Immigrants*, London & Basingstoke: Macmillan, pp 51-51.

1045 Playback No: 17, First Generation Lithuanian woman.

1046 Tannahill noted that one way of saving, reputedly practised among many male EVWs was to have an extremely close haircut. This made them so self-conscious that they were not tempted into having 'a night out' and were forced to withdraw from social life until their hair grew again. Footnote 1, Tannahill, *European Volunteer Workers*, p 86.

1047 Tannahill, *European Volunteer Workers*, pp 85-86.

1048 Ibid., p 86.

1049 National Coal Board.

1050 Tannahill, *European Volunteer Workers*, p 86.

1051 Ibid.

1052 Ibid., p 87.

1053 Ibid.

1054 Ibid.

1055 Ibid.

1056 These statistics are based on an analysis by the Superintendent Registrar of Births, Marriages and Deaths of marriages of refugees in his district for the years 1951-55. The figures excluded men who had been naturalised; thus Tannahill concludes, the proportion of British brides may be even higher. (Tannahill, *European Volunteer Workers*, p 88)

421

[1057] Playback No: 17, First Generation Lithuanian woman.

[1058] For example, one Lithuanian woman from Manchester stated that she could not think of any Lithuanian women in the Manchester area who had married outside their own nationality. (Playback No: 17, First Generation Lithuanian woman)

[1059] Tannahill, *European Volunteer Workers*, 1958, p 90.

[1060] Ibid.

[1061] Ibid.

[1062] Ibid.

[1063] Ibid.

[1064] One Latvian woman stated that the refugees began sending letters in 1953. They also received letters from family in the homeland, although sometimes letters were sent via Germany to avoid identification of relatives in Great Britain. Letters received and sent were reportedly opened by the Soviet authorities, and often doctored, with black lines concealing sections of the letters.

[1065] Foreign Minister, 1957-1985.

[1066] It is impossible to state accurately how many exit visas were granted to Latvians, Lithuanians and Estonians to join relatives in Britain as records are incomplete, as far as I can tell. One document states that 35 exit visas were granted on 13 May 1959, mainly to the elderly. This number included 14 (1 man & 13 women) who wished to join relatives in the UK. 19 of the 35 were Latvians, 11 Estonians and 2 Lithuanians. It is possible that further exit visas were granted. (FO371/143521, 'Soviet Nationals wishing to join relatives in the UK and Australia').

[1067] 'Sodyba', *Lynes*, No 13, August 1980, p 2.

[1068] Andrups, J. (1995) 'A History of Latvians in Great Britain', English summary by Andris Abakus, , *Latvieši Lielbritanijā*, Latvian National Council in Great Britain, p 452.

[1069] Ibid.

[1070] 'DBLS History: Birth of Lithuanian youth organisations', *LYNES* (Lithuanian Youth News Sheet), 11(January 1997) p 1.

[1071] Bülbring, 'Post-War Refugees in Britain', p 109.

[1072] Blodnieks, A. (1960) *The Undefeated Nation*, New York: Robert Speller & Sons, p 280.

[1073] FO371/106114, 'Estonian Government–in-Exile in Stockholm', NB 1821/1, From BBC Monitor, 23/1/53.

[1074] This contained a variety of information relating to communist activities in the Baltic States and other East European countries, for example, copies from 1952 and 1953 contained information relating to religious suppression in Lithuania. *Newsletter from Behind the Iron Curtain: Reports on Communist Activities in Eastern Europe*, compiled by the Baltic Review, Stockholm, Sweden, Estonian Information Centre, Stockholm. Information from FO371/106114, NB 1821/7.

[1075] FO371/106114, NB1821/12, Letter from Chairman of Lithuanian Association in Great Britain, M. Bajorinas to PM, Churchill, 4/1/53.

[1076] FO371/11379, C. Zarine to Anthony Eden, Sec. of State, 19/1/54.

[1077] Chairman of the USSR Council of Ministers (1955-58). Source: Brown, A. (ed.) (1990) *The Soviet Union: A Biographical Dictionary*, London: Weidenfeld and Nicolson, p 61

[1078] Appeals were sent by the diplomatic representatives of all three Baltic nations based in Britain: A. Torma (Estonian Legation), C. Zarine (Latvian Legation), B. K. Balutis (Lithuanian Legation). FO371/121133, 'Political Relations between UK and Members of Former Missions of Baltic States in London', 1956.

[1079] Paul, P. (1997) *Whitewashing Britain: Race and Citizenship in the Postwar Era*, Ithaca and London: Cornell University Press, p 132.

[1080] Ibid.

[1081] See Chapter Six for discussion of H B M Murphy's definition of resettlement. Also see: Murphy, H. B. M. (1955) 'The Conditions of Resettlement', in Murphy, H. B. M. (ed) *Flight and Resettlement*, Switzerland: UNESCO, p 91.

[1082] Playback No: 16, First Generation Estonian man.

[1083] John Brown, *Un-Melting Pot*, p 50.

[1084] BHRU, BO 122/1, First Generation Latvian woman.

[1085] BHRU, BO 127/01, First Generation Estonian man.

[1086] As defined by Berry, integration 'implies some maintenance of the cultural integrity of the group (that is, some reaction or resistance to change as well as the movement to become an integral part of a larger societal framework (that is, some adjustment). (Berry, J. W. 'Acculturation and Adaptation in a New Society', *International Migration*, 30, p 72)

[1087] Brown, *The Un-Melting Pot*, p 44.

[1088] Ibid.

[1089] Men formed approximately three-quarters of the original Latvian EVW population.

[1090] Brown, *Un-Melting Pot*, p 50.

[1091] Playback No: 05, First Generation Latvian man.

[1092] Berry, 'Acculturation and Adaptation in a New Society', p 73.

[1093] Ibid.

[1094] There were no single refugees from the older cohort interviewed for this study, primarily since many have already died. I did however, interview one younger Latvian man who never married. However, he lived with his parents who had come to Britain as dependants, and was thus less isolated than single refugees without dependants. He also successfully integrated into British society, while at the same time, maintaining some aspects of homeland culture.

[1095] From discussions with a Social Worker of the East European communities in West Yorkshire.

[1096] Playback No: 05, First Generation Latvian man.

[1097] From the mid-sixties onwards, trips to the homeland were organised with Intourist, the Soviet travel agency. These were tightly structured package tours to the capital and one or two 'tourist' destinations, such as Sigulda or Jurmala in Latvia. Visitors were not allowed to diverge from the schedule and forbidden to travel independently outside the capital. They were therefore unable to return to their pre-war homes and villages. There were rumours about hotel rooms being bugged, and tourists being followed when they left their hotel.

[1098] Brown, *Un-Melting Pot*, p 52.

[1099] Ibid.

[1100] According to Marwick, the total numbers in manufacturing employment declined by 2.2 per cent between 1971 and 1974 and by a further 6.1 per cent between 1974 and 1977. Marwick, A. (1990) *British Society since 1945*, London: Penguin, p 186.

[1101] According to one Latvian refugee I spoke to in Leeds.

[1102] Playback No: 16, First generation Estonian man.

[1103] Playback No: 03, First Generation Latvian woman.

[1104] 'Lithuanian Charter', Insert in *LYNES*, 27(July 1982).

[1105] *LYNES*, 20 (June 1981).

[1106] Playback No: 03, First Generation Latvian woman.

[1107] Ibid.

[1108] Ibid.

[1109] Playback No: 04, First generation Latvian man.

[1110] Playback No: 03, First Generation Latvian woman.

[1111] *LYNES*, 11(January 1997).

[1112] Lithuanian Youth Association in Great Britain (*Didžiosios Britanijos Lietuvių Jaunimo Sąjunga*), Constitution, Insert in *LYNES*, 27(July 1982).

[1113] 'Lithuanian Youth Association in Great Britain – Constitution', Insert in *LYNES*, 27(July 1982).

[1114] Information provided by a first generation Estonian man.

[1115] Anon. (1978) *Latvians in Great Britain*, London: The Latvian National Council in Great Britain.

[1116] *LYNES*, 20(June 1981).

[1117] 'Lithuanian Youth Association in Great Britain (*Didýiosios Britanijos Lietuvių Jaunimo Sąjunga) CONSTITUTION*', accepted at the DBLJS General Meeting in Manchester, 31/1/81 reprinted in *LYNES*, 27(July 1982 (Insert)).

[1118] *LYNES*, 12(June, 1980) and 13(August 1980).

[1119] *LYNES*, 38b(December 1986).

[1120] Ibid.

[1121] *LYNES*, 36(June 1985).

[1122] *LYNES*, 36(June 1985).

[1123] *LYNES*, 31(June 1983).

[1124] *LYNES*, 4(May-June 1978).

[1125] *LYNES*, 32 & 33(November 1983).

[1126] *LYNES*, 38b(December 1986).

[1127] Obviously, the degree to which the home retained Lithuanian influences was extremely variable, and was usually greater in all-Lithuanian household.

[1128] Esther Davis, 'Why be Lithuanian?' *LYNES*, 20(June 1981), p 3.

[1129] Ibid.

[1130] Ibid.

[1131] *LYNES*, 31(June 1983).

[1132] *Lithuania 6 (Lietuva): How Much Do We Know About Her?*, 6(1989), Lithuanian Scouting in Great Britain, London: Lithuanian House Ltd.

[1133] *LYNES*, 20(June 1981).

[1134] *LYNES*, 17(February 1981).

[1135] *LYNES*, 36(June 1985). *LYNES* later revived partly as a result of increased interest brought about by the onset and declaration of homeland independence.

[1136] *LYNES*, 36(June 1985).

[1137] Ibid.

[1138] Correspondence from first generation Estonian.

[1139] Playback No: 16, First Generation Estonian man.

[1140] BO127/01, First Generation Estonian.

[1141] Playback No: 14, First Generation Latvian man.

[1142] Playback No: 21, First generation Estonian man.

[1143] Playback No: 16, First Generation Estonian man.

[1144] Among all three communities, Deportations Day (13-14 June) and National Independence Day (18 November – Latvia, 16 February – Lithuania, 24 February - Estonia, were very important. For Latvians and Estonians, St. John's Day (24 June – midsummer) was also an important date in the exile calendar. Among the Latvian community, Kalpak's Day – 6 March was also important, marking the date that Colonel Oskars Kalpaks, the first Commander-in-Chief of the Latvian Army died in battle in 1919. The day also commemorates all those who in both world wars died fighting for the independence of Latvia. Mother's Day was important among all three communities and was celebrated on the first Sunday in May. Among the Estonian community Rebirth Day on 16 November and Victory Day on 23 June, which was commemorated with Deportations Day, were significant. Among Lithuanians some religious days were particularly important, including Kučios (Christmas Eve) and All Saint's Day on 1 November. Other important days included Statehood Day on 6 July, and National Day on 8 September.

[1145] Lithuanian Charter, adopted by The Supreme Committee for the Liberation of Lithuania, 14 June 1949. Reproduced as an insert in *LYNES*, 27(June 1982).

[1146] Among the Latvian community an annual appeal in aid of schools held on or around 28 January became a popular tradition in the Latvian exile calendar. Various events were organised with the aim of raising money to provide books and other teaching aids for weekend schools and to support Latvian education in general. The tradition had originated in 1935 when Prime Minister Ulmanis invited people to remember their first school and present it with a gift. (Anon. (1978) *Latvians in Great Britain*, The Latvian National Council in Great Britain, London, part 10: 'Annual Events')

[1147] Playback No: 14, First Generation Latvian man.

[1148] For example, the centre of the Lithuanian community in Nottingham – Lithuanian Marian Fathers, in Hounds Road was a site for the circulation of samizdat material.

[1149] *Lithuania (Lietuva): How much Do We Know about Her?*, 6(1989), Lithuanian Scouting in Great Britain, London: Lithuanian House, p 11.

[1150] Sinka, J. (1988) *Latvia and Latvians*, Central Board "Daugavas Vanagi", , London: Nida Press.

[1151] *LYNES*, no 13, August 1980.

[1152] The other nations in the Captive Nations' Committee were Byelorussia, Hungary, Ukraine.

[1153] An example was VLIKas (*Vyriausias Lietuvos Išlaisvinomo Komitetas* – Supreme Committee for the Liberation of Lithuania), the Lithuanian underground political organisation which moved to the West in 1944, setting up headquarters in the USA in 1955. VLIKas was established during the Second World War as a representative organisation of all political underground groups. VLIKas urged Lithuanians to resist German efforts to yoke it to the German war machine. When President Smetona died in the US in 1944, VLIKas announced that as the supreme organ of the Lithuanian resistance it was assuming legitimate national leadership and carrying out the constitutional functions of government. However, it remained confined to the underground although succeeded in maintaining links with the west through Sweden. It withdrew to the west in 1944 when the Russians took over. Here it resuscitated the Lithuanian Red Cross and drafted a charter of the World Lithuanian Community, before moving to the US in 1955. (*LYNES*, 4(May-June 1978))

[1154] This was commemorated by all three communities annually to mark the mass deportations of thousands of Latvians, Lithuanians and Estonians on the night of 13-14 June 1941. The commemoration was and continues to be one of the most important events in the Baltic exile calendar in Britain, and indeed globally.

[1155] Before the re-establishment of independence in 1991, Independence Day marked the date of the establishment of independence during the inter-war period. Lithuanian Independence Day - 16 February; Estonian Independence Day - 24 February; Latvian Independence Day - 18 November.

[1156] See the section on Citizenship later in this chapter.

[1157] *Bradfordo Lietuvių Veikla Didžiojoje Britanijoje* (Lithuanians in Bradford), Lithuanian Club "*Vytis*", *Lieutuvos literatųros fondas* – "*Litfondas*", Vilnius, 1995, pp 117-118.

[1158] *LYNES*, 29(January 1983).

[1159] Anon. (1978) *Latvians in Great Britain*, London: The Latvian National Council in Great Britain, part 13: The aims of Latvian organisations.

[1160] Ibid.

[1161] King, V. & Wilson, R. (1988) 'Latvian Residential Homes for Retired People', in '*Age in Exile: A Report on Elderly exiles in the United Kingdom*', August 1988, British Refugee Council, for the Age in Exile Conference, Noordwijkerhout, the Netherlands, p 55.

[1162] Ibid.

[1163] Ibid.

[1164] Ibid., p 56.

[1165] Further buildings were added in 1996.

[1166] King & Wilson, '*Age in Exile: A Report on Elderly exiles in the United Kingdom*', p 76.

[1167] Ibid.

[1168] *LYNES*, no 13, August 1980.

[1169] Ibid.

[1170] King, V. (1988) 'Talking Books in Latvian', in *Age in Exile: A Report on Elderly exiles in the United Kingdom'*, August 1988, British Refugee Council, for the Age in Exile Conference, Noordwijkerhout, the Netherlands, p 36.

[1171] Playback No: 16, First Generation Estonian.

[1172] Ibid.

[1173] Extracts from *Britanijos Lietuviai, 1947-1973* edited by Barėnas, K., reprinted in *LYNES*, 9(November 1996).

[1174] King, V. & Wilson, R. (1988) 'Latvian Residential Homes for Retired People', in *'Age in Exile: A Report on Elderly exiles in the United Kingdom'*, August 1988, British Refugee Council, for the Age in Exile Conference, Noordwijkerhout, the Netherlands, p 55.

[1175] For example, the Latvian *Daugavas Vanagi* club branch in Leeds.

[1176] *Bradfordo Lietuvių Veikla Didžiojoje Britanijoje* (Lithuanians in Bradford), Lithuanian Club 'Vytis', p 117.

[1177] *LYNES*, 12(June 1980).

[1178] Anon. (1978) *Latvians in Great Britain*, London: The Latvian National Council in Great Britain, part 6: The Latvian Welfare Fund.

[1179] *LYNES*, no 34, January 1999, p 5.

[1180] Ibid.

[1181] The original club in Mossend had been bought in 1950 by both Lithuanian DPs and the 'old' Lithuanian refugees from the late nineteenth and early twentieth century who joined forces and raised funds by voluntary contributions to buy St Margaret's Episcopal church, to use as their meeting hall. The club moved to new premises in 1979, due to redevelopment plans by Monklands District Council, who agreed to erect new premises. During the early 1980's an extension was built. (Excerpt from interview with Joseph Blue (Bliudzius, in Millar, J. (1998) *The Lithuanians in Scotland*, Isle of Colonsay: House of Lochar, 1998, pp 147-148).

[1182] *I.E.U ia Eesti Haal: 50a Inglismaal* (Inglismaa Eestlaste Ühing, Association of Estonians in Great Britain: Fifty Years in Britain).

[1183] Playback No: 05, First Generation Latvian man.

[1184] Tannahill, *European Volunteer Workers*, p 99, outlined the provisions of the British Nationality Act of 1948 under which EVWs were considered for naturalisation. In brief, the Second Schedule of the Act stated that the qualifications for naturalisation of an alien who applied were:

that he had either resided in the United Kingdom or been in Crown service under Her Majesty's government in the United Kingdom, or partly the one and partly the other, throughout the period of twelve months immediately preceding the date of the application; and

that during the seven years immediately preceding the said period of twelve months he had either resided in the United Kingdom or any colony, protectorate, United kingdom or any colony, protectorate, United Kingdom mandated territory or United Kingdom trust territory or been in Crown service as aforesaid, or partly the one and partly the other, for periods amounting in the aggregate to not less than four years;

that he was of good character; and

that he had sufficient knowledge o f the English language; and

that he intended in the event of a Certificate being granted to him-

to reside in the United Kingdom or in any colony, protectorate or United kingdom trust territory or in the Anglo-Egyptian Sudan; or

to enter into or continue in Crown service under His Majesty's Government in the United Kingdom, or under the government of the Anglo-Egyptian Sudan, or service in the employment of a society, company or body of persons established in the United Kingdom or established in any colony, protectorate or United Kingdom trust territory.

[1185] Tannahill, *European Volunteer Workers*, p 98.

[1186] Ibid., p 99.

[1187] Playback No: 03, First Generation Latvian woman.

[1188] Tannahill, *European Volunteer Workers*, p 100.

[1189] Playback No: 12, First Generation Latvian man.

[1190] Playback No 06, First Generation Latvian man.

[1191] Playback No: 08, First Generation Latvian woman.

[1192] Ibid.

[1193] Playback No: 04, First Generation Latvian man.

[1194] Berry, 'Acculturation and Adaptation', *International Migration*, p 72.

[1195] See the Glossary of Terms for definitions.

[1196] These sources only discuss Latvians and Estonians. However, a similar character and process of integration could also been discerned among Lithuanians.

[1197] Brown, *Un-Melting Pot*.

[1198] Ibid, p 49.

[1199] Okamura, J. (1981) 'Situational Ethnicity', *Ethnic and Racial Studies*, 4(4).

[1200] Brown, *Un-Melting Pot*, pp 49-50.

[1201] Ibid., p 53.

[1202] Ibid.

[1203] Ibid., p 54.

[1204] Ibid.

[1205] Ibid., p 52.

[1206] Ibid.

[1207] BHRU BO 122/1, First Generation Latvian woman. I have given this woman a pseudonym.

[1208] BHRU BO 127/01, First Generation Estonian man. Lennart is a pseudonym.

[1209] BHRU, BO 0060, First Generation Latvian woman. I have given this woman a pseudonym.

[1210] BHRU BO 122/1, First Generation Latvian woman.

[1211] BHRU BO 127/01, First Generation Estonian man.

[1212] BHRU, BO 0060, First Generation Latvian woman.

[1213] BHRU, BO 0060, First Generation Latvian woman.

[1214] BHRU BO 122/1, First Generation Latvian woman.

[1215] BHRU BO 127/01, First Generation Estonian man.

[1216] BHRU BO 122/1, First Generation Latvian woman.

[1217] BHRU BO 127/01, First Generation Estonian man.

[1218] BHRU, BO 0060, First Generation Latvian woman.

[1219] Brown, *Un-Melting Pot*, p 50.

[1220] Playback No: 14, First Generation Latvian man.

[1221] Brown, *The Un-Melting Pot*, p 34.

[1222] Esther Davis, 'Why be Lithuanian?', *LYNES*, 20(June 1981), p 3.

[1223] Hiden & Salmon, *The Baltic Nations and Europe*, p 137.

[1224] Anon. (1978) *Latvians in Great Britain*, The Latvian National Council in Great Britain, part 13. 'The aims of Latvian organisations'.

[1225] Mockūnas, L. (1985)'The Dynamics of Lithuanian Émigré – Homeland Relations', *Baltic Forum*, 2(1), p 66.

[1226] Playback No: 13, First Generation Lithuanian woman and child dependant.

[1227] *LYNES*, No 40, August 1989, p 1.

[1228] Playback No: 01, First Generation Latvian woman.

[1229] Miezitis, S. (1990) 'Preface', *Journal of Baltic Studies*, 11(3), p 191.

[1230] Richard Krickus noted the support provided to Sajudis (Lithuanian Popular Front) by the American and Canadian Lithuanian diaspora: 'Young Canadians and Americans of Lithuanian descent worked for *Sajudis* as translators, press aides, and liaisons with the Western media. Lithuanian organizations in North America provided fax machines, computers, and financial assistance to *Sajudis*. The Brooklyn-based Lithuanian Information Center established a press office for the organization'. The diaspora also planned trips for leaders of *Sajudis* to travel to the US and organised translators for their meetings with the US President and Congress. Richard Krickus, 'Lithuania: nationalism in the modern era' in Bremmer, I. & Taras, R. (eds.) (1993) *Nations and Politics in the Soviet Successor States*, Cambridge: Cambridge University Press, p 173.

[1231] *LYNES*, 40(August 1989).

[1232] Anthony Daniels, 'Chill pervades the Baltic Spring', *Sunday Telegraph*, 27/11/88.

[1233] Sinka, J. (1988) *Latvia and Latvians*, Central Board "Daugavas Vanagi", London: Nida Press, pp 3-4..

[1234] Ibid., p 4.

[1235] Playback No: 17, First Generation Lithuanian woman.

[1236] Playback No: 07, First Generation Latvian man.

[1237] Playback No: 07, First Generation Latvian man.

[1238] Sinka, J. (1992) *Latvia and Latvians*, Central Board 'Daugavas Vanagi', London: Nida Press (Revised Second Edition for Australian audience), p 4.

[1239] Sinka, J. (1996) *Latvia and Latvians*, Third Edition, p 4.

[1240] The Freedom Monument was erected in the 1930's, during the inter-war period of independence. It became the symbol of Latvian freedom. Its significance as a symbol of Latvian independence was furthered during the Soviet period, when the Soviet authorities attempted to tear it down on several occasions. It was categorically forbidden to approach it. Since the declarations of independence not only have honour guards stood at the base of the monument, there is always a carpet of flowers at its foot. (Source: Dāboliņš, A. & Shipman, S. (1993) *Latvia: A Guide Book*, Latvia: PUSE, p 107)

[1241] Playback No: 08, First Generation Latvian woman.
[1242] Playback No: 20, First Generation Lithuanian man.
[1243] Ibid.
[1244] Playback No: 13, Lithuanian child dependant.
[1245] Playback No: 13, First Generation Lithuanian woman.
[1246] Playback No: 07, First Generation Latvian man.
[1247] Playback No: 05, First Generation Latvian man.
[1248] Playback No; 06, First Generation Latvian man.
[1249] Ibid.
[1250] Playback No: 09, First Generation Lithuanian returnee.
[1251] Playback No: 01, First Generation Latvian woman.
[1252] Ibid.
[1253] Ibid.
[1254] Playback No: 08, First Generation Latvian woman.
[1255] Playback No: 03, First Generation Latvian woman.
[1256] Playback No: 02, First Generation Estonian man.
[1257] Ibid.
[1258] Playback No: 14, First Generation Latvian man.
[1259] Playback No: 03, First Generation Latvian woman.
[1260] From a conversation with a Latvian woman.
[1261] This is my own opinion, derived from experience in the Baltic States. Altogether the number of returnees I have met and known about via the diaspora in Britain or through fieldwork equal more than 10 returnees in Latvia. It is likely that there are many more Latvian returnees of whom I am unaware.
[1262] *Vincents* was opened by a Latvian man from Corby, Leicestershire. Information provided by a Latvian in Britain. It has been an extremely successful, upmarket restaurant, located in the centre of Riga on *Elizabetes iela.*
[1263] In the 1993 elections to the Fifth Saiema, 'Latvia's Way' won the most seats out of all the political parties – 36. Of these, eight members were members of the diaspora from abroad. Of the hundred deputies elected to the Saiema, 18 were Western émigrés (Dreifelds, J. (1996) *Latvia in Transition*, Cambridge: Cambridge University Press, pp 88-90).
[1264] The current Latvian President is Vaira Vike-Freiberga, age 61, a member of the Canadian-Latvian diaspora. She was elected President in June 1999. The current Lithuanian President is a Lithuanian-American – Valdas Adamkus, voted in as President in January 1998.
[1265] Reclamation of property, which had been expropriated by the Soviet authorities during the war, became possible after independence, although it was often a lengthy and complex procedure.
[1266] Playback No: 13, Lithuanian child dependant.
[1267] Playback No: 10, First Generation Latvian man (Returnee based in Riga).
[1268] Playback No: 10, First Generation Latvian man (Returnee based in Riga).

[1269] Playback No: 09, First Generation Lithuanian man (Returnee based in Vilnius).

[1270] Ibid.

[1271] When I interviewed him, his wife and one child had since returned to England, and he was uncertain about whether they would return, of if he would return to Britain.

[1272] Playback No: 11, First Generation Latvian man (Returnee in Latvia).

[1273] Playback No: 09, First Generation Lithuanian returnee.

[1274] Ibid.

[1275] Playback No: 07, First Generation Latvian man.

[1276] Playback No: 08, First Generation Latvian woman.

[1277] Ibid.

[1278] Playback No: 04, First Generation Latvian man.

[1279] Playback No: 16, First Generation Estonian man.

[1280] Playback No: 05, First Generation Latvian man.

[1281] Ibid.

[1282] Playback No: 05, First Generation Latvian man.

[1283] Information provided by a Latvian in Britain.

[1284] Playback No: 13, First Generation Lithuanian woman.

[1285] Playback No: 15, First Generation Estonian man.

[1286] Ibid.

[1287] Playback No: 07, First Generation Latvian man.

[1288] Ibid.

[1289] Playback No: 13, First Generation Lithuanian woman.

[1290] Playback No: 01, First Generation Latvian woman.

[1291] Playback No: 01, First Generation Latvian woman.

[1292] Playback No: 16, First generation Estonian man.

[1293] Playback No: 04, First Generation Latvian woman.

[1294] Playback No: 12, First Generation Latvian man.

[1295] Playback No: 07, First Generation Latvian man.

[1296] Playback No: 16, First Generation Estonian man.

[1297] Playback No: 08, First Generation Latvian woman.

[1298] Ibid.

[1299] Ibid.

[1300] Playback No: 17, First Generation Lithuanian woman.

[1301] Playback No: 16, First Generation Estonian man.

[1302] Playback No: 07, First Generation Latvian man.

[1303] Ibid.

[1304] Playback No: 08, First Generation Latvian woman.

[1305] Playback No: 13, Lithuanian child dependent.

[1306] Rubchak, M. J. (1993) 'Dancing with the Bones: A Comparative Study of Two Ukrainian Exilic Societies', *Diaspora*, 2(3), p 353.

[1307] Playback No: 05, First Generation Latvian man.

[1308] Playback No: 01, First generation Latvian woman.

[1309] Playback No: 01, First Generation Latvian woman.

[1310] The *Saiema* is the Latvian Parliament.

[1311] Playback No: 08, First Generation Latvian woman.

[1312] Ibid.

[1313] Ibid.

[1314] Playback No: 05, First Generation Latvian man.

[1315] Bradford Lithuanian Club "Vytis" (ed.) (1995) *Bradfordo Lietuvių Veikla* Didžiojoje Britanijoje, 1947-1995 (Lithuanians in Bradford, 1947-1995), Vilnius: 'Litfondas'.

[1316] Lithuania Assessment, Version 4, September 1999, Country Information and Policy Unit, Home Office, p 4. (http://www.homeoffice.gov.uk/ind/lit4.htm)

[1317] 'Lithuanian Asylum Applications Declined Significantly in the UK', *UNHCR Asyl Nord* No. 9, 19 April 1999. Information collated by UNHCR from: *ELTA* 31 March 1999. (http://www.immi.se/asyl/nord9.htm)

[1318] 'Tighter Control on Travellers to London from Lithuania', *UNHCR Asyl Nord* No. 7, 16 February 1999. Information collated by UNHCR from: *ELTA*, 20 January 1999; *ELTA*, 26 January 1999; *The Baltic Times*, 10 February 1999. (http://ww.immi.se/asyl/nord7.htm)

[1319] 'Lithuanian Asylum Applications Declined Significantly in the UK', *UNHCR Asyl Nord* No. 9, 19 April 1999. Information collated by UNHCR from: *ELTA* 31 March 1999. (http://www.immi.se/asyl/nord9.htm)

[1320] 'Tighter Control on Travellers to London from Lithuania', *UNHCR Asyl Nord* No. 7, 16 February 1999. Information collated by UNHCR from: *ELTA*, 20 January 1999; *ELTA*, 26 January 1999; *The Baltic Times*, 10 February 1999. (http://ww.immi.se/asyl/nord7.htm)

[1321] Ibid.

[1322] *LYNES*, 35(February 1999).

[1323] Ibid.

[1324] Virginia Juras, 'Eligibility for membership of DBLS', Ibid., p 6.

[1325] 'Vytautas Landsbergis meets DBLS directors', *LYNES*, 36(February 1999), p 1.

[1326] 'DBLS Members Beware', *LYNES*, 37(March 1999), pp 1 &5.

[1327] Ibid.

[1328] Playback No: 13, Lithuanian child dependant.

[1329] Ibid.

[1330] Ibid.

[1331] 'Conflict of Interest', *LYNES*, 38(April 1999), p 1.

[1332] 'A Clean Sweep', *LYNES*, 39(May 1999), pp 1-2.

[1333] Alkis, J. (Chairman of DBLS), 'Lithuanian Association in Great Britain', *LYNES*, 40(June 1999), p 1.

[1334] Ibid.

[1335] O'Brien, V. (Chairman, DBLS Taryba) 'DBLS Regeneration: A time to heal, a time to move forward: A discussion Document', *LYNES*, 41(July 1999), pp 1-2.

[1336] Playback No: 12, First Generation Latvian couple.

[1337] Playback No: 03, First Generation Latvian woman.

[1338] Tölöyan, K. (1996) 'Rethinking Diaspora(s): Stateless Power in the Transnational Movement, *Diaspora*, 5(1), pp 14-15.

[1339] Correspondence from first generation Estonian man.

[1340] Gilbert, E. (2002) 'The Impact of Homeland Independence on the Latvian Community in Great Britain', *Journal of Baltic Studies*, 33(3): 280-306.

[1341] Playback No: 10, First Generation Latvian man, a returnee living in Riga, at the date of the interview in 1997.

[1342] Playback No: 16, First Generation Estonian man.

[1343] Playback No: 21, First Generation Estonian man.

[1344] Playback No: 06, First Generation Latvian man.

[1345] Playback No: 01, First Generation Latvian woman.

[1346] *I.E.Ü ia Eesti Hääl: 50a Inglismaal* (1997) Association of Estonians in Great Britain.

[1347] Home Office files suggest that by 31 December 1950, a total of 5154 Estonians, with 504 dependants had arrived in Britain. Source: HO213/596, cited by Kay, D. and Miles, R. (1992) *Refugees or Migrant Workers?: European Volunteer Workers in Britain, 1946-51*, London: Routledge, p 43.

[1348] A few of the refugees may have been recruited onto the EVW schemes younger than the specified minimum age of 18. It was difficult for Camp authorities to verify ages due to lack of identifying documentation.

[1349] Older refugees were more likely to remain single, and tended to remain in areas of high Baltic settlement. The younger refugees were more likely to inter-marry and felt less need to live near a centre of Baltic community.

[1350] The full questionnaire study involved about 40 participants.

[1351] In December 1996, newspapers revealed that the German authorities were paying annual pensions of £2,800 to former soldiers living in Britain. This supplements their British state pensions. They included former soldiers from the Baltic States who were enlisted in the national units of the SS, including the Latvian Legion. However, the numbers receiving payments is very small. A total of 459 former soldiers mainly from Ukraine and the Baltic States were reported to be receiving payment. These pensions are administered through the DSS. See: Bennett, W., 'Nazi war pensions are supplied through DSS', *The Daily Telegraph*, 16/12/96; Chaudhary, V., 'UK "assisting SS claimants for pensions"', *The Guardian*, 16/12/96; Evans, M., 'Call for enquiry into pensioners' war crime record', *The Times*, 16/12/96.

[1352] Anon., (1978) *Latvians in Great Britain*, The Latvian National Council in Great Britain, London, Section 6: The Latvian Welfare Fund.

[1353] Information provided on a visit to the DVF branch in Leeds on 28/3/95.

[1354] Information provided by a Latvian man in Leeds in February 1997.

[1355] *LYNES*, 34 (January 1999), p 6. *LYNES*, 41 (July 1999), p 1 noted 'some 19 branches of the Lithuanian Association in Great Britain'. This figure may not have taken into account the new branches, as I am unaware of any branch closing in 1999, only the closing and re-opening of the Sodyba branch.

[1356] *LYNES*, 34 (January 1999), p 6.

[1357] *LYNES*, 35 (February 1999), p 1.

1358 Lithuanian House Hotel at Freeland Road was sold in late 1999. As of the date of writing the future of the Freeland Road branch was uncertain, despite being newly opened.

1359 See: *LYNES*, 34 (January 1999), p 5.

1360 Inglismaa Eestlaste Ühing – Association of Estonians in Great Britain, Information Leaflet.

1361 *LYNES*, 46 (December 1999), pp 2 & 4.

1362 Information gained from fieldwork at the Bradford Estonian club in 1997.

1363 *LYNES*, 34 (January 1999), p 1.

1364 Playback No: 17, First Generation Lithuanian woman.

1365 Ibid.

1366 From fieldwork at the Manchester Lithuanian club in 1997 and 1998.

1367 Playback No: 01, First Generation Latvian woman.

1368 Visit to Latvian club in Leeds on 28/3/95.

1369 *LYNES*, 34(January 1999), p 5.

1370 *LYNES*, 39 (June 1999), p 5.

1371 *LYNES*, 34 (January 1999), p 1.

1372 Playback No: 01, First Generation Latvian woman.

1373 Playback No: 07, First Generation Latvian man.

1374 *LYNES*, 45 (November 1999), p 4.

1375 Ibid.

1376 Ibid.

1377 Danys, M. (1986) *DP: Lithuanian Immigration to Canada after the Second World War*, Toronto: Multicultural History Society of Ontario, p 299.

1378 Stuart Hall used the term 'translation' to describe the process whereby cultures and identities are modified as a result of migration and settlement in a new country. (Hall, S (1992) 'The Question of Cultural Identity', in Hall, S., Held, D. & McGrew, T. (eds.) *Modernity and its Futures*, Cambridge and Oxford: Polity Press in association with The Open University, p 310)

1379 Playback No: 17, First Generation Lithuanian woman.

1380 Playback No21, First Generation Estonian man.

1381 Playback No: 18, First Generation Lithuanian man.

1382 Playback No: 17, First Generation Lithuanian woman.

1383 Playback No: 12, First Generation Latvian man.

1384 From a visit to the Latvian club in Leeds,

1385 See Chapter Five

1386 See Chapter Five.

1387 The majority of the third generation can be said to have assimilated, even though there was some residual symbolic cultural maintenance among a minority.

1388 See: LAB26/247, 'Regional Reports on the Progress of the Assimilation of the European Volunteer Workers', February 1950.

1389 Playback No: 05, First Generation Latvian man.

1390 Winland, D. (1995) ' "We are Now an Actual Nation": The Impact of National Independence on the Croatian Diaspora in Canada', *Diaspora*, 4(1), p24.

[1391] Playback No: 01, First Generation Latvian woman.

[1392] Connor, W. (1986) 'The Impact of Homelands Upon Diasporas', in Sheffer, G. (ed.) *Modern Diasporas in International Politics*, London & Sydney: Croom Helm.

[1393] Ibid., p 16.

[1394] Playback No: 17, First Generation Lithuanian woman.

[1395] Playback No: 01, First Generation Latvian woman.

[1396] Playback No: 14, First Generation Latvian man.

[1397] Playback No: 04, First Generation Latvian man.

[1398] Playback No: 14, First Generation Latvian man.

[1399] Playback No: 21, First Generation Estonian man.

[1400] Playback No: 18, First Generation Lithuanian man.

[1401] Playback No: 13, First Generation Lithuanian woman.

[1402] Playback No: 04, First Generation Latvian man.

[1403] Playback No: 01, First Generation Latvian woman.

[1404] Playback No: 02, First Generation Latvian woman.

[1405] The potential impact of children upon their parent's culture and identity is an area which has not yet been studied, and is a possible area for future investigation.

[1406] Playback No: 17, First Generation Lithuanian woman.

[1407] Playback No: 03, First Generation Latvian woman.

[1408] *LYNES*, 41 (July 1999), p 1.

[1409] Ibid.

[1410] BO122/1, First Generation Latvian woman, BHRU.

[1411] Playback No: 01, First Generation Latvian woman.

[1412] *LYNES*, 44 (October 1999), p 2.

[1413] LYNES, 46(December 1999), p 5.

[1414] This chapter deals both with the UK (Great Britain and Northern Ireland) and Britain (England, Scotland, Wales) and with just England Wales depending on the statistical data used. For example, the 2011 Census was only undertaken in England and Wales whereas National Insurance data and Worker Registration Scheme data is from the whole of the UK. The correct geographical unit of measurement is cited for each type of data used.

[1415] Population Trends, (2007) *Migrants from Central and Eastern Europe: local geographies*, Office for National Statistics, Autumn 2007.

[1416] Ibid: p 11.

[1417] Ibid., pp 11-17.

[1418] Ibid., p 18.

[1419] McCollum, D., Cook, L., Chiroro., Platts, A., McLeod, F., Findlay, A., (2012) *Spatial, sectoral and temporal trends in A8 migration to the UK 2004-2011: Evidence from the Worker Registration Scheme*, Centre for Population Change, March 2012, p 14.

[1420] Ibid.

[1421] Population Trends, (2007) *Migrants from central and eastern Europe: local geographies*, Office for National Statistics, Autumn 2007.

[1422] McCollum et al', As above.

[1423] Population Trends, (2007) *Migrants from central and eastern Europe: local geographies*, Office for National Statistics, Autumn 2007, p 18.

[1424] Pidd, H., (2013) *Baltic Exchange: meet the Lithuanians who have made Britain their home*, The Guardian, 7 January 2013.

[1425] Ibid.

[1426] Ibid.

[1427] According to the Office for National Statistics the number of Lithuanians in the UK registering on the Worker registration Scheme between May 2004 and December 2006 was 54,529, which compares to a far larger figure of 327,538 Poles during the same period (Population Trends, (2007) *Migrants from central and eastern Europe: local geographies*, Office for National Statistics, Autumn 2007).

[1428] Citing Pidd, H. (As above) – she staes that this is an increase of almost 93,000 on 2001 levels.

[1429] Ibid.

[1430] www.global.truelithuania.com/category/western-europe/united-kingdom/

[1431] Straumanis, A. *'Migration to the U.K. rising, data show'*, Latvians Online Website, (www.latviansonline.com).

[1432] Article on The Economist website, *Migration and Latvia: Far From Home*, 1 October 2010. (www.economist.com/easternapproaches/2010/10/migration_and_latvia)

[1433] Ibid.

[1434] Department for Work and Pensions, *Statistical Bulletin: National Insurance Number Allocations to Adult Overseas Nationals Entering the UK – registrations to March 2012*, Sheffield: August 2012, p 5.

[1435] Ibid

[1436] Ibid.

[1437] Information cited in Pidd, H., as above.

[1438] Department for Work and Pensions, *Statistical Bulletin: National Insurance Number Allocations to Adult Overseas Nationals Entering the UK – registrations to March 2012*, Sheffield: August 2012.

[1439] Pidd., As above.

[1439] See in particular the references in this section as well as work by Linda McDowell (see bibliography).

[1440] See in particular the references in this section as well as work by Linda McDowell (see bibliography). In February 2013 a conference was held at the University of Glasgow entitled 'A Long Way from Home: The Baltic People in the United Kingdom', which showcased the range of research taking place on this subject. Information available at: http://www.gla.ac.uk/schools/socialpolitical/crcees/newsevents/pastevents/headline_248242_en.html

Interview Schedule for First Generation Latvians, Lithuanians and Estonians in Great Britain

A different interview schedule was used for interviewing second generation participants

N.B. LLE is short for Latvia(n)(s), Lithuania(n)(s), Estonia(n)(s)

Interview Schedule

A Guide for a Semi-Structured Interview with First generation Latvians, Lithuanians and Estonians

Background

1) Can you give me some background about the circumstances under which you left LLE, and how you came to Great Britain?
2) Why did you choose to accept the offer to come to Britain?
3) How did you feel when you first came to Britain?
4) Where did you live initially?
5) In the first five or ten years how did you adjust to life in Britain?
6) Initially, did you mix mainly with LLE?
7) When you first came to Britain did you think it would be only a temporary stay? When did you realise that you wouldn't be returning to LLE? How did you feel?
8) Can you tell me what job you did when you first came over and what jobs you have done since?

Identity Issues

9) How would you describe your identity when you first came to Britain? What were the main elements of this identity?
10) How would you describe your sense of ethnic identity at present?
11) Has your identity changed over your lifetime, and if so, how?
12) How do you maintain a sense of LLE…ness?
13) Have you maintained strong LLE cultural traditions? How?
14) Do you feel fully integrated into British society? Can you explain how you feel?
15) Do you feel like an outsider? Why/why not?
16) Do you think you have a stronger or weaker sense of LLE identity now than you did when you first came to Britain or just the same?

17) Are there times when you feel especially aware of being a LLE? When?
18) Are there times when you feel British and forget about your LLE identity?
19) Do people comment on your ethnic background? Can you recall the last time someone commented on it?
20) Have you ever suffered discrimination or hostility for being a LLE?
21) How would you describe the LLE national character? How does it differ from the british national character?
22) Do you think the English and the LLE are quite similar or different?
23) What are the main differences between the LLE way of life and the English way of life?
24) What is your opinion of Britain and the British people?
25) Was it easy to integrate into the British way of life?
26) What are your attitudes towards Russia?
27) During the Soviet period, what were the motivations for maintaining LLE identity and culture in Britain?
28) Was it primarily to bond the community in Britain, or was it to maintain LLE identity and culture on behalf of the homeland, so that it could be transplanted once Russia had been ousted from LLE? Or both?
29) Now that LLE is independent, what are the motivations for maintaining LLE culture and identity in Britain?

Restoration of LLE independence

30) How has the restoration of independence changed your life as a LLE in Britain? Has it?
31) What changes if any have occurred within the LLE community in .... as a result of LLE independence?
32) Can you remember how you felt when LLE became free?
33) Have you been back to LLE? How did you feel when you went back?
    Have you thought about returning to live there?
    Do you have any relatives or friends who live there?
    Do you know anyone who has returned to live? Why did they return?
34) What are your thoughts about present-day LLE?
35) Do you identify with LLE in LLE today or do you feel different from them?

36) Do you identify more with LLE in LLE today than with British people?
37) How would you describe contemporary LLE national identity and culture? Does it differ from the identify and culture of LLE emigrants?

Retirement

38) How has retirement changed your life as a LLE in Britain?
39) Do you reminisce more about life in LLE now that you are retired?

LLE community in Great Britain and community participation

40) How has the LLE community in Great Britain changed since you first arrived?
41) What do you think will happen to the LLE community in Britain in the future?
42) What percentage of the LLE community in GB is actively involved in the LLE community?
43) Do you know many LLE who do not attend clubs or take part in celebration of festivals?
44) Would you say that you are typical of the average LLE in GB in terms of levels of ethnic i.d. and cultural adaptation?
45) Tell me about the LLE community in.......? How large is it, and what kinds of activities are there?
46) How has the LLE community in........ changed in the last fifty years? What was it like in the 1950's, 1960's, 1970's and 1980's?
47) Tell me about your involvement in the LLE community in ....?
48) Have you been on any committees or helped with any organisation of cultural events etc.?
49) Did you take part in any of the campaigns for independence? Was the LLE community in GB actively involved in any political campaigns?
50) During the Soviet period did the LLE community in GB have strong links with other LLE abroad in other countries, e.g. USA?
51) What has happened to these links since independence?
52) Tell me about the links between the LLE community in Great Britain and the homeland during the Soviet period? What sort of contact was there?
53) How important is belonging to a LLE club to you?
54) Have there been times when it has been less important?

55) Has a desire to remain within reach of a LLE club or community motivated you to stay in this area?

56) Is it important to you to live near to a LLE club?/How do you feel about living far away from a LLE club?

57) How frequently do you attend a LLE club? Why do you attend?

58) Do you have mainly LLE friends or do you have English friends/friends from other nationalities?

59) Do you mix with other East European groups?

60) Do you identify with LLE to some degree?

61) What are the main differences and similarities between the ELL communities and the LLE communities?

Children (If have children – check questionnaire)

62) Do your children have strong LLE identities or do they feel more British?
Do they maintain any aspects of the culture of LLE?

63) Did you try to bring up your children as LLE's? How?

Marriage & gender issues

64) (If intermarried) How has intermarriage affected your LLE identity and maintenance of LLE culture? Has it affected your involvement in the LLE community?

65) (If married to a LLE) Do you think that being married to a LLE has helped you to maintain a strong sense of LLE identity and culture?

66) Can you tell me about the different experiences of LLE men and women in GB?

67) What have been the effects of the disproportionate numbers of men and women?

68) Did most women marry within their ethnic group?

69) Can you tell me about the role of women in the inter-war period in the homeland?
Were these gender relations/ roles continued in Great Britain?

Culture

70) Which LLE festivals and events do you participate in?

70) How do you celebrate Christmas?

71) How do you celebrate Easter?

72) (Latvians/Estonians) Do you celebrate St. John's Day? Every year? How do you celebrate it?

73) (Latvians) Do you celebrate name days?

Food
74) Do you eat LLE foods?
75) What is the traditional LLE diet?
76) What food did you eat in the inter-war LLE?
77) Are there differences between L & L & E food?
78) Are there any typically national dishes or foods?
79) What food do you eat at Christmas?
80) Do Latvians eat St. John's cheese on St. John's day in GB?
81) What sort of bread do you eat in Britain?
82) Has your diet changed since first coming to GB?
83) Did you eat more LLE food when you first came to Britain?
84) Do you eat traditional English foods?

Religion
85) Are you religious? Does religion form part of your identity? How often do you attend   services?
86)   Do you remember being religious as a child/attending church?
87) (Lithuanians) Tell me about the importance of the Catholic Church as an element of Lithuanian identity?
88)   (Lithuanians) How important is the Catholic religion among Lithuanian communities abroad?
Language
89) When did you learn English
90) When do you speak LLE?
91) When do you speak English?
92) Do you read LLE books and newspapers?
93) Do you read English books and newspapers?

94) Do you keep LLE artefacts and objects in the house? Why?

Childhood/Inter-war LLE

95) Can you tell me about your childhood?
96) How would you describe LLE national identity during the inter-war period? What were the main components of this identity?
97) Did you have a sense of a national identity when you were growing up?
98) Do you remember celebrating national festivals before the war? Which ones?
99) Tell me about LLE culture during the inter-war period?

100) Can you describe your day to day life in the inter-war period?
101) Can you tell me about attitudes towards Russian and Germany during the inter-war period?
102) Can you tell me about attitudes towards the Jewish population during the inter-war period?

Second World War

103) Do you remember the first Russian occupation? How did it change things?
104) Do you remember the German occupation?
105) What was your attitude towards the Germans and the Russians during the war?
106) What happened to your family and friends during the war?
107) What happened to you personally? (Check experiences of displacement, recruitment in German/Russian army & experiences if not already covered by Q1)
108) Did the war change your national identity? Did it strengthen it?

DP Camps

109) How did you reach the DP Camps?
110) Which Camp(s) were you in?
111) What were the conditions like?
112) What LLE cultural activities took place?
113) Which nationalities were in the Camp(s)?
114) How did you feel when you were in the DP Camps?
115) Did you think you would be able to return to LLE shortly?
116) When did you realise that this would not happen?
117) Can you tell me about your recruitment onto the EVW scheme (If not covered in Q1)?

Other Questions

118)   Have you taken up British citizenship? When? Why/why not?
119) How would describe your status when you first came to Great Britain? (alien, foreigner, refugee, member of diaspora, immigrant, political refugee, labour migrant etc.)
120) How would you describe your status now?
121) Do you feel like you are a member of a world-wide LLE community?

122) Is your identity as a LLE in Britain stronger than your feeling of belonging to a world-wide community? Has this always been the case?

123) At the present time how strong is your bond to Britain, and how strong is your bond to LLE?

124) Where is home?

At end of interview check responses in questionnaire – check for any contradictions & areas not covered

Abbreviations

BHRU	Bradford Heritage Recording Unit
CAB	Cabinet Papers
CCG	Control Commission for Germany
DBLS	*Didžiosios Britanijos Lietuvių Sąjunga* (Lithuanian Association in Great Britain)
DBLJS	*Didžiosios Britanijos Lietuvių Jaunimo Sąjunga* (Lithuanian Youth Association in Great Britain)
DP	Displaced Person
DVF	*Daugavas Vanagi Fondas*
EVW	European Volunteer Worker
FO	Foreign Office
HC Debs	House of Commons Debates
HL Debs	House of Lords Debates
HO	Home Office
IMR	International Migration Review
IRO	International Refugee Organisation
JBS	Journal of Baltic Studies
LAB	Ministry of Labour
LYNES	Lithuanian Youth News-sheet
PRO	Public Record Office
UNHCR	United Nations High Commissioner for Refugees
UNNRA	United Nations Refugee and Rehabilitation Administration

Glossary of Terms

As the reader will be aware, there is an unwieldy supply of books and journal articles on terms and theories relating to immigration, race and ethnicity. The below, is necessarily very brief, focusing on the definitions I have used for this book. For more information on many of these terms, see: Cashmore, E. (ed.) (1997) *Dictionary of Race and Ethnic Relations*, Fourth Edition, London NA New York: Routledge, and other works listed in the bibliography. Guibernau, M. & Rex. J. (eds.) (1997) *The Ethnicity Reader: Nationalism, Multiculturalism and Migration*, Cambridge: Polity, provides a useful introduction. All the references cited below are listed in the bibliography.

absorption

'Absorption' is a rather ill-defined term, which has been used in many different ways, both general and specific. It was a term used by the British Government in the 1940's to refer primarily to a process by which it hoped, assimilation would be reached. (See for example, the use of the terms in the following statement: 'Although this nation has a genius for absorbing foreigners into its system in small doses, and to the mutual advantage of both parties, the present influx is so enormous...that an especial effort is imperative: the gradual absorption of these thousands of foreigners into our community will not occur automatically'. (LAB 26/247, 'English for foreign Workers', Report of an Enquiry made by one of HM Inspectors of Schools during January, February and April 1049 into the teaching of English to Foreign Workers, with special reference to the relevant social and labour problems involved). As this statement implies, absorption can also be seen as an end product. Absorption can be used in a general sense, e.g. the overall absorption of immigrants into British society, or in a more specific sense. For example, industrial absorption refers to absorption into British labour. Sheila Patterson used the term absorption in a fairly general sense, to mean 'the whole range of the reciprocal processes of "adaptation and acceptance"'. According to Patterson, absorption refers both to a process and an end product. Patterson was particularly interested in 'industrial absorption', which referred to the range of processes referring to the adaptation of the immigrant to British labour, and acceptance by British labour. (Patterson, S. (1968) *Immigrants in*

Industry, London and New York: OUP, pp 6-7) The latter aspect 'acceptance' by British labour has also been referred to as *accommodation*. Patterson defines accommodation as the first stage in the process of industrial absorption, generally taking place during the first years of settlement. (Patterson, S. *Ibid.*, pp 7-8) In this book, I will be using the term infrequently, and only in the context of British Government policy.

acculturation

Like many of the words listed in this glossary, the term 'acculturation' has been used in many different senses, and has been defined differently during various phases of British immigration history. In 1972, Krausz defined acculturation in the following way: 'While assimilation implies changes that bring about the disappearance of the minority group, acculturation is regarded as a process whereby the minority becomes more akin to the dominant group although it continues to exist as a separate entity'. (Krausz, E. (1972) 'Acculturation and pluralism: a clarification of concepts', *New Community*, 1(4), p 251) In this book, I will be adopting a slightly different definition provided by J. W. Berry, in his theoretical study of refugee adaptation: 'Acculturation and Adaptation in a New Society', *International Migration* (1992). Berry defines acculturation as 'culture change that results from continuous, first-hand contact between two distinct cultural groups'. Further, 'while changes to both groups are implied in the definition, most changes in fact occur in the non-dominant (society of settlement) group'. (Berry, J. W. (1992), pp 69-70) According to Berry, there are four possible outcomes of the acculturation process, not just one, as suggested by Krausz. The four outcomes are: assimilation, integration, separation and marginalization.

adaptation

Adaptation has been used in many senses by immigration specialists, both general and specific. In a 1974 article about immigrant adaptation, Goldlust noted the benefits for using the term in preference to assimilation. Although lacking specificity, 'the term adaptation has the advantage of not involving a priori value judgements concerning desirable outcomes or conveying the same ideological overtones that come to be associated with the notion of assimilation'. (Goldlust, J. (1974) 'A Multivariate Model of Immigrant Adaptation', *IMR*, 8(2), p

195) For this book, I will use the term adaptation in a rather broad sense, to refer primarily to the process through which the immigrant changes his or her way of living and culture to fit in to the new country of residence. Patterson defines the process of 'immigrant-host adaptation' as a reciprocal process, in which both immigrant and host society adapts. (Patterson, S. (1968), pp 6-7) However, I will be using the term primarily in the context of the process of immigrant adaptation. (For other uses of the term adaptation, see: Berry, J.W. (1992) 'Acculturation and Adaptation in a New Society', *International Migration*, 30, pp 69-85; Cohon Jr., J. R. (1981) 'Psychological Adaptation and Dysfunction among Refugees', *IMR*, 15(1), pp 255-275).

adjustment

Like the term adaptation, in this book, I have used the term adjustment in a broad sense, to refer to the response of the immigrant upon meeting with the receiving society, and how he or she 'adjusts' to the new country of residence. Adjustment occurs in different spheres, for example, cultural or psychological. Like adaptation, adjustment can be a reciprocal process, where both immigrant and receiving society adjusts. However, in this book, I will use the term to refer primarily to the process of immigrant adjustment, with a particular focus on cultural adaptation.

assimilation

Assimilation was the goal of many western receiving societies in the immediate post-war period. Banton defines it as 'the process of becoming similar'. (Banton, M. (1997), p 43). In 1940's Britain, a country with little experience of large-scale immigration, assimilation referred to a straight-line process whereby one ethnic group (usually a minority group) merges into another (usually the dominant group). Assimilation can occur in many spheres. As Danys noted, it is possible to assimilate 'economically, psychologically or culturally'. (Danys, M. (1986), p 299) In discussing assimilation, the British Government envisaged assimilation in all areas, but referred primarily to the merging of cultures and identities. It hoped that immigrant groups would not only become British in a cultural sense, they would also assume British identities. Britain's growing experience of immigration in the 1950's, particularly the large-scale immigration of colonial newcomers, led to an increasing awareness both in governmental and academic circles of the complexity of the assimilation process, and a realisation that it would not be as straightforward as previously envisaged. This led to an increasing sophistication in theories of assimilation from the 1950's onwards. Assimilation became increasingly viewed as a two-way process, whereby both newcomers and the receiving society would have to accommodate each other. In 1968, there remained no clear definition of assimilation. Sheila Patterson's definition reflected contemporary thinking. Patterson used assimilation, 'to denote complete adaptation by the incoming individual or groups and complete acceptance by the receiving society. The process is a reciprocal one, in that the receiving society may move some way towards the newcomers, but the main effort of adaptation falls on the latter, particularly in such a relatively homogenous and stable society as Britain'. (Patterson, S. (1968) *Immigrants in Industry*, p 7). Although assimilation came to be identified with Anglicization, theorists in America distinguished three models of assimilation. The first was Anglo-conformity, in which immigrants were brought to conform to the practices of the dominant Anglo-Saxon groups. The second was the 'Melting Pot' in which all groups pooled their characteristics and produced a new society. Finally, the third model comprised elements of pluralism – cultural and structural, depending on whether the minority 'while resembling the majority in many respects, retained elements of distinctive culture or could be distinguished by the way its members continued to associate with one another'. (Banton, M. 'Assimilation', in Cashmore, E. (ed.) *Dictionary of Race and Ethnic Relations*, p 44). The first model was the closest to that which the government had envisaged in the late-1940's. In 1960's Britain, the British Government and local authorities were accused of racism and discontented minorities protested in disturbances such as the 1968 Notting Hill Riots. The growing black and Asian populations were dissatisfied with the concept of assimilation since they felt that it left no room for the maintenance and expression of cultures and identities. The lack of 'complete acceptance' on the part of the receiving society was also becoming clear. This led to a move away from the concept of assimilation from the mid-sixties onwards towards the concept of *integration* (see below), although the term lingered on among some academic studies. Berry provides a contemporary definition of assimilation, which he defines as 'relinquishing one's cultural identity and moving into the larger society. It can take place by way of absorption of a non-dominant group into an established dominant group, or it can be by way of the merging of many groups to form a new society, as in the "melting pot" concept'. (Berry, J. W. (1992)

'Acculturation and Adaptation in a New Society', *International Migration*, p 72).

culture

Culture is a particularly difficult term to define. Popular understanding of culture ranges from the focus on 'ethnic' culture or traditions, i.e. the particular customs of a society or ethnic group, to its meaning as creative, artistic or musical endeavours, and finally, its more simple meaning as 'way of life'. Culture is all of these, and more. According to Boyle, Halfacree and Robinson, in 'recent years academic understanding of the term has shifted from an emphasis upon highly skilled and distinctive human activities to a concentration on overall ways in which groups of people live their lives – their actions, their motivations, their feelings'. Further, 'culture' exists 'through the shared and negotiated practices of everyday life'. (Boyle, P., Halfacree, K. & Robinson, V. (1998) *Exploring Contemporary Migration*, London: Longman, p 207) Sir Edward Tylor's definition in 1871 is also quite useful. He wrote that when 'taken in its wide ethnographic sense', culture is the 'complex whole which includes knowledge, belief, art, morals, law, custom and any other capabilities and habits acquired by man as a member of society'. (Source: Banton, M. (1997) 'Culture', in Cashmore, E. *Dictionary of Race and Ethnic Relations*, p 91) These broad definitions have guided the use of the term 'culture' in this book.

diaspora

The word diaspora is drawn from ancient Greek terms *dia* (through) and *speirō*, which means dispersal or to scatter. (Vertovec, S. (1997) 'Diaspora', in Cashmore, E. (ed.) *Dictionary of Race and Ethnic Relations*, pp 99-100) Originally, diaspora referred exclusively to the Jewish diaspora, exiled from their homelands and dispersed through many lands. Over the last decade, the growth of the field of diaspora studies, influenced by transnationalism and globalisation has led to a wider definition of the term, which now encompasses a broader range of groups. Using broader definitions such as that introduced by William Safran has resulted in many groups now being characterised as diaspora, including Armenians, Africans, Poles, and also, as in this study, Latvians, Lithuanians and Estonians. William Safran composed the following criteria for the existence of a diasporic community (my additions to his definitions are in brackets):

1) they or their ancestors have been dispersed from an "original" centre to two or more "peripheral" or foreign regions (some theorists suggest that the circumstances of the dislocation are highly significant – usually displacement occurs as flight from, or expulsion by, a new political regime or oppression);

2) they retain a collective memory, vision or myth about their original homeland – its physical location, history, and achievements (this is usually manifested in the establishment of an exile culture and identity, which is based upon the perceived 'true' culture and identity of the homeland);

3) they believe that they are not – and perhaps cannot be – fully accepted by their host society and therefore feel partly alienated from it (this point has been qualified by some theorists who suggest that experiences vary depending upon whether there is strong pressures to assimilate within the receiving society, or whether it is a more pluralistic and accepting society);

4) fourth, they regard their ancestral homeland as their true, ideal home and as such the place to which they or their descendants would (or should) eventually return – when conditions are appropriate (this is the infamous myth or return, a key feature of diaspora);

5) they believe that they should, collectively, be committed to the maintenance or restoration of their original homeland and to its safety and prosperity (they are in a sense, the 'guardians' of the homeland, and this responsibility provides motivation for political campaigning and the maintenance of ethnic identity and culture);

6) they continue to relate, personally or vicariously, to that homeland in one way or another, and their ethnocommunal consciousness and solidarity are importantly defined by the existence of such a relationship.

(Safran, W. (1991) 'Diasporas in Modern Societies: Myths of Homeland and Return, *Diaspora*, 1(1), p 83)

Safran's definition and even broader ones, such as Walker Connor who defined diaspora as 'that segment of a people living outside the homeland' (Connor, W. (1986) 'The Impact of Homelands upon Diaspora', in Sheffer, G. (ed.) *Modern Diasporas in International Politics*,

London & Sydney: Croom Helm, p 16) have been criticised by some theorists who feel that the definition of diaspora should be tightened up, and have added extra criteria to those suggested by Safran (some of which I included in brackets). These debates can be found in the new journal *Diaspora*, published since 1997, quickly establishing itself as one of the main vehicles for discussion of the concept of diaspora. Finally, it is noteworthy to stress, as Vertovec does, that 'diaspora' does not only refer to a particular form of community characterised by physical dislocation, it also refers to a form of consciousness, a feeling of being 'here and there', and of multiple attachments (See diasporic identity below). (Source: Vertovec, S. (1997) 'Diaspora', in Cashmore, E. (ed.) *Dictionary of Race and Ethnic Relations*, pp 99-100) For further information about the concept of diaspora, see articles in the journal *Diaspora* and Cohen, R. (1997), *Global Diasporas: An Introduction*, London: UCL Press.

diasporic identity

Diasporic identity or 'diasporan identity' are relatively new terms derived from the term 'diaspora', and which relate to the term '*diasporan consciousness*' (See '*exile identity*' below). All these terms stress the decentred, dual or multiple location consciousness common to diaspora, as well as their identification as members of a diaspora. Discussions of diasporic identity depict individuals being simultaneously 'home away from home', 'here and there', or being British and something else. (Source: Vertovec, S. (1997) 'Diaspora', in Cashmore, E. (ed.) *Dictionary of Race and Ethnic Relations*, pp 99-100) Diasporic identity stresses the continuing orientation towards the homeland, a feature which distinguishes diaspora from other immigrant groups. Diasporic identities often consist of multiple identities and connections to different nations. For further reading, see: Mankekar, P. (1994) 'Reflections on Diasporic Identities: A Prolegomenon to an Analysis of political Bifocality', *Diaspora*, 3(3), pp 349-371.

ethnic group

Like ethnic identity and ethnicity, ethnic group is derived from the Greek term *ethnos*, 'the Greek word for "nation" in the sense of a group characterised by common descent'. (Eriksen, T. H. (1993) *Ethnicity and Nationalism: Anthropological Perspectives*, p 3) Although the term ethnic group initially referred to a basic human category and not a sub-group, it came to be employed by American sociologists to refer to 'a group with a common cultural tradition and a sense of identity which exists as a subgroup of a larger society'. (Eriksen, T. H. (1993), p 4) The result was that the term ethnic group became synonymous with the idea of a minority group, although of course, an ethnic group need not be a sub-group. It may be a dominant group, for example, the English.

ethnic identity

Ethnic identity is a notoriously contested term, and there are many, quite different definitions. Ethnic identity is distinct from national identity, and has been broadly defined by Alba as 'the subjective orientation towards ethnic origins'. (Alba, R. (1990) *Ethnic Identity: The Transformation of White America*: 20) David Levinson points out that ethnic identity also involves external ascription by others. (Levinson, D. (1994) *Ethnic Relations: A Cross-Cultural Encyclopedia*, Santa Barbara, CA: ABC-CLIO, p 73) Ethnic identity derives from ideas about 'identity', a term which first came into use as a popular social science term in the 1950's. Identity is not just about Who am I?, but critically, Who am I in relation to others? In simplistic terms, it denotes not just the self-ascribed similarities to others, but more importantly, the self-ascribed differences with others. Eriksen defines identity as an individual's personal identification with the prototypes available. Ethnic identity adds the ethnic element to identity, and denotes ones identity as a member of an ethnic group. According to Eriksen, it is 'the notion, or the belief in a shared culture' which distinguished ethnic identity from other social identities. (Eriksen, T. H. (1994*) Ethnicity and Nationalism: Anthropological Perspectives*: 35) Wallerstein and Wolf consider an ideology of common decent, substance and/or history as the main differentiating characteristics. (Vermeulen, H. & Govers, C. (1994) (eds.) 'Introduction'*, The Anthropology of Ethnicity: Beyond 'Ethnic Groups and Boundaries'*, p 3) An important area of contention among theorists of ethnic identity is whether ethnic identity is primordial or optional. According to Gleason, the difference between the two approaches is that primordialists regard ethnic identity as a given, a basic element in one's personal identity that is simply there and cannot be changes, while optionalists argue that ethnic identity is 'not an indelible stamp impressed on the psyche but a dimension of individual and group existence that can be consciously emphasised or de-emphasised as the situation requires'. (Gleason, P. (1983) Identifying Identity: A Semantic history', in Sollors, W. (1996) (ed.), *Theories of Ethnicity: A Classical Reader*: 469). (In the 1960's, theorists of the 'optionalist' school in both Britain and America began to cultivate new theories which tended to focus on ethnic identity as fluid, malleable, situational and complex. Various ideas were put forward, including the idea of ethnic identity as symbolic and situational. However, the debate between the primordialists and the essentialists continues and has yet to be resolved. In recent years, there have been several criticisms of the term 'ethnic identity'. Firstly, because of its ill-defined, contested nature it is an extremely problematic term to employ, and is ridden with assumptions and connotations. Second, the use of the term 'ethnic' has been criticised for being originally adopted and used primarily by dominant groups within society, mainly the dominant ethnic group. Solomos and Black outlined the problem: '...ethnic identity is almost uniformly viewed as only relevant to minority populations who have to resolve "their" contradictory position within British society. With some notable exceptions...there are very few discussions of the nature of majority identities', which are assumed to be 'less problematic and by implication homogenous'. (Solomos, J. & Black, L. (1996) *Racism and Society*, Basingstoke & London: Macmillan, p 131) The stress on minority populations has given rise to a host of assumptions and arguably, racist ideas, in discourses of ethnic identity. Another outcome of the use of ethnic identity mainly by dominant ethnic groups, has been an over-emphasis on the immigrant-receiving society relationship, to the neglect of an often, on-going relationship with the home country.

In this book, I will define ethnic identity as *self-identification as a member of an ethnic group, ethnic group being defined above, as a group with shared descent and culture.*

ethnicity

Although ethnicity is closely related to ethnic identity, the two terms have different meanings. Alba defines ethnicity as the articulation of ethnic identity or how ethnic identity manifests itself. (Alba, R. (1990) *Ethnic Identity: The Transformation of White America*, New Haven & London: Yale University Press, p 20) In this sense, it is the 'doing' or expression of ethnic identity, ethnic identity in practice. De Vos defines ethnicity as 'the subjective, symbolic or emblematic use by a group of people...of any aspect of culture, in order to differentiate themselves from other groups'. (De Vos, (1975), p 16, quoted in Vermeulen, H. & Govers, C. (1994) 'Introduction', in Vermeulen, H. & Goovers, C. (eds.) (1994) *The Anthropology of Ethnicity: Beyond 'Ethnic Groups and Boundaries'*: 4)

Finally, in Stuart Hall's view, ethnicity 'is the term we give to cultural features – language, religion, custom, traditions, felling for 'place' – which are shared by people'. (Hall, S. (1992) 'The Question of Cultural Identity', in Hall, S., Held, D. & McGrew, T. (eds.) *Modernity and its Futures*, Cambridge: Polity Press, p 297)

exile identity

'Exile identity' refers to the identity of exiles, an identity characterised by feelings of dislocation and displacement from the homeland, together with feelings of responsibility towards that homeland. Exiles are political refugees, in that they have been forced to leave, and/or are unable to return to the homeland, due to political reasons. In the case of the Baltic refugees and for many other exiles, they were unable to return to the homeland due to a change in political power, which led to an undesirable political regime. Due to the reasons of their dislocation, exiles feel a responsibility towards the homeland: they feel that they are the guardians of the homeland and therefore, have a responsibility to maintain cultures and identities on behalf of the homeland. Due to the circumstance of their uprooting from the homeland, many diasporic groups are also exiles, although not all exiles can be classified as diaspora. For example, an exile could be an individual political refugee, and not a member of a diaspora. However, because so many exiles are also diaspora, there are similarities between the terms 'exile identity' and 'diasporan consciousness'. Like exile identity, diasporan consciousness can be used to describe, 'individuals who view themselves as the only ones at liberty to preserve and perpetuate "true culture" during a period of "foreign occupation" of the homeland'. (Carpenter, I. G. (1996) 'Festival as Reconciliation: Latvian Exile Homecoming in 1990', *Journal of Folklore Research*, 33(2), p 93) Both exile and diasporan identity also encompass the feelings of dislocation, experienced by exiles and diaspora. For more on exile identity, see also: Carpenter, I. G. (1992) 'From Lecture to Debate: Generational Contestation in Exile', *Selected Papers on Refugee Issues*, Committee on Refugee Issues; Carpenter, I. G. (1988) 'Exile as Life Career Model', in Hofer, T. and Neidermüller, P. (eds.) *Life History as Cultural Construction/Performance*, Budapest: Ethnographic Institute.

integration

Integration first gained currency in Great Britain in the mid-1960's, when it superseded assimilation as the British Government's favoured goal. The replacement of assimilation with integration was influenced by increasing evidence of racial discrimination towards Britain's black and Asian communities, and a rejection of assimilation by these communities, who felt that it left little room for cultural maintenance or expression. In a frequently quoted speech, Roy Jenkins, the then Home Secretary argued against the flattening process of assimilation, in favour of integration. In Jenkins' view, the latter should be regarded, not as a 'flattening process of assimilation but as equal opportunity, accompanied by cultural diversity, in an atmosphere of mutual trust'. (Brah, A. (1996) *Cartographies of Diaspora: Contesting Identities*, p 25) Like assimilation, the use of the term integration underwent many metamorphoses in subsequent years. Cashmore defines integration as 'a condition in which different ethnic groups are able to maintain group boundaries and uniqueness, while participating equally in the essential processes of production, distribution and government'. (Cashmore, E. 'Integration' in Cashmore, E. (ed.) *Dictionary of Race and Ethnic Relations*, p 172) This definition paints a helpful picture of an integrated society. In this book, I have also used the definition provided by Berry. In his view, integration, 'implies some maintenance of the cultural integrity of the group (that is, some reaction or resistance to change as well as the movement to become an integral part of a larger societal framework (that is, some adjustment). Therefore, in the case of Integration, the option is to retain cultural identity and move to join the dominant society. When this strategy is widely adopted, there are a number of distinguishable ethnic groups, all co-operating within a larger social system'. (Berry, J. W. 'Acculturation and Adaptation in a New Society', *International Migration*, 30, p 72)

marginalization

In this book, I have adopted Berry's definition of marginalization, which he describes as one of four outcomes of the acculturation process (the others being *integration*, *assimilation* and *separation*). According to Berry, marginalization 'is characterised by striking out against the larger society and by feelings of alienation, loss of identity....' Marginalized groups and individuals 'lose cultural and psychological contact with both their traditional culture and the larger society, either by exclusion or withdrawal)'. Marginalization differs from separation, also known as *segregation*, when ethnic identity and traditions are maintained, but with no substantial relations with the larger society. (Berry, J. W. (1992) Acculturation and Adaptation in a New Society' *International Migration*, 30, pp 72-73).

multiculturalism

Multiculturalism has emerged in recent years, in popular and political discourses to describe the society Britain, as an immigrant country, is moving towards. Multiculturalism has not replaced the goal of integration, but it has supplemented it, and has perhaps become a more popularly used term by the British Government to describe its policies towards ethnic minorities in Britain. At its core, multiculturalism 'has the idea, or ideal of the harmonious coexistence of differing cultural or ethnic groups in a pluralist society at its core'. ('Multiculturalism' in Cashmore, E. (ed.) *Dictionary of Race and Ethnic Relations*, p 244) Multiculturalism has a range of meanings, as an ideology, a discourse and as a cluster of policies and practices. The image of a multicultural society is as a mosaic or salad bowl, with each component group having distinctive forms, but together making a unified whole, with all groups having equal rights. This image can be contrasted with the image of the 'melting pot' used to illustrate an assimilating society.

national identity

National Identity differs from ethnic identity, in that it refers not to identification as a member of an ethnic group, but identification as a member of a nation state or other form of national unit, as well as identification with national culture. In some cases however, ethnic and national identity are the same, primarily for the majority ethnic group, in countries where the nation state is defined on the basis of the majority ethnic group. For example, in present-day Latvia, the national and ethnic identity of a resident Latvian are the same. In Great Britain, the national identity and ethnic identity of some residents may be different. For example, a West Indian may have a West Indian ethnic identity, but have a British national identity. National identity is closely linked to nationality, and also with citizenship. I have used the term national identity in Chapter Two: *The Homeland*, where I investigate the development of national identities among the populations of the newly independent Baltic States. In later chapters of the study, I have examined whether the national identities of Latvians, Lithuanians and Estonians in Britain changed after several decades in Britain, and whether or not the acquisition of citizenship and thus of British nationality altered their national identities. I have attempted to separate the concepts of national and ethnic identity. Confusion over the meaning of the term national identity often stems from the fuzzy meaning of 'nation', which can refer both to nation in the sense of a nation state or to nation in the sense of an ethnic nation or ethnic group. According to Timothy Brennan, the word nation can refer 'both to the modern nation-state and to something more ancient and nebulous – the *natio* – a local community, domicile, family, condition of belonging'. (Brennan, T. (1990) 'The National Longing for Form', in Bhabba, H. (ed.) *Narrating the Nation*, London: Routledge, p 45) In Stuart Hall's view, the concept of national identity 'represented precisely the result of bringing these two halves of the national equation together, offering both membership of the political nation-state and identification with the national culture'... (Hall, S. (1992) 'The Question of Cultural Identity', in Hall, S., Held, D. & McGrew, T. (eds.) *Modernity and its Futures*, Cambridge: Polity Press, p 296) In this way, national identity is different to ethnic identity, and refers to identification with both a national state and a national culture, i.e. a shared cultural identity.

nationality

The most common use of nationality is as a legal term denoting citizenship. Although one's nationality is usually determined by citizenship, this is not true in every case, for example, for Latvians living in the Latvian SSR in the 1960's, although they had Latvian nationality, they were Soviet citizens. Nationality differs from ethnic identity in many cases. For example, in Britain, an English man or woman has an English ethnic identity, but a British national identity and nationality. In a devolving Scotland, inhabitants may have a Scottish and/or British national identity.

racialization

I have used the term racialization within the book, to refer to the government's categorisation of different nationalities for the EVW schemes. The idea of a racialized hierarchy of recruits was formulated by Kay and Miles in their 1992 work, *Refugees or Migrant Workers?*. But what does racialization mean? Miles defines racialization as a 'term that emerged in analysis in the 1970's to refer to a political and ideological process by which particular populations are identified by direct or indirect reference to their real or imagined pheno-typical characteristics in such a way as to suggest that the population can only be understood as a supposedly biological unity. This process usually involved the direct utilization of the idea of "race" to describe or refer to the population in question'. (Miles, R. 'Racialization', in Cashmore, E. (ed.) (1997) *Dictionary of Race and Ethnic Relations*, pp 306-7) There is some discussion of racialization within the book: See Chapter 5.

receiving society

'Receiving Society' refers to the country which 'receives' the refugees or immigrants, i.e. the country of settlement, in this case, Great Britain. The term has been used by some immigration specialists in preference to the term '*host society*', which formed part of earlier discourse relating to assimilation and integration. Host society infers two things. First, that the society is playing host to the immigrant, and therefore welcoming them, although perhaps only for a short period. Second, and this is where the criticisms have been directed, host brings up connotations of the biological relationship between a parasite and host, i.e. inferring that the immigrant is a parasite which feeds off, and drains the host. Receiving society could be criticised in that it suggests that all immigrants are received (clearly they are not), but in the case of the European Volunteer Workers, who were invited to enter Britain, it appears to be a more suitable term to use.

transnationalism

Transnationalism is a relatively new term emerging from the field of diaspora studies, and influenced by theories of globalisation, although as a phenomenon it has existed in earlier periods of immigration. Transnationalism emphasises the increasingly global links of immigrant groups and the continuous exchange of wealth and people between the homeland, the country of residence, and diaspora in different receiving societies. The term transnationalism refers to the processes by which immigrants 'forge and sustain multi-stranded social relations that link together their societies of origin and settlement'. (Basch, l., Glick Shiller,

N. and Szanton Blanc, C. (1994) *Nations Unbound: Transnational Projects, Postcolonial Predicaments, and Deterritorialized Nation States*, Langhorne, PA: Gordon and Breach, p 7) According to Foner, in a transnational perspective, 'contemporary immigrants are seen as maintaining familial, economic, political, and cultural ties across international borders, in effect making the home and host societies a single arena of social action'. (Foner, N. (1997) 'What's New about Transnationalism? New York Immigrants Today and as the Turn of the Century', *Diaspora*, 6(30), p 355).

BIBLIOGRAPHY

A NOTE ON SOURCES

The oral history interviews recorded for this project constitute the core source material in this book, together with supplementary material from questionnaires, participant observation and fieldwork trips to the Baltic States. Although the material from the interviews forms the backbone of the research, a variety of other sources have also been utilised. Several interviews with Latvians, Lithuanians and Estonians in Bradford carried out by Bradford Heritage Recording Unit in the 1980's provided a useful pre-independence perspective on the Baltic communities. British Government files in the Public Record Office (PRO) in London were a particularly important source of material relating to British Government policy vis-à-vis DP's in Europe and the EVW schemes, contained principally in Ministry of Labour and Foreign Office (FO) files, although Cabinet and Prime Minister's files were also consulted. 125 separate files were consulted, of which some of the most important were contained within the following record classes: CAB 9; PREM 9; HO 213; LAB 8; LAB 26; FO 371; FO 945; FO 1006; FO 1032; FO 1049; FO 1052; FO 1056; FO 1110. The PRO also provided useful source materials written by the refugees themselves, and representatives of the refugee communities. Often these were in the form of appeals, requesting the British Government to ameliorate the situation of DP's in the Camps, and to improve conditions for EVW's. Soviet propaganda material and evidence of Britain's shifting foreign relations and policy towards the Baltic States can also be found in FO files. Information about the first years of settlement within Britain, the development of community structures, government assimilation policies and the reported progress of the EVW's were also found in these files. Other government publications consulted outside the PRO included House of Commons and House of Lords debates. In addition to the PRO, other archives were consulted, including the Weiner Library in London, and the Northern Refugee Centre in Sheffield. These archives provided a miscellany of materials, including sources from the DP camps and newspaper articles. Sources published by the Latvian, Lithuanian and Estonian communities in Britain were invaluable. These ranged from community newspapers, newsletters, and books, to personal memoirs and other sources provided by individuals. A detailed personal memoir by an Estonian in Britain, *Remembering Pussa*, provided a useful English language account of a childhood on Saaremaa island in Estonia. Although most of the publications of the Baltic communities are written in the homeland language, there are some notable exceptions and some books have English summaries. The newsletter, *LYNES*, intended for second and third generation Lithuanians and written mainly in English was a key source of information relating to younger generations. A publication of Lithuanian Scouting in Great Britain, intended for Lithuanian children, called *Lithuania: How Much Do We Know About Her?* was also very useful. For example, number 10(1993) contains an article, 'The Lithuanians in Britain': 4-20, which provides a useful overview of Lithuanians in different regions of Britain. I received many of the publications written by the Baltic communities in Britain by individuals from the communities. Many of these publications are unavailable elsewhere. The publications of the world-wide Baltic diaspora were also useful, including publications written in the DP Camps. A variety of secondary sources were consulted, including general British immigration histories, theories of immigration and refugee settlement, studies of the Baltic diasporas in other countries, novels about Baltic migrants, and works examining aspects of the history of the Baltic States. Various unpublished theses and dissertations were consulted, and several important publications were purchased during fieldwork trips to the Baltic States, many of which are unavailable elsewhere. These included publications concerning cultures and identities in the Baltic States, and the following useful volume: Ezergailis, A. (ed.) (1997) *The Latvian Legion: Heroes, Nazis or Victims? – A Collection of Documents from OSS War-Crimes investigation files, 1945-50*, Riga: The Historical Institute of Latvia.

BRADFORD HERITAGE RECORDING UNIT INTERVIEWS (BHRU)

1) ACC.No. BO 060, 5.3.84, (First Generation Latvian), Sound Recording.

2) ACC.No. BO 122, 21.8.84, (First Generation Latvian), Sound Recording.

3) ACC.No. BO 127, 30.8.84, (First Generation Estonian), Sound Recording.

4) ACC.No. BO 166, 7.8.85, (First Generation Lithuanian), Transcript.

GOVERNMENTAL PAPERS

12 Dec 1989, *'War Crimes' Debate*, HC Debs, vol 163, 1989-1990, Dec 4 - Dec 15, pp 868-910.

4 June 1990, *'War Crimes Bill'*, HL Debs, vol. 519, 1989-90, May 14 1990 - June 7 1990, cols 1080-1280,

'Report on the Entry of Nazi War Criminals and Collaborators into the UK, 1945-50', The All-Party Parliamentary War Crimes Group, November 1988.

SECONDARY SOURCES

Abrahams, M. (1995) 'Dad, Why do people say these things about you?', *The Independent Magazine*, Saturday 1 January 1995: 22-26.

Abramson, P. R. & Neslek, J. B. (1994) 'A Case for Case Studies – An Immigrant's Journal', *Contemporary Psychology*, 39(6): 663-664.

Alba, R. (1990) *Ethnic Identity: the Transformation of White America*, New Haven & London: Yale University Press.

Alderman, G. & Holmes, C. (eds.) (1993) *Outsiders and Outcasts : Essays in honour of William J Fishman,* London: Duckworth.

Alexander, T. (1987) *An Estonian Childhood*, London: Heinemann.

Ambrazevičus, R. (1994) *Lithuanian Roots: An Overview of Lithuanian Traditional Culture*, Vilnius: Lithuanian Folk Culture Centre.

Amos Hatch, J. & Wisneiewski, R. (1995) 'Life history and narrative: questions, issues, and exemplary works', in Amos Hatch, J. & Wisniewski, R. (eds.) *Life History and Narrative*, London: Falmer.

Anderson, B. (1991) *Imagined Communities: Reflections on the Origin and Spread of Nationalism*, Revised Edn., L & NY: Verso.

Anderson, R. J., Hughes, J. A., & Sharrock, W. W. (1986) *Philosophy and the Human Sciences,* London: Croom Helm.

Andrups, J., (1995) 'A History of Latvians in Great Britain', (English translation by Andris Abakus), in Auziņa-Smita, I. (1995*) Latvieši Lielbritanijā(Latvians in Great Britain*), vol 1, London: Latvian National Council in Great Britain and Daugavas Vanagi.

Anon., (1981) *Latvian Committee for Cultural Relations with Countrymen Abroad*, Riga: Avots.

Anon., (1982) *Migration and Settlement*, Milton Keynes: Open University Press.

Anon., (1985) 'The Church in Lithuania', *Europe-North America Dossier, Pro-Mundi Vita : Dossiers,* 30(3).

Anon. (1988) 'Age in Exile : A Report on Elderly Exiles in the United Kingdom', The British Refugee Council for the Age in Exile Conference, August 1988, Noordwijkerhaut, the Netherlands, 25-27 November 1988.

Anon., (1995) Lithuania in March 1941: An American Diplomat's Report, xxvi(2): 151-158.

Anon. (1996) War Crimes Committal Starts, The Guardian, 20 February 1996: 4.

Anwar, M. (1979) The Myth of Return: Pakistanis in Britain, London: Heinemann.

Anwar, M. (1995) '"New Commonwealth" : Migration to the UK', in Cohen, R. The Cambridge Survey of World Migration, Cambridge: CUP: 274-278.

Appignanesi, R. & Garratt, C. (1995) Postmodernism for Beginners, Cambridge: Icon Books.

Armstrong, J. (1994) 'Nations before Nationalism', in Hutchinson, J. & Smith, A. D. (eds.), Nationalism, Oxford & NY: O.U.P.

Ashton, R. (1986) Little Germany: Exile and Asylum in Victorian Britain, Oxford.

Aun, K. (1985) The Political Refugees: A History of the Estonians in Canada, Toronto: McClleland and Steward Ltd.

Auziņa-Smita, I. (1995) Latvieši Lielbritanijā (Latvians in Great Britain), vol 1, London: Latvian National Council in Great Britain and Daugavas Vanagi.

Avizienis, R. & Hough, W. (1995) Guide to Lithuania, London: Bradt.

Baker, R. (ed.) (1985) The Psychosocial Problems of Refugees, The Refugee Council and European Consultation on Refugees and Exiles.

Baldwin-Edwards, M. & Schain, M. A. (eds.) (1994) The Politics of Immigration in Western Europe, Newbury Park: Frank Cass.

Balys, J, P. (1976) 'The American Lithuanian Press', Lituanus, 22(1): 42-53.

Banks, M. (1996) Ethnicity: Anthropological Constructions, London & New York: Routledge.

Banton, M. (1988) Racial Consciousness, Longman Singapore Publishers.

Banton, M. (1997) 'Assimilation' in Cashmore, E. (ed.) Dictionary of Race and Ethnic Relations, London & New York: Routledge.

Basch, L., Glick Shiller, N. and Szanton Blanc, C. (1994) Nations Unbound: Transnational Projects, Postcolonial Predicaments, and Deterritorialized Nation States, Langhorne, PA: Gordon and Breach.

Baškauskas, L. (1977) 'Multiple Identities : Adjusted Lithuanian Refugees in Los Angeles', Urban Anthropology, 6(2): 141-154.

Baškauskas, L. (1981) 'The Lithuanian Refugee Experience and Grief', *IMR*, 15(1): 276-291.

Barėnas, K. (1978) *Britanijos Lietuviai, 1947-1973 (Lithuanians in Britain, 1947-1973)*, London: Lithuanian Association in Great Britain.

Barth, F. (ed.) (1969) *Ethnic Groups and Boundaries: The Social Organisation of Culture Difference*, Bergen: Scandinavian University Press.

Benmayor, R. & Skotnes, A. (1994) *Migration and Identity*, International Yearbook of Oral History and Life Stories, vol II, Oxford: OUP.

Berghahn, M. (1984) 'German Jews in England : Aspects of the Assimilation and Integration Process', in Hirschfeld, G. (1984) *Exile in Great Britain*, London.

Berry, J. W. (1992) 'Acculturation and Adaptation in a New Society', *International Migration*, 30: 69-83.

Bertaux, D. (1981) 'From the Life History Approach to the Transformation of Sociological Practice', in Bertaux, D. *Biography and Society: The Life History Approach in the Social Sciences*, ch 2: 29-45.

Bertaux, D. (1981) *Biography and Society: The Life History Approach in the Social Sciences*, London: Sage.

Beyer, G. (1981) 'The Political Refugee: 35 Years Later', *IMR*, 15(1): 26-41.

Bhabbha, H. (ed.) (1990) *Narrating the Nation*, London: Routledge.

Bilmanis, A. (1970) *A History of Latvia*, Westport, Connecitut: Greenwood Press.

Blakemore, K. & Boneham, M. (1994) *Age, Race and Ethnicity: A Comparative Approach*, Buckingham: O.U.P.

Blodnieks, A. (1960) *The Undefeated Nation*, New York: Robert Speller & Sons.

Bornat, J. (1989) 'Oral History as a Social Movement: Reminiscence and Older People', *Oral History*, 17(22): 16-24.

Bornat, Joanna. (ed.) (1994) *Reminiscence Reviewed : Perspectives, Evaluations, Achievements*, Buckingham: OUP.

Bourdeaux, M. (1979) *Land of Crosses: The Struggle for Religious Freedom in Lithuania, 1939-1978*, Devon: Augustine Publishing Company.

Bower, T. (1981) *Blind Eye to Murder: Britain, America and the Purging of Nazi Power*, Deutsch.

Bower, T. (1989) *The Red Web: MI6 and the KGB Master Coup*, London: Aurum.

Boyle, P., Halfacree, K. & Robinson, V. (1998) *Exploring Contemporary Migration*, London: Longman.

Bradford Heritage Recording Unit (1987), *Destination Bradford: A Century of Immigration*, Bradford.

Bradford Lithuanian Club "Vytis" (ed.) (1995) *Bradfordo Lietuvių Veikla Didžiojoje Britanijoje, 1947-1995 (Lithuanians in Bradford, 1947-1995)*, Vilnius: 'Litfondas'.

Brah, A. (1996) *Cartographies of Diaspora: Contesting Identites*, London: Routledge.

Bramwell, A. C. (ed.) (1988) *Refugees in the Age of Total War*, London: Unwin Hyman.

Brass, P. R. (1994) 'Elite competition and Nation-Formation', in Hutchinson, J. & Smith, A. D. *Nationalism,* Oxford & New York: O.U.P..

Bremmer, I. & Taras, R. (eds.) (1993) *Nations and Politics in the Soviet Successor States*, Cambridge: Cambridge University Press.

Brennan, T. (1990) 'The national longing for form', in Bhabbha, H. (ed.) *Narrating the Nation*, London: Routledge.

Bringeús, N-A. (1970), Man, Food and Milieu, *Folk Life*, 8: 45-56.

Brivati, B., Buxton, J. & Seldon, A. (eds) (1996) *The Contemporary History Handbook*, Manchester: Manchester University Press.

Brooke, S. (1995) *Reform and Reconstruction: Britain after the War, 1945-51*, Manchester: Manchester University Press.

Brown, J. (1970) *The Un-Melting Pot: An English Town and its Immigrants*, London & Basingstoke: Macmillan.

Bruner, J. (1995) 'The Autobiographical Process', *Current Sociology*, Special Issue: 'Biographical Research', 43(2/3): 161-177.

Budreckis, A. M. (1976) *The Lithuanians in America, 1651-1975 : A Chronology and Fact Book*, New York: Oceana.

Budreckis, A. M. (1976) *The Lithuanians in America, 1651-1975 : A Chronology and Fact Book*, New York: Oceana.

Buijs, G. (1981) *Migrant Women: Crossing Boundaries and Changing Identities*, Oxford: Berg.

Bülbring, M. (1954) 'Post-war Refugees in Great Britain', *Population Studies*, viii(2): 99-112.

Bulmer, M. & Solomos, J. (eds.) (1999) *Ethnic and Racial Studies Today*, Routledge: London & New York.

Cairncross, A. (1985) *Years of Recovery: British Economic Policy, 1945-51*, London: Methuen.

Campani, G. (1995) 'Women Migrants: From Marginal Subjects to Social Actors', in Cohen, R. *The Cambridge Survey of World Migration*, Cambridge: Cambridge University Press.

Canadian Committee for Human Rights in Latvia, (1983) *'Genocide? Destruction? Annihilation?: time is running out for the threatened Latvian nation'*, Toronto: Canadian Committee for Human Rights in Latvia.

Carpenter, I. G. (1988) 'Exile as Life Career Model', in Hofer, T. & Niedermüller, P. *Life History as Cultural Construction*, Budapest: Ethnographic Institute.

Carpenter, I. G. (1988) *Being Latvian in Exile: Folklore as Ideology*, Unpublished PhD thesis, Indiana University.

Carpenter, I. G. (1992) 'From Lecture to Debate: Generational Contestation in Exile', in DeVoe, P. A. (ed.) *Selected Papers on Refugee Issues*, Committee on Refugee Issues.

Carpenter, I. G. (1996) 'Baltic Peoples: Lithuanians, Latvians and Estonians', in Taylor JR., R. M. & McBirney, C.A. *Peopling Indiana: the Ethnic Experience*, Indianopolis: Indiana Historical Society.

Carpenter, I. G. (1996) 'Festival as Reconciliation: Latvian Exile Homecoming in 1990', *Journal of Folklore Research*, 33(20.

Carpenter, I.G. (1990) 'A Detour through America: The Latvian Émigré experience in Jānis Jaunsudrabiņš' Tā Mums Iet, in Metuzāle-Kangere, B. & Rinholm, H. D. (eds.) *Symposium Balticum: A Festschrift to honour Professor Velta Rūķe-Draviņa*, Hamburg: Helmut Buske Verlag.

Carter, R. (1994) 'A Turbulent History', in Williams, R. (ed.), *Baltic States*, London: APA Publications.

Cashmore, E. (ed.) (1997) *Dictionary of Race and Ethnic Relations*, Fourth Edition, London and New York: Routledge.

Castles, S. () 'The Guest-Worker in Western Europe - An Obituary', *IMR*, 20(4): 761-778.

Castles, S. (1984) *Here for Good : Western Europe's New Ethnic Minorities*, London: Pluto.

Castles, S. (1995) 'Contract Labour Migration', in Cohen, R. (ed.) *The Cambridge Guide to World Migration* Cambridge: CUP.

Castles, S. (1995) 'Contract Labour Migration', in Cohen, R. *The Cambridge Survey of World Migration*, Cambridge: CUP: 274-278.

Caunce, S. (1994) *Oral History and the Local Historian*, London & New York: Longman.

Cesarani, D. & Fulbrook, M. (eds.) (1996) *Citizenship, Nationality and Migration in Europe*, London & New York: Routledge.

Cesarani, D. (1992) *Justice Delayed: How Britain became a refuge for Nazi War Criminals*, London: Heinemann.

Cesarani, D. (1994) *The Final Solution: Origins and Implementation*, London & New York: Routledge.

Cesarani, D. (1996) 'The Changing Character of Citizenship in Britain', in Cesarani, D. & Fulbrook, M. (eds.) *Citizenship, Nationality and Migration in Europe*, London & New York: Routledge.

Chamberlain, M. (1994) 'Family and Identity: Barbadian Migrants to Britain', in Benmayor, R. & Skotnes, A. *Migration and Identity*, International Yearbook of Oral History and Life Stories, vol II, Oxford: OUP.

Chamberlain, M. (1997) 'Gender and the Narratives of Migration', *History Workshop Journal*, 43: 87-108.

Chave, R. (ed.) (1988) *Lucy Addison: Letters from Latvia*, London: Futura.

Chiswick, B. R. & Miller, P. W. (1994) 'Language choice among Immigrants in a Multi-lingual destination', *Journal of Population Economics*, 7(2): 119-131.

Clifford, J. (1997) 'Diasporas', in Guibernau, M. & Rex, J. (eds.) *The Ethnicity Reader: Nationalism, Multiculturalism and Migration*, Cambridge: Polity.

Cohen, A. P. (1989), 'Symbolising Boundaries - Identity & Diversity in British Cultures', *Journal of Historical Geography*, 15(2): 219-220.

Cohen, R. (1994) *Frontiers of Identity: The British and Others*, London: Longman.

Cohen, R. (1995) 'Rethinking "Babylon": iconoclastic conception of the diasporic experience', *New Community*, 21(1): 5-18.

Cohen, R. (1997) *Global Diasporas: An Introduction*, London: UCL Press.

Cohen, R. (ed.) (1995) *The Cambridge Survey of World Migration*, Cambridge: CUP.

Cohon Jr. J. D. (1981) 'Psychological Adaptation and Dysfunction among Refugees', *IMR*, 15(1): 255-275.

Coleman, D. & Salt, J. (eds.) (1996) *Ethnicity in the 1991 Census. Vol One: Demographic Characteristics of the ethnic minority populations*, London: Office of Population Censuses & Surveys, HMSO.

Coleman, P. (1986) *Ageing and the Reminiscence Process : Social and Clinical Implications*, Wiley.

Colpi, T. (1991) *The Italian factor: the Italian Community in Great Britain*, Edinburgh.

Connor, W. (1994) 'A Nation is a nation, is a state, is an Ethnic Group, is a ...', in Hutchinson, J. & Smith, A. D. (eds.), *Nationalism*, Oxford & New York: Oxford University Press.

Cooper, K. (1979) *The Uprooted: Agony and Triumph among the Debris of War*, London: Quartet Books.

Cordasco, F. & Alloway, P. N. (1981) *American Ethnic Groups : The European Heritage : A Bibliography of Doctoral Dissertations Completed at American Universities*, London: The Scarecrow Press.

Crick. B. (1995) 'The sense of identity of the indigenous British', *New Community*, 21(2): 167-182.

Crowe Jr. D. M. (1978) 'The Contemporary Baltic Press in the Non-Soviet World', *Lituanus,* 24(2): 57-71.

Crowe, D. (1988) 'Baltic émigré publishing and scholarship in the Western World', *Nationalities Papers,* 16(2): 225-241.

Daboliðø, S. & Shipman, S. (1993) *Latvia: A Guide Book,* Latvia: PUSE.

Dahlstrom, E. (1965) 'Esthonian Refugees in a Swedish Community', in Rose, A, M. & Rose, C. B. (eds.), *Minority Problems,* New York: Harper & Row: 98-107.

Danys, M. (1983) 'The Emigrant Experience: Contract Hiring of Displaced Persons in Canadian Domestic Employment', *Lituanus,* 29(2): 40-51.

Danys, M. (1986) *DP: Lithuanian Immigration to Canada after the Second World War,* Toronto: Multicultural History Society of Ontario.

Dashefsky, A. (1976) *Ethnic Identity in Society,* Rand Mcnally.

Denzin, N. (1989) *Interpretive Biography,* Qualitative Research Methods Series (17), London: Sage.

Denzin, N. K. & Lincoln, Y. S. (eds.) (1994) *Handbook of Qualitative Research,* London: Sage.

Denzin, N. K. (1978) *Sociological Methods: A Sourcebook,* New York: Mcgraw-Hill.

Dex, S. (ed.) (1991) *Life and Work History Analyses : Qualitative and Quantitative Developments,* London & New York: Routledge.

Donald, J. & Rattansi. A. (eds.) (1994) *'Race', Culture and Difference,* London: Sage.

Drake, M. (ed.) (1995) *Time, Family and Community: Perspectives on Family and Community History,* 2nd Edn., Oxford: OUP in association with Blackwell.

Dreifelds, J. (1996) *Latvia in Transition,* Cambridge: Cambridge University Press.

Dzerzins, I. (1988) 'Leaving Latvia: A Case Study of Immigration from the Baltic States to the United Kingdom after the Second World War', Unpublished dissertation for BSc in Soc. Sc. with History and Philosophy, School of Humanities and Social Sciences, University of Bath, June 1988.

Elliott, M. R. (1982) *Pawns of Yalta: Soviet Refugees and America's Role in their Repatriation,* London & Chicago: University of Illinois Press.

Eriksen, T. H. (1993) *Ethnicity and Nationalism: Anthropological Perspectives,* London: Pluto Press.

Esman, M. J. (1986) 'Diasporas and International Relations', in Sheffer, G. (ed.) *Modern Diasporas in International Politics,* London & Sydney: Croom Helm.

Estonian Committee in Göttingen, *Estonia: My Beautiful Land,* 1946.

Ezergailis, A. (ed.) (1997) *The Latvian Legion: Heroes, Nazis or Victims? – A Collection of Documents from OSS War-Crimes investigation files, 1945-50*, Riga: The Historical Institute of Latvia.

Farraday, A. & Plummer, K. (1979) 'Doing Life Histories', *Sociological Review*, 27(4): 773-798.

Fassmann, H. & Munz, R. (1994) 'European East-West Migration 1945 –1992', *IMR*, 28(3): 520-538.

Fassmann, H. & Munz, R. (1995) 'European East-West Migration, 1945-1992', in Cohen, R. (ed.) *The Cambridge Survey of World Migration*, Cambridge: CUP.

Feagin, J. R., Orum, A. M. & Sjoberg, G. (eds.) (1991) *A Case for the Case Study*, University of North Carolina Press.

Ferrarotti, F. (1981) 'On the Autonomy of the Biographical Method', in Bertaux' D. *Biography and Society*.

Field, S. J. (1994) 'Becoming Irish - Personal Identity Construction among first-generation Irish Immigrants', *Symbolic Interaction*, 17(4): 431-452.

Finnan, C. R. 'Occupational Assimilation of Refugees', *IMR*, 15(1): 292-309.

Fishman, J. A. (ed.) (1985) *The Rise and Fall of the Ethnic Revival: Perspectives on Language and Ethnicity*, Berlin, New York & Amsterdam: Mouton Publishers.

Fjuck, I. & Aarend-Mihkel, R. (eds.) (1994) *Estonia: Free and Independent*, Tallinn: Estonian Encyclopaedia Publishers & Ignar Fujk Architects and Publishers.

Flick, U.(1998) *An Introduction to Qualitative Research*, London: Sage.

Foner, N. (1997) 'What's New about Transnationalism? New York Immigrants Today and at the Turn of the Century', *Diaspora*, 6(3): 355-375.

Fontana, A. & Frey, J. H. (1994) 'Interviewing: The Art of Science', in Denzin, N. K. & Lincoln, Y. S. (eds.) *Handbook of Qualitative Research*, London: Sage.

Fortier, A-M. (1998) 'the Politics of "Italians Abroad": Nation, Diaspora and New Geographies of Identity', *Diaspora*, 7(2): 197-224.

Gans, H. J. (1979) 'Symbolic ethnicity: the future of ethnic groups and cultures in America', *ERS*, 2(1): 1-20.

Gans, H. J. (1994) 'Symbolic Ethnicity and symbolic religiosity: towards a comparison of ethnic and religious acculturation', *ERS*, 17(4): 577-592.

Gartner, L. P. (1973) *The Jewish Immigrant in England, 1870-1914*, Reprint of 1960 edn., London: Allen & Unwin.

Gedmintas, A. (1980) 'Organisational Relationships in the Development of the Binghampton Lithuanian Community', *JBS*, xi(4): 315-324.

Gedmintas, A. (1989) *An Interesting Bit of Identity: The Dynamics of Ethnic Identity in a Lithuanian-American Community*, New York: AMS Press.

Gellner, E. (1983) *Nations and Nationalism*, Oxford: Blackwell.

Gilbert, E. (2000) *Latvian, Lithuanian and Estonian Displaced Persons in Great Britain*, PhD Thesis, University of Sheffield: Sheffield.

Gilbert, E. (2002) 'The Impact of Homeland Independence on the Latvian Community in Great Britain', *Journal of Baltic Studies*, 33(3): 280-306.

Girnius, K. K. (1985) 'Soviet Version of Lithuanian History', *Index on Censorship*, 6: 17-19.

Glaser, B. G. & Strauss, A.L (1967) *The Discovery of Grounded Theory: Strategies for qualitative research*, New York: Aldine de Gruyter.

Glaser, D. (1958) 'Dynamics of Ethnic Identification', *American Sociological Review*, 1958, 23(1): 31-40.

Glazer, N. & Moynihan, D. P. (1963) *Beyond the Melting Pot: the Negroes, Puerto Ricans, Jews, Italians and Irish of New York City*, Cambridge, Mass.: MIT Press.

Gleason, P. (1983) 'Identifying Identity: A Semantic History', in Sollors, W. (ed.) (1996) *Theories of Ethnicity: A Classical Reader*, Basingstoke & London: Macmillan.

Goldlust, J. & Richmond, A. H. (1974) 'Multivariate Model of Immigrant Adaptation', *IMR*, 8(2): 193-225.

Green, A. & Troup, K. (1999) *The Houses of History: A critical reader in twentieth century history and theory*, Manchester, Manchester University Press.

Greene, V. (1975) *For God and Country: The rise of Polish and Lithuanian Ethnic Consciousness in America, 1860-1910*, Madison: The State Historical Society of Wisconsin.

Guibernau, M. & Rex, J. (eds.) (1997) *The Ethnicity Reader: Nationalism, Multiculturalism and Migration,* Cambridge: Polity.

Gutting, D. (1996) 'Narrative Identity and residential history', *Area*, 28(4): 482-490.

Hall, C. (1992) *White, Male and Middle-Class : Explorations in Feminism and History*, Cambridge: Polity.

Hall, S. (1992) 'New Ethnicities' in Donald, J. & Rattansi, A. (eds.) *'Race', Culture and Difference*.

Hall, S., Held, D. & McGrew, T. (eds.) (1992) *Modernity and its futures*, Cambridge: Polity Press in association with The Open University.

Handley, J. E. (1947) *The Irish in Modern Scotland*, Cork: Cork University Press.

Haynes, J. (1993) *People to People: Lithuania/Latvia/Estonia*, Edinburgh: Canongate Press & Boston: Zephyr Press, Boston.

Hiden, J. & Salmon, P. (1991) *The Baltic Nations and Europe: Estonia, Latvia and Lithuania in the Twentieth Century*, London & NY: Longman.

Hinds, D. (1966) *Journey to an Illusion: The West Indian in Britain*, London: Heinemann.

Hindo, N. (1968) *Eesti organisatsioonid Inglismal, 1918-1968* (reference provided by an Estonian in Britain).

Hobsbawm, E. J. (1992) *Nations and Nationalism since 1780: Programme, Myth and Reality*, Second Edn., Cambridge: Cambridge University Press.

Hoffman, E. (1991) *Lost In Translation*, London: Minerva.

Holmes, C. (ed.) (1978) *Immigrants and Minorities in British Society*, London: Allen & Unwin.

Holmes, C. (1985) 'Immigration into Britain', *History Today*, June 1985: 16-17.

Holmes, C. (1991) 'Building the Nation: the contributions of immigrants and refugees to British society', *RSA Journal*, November 1991: 725-733.

Holmes, C. (1994) *John Bull's Island: Immigration and British Society, 1871-1971*, Basingstoke and London: Macmillan.

Holmes, C. (1995) 'Historians and Immigration', Drake, M. (ed), *Time, Family and Community: Perspectives on Family and Community History*, 1995.

Hope, N. (1994) 'Interwar Statehood: Symbol and Reality', in Smith, G. (ed.) *The Baltic States: The National Self-Determination of Estonia, Latvia and Lithuania*, Basingstoke & London: Macmillan.

Hosking, G. (1993) (Book review) 'A Will to Survive: the Baltic peoples' struggle to recover nationhood', *The Times Literary Supplement*, 4710(9 July 1993): 5.

Howarth, K. (1984) *Remember, Remember: Tape Recording Oral History*, Pennine Heritage Network.

Hughes, C. (1991) *Lime, Lemon and Sarsparilla: the Italian Community in South Wales, 1881-1945*, Bridgend.

Humphrey, R. (1993) 'Life Stories and Social Careers: Ageing and Life Stories in an Ex-Mining Town', *Sociology*, 27(1): 166-178.

Humphries, S. (1984) *The Handbook of Oral history: Recording Life stories*, Inter-Action imprint.

Husband, C. (ed.) (1982) *'Race' in Britain: Continuity and Change*, London: Hutchinson.

Hutchinson, J. & Smith, A. D. (eds.) (1994) *Nationalism*, Oxford & New York: O.U.P.

Hutchinson, J. & Smith, A.D. (eds.) (1996) *Ethnicity*, Oxford: O.U.P.

Isaac, J. (1954) *British Post-War Migration*, Cambridge: CUP.

Isajiw, W. W. (1990) 'Ethnic Identity Retention in Four Ethnic Groups: Does it Matter?' *JBS*, XXI(3): 289-304.

Jackson, J. A. (1963) *The Irish in Britain*, London: Routledge and Kegan Paul.

Jackson, P. & Penrose, J. (eds.) (1993) *Constructions of Race, Place and Nation*, London: UCL Press.

Jackson, P. (1988) 'Beneath the Headlines: Racism and Reaction in Contemporary Britain', *Geography*, 202-207.

Jackson, P. (1992) 'The racialization of labour in post-war Bradford', *Journal of Historical Geography*, 18(2): 190-209.

Jaksic, I. (1994) 'In Search of Safe Haven: Exile, Immigration and Identity', in Benmayor, R. & Skotnes, A. *Migration and Identity*, International Yearbook of Oral History and Life Stories, vol II, Oxford: OUP.

Jansen, C. J. (1994) (Book review), Luciuk L & Hryniuk S (ed), Canada's Ukrainians: Negotiating an Identity, *IMR*, 28(3): 601-602.

Jeffcoate, R. & Mayor, B. (1982) *Bedford - Portrait of a Multi - Ethnic Town*, Milton Keynes: Open University.

Jeffery, P. (1976) *Migrants and Refugees: Muslim and Christian Pakistani Families in Bristol*, Cambridge: Cambridge University Press.

Jenkins, K. (1997) *The Postmodern History Reader*, London: Routledge.

Jenkins, R. (1994) 'Rethinking ethnicity: Identity, Categorisation and Power', *ERS*, 17(2): 197-223.

Jerabek, I. & Deman, A. F. (1994) 'Social Distance among Caucasian-Canadians and Asian, Latin American and Eastern-European Immigrants in Quebec', *Social Behaviour and Personality*, 22(3): 297-304.

Jõeste, M., Kaevats, U., Urdziņš, A., Vilks, A., Demskis, K. and Mikalajūnas, M. (eds.) (1991) *The Baltic States: A Reference Book*, Tallinn, Riga, Vilnius: Estonian Encyclopaedia Publishers, Latvian Encyclopaedia Publishers, Lithuanian Encyclopaedia Publishers.

Johansons, A. (1951) 'Latvian Literature in Exile', *Slavonic and East European Review,* 29-30: 465-475.

Joly, D. (1992) *Refugees : Asylum in Europe?*, London: Minority Rights Publications.

Joly, D. (1993) (Book Review) Kay, D. & Miles, R. (1992) 'Refugees or Migrant Workers?: European Volunteer Workers in Britain, 1946-1951' *ERS*, 16(3): 563-564.

Juøkaitė, A. (1980) 'The Contemporary Identity Problem of Baltic Youth in Australia', *Lituanus*, 26(4): 7-17.

Kalnins, I. V. (1990) Patterns of Ancestral Language Knowledge and use among Estonians, Latvians and Lithuanians in Canada, *JBS*, XXI(3): 193-200.

Karklis, M., Streips, L. & Streips, L. (1974) *The Latvians in America, 1640-1973: A Chronology and Fact Book*, New York: Oceana.

Karklis, M., Streips, L. & Streips, L. (eds.) (1974) *The Latvians in America, 1640-1973: A Chronology and Fact Book*, New York: Oceana.

Karnups, V. P. (1980) 'The Role of the Ethnic Family in Maintaining Ethnic Identity', *Lituanus*, 26(4): 18-24.

Karpinski, J. (1997) 'Poland and Lithuania look towards a common future', *Transition*, 3(6).

Kay, D. & Miles, R. (1988) 'Refugees or Migrant Workers?: The case of the European Volunteer Workers', *Journal of Refugee Studies*, 1(3): 214-36.

Kay, D. & Miles, R. (1992) *Refugees or Migrant Workers?: European Volunteer Workers in Britain, 1946-1951*, London: Routledge.

Kay, D. (1995) 'The Resettlement of Displaced Persons in Europe, 1946-1951', in Cohen, R. *The Cambridge Survey of World Migration*, Cambridge: Cambridge University Press.

Kelemen, P. (Book Review), Kay, D. & Miles, R. 'Refugees or Migrant Workers?: European Volunteer Workers in Britain, 1946-1951', *Sociology*, 26(4): 712-713.

Keramida, F. (1999) 'The Way to the Homeland: A 'Repatriated' Migrant's Life Story', *Oral History*, Spring 1999: 75-85.

Kershen, A. J. (ed.) (1997) *London: the promised land?*, Aldershot & Brookfield: Avebury.

Kincheloe, J. K. & McClaren, P. L. (1994) 'Rethinking Critical Theory and Qualitative Research' in Rattansi, A. & Westwood, S. (eds.) *Racism, Modernity and Identity on the Western Front*, Cambridge: Polity Press.

King, V. & Wilson, R. (1988) 'Latvian Residential Homes for Retired People' in *Age in Exile: A Report on Elderly Exiles in the United Kingdom*, (Unpublished), British Refugee Council for the Age in Exile Conference, Noordwijkerhout, the Netherlands.

Kionka, R. (1990) 'Estonians', in Smith, G. *The Nationalities Question in the Soviet Union*, London & New York: Longman.

Kirby, D. (1994) 'Incorporation: the Molotov-Ribbentrop Pact', in Smith, G. (ed.) *The Baltic States: The National Self Determination of Estonia, Latvia and Lithuania*, Basingstoke & London: Macmillan.

Kivosto, P. (1989) *The Ethnic Enigma: The Salience of Ethnicity for European-Origin Groups*, London & Toronto: Associated University Press.

Klier, J. (1995) *Imperial Russia's Jewish Question, 1855-1881*, Cambridge: Cambridge University Press.

Kmita, M. (1992) 'Working with the Polish Immigrant Community: Issues and Ways Forward', (*Unpublished*), Lynfield Mount Hospital, April 1992, Avail. from NRC.

Krausz, E. (1972) 'Acculturation and pluralism: a clarification of concepts', *New Community*, 1(4):250-255.

Kreutzwald, Fr. R. (1982) *Kalvipoeg: An Ancient Estonian Tale*, English Edn., Transl. by Kurman, J., Moorestown, New Jersey.

Krickus, R. (1993) 'Lithuania: nationalism in the modern era', in Bremmer, I. & Taras, R. (eds.) *Nations and Politics in the Soviet Successor States*, Cambridge: Cambridge University Press.

Krisciunas, R. G. (1983) 'The Emigrant Experience: The Decision of Lithuanian Refugees to Emigrate, 1945-1950', *Lituanus*, 29(2): 30-39.

Kudirka, J. (1991) *The Lithuanians: An Ethnic Portrait*, Vilnius: Lithuania Folk Culture Centre.

Kulischer, E. M. (1943) *The Displacement of Population in Europe*, Montreal.

Kulischer, E. M. (1948) *Europe on the Move: War and Population Changes, 1917 - 1947*, New York: Columbia University Press.

Kunz, E. F. (1973) 'The Refugee in Flight : Kinetic Models and Forms of Displacement', *IMR*, 7(2): 125-146.

Kunz, E. F. (1981) 'Exile and Resettlement: Refugee Theory', *IMR*, 15(1): 42-51.

Kushner, T. (1995) 'Holocaust Survivors in Great Britain: An Overview and research Agenda', *Journal of Holocaust Education*, 4(2).

Laar, K-A. (1990) 'Estonian Ethnic Identity: Language Maintenance and Shift', *JBS*, XXI(3): 239-258.

Lane, T. (2004) *Victims of Stalin and Hitler: The Exodus of Poles and Balts to Britain*, Hampshire and New York, Palgrave Macmillan

Laslett, J. H. M. (Book Review), Wyman, M. DP: Europe's Displaced Persons, 1945-1951, *IMR*, 24(4): 839-40.

Latvian National Council in Great Britain (1995) *Latvians in Great Britain*, London: Latvian National Council in Great Britain.

Latvian National Foundation. (undated) *These Ruins Accuse: A Record of Religious Suppression of the Evangelical Lutheran Church in Occupied Latvia*, Sweden: Latvian National Foundation.

Lavie, S. & Swedenburg, T. (eds.) (1996) *Displacement, Diaspora and Geographies of Identity*, Durham, North Carolina: Duke University Press.

Levin, D. (1975) 'Participation of the Lithuanian Jews in the Second World War', *JBS*, vi(4): 300-310.

Levinson, D. (1994) *Ethnic Relations: A Cross-Cultural Encyclopedia*, Santa Barbara, CA: ABC-CLIO.

Lieven, A. (1993) *The Baltic Revolution: Estonia, Latvia, Lithuania and the Path to Independence*, New Haven & London: Yale University Press.

Lieven, A. (1994) 'Ethnic Diversity', in Williams, R. (ed.) *Baltic States*, London: APA Publications.

Lieven, A. (1994) 'Folklore', in Williams, R. (ed), *Baltic States*, London: APA Publications.

Linda Kivi, K. (1995) *If Home is a Place*, Vancouver: Polestar.

Lipman, V. D. (1954) *Social History of the Jews in England, 1850-1950*, London: Watts.

Lithuania: How Much Do We know About Her?, Lithuanian Scouting in Great Britain & Lithuanian House, London, vols 1-10.

Lorencs, J. (1994) 'The Church and Religion', in Williams, R. (ed.) *Baltic States*, Basingstoke: APA Publications.

Lucas, E. & Tammerk, T. (1992), 'Ghost from the past returns to Estonia', *The Baltic Independent*, 3(116): 11.

Lucas, E. (1994) 'People of the Baltics', in Williams, R. (ed.), *Baltic States*, Basingstoke: APA Publications.

Luciuk, L. & Hryniuk, S. (ed.) (1991) *Canada's Ukrainians: Negotiating an Identity*, Toronto: University of Toronto Press.

Luciuk, L. Y. 'Unintended Consequences in Refugee Resettlement: Post-War Ukrainian Refugee Immigration to Canada', *IMR*, 20(2): 467-482.

Lummis, T. (1987) *Listening to History: the Authenticity of Oral History*, London: Hutchinson.

Lunn, K. (1980), 'Reactions to Lithuanian and Polish Immigrants in the Lanarkshire Coalfield, 1850-1914', in *Hosts, Immigrants & Minorities: Historical Responses to Newcomers in British Society, 1870-1914*, Kent: Dawson.

Lunn, K. (1985) 'Immigrants and British Labour's Response, 1870-1950', *History Today*, November 1985: 48-52.

Lunn, K. (1992) 'The Employment of Polish and European Volunteer Workers in the Scottish Coalfields, 1945-1950', in Tenfelde, K. (ed.) *Towards a Social History of Mining in the Nineteenth and Twentieth Centuries*, Munich: C. H. Beck.

Lunn, K. (ed.) (1980) *Hosts, Immigrants & Minorities: Historical Responses to Newcomers in British Society, 1870-1914*, Kent: Dawson.

LYNES, Lithuanian Youth News-sheet, Lithuanian Youth Association in Great Britain, 1 (1978) – 54 (August 2000) (some missing).

MacDonald, I. A. (1987) *Immigration Law and Practice in the United Kingdom*, Second Edn., London: Butterworths.

Malik, K. (1996) 'Universalism and difference: race and the postmodernists', *Race & Class*, Special Issue: 'Paradigms of Racism', 37(3): 1-17.

Mankekar, P (1994) 'Reflections on Diasporic Identities: A Prolegomenon to an Analysis of Political Bifocality', *Diaspora*, 3(3): 349-371.

Markides, K. S. (1983) 'Minority Ageing', in Riley, Hess, & Bond, *Ageing in Society: Selected Reviews of Recent Research*, London: Lawrence Erlbaum Assoc.

Marwick, A. (1990) *British Society since 1945*, Second Edn., London: Penguin.

Mason, D. (1995) *Race and Ethnicity in Modern Britain*, Oxford: Oxford University Press.

Massey et al., D. S. (1997) 'Causes of Migration', in Guibernau, M. & Rex, J. (eds.) *The Ethnicity Reader: Nationalism, Multiculturalism and Migration*, Cambridge: Polity.

McDowell, L., (2003) 'The particularities of place: geographies of gendered moral responsibilities among Latvian migrant workers in 1950s Britain,' *Transactions of the British Institute of British Geographers*, 28(1):19-34.

McDowell. L., (2005) *Hard Labour: The Forgotten Voices of Latvian migrant 'Volunteer' Workers,* London, UCL.

Melderis, V. (1982) *Latvia,* Moscow: Novosti Press Agency.

Merrimann, N. (ed.) (1993) *The Peopling of London: Fifteen Thousand Years of Settlement from Overseas*, London: Museum of London.

Miezitis, S. (1990) 'Ethnic Identity Development: A Comparative Study of Active and Non-Active second Generation Youth in the Latvian Community', *JBS*, XXI(3): 259-288.

Miezitis-Matiss, I. A. (1990) Patterns of Language use in Second Generation Families of Latvian Origin, *JBS*, XXI(3): 231-238.

Miles, R. & Kay, D. (1994) 'The Politics of Immigration into Britain: East-West Migrations in the Twentieth Century', in Baldwin-Edwards, M. & Schain, M. A. (eds.) *The Politics of Immigration in Western Europe*, Newbury Park: Frank Cass.

Miles, R. & Phizacklea, A. (1979) *Racism and Political Action in Action*, London: Routledge & Kegan Paul.

Miles, R. & Phizacklea, A. (1980) *Labour and Racism*, London: Routledge and Kegan Paul.

Miles, R. (1982) *Racism and Migrant Labour*, London: Routledge & Kegan.

Miles, R. (1987) *Capitalism & Unfree Labour: Anomaly or Necessity?*, London: Tavistock.

Miles, R. (1989) *Racism*, London: Routledge.

Miles, R. (1995) *Racism after 'Race Relations'*, London: Routledge.

Millar, J. (Jonas Stepšis) (1998) *The Lithuanians in Scotland: A Personal View*, Isle of Colonsay: House of Lochar.

Miller, D. (1995) 'Reflections on British national identity', *New community*, 21(1): 153-166.

Miller, W. C. (ed.) (1976) *A comprehensive Bibliography for the Study of American Minorities*, vol. 1, New York: New York University Press.

Miller, W. C. (ed.) (1977) *Minorities in America: The Annual Bibliography*, University Park and London: The Pennsylvania University Press.

Mills, J. (1963), 'Britain's Community of Poles', *New Society*, 18 July 1963: 13-14.

Milosz, C. (1984) 'Lithuania, Latvia and Estonia 1940-1980: Similarities and Differences', *Baltic Forum*, 1(1).

Milosz, C. (1984) 'The Lessons of the Baltics', *Baltic Forum*, 1(1).

Misiunas, R. & Taagepera, R. (1993) *The Baltic States: Years of Dependence, 1940-1990*, 2nd Edn., London: Hurst & Co.

Misiunas, R. J. (1982) 'Baltic Identity and Sovietization', Review Article, *Problems of Communism*, March-April 1982: 39-41.

Mockūnas, L. (1985) 'The Dynamics of Lithuanian Émigré – Homeland Relations', *Baltic Forum*, 2(1).

Modood, T., Beishon, S. & Virdee, S. (1994) *Changing Ethnic Identities*, London: Policy Studies Institute.

Modood, T. & Berthoud, R. (1997) *Ethnic Minorities in Britain: Diversity and Disadvantage*, London: Policy Studies Institute.

Morris, L. (1993) 'Migrants and Migration', Review Article, *Work, Employment and Society*, 7(3): 473-492.

Muiznieks, N. (1993) 'Latvia: origins, evolution and triumph' in Bremmer, I. & Taras, R. (eds.) *Nations and Politics in the Soviet Successor States*, Cambridge: Cambridge University Press.

Murphy, H. B. M. (1952) 'The Assimilation of Refugee Immigrants in Australia', *Population Studies*, March 1952, part 3: 179-206.

Murphy, H. B. M. (ed.) (1955) *Flight and Resettlement*, Switzerland: UNESCO.

Muzikants, B. (1980) 'Reflections on the Implications of Bilingualism and Biculturalism', *Lituanus*, 26(4): 25-31.

Nagel, J. (1994) 'Constructing Ethnicity: Creating and Recreating Ethnic Identity and culture', *Social Problems*, 41(1): 152-176.

Nesaule, A. (1995) *A Woman in Amber: Healing the Trauma of War and Exile*, New York & London: Penguin.

Neuman, W. L. (1994) *Social Research Methods: Qualitative and Quantitative Approaches*, 2nd Edn., London: Allyn & Bacon.

Niczyperowicz, J. (1987) 'The Polish Community in Leeds: A social Perspective', (*Unpublished*), Social Services, Leeds City Council, March 1987, Avail. from NRC.

Niederhauser, E. (1981) *The Rise of Nationality in Eastern Europe*, Gyoma, Hungary: Corvina Kiadó.

Noble, J. (1994) *Baltic States and Kaliningrad: a travel survival kit*, London: Lonely Planet.

Nocon, A. (1996) 'A Reluctant Welcome?: Poles in Britain in the 1940's', *Oral History*, Spring 1996: 79-87.

Noiriel, G. (1996) *The French Melting Pot: Immigration, Citizenship, and National Identity*, Minneapolis & London: University of Minnesota Press.

Nõmme, E. (1980) 'The Adjustment of Second Generation Estonians in Australia', *Lituanus*, 26(4): 32-38.

Norman, A. (1985) *Triple Jeopardy: Growing Old in a Second Homeland*, London: Centre for Policy on Ageing.

Norris, A. (1989) 'Clinic or Client?: A Psychologists Case for Reminiscence', *Oral History*, 17(2): 26-30.

Okamura, J. Y. (1981) 'Situational Ethnicity', *ERS*, 4(4): 452-465.

Olsson, L. (1997) *On the Threshold of the People's Home of Sweden : A Labor Perspective of Baltic Refugees and relieved Polish Concentration Camp Prisoners in Sweden at the End of World War II*, New York: Centre for Migration Studies.

Olwig, K. F. (1999) 'Narratives of the children left behind: home and identity in globalised Caribbean families', *Journal of Ethnic and Migration Studies*, 25(2): 267 -284.

Švabe, A., Balodis, Fr., Blese, E., Sīlis, O. & Korsts, K. (1947) *Latvia on the Baltic Sea*, DP Camp, Hanau: Gaismas Pils.

Owen, D. *Country of Birth: Settlement Patterns, 1991 Census Statistical Paper*, National Ethnic Minority Data Archive, Warwick University.

Pajaujas-Javis, J. (1980) *Soviet Genocide in Lithuania*, New York: Maryland Books.

Pallister, D. (1996) 'Man, 85, to face war crimes trial', *The Guardian*, 16 April 1996: 3.

Panayi, P. (1988) *The Enemy in our Midst: Germans in Britain in the First World War*, Oxford.

Panayi, P. (1994) *Immigration, Ethnicity and racism in Britain, 1815-1945*, Manchester: M.U.P.

Panayi, P. (1999) 'The historiography of immigrants and minorities: Britain compared with the USA', in Bulmer, M. & Solomos, J.

(eds.) *Ethnic and Racial Studies Today*, Routledge: London & New York.

Patterson, S. (1968) *Immigrants in Industry*, London: O.U.P.

Patterson, S. (1977) 'The Poles: An Exile Community in Britain', in Watson, J. L. (ed.), *Between Two Cultures Cultures: Immigrants and Minorities in Britain*, Oxford: Blackwell..

Pattie, S. (1994) 'At Home in Diaspora: Armenians in America', *Diaspora*, 3(2): 185-198.

Paul, K. (1997) *Whitewashing Britain: Race and Citizenship in the post-war era*, Ithaca and London: Cornell University Press.

Pennar, J. (ed.) (1975) *The Estonians in America, 1627-1975*, New York: Oceana.

Pennar, J. (ed.) (1975) *The Estonians in America, 1627-1975: A Chronology and Fact Book*, New York: Oceana.

Penrose, J. & Jackson, P. (eds.) (1993) *Constructions of Race, Place and Nation*, London: UCL Press.

Perks, R. & Thomson, A. (eds.) (1997) *The Oral History Reader*, London: Routledge.

Perks, R. (1987) 'European Migrants to Bradford - The Oral Evidence', in *Moving Stories: Towards a History of the Many Peoples of the English Cities*, Multicultural Education Centre, Leeds City Council.

Perks, R. (1987) 'Immigration to Bradford : the Oral testimony', *Immigrants And Minorities*, 6: 362-68.

Perks, R. (1990) *Oral History: An Annotated Bibliography*, London: The British Library.

Perks, R. (1992) *Oral History: Talking about the Past*, London: The Historical Association.

Perks, R. (1993) 'Ukraine's Forbidden History: Memory and Nationalism', *Oral History*, Spring 1993: 43-53.

Perks, R. B. (1984) 'A Feeling of not belonging?: Interviewing European Immigrants in Bradford', *Oral History*, 12(2):64-67.

Pernice, R. (1994) 'Methodological Issues in Research with Refugees and Immigrants', *Professional Psychology - Research & Practice*, 25(3): 207-213.

Peterson Royce, A. (1982) *Ethnic Identity: Strategies of Diversity*, Bloomington: Indian University Press.

Plakans, A. (1995) *Latvia: A Short History*, Stanford: Hoover University Press.

Plensners, A. (1955) *A Small Nation's Struggle for Freedom: Latvian Soldiers in World War II*, Stockholm: Latvian National Foundation.

Plummer, K. (1983) *Documents of Life: An Introduction to the problems of a humanistic method*, London: George Allen & Unwin.

Poopuu, H. (1985-86) *Remembering Pussa* (Unpublished personal memoirs).

Popham, P. (1995) 'The Unknown Quantity', *Independent Magazine*, 14 October 1995: 8-14.

Porat, D. (1994) 'The Holocaust in Lithuania', in Cesarani, D. *The Final Solution: Origins and Implementation*, London and New York: Routledge.

Priedkalns, J. (1982) 'The Latvians in Australia: Comments on Demographic Studies', *JBS*, XIII(2): 128-133.

Priedkalns, J. (1994) 'Language as the Core Value of Latvian Culture: The Australian Experience', *JBS*, XXV(1): 29-42.

Proudfoot, M. (1957) *European Refugees: 1939-52, A Study in Forced Population Movement*, London: Faber & Faber.

Putniņš, A. L. (1979) 'Latvian Identification: Second Generation Youth in Australia and North America', *JBS*, X(1): 60-63.

Putniņš, A. L. (1981) *Latvians in Australia: Alienation and Assimilation*, Canberra: Australian National University Press.

Putniņš, A. L. (1985) 'Latvians in Australia: A Problem in Baltic Demography', *JBS*, XVI(1): 73-82.

Racevskis, K. (1993) 'Voices from the Gulag: A Review Essay', *JBS*, xxiv(3): 299-306.

Ragin, C. C. & Hein, J. (1993) 'The Comparative Study of Ethnicity : Methodological and Conceptual Issues', in Stanfield, J. H. II. & Dennis, R. M. *Race & Ethnicity in Research Methods*, London: Sage.

Rattansi, A. & Westwood, S. (eds.) (1994) *Racism, Modernity and Identity on the Western Front*, Cambridge: Polity Press.

Rattansi, A. (1994) '"Western" Racisms, Ethnicities and Identities in a "Postmodern" Frame', in Rattansi, A. & Westwood, S. (eds.) *Racism, Modernity and Identity on the Western Front*, Cambridge: Polity Press.

Raud, V. (1953) *Estonia: A Reference Book*, New York: Nordic Press.

Rawicz, S. (1956) *The Long Walk*, London: Chiswick Press.

Rebas, H. (1980) 'Baltic Minorities: Problems of Method and Documentation', *JBS*, 1: 37-48.

Rees, T. (1982) 'Immigration Policies in the United Kingdom', in Husband, C. (ed.) *'Race' in Britain: Continuity and Change*, London: Hutchinson.

Rex, J. (1995) 'Ethnic Identity and the Nation State: the Political Sociology of Multi-Cultural Societies', *Social Identities*, 1(1).

Rex, J. (1997) 'The Concept of a Multicultural Society', in Guibernau, M. & Rex, J. (eds.) *The Ethnicity Reader: Nationalism, Multiculturalism and Migration*, Cambridge: Polity.

Rex, J. (1997) 'The nature of ethnicity in the project of migration', in Guibernau, M. & Rex, J. (eds.) *The Ethnicity Reader: Nationalism, Multiculturalism and Migration,* Cambridge: Polity.

Richardson, A. (1967) 'A Theory and Method for the Psychological Study of Assimilation', *IMR,* II(1): 3-28.

Richardson, J. (1992) 'The Needs of Refugees from Central and East Europe', *(Unpublished),* Draught Typescript of section from The Elderly Refugee Project report.

Richmond, A. H. (1967) *Immigrants and Ethnic groups in Metropolitan Toronto,* Toronto: Institute for Behavioural Research.

Riley, M. W., Hess, B. B. & Bond, K. (eds.) (1983) *Ageing in Society: Selected Reviews of Recent Research,* London: Lawrence Erlbaum Associates.

Robinson, B. (1990) 'The Plight and prospects of Elderly Exiles in Developed Nations', *Ageing International,* June 1990: 11-15.

Rodgers, M. (1982) 'The Anglo-Russian Military Convention and the Lithuanian Immigrant Community in Lanarkshire, Scotland, 1914-20', *Immigrants and Minorities,* 1:

Rodgers, M. (1984) 'Political Developments in the Lithuanian Community in Scotland, c. 1890-1923', in Slatter, J. (ed.) *From the Other Shore: Russian Political Emigrants in Britain, 1880-1917, London:* Cass.

Rodgers, M. (1985) 'The Lithuanians', *History Today,* 35: 15-20

Roos, A. (1985) *Estonia: A Nation Unconquered,* Baltimore: Estonian World Council.

Roper, M. (1996) 'Oral History', in Brivati, B., Buxton, J. & Seldon, A. (eds) *The Contemporary History Handbook,* Manchester: Manchester University Press.

Rose, A. M. & Rose, C. B. (eds.) (1965) *Minority Problems: A textbook of Readings in Intergroup Relations,* New York: Harper and Row.

Rose, R. & Maley, W. (1994) *Nationalities in the Baltic States: A Survey Study,* University of Strathclyde, Glasgow: Centre for the Study of Public Policy.

Rothschild, J. (1974) *East-Central Europe between the Two World Wars,* Seattle and London: University of Washington Press.

Rothwell, V. (1982) *Britain and the Cold War,* London: Jonathon Cape.

Rubchak, M. J. (1993) 'Dancing with the Bones: A Comparative Study of Two Ukrainian Exilic Societies', *Diaspora,* 2(3).

Rubulis, A. (1970) *Baltic Literature: A survey of Finnish, Estonian, Latvian and Lithuanian Literatures,* Notre Dame & London: The University of Notre Dame.

Rumbaut, R. G. 'The Crucible Within: Ethnic Identity, Self Esteem and Segmented Assimilation Among Children of Immigrants', *IMR*, xxvii(4): 748-794.

Safran, W. (1991) 'Diasporas in Modern Societies: Myths of Homeland and Return', *Diaspora*, 1(1): 83-99.

Schochat, A. (1974) 'Jews, Lithuanians and Russians, 1939-1941', in Vago, B. & Mosse, G. L. *Jews and non-Jews in Eastern Europe*, Jerusalem: Keter Publishing House.

Senn, A. E. (1990) 'Perestroika in Lithuanian Historiography: The Molotov-Ribbentrop Pact', *Russian Review*, 49: 43-56.

Sheffer, G. (ed.) (1986) *Modern Diasporas in International Politics*, London & Sydney: Croom Helm.

Sherman, A. J. (1973*) Island Refuge: Britain and Refugees from the Third Reich, 1933-1939*, Paul Elek.

Sieber, J. E. (1992) *Planning Ethically Responsible Research: A Guide for Students and Internal Review Boards*, London: Sage.

Silgailis, A. (1986) *Latvian Legion*, San Jose, California: James Bender.

Simanis, V. V. (ed.) (1984) *Latvia*, St. Charles: The Book Latvia Inc.

Simeoni, D. & Diani, M. (1995) 'Introduction : Between Objects and Subjects: the Nation-bound Character of Biographical Research', *Current Sociology*, Special Issue : 'Biographical Research', 43(2/3): 1-10.

Sinka, J. (1988) *Latvia and Latvians*, Central Board "Daugavas Vanagi", London: Nida Press.

Skultans, V. (1996) 'Latvian Identity in Text and Memory : Looking for a Subject', (*Unpublished*), Paper presented at the 'Auto/Biography, Education and Culture Conference', University of Southampton, 29 June 1996.

Skultans, V. (1996) 'Looking for a subject: Latvian memory and narrative', (*Unpublished*), School of Mental Health, University of Bristol.

Skultans, V. (1996) 'Theorising Latvian lives : The Quest for Identity', (*Unpublished*), School of Mental Health, University of Bristol.

Skultans, V. (1998) 'Remembering Time and Place: A Case Study in Latvian narrative', *Oral History*, 55-63.

Skultans, V. (1998) *The Testimony of Lives: Narrative and Memory in post-Soviet Latvia*, London & New York: Routledge.

Slatter, J. (1984) *From the Other Shore : Russian Political Emigrants in Britain, 1880 - 1917,* London: Cass.

Smith, A. D. (1988) 'The Myth of the "Modern Nation" and the myths of nations', *ERS*, 11(1): 1-26.

Smith, A. D. (1994) 'The Origins of Nations', in Hutchinson, J. & Smith, A. D. (eds.) *Nationalism*, Oxford & New York: O.U.P.

Smith, G. (1990) 'Latvians', in Smith, G. *The Nationalities Question In the Soviet Union*, London & New York: Longman.

Smith, G. (ed.) (1990) *The Nationalities Question in the Soviet Union*, London & New York: Longman.

Smith, G. (ed.) (1994) *The Baltic States: The National Self-Determination of Estonia, Latvia and Lithuania*, Basingstoke & London: Macmillan.

Smith, T., Perks, R. & Smith, G. (1998) *Ukraine's Forbidden History*, Stockport: Dewi Lewis Publishing.

Smolicz, J. (1981) 'Core Values and cultural identity', *ERS*, 4(1): 75-90.

Solomos, J. & Black, L. (1996) *Racism and Society*, Basingstoke & London: Macmillan.

Sponza, L. (1988) *Italian Immigrants in Nineteenth Century Britain: Realities and Images*, Leicester.

Stadulis, E. (1952) 'The Resettlement of Displaced Persons in the UK', *Population Studies*, March 1952: 207-237.

Stanfield II, J. H. (1994) 'Ethnic Modelling in Qualitative Research', in Denzin, N. K. & Lincoln, Y. S. *Handbook of Qualitative Research*, London: Sage.

Stanfield, J. H. & Dennis, R. M. (eds.) (1993) *Race and Ethnicity in Research Methods*, London: Sage.

Stano, R. (1989) 'The Refugee', (*Unpublished*), I.C.S.C. Project, 17 May 1989, Avail. from NRC.

Stein, B. N. (1981) 'The Refugee Experience: Defining the Parameters of a Field of study', *IMR*, 15(1): 320-330.

Stola, D. 'Forced migrations in Central European History', *IMR*, 26(2): 324-341.

Stuart, M. (1993) 'And how was it for you Mary?: Self, Identity and Meaning for Oral Historians', *Oral history*, 21(2): 80-83.

Sword, K. (1993) 'The Poles in London', in Merrimann, N. (ed.) *The Peopling of London*, London: Museum of London.

Sword, K. (1995) 'The Repatriation of Soviet Citizens at the end of the Second World War', in Cohen, R. *The Cambridge Survey of World Migration*, Cambridge: Cambridge University Press.

Sword, K., Davies, N. & Ciechanowski, J. (1989) *The Formation of the Polish Community in Great Britain, 1939-1950*, London: SEES.

Taagepera, R. (1993) *Estonia: Return to Independence*, Westview Press: Boulder.

Tannahill, J. A. (1958) *European Volunteer Workers in Britain*, Manchester: Manchester University Press.

Teczarowska, D. (1985) *Deportation into the Unknown*, Devon: Merlin Books Ltd.

Tedre, U. (1991) *Estonian Customs and Traditions*, (English Edn., translated by Victoria Hain and Kristi Tarand), Tallinn: Perioodika.

Temple, B. (1995) 'Telling Tales: Accounts and Selves in the Journeys of British Poles', *Oral History*, Autumn 1995: 60-64.

The Latvian National Foundation in co-operation with the World Federation of Free Latvians (1982) *These Names Accuse : Nominal List of Latvians Deported in Soviet Russia in 1940-41*, 2nd. Edn. with supplementary list, Stockholm: Latvian National Foundation.

Thompson, P. & Perks, R. (1989) *Telling it How it was: A Guide to Recording Oral History*, London: BBC.

Thompson, P. (1988) *The Voice of the Past: Oral History*, O.U.P, 2nd Edn.

Thomson, A. (1999) 'Moving Stories: Oral History and Migration Studies', *Oral History*, Spring 1999: 24-38.

Thomson, C. (1992) *The Singing Revolution: A Journey through the Baltic States*, London: Michael Joseph.

Tölöyan, K. (1996) 'Rethinking Diaspora(s): Stateless Power in the Transnational Movement, *Diaspora*, 5(1).

Tolstoy, N. (1986) *Victims of Yalta*, London: Corgi.

Tonkin, E. (1992) *Narrating our pasts: The social construction of oral history*, Cambridge: Cambridge University Press.

Tuchman, G. (1994) 'Historical Social Science: Methodologies, Methods and Meanings', in Denzin, N. K. & Lincoln, Y. S. (eds.) *Handbook of Qualitative Research*, London: Sage.

Tupeøu, J. (1984) 'Ancient Latvian Religion', in Simanis, V. V. (ed.) (1984) *Latvia*, St. Charles: The Book Latvia Inc.

Vago, B. & Mosse, G. (eds.) (1974) *Jews and non-Jews in Eastern Europe, 1918-1945*, Jerusalem: Keter Publishing House.

Vairogs, D. (trans. and ed. Hildebrants, M. T.) (Undated) *Latvian Deportations 1940 - Present,* Rockville: The World Federation of Free Latvians.

Valantiejus, A. (1996) 'Changes in Identity: Memory and Forgetfulness' in Taljunaite, M. (ed.) *Changes of Identity in Modern Lithuania*, Vilnius: Lithuanian Institute of Philosophy and Sociology.

Van Den Berghe, P. L. (1984) 'Ethnic Cuisine: culture in nature', *ERS*, 7(3): 387-397.

Van der Berghe, P. (1994) 'A Socio-Biological Perspective', in Hutchinson, J. & Smith, A. D. *Nationalism*, Oxford & New York: O.U.P.

Van Hear, N. (1998) *New diasporas: the mass exodus, dispersal and regrouping of migrant communities*, London: UCL Press.

Van Reenan, A. J. (1990) *Lithuanian Diaspora: Königsberg to Chicago*, New York: University Press of America.

Vardys, V. S. & Sedaitis, J. (1997) *Lithuania: The Rebel Nation*, Boulder, Colorado: Westview Press.

Vardys, V. S. (1975) 'Modernization and Baltic Nationalism', *Problems of Communism*, 24(5).

Vardys, V. S. (1981) 'Freedom of Religion, Lithuania and the Chronicle: An Introduction', *Chronicle of the Catholic Church in Lithuania*, 1(1-9), Chicago: Loyola University Press and Society for the Publication of the Chronicle of the Catholic Church in Lithuania.

Vardys, V. S. (1983) 'Polish Echoes in the Baltic', *Problems of Communism*, July-August 1983.

Vardys, V. S. (1990) 'Lithuanians', in Smith, G. (ed.) *The Nationalities Question in the Soviet Union*, New York: Longman.

Vardys, V.S. & Misiunas, R. J. (eds.) (1978) *The Baltic States in Peace and War, 1917-45*, Pennsylvania and London: University Park.

Veidemanis, J. (1982) *Social Change, Major Value Systems of Latvians at Home, as Refugees, and as Immigrants*, Colorado: University of Northern Colorado, Museum of Anthropology, Occasional Publications in Anthropology, Ethnology Series, 38(1).

Vermeulen, H. & Govers, C. (eds.) (1994) *The Anthropology of Ethnicity: Beyond 'Ethnic Groups and Boundaries'*, Amsterdam: Het Spinhuis.

Vernant, J. (1953) *The Refugee in the Post-War World*, London: Allen & Unwin.

Vertovec, S. (1997) 'Diaspora', in Cashmore, E. (ed.) *Dictionary of Race and Ethnic Relations*, London and New York: Routledge.

Vertovec, S. (1997) 'Three Meanings of "Diaspora," exemplified among South Asian Religions, *Diaspora*, 6(3): 277299.

Vertovec, S. (1999) 'Conceiving and researching transnationalism', *ERS*, 22(2): 447-462.

Vizulis, I. J. (1985) *Nations under Duress: The Baltic States*, New York: Port Washington.

Von Rauch, G. (1995) *The Baltic States: The Years of Independence : Estonia, Latvia, Lithuania, 1917-1940*, First Pbk. Edn., London: Hurst & Co.

Ward, A. (1995) *Copyright Ethics and Oral History*, Colchester: Oral History Society.

Ward, S. (1995) 'War Crimes case thrown into chaos', *The Independent*, 27 Sept 1995: 2.

Waters, M. C. (1990) *Ethnic Options: Choosing Identities in America*, Berkeley, LA, Oxford: University of California Press.

Watson, J. L. (1977) 'Introduction: Immigration, Ethnicity and Class in Britain', in Watson, J. L. (ed.) *Between Two Cultures*, Oxford: Blackwell.

Watson, J. L. (ed.) (1977) *Between Two Cultures : Immigrants and Minorities in Britain*, Oxford: Blackwell.

Weber, M. 'What is an ethnic group?', in Guibernau, M. & Rex, J. (eds.) *The Ethnicity Reader: Nationalism, Multiculturalism and Migration*, Cambridge: Polity.

White, J. D. (1975) 'Scottish Lithuanians and the Russian Revolution', *JBS*, 6(1): 1-8.

Williams, R. (1994) 'Country Life', in Williams, R. (ed.) *Baltic States*, Basingstoke: APA Publications.

Williams, R. (ed.) (1994) *Baltic States*, Basingstoke: APA Publications.

Williams, R. C. (1970) 'European Political Emigrations: A Lost Subject', *Comparative Studies in Society and History*, 12:140-48.

Wilson, F. (1947) 'Displaced Persons: Whose Responsibility?', *Current Affairs*, 28 June 1947(31).

Winland, D. N. (1995) '"We are Now an Actual Nation": The Impact of National Independence on the Croatian Diaspora in Canada', *Diaspora*, 4(1): 29.

Winslow, M. (1995) '"Scarred for Life": The Effect of War trauma upon an ageing Polish Population', (*Unpublished*) Dissertation, BA Hons Historical Studies, School of Cultural Studies, Sheffield Hallam University, June 1995.

Winslow, M. (1999) 'Polish Migration to Britain: War, Exile and Mental Health', Oral History, Spring 1999: 57-64.

Woods, T. (1998) 'Mending the Skin of Memory: Ethics and history in contemporary narratives', *Rethinking History*, 2(3): 339-348.

Wyman, M. (1989) *DP: Europe's Displaced Persons, 1945-1951*, Philadelphia: The Balch Institute.

Yinger, J. M. (1981) 'Towards a theory of Assimilation and Dissimilation', *ERS*, 1981, 4(3): 249-264.

Yow, V. R. (1994) *Recording Oral History: A Practical Guide for Social Scientists*, London & New York: Sage.

Zaborowska, M. J. (1995) *How we Found America: Reading Gender through East European Immigrant Narratives*, Chapel Hill and London: The University of North Carolina Press.

Zaleski, Z. (1992) 'Ethnic identity and Prosocial Attitudes', *The Journal of Psychology*, 126(6): 651-659.

Zubrzycki, J. (1956) *Polish Immigrants in Britain*, The Hague.

Printed in Great
Britain
by Amazon